African American Mosaic

A Documentary History
from the Slave Trade
to the Twenty-First Century
Volume Two:
From 1865 to the Present

The Reverend Martin Luther King, Jr. joins hands with other leaders in the civil rights movement at the head of a street procession during the 1963 March on Washington. (*Source:* The National Archives and Records Administration.)

African American Mosaic
A Documentary History
from the Slave Trade
to the Twenty-First Century
Volume Two:
From 1865 to the Present

John H. Bracey, Jr.
Manisha Sinha

University of Massachusetts, Amherst

PEARSON
Prentice
Hall

Upper Saddle River, New Jersey 07458

Library of Congress Cataloging-in-Publication Data

African American mosaic: a documetary history from the slave trade to
the twenty-first century / [compiled by] John H. Bracey, Jr., Manisha
Sinha.

    p. cm.

Includes bibliographical references and index.

  ISBN 0-13-092287-0—ISBN 0-13-092288-9

  1. African Americans—History—Sources. I. Bracey, John H.   II. Sinha,
Manisha.

  E184.6.A333 2004

  973'.0496073—dc22

                               2003022536

Editorial Director: Charlyce Jones-Owen
Senior Acquisitions Editor: Charles Cavaliere
Editorial Assistant: Shannon Corliss
Marketing Manager: Heather Shelstad
Senior Marketing Assistant: Jennifer Bryant
Production Liaison: Marianne
  Peters-Riordan
Production Editor: Bruce Hobart
Permissions Coordinator: Ronald Fox
Manufacturing Buyer: Tricia Kenny

Cover Image: "Oneness" by Nelson Stevens. By
  permission of the artist, Nelson Stevens, Pro-
  fessor of Afro-American Studies, University of
  Massachusetts, Amherst
Cover Design: Bruce Kenselaar
Composition/Full-Service Project
  Management: Pine Tree Composition

Pearson Education LTD., London
Pearson Education Singapore, Pte. Ltd
Pearson Education, Canada, Ltd
Pearson Education–Japan
Pearson Education Australia PTY,
  Limited
Pearson Education North Asia Ltd

Pearson Educación de Mexico,
  S.A. de C.V.
Pearson Education Malaysia, Pte. Ltd
Pearson Education, Upper Saddle River,
  New Jersey

ISBN: 0-13-092288-9

Dedicated to the Spirit and Courage of the People of African Descent

and

To the memory of three pioneering scholars of the black experience
and veterans of the struggle to end racial oppression:

Herbert Aptheker
August Meier
Meyer Weinberg

Contents

SEVEN
THE ONSET OF JIM CROW   79

INTRODUCTION   79

EIGHT
THE AGE OF MIGRATIONS   159

INTRODUCTION   159

NINE
A NEW DEAL FOR BLACKS   **233**

INTRODUCTION   233

Ten
Eyes on the Prize   331

Introduction   331

Eleven
And Still We Are Not Saved   415

Introduction   415

Acknowledgments

We would like to acknowledge the help and support of several people who helped bring this volume to fruition. First and foremost, we thank Tricia Loveland, our department secretary, who greatly assisted us at every stage in the preparation of this manuscript. We also thank Sarah Fitzgerald, our work study student, for copying documents for us. It gives us great pleasure to acknowledge the support of all our colleagues and graduate students at the W. E. B. Du Bois Department of Afro-American Studies. We also thank the scores of undergraduate students at the University of Massachusetts, Amherst, whose needs inspired us to substantially revise an early edition of these volumes. We are particularly grateful to two of the original co-editors, the late Professors August Meier and Elliot Rudwick. Darlene Clark Hine, David W. Blight, and Eric Foner reviewed the table of contents and provided invaluable suggestions, for which we are indebted. We thank our editor at Prentice Hall, Charles Cavaliere, for his patience and gentle prodding to complete this manuscript. Finally, we thank our families for their forbearance while we were putting this book together.

Introduction

In the past few decades, the field of African American history has come of age. Not only is it one of the most dynamic areas in American history, containing some of the most exciting contemporary historical debates, but it is also changing the very way in which we view American history as a whole. African American history is not merely the addition of black people to a larger American historical narrative; it has its own issues and concerns. It is not merely the history of oppression and suffering but also one of overcoming against tremendous odds. Finally, African American history leads us to reevaluate the "consensus" view of American history and highlights contradiction and conflict.

Keeping these ideas in mind, we have selected some of the most significant primary documents on the black experience in a two-volume collection. These documents illustrate enduring themes in African American history, the enslavement of black people and growth of a strong black protest tradition. They also reflect the latest research in the field such as the distinct experience of black women and the development of African American culture and communities. The present volume, which deals with the period from Reconstruction to the present, covers the rise and fall of Reconstruction, the segregation and disfranchisement of African Americans that confined them to the ranks of second-class citizens until the triumph of the Civil Rights movement, and the more intractable problems of racial and economic inequality that still confront African Americans today.

The documents are arranged topically and chronologically in six chapters. These volumes may be used in conjunction with a secondary text on black history or by themselves. They are meant to stimulate students into understanding that history is not merely the rote memorization of facts, but the critical reading and interpretation of historical data. As much as possible we have used complete documents or substantial selections from longer documents. We have deliberately kept introductory commentary to a minimum, preferring to let the various "voices" speak for themselves. Documents have been reprinted without revision, except for obvious typographical errors and the fact that the word "Negro" has been capitalized throughout.

In seeking to revise the original one-volume selection of primary documents in African American history, *The Afro-Americans: Selected Documents*, edited by John H. Bracey, Jr., August Meier and the late Elliot Rudwick, we realize that we are following the footsteps of generations of black and white scholars. Despite the common misperception, there is nothing new or faddish about black history. African American leaders and writers such as William Wells Brown and William C. Nell tried to chronicle the role of black people in American history in the face of unremitting racial hostility as early as the nineteenth century. Much of this work was "contributionist" in tone, stressing the contributions of African Americans to the making of the American nation. The first formal work in African American history, George Washington William's *History of the Negro Race in America, 1619–1880,* was published in 1882. By the turn of the century, when the mainstream American academy and universities ignored or caricatured the black historical experience, institutes and associations for the study of black history—such as the Banneker Institute and the Negro Historical Society in Philadelphia, the American Negro Academy in Washington D.C. and the Negro Society for Historical Research founded by Arthur Schomburg in 1911, which lives on as the famous Schomburg Library in New York City—proliferated among African American intellectuals and historians.

The "professionalization" of the field was completed under Carter G. Woodson, the father of black history. Woodson founded the Association for the Study of Negro Life and History in 1915 (now known as the Association for the Study of African American Life and History), the *Journal of Negro History,* and the Negro History Week, which is now Black History Month. A generation of black historians, trained at historically black colleges such as Howard, Fisk, and Atlanta, devoted themselves to writing an objective history of black people following the most rigorous "scientific" standards of the day. The most original and talented of course was the great W. E. B. Du Bois, whose ideas and interpretations prefigured the contours of modern African American history. During the Second World War, when Nazism completely discredited racism in the academy and society, a new generation of black and white "revisionist" historians such as John Hope Franklin and Kenneth Stampp challenged dominant historical interpretations of slavery as a beneficent institution and Reconstruction, when former slaves acquired the right to vote briefly, as a period of corruption and black misrule.

However, it was only with the rise of the Civil Rights Movement and the explosion of social history, or the effort to write history from "the bottom up," that African American history came into its own. Increasingly, African Americans were viewed as the legitimate subjects of history or as historical actors rather than as objects or victims of history. New methodologies borrowed from the social sciences and the use of oral testimony uncovered the history of ordinary African Americans. This last phase in the maturation of black history has also been marked by its "institutionalization" in various departments and institutes in universities and colleges across the country.

Today African American history occupies a central position in American history and is instrumental in the construction of new historical synthesis in the United States. Indeed, the international dimensions of the Atlantic slave trade, the hemispheric nature of racial slavery and its aftermath, and the problem of race throughout the western world suggests—to use a phrase popularized by Hegel who sanguinely claimed that Africans had no history—"the world historical significance" of African American history. We offer this collection of primary documents as part of a long and ongoing effort to uncover the history of people of African descent and to reevaluate American history from the black perspective. We hope it proves useful to students of African American and United States history.

John H. Bracey, Jr.
Manisha Sinha
W. E. B. Du Bois Department of Afro-American Studies
University of Massachusetts, Amherst

African American Mosaic

A Documentary History

from the Slave Trade

to the Twenty-First Century

Volume Two:

From 1865 to the Present

THE FIRST COLORED SENATOR AND REPRESENTATIVES,

In the 41st and 42nd Congress of the United States.

The first seven African Americans to serve in the U.S. Senate and the U.S. House of Representatives. (Courtesy of the Library of Congress.)

Chapter 6

Black Reconstruction

The end of the Civil War and the destruction of slavery raised black hopes to unprecedented levels. African Americans actively sought to define the contours and content of their freedom during Reconstruction. Lincoln's assassination led to a brief period of Presidential Reconstruction under Andrew Johnson. During this time, white southerners, taking advantage of Johnson's pardons, attempted to push freed people back into conditions as close to slavery as possible by instituting "Black Codes" that denied them basic civil and political rights. However, by 1866, black southerners and their radical Republican allies inaugurated Congressional Reconstruction, which nullified the Black Codes and established the legal foundations for African American citizenship. African Americans sought to give meaning to their freedom by reconstituting families that had been torn apart by slavery; acquiring education; developing their own institutions, such as the church and benevolent and fraternal associations; and demanding all the rights of American citizenship and property ownership.

The Freedmen's Bureau, established by the federal government to ease the transition from slavery to freedom, was the first large-scale government agency created to address social problems. One of the most remarkable achievements of Reconstruction was black enfranchisement (excluding women) and the rapid ascension of African Americans to positions of power in local, state, and federal government. Despite black demands and the support of some radical politicians, land in the south was not redistributed to the freed people, and African Americans, though legally free, were forced to labor as agricultural workers, tenants, and sharecroppers. Moreover, most white southerners resisted black rights by every means possible, including the employment of wholesale vigilante violence and racial intimidation through newly founded organizations such as the Ku Klux Klan. The fall of Reconstruction and the disfranchisement of African Americans put an end to the promise of an interracial democracy in the south.

The first document on the Colloquy with black ministers shows how former slaves tried to define their freedom by demanding political rights and economic autonomy. This conversation led to Sherman's famous Field Order Number 15, which settled African Americans in lowcountry South Carolina and Georgia on forty acres of land and gave them a mule. Johnson revoked this order. The role of the Freedman's Bureau and northern "Gideonites," who traveled to the south to teach in freedmen's schools, is amply illustrated by the selection from J.W. Alvord's book. The three Reconstruction amendments and the

Civil Rights Act of 1875 dramatically expanded citizenship and civil rights for black people. The selection from the proceedings of the South Carolina Constitutional Convention of 1868 that inaugurated Reconstruction there reveals the debate over land reform. Racial violence during Reconstruction is epitomized by the description of the famous Hamburg Riot of 1876. The speeches by Henry Turner and George White protesting their expulsion from the Georgia legislature and Congress are examples of the feeling of betrayal among African Americans once Reconstruction came to an end, accompanied by the demise of black political power. In 1883, the Supreme Court overturned the Civil Rights Act of 1875, prompting Frederick Douglass to protest this betrayal of the legacy of the Civil War and Reconstruction. This retreat paved the way for the instituting of racial segregation in the south. Two documents, the memorial from former slaves in Indian territory and noted black Senator Blanche K. Bruce's speech, illustrate the complex interaction between African Americans and Native Americans. Frances Ellen Watkins Harper's speech to the Women's Congress affirms the role of African American women in the struggle for black equality during Reconstruction.

Colloquy with Colored Ministers[1]

On the evening of Thursday, the 12th day of January, 1865, the following persons of African descent met, by appointment, to hold an interview with Edwin M. Stanton, Secretary of War, and Major-General Sherman, to have a conference upon matters relating to the freedmen of the State of Georgia, to wit:

1. *William J. Campbell*, aged fifty-one years, born in Savannah; slave until 1849, and then liberated by will of his mistress, Mrs. Mary Maxwell; for ten years pastor of the First Baptist Church of Savannah, numbering about eighteen hundred members; average congregation nineteen hundred; the church property belonging to the congregation (trustees white) worth eighteen thousand dollars.

2. *John Cox*, aged fifty-eight years, born in Savannah; slave until 1849, when he bought his freedom for eleven hundred dollars; pastor of the Second African Baptist Church; in the ministry fifteen years; congregation twelve hundred and twenty-two persons; church property worth ten thousand dollars, belonging to the congregation.

3. *Ulysses L. Houston*, aged forty-one years, born in Grahamsville, South Carolina; slave 'until the Union army entered Savannah'; owned by Moses Henderson, Savannah; and pastor of Third African Baptist Church, congregation numbering four hundred; church property worth five thousand dollars, belongs to congregation; in the ministry about eight years.

Source: "Colloquy with Colored Ministers," *Journal of Negro History*, vol. XVI, No. 1, January 1931, pp. 88–94. Copyright 1931 Journal of Negro History.

[1]This colloquy is valuable not only for the information concerning the war but for understanding the status of Negroes in Georgia: the effect of the war on them, and their prospects in 1865.

4. *William Bentley,* aged seventy-two years, born in Savannah; slave until twenty-five years of age, when his master, John Waters, emancipated him by will; pastor of Andrew's Chapel, Methodist Episcopal Church (only one of that denomination in Savannah), congregation numbering three hundred and sixty members; church property worth about twenty thousand dollars, and is owned by the congregation; been in the ministry about twenty years; a member of Georgia Conference.

5. *Charles Bradwell,* aged forty years, born in Liberty County, Georgia; slave until 1851; emancipated by will of his master, J. L. Bradwell; local preacher, in charge of the Methodist Episcopal congregation (Andrew's Chapel) in the absence of the minister; in the ministry ten years.

6. *William Gaines,* aged forty-one years, born in Wills County, Georgia; slave 'until the Union forces freed me'; owned by Robert Toombs, formerly United States Senator, and his brother, Gabriel Toombs; local preacher of the Methodist Episcopal Church (Andrew's Chapel); in the ministry sixteen years.

7. *James Hill,* aged fifty-two years, born in Bryan County, Georgia; slave 'up to the time the Union army come in'; owned by H. F. Willings, of Savannah; in the ministry sixteen years.

8. *Glasgow Taylor,* aged seventy-two years, born in Wilkes County, Georgia; slave 'until the Union army come'; owned by A. P. Wetter; is a local preacher of the Methodist Episcopal Church (Andrew's Chapel); in the ministry thirty-five years.

9. *Garrison Frazier,* aged sixty-seven years, born in Granville County, North Carolina; slave until eight years ago, when he bought himself and wife, paying one thousand dollars in gold and silver; is an ordained minister in the Baptist Church, but, his health failing, has now charge of no congregation; has been in the ministry thirty-five years.

10. *James Mills,* aged fifty-six years, born in Savannah; freeborn, and is a licensed preacher of the First Baptist Church; has been eight years in the ministry.

11. *Abraham Burke,* aged forty-eight years, born in Bryan County, Georgia; slave until twenty years ago, when he bought himself for eight hundred dollars; has been in the ministry about ten years.

12. *Arthur Wardell,* aged forty-four years, born in Liberty County, Georgia; slave until 'freed by the Union army'; owned by A. A. Solomons, Savannah, and is a licensed minister in the Baptist Church; has been in the ministry six years.

13. *Alexander Harris,* aged forty-seven years, born in Savannah; free-born; licensed minister of Third African Baptist Church; licensed about one month ago.

14. *Andrew Neal,* aged sixty-one years, born in Savannah; slave 'until the Union army liberated me'; owned by Mr. William Gibbons, and has been deacon in the Third Baptist Church for ten years.

15. *James Porter,* aged thirty-nine years, born in Charleston, South Carolina; free-born, his mother having purchased her freedom; is lay-reader and president of the board of wardens and vestry of St. Stephen's Protestant Episcopal Colored Church in Savannah; has been in communion nine years; the congregation numbers about two hundred persons; the church property is worth about ten thousand dollars, and is owned by the congregation.

16. *Adolphus Delmotte,* aged twenty-eight years, born in Savannah; free-born; is a licensed minister of the Missionary Baptist Church of Milledgeville, congregation numbering about three or four hundred persons; has been in the ministry about two years.

17. *Jacob Godfrey,* aged fifty-seven years, born in Marion, South Carolina; slave 'until the Union army freed me'; owned by James E. Godfrey, Methodist preacher, now in the rebel army; is a classleader, and steward of Andrew's Chapel since 1836.

18. *John Johnson,* aged fifty-one years, born in Bryan County, Georgia; slave 'up to the time the Union army came here'; owned by

W. W. Lincoln, of Savannah; is class-leader, and treasurer of Andrew's Chapel for sixteen years.

19. *Robert N. Taylor,* aged fifty-one years, born in Wilkes County, Georgia; slave 'to the time the Union army come'; was owned by Augustus P. Wetter, Savannah, and is class-leader in Andrew's Chapel—for nine years.

20. *James Lynch,* aged twenty-six years, born in Baltimore, Maryland; free-born; is presiding elder of the Methodist Episcopal Church, and missionary to the Department of the South; has been seven years in the ministry, and two years in the South.

Garrison Frazier being chosen by the persons present to express their common sentiments upon the matters of inquiry, makes answers to inquiries as follows:

1. State what your understanding is in regard to the acts of Congress, and President Lincoln's proclamation, touching the condition of the colored people in the rebel States.

Answer. So far as I understand President Lincoln's proclamation to the rebellious States, it is, that if they would lay down their arms and submit to the laws of the United States before the 1st of January, 1863, all should be well; but if they did not, then all the slaves in the rebel States should be free, henceforth and forever: that is what I understood.

2. State what you understand by slavery, and the freedom that was to be given by the President's Proclamation.

Answer. Slavery is receiving by irresistible power the work of another man, and not by his consent. The freedom, as I understand it, promised by the proclamation, is taking us from under the yoke of bondage and placing us where we could reap the fruit of our own labor, and take care of ourselves, and assist the Government in maintaining our freedom.

3. State in what manner you think you can take care of yourselves, and how can you best assist the Government in maintaining your freedom.

Answer. The way we can best take care of ourselves is to have land, and turn in and till

it by our labor—that is, by the labor of the women, and children, and old men—and we can soon maintain ourselves and have something to spare; and to assist the Government, the young men should enlist in the service of the Government, and serve in such manner as they may be wanted (the rebels told us that they piled them up and made batteries of them, and sold them to Cuba, but we don't believe that). We want to be placed on land until we are able to buy it and make it our own.

4. State in what manner you would rather live, whether scattered among the whites, or in colonies by yourselves.

Answer. I would prefer to live by ourselves, for there is a prejudice against us in the South that will take years to get over; but I do not know that I can answer for my brethren.

[*Mr. Lynch* says he thinks they should not be separated, but live together. All the other persons present being questioned, one by one, answer that they agree with 'brother *Frazier.*']

5. Do you think that there is intelligence enough among the slaves of the South to maintain themselves under the Government of the United States, and the equal protection of its laws, and maintain good and peaceable relations among yourselves and with your neighbors?

Answer. I think there is sufficient intelligence among us to do so.

6. State what is the feeling of the black population of the South toward the Government of the United States; what is the understanding in respect to the present war, its causes and object, and their disposition to aid either side; state fully your views.

Answer. I think you will find there is thousands that are willing to make any sacrifice to assist the Government of the United States, while there is also many that are not willing to take up arms. I do not suppose there is a dozen men that is opposed to the Government. I understand as to the war that the South is the aggressor. President Lincoln was elected President by a majority of the

United States, which guaranteed him the right of holding the office and exercising that right over the whole United States. The South, without knowing what he would do, rebelled. The war was commenced by the rebels before he came into the office. The object of the war was not, at first, to give the slaves their freedom, but the sole object of the war was, at first to bring the rebellious States back into the Union, and their loyalty to the laws of the United States. Afterwards, knowing the value that was set on the slaves by the rebels, the President thought that his proclamation would stimulate them to lay down their arms, reduce them to obedience, and help to bring back the rebel States; and their not doing so has now made the freedom of the slaves a part of the war. It is my opinion that there is not a man in this city that could be started to help the rebels one inch, for that would be suicide. There was two black men left with the rebels, because they had taken an active part for the rebels, and thought something might befall them if they staid behind, but there is not another man. If the prayers that have gone up for the Union army could be read out, you would not get through them these two weeks.

7. State whether the sentiments you now express are those only of the colored people in the city, or do they extend to the colored population through the country, and what are your means of knowing the sentiments of those living in the country?

Answer. I think the sentiments are the same among the colored people of the State. My opinion is formed by personal communication in the course of my ministry, and also from the thousands that followed the Union army, leaving their homes and undergoing suffering. I did not think there would be so many; the number surpassed my expectation.

8. If the rebel leaders were to arm the slaves, what would be its effect?

Answer. I think they would fight as long as they were before the bayonet, and just as soon as they could get away they would desert, in my opinion.

9. What, in your opinion, is the feeling of the colored people about enlisting and serving as soldiers of the United States, and what kind of military service do they prefer?

Answer. A large number have gone as soldiers to Port Royal to be drilled and put in the service, and I think there is thousands of the young men that will enlist; there is something about them that, perhaps, is wrong; they have suffered so long from the rebels, that they want to meet and have a chance with them in the field. Some of them want to shoulder the musket, others want to go into the quartermaster or the commissary's service.

10. Do you understand the mode of enlistment of colored persons in the rebel States, by State agents, under the act of Congress; if yea, state what your understanding is?

Answer. My understanding is that colored persons enlisted by State agents are enlisted as substitutes, and give credit to the States, and do not swell the army, because every black man enlisted by a State agent leaves a white man at home; and, also, that larger bounties are given or promised by the State agents than are given by the States. The great object should be to push through this rebellion the shortest way, and there seems to be something wanting in the enlistment by State agents, for it don't strengthen the army, but takes one away for every colored man enlisted.

11. State what in your opinion is the best way to enlist colored men for soldiers.

Answer. I think, sir, that all compulsory operations should be put a stop to. The ministers would talk to them, and the young men would enlist. It is my opinion that it would be far better for the State agents to stay at home, and the enlistments to be made for the United States under the direction of General Sherman.

In the absence of General Sherman, the following question was asked:

12. State what is the feeling of the colored people in regard to General Sherman, and how far do they regard his sentiments and

actions as friendly to their rights and interests, or otherwise?

Answer. We looked upon General Sherman, prior to his arrival, as a man, in the
providence of God, specially set apart to accomplish this work, and we unanimously
felt inexpressible gratitude to him, looking
upon him as a man that should be honored
for the faithful performance of his duty.
Some of us called upon him immediately
upon his arrival, and it is probable he did
not meet the Secretary with more courtesy
than he met us. His conduct and deportment
towards us characterized him as a friend
and a gentleman. We have confidence in
General Sherman, and think that what concerns us could not be under better hands.
This is our opinion now from the short acquaintance and intercourse we have had.

[*Mr. Lynch* states that, with his limited acquaintance with General Sherman, he is unwilling to express an opinion. All others
present declare their agreement with Mr.
Frazier about General Sherman.]

Some conversation upon general subjects
relating to General Sherman's march then
ensued, of which no note was taken."

From the Journals of Charlotte Forten Grimke

Charlotte Forten Grimke

Tuesday, October 28, 1862. It was nearly
dark when we reached St. Helena's, where
we found Miss T. [owne]'s carriage awaiting
us, and then we three and our driver, had a
long drive along the lonely roads in the dark
night. How easy it sh'ld have been for a
band of guerillas—had any chanced that
way—to seize and hang us. But we found
nothing of the kind. We were in a jubilant
state of mind and sang "John Brown" with a
will as we drove through the pines and pal-
mettos. Arrived at the Superintendent's
house[;] we were kindly greeted by him and
the ladies and shown into a lofty *ceilinged*
parlor where a cheerful wood fire glowed in
the grate, and we soon began to feel quite at
home in the very heart of Rebeldom; only
that I do not at all realize yet that we are in
S.[outh] C.[arolina]. It is all a strange wild
dream, from which I am constantly expecting to awake.

Wednesday, October 29. We left Oaklands
and drove to the school. It is kept by Miss
[Ellen] Murray and Miss Towne in the little
Baptist Church, which is beautifully situated
in a grove of live oaks. Never saw anything
more beautiful than these trees. It is strange
that we do not hear of them at the North.
They are the first objects that attract one's attention here. They are large, noble trees with
small glossy green leaves. Their beauty consists in the long bearded moss with which
every branch is heavily draped. This moss is
singularly beautiful, and gives a solemn almost funeral aspect to the trees.

We went into the school, and heard the
children read and spell. The teachers tell us
that they have made great improvement in a
very short time, and I noticed with pleasure
how bright, how eager to learn many of
them seem. The singing delighted me most.
They sang beautifully in their rich, sweet

Source: From *The Journals of Charlotte Forten Grimke,* 1854–1892. Ms. Moorland-Spingarn Library, Howard University.

clear tones, and with that peculiar swaying motion which I had noticed before in the older people, and which seems to make their singing all the more effective. Besides several other tunes they sang "Marching Along" with much spirit, and then one of their own hymns "Down in the Lonesome Valley," which is sweetly solemn and most beautiful. Dear children! born in slavery, but free at last? May God preserve to you all the blessings of freedom, and may you be in every possible way fitted to enjoy them. My heart goes out to you. I shall be glad to do all that I can to help you.—

Sunday, November 2. Drove to church to-day—to the same little Baptist Church that the school is held in. The people came in slowly. They have no way of telling the time. About eleven they had all assembled; the church was full. Old and young were there assembled in their Sunday dresses. Clean gowns on, clean head handkerchiefs, bright colored, of course, I noticed that some had even reached the dignity of straw hats, with bright feathers. The services were very interesting. The minister, Mr. P.[hillips?] is an earnest N.[ew] E.[ngland] man. The singing was very beautiful, sat there in a kind of trance and listened to it, and while I listened looked through the open windows into the beautiful grove of oaks with their moss drapery. "Ah w'ld that my tongue c'ld utter the thoughts that arise in me." But it cannot. The sermon was quite good. But I enjoyed nothing so much as the singing—the wonderful, beautiful singing. There can be no doubt that these people have a great deal of musical talent. It was a beautiful sight,— their enthusiasm. After the service two couples were married. Then the meeting was out. The various groups under the trees forming a very pretty picture. We drove to the Episcopal Church afterward where the aristocracy of Rebeldom was to worship.

Saturday, November 8. Spent part of the morn. in the store which was more crowded than ever. So much gold and silver I've not

seen for many months. These people must have been hoarding it up for a long time. They are rather unreasonable, and expect one to wait on a dozen at once. But it is not strange. Miss T.[owne] came this afternoon, and gave medicine to Tilla's baby, which seems, I think, a little better; and all the other children. Everyone of them has the whooping cough.'

Monday, November 10. We taught—or rather commenced teaching the children "John Brown" which they entered into eagerly. I felt to the full the significance of *that* song being sung here in S.[outh] C.[arolina] by little negro children, by those whom he— the glorious old man—died to save. Miss [Laura] T.[owne] told them about him. A poor mulatto man is in one of our people's houses, a man from the North, who assisted Mr. [Samuel D.] Phillips (a nephew of Wendell P. [hillips]) when he was here, in teaching school; he seems to be quite an intelligent man. He is suffering from fever. I shall be glad to take as good care of him as I can. It is so sad to be ill, helpless and poor, and so far away from home.

Thursday, November 13. Talked to the children a little while to-day about the noble Toussaint. They listened very attentively. It is well that they sh'ld know what one of their own color c'ld do for his race. I long to inspire them with courage and ambition (of a noble sort), and high purposes. It is noticeable how very few mulattoes there are here. Indeed in our school, with one or two exceptions, the children are all black.

A little mulatto child strayed into the school house yesterday—a pretty little thing with large beautiful black eyes and lovely long lashes. But so dirty! I longed to seize and thoroughly cleanse her. The mother is a good-looking woman, but quite black. "Thereby," I doubt not, "hangs a tale."

This eve. Harry, one of the men on the place, came in for a lesson. He is most eager to learn, and is really a scholar to be proud of. He learns rapidly. I gave him his first lesson in writing to-night, and his progress was wonderful. He held his pen almost perfectly right the first time. He will very soon learn to write, I think. I must inquire who w'ld like to take lessons at night. Whenever I am well enough it will be a real pleasure to teach them.

Monday, November 17. Had a dreadfully wearying day in school, of which the less said the better. Afterward drove the ladies to "The Corner," a collection of negro houses, whither Miss T.[owne] went on a doctoring expedition. The people there are very pleasant. Saw a little baby, just borne [sic] today—and another—old Venus' great grandchild for whom I made the little pink frock. These people are very grateful. The least kindness that you do them they insist on repaying in some way. We have had a quantity of eggs and potatoes brought us despite our remonstrances. Today one of the women gave me some Tanias. Tania is a queer looking root. After it is boiled it looks a little like potato, but is much larger. I don't like the taste.

Tuesday, November 18. After school went to the Corner again. Stopped at old Susy's house to see some sick children. Old Susy is a character. Miss T.[owne] asked her if she wanted her old master to come back again. Most emphatically she answered. "No *indeed,* missus, no indeed dey treat we too bad. Dey tuk ebery one of my chilen away from me. When we sick and c'ldnt work dey tuk away all our food from us; gib us nutten to eat. Dey's orful hard Missis." When Miss T.[owne] told her that some of the people wanted their old masters to come back, a look of supreme contempt came to old Susy's withered face. "That's cause dey's got no sense den, missus," she said indignantly. Susy has any quantity of children and grandchildren, and she thanks God that she can now have some of them with her in her old age. To-night gave Cupid a lesson in the alphabet. He is not a brilliant scholar, but he tries hard to learn, and so I am sure will succeed in time. A man from another plantation

came in for a lesson. L.[izzie Hunn] attended to him while I had Cupid. He knows his letters, and seems very bright.

Sunday, November 23. Attended church to-day. T'was even a pleasanter experience than before. Saw several new arrivals there—old ones returned, rather—among them Mr. S.[amuel] Phillips, a nephew of *the* Phillips. He has not the glorious beauty of his illustrious relative, but still has some-what the Phillips style of face. He is not at all handsome; has bright red hair, but a pleasant face, and an air *distingue.* After the sermon an old negro made a touching and most effective prayer. Then the minister read Gen. Saxton's Proclamation for Thanksgiving—which is grand—the very best and noblest that c'ld have been penned. I like and admire the Gen.[eral] more than ever now. Six couples were married to-day. Some of the dresses were unique. Am sure one must have worn a cast-off dress of her mistress's. It looked like white silk covered with lace. The lace sleeves, and other trimmings were in rather a decayed state and the white cotton gloves were well ventilated. But the bride looked none the less happy for that. Only one had the slightest claim to good looks, and she was a demure little thing with a neat, plain silk dress on. T'was amusing to see some of the headresses. One, of tattered flowers and ribbons, was very ridiculous. But no matter for that. I am *truly* glad that the poor creatures are trying to live right and virtuous lives. As usual we had some fine singing. It was very pleasant to be at church again. For two Sundays past I had not been, not feeling well.

This eve. our boys and girls with others from across the creek came in and sang a long time for us. Of course we had the old favorites "Down in the Lonesome Valley," and "Roll, Jordan, Roll," and "No man can hender me," and beside those several shouting tunes that we had not heard before; they are very wild and strange. It was impossible for me to understand many of the words although I asked them to repeat them for me. I only know that one had something about "De Nell Am Ringing." I think that was the refrain; and of another, some of the words were "Christ build the church widout no hammer nor nail." "Jehovah Halleluhiah," which is a grand thing, and "Hold the light," an especial favorite of mine—they sang also with great spirit. The leader of the singing was Prince, a large black boy, from Mr. R. [uggle]'s place. He was full of the shouting spirit, and c'ld not possibly keep still. It was amusing to see his gymnastic performances. They were quite in the Ethiopian Methodists' style. He has really a very fine bass voice. I enjoyed their singing so much, and sh'ld have enjoyed it so much more if some dear ones who are far away c'ld have listened it to [sic] with me.

How delighted they would have been. The effect of the singing has been to make me feel a little sad and lonely to-night. A yearning for congenial companionship *will* sometimes come over me in the few leisure moments I have in the house. 'Tis well they are so few. Kindness, most invariable,—for which I am most grateful—I meet with constantly, but congeniality I find not at all in this house. But silence, foolish murmurer. He who knows all things knows that it was for no selfish motive that I came here, far from the few who are so dear to me. Therefore let me not be selfish now. Let the work to which I have solemnly pledged myself fill up my whole existence to the exclusion of all vain longings.

Thursday, November 27. Thanksgiving Day. This, according to Gen. [Rufus] Saxton's noble Proclamation, was observed as a day of "Thanksgiving and praise." It has been a lovely day—cool, delicious air, golden, gladdening sunlight, deep blue sky, with soft white clouds floating over it. Had we no other causes the glory and beauty of the day alone make it a day for which to give thanks. But we have other causes, great and glorious, which unite to make this peculiarly a day of thanksgiving and praise. It has been a general holiday. According to Gen. Saxton's

orders an animal was killed on each plantation that the people might to-day eat fresh meat, which is a great luxury to them, and indeed to all of us here. This morning a large number—Superintendents, teachers, and freed people, assembled in the little Baptist church. It was a sight that I shall not soon forget—that crowd of eager, happy black faces from which the shadow of slavery had forever passed. "Forever free!" "Forever free!" Those magical words were all the time singing themselves in my soul, and never before have I felt so truly grateful to God. The singing was, as usual, very beautiful. I thought I had never heard my favorite "Down in the Lonesome Valley" so well sung. After an appropriate prayer and sermon by Rev. Mr. Phillips, Gen. Saxton made a short but spirited speech to the people—urging the young men to enlist in the regiment now forming under Col. T. [homas] W. [entworth] Higginson. That was the first intimation I had had of Mr. H. [igginson]'s being down here. I am greatly rejoiced thereat. He seems to me of all fighting men the one best fitted to command a regiment of colored soldiers. The mention of his [name] recalled the happy days passed last summer in Mass. [achusetts], when day after day, in the streets of W. [orcester] we used to see the indefatigable *Capt. H.* [igginson] drilling his white company. I never saw him so full of life and energy—entering with his whole soul into his work—without thinking what a splendid general he w'ld make. And that too may come about. Gen. Saxton said today that he hoped to see him commander of an army of black men. The Gen. told the people how nobly Mr. H. [igginson] had stood by Anthony Burns, in the old dark days, even suffering imprisonment for his sake; and assured [them] that they might feel sure of meeting with no injustice under the leadership of such a man; that he w'ld see to it that they were not wronged in any way. Then he told them the story of Robert Small[s], and added "Today Robt. came to see me. I asked him how he was getting on in the store which he is keeping for the freed people. He said he was doing very well—making fifty dollars a week, sometimes. 'But,' said he[,] 'Gen. I'm going to stop keeping store. I'm going to enlist!' When you can make fifty doll[ar]s. a week keeping store? 'Yes Sir,' he replied, 'I'm going to enlist as a private in the black regiment. How can I expect to keep my freedom if I'm not willing to fight for it? Suppose the Secesh sh'ld get back here again? what good w'ld my fifty doll[ar]s. do me then? Yes, Sir, I sh'ld enlist if I were making a thousand dollars a week.' " Mrs. [Francis] Gage then made a few beautiful and earnest remarks. She told the people about the slaves in Santa Cruz, how they rose and conquered their masters, and declared themselves free, and no one dared to oppose them. And how, soon after, the governor rode into the market-place and proclaimed emancipation to all the people of the Danish W.[est] I.[ndies]. She then made a beautiful appeal to the mothers, urging them not to keep back their sons from the war fearing they might be killed but to send them forth willingly and gladly as she had done hers, to fight for liberty. It must have been something very novel and strange to them to hear a woman speak in public, but they listened with great attention and seemed much moved by what she said. Then Gen. Saxton made a few more remarks. I think what he said will have much effect on the young men here. There has been a good deal of distrust about joining the regiment[,] the soldiers were formerly so unjustly treated by the Government. But they trust Gen. Saxton. He told them what a victory the black troops had lately won on the Georgian coast, and what a great good they had done for their race in winning: they had proved to their enemies that the black man can and will fight for his freedom. After the Gen. had done speaking the people [sang] "Marching Along," with great spirit. After church there was a wedding. This is a very common occurrence here. Of course the bridal costumes are generally very unique and comical, but the principal actors are fortunately quite unconscious of it, and look so proud and

happy while enjoying this—one of the many privileges that freedom has bestowed upon them—that it is quite pleasant to see them. Beside the Gen. and Miss. G.[age] there were several other strangers present;—ladies from the North who come down here to teach. In Miss T.[owne]'s box came my parcel—so long looked for—containing letters from my dear Mary S.[hepard], Aunt M.[argaretta], Nellie A.[lexander?] and Mrs. J. and a "Liberator," the first that I have seen since leaving home. How great a pleasure it is to see it. It is familiar and delightful to look upon as the face of an old friend. It is of an old date—October 31st—but it is not the less welcome for that. And what a significant fact it is that one may now sit here in safety—here in the rebellious little Palmetto State and read the "Liberator," and display it to one's friends, rejoicing over it in the fulness of one's heart as a very great treasure. It is fitting that we sh'ld give to this—the pioneer paper in the cause of human rights—a hearty welcome to the land where, until so recently, those rights have been most barbarously trampled upon. We do not forget that it is in fact directly traceable to the exertions of the editor of this paper and those who have labored so faithfully with him, that the Northern people now occupy in safety the S.[outh] C.[arolina] shore; that freedom now blesses it, that it is, for the first time, a place worth living in. This eve. commenced a long letter to Mr. [William Lloyd] Garrison. Composed partly of to-day's journalism, and partly of other things that I thought w'ld interest him. He can publish it in the "Liberator," if he thinks it worth printing, which I do not. Truly this has been a delightful day to me. I recal [sic] with pleasure the pleasant Thanks-giving days passed in N.[ew] E.[ngland] in Mass.[achusetts], which I believe I am in the habit of considering as *all* N.[ew] E.[ngland]. But this has been the happiest, the most jubilant Thanksgiving day of my life. We hear of cold weather and heavy snow-storms up in the North land. But here roses and oleanders are blooming in the open air. Figs and oranges are ripening, the sunlight is warm and bright, and over all shines gloriously the blessed light of Freedom—Freedom forevermore!

Sunday November 30. Am in a writing mood to-night, and think I will give to you, my dearest A.[,] a more minute description of the people around than I've yet given to anyone. I shall write down their names too, that I may remember them always. Don't know them thoroughly enough yet to say much about their characters. To begin with the older ones.

First there is old Harriet. She is a very kind, pleasant old soul. Comes from Darien G.[eorgia]. Her parents were Africans. She speaks a *very* foreign tongue. Three of her children have been sold from her. Her master's son killed somebody in a duel, and was obliged to "pay money" H.[arriet] says. I suppose she means to give bail. And she and her children were sold to this place, to raise the money. Then there is her daughter Tillah. Poor creature, she has a dear little baby, Annie, who for weeks has been dangerously ill with whooping cough and fever. Our good Miss T.[owne] attends it, and does all that can be done, but the baby is still very ill. For Tillah's sake I hope it will get well. She is devoted to it night and day. T.[illah]'s husband is a gallant looking young soldier—a member of the black regiment. H.[arriet]'s mother, Bella, is rather a querulous body. But who can blame her? She has had enough to try her sorely. One by one her children at a tender age have been dragged from her to work in the cotton fields. She herself has been made to work when most unfit for it. She has had to see her own children cruelly beaten. Is it strange that these things sh'ld have embittered her? But she has much of the milk of human kindness left her yet. She nurses her poor baby faithfully, and often, old as she is, sits up the entire night with it. Harry is another of her sons. I have told you, dear A., how bright, how eager to learn, he is. His wife, Tamar, is a good-natured easy soul. She has several nice little children, and

the baby—Mary Lincoln—as Mr. [T. Edwin] R.[uggles] the Superintendent has named her—is a very cunning little creature, an especial pet of ours. Celia is one of the best women on the place. She is a cripple. Her feet and limbs were so badly frozen by exposure that her legs were obliged to be amputated just above the knees. But she manages to get about almost as actively as any of the others. Her husband, Thomas, has been a soldier, and is now quite ill with pneumonia. She has several children—Rose, who is our little maid, Olivia the eldest, Dolly, a bright little thing who goes to school with me every morn. and who likes to go. Lastly Aikin, whose proper name is Thomas. He is an odd little fellow, very much spoiled. Amaretta, Celia's sister is our laundress and cook. I like her very much. Then there is Wilhelmina, a mulatto (the others are all black). She comes from Virginia, and speaks therefore quite intelligibly. She is a good sensible woman, and both she and her husband Robt.,—who is one of my night pupils—are most anxious for their three little ones to learn. Cupid our major-domo. is as obliging as possible. A shrewd fellow, who knows well what he is about. His wife Patience, is Tamar's sister, and lives across the creek at Pollywana. Their children—two of them—come to our school. They are good scholars. I do enjoy hearing Cupid and Harry tell about the time that the Secesh had to flee. The time of the "gun shoot," as they call the taking of Bay Point, which is opposite Hilton Head. It delights them greatly to recall that time. Their master had the audacity to venture back even while the Union troops were occupying Beaufort. H.[arry] says he tried to persuade him to go back with him, assuring him that the Yankees w'ld shoot them all when they came. "Bery well sur," he replied[,] "if I go wid you I be good as dead, so if I got the dead, I might's well dead here as anywhere. So I'll stay and wait for the Yankees." He told me that he knew all the time that his master was not telling the truth. Cupid says the master told the people to get all the furniture together and take it over to Pollywana, and to stay on that side themselves, "so" says Cupid, "dey c'ld jus' swap us all and put us in de boat. And he telled me to row Patience and de chilens down to a certain pint, and den I c'ld come back if I choose." "Jus' as if I was gwine to be sich a goat" adds Cupid, with a look and gesture of ineffable contempt. The *finale* of the story is that the people left the premises and hid themselves so that when the master returned not one of all his "faithful servants" was to be found to go into slavery with him, and he was obliged to return, a disappointed, but it is to be hoped, a wiser man.

As I sat on the stand and looked around on the various groups, I thought I had never seen a sight so beautiful. There were the black soldiers, in their blue coats and scarlet pants, the officers of this and other regiments in their handsome uniforms, and crowds of lookers-on, men, women and children, grouped in various attitudes, under the trees. The faces of all wore a happy, eager, expectant look. The exercises commenced by a prayer from Rev. Mr. [James H.] Fowler, Chaplain of the Reg. An ode written for the occasion by Prof. [John] Zachos, originally a Greek, now Sup.[erintendent] of Paris Island, was read by himself, and then sung by the whites. Col. H.[igginson] introduced Dr. [William] Brisbane in a few elegant and graceful words. He (Dr. B.[risbane]) read the President's Proclamation, which was warmly cheered. Then the beautiful flags presented by Dr. [George] Cheever's Church were presented to Col. H.[igginson] for the Reg. in an excellent and enthusiastic speech, by Rev. Mr. [Mansfield] French. Immediately at the conclusion, some of the colored people—of their own accord sang "My Country Tis of Thee." It was a touching and beautiful incident, and Col. Higginson, in accepting the flags made it the occasion of some happy remarks. He said that *that* tribute was far more effecting than any speech he c'ld make. He spoke for some time, and all that he said was grand, glorious. He seemed inspired. Nothing c'ld have been better, more perfect. And Dr. R.[ogers] told

me afterward that the Col. was much affected. That tears were in his eyes. He is as Whittier says, truly a "sure man." The men all admire and love him. There is a great deal of personal magnetism about him, and his kindness is proverbial. After he had done speaking he delivered the flags to the color-bearers with a few very impressive remarks to them. They each then, Prince Rivers, and Robert Sutton, made very good speeches indeed, and were loudly cheered. Gen. Saxton and Mrs. Gage spoke very well. The good Gen. was received with great enthusiasm, and throughout the morning—every little while it seemed to me three cheers were given for him. A Hymn written I believe, by Mr. Judd, was sung, and then all the people united with the Reg. in singing "John Brown." It was grand. During the exercises, it was announced that [John C.] Fremont was appointed Commander-in-Chief of the Army, and this was received with enthusiastic and prolonged cheering.

Saturday January 31. In B.[eaufort] we spent nearly all our time at Harriet Tubman's otherwise [*sic*] "Moses." She is a wonderful woman—a real heroine. Has helped off a large number of slaves, after taking her own freedom. She told us that she used to hide them in the woods during the day and go around to get provisions for them. Once she had with her a man named Joe, for whom a reward of $1500 was offered. Frequently, in different places she found handbills exactly describing him, but at last they reached in safety the Suspension Bridge over the Falls and found themselves in Canada. Until then, she said, Joe had been very silent. In vain had she called his attention to the glory of the Falls. He sat perfectly still—moody, it seemed, and w'ld not even glance at them. But when she said, "Now we are in Can.[ada]" he sprang to his feet—with a great shout and sang and clapped his hands in a perfect delirium of joy. So when they got out, and he first touched *free* soil, he shouted and hurrahed "as if he were crazy"—she said. How exciting it was to hear her tell the story. And to hear her sing the very scraps of jubilant hymns that he sang. She said the ladies crowded around them, and some laughed and some cried. My own eyes were full as I listened to her—the heroic woman! A reward of $10,000 was offered for her by the Southerners, and her friends deemed it best that she sh'ld, for a time find refuge in Can.[ada]. And she did so, but only for a short time. She came back and was soon at the good brave work again. She is living in B.[eaufort] now; keeping an eating house. But she wants to go North, and will probably do so ere long. I am glad I saw her—*very* glad.

United States Constitution: Reconstruction Amendments

AMENDMENT XIII [1865]

Section 1. Neither slavery nor involuntary servitude, except as a punishment for crime whereof the party shall have been duly convicted, shall exist within the United States, or any place subject to their jurisdiction.

Section 2. Congress shall have power to enforce this article by appropriate legislation.

AMENDMENT XIV [1868]

Section 1. All persons born or naturalized in the United States, and subject to the jurisdiction thereof, are citizens of the United States and of the State wherein they reside. No State shall make or enforce any law which shall abridge the privileges or immunities of citizens of the United States; nor shall any State deprive any person of life, liberty, or property, without due process of law; nor deny to any person within its jurisdiction the equal protection of the laws.

Section 2. Representatives shall be apportioned among the several States according to their respective numbers, counting the whole number of persons in each State, excluding Indians not taxed. But when the right to vote at any election for the choice of electors for President and Vice President of the United States, Representatives in Congress, the Executive and Judicial officers of a State, or the members of the Legislature thereof, is denied to any of the male inhabitants of such State, being twenty-one years of age, and citizens of the United States, or in any way abridged, except for participation in rebellion, or other crime, the basis of representation therein shall be reduced in the proportion which the number of such male citizens shall bear to the whole number of male citizens twenty-one years of age in such State.

Section 3. No person shall be a Senator or Representative in Congress, or elector of President and Vice President, or hold any office, civil or military, under the United States, or under any State, who, having previously taken an oath, as a member of Congress, or as an officer of the United States, or as a member of any State legislature, or as an executive or judicial officer of any State, to support the Constitution of the United States, shall have engaged in insurrection or rebellion against the same, or given aid or comfort to the enemies thereof. But Congress may by a vote of two-thirds of each House, remove such disability.

Section 4. The validity of the public debt of the United States, authorized by law, including debts incurred for payment of pensions and bounties for services in suppressing insurrection or rebellion, shall not be questioned. But neither the United States nor any State shall assume or pay any debt or obligation incurred in aid of insurrection or rebellion against the United States, or any claim for the loss or emancipation of any slave; but all such debts, obligations and claims shall be held illegal and void.

Section 5. The Congress shall have power to enforce, by appropriate legislation, the provisions of this article.

AMENDMENT XV [1870]

Section 1. The right of citizens of the United States to vote shall not be denied or abridged by the United States or by any State on account of race, color, or previous condition of servitude.

Section 2. The Congress shall have power to enforce this article by appropriate legislation.

Excerpts from the Proceedings of the Constitutional Convention of South Carolina

The Committee on Petitions, to whom was referred the preamble and resolution relative to petitioning Congress for a grant of one million dollars to be appropriated for the purchase of lands in this State, ask leave to report that they have duly considered the same, and are of the opinion that the prayer of your petitioner should be granted, and that the President of this Convention be requested to transmit a copy of the preamble and resolution to the Congress of the United States at as early a date as practicable.

W. E. Rose, *Chairman.*

. . . **Mr. Cain.** I offer this resolution with good intentions. I believe there is need of

Source: From *Proceedings of the Constitutional Convention of South Carolina.* (Charleston: Denny and Perry, 1868), Vol. I, pp. 376, 378–82, 400–406, 419–24, 438.

immediate relief to the poor people of the State. I know from my experience among the people, there is pressing need of some measures to meet the wants of the utterly destitute. The gentleman says it will only take money out of the Treasury. Well that is the intention. I do not expect to get it anywhere else. I expect to get the money, if at all, through the Treasury of the United States, or some other department. It certainly must come out of the Government. I believe such an appropriation would remove a great many of the difficulties now in the State and do a vast amount of good to poor people. It may be that we will not get it, but that will not debar us from asking. It is our privilege and right. Other Conventions have asked from Congress appropriations. Georgia and other States have sent in their petitions. One has asked for $30,000,000 to be appropriated to the Southern States. I do not see any inconsistency in the proposition presented by myself.... This is a measure of relief to those thousands of freed people who now have no lands of their own. I believe the possession of lands and homesteads is one of the best means by which a people is made industrious, honest and advantageous to the State. I believe it is a fact well known, that over three hundred thousand men, women and children are homeless, landless. The abolition of slavery has thrown these people upon their own resources. How are they to live. I know the philosopher of the New York Tribune says, "root hog or die;" but in the meantime we ought to have some place to root. My proposition is simply to give the hog some place to root. I believe if the proposition is sent to Congress, it will certainly receive the attention of our friends. I believe the whole country is desirous to see that this State shall return to the Union in peace and quiet, and that every inhabitant of the State shall be made industrious and profitable to the State. I am opposed to this Bureau system. I want a system adopted that will do away with the Bureau, but I cannot see how it can be done unless the people have homes. As long as people are working on shares and contracts, and at the end of every year are in debt, so long will they and the country suffer. But give them a chance to buy lands, and they become steady, industrious men. That is the reason I desire to bring this money here and to assist them to buy lands. It will be the means of encouraging them to industry if the petition be granted by Congress. It will be the means of meeting one of the great wants of the present among the poor. It will lay the foundation for the future prosperity of the country as no other measure will at this time, because it will bring about a reconciliation in the minds of thousands of these helpless people, which nothing else can. This measure, if carried out, will bring capital to the State and stimulate the poor to renewed efforts in life, such as they never had before. Such a measure will give to the landholders relief from their embarrassments financially, and enable them to get fair compensation for their lands. It will relieve the Government of the responsibility of taking care of the thousands who now are fed at the Commissaries and fostered in laziness, I have gone through the country and on every side I was besieged with questions: How are we to get homesteads, to get lands? I desire to devise some plan, or adopt some measure by which we can dissipate one of the arguments used against us, that the African race will not work. I do not believe the black man hates work any more than the white man does. Give these men a place to work, and I will guarantee before one year passes, there will be no necessity for the Freedman's Bureau, or any measure aside from those measures which a people may make in protecting themselves.

But a people without homes become wanderers. If they possess lands they have an interest in the soil, in the State, in its commerce, its agriculture, and in everything pertaining to the wealth and welfare of the State. If these people had homes along the lines of railroads, and the lands were divided and sold in small farms, I will guarantee our railroads will make fifty times as much money, banking systems will be advanced by virtue of the settlement of the people throughout the whole State. We want these large tracts of land cut up. The land is productive, and there is nothing to prevent the greatest and highest prosperity. What we need is a system of small farms. Every farmer owning his own land will feel he is in possession of something. It will have a tendency to settle the minds of the people in the State and settle many difficulties. In the rural districts now there is constant discontent, constant misapprehension between the parties, a constant disregard for each other. One man won't make an engagement to work, because he fears if he makes a contract this year, he will be cheated again as he thinks he was last year. We have had petitions from planters asking the Convention to disabuse the minds of the freedmen of the thought that this Convention has any lands at its disposal, but I do desire this Convention to do something at least to relieve the wants of these poor suffering people. I believe this measure, if adopted and sent to Congress, will indicate to the people that this Convention does desire they shall possess homes and have relief.

Some of my friends say that the sum is too small, and ask why I do not make it more. I made it a million, because I thought there would be more probability of getting one million than five. It might be put into the hands of the Bureau, and I am willing to trust the Bureau. . . . I do not desire to have a foot of land in this State confiscated. I want every man to stand upon his own character. I want these lands purchased by the government, and the people afforded an opportunity to buy from the government. I believe every man ought to carve out for himself a character and position in this life. I believe every man ought to be made to work by some means or other, and if he does not, he must go down. I believe if the same amount of money that has been employed by the Bureau in feeding lazy, worthless men and women, had been expended in purchasing lands, we would to-day have no need of the Bureau. Millions upon millions have been expended, and it is still going on *ad infinitum.* I propose to let the poor people buy these lands, the government to be paid back in five years time. It is one of the great cries of the enemies of reconstruction, that Congress has constantly fostered laziness. I want to have the satisfaction of showing that the freedmen are as capable and willing to work as any men on the face of the earth. This measure will save the State untold expenses. I believe there are hundreds of persons in the jail and penitentiary cracking rock to-day who have all the instincts of honesty, and who, had they an opportunity of making a living, would never have been found in such a place. I think if Congress will accede to our request, we shall be benefited beyond measure, and save the State from taking charge of paupers, made such by not having the means to earn a living for themselves.

I can look to a part of my constituency, men in this hall, mechanics, plasterers, carpenters, engineers, men capable of doing all kind of work, now idle because they cannot find any work in the city. Poverty stares them in the face, and their children are in want. They go to the cotton houses, but can find no labor. They are men whose honesty and integrity has never been called in question. They are suffering in consequence of the poverty-stricken condition of the city and State. I believe the best measure is to open a field where they can labor, where they can take the hoe and the axe, cut down the forest, and make the whole land blossom as the Garden of Eden, and prosperity pervade the whole land.

Now, the report of Major General Howard gives a surplus of over seven millions in the Freedman's Bureau last year. Out of that seven millions I propose we ask Congress to make an appropriation of one million, which will be properly distributed and then leave several millions in that Department, my friend from Barnwell notwithstanding.

I think there could be no better measure for this Convention to urge upon Congress. If that body should listen to our appeal, I have no doubt we shall be benefited. This measure of relief, it seems to me, would come swiftly. It is a swift messenger that comes in a week's time after it is passed; so that in the month of February or March the people may be enabled to go to planting and raising crops for the ensuring year. One gentleman says it will take six months or a year, but I hope, with the assistance of the Government, we could accomplish it in less time. . . . If this measure is carried out, the results will be that we will see all along our lines of railroad and State roads little farms, log cabins filled with happy families, and thousands of families coming on the railroads with their products. There will also spring up depots for the reception of cotton, corn and all other cereals. Prosperity will return to the State, by virtue of the people being happy, bound to the Government by a tie that cannot be broken. The taxes, that are so heavy now that men are compelled to sell their horses, will be lightened. I want to see the State alive, to hear the hum of the spindle and the mills! I want to see cattle and horses, and fowls, and everything that makes up a happy home and family. I want to see the people shout with joy and gladness. There shall then be no antagonism between white men and black men, but we shall all realize the end of our being, and realize that we are all made to dwell upon the earth in peace and happiness. The white man and the black man then work in harmony, and secure prosperity to all coming generations. . . .

Mr. W. J. Whipper. In attempting to speak upon this question, it is with no view of defeating the resolution or adoption of the report of the Committee. I intend to vote against the measure, and take this opportunity of saying so. I am the more zealous to do so when I find members of this body oscillating as they are, and openly declaring that they are going to vote for it, though believing it wrong. I am the more zealous of doing so when I find members afraid to follow their honest convictions; and then meet their constituency. Whatever may be my conviction as to the policy of this measure, I, in my heart of hearts, believe it will be detrimental to the people and detrimental to the State, and for that reason shall record my vote against it. I am not afraid to meet my constituents, nor afraid to meet the people of South Carolina, and answer for all that I shall do here, believing it to be for their best interest. I am willing that time should decide as to the propriety of the course I pursue in this body. I say it is my earnest desire that that petition should be voted down, as it should have been without discussion.

With regard to the gentleman from Barnwell, upon whom it has been the province of the delegates to pounce so wickedly, I would say he has told much that is true, and much that they will find hereafter incontrovertible.

As to the office seeking of the Charleston delegates, I have nothing to do.

In the first place, I regard the petition a failure. I am opposed to one million of dollars being brought to the State of South Carolina to be disposed of as that petition proposes. I am in favor of any measure of relief that will affect the people permanently; but if we can devise no other measure than this, then I am opposed to it. Admitting it can be done, that Congress may appropriate one million of dollars, what will be the result? The gentleman from Charleston tells you it will give homes to one-fourth of the people of the State. What kind of homes would they be? It would place them in possession of five and one-seventh acres; just about enough to starve to death decently that one-fourth of the people. If you want to make a man an everlasting pauper, do as the United States did in my district, make him the owner of some ten acres. He cannot raise more than enough to feed his babies upon it. Men in this State must have more land. . . . I claim that this measure will not benefit the people of South Carolina, and upon that ground I oppose it. The very moment this resolution passes and the papers publish that a petition has been sent to Congress to buy lands for the poor of this State, a clamor for land will at once arise, the freedmen will forsake their contracts and at once leave their places of employment. You raise the hopes of the entire poor people of the country, you draw around the land offices, which they will inevitably create, a multitude, three fourths of whom will be compelled to go away with shattered hopes. Let me give you an illustration. In my district quite a scarcity of provisions existed. The Bureau, in its wisdom and charity, sent to that district twelve hundred bushels of corn, and I know that I am speaking the sentiments of my constituents when I say that that distribution of corn had an injurious effect upon labor.

This miserable meagre measure of relief but looses the laborer from the land and raises his hopes, leading him to believe he is to realize all he has longed for for years, and with that object in view goes to the land office perhaps, only to return to his house disappointed, and see his prospects for another year frustrated. You will have three-fourth without an inch of land, and another fourth with but five and one-seventh acres. If you wish to see such a state of affairs, vote for that petition. If Congress does not, in its wisdom, see fit to withhold this loan, you will see that condition of affairs to your satisfaction.

It is said we must do something here, or the people will never ratify the Constitution. There is no one would be prouder to do something that would give permanent relief than I would. If we can give any thing, give the poor man property in his labor, and we will have effected that relief. There cannot be a delegate from the coast but knows of the dire effect of holding out inducements to hold land, produced upon the laborers on the adjacent islands. Only about two years ago the Commissioner was compelled, with the bayonet, to force the people to go to work for the very reason that these inducements, with regard to owning land, had been held out to them. They had been made to believe they should hold them. The sooner the public mind is disabused of that impression, the sooner every man knows that to acquire land he must earn it; the sooner he feels the Government has no lands to dispose of or to give him, the better. Do what is necessary to protect the laborer in his labor and you will effect the greatest possible good. All these temporary and meagre measures of relief that are gotten up, I fear are too much for political purposes. I believe a majority of the members of this body do not believe this measure is permanent in its character. They look upon it as a measure of relief that in its details must fail. But they ask, must we face our constituency—go home and say we voted against that which certain members said was calculated to relieve the poor? Must we say we voted against a donation? No, it will frustrate our future prospects. But to whatever political

death it may consign me, I shall vote against it.

I know members upon this floor have said in the last twenty-four hours that they intend to swim with the tide. I regret to see this disposition, for in my judgment if a measure does not meet the conscientious convictions of the members, they should vote against it and take the consequences. I believe the adoption of this measure would bring interminable difficulties upon the Assistant Commissioner of your district. But I warn you, gentlemen, against the final results. Are you not going to disappointment the people beyond all expectation? I warn you against the indignation of the people whom you may deceive by that measure, and whose hopes you raise only to be blasted a few months hence. You may establish a measure giving to the poor man property in his labor. Do that, and you further the permanent interests of the State, build up the waste places, erect school houses, give encouragement to the mechanic and the laborer, and furnish the means for the cultivation of those lands.

If you create property in labor, the landholder will be compelled to divide and sell his lands, and the laborer will be able to purchase a home for himself. I desire to see established a system of taxation which will make it unprofitable for a man to keep lands uncultivated. We are not here to enter into any begging scheme, even if expedient to do so. I do not believe that it is for the interest of the people of this State. But protect labor and secure the laborer in all his right, and with their own strong arms and willing hands the people will accumulate property for themselves, and purchase homesteads with the results of honest industry. . . .

. . . **Mr. F. L. Cardozo.** This question has been mingled by some of the opposition with a great deal of personality. They freely imputed the most malicious motives to their opponents, and while I sat listening to those imputations I was forcibly reminded of the proverb, "It takes a rogue to catch a rogue." I will make one remark, and then will be done with personalities. The gentleman from Barnwell has referred constantly to the gentleman from Charleston; but it is believed that the gentleman from Barnwell is an old cast off Charleston politician. I remember his obtaining a hall of me and asking me to go help him at Barnwell. I positively refused to do it, because I thought, as the gentleman from Edgefield has said, that he (Leslie) was *non compos mentis.*

I am surprised at the gentleman from Beaufort, who just about two weeks ago rose in this Convention and advocated two measures of relief for the planters of this State, to save their property from going under the hammer of the auctioneer for debts contracted for the purchase of slaves. He was very eloquent in favor of those two measures of relief that would save to the rebel planters their old estates. But now, when a measure comes up to request help for the poor colored people, the very same eloquence is employed on the opposite side.

I would only say to him who imputed improper motives to the gentleman who originated this measure, it is currently reported that he is the tool of rebels, and his course has certainly justified that report. I opposed those two measures of relief that he favored, for two reasons; first, I said they were unjust in themselves. Men had contracted debts with their eyes wide open, knew the risks they run, took those risks, and if they were honest men, would pay their debts; but if they were dishonest, I claim they ought to be made to pay their debts. They contracted those debts in the rebel cause, to keep poor colored people down, to perpetuate slavery, and, having done that, they should suffer the consequences. Let their large estates be divided, and the poor colored people would have a better opportunity of buying lands. Those measures of relief were passed. This Convention refused to give the colored people that legal opportunity, and I would say to the gentlemen who voted for those measures of relief, if they are consistent, if they are the friends of the colored man, they may,

with equal consistency, vote for this measure. The argument is used that we are not likely to get the money asked for. But how can they tell? I think we are just as likely to get it, and more likely to obtain it, than the thirty millions asked by the Georgia Convention for the planters of the South, who have tried to reduce the colored man again to slavery or its equivalent condition—serfdom.

The gentleman from Beaufort argued that this was an impolitic measure, because it would not give all the colored people lands, and I would say better that than none at all. It will do a great deal of good. It is precisely what the Assistant Commissioner of this State has been doing in this District. No later than last night he told me that he had a large quantity of provisions, amounting to a large sum, to aid the people of this State, and had been told to give it out freely. He wrote to General Howard, stating that it would be better to assist the planters, taking a lien on the crops, and he sent him word to do so: took a lien upon the crops, and said when he got the money he would build school houses with it. But the crops have failed, and it is probable he will have no return. That was a help to the white planter. The Assistant Commissioner, however, made no invidious distinction, for a truer and nobler friend, both to the colored and white man does not exist in our State. He helps all alike, and assists all alike. The poor freedmen were induced, by many Congressmen even, to expect confiscation. They held out the hope of confiscation. General Sherman did confiscate, gave the lands to the freedmen; and if it were not for President Johnson, they would have them now. The hopes of the freedmen have not been realized, and I do not think that asking for a loan of one million, to be paid by a mortgage upon the land, will be half as bad as has been supposed. I have been told by the Assistant Commissioner that he has been doing on a private scale what this petition proposes to do. I say every opportunity for helping the colored man should be seized upon. I think the adoption of this measure will do honor to the Convention. We should certainly vote for some measure of relief for the colored men, as we have to the white men, who mortgaged their property to perpetuate slavery, and whom they have liberated from their bonds.

. . . [Mr. R. H. Cain.] The appropriations could be made in three directions; first, to the purchase of lands; second, to the purchase of sites; third, to the purchase of necessary agricultural implements. It was said that this appropriation, if carried out, would give homes to but few. I think it was said that it would give one hundred and twenty-five thousand persons homes. According to my friend from Beaufort (Mr. Whipper), it would allow but five and one-seventh acres to each head of a family, and he claims that that would not be sufficient to do any good. Well, if we can give homes to one hundred and twenty-five thousand persons, we shall thereby take out from the jurisdiction of the Freedman's Bureau that number who still linger at the door of the Commissary, waiting for something to eat. It will, therefore, be a measure of relief to three parties; first, a measure of relief to the poor; second, to the Freedman's Bureau; third, to the landholders who will receive just compensation for the lands they own, and thus spread a million of dollars in circulation, giving to every class of men something to eat and something to do. That much good will be accomplished. But to answer the gentleman, that it will give discontent to the poor colored people, is it not better to give one hundred and twenty-five thousand people homes by a measure so judicious, so complete and so swift as this will be, than to let four hundred thousand go without any homes at all. It is objected by the gentleman also, that it will create discontent in the minds of others. I prefer to cut off one hundred and twenty-five thousand grumblers than none at all. I believe it a measure of relief, such as the people do need, such as they want, and such as they shall have.

I can see no reason why any gentleman should object to the proposition; I believe the Government will be benefited by it, and I reiterate what I said last week. I am opposed to the people constantly going up to the Commissary Department and receiving rations; I believe that if the money expended by the Commissary Department of the Freedman's Bureau was given for the purchase of land it would have a more permanent and beneficial effect. Four hundred and fifty thousand dollars has been expended in that Bureau in five months for the simple item of rations, yet that Bureau has not reached one-tenth of the people in this State. Again, I would not call into question the honesty of the officers of the Bureau, I believe there are some honest men there at any rate. . . . I believe that the gentlemen at the head of that Bureau, from their antecedents and long experience in these matters, will do justice in this case.

The gentleman from Beaufort opposed the measure on the ground that it would create discontent, but was in favor of bringing up a resolution either in the Convention or by the Legislature, fixing such a tax upon the lands as to compel the sale of those lands, whether the owners wanted to or not.

Mr. W. J. Whipper. I deny it.

Mr. R. H. Cain. I may be mistaken, but I watched very closely the arguments made by the gentleman last Saturday, and I distinctly understood him to say he was in favor of taxing the lands so as to compel the sale of them, and throw them into the market. The poor would then have a chance to buy. I am unqualifiedly opposed to any measure of taxation for the simple purpose of compelling the owners to sell their lands. I believe the best measure to be adopted is to bring capital to the State, and instead of causing revenge and unpleasantness, I am for even-handed justice. I am for allowing the parties who own lands to bring them into the market and sell them upon such terms as will be satisfactory to both sides. I believe a measure of this kind has a double effect: first, it brings capital, what the people want; second, it puts the people to work; its gives homesteads, what we need; it relieves the Government and takes away its responsibility of feeding the people; it inspires every man with a noble manfulness, and by the thought that he is the possessor of something in the State; it adds also to the revenue of the country. By these means men become interested in the country as they never were before. It was said that five and one-seventh acres were not enough to live on. If South Carolina, in its sovereign power, can devise any plan for the purchase of the large plantations in this State now lying idle, divide and sell them out at a reasonable price, it will give so many people work. I will guarantee to find persons to work every five acres. I will also guarantee that after one year's time, the Freedman's Bureau will not have to give any man having one acre of land anything to eat. This country has a genial clime, rich soil, and can be worked to advantage. The man who can not earn a living on five acres, will not do so on twenty-five. I regret that another position taken by gentlemen in the opposition, is that they do not believe that we will get what we ask for. I believe that the party, now in power in the Congress of the United States, will do whatever they can for the welfare of the people of this State and of the South. I believe that the noble men who have maintained the rights of the freedmen before and since their liberation, will continue to do everything possible to forward these great interests. I am exceedingly anxious, if possible, to allay all unpleasant feeling—I would not have any unpleasant feeling among ourselves.

I would not have any unpleasant feelings between the races. If we give each family in the State an opportunity of purchasing a home, I think they will all be better satisfied.

But it is also said that it will disturb all the agricultural operations in the State. I do not believe if the Congress of the United States shall advance one million of dollars to make purchase of lands, the laborers will abandon their engagement and run off. I have more confidence in the people I represent. I believe all who have made contracts will fulfill those contracts, and when their contracts have expired, they will go on their own lands, as all freemen ought to go. I claim it would do no harm. It would be a wonderful concatenation of circumstances indeed, to find that because the Government had appropriated one million of dollars for the purchase of lands, to see all of four hundred thousand people, rushing pell mell down to Charleston to get a homestead. I know the ignorance of the people with whom I am identified is great. I know that four hundred years of bondage has degraded them, but I have more confidence in humanity then to believe the people will leave their homes and their families to come to Charleston just to get five acres of land.

If I understood the speaker in the opposition this morning, he offered it because he said it was simply a scheme for colored men. I wish to state this question right. If there was one thing on which I thought I had been specific, it was on that point. The clock had struck two and I had dashed down my pen when the thought struck me it might be misunderstood. I retraced my steps and so shaped the petition as simply to state the poor of any class. I bore in mind the poor whites of the upper districts. I saw, not long ago, a poor white woman walk eighteen miles barefooted to receive a bag of corn and four pounds of meat, resting all night on the roadside, eating one-half and then go away, living on roots afterwards and half starved. I desire that class of people to have homes as well as the black man. I have lost long since that hateful idea that the complexion of a man makes any difference as far as rights are concerned. The true principle of progress and civilization is to recognize the great brotherhood of man, and a man's wants, whatever he may be, or whatever clime he comes from, are as sacred to me as any other class of men. I believe this measure will advance the interests of all classes.

A few more words and I am done. Gentlemen of the Convention, I wish to appeal to you and ask have we not had suffering enough in this country? Has not the rude hands of war, with its fiery sword, trampled out the commercial interests of the States? Hath not the rude hand of war laid up the ships in our harbors, torn down fences and barns, and left our country almost a wilderness? Hath not war set the whole country in commotion? Look at the former rich white man, now walking poor and penniless; look at those formerly in opulence, now poor and brought down low. Can the gentleman from Barnwell, formerly from New York, last from Charleston, understand the fact that the people of the State want relief? I came to identify myself with the interests of the country. If she falls, I fall with her. If she rises, I rise with her. I have a kind of South Carolina pride, because my broad heart reaches out to all men's interests wherever I am. I have identified myself with the country, and I claim it is no time in the reconstruction of the State to seek revenge upon the head of any person, or to disregard the cries of millions for relief. The freed people, in connection with the poor whites of this State, are in great want. Let us see the number of destitute in this State. General Howard reports in South Carolina five thousand colored and five thousand whites, March 7th, 1867. There are other reports here which show a larger number of persons, and as I before remarked, the Bureau hath not met one-tenth of the wants of the people. This measure, if carried out, therefore, will meet a want which the Bureau never can meet. A man may have rations to-day and not tomorrow, but when he gets land and a homestead, and is once fixed on that land, he never will want to go to the Commissary again. It is said that I depicted little farms by the roadside, chickens roosting on the fence, and all those poetical beauties. But however poetical the gentlemen may be in his remarks, I prefer to see chickens roosting on the fence, and the lambs frisking round the place, and all other things which may be desired, than to see four hundred thousand people without homes, without owning even the sand they carry in their shoes. I prefer to see each one of them the owner of a log cabin, than to be compelled to work for five or ten dollars per month. I prefer to see that than to see the bayonets of the United States brought into requisition to drive poor, helpless men, women and children, because of the relentless hearts of those planters who will not pay. I prefer this to seeing strong men working for the paltry sum of five or ten dollars a month, and some for even three dollars a month. How can a man live at that rate. I hate the contract system as I hate the being of whom my friend from Orangeburg (Mr. Randolph) spoke last week (the devil). It has ruined the people. After fifty men have gone on a plantation, worked the whole year at raising twenty thousand bushels of rice, and then go to get their one-third, by the time they get through the division, after being charged by the landlord twenty-five or thirty cents a pound for bacon, two or three dollars for a pair of brogans that costs sixty cents, for living that costs a mere song, two dollars a bushel for corn that can be bought for one dollar; after I say, these people have worked the whole season, and at the end make up their accounts, they find themselves in debt. The planters sell their cotton, for it is said that a Negro has not brain enough to sell his own cotton. He can raise anything; he can dig ditches, pick cotton, but has not the sense to sell it. I deprecate that idea. I would rather see these people have little cottages and farms for themselves.

It is but a few days ago I went to a plantation on Cooper river. The first place I visited, I said to the men there, go to work, work honestly, stay on the plantation, do the best you can, make yourselves as comfortable as possible. After awhile your old masters may do you justice. Those people have remained on those plantations. What was the result.

Week before last they came and said to me, we took your advice, have worked hard, but as God is our judge, we have not as much as when these men got back their place again. I looked and saw four mule teams rolling off bales of cotton. I saw corn cribs piled with corn, and fodder houses filled with fodder. I went into the cabin of the Negroes and found but a scanty morsel of corn dodger and a scanty ration of bacon.

I say, therefore, it is time to relieve these people, and if this is not a measure of relief I know not what is. I desire to relieve all classes. I desire to relieve the planters of the large plantations they cannot attend to, and which must be so great a burden on their minds. They are pressed down; do now know what to do with their great plantations. I propose to bring money and say to them, "here gentlemen, you want to sell, we want to buy; we will give you a reasonable price; you will have the greenbacks, we will have the land; you can apply that money to banking purposes or buy bank stock, we will deposit the money with you." I want to see a change in this country. Instead of the colored people being always penniless, I want to see them coming in with their mule teams and ox teams. I want to see them come with their corn and potatoes and exchange for silks and satins. I want to see school houses and churches in every parish and township. I want to see children coming forth to enjoy life as it ought to be enjoyed. This people know nothing of what is good and best for mankind until they get homesteads and enjoy them.

With these remarks, I close. I hope the Convention will vote for the proposition. Let us send up our petition. The right to petition is a jealous right. It was a right guaranteed to the Barons of England. The American people have always been jealous of that right, and regarded it as sacred and inviolate. That right we propose to maintain. It is said here that some high officers are opposed to it. I do not care who is opposed to it. It is none of their business. I do not care whether General Scott, General Grant, or General anybody else is opposed to it, we will petition in spite of them. I appeal to the delegates to pass this resolution. It will do no harm if it does no good, and I am equally confident that some gentleman will catch what paddy gave the drum when they go back to their constituents. . . .

[After further debate, the resolution was finally passed in an amended and watered-down form.]

Resolved, That the President of the Convention be authorized to telegraph to the President of the United States Senate and Speaker of the national House of Representatives, and request them to present before their respective branches of Congress the great need of our people, and their homeless and landless condition, with the view of securing an early expression from the Government as to whether a petition of every member of this Convention would be productive of a loan from the national Treasury to enable our people to buy farms on a reasonable credit, and if so, how large an amount should be petitioned for.

Speech on the Eligibility of Colored Members to Seats in the Georgia Legislature

Henry M. Turner

Mr. Speaker: Before proceeding to argue this question upon its intrinsic merits, I wish the Members of this House to understand the position that I take. I hold that I am a member of this body. Therefore, sir, I shall neither fawn nor cringe before any party, nor stoop to *beg* them for my rights. Some of my colored fellow-members, in the course of their remarks, took occasion to appeal to the *sympathies* of Members on the opposite side, and to eulogize their character for magnanimity. It reminds me very much, sir, of slaves begging under the lash. I am here to demand my rights, and to hurl thunderbolts at the men who would dare to cross the threshold of my manhood. There is an old aphorism which says, "Fight the Devil with fire," and if I should observe the rule in this instance, I wish gentlemen to understand that it is but fighting them with their own weapon.

The scene presented in this House, to-day, is one unparalleled in the history of the world. From this day, back to the day when God breathed the breath of life into Adam, no analogy for it can be found. Never, in the history of the world, has a man been arraigned before a body clothed with legislative, judicial or executive functions, charged with the offence of being of a darker hue than his fellow-men. I know that questions have been before the Courts of this country, and of other countries, involving topics not altogether dissimilar to that which is being discussed here to-day. But, sir, never, in all the history of the great nations of this

Source: Henry M. Turner, *Speech on the Eligibility of Colored Members to Seats in the Georgia Legislature, . . . September 3, 1868.* (Augusta: E. H. Pughe, 1868).

world—never before—has a man been arraigned, charged with an offence committed by the God of Heaven himself. Cases may be found where men have been deprived of their rights for crimes and misdemeanors; but it has remained for the State of Georgia, in the very heart of the nineteenth century, to call a man before the bar, and there charge him with an act for which he is no more responsible than for the head which he carries upon his shoulders. The Anglo-Saxon race, sir, is a most surprising one. No man has ever been more deceived in that race than I have been for the last three weeks. I was not aware that there was in the character of that race so much cowardice, or so much pusillanimity. The treachery which has been exhibited by gentleman belonging to that race has shaken my confidence in it more than anything that has come under my observation from the day of my birth.

What is the question at issue? Why, sir, this Assembly, to-day, is discussing and deliberating on a matter upon which Angels would tremble to sit in judgment; there is not a Cherubim that sits around God's Eternal Throne, to-day, that would not tremble—even were an order issued by the Supreme God himself—to come down here and sit in judgment on my manhood. Gentlemen may look at this question in whatever light they choose, and with just as much indifference as they may think proper to assume, but I tell you, sir, that this is a question which will not die to-day. This event shall be remembered by posterity for ages yet to come, and while the sun shall continue to climb the hills of heaven.

Whose Legislature is this? Is it a white man's Legislature, or is it a black man's legislature? Who voted for a Constitutional

Convention, in obedience to the mandate of the Congress of the United States? Who first rallied around the standard of Reconstruction? Who set the ball of loyalty rolling in the State of Georgia? And whose voice was heard on the hills and in the valleys of this State? It was the voice of the brawny-armed Negro, with the few humanitarian-hearted white men who came to our assistance. I claim the honor, sir, of having been the instrument of convincing hundreds—yea, thousands—of white men, that to reconstruct under the measures of the United States Congress was the safest and the best course for the interest of the State.

Let us look at some facts in connection with this matter. Did half the white men of Georgia vote for this Legislature? Did not the great bulk of them fight, with all their strength, the Constitution under which we are acting? And did they not fight against the organization of this Legislature? And further, sir, did they not *vote* against it? Yes, sir! And there are persons in this Legislature, to day, who are ready to spit their poison in my face, while they themselves opposed, with all their power; the ratification of this Constitution. They question my right to a seat in this body, to represent the people whose legal votes elected me. This objection, sir, is an unheard of monopoly of power. No analogy can be found for it, except it be the case of a man who should go into my house, take possession of my wife and children, and then tell me to walk out. I stand very much in the position of a criminal before your bar, because I dare to be the exponent of the views of those who sent me here. Or, in other words, we are told that if black men want to speak, they must speak through white trumpets; if black men want their sentiments expressed, they must be adulterated and sent through white messengers, who will quibble, and equivocate, and evade, as rapidly as the pendulum of a clock. If this be not done, then the black men have committed an outrage, and their Representatives must be denied the right to represent their constituents.

The great question, sir, is this: Am I a man? If I am such, I claim the rights of a man. Am I not a man, because I happen to be of a darker hue than honorable gentlemen around me? Let me see whether I am or not. I want to convince the House, to-day, that I am entitled to my seat here. A certain gentleman has argued that the Negro was a mere development similar to the ourang-outang or chimpanzee, but it so happens that, when a Negro is examined, physiologically, phrenologically and anatomically, and, I may say, physiognomically, he is found to be the same as persons of different color. I would like to ask any gentleman on this floor, where is the analogy? Do you find me quadruped, or do you find me a man? Do you find three bones less in my back than in that of the white man? Do you find less organs in the brain? If you know nothing of this, I do, for I have helped to dissect fifty men, black and white, and I assert that by the time you take off the mucous pigment—the color of the skin—you cannot, to save your life, distinguish between the black man and the white. Am I a man? Have I a soul to save, as you have? Am I susceptible of eternal development, as you are? Can I learn all the arts and sciences that you can—has it ever been demonstrated in the history of the world? Have black men ever exhibited bravery, as white men have done? Have they ever been in the professions? Have they not as good articulative organs as you? Some people argue that there is a very close similarity between the larynx of the Negro and that of the ourang-outang. Why, sir, there is not so much similarity between them as there is between the larynx of the man and that of the dog, and this fact I dare any Member of this House to dispute. God saw fit to vary everything in Nature. There are no two men alike—no two voices alike—no two trees alike. God has weaved and tissued variety and versatility throughout the boundless space of His creation.— Because God saw fit to make some red, and some white, and some black, and some brown, are we to sit here in judgment upon what God has seen fit to do? As well might one play with the thunderbolts of heaven as with that creature that bears God's image—God's photograph.

The question is asked: "What is it that the Negro race has done?" Well, Mr. Speaker, all I have to say upon the subject is this: that if we are the class of people that we are generally represented to be, I hold that we are a very great people. It is generally considered that we are the Children of Canaan, and that the curse of a father rests upon our heads, and has rested, all through history. Sir, I deny that the curse of Noah has anything to do with the Negro. We are not the Children of Canaan; and if we were, sir, where should we stand? Let us look a little into history. Melchisedeck was a Canaanite; all the Phœnicians—all those inventors of the arts and sciences—were the posterity of Canaan; but, sir, the Negro is not. We are the children of Cush, and Canaan's curse has nothing whatever to do with the Negro. If we belong to that race, Ham belonged to it, under whose instructions Napoleon Bonaparte studied military tactics. If we belong to that race, St. Augustine belonged to it. Who was it that laid the foundation of the great Reformation? Martin Luther, who lit the light of Gospel Truth—a light that will never go out until the sun shall rise to set no more; and, long ere then, Democratic principles will have found their level in the regions of Pluto and of Proserpine.

The Negro is here charged with holding office. Why, sir, the Negro never wanted office. I recollect that when we wanted candidates for the Constitutional Convention, we went from door to door in the "Negro belt," and begged white men to run. Some promised to do so; and yet, on the very day of election, many of them first made known their determination not to comply with their promises. They told black men, everywhere, that they would rather see *them* run; and it was this encouragement of the white men that induced the colored man to place his name upon the ticket as a candidate for the Convention. In many instances, these white men voted for us. We did not want them, nor ask them, to do it. All we wanted them to do was, to stand still and allow us to walk up to the polls and deposit our ballots. They would not come here themselves, but would insist upon sending us. Ben. Hill told them it was a nigger affair, and advised them to stay away from the polls—a piece of advice which they took very liberal advantage of. If the "niggers" had "office on the brain," it was the white man that put it there—not carpet-baggers, either, nor Yankees, nor scalawags, but the high-bred and dignified Democracy of the South. And if any one is to blame for having Negroes in these Legislative Halls—if blame attaches to it at all—it is the Democratic party. Now, however, a change has come over the spirit of their dream. They want to turn the "nigger" out; and, to support their argument, they say that the black man is debarred from holding office by the Reconstruction measures of Congress. Let me tell them one thing for their information. Black men have held office, and are now holding office, under the United States Government. Andrew Johnson, President of the United States, in 1865, commissioned me as United States Chaplain, and I would have been Chaplain today, had I not resigned—not desiring to hold office any longer. Let the Democratic party, then, go to Mr. Johnson, and ask him why he commissioned a Negro to that position? And if they inquire further, they will ascertain that black men have been commissioned as Lieutenants, Captains, Majors, Brevet Colonels, Surgeons, and other offices of trust and responsibility, under the United States Government. Black men, today, in Washington City, hold positions as Clerks, and the only reason why Mr. Langston is not at this time a Consul Diplomat or Minister Plenipotentiary in some foreign country, is, because he would not be corrupted by President Johnson and made to subscribe to his wicked designs. Is not that an office, and is it not a great deal better office than any seat held in this body?

The honorable gentleman from Whitfield (Mr. Shumate), when arguing this question, a day or two ago, put forth the proposition that to be a Representative was not to be an officer—"it was a privilege that citizens. had a right to enjoy." These are his words. It was not an office it was a "privilege." Every gentleman here knows that he denied that to be a Representative was to be an officer. Now, he is recognized as a leader of the Democratic party in this House, and generally cooks victuals for them to eat; makes that remarkable declaration, and how are you, gentlemen on the other side of the House, to ignore that declaration? Are you going to expel me from this House, because I am an officer, when one of your great lights says that I am *not* an officer? If you deny my right—the right of my constituents to have representation here—because it is a "privilege," then, sir, I will show you that I have as many privileges as the whitest man on this floor. If I am not permitted to occupy a seat here, for the purpose of representing my constituents, I want to know how white men can be permitted to do so? How can a white man represent a colored constituency, if a colored man cannot do it? The great argument is: "Oh, we have inherited" this, that and the other. Now, I want gentlemen to come down to cool, common sense. Is the created greater than the Creator? Is man greater than God? It is very strange, if a white man can occupy on this floor *a seat created by colored votes,* and a black man cannot do it. Why, gentlemen, it is the most shortsighted reasoning in the world. A man can see better than that with half an eye; and even if he had no eye at all, he could forge one, as the Cyclops did, or punch one with his finger, which would enable him to see through that.

It is said that Congress never gave us the right to hold office. I want to know, sir, if the Reconstruction measures did not base their action on the ground that no distinction should be made on account of race, color, or previous condition! Was not that the grand fulcrum on which they rested? And did not every reconstructed State have to reconstruct on the idea that no discrimination, in any sense of the term, should be made?

There is not a man here who will dare say, "No." If Congress has simply given me merely sufficient civil and political rights to make me a mere political slave for Democrats, or anybody else—giving them the opportunity of jumping on my back, in order to leap into political power—I do not thank Congress for it. Never, so help me, God, shall I be a political slave. I am not now speaking for those colored men who sit with me in this House, nor do I say that they endorse my sentiments [cries from the colored Members, "We do!"], but I am speaking simply and solely for myself. Congress, after assisting Mr. Lincoln to take me out of servile slavery, did not intend to put me and my race into *political* slavery. If they did, let them take away my ballot—I do not want it, and shall not have it. [Several colored Members: "Nor we!"] I don't want to be a mere tool of that sort. I have been a slave long enough already.

I tell you what I would be willing to do: I am willing that the question should be submitted to Congress for an explanation as to what was meant in the passage of these Reconstruction measures, and of the Constitutional Amendment. Let the Democratic party in this House pass a Resolution giving this subject that direction, and I shall be content. I dare you, gentlemen, to do it. Come up to the question openly, whether it meant that the Negro might hold office, or whether it meant that he should merely have the right to vote. If you are honest men, you will do it. If, however, you will not do that, I would make another proposition: Call together, again, the Convention that framed the Constitution under which we are acting; let them take a vote upon the subject, and I am willing to abide their decision.

In the course of this discussion, a good deal of reference has been made to the Constitution of the United States. I hold, sir, that, under that Constitution, I am as much a man as anybody else. I hold that that document is neither proscripted, or has it ever, in the first instance, sanctioned slavery.

The Constitution says that any person escaping from service in one State, and going to another, shall, on demand, be given up. That has been the clause under which the Democratic fire-eaters have maintained that that document sanctioned slavery in man. I shall show you that it meant no such thing. It was placed there, according to Mr. Madison, altogether for a different purpose. In the Convention that drafted the Constitution,

> Mr. Madison declared, he "thought it wrong to admit in the Constitution the idea that there could be property in man." On motion of Mr. Randolph, the word "servitude" was struck out, and "service" unanimously inserted—the former being thought to express the condition of SLAVES, and the latter the obligation of free persons.—3D MAD. PAP., 1429 and 1569.

Now, if you can, make anything out of that that you find in it. It comes from one of the fathers of the Constitution. Sir, I want the gentleman to know that the Constitution, as Mr. Alexander H. Stephens said, I think, in 1854, so far as slavery is concerned, is neutral. He said, that if slavery existed in Georgia, it existed under the Constitution and by the authority of the Constitution; that if slavery did not exist in Pennsylvania, or in New York, *it was equally under the Constitution.*

That is a distinct avowal that the Constitution was neutral, and it is the opinion of a man who is acknowledged to be a man of great mind and large acquaintance with political affairs. Again: the Constitution of the United States has the following clause:

> This Constitution, and *and all laws made in pursuance thereof,* shall be the supreme law of the land.

Every law, therefore, which is passed under the Constitution of the United States, is a portion of the supreme law of the land, and you are bound to obey it.

But gentlemen say that the Democrats did not pass the Reconstruction measures. I know they did not. Such Democrats as we are having in this State come pretty well under the description given of the Bourbons by Napoleon Bonaparte, who said that they never originated a new idea, nor ever forgot an old one. They certainly never would pass such measures. Did the Revolutionary Fathers intend to perpetuate slavery? Many say they did; I say they did not. What was meant by the clause which states that no bill of attainder or *ex-post facto* law shall be passed? I will tell you what I believe the Revolutionary Fathers meant: I believe it was intended to put a clause there which should eventually work out the emancipation of the slaves. It was not intended that because the father has served in slavery the curse should descend.

One of the strongest objections to the Negro holding office is based upon the fact that he has been a slave, and had no rights; but the Fathers of this country framed a Constitution and Laws, whose spirit and letter condemn this everlasting proscription of the Negro.

Let us take, for example, an extract from a memorial sent to Congress in 1794. It was written by a Committee of which Dr. Rush was Chairman, and is signed by such men as Samuel Adams, John Adams, Isaac Law, Stephen Hopkins, and a host of other prominent gentlemen. This memorial says:

> Many reasons concur in persuading us to abolish slavery in our country. It is inconsistent with the safety of the liberties of the United States. Freedom and slavery cannot long exist together.

Let it be remembered that some of the gentlemen who signed this memorial had been Presidents of the United States. It is also well known that General Washington, in his will, earnestly expresses a desire that all his slaves should receive their freedom upon the death of his wife. He says:

> Upon the decease of my wife, it is my will and desire that all the slaves held by me in my own right should receive their freedom. And I do

most pointedly and solemnly enjoin on my Executors to see that the clause regarding my slaves, and every part thereof, be religiously fulfilled.

Did *he* intend to perpetutate slavery or Negro proscription? What says he, when writing to General Lafayette?—

There is not a man living who wishes more sincerely than I do, to see a plan adopted for the abolition of slavery, but there is only one plan by which it can be accomplished. That is by legislative authority, and this, so far, as my suffrage will go, shall not be wanting.

General Lafayette once said:

I never thought, when I was fighting for America, that I was fighting to perpetuate slavery. I never should have drawn my sword in her defence, if I suspected such a thing.

Jefferson says:

And can the liberties of the nation be thought secure, when we have removed the only firm basis—the conviction of the minds of the people that liberty is the gift of God? Indeed, I tremble for my country, when I reflect that God is just, and that injustice cannot last forever.

I could quote from such men for days and weeks together, to show the spirit that was in them upon this subject, if I thought it necessary to my cause.

We are told that we have no right to hold office, because it was never conferred upon us by "specific enactment." *Were we ever made slaves by specific enactment?* I hold, sir, that there never was a law passed in this country, from its foundation to the Emancipation, which enacted us slaves. Even the great Mr. Calhoun said: "I doubt whether there is a single State in the South that *ever enacted them slaves.*" If, then, you have no laws enacting me a slave, how can you question my right to my freedom? Judge Lump-

kin, one of the ablest jurists that Georgia ever had, said that there never was any positive law in the State of Georgia that forbade Negroes from testifying in Courts; "and they are," said he, "only debarred by their ignorance and ignoble status." Neither did Queen Elizabeth, when she gave to Sir John Hawkins a charter to bring Negroes to this country, give him that right with any other understanding than that no violence or force should be used therefor; and she never intended that they should be anything more than apprentices. Mr. Madison, in speaking upon the subject of jury-trials for Negroes, says: "Proof would have to be brought forward that slavery was established by preexisting laws;" "and," said he, "it will be impossible to comply with such a request, *for no such law could be produced.*" Why, then, do gentlemen clamor for proof of our being free "by virtue of specific enactment?" Show me any specific law of Georgia, or of the United States, that enacted black men to be slaves, and I will then tell you that, before we can enjoy our rights as free men, such law must be repealed.

I stand here to-day, sir, pleading for ninety thousand black men—voters—of Georgia; and I shall stand and plead the cause of my race until God, in His providence, shall see proper to take me hence. I trust that He-will give me strength to stand, and power to accomplish the simple justice that I seek for them.

Why did your forefathers come to this country? Did they not flee from oppression? They came to free themselves from the chains of tyranny, and to escape from under the heel of the Autocrat. Why, sir, in England, for centuries together, men—and *white* men at that—wore metal collars around their necks, bearing, in graven characters, the names by which they were known. Your great and noble race were sold in the slave-marts of Rome. The Irish, also, held many white slaves, until 1172; and even Queen Elizabeth, in her day, had to send a deputation to inquire into the condition of such white slaves as had been born in England.

King Alfred the Great, in his time, provided that for seven years' work the slave should be set free. And, going back to more ancient and more valuable authority, did not God himself, when he had brought the Children of Israel out of Egypt, say unto them: "Remember that you were slaves in Egypt?" I say to you, white men, to-day, that the great deliverance of the recent past is not altogether dissimilar to the great deliverance of ancient times. Your Democratic party may be aptly said to represent Pharaoh; the North to represent one of the walls, and the South the other. Between these two great walls the black man passes out to freedom, while your Democratic party—the Pharaoh of to-day—follows us with hasty strides and lowering visage.

The gentleman from Floyd (Mr. Scott) went down amid the chambers of the dead, and waked up the musty decision of Judge Taney in the Dred Scott case. Why, the very right on which he denied citizenship to Dred Scott, was, that if he were a citizen, he would be a free man, and invested with all rights of citizenship. The Constitution says that

All persons born or naturalized in the United States, and residents in this State, are hereby declared citizens of this State; and no law shall be made or enforced that shall abridge the privileges or immunities of citizens of the United States, or of this State, or deny to any person within its jurisdiction the equal protection of its laws.

For what purpose was this clause inserted in that Constitution? It was placed there, sir, to protect the rights of every man—the Heaven-granted, inalienable, unrestricted rights of mine, and of my race. Great God, if I had the voice of seven thunders, to-day, I would make the ends of the earth to hear me. The Code of Laws known as Irwin's Code of Georgia, clearly states the rights of citizens. Section 1648 is as follows:

Among the rights of citizens are the enjoyment of personal security, of personal liberty, private

property and the disposition thereof, the elective franchise, the right to hold office, to appeal to the Courts, to testify as a witness to perform any civil function, and to keep and bear arms.

Section 1649 of the same Code says:

All citizens are entitled to exercise of their right as such, unless specially prohibited by law.

I would like to ascertain, Mr. Speaker, what prohibition has been put upon me, or upon my race, and what can be put upon it, under the provision of the Constitution, which would deprive us of holding office. The Constitution of Georgia, Article 2, Section 2, says that

Every male person who has been born or naturalized, or who has legally declared his intention to become a citizen of the United States, twenty years old or upward, who shall have resided in this State six months next preceding the election, and shall have resided thirty days in the county in which he offers to vote, and shall have paid all taxes which may have been required of him, and which he may have had an opportunity of paying, agreeably to law, for the year next preceding the election (except as hereinafter provided), shall be declared an elector; and every male citizen of the United States, of the age aforesaid (except as hereinafter provided), who may be a resident of the State at the time of the adoption of this Constitution, shall be deemed an elector, and shall have all the rights of an elector as aforesaid.

Now let me read to you the meaning of the word "citizen," as given by Mr. Bouvier in his Law Dictionary:

In American law, one who, under the Constitution and Laws of the United States, has a right to vote for Representatives in Congress and other public officers, and who is qualified to fill offices in the gift of the people. Any white person born in the United States, or naturalized persons born out of the same, who has not lost his right as such.

Now, sir, I claim to be a citizen, I claim to be an elector, and I claim to be entitled to hold office.

We have heard a good deal said about Greece and Rome, and the great nations of antiquity, and of such great men as Socrates, Seneca, Aristotle, Plato, Herodotus, Horace, and Homer. Well, I make a reference or two to these times and nations. A freedman among the Romans was nothing more than, in the time of slavery in this country, a free Negro would be. He could not come in contact with the citizen upon an equal footing, but when the Empire came under the sway of Constantine, he provided that all slaves who were made free upon account of meritorious conduct should be enfranchised. Go back, then, Georgians, to the days of Constantine, and learn from him a lesson of wisdom. In the days of Justinian, too, provision was made that every slave who was made free should be enfranchised and made a full citizen of Rome. The celebrated Roman writer, Horace, boasted that he was the son of a freedman; and I would remind you, also, that one of the Emperors and rulers of Rome had a slave mother. Another provision of those times was, that a slave could become free and a citizen by the consent of six thousand other citizens. Now, sir, even following the example of Rome, am I not a citizen? Have not more than six thousand white citizens voted me my rights as such? And have not forty thousand white citizens voted for the Constitution which grants me my rights as such?

We learn some peculiar points in regard to slavery from many of the writers of ancient times. Tacitus, for instance, tells us that, amongst the ancient Germans, if, in gaming, the slave should win, the master became his property and and slave, while he became master. Mohammed gave political rights to all slaves who defended his religion; and so, indeed, in general, did the Crusaders; and the Popes of Rome used to teach their flocks that all men were the Lord's freemen. St. Jerome once remarked that a man's right to enfranchisement existed in his knowledge of the truth. I might quote for hours from such authorities as these upon the rights which rested in, and were acquired by, the slaves of old, but I deem it unnecessary to do so at this time.

These colored men, who are unable to express themselves with all the clearness, and dignity, and force of rhetorical eloquence, are laughed at in derision by the Democracy of the country. It reminds me very much of the man who looked at himself in a mirror, and, imagining that he was addressing another person, exclaimed: "My God, how ugly you are!" [Laughter.] These gentlemen do not consider for a moment the dreadful hardships which these people have endured, and especially those who in any way endeavored to acquire an education. For myself, sir, I was raised in the cotton field of South Carolina, and, in order to prepare myself for usefulness, as well to myself as to my race, I determined to devote my spare hours to study. When the overseer retired at night to his comfortable couch, I sat and read, and thought, and studied, until I heard him blow his horn in the morning. He frequently told me, with an oath, that if he discovered me attempting to learn, he would whip me to death, and I have no doubt he would have done so, if he had found an opportunity. I prayed to Almighty God to assist men, and He did, and I thank Him with my whole heart and soul.

Personally, I have the highest regard for the gentleman from Floyd (Mr. Scott), but I need scarcely say that I heartily despise the political sentiments which he holds. I would pledge myself to do this, however: To take the Holy Bible and read it in as many different languages as he will. If *he* reads it in English, *I* will do it; if *he* reads it in Latin, *I* will do the same; if in Greek, *I* will read it in that language, too; and if in Hebrew, *I* will meet *him*, also, there. It can scarcely, then, be upon the plea of ignorance that he would debar me from the exercise of political rights.

I must now direct your attention to a point which shows the intention of the framers of the Constitution of Georgia, which you have sworn to support. In the "Proceedings of the Constitutional Convention," which framed this Constitution, I find, under date of March 3d, 1868, that, on motion of Mr. Akerman, the report of the Judiciary Committee on the subject of the qualifications of persons for membership to the first General Assembly, after the ratification and adoption of the Constitution, was taken up, and, without amendment, adopted. That report is as follows:

Be it ordained by the people of Georgia, in Convention assembled, That the persons eligible as members of the General Assembly, at the first election held under the Constitution framed by this Convention, shall be citizens of the United States who shall have been inhabitants of this State for six months, and of the district or county for which they shall be elected for three months next preceding such election, and who, in the case of Senators, shall have attained the age of twenty-five years, and, in the case of Representatives, the age of twenty-one years, at the time of such election.

Gentlemen will observe the word "inhabitant" in that Ordinance; and it was put there especially, in order that no question could arise as to who were eligible to fill the positions of Senator and Representative.

So far as I am personally concerned, no man in Georgia has been more conservative than I. "Anything to please the white folks" has been my motto; and so closely have I adhered to that course, that many among my own party have classed me as a Democrat. One of the leaders of the Republican party in Georgia has not been at all favorable to me for some time back, because he believed that I was too "conservative" for a Republican. I can assure you, however, Mr. Speaker, that I have had quite enough, and to spare, of such "conservatism."

The "conservative" element has pursued a somewhat erratic course in the reconstruction of Georgia. In several instances—as, for instance, in Houston county—they placed Negroes on their tickets for county offices, and *elected* them, too, and *they are holding office to-day.* And this policy is perfectly consistent with the doctrine taught, in public and in private, by the great lights of Democracy, all through the last canvass. They objected to the Constitution, "because," said they, "it confers upon the niggers the right to hold office." Even Mr. Alexander H. Stephens—one of the greatest men, if not *the greatest* man, in the South, to-day, and one for whom I have the utmost respect—in a conversation that I had with him before the Legislature convened (Governor Brown's Marietta speech being one of the topics under consideration very generally throughout the State at the time), said: "Governor Brown says that the black man cannot hold office under that Constitution, but he *knows* that he can."

But, Mr. Speaker, I do not regard this movement as a thrust at me. It is a thrust at the Bible—a thrust at the God of the Universe, for making man and not finishing him; it is simply calling the Great Jehovah a fool. Why, sir, though we are not white, we have accomplished much. We have pioneered civilization here; we have built up your country; we have worked in your fields, and garnered your harvests, for two hundred and fifty years! And what do we ask of you in return? Do we ask you for compensation for the sweat our fathers bore for you—for the tears you have caused, and the hearts you have broken, and the lives you have curtailed, and the blood you have spilled? Do we ask retaliation? We ask it not. We are willing to let the dead past bury its dead; but we ask you, now, for OUR RIGHTS. You have all the elements of superiority upon your side; you have our money and your own: you have our education and your own; and you have our land and your own, too. We, who number hundreds of thousands in Georgia, including our wives and families, with not a foot of land to call our own—strangers in the land of our birth; without money, without education, without aid, without a roof to cover us while we live, nor sufficient clay to cover us when we die! It is extraordinary that a race such as yours, professing gallantry, and chivalry, and education, and superiority, living in a land where ringing chimes call child and sire to the Church of God—a land where Bibles are read and Gospel truths are spoken, and where courts of justice are presumed to exist; it is extraordinary, I say, that, with all these advantages on your side, you can make war upon the poor defenceless black man. You know we have no money, no railroads, no telegraphs, no advantages of any sort, and yet all manner of injustice is placed upon us. You know that the black people of this country acknowledge you as their superiors, by virtue of your education and advantages.

There was a Resolution passed here at the early part of this session stating that all persons who were in their seats were eligible thereto, What are gentlemen going to do, with that Resolution staring them in the face? Your children and my children will read that Resolution, and they will be this House that is contemplated to-day, I will call a colored Convention, and I will say to my friends: Let us send North for carpet-baggers and Yankees, and let us send to Europe and all over the world for immigrants, and when they come here, we will give them every vote we have, and send them to the Legislature, in preference to sending a Georgian there.

Go on with your oppressions. Babylon fell. Where is Greece? Where is Nineveh? and where is Rome, the mistress Empire of the world? Why is it that she stands, to-day, in broken fragments throughout Europe? Because oppression killed her. Every act that we commit is like a bounding ball. If you curse a man, that curse rebounds upon you; and when you bless a man, the blessing returns to you; and when you oppress a man, the oppression, also, will rebound. Where have you ever heard of four millions of freemen being governed by laws, and yet have no hand in their making? Search the records of the world, and you will find no example. "Governments derive their just powers from the consent of the governed." How dare you to make laws by which to try me and my wife and children, and deny me a voice in the making of these laws? I know you can establish a monarchy, an autocracy, an oligarchy, or any other kind of an "ocracy" that you please: and that you can declare whom you please to be sovereign; but tell me, sir, how you can clothe me with more power than another, where all are sovereigns alike? How can you say you have a Republican form of Government, when you make such distinction and enact such proscriptive laws?

Gentlemen talk a good deal about the Negroes "building no monuments." I can tell the gentlemen one thing that is, that we could have built monuments of fire while the war was in progress. We could have fired your woods, your barns and fences, and called you home. Did we do it? No, sir! And God grant that the Negro may never do it, or do anything else that would destroy the good opinion of his friends. No epithet is sufficiently opprobrious for us now. I say, sir, that we have built a monument of docility, of obedience, of respect, and of self-control, that will endure longer than the Pyramids of Egypt.

We are a persecuted people. Luther was persecuted; Galileo was persecuted; good men in all nations have been persecuted; but the persecutors have been handed down to posterity with shame and ignominy. If you pass this Bill, you will never get Congress to pardon or enfranchise another rebel in your lives. You are going to fix an everlasting disfranchisement upon Mr. Toombs and the other leading men of Georgia. You may think you are doing yourselves honor by expelling us from this House; but when we go, we will do as Wickliffe and as Latimer did. We will light a torch of truth that will never be extinguished—the impression that will run through the country, as people picture in their mind's eye these poor black men, in all parts of this Southern country, pleading for their rights. When you expel us, you make us forever your political foes, and you will never find a black man to vote a Democratic ticket again; for, so help me, God, astonished that persons, claiming to be men, with souls and consciences, should, contrary to the express provision of that Resolution, turn the colored man out of his seat in this Hall. Another Resolution came before this House, a short time ago, praying Congress to remove all political disabilities from the white people of Georgia. I stood up in my place here, sir, and advocated that Resolution, and advised all colored Members to do the same; and almost every one of them voted for it. We were willing to give the white man every right which he ever rightfully possessed, and, were there forty Negroes in this country to one white man, I would have precisely the same feeling, and act precisely the same way. The action of the House reminds me very much of a couple of lines of verse which we occasionally read:

> "When the Devil was sick, the Devil a saint would be;
> When the Devil was well, the Devil a saint was he."

When this House was "sick" with fear for the safety of the seats of ineligible Democrats, they were all very gracious and polite. But, when the Resolution was passed, declaring, in the face of facts, that all who were in their seats were eligible, then the foot was raised which was to trample on the poor Negro, and that, too, by those who claim bravery and chivalry.

You may expel us, gentlemen, but I firmly believe that you will some day repent it. The black man cannot protect a country, if the country doesn't protect him; and if, to-morrow, a war should arise, I would not raise a musket to defend a country where my manhood is denied. The fashionable way in Georgia, when hard work is to be done, is, for the white man to sit at his ease, while the black man does the work; but, sir, I will say this much to the colored men of Georgia, as, if I should be killed in this campaign, I may have no opportunity of telling them at any

other time: Never lift a finger nor raise a hand in defence of Georgia, unless Georgia acknowledges that you are men, and invests you with the rights pertaining to manhood. Pay your taxes, however, obey all orders from your employers, take good counsel from friends, work faithfully, earn an honest living, and show, by your conduct, that you can be good citizens.

I want to take your memories back to 1862. In that year, the Emperor of Russia, with one stroke of his pen, freed twenty-two millions of serfs. What did Russia do, then? Did she draw lines of distinction between those who had been serfs and her other citizens? No! That noble Prince, upon whose realm the sun never sets, after having freed these serfs, invested them with all the political rights enjoyed by his other subjects. America boasts of being the most enlightened, intelligent and enterprising nation in the world, and many people look upon Russia as not altogether perfectly civilized. But, look at what Russia has done for her slaves; there were twenty-two millions of them, while there are but four millions of us in the whole South, and only half a million in Georgia. If the action is taken in I will go through all the length and breadth of the land, where a man of my race is to be found, and advise him to beware of the Democratic party. Justice is the great doctrine taught in the Bible. God's Eternal Justice is founded upon Truth, and the man who steps from Justice steps from Truth, and cannot make his principles to prevail.

I have now, Mr. Speaker, said all that my physical condition will allow me to say. Weak and ill, though I am, I could not sit passively here and see the sacred rights of my race destroyed at one blow. We are in a position somewhat similar to that of the famous "Light Brigade," of which Tennyson says, they had

> "Cannon to right of them,
> Cannon to left of them,
> Cannon in front of them,
> Volleyed and thundered."

I hope our poor, down-trodden race may act well and wisely through this period of trial, and that they will exercise patience and discretion under all circumstances.

You may expel us, gentlemen, by your votes, to-day; but, while you do it, remember that there is a just God in Heaven, whose All-Seeing Eye beholds alike the acts of the oppressor and the oppressed, and who, despite the machinations of the wicked, never fails to vindicate the cause of Justice, and the sanctity of His own handiwork.

Letters from the South, Relating to the Condition of the Freedman

J. W. Alvord

Major General O. O. Howard.
        Columbia, S. C., *January 7*, 1870.

Dear General: I will not report in detail the Schools in Columbia, as you were an eye witness to their condition.

The absence of advanced and older pupils, is said to be from the fact that young colored men here, who were boys during the war, grew up especially vicious, and are now, therefore, comparatively indifferent to an education. From the younger class we are undoubtedly to expect the largest results in all parts of the South, as well as in this city.

These colored schools are the only public schools of the Capital of South Carolina, and in their well arranged and spacious building, under the fine direction of so efficient a corps of teachers, will certainly accomplish great good.

The older colored people of the city and surrounding country, as I learned, are unusually intelligent and prosperous—one man, a skillful mechanic, being worth $50,000. More than forty heads of families have within the last six months purchased city property for homes, at from $500 to $1,200 each. It is the testimony of well-informed gentlemen that the whole colored population of upper South Carolina is, in general, in a thriving condition—with better houses, clothing, and family comforts from year to year.

South Carolina appropriated last year $200,000 to buy land in the upper part of the State which has been sold to Freedmen for homesteads. Upwards of 40,000 acres of this land have been actually sold during the year to poor men of all colors. The Governor says he intends this year to recommend for the same purpose an appropriation of $400,000. Colored members of the Legislature, whom I met in the interior counties, asked me earnestly for more schools for their children, which were promised as strongly as I dared.

I have been much interested in witnessing the social elevation of the Freedmen at this place. The Governor, General R. K. Scott, in his receptions makes no distinction among the members of the Legislature, (125 of whom are colored); all are taken equally by the hand with the graceful urbanity for which his honor is distinguished. All alike, on such occasions, crowd around his luxurious refreshment tables, where, as his accomplished lady told me, no invidious distinctions are made.

Source: From J. W. Alvord, *Letters from the South, Relating to the Condition of the Freedman* (Washington: Howard University Press, 1870), pp. 5–28.

You will remember at the dinner party given on your account by the Governor, and at which I had the honor of being a guest, his Secretary of State, the Hon. F. L. Cardozo and lady, (both colored,) received equal attention with other officials, and ladies and gentlemen of the highest standing. I could but feel as I looked around upon that agreeable circle that *equality of character and culture were the true conditions of equality in social life.* I learned of other occasions when the Governor had followed the same rule, and in conversation he assured me he could allow himself to adopt none other.

His opinion is that in our higher institutions of learning *cultured* youth of both colors will come, at length, to associate on equal terms, and that scholarship and general refinement on each side will gradually settle the whole question of mixed schools.

At Orangeburg I found the Claflin University in the large and beautiful building (late the Orangeburg Female Academy, bought recently by the Methodist Episcopal Society, and repaired by Major Deane, of the Bureau, at an expense of $2,500,) with about one hundred students, under the efficient training of Dr. Webster. This is a very promising Institution, and in a commanding and well chosen locality. It will probably ask for further assistance from the Bureau.

Will write you next from Charleston.

I have the honor to be yours, &c., very respectfully,

J. W. Alvord,
Gen. Supt. Ed., Bu. R., F., & A. L.

Major General O. O. Howard.

Charleston, S. C., *January* 11, 1870.

Dear General: In Charleston I have visited the schools, eight in number, with, in all, about 2,500 pupils, and, with one or two exceptions find them in good condition. The "Avery Institute" and the "Shaw Memorial" rank first. Each of these have an enrollment of about 300 pupils. The Morris Street School, with 800 pupils, in charge of the City Board, is conducted on the Southern plan; strict in discipline, but with less that cultivates the mind and heart. It is, however, an honor to the city. The Orphan School, (100 inmates,) now in charge of the State, is much neglected. The lady manager, Miss Boorn, is energetic, but needs assistants and more means. I have directed Mr. Cook to send her books, and will see the trustee to-day. South Carolina is at present too much immersed in politics to care thoroughly for orphans.

The "Freedmen's *Pay* School," (150 pupils,) with colored teachers, is a landmark, showing the progress of these people. All its expenses are met by *the Freedmen.* The school of the Episcopal Society, in the old Marine Hospital, is respectable in conduct and attainment, with 160 pupils, but the building needs repairs. I went thoroughly through Rev. A. T. Porter's "Parochial Orphan School" with much interest; eighty boys, well kept and taught, and the whole Institution on a larger scale than I expected. Mr. Porter deserves much credit for his earnest labors, and in my judgment what you have done for him has been within the law and well deserved.

Since I was in Charleston, three years ago, there has been great progress in our educational work, seen not only in the schools themselves, but in the *general* elevation of the whole colored population.

We are not to contrast these people with the white race, long favored with opportunities. Their history of utter demoralization is to be constantly kept in mind, and progress only (in comparison) from that stand-point noted.

In this advancing civilization, nothing is more apparent than the altered *apparel* of the Freedmen. From linsey wolsey, ragged garments, clumsy brogans, or bare feet of former times, we notice the change to clothes of modern material; shoes or gaiters on the feet of boys and girls; whole schools as tidily dressed as most of the common schools at the North. While the same make of clothing, bought with their own money from the shops, or skillfully made with their own hands, is everywhere to be seen. It gives the adult population in the streets and churches an air strikingly in contrast with the menial raiment with which slavery had clothed them. It is the costume of freedom, each choosing his or her dress, according to taste, and all mainly in the respectable raiment of society around them.

The point to be gained in our schools is to retain more permanently the advanced pupils; they pass away two [sic] soon, called by the stern necessities of life.

Some *liberal fund* is needed to keep choice, select scholars for two or three years until they can be thoroughly prepared as teachers and leaders of the people.

The *Normal* Schools and classes, of all the Northern Associations, should be more thorough, with special effort and expenditure to carry pupils entirely through the course.

On the whole, I am satisfied that educational matters in this State are running in the *right direction,* and if the new State school bill passes, we shall be able to accomplish much more than at present.

With respect, yours, &c.,

J. W. Alvord,
General Superintendent of Education.

Major General O. O. Howard.

Savannah, Ga., *January* 13, 1870.

Dear General: In Charleston and on Sea Island plantations I had excellent opportunity of seeing the Freedmen's condition. The statements of Mr. Pillsbury are exaggerations; extreme cases, as there are, would not justify his account of things.

I have visited the same class of plantations and Negroes, and from all parties, have usually, a flat contradiction and denial of such allegations as he made, especially from the old planters and the more intelligent Freedmen. As a very respectable old colored preacher said to me, "Whoever say such tings don't speak de trut." Possibly, mothers and babes do not have the care which slavery gave them when the birth and life of the latter was of such pecuniary advantage; but in spite of neglect and poverty, I have invariably seen around cabin doors respectable

squads of juveniles—"children enough," everybody says.

Infanticide, as such, is never known. An eminent Southern physician, whom I consulted, remarked that "the Negroes, with their strong domestic affection, were incapable of such a crime."

Similar testimony comes from planters, freedmen, preachers, cottonfactors on the wharves, and officials of both parties. Among the latter are the mayors and both chiefs of police in Charleston and this city. The people are poor, and their children die, as do the suffering poor everywhere, but not as the result of deliberate barbarity.

As to intemperance there is certainly quite too much of it among the Freedmen. Three reasons have been given me for its prevalence: 1st. In the interior the "whiskey wagons" perambulating the country; 2d. The unrestrained sale of liquors in towns and cities; 3d. The Negroes now have money. The general admission, however, is that there is not as much drunkenness among the blacks as whites. Your friend, Gen. Robt. Anderson, chief of police of this city, (as did his first lieutenant,) assured me that this was so. The arrests for this crime may be greater among the Negroes, for as these officers said, "they are usually boisterous when intoxicated." "We do not," said they, "arrest a drunken man who is quietly trying to get home.

I will send you soon a synopsis of the police reports of crime from Charleston and Savannah for the last three months as in comparison between the whites and blacks. It will show you the precise facts, which are vouched for respectively as correct by both the mayors. Also, I will send the mortuary reports from the officers of the city clerks showing how Freedmen do not "die off" as reported.

It is remarkable what a general reputation the Freedmen have for good behavior and industry. "They work well when paid," is a universal remark. "We don't want Chinamen," said a planter to me, and he pointed around to the cabins of his laborers, saying, "these people are used to our work, and we are used to them." Mr. Wm. Whaley, acknowledges that "the people on Edisto are industrious and well behaved," and, said he, "we are satisfied with their labor." He will plant next season six hundred acres.

The Freedmen are very eager for land. The savings they have placed in our Banks, and the profits of cotton this year, are enabling them to make large purchases. In Orangeburg County, South Carolina, hundreds of colored men have bought lands and are building and settling upon them. In a single day, in our Charleston Savings Bank, I took the record of seventeen Freedmen who were drawing their money to pay for farms they had been buying, generally forty or fifty acres each, paying about $10 per acre. I met at a cotton merchant's in that city ten Freedmen who had clubbed together with the proceeds of their crop and bought a whole Sea Island plantation of seven hundred acres. The merchant was that day procuring their deed. He told me that the entire purchase price was paid in cash from the balance due them on the crop of the season. Here, then, besides supporting their families with provisions raised, these men had each, by the profits of a single year, bought a farm of seventy acres. What northern laborer could do better?

I found on the Islands other clubs forming to do the same thing, and this in a season when the caterpillar has destroyed one-half their cotton. A leading cotton broker in Charleston told me that he thought nearly half the cotton on the Islands belonged to colored men. He had himself already 126 consignments from them, and the amount of his sales on their account had reached over $30,000. As I learned, the average of the Freedmen's crop, or share of crop, of Sea Island cotton is from three to six hundred pounds each.

Much excitement prevails here in political matters, and we are seeing the worse side of things. Much, indeed, to be deplored among all classes, but leading men are preparing, as I can see, to accept what Congress will give them; these men will gradually allow the Freedmen all their immunities. Wages for labor are too low, but prices must improve as the large cotton crop of the next season goes in.

The planters beg off strongly on payment for the "supplies," yet acknowledge that this is a debt of honor, and must be met, unless Congress grant them relief. Mr. Bennett, your agent, is hopeful of immediate collections.

General Anderson sends his compliments to you—a fellow student, I believe, at West Point—and assures me that he is interested in our work. He has aided me most cheerfully in obtaining facts, and testifies strongly to what he says is "the magnificent conduct of the Negroes." I presented him with your last report.

I have the honor to be yours, &c., very respectfully,

J. W. Alvord,
Gen. Supt. Ed. Bu. R., F., & A. L.

Major General O. O. Howard,
Commissioner, &c.

Savannah, Ga., *January*, 14, 1870.

Dear General: I find in this city the "Beach Institute," with three hundred pupils and seven teachers in the different departments, all in excellent condition and making good progress. The building is large, (erected by the Bureau,) of the most improved modern construction, and well kept. Although the children and colored population generally here, are not as far advanced as in Charleston, yet this Institute is a credit to our work, and seems to command the respect of all classes.

This is a continuation of the schools we started when your army from Atlanta met us on the coast. Changes have taken place but the organization, as you recollect, with a colored educational committee and ten colored teachers, was placed under the general patronage of the American Missionary Association, occupying, by leave of General Geary, who was left in command of the city, the old "Bryan Slave Mart." *Now* we have a *permanent Institution,* under the best possible direction and well endowed, having had a total expenditure by the Association and Bureau of over $40,000. One thousand dollars were given by the Freedmen at the time of starting.

I called together the old colored educational committee (these are the men whom Secretary Stanton met and conferred with when at Savannah in 1865,) for examination of these schools. These fathers were highly gratified with the wonderful exhibition and progress made, and promised to visit the Institution, in an advisory way, on the first Tuesday of each month. This will continue their own interest and help the association in the estimation of all the colored people.

I visited the private schools taught by colored men. They are quite respectable, with, in all, about one hundred and twenty pupils.

The Catholics have a school of sixty pupils, managed by the Bishop and taught by the St. Joseph Sisters, an order in France trained expressly for African missions. By especial dispensation of the Pope a band of them have been sent here, and others to St. Augustine and Jacksonville, Florida; they have a small school, as I should have informed you, at Charleston. After looking in upon one of these schools, with very polite reception by the teacher, I called upon the acting bishop. The call was in every way agreeable. He complained, however, that your officers had refused to their church the aid given, under the law, to other parties.

I promised, on his invitation, to examine the school more thoroughly, and if found to be teaching the *elements of an English education* would report in favor of its receiving such assistance. But knocking for admission next morning, the teacher held the door partly open and positively forbade my entrance—said "*the father* (after my call) had ordered her so to do." I was of course surprised, but parleyed pleasantly; told her that "the father" *had invited me to "visit the school whenever I wished,"* but in vain. She "presumed the permission had been reconsidered," and said that "the teachers were a

priesthood," "took no pay," "were mainly teaching religion," &c., and reiterated her positive refusal to admit me. I could only express my regrets, and on leaving sent my official card to "Father Hamilton," with the message that I was very sorry not to be able to see the school; that our government made no distinction in religious denominations, and that if the school could *be reported on our blanks,* the usual Bureau aid would be most cheerfully granted. On the back of the card I noted that I should be happy to see him at the Beach Institute at any time during the day, but he did not call. This bishop should not complain of you hereafter.

The general testimony of the citizens of Savannah (I saw all classes) is that our schools are a great benefit to the Freedmen. Old families exclude our teachers from their social circles, yet no longer denounce their Christian work.

The industry of the Freedmen is also admitted, and the good influence of the Savings Bank. The mayor and other officials were quite surprised when I told them the branch in their city had on deposit over $80,000. A prominent physician assured me that in constitutional health Negroes had suffered from the influences of slavery; that in their extreme poverty, no doubt, many infants died from want of care. "In the old time," he said, *"they were cared for as animals to be bred."*

I went through the public market, along the wharves, out into the suburbs, noting carefully the conduct of the colored population, and can only say there are signs of constant improvement. I was in business in this city when a young man, nearly forty years ago; often visiting the place since, and cannot be mistaken.

The *general* condition of the Freedmen along all this coast, (city, county, and islands,) is comparatively low, but so far as my observation goes, they compare favorably with other laboring classes in moral conduct, temperance, chastity, especially in a desire for quiet home-life, wherever they can buy and settle upon lands. The taxes upon their accumulating property and homesteads are already swelling the revenue of both the city and surrounding parishes. And these Freedmen have just reached a condition to make, if elevating influences are continued, still more rapid progress.

I have the honor to be yours, &c., very respectfully,

J. W. Alvord,
General Superintendent of Education.

Major General O. O. Howard.
Commissioner, &c.

Augusta, Ga., *January* 17, 1870.

Dear General: Arrived at this place, by night train, yesterday morning.

The schools in Augusta are among the best I have seen, not so much in advancement as in high tone and enthusiasm. The older classes are well sustained.

They are under the care, as you know, of the "Baptist Home Mission Society," with the exception of one (sixty pupils) supported by county commissioners, and two smaller schools, the expenses of which are paid by the Freemen themselves. I am happy to report the above society as doing so well. The superintendent, Rev. W. D. Seigfried, appears, in all ways to be the right man. Their seven teachers (three of whom are colored) are accomplished and thorough. Mr. S. has also a class of seventeen men who are studying the Scriptures, in order to become preachers. The county school is well conducted by one of the excellent teachers of the American Missionary Association, but she fails of prompt pay from the county commissioners. Excellent singing was noted in this school.

In the evening we had an enthusiastic meeting in one of the churches, when the subjects of education, savings bank, and general prosperity of the Freedmen were the themes; a number of the speakers were colored; audience deeply interested.

One half the population of Augusta, numbering in all 12,000, is colored. With much to struggle against, and some division among themselves in religious matters, the Freedmen here are fully meeting our expectations. As a body they are more intelligent and enterprising than those on the coast.

Just out of the city is a settlement of about one hundred families—something like the Barry Farm at Washington—where small homesteads have been purchased and are being paid for; average value of each from $100 to $500. These families are joyously cultivating their own gardens and provision grounds, also finding work in the city. The Bureau has erected for them a convenient house, now used for a school and chapel.

Further in the interior the Freedmen are buying or renting land and raising their own crops. A community of such families, about thirty miles out, (in South Carolina,) came in, a few days since, to market their crops for the season. They had chartered a railroad car for $140 the round trip, and loading it with cotton, corn, &c. exchanged the same for clothing, furniture, implements of husbandry, and supplies for putting in their next crop. They came to us on returning, and begged very hard that a teacher might be sent to their settlement, promising to pay all expenses. These are indications of the *drift* of these people towards independent home life and profitable labor. Although the savings bank here is one of the most recently established, it has had deposited over $60,000, of which 31,000 is still to their credit.

One of the worse habits of Freedmen in Augusta is spending money for lottery tickets. Lottery offices are on every business street, tempting the unwary, and by an occasional prize, these ignorant people (not all of them) are lured to this species of gambling Mr. Ritter, the cashier of the bank, told me that probably more was thus wasted than is brought to the bank.

A trifling incident at the above meeting may interest you. Without my expecting it, one of the prominent colored men rose at the close of the addresses, and said he had heard that "the Bureau was to be abolished," and wished all who were opposed would raise their hands. Instantly their came up a whole forest of *arms* from all parts of the house. Of course I gave assurances that their request should be reported to Congress.

I regret to find that the educational association in Georgia, spoken of in my former reports, composed of both white and colored men, is embarrassed by the political conflicts of the State. The colored men are greatly incensed that some of their leaders are tampering with the rebel element. Almost to a man the entire freed people of the State are intensely loyal; and colored members-elect of the approaching Legislature will vote to sustain the action of Congress, and the enactment of a code of laws providing for universal education.

I have the honor to be yours, &c.,

J. W. Alvord,
General Superintendent of Education.

Major General O. O. Howard.

Macon, Ga., *January* 18, 1870.

Dear General: I enclose to you a synopsis of criminal arrests from records of the Mayor's court in Savannah. You perceive cases marked "colored" predominate. This differs from the record at Charleston, a copy of which, made with great care, I sent you, which showed nearly an equality as to color. The disparity is more apparent than real: 1. At this season of the year laborers come, in great numbers, from the plantations outside of Savannah to help in shipping cotton. They become what are called "long-shoremen," have small jobs on the wharves at twenty-five-cents per hour, and are exposed to every species of temptation. I counted twenty-five square-rigged cotton ships in port, with crews of idle sailors on shore demoralizing both sexes. This greatly swells the criminal calender of the city at the present time.

2. The authorities and police in Savannah are of the old rebel class, (Charleston has Northern men,) and the colored race in court suffers in comparison with the white. You notice the record is one of "*arrests.*" A Negro with firearms about him, and many now feel obliged to carry them, or any considerable sum of money in his hand, is liable to arrest on suspicion. Not so with white men. The latter also, when intoxicated, are often conveyed home, while the former are sure to be held for trial, when comparatively far less testimony convicts the black. The old slavery feeling remains, and, from past Negro habit and character, presupposes that the accused is surely guilty; respectable parties declare that in Southern cities, if still governed by a native magistracy, at least twenty-five per cent. should on this account be abated from the colored criminal list. It has been to me a noticeable fact that where recorded crime is against color, the verbal admission of magistrates has been that "there is less drunkenness with Freedmen than among the white population."

Allow me to add my own observation. I have now travelled 1,200 miles, through city and country, conversing with fellow passengers, mingling with numerous colored assemblies, making excursions on the coast and islands by row-boat, carriage, and on foot, always going in the lowest purlieus and carefully observing all classes, and I declare to you, General, I have not seen one colored man or woman who appeared intoxicated. I did see white men in this condition. Before reaching my hotel, as I entered Charleston, two gentlemen of high (political) standing, whose names I could give, were pointed out to me reeling in locked arms along the street, helping each other home!

I beg you will note that those who make statements in regard to the morality of Freedmen seem to have forgotten the deplorable influences of slavery; the embruted condition from which these people have been so lately taken. A few months, or years, even, are only sufficient to make the first stand against such moral ruin. Give us time to rally them, so as to start fair in the race with the hitherto privileged class. A generation at least should be granted for an even chance, and all judgment (as to comparison at present) should be stayed, or else made with this reasonable allowance.

Those of us who have often seen the Negro, both before and since emancipation, feel assured that such progress as has already been made is evidence of a *vitality* prophetic of a rapidly rising people. Notwithstanding delinquencies and admissions, we must not ignore the evidences of improvement in all private, social, industrial, educational, moral, and religious life.

The following is the abstract above referred to:

To J. W. Alvord:

Arrests by police force of the City of Savannah, from October 1 to December 31, 1868, inclusive:

Month	No. White.	No. Colored.	Total
October	61	90	151
November	101	156	257
December	144	173	317
	306	419	725

R. H. Anderson, *Chief of Police*

If space permitted I would state in specific detail the various crimes in the abstract here given.

Yours, &c., very respectfully,

J. W. Alvord,
General Superintendent of Education.

Major General O. O. Howard.

Atlanta, *January* 18, 1870.

Dear General: My Sabbath was in Macon visiting colored schools and congregations, observing the religious habits of this people, and addressing them. On Monday examined schools, banks, business marts, police stations, &c.

More general prosperity is apparent than in the lower part of the State; cotton crop abundant, and of the 80,000 bales already sent to the Macon market, 10,000 bales are the property of Freedmen. Not less than $1,000,000 (as the brokers say) have been paid them in that city for this crop the present season. It is supposed by good judges that one-third of the cotton in all upper Georgia belongs to colored men. This has been raised generally on shares or rented land. There are three methods of working on shares: 1. The laborer has one-third of the corn and one-fourth of the cotton, with all supplies found. 2. He has one-third of all crops and found. 3. One-half of all, and shares equally in expenses.

Rents of land are from $1 to $2 per acre. These rentals are much more common than heretofore. With the proceeds of the present crop a large amount of land will be purchased.

I find the following history of the Freedmen's labor: The first year they worked for bare subsistence; second year they bought stock—mules, implements, &c.; third year many rented lands; and now, the fourth year, large numbers are prepared to buy. This is the record of the most industrious, others are following at a slower pace. In this process difficulties have been encountered—low wages, fraud, ill-treatment, &c., some becoming discouraged, but the majority are determined to rise. As illustrations: Several Freedmen in Houston county have bought from 100 to 600 acres of land each. One man is now planting for fifty bales of cotton. A colored company (called Peter Walker's) own 1,500 acres. Two brothers (Warren) saved in the bank $600, and with it obtained a title to 1,500 acres, having credit for the balance, and both are now building houses and preparing to make a crop which they expect will clear off their whole debt. In Americus fully one hundred houses and lots belong to colored people.

Wages in this part of the State are better than below, usually $12 per month, and for the coming season promise to be still higher. I saw a group of laborers at the mart contracting with planters for from $150 to $175 per year. Emigration for laboring purposes is rapidly going from Georgia to the west and southwest especially to the lower Mississippi. The train on which I came to this city had a large company—poor whites as well as blacks. This will soon relieve the depressed population of the coast, and help to increase wages throughout the State.

The testimony of all parties in Macon is that the freed people are industrious, more sober than the whites; though there are worthless characters, and all spend too much money in childish shows, circuses and lotteries, yet as a people they are becoming saving and thrifty. Mr. William P. Goodall, cashier of the city bank—a southern man— with whom I conferred on banking affairs, spoke of the Freedmen, as a whole, in terms of high commendation.

The Speaker of the State Senate, Mr. Conly, of Augusta, said to me: "I have been in this State forty years, and I never knew a Christmas and New Years pass off with so little intemperance among the colored population as the recent one." I was travelling," he said, "and saw hundreds about the depots, but none were drunk."

Our schools in Georgia have silenced open opposition, even in this time of fearful political excitement. I, as yet, hear of no increased violence to teachers. In Macon the schools of the American Missionary Association, (five hundred pupils,) under the care of Mr. Sawtell, are in excellent order, and the large and substantial building which the Bureau has erected, is admirably arranged and kept in good repair. I could not find a pin scratch on a single desk. Some others, especially the private schools, are not in as good condition.

The thing to be deplored is that the *older* classes cannot be retained and carried forward to the completion of their studies. The "fund," to which I alluded in a former letter, for the support of worthy youth is greatly needed. These are almost sure now to be forced away by the incessant calls of actual life. Who can be drawn upon? Will the Northern people do this or the General Government? I asked Mr. C. R. Robert, of New York, whom I met at Macon, if he could not start such an educational fund. He admitted its urgent necessity, but pointed to his "Lookout Mountain" enterprise. These Southern States may do well in *legislation*, but if left to themselves will not take earnest hold of this school work for years to come.

The bank is starting well—a colored cashier of good ability. On deposit, $15,000. Chapel and church enterprise by the American Missionary Association promising. We had delightful services on the Sabbath, with more special religious interest than I have before seen.

Of the political status in this city (Atlanta) you are, of course, informed by the daily press. General Terry is very firm and the commission on membership is earnestly at work. One old friend of ours (I need not give his name) seems to be foolishly selling himself and his party, if he can, to the opposition. Not a colored member goes with him in either House. Even though he were honest in saying that he "can now hold the balance of power and afterwards turn it into the hands of the Republicans," he greatly overestimates his strength. His best friends in all the State will drop him.

Passing through the halls of the House, I overheard a group of Democratic leaders cursing him in the most blasphemous terms, and then, in an undertone, saying, "but we've got to use him; can then throw him out," &c. Don't credit his telegrams and letterwriters. I have had a number of interviews with him, and he told me distinctly "he'd rather the whole Republican party in Georgia should be a failure than that Bullock should triumph." His more intimate advisers, I have seen, and know their character, and can assure you that no true Republican here stands by him.

Yours, &c., very respectfully,

J. W. Alvord,
General Superintendent of Education.

Major General O. O. Howard,
Commissioner, &c.

Atlanta University, *January* 22, 1870.

Dear General: I look out upon these entrenchments, which flank the grounds of this university, in wonder at the change which four short years have made. These earthworks, where rebels defied the approach of freedom, have now risen in walls of brick and stone to shelter the children of the free, and endow them with the power of knowledge. The roar of batteries is now exchanged for the music of school songs and recitations.

We are asked for progress! Such altered position is enough. Is not this progress? The institution of such a school in such a place and these fine classes of students, is but the beginning of the end. I have listened to them from the model department to the highest in languages and mathematics, and can testify to the accuracy and enthusiasm of both pupils and teachers. Blackboard demonstrations especially showed ready brains and skillful fingers.

At the opening of the evening session in the large public hall the pupils requested in childlike simplicity permission to sing for me *"We are rising,"* evidently supposing the song at least, if not the incident, to which the genius of Whittier has given world-wide fame, would be new to me. They rendered it in exact time and with much spirit. At the close, I suggested that this must not merely be true in *song* but in *fact;* that it *is true,* perhaps, far beyond what they were aware of. I then made a brief statement of our three thousand or four thousand colored schools of different kinds, varying grades, advancement, &c., from the lowest primary to those of full college classes. I described commencement graduations of such classes which I had witnessed, and positions which the graduates are now occupying; mentioned your honored name as commissioner, and the interest you feel in regard to all especially Atlanta University.

The whole school bent forward as I spoke, every face beaming with intense interest. I could not avoid the remark, in closing, that if any had message to send you I should be most happy to bear them. A silent pause of about half a minute, and a tall boy, in a distant corner, slowly arose, stood a moment in thought, and then said, "Tell General Howard we are all thankful for what he is doing for us. We will endeavor to improve these privileges, and prepare ourselves for usefulness;" a short pause, and he added, *"socially, religiously,* and *politically."* I give his exact words as pencilled at the moment, uttered with deliberation and most appropriate emphasis.

Before leaving next morning the enclosed written messages, each in the handwriting of its author, accumulated in my hands. I send them without correction, expressed as you see in great simplicity, but they are the voice of those young hearts to yours.

The lad who in this school two years ago gave you the message immortalized by Whittier, is now a half-grown young man and a promising scholar. I am sorry to say he was not present. His mother aids him all in her power, but a step-father (an intemperate man) has taken him from school, insisting that he help support himself and the family. I did not hesitate to sanction measures to have him returned. Will not some one become patron of this interesting boy? His name is Richard B. Wright. He was pointed out to me to-day in front of our Savings bank, (just being opened,) gazing up at the new sign. "Have you any money here?" I inquired. "No, sir," said he, "but I mean to have."

To Chattanooga in the morning.

Yours, &c., very respectfully,

J. W. Alvord,
General Superintendent of Education.

The following are specimens of the messages to General Howard referred to in the above letter:

FROM THE MODEL SCHOOL

Atlanta, Ga., 21*st. January.*

Gen. Howard—*Sir:* It is true that we were in bondage, and if it had not been for the kind people of the North we should have been slaves this day. Instead we are free. Oh, how thankful I feel because we have learned to pray.

Wright Kemp.

[Wright Kemp, the above boy, has lost his right arm, and is about fourteen years old.]

Atlanta, Ga., *Jan.* 21, 1870.

Sir: You will please tell Gen. Howard we are trying to rise as fast as possible, and I hope we shall soon be able to do much good among our people. And I hope his name will ever be remembered among our people as one that has done much good.

Yours respectfully,

Melinda A. Griffin.
Of Augusta, Ga.

Atlanta University, *Jan.* 21, 1870.

Sir: Will you please to tell the General that we have been expecting him for some time in our city with great joy. I hope we *are* rising as a people. We are striving with all our strength and minds to progress, both in our books and also in our duty to God. We will ever remember him in our prayers, and do return him sincere thanks for his kindness in aiding us so much.

Respectfully,

Lucy Sauey, *Of Macon, Ga.*

Atlanta, Ga., *Jan.* 21.

Dear Sir: We are glad to hear you have done so much for us, and we will never forget you so long as the world stands.

Your friend.

J. W. Marlow.

Major General O. O. Howard.

Marietta, Ga., *January* 22, 1870.

Dear General: Left Atlanta a few hours since, and here under the shadow of Kenesaw and Lost mountains, still bearing on their flanks the greatest scars of your victories, I stop to look about and make a few notes. The town (county seat of Cobb county) was much torn by troops in the rebellion, but is now rebuilding, in a region, as you remember, beautifully picturesque, and by the war made classic ground. This mountains region (so New England like) gives to the traveler refreshing relief from the piney levels or slightly rolling country on the coast, and slopes of this Alleghany range. From Atlanta the way is thick with localities

of interest. Tourists will hereafter often trace its scenes of thrilling history. Marietta has two colored day schools and two on the Sabbath. They are not large, but will increase as the town recovers its former population.

We have seen along the road more emigration to the West and Southwest. Yesterday a train with 150 freedmen passed through the capital, and to-day we met another train, well loaded. Labor agents go through the country, contract with and conduct these laboring people to their destination. These agents have much opportunity for fraud. Some, with whom I conversed, appeared heartily interested in their welfare—told me that firstclass hands would get $15 per month. One had them in families, and his whole company were stopping a day for the funeral of one of their children.

A recent tour of Colonel Lewis, superintendent, to the States on the Mississippi river, reveals some contrasts to what is found in Georgia. More general immorality prevails. Frauds on colored soldiers having claims against the Government are attempted, and so complicated that their fellow-freedmen are often involved in them. As accomplices of dishonest men, they are taught to deceive and cheat each other. Would it not be wise to have pensions and bounties for colored soldiers, which sharpers are so apt to get from them, (even after the money is in their own hands,) placed, in some way, in the savings bank as a depositary or receiver, thus affording these soldiers its friendship and some legal hinderance against their enemies?

Your officers in Georgia are excellent and efficient men, diligently at work in all the interests of the freedmen.

On that most interesting of questions, the industry and economy of these people, permit me to add another fact: Mr. Harris, our inspector, who resides at Beaufort, S.C., and whom I find earnestly examining the freedmen's banks in this region, has given me the record of nearly two thousand families now settled on Sea Island lands owned by themselves. For these purchases most of them had saved their money in the savings bank, at Beaufort.

I distributed bank papers to-day from the cars which were eagerly taken by the younger freedmen who could read.

Our train is off in a few minutes.
Yours, &c., very respectfully,

J. W. Alvord,
General Superintendent of Education.

Civil Rights Act of 1875

AN ACT TO PROTECT ALL CITIZENS IN THEIR CIVIL AND LEGAL RIGHTS*

Whereas, it is essential to just government we recognize the equality of all men before the law, and hold that it is the duty of government in its dealings with the people to mete out equal and exact justice to all, of whatever nativity, race, color, or persuasion, religious or political; and it being the appropriate object of legislation to enact great fundamental principles into law: Therefore,

Be it enacted by the Senate and House of Representatives of the United States of America in Congress assembled, That all persons within the jurisdiction of the United States shall be entitled to the full and equal enjoyment of the accommodations, advantages, facilities, and privileges of inns, public conveyances on land or water, theaters, and other places of public amusement; subject only to the conditions and limitations established by law, and applicable alike to citizens of every race and color, regardless of any previous condition of servitude.

Sec. 2. That any person who shall violate the foregoing section by denying to any citizen, except for reasons by law applicable to citizens of every race and color, and regardless of any previous condition of servitude,

the full enjoyment of any of the accommodations, advantages, facilities, or privileges in said section enumerated, or by aiding or inciting such denial, shall, for every such offense, forfeit and pay the sum of five hundred dollars to the person aggrieved thereby, to be recovered in an action of debt, with full costs; and shall also, for every such offense, be deemed guilty of a misdemeanor, and, upon conviction thereof, shall be fined not less than five hundred nor more than one thousand dollars, or shall be imprisoned not less than thirty days nor more than one year: *Provided,* That all persons may elect to sue for the penalty aforesaid or to proceed under their rights at common law and by State statutes; and having so elected to proceed in the one mode or the other, their right to proceed in the other jurisdiction shall be barred. But this proviso shall not apply to criminal proceedings, either under this act or the criminal law of any State: *And provided further,* That a judgment for the penalty in favor of the party aggrieved, or a judgment upon an indictment, shall be a bar to either prosecution respectively.

Sec. 3. That the district and circuit courts of the United States shall have, exclusively of the courts of the several States, cognizance of all crimes and offenses against, and violations of, the provisions of this act; and actions for the penalty given by the preceding section may be prosecuted in the territorial,

---

*18 Stat. 335 (1875).

district, or circuit courts of the United States wherever the defendant may be found, without regard to the other party; and the district attorneys, marshals, and deputy marshals of the United States, and commissioners appointed by the circuit and territorial courts of the United States, with powers of arresting and imprisoning or bailing offenders against the laws of the United States, are hereby specially authorized and required to institute proceedings against every person who shall violate the provisions of this act, and cause him to be arrested and imprisoned or bailed, as the case may be, for trial before such court of the United States, or territorial court, as by law has cognizance of the offense, except in respect of the right of action accruing to the person aggrieved; and such district attorneys shall cause such proceedings to be prosecuted to their termination as in other cases: *Provided,* That nothing contained in this section shall be construed to deny or defeat any right of civil action accruing to any person, whether by reason of this act or otherwise; and any district attorney who shall willfully fail to institute and prosecute the proceedings herein required, shall, for every such offense, forfeit and pay the sum of five hundred dollars to the person aggrieved thereby, to be recovered by an action of debt, with full costs, and shall, on conviction thereof, be deemed guilty of a misdemeanor, and be fined not less than one thousand nor more than five thousand dollars: *And provided further,* That a judgment for the penalty in favor of the party aggrieved against any such district attorney, or a judgment upon an indictment against any such district attorney, shall be a bar to either prosecution respectively.

Sec. 4. That no citizen possessing all other qualifications which are or may be prescribed by law shall be disqualified for service as grand or petit juror in any court of the United States, or of any State, on account of race, color, or previous condition of servitude; and any officer or other person charged with any duty in the selection or summoning of jurors who shall exclude or fail to summon any citizen for the cause aforesaid shall, on conviction thereof, be deemed guilty of a misdemeanor, and be fined not more than five thousand dollars.

Sec. 5. That all cases arising under the provisions of this act in the courts of the United States shall be reviewable by the Supreme Court of the United States, without regard to the sum in controversy, under the same provisions and regulations as are now provided by law for the review of other causes in said court.

Approved, March 1, 1875.

Hamburg Riot of 1876

D. L. ADAMS—AIKEN COUNTY

Columbia, S. C., *December 16, 1876.*

D. L. Adams (colored) sworn and examined. By Mr. Cameron:

Question. Where do you live?—*Answer.* I live in Hamburgh.

Q. How long have you lived there?—*A.* I have been living in Hamburgh about two years and six months, I guess.

Q. What is your age?—*A.* I was thirty-eight years old on the 4th day of July.

Q. Where did you live before you went to Hamburgh?—*A.* In Augusta, Ga.

Q. How long did you live there?—*A.* I have lived there about twenty-five or twenty-six years—about twenty-six years, I guess.

Q. Of what State are you a native?—*A.* I was born in the upper part of Georgia, Talbot County.

Q. Where had you worked or lived?—*A.* I generally have worked in Augusta, Ga., up to the 8th of July. I haven't been in Augusta since that time.

Q. On what day did the Hamburgh massacre take place?—*A.* On the 8th of July.

Q. Where were you on the 4th of July?—*A.* I was also in Hamburgh.

Q. I will ask you if you were captain of the colored militia company in Hamburgh at that time?—*A.* Yes, sir.

Q. Of how many men did that company of militia consist?—*A.* It consisted of eighty-four members. It was called Company A, Eighteenth Regiment National Guards.

Q. State whether or not it was organized under the State laws?—*A.* It was organized under the State laws.

Source: Hamburg Riot of 1876. From *South Carolina in 1876*, 44th Congress, 2nd Session, Senate Miscellaneous Document # 48 (Washington: 1887), Volume I, pp. 34–45, 47.

Q. How long had it been an organized company?—*A.* It had been an organized company some five or six years, I think, or probably more.

Q. How long had you been captain of the company?—*A.* I had been captain of the company, I guess, about seven or eight months—somewhere about that, as near as I could come at it.

Q. Who were the other commissioned officers of the company?—*A.* Louis Cartiledge was first lieutenant; A. T. Attaway was second lieutenant.

Q. How frequently did the company meet for military drill or exercise?—*A.* According to the rule and according to the law we drilled once every month; but after I got to be captain of the company I drilled them about once or twice a week.

Q. State whether or not the company had a hall or armory?—*A.* It had a hall; we called it an armory.

Q. How was the company armed?—*A.* With thumb-loading rifles.

Q. State what occurred in the fourth day of July; begin with the beginning and go through with the narrative.—*A.* On the fourth day of July, about six o'clock in the evening, or probably half past five, to be sure of it, I took the company out on parade. As we were going up a street in Hamburgh called Market street, about six or half past six o'clock, I guess it was, there was a man by the name of Henry Getsen, and Tom Butler, son of R. J. Butler, and also a son-in-law of R. J. Butler, all white men. They had been on one side of the street, sitting in a buggy, looking at us drill up and down the street, I reckon, for about half an hour. After a while they went back down the street from where we were drilling, and went around on the street called Main street. Afterward they came back on the street. I was at the upper part of the street, and we were going down, marching by fours, in what is called an interval march, open order, having an interval between ranks, I suppose, of twenty or thirty feet.

Q. How wide was the street?—*A.* It was one hundred and fifty-eight feet wide, and we were about the center of the street going down. They turned the corner and came up the street in a slow trot. I saw that they intended to drive through the company, and I halted the company, and then they stopped. I was at the head of the company, and I went around in front of their buggy and said to him, "Mr. Getsen, I do not know for what reason you treat me in this manner." He asked me "What?" I said, "Aiming to drive through my company, when you have room enough on the outside to drive in the road." He said, "Well, this is the rut I always travel." Said I, "That may be true; but if ever you had a company out here I should not have treated you in this kind of a manner." Said I, "I would have gone around and showed some respect to you." 'Well," said he, "this is the rut that I always travel, and I don't intend to get out of it for no d—d niggers." Said I, "All right; I won't hold any contention with you; I will let you through." So I gave command to the company to "open order," and let him go through; so he went on through, and I then went on down to the hall. Some of the men seemed to have got a little flustrated because they drove through the company, and commenced talking, but I ordered them to hush, and carried them in the hall and dismissed the company. On Monday his father-in-law came down and took out a warrant.

Q. Mr. Getson's father-in-law?—*A.* Yes, sir.

Q. What was his name?—*A.* Robert J. Butler. He took out a warrant, and on Tuesday morning I received a summons. The constable brought it to me, and, after looking at it, I told him that it was all right; I would be there at the time designated. Sure enough I went.

Q. Before what justice?—*A.* Before Trial-Justice Prince Rivers. So I went down to the court at the time designated, and when I got there Rivers read—I don't know what you call it—but anyhow he did not say that it was a warrant. I asked him if it was a warrant, and he said it was not. He was general of the militia organization, major-general of the State.

Q. Butler was?—*A.* Rivers was. And he said he wanted to find out from the evidence in the case—he wanted to hear the officers' testimony and afterward he wanted to find out whether it would be a case that would be suitable or a case calling for his court-martialing officers, or whether it would be a case to prosecute them before a court. He went on to hear

Getsen's testimony, and after he got through, if I mistake not, he heard Tommy Miller's evidence—no, he had just heard Getsen's evidence. After he got through, he told me, "As you have no counsel you can ask any question of the witness you desire." So I asked him a few questions, and at the same time, said I, "Mr. Gesten, did I treat you with any disrespect when I spoke to you or didn't I treat you politely?" He said, "I can't say that you treated me with any disrespect, but I can say this much, that there was one or two members of the company that showed some impudence to me, and also I saw them load their guns." I said, "Mr. Getsen, didn't you see me examining the cartridge-boxes and also the pockets of the members of the company to see if they had any ammunition, before they went on drill?" He said, "Yes," he did. Said I, "Did you see any?" He said "No, I didn't." I made him recollect this; said I, "Didn't you know that I found one man with a cartridge in his pocket and I took it away from him and scolded him about it?" He said "Yes," he did. Said I, "Well, then, are you certain that these men loaded their guns?" He said, "I saw them move their guns and I thought they loaded." Whilst I was asking that question, Rivers, the trial justice, said to me, says he, "I don't want you to treat my court with contempt." Said I to him, "Judge, I don't mean to do that, if I know myself. I never expect to treat any lawful officer with any contempt," and said I, "I was only asking the question, and if the question is not legal then I don't want to ask him." Before he could say anything to me I was taking my seat, and said I, "I will ask the witness no more questions, but will leave it to your discretion." He then said that sitting down was contempt of court. I told him if it was he must excuse me, as I was not accustomed to law, and if it was any contempt I was then asking his pardon for it, for I did not mean contempt of the court. He said it was contempt and he would put me under arrest, and he dismissed the court until Thursday; I think it was Thursday; it was on the 8th of July, anyhow. I was also, then, under arrest with the constable. He went out to his dinner and came back again, and when he came back he asked me if I would retract. I told him I did not know what he meant. He said if I was willing to beg pardon of the court he would excuse me from the fine. I told him, well, if I had contempted the court I was willing to ask pardon of the court. He said, well he would relieve me of the fine, and I was to appear again on the 8th of July, at half past four o'clock. I told him all right, I would appear. So it passed off, then, until the 8th of July. During that time I heard a great many threats that were made. These persons would send me notice at different times of what they had heard; what they were going to do with me on that day. I did not pay any attention to them; did not give no notice to them at all. The day before the trial, (on the 7th of July,) I went home to dinner at one o'clock, and when I got home to dinner it was not ready, and it was very warm, and the company's drill-room was joining my house where I lived; it was a part of the house, and I could pass right out of my bed-room into the drill-room; so I went out of my bed-room into the drill-room, and I was sitting by the window when a man by the name of Mr. Melen, [Meling,] (a white man and a preacher,) him and some other white man were together, and were right by the drill-room, and I got up and looked out of my window and I heard them say, "That's where that d——d militia company drills;" and, said he, "To-morrow thay are going to have a trial, and we intend to kill the captain of that company before he gets away from that court." Well, I heard a great deal of big talk and of threats, but I did not pay any attention to them. Sure enough, on the 8th of July I came home from work as usual, and I did not go back with the expectation of attending to court. About two o'clock R. J. Butler and Tommy Butler, his son, and Henry Getsen, his son-in-law, and Harrison Butler, another son of his, were there, and I was standing out before my door when they came on down. Henry Getsen had a gun; I supposed it to be a sixteen-shooter; it might not have been; there was another fashion of gun at that time, but it appeared to be a sixteen-shooter which he had across his saddle. R. J. Butler and his son Tommy were in the buggy together, and had a sixteen-shooter in the buggy. I supposed from the looks of it they had about seven or eight pistols in the buggy; large Navy pistols. They went on down in the town, and yet I did not pay much attention to that. In a little while there was about thirty men came, armed with sixteen-shooters and double-barreled shot-guns; they were coming in from Edgefield.

Q. How far does R. J. Butler live from Hamburgh?—A. One part of his place is in Hamburgh and the other just out; I guess from the main part of town he lives three-quarters of a mile, or it may be a mile. I saw about thirty of these men come in, but I did not get scared yet; so about half past two o'clock I reckon there was about one hundred men in the town of Hamburgh, all armed, some with pistols and some with guns also.

Q. White men?—A. White men; they were getting drunk very fast, or drinking liquor and appearing like they were drunk, and saying they were going to kill every God damned nigger in Hamburgh that day, and especially Dock Adams; that was myself. So, hearing all this, I went down to Judge Rivers's house and told him, said I, "Judge Rivers, I can't appear before your court to-day for I feel that you are unable, and your court is unable, to protect my life, and I believe my life to be unsafe; I am willing that you should go to work and draw up a bond that you think proper and I am willing to give bond to a higher court, where I think my life will be safe. The reason I come to you to tell you, is because I don't want you to suppose that I treated your court with any disrespect by not coming, but it is because I don't think my life is safe." He stopped and said to me, "Well, you must use your own judgment of course, if your life is unsafe, and if these men intended to take your life of course I can't protect you. I haven't protection enough to protect you; my constable can't do much." Said I, "That is my belief, and for that reason I don't want to go before your court without you force me to, and then if I am killed you will be responsible." He said, "You can use your own judgment; I shall go to court at the usual time; your name, of course, will be called, and if you don't answer to your name—well," he says, "you won't be there; that is all; you won't be there to answer." So, sure enough, before I got through talking with him a white man by the name of Sparnick—I forget his other name—before I got out of the house this man Sparnick came up to his house and knocked at the door and came in. He said that Mr. M. C. Butler had met him at the store that they call George Damm's, and he said that he would like to see me; that he appeared as counsel for R. J. Butler, and he would like to settle the matter without any difficulty and without going before the court, if it could be settled. I told him, "Well, there is no one more readier to settle it than I am." He said that Mr. Butler wanted the officers of the company, in fact, to meet him. Whilst he was talking another man came in, by the name of Sam. P. Spencer, and said that M. C. Butler also had said that he would like to have a conference with the officers of the company. I told him, "Well, I will go;" but afterward I went to the door and I saw a great crowd down at his place, all armed men, and they were drunk, or playing off drunk; they appeared to be drunk, any way. I went back and told Mr. Spencer to go and tell General Butler that I would meet him, but I would like for him to come away from where those men were, and that I was willing to meet him at Spencer's house. So Spencer went back and told him, and he agreed to meet me there. In this time I was in my shirt-sleeves; I had just come from work and had pulled off my coat; so I went back and put on my coat to go down there, and sent word that I would come and meet him. One of the officers refused to go. I told him, well, I would go, and I supposed if I went it would be sufficient; and the first lieutenant agreed to go, but the second lieutenant wouldn't go, because he believed he would be killed; he expressed the reason in that way. I went on down to meet Mr. Butler. Before getting there Mr. Butler left; in fact he didn't go to Spencer's house; he left Mr. Damm's store, after promising to meet me, but he did not go. He got in the buggy and went on across the river to Augusta. I desire to alter that; he didn't go to Augusta at that time; he went on to the court, where we were to meet the court at. He came on up where Rivers lived and said that the time to meet the court had come and he was ready to go to court and he was going on there. Rivers got his book and went on down to the court. I didn't go, but they went. I couldn't tell you—I couldn't tell you, but if I was to tell you it would be what I heard, and that wouldn't be relative, I suppose. General Butler came back from the court and sent word for me to meet him at the council-chamber; that was at the town hall. I sent word back expressing more reasons, that the men were still gathering in the town and that they had expressed themselves as going to kill me on sight, but that I was willing to meet him to settle the matter any way that it could be settled, that was right, but that I couldn't go down to

the council-chamber; that his men were all around him, and he had already expressed himself that he couldn't control them; that they were drunk, and that I wouldn't be able to go to him, but that if he was willing and wanted to see me of course he could go where I could make it convenient to see him. He said he wasn't going nowhere else, and right there I had to come. So I said I wasn't going to that place. Then he left the council chamber and went on around to Augusta.

Q. About what time did he go to Augusta?—A. He went to Augusta about 5 o'clock in the afternoon, as near as I can guess at it. He came back from Augusta with a man by the name of S. B. Picksley, who, I think, was on the committee; and he met him and had a talk with him. I don't know what that talk was.

Q. How long did he remain at Augusta?—A. He remained, I suppose about twenty-five or thirty minutes. He came on back. The intendant of the town went to him and told him that there was a great many women and children, and he believed there was going to be a fuss, and he would like to have some time to get the women and children out. He told me, I think, that he would give him fifteen minutes to get them out. He asked him, then, wasn't there any way in the world that that matter could be settled without a difficulty. He said the only thing that would settle the matter was for the company to surrender the arms and the officers to him, and he wanted an answer from me. I sent word back to him that the arms that were borne by that company belonged to the State; that I had received those arms in my charge, and was responsible for them, and I couldn't give them up to no private citizen; but if any officer who had a right to take them would come to me for them, I would give them to him. The intendant of the town asked him, in case the arms were surrendered to him, would he guarantee the safety of the town. He said it depended entirely upon how they behaved. He afterward turned around and said he wouldn't vouch for anything; he had nothing to do with that part. So I sent word, in reply to his answer, that I couldn't give them to him; that I had no right, but he could send any officer that had a right to receive them that would relieve me from responsibility, and I would give them to him. So the major-general came, (that is, Rivers,) and told me what Mr. Butler had said, and all about it, and what he said he would do, and that if we didn't give them up he was going to melt the ball down before 10 o'clock that night. I said to him, "General, I see you are major-general of this State, are you not?" He said, "Yes, I am." I said, "Do you demand these arms? If you do, I will give them to you." He says, "I have no right to do it under the law." I says, "Well, I know, come down to the law about a matter of law, of course I don't believe you have a right to do it; but if you do demand them, to relieve the responsibility of any blood being shed in the town from me, I will give them to you." He said, "No, I don't demand them; I have no right to do it; you must use your own discretion about it." I said, "Well, if that is the way you leave me, I am not going to give them to General Butler." I then wrote a note to General Butler, saying in the note: "General Butler, these guns are placed in my hands, and I am responsible for them, and I have no right to give them up to no private citizen; I can't surrender them to you." He sent me word back that he was going to have them in fifteen minutes. I told him, well, then he would have to take them by force, and then I would not be responsible for them. So then, after that, he commenced placing his men; in the first place, about twenty-five or thirty horsemen—men mounted on horses—in front of the drill-room, near the river bank.

Q. How far from the drill-room were they?—A. I suppose they were about seventy-five or eighty yards. Then he placed behind the first abutment of the N. and C. C. R. R., he placed about fifteen or twenty, as near as I can guess at it without counting. Down below, on the river, under a large tree, he had some thirty or forty. And there was a well about two hundred yards from the drill-room, and just beyond the well, about fifty or sixty feet, there stood, I suppose, 800 men, all in arms. He placed them all around the square, back of the drill-room, on the street. I forget the name of the street; but it was back of the drill-room. He had men placed all around there, and up on a hill, about five hundred or six hundred yards—may be a little more. I could see him placing men all around town.

Q. He was stationing them there himself?—A. Yes, sir. He was with the men that was doing it. Pick Butler was also in the crowd. Colonel Butler was also carrying out the orders. I could go up on top of the drill-room and see them,

and I did so. Then I came down off the top of the drill-room into the drill-room, and I placed my men then where they wouldn't get hurt.

By Mr. Christiancy

Q. How many had you in the drill-room?—A. Thirty-eight; I suppose about twenty-five were members of the company, and some others were taking refuge there. Those I didn't call in myself, I only had twenty-five members of the company in the drill-room. After he got all the men placed he sent word back to me to know if I was going to give the guns up; that the time was out. I sent word back to him that I could not give them up; that I didn't desire any fuss, and we had gone out of the streets into our hall for the safety of our lives, and there I was going to remain; that I was not going to give the guns to anybody. He did not send no more answer then. About the time he must have got the word his men commenced firing. There was a signal-gun fired; I suppose it was a signal-gun; it was down the river, sorter. It looked like it fired right up into the air. These horsemen that I was telling you about, that had been placed in front of the drill-room, they were removed before the firing commenced, and went down the street back of the square. I didn't see them after they got out of sight, and don't know where they went; and these men, when that signal-gun was fired behind the abutment of the bridge, fired upon the drill-room. They fired rapidly, I suppose, for about half an hour. They shot out nearly all the window-panes in the building. There were four windows in front, and they shot mighty near all the panes out; I don't think there were two panes left standing in each one of the windows, but there may be three; anyhow, the most of them was shot out; the glass rattled all over the floor. There was side glass and transom lights over the door, and all those were shot out; the men were standing between the windows and behind the wall. After awhile, just about half past six o'clock, I guess, they kept closing up like they were coming up to the drill-room, and after awhile I gave orders to fire, for it was the only chance of our lives to fire, and they commenced firing then. The firing was kept up, I suppose, for about a half an hour from the drill-room, but only every now and then; not regularly. During that time this man that was said to have been shot (Mackey Merrivale) was killed. He was one of the men that was firing from behind this abutment. Then I went upon the top of the drill-room to see where the largest body of men was. I had heard somebody holler down the street, and I recognized it to be A. P. Butler's voice; I was very familiar with it; he hollered to a man by the name of Walker McFeeny to go over the river and bring two kegs of powder; that they were going to blow that building up. There was one part of the building that we couldn't see nobody from it. It had then got sort of dark anyway; it was moonshiny, but it was so dark from the trees and houses that were handy to it that we couldn't see them. Of course, then I was afraid that they might do something of that kind, believing that they could do it. I then went to work, and tore up some lumber, and made a ladder, and got out of the back way of the building; there was no way to get down without a ladder; and we escaped from the building the back way.

Q. All of you went out?—*A.* Yes, sir; we all went out. But before I went out of the building I sent the men out. I seen that in the back part of the yard there was no firing; everything was perfectly still. I had been outside of the building, and went down the street, I suppose, between 200 and 300 yards, to see where the men were, and went all around. I went back in front of the building, and went through front door, the entrance leading up in the hall, and told this Ataway, the first lieutenant; he had got outside somehow or other; he had got scared, and left the building before I knew it. I told him to go down first and receive all the men that were in the building, and keep them together till I came out; that I would stay up there with two or three men, and every once in a while fire and make them think we were in the building, while they were escaping. So he went out, and he got scared, and, I suppose, got excited—I couldn't allege it to be anything else—and controlled off the best part of the company; so when I got to them there wasn't but fifteen men with myself. So I asked for Lieutenant Ataway and the balance of the men, and they told me that he had gone off and tried to carry them off. They said they couldn't tell me where he had gone. Said I, "Men, we are surrounded." I think there was over three thousand men there; they were coming from Augusta at all times, three and four hundred

together, all around; the lower part of Market street had been completely blocked up with them for about 200 yards; it looked like just as thick as they could stand; and in the rear street it was the same way, and also on the street called Main street, which runs across. So I told these few men that were there, said I "Men, I don't know how we will get out of here, and there is but one way;" and said I, "You will have to fight pretty rapidly to get out that way."

Q. Had you your guns with you?—*A.* Yes, sir; we all had our guns. We went out that way, and got out on the street, and had to fight pretty rapidly; in fact, the fight lasted until about half past one o'clock that night before we did get out. None of the men that was with me got killed. One of them got wounded in the thigh, but he managed to get away; he didn't fall or anything of the sort. I carried them away in the upper part of the street and put them down next to the river in R. J. Butler's field. Of course they didn't expect us to go there, he being such an enemy to us. I carried them in there, and put them over by the side of a little branch, where it was very thick with bushes. I was very troubled about these men that had hid themselves, and wanted to get them out. I believed if they were caught they would be killed; the men with the second lieutenant. So after I got these men safe—they were out of ammunition then; they hadn't had very much any way—said I, "You stay here now, and I will go back and find the men, if I can. I will try to work my way back, and will try to bring them out." So I did go back. I was shot at, I reckon, over two hundred times before I got in the square; however, I didn't turn my course; I went on. I went back in the square, and I went under most every house there was in the square; that is, I went far enough to call under-it. Some one or two, probably three, men answered; the balance wouldn't answer. They were scared, I suppose, and wouldn't answer. I got three of them. By that time I was surrounded and couldn't get out on more, but I carried those three men where I thought they would be safe. I knocked out some bricks under a brick house with the butt of my gun, and told them to crawl under there. That was under a house that was very near to the ground, and was bricked up all the way from the ground. After they got in there I placed the bricks all back all back just like they were before, very smooth so you couldn't discover any hole, especially in the night. Then I went back in pursuit of these other men, but I didn't find them. While standing in a little corner field, near a garden, looking out, one of the men, which was the town marshal, run across the garden, and I called him, but I suppose he didn't recognize my voice, as he didn't stop. He ran on and jumped over the fence, and I managed to get up on some part of the trestle of the railroad and could see through it. The moon was shining very bright, The corn made a shade where I was, and of course they didn't see me. They stopped the town marshal; his name was Jeems Cook. Henry Getsen, a man by the name of Bill Morgan, and I recognized one of the men I thought to be Kenlo Chaffee, but I was not certain whether it was him or not, but I knew Henry Gibson and Bill Morgan. I recognized their voices. They stopped him and told him "God damn you! we have got you. You have been town marshal here going about here arresting democrats, but you won't arrest any more after tonight." Said he, "Mr. Getsen, I know you and will ask you to save my life. I haven't done anything to you. I have only done my duty as town marshal." "Yes," says he, "God damn you, your knowing me ain't nothing; I don't care anything about your marshalship; we are going to kill you;" and they fired. There was four or five men in the crowd, and all of them shot him. He fell. I staid there and saw them taking his boots off, and they took his watch out of his pocket.

By Mr. Cameron:

Q. Who did that?—A. They were all down in a huddle and I couldn't see who it was took the watch. So some of them said. "By God, I reckon some of us had better go over in the corn-field." Then I moved out of the corn field. Louis Shiller—his house was in the same square—I went then in his office.

Q. Was Shiller a white man?—A. Shiller was a white man, and a trial-justice also. I went in his office, right under his house. I remained there, I suppose, about an hour. They were breaking in the houses everywhere and shooting people. This time they came to the front door, and broke in the front door of the office. So I went out of the back door into the back yard. They came in there, and they looked around and found what I didn't find the

whole hour that I was in there. I suppose they had lights, and found these men that were in there who wouldn't answer me when I called them. They found one of two colored men in there and took them out. I heard them cursing and say, "God damn you, we have got you." They were beating them with sticks and guns, or something.

Q. Did you know any of the men that went into Shiller's house?—A. No; I didn't know any of them. Whilst I was standing in the back yard I could look right into my bed-room window, and also into my sitting-room window, and I saw them taking down my pictures and breaking up the furniture. They broke up everything I had in the world; took all my clothes, my mattresses and feather-bed, and cut it in pieces and scattered it everywhere, destroying everything that I had. I didn't have a suit of clothes only what I had on my back. They took all my wife's clothes, and broke up all my furniture and everything. By that time they commenced getting very thick in the square, and as they commenced getting thick, I jumped over a little cross fence in Shiller's yard; and as I got up on the fence I heard somebody say "Halt!" and I looked over the fence and I saw old man R. J. Butler run out the back part of Lafayette Davis's store, and he shot and I heard him say, "God damn him! I have got him." This was a man by the name of Moses Parks. So he shot him. He turned around and said, "God damn him! I have got him," and shot Parks and killed him. I went then up in the post-master's house, where he lived. His name is Rawles. I forget his other name. It was a two-story house, and I went up stairs in the veranda, and it had slats all along on the top of the banisters along there in front. It was like the house fronted one street, this way. (Illustrating by diagram on paper.) I was on the back part of it, and here came another street. Right on this street, I suppose, there was over a thousand men. They had their head-quarters there, and Gen. M. C. Butler was among that crowd, and every time a party would come in and bring a colored man that they had captured they would bring him right up there to what they called the "dead-ring." They had a "dead-ring" down below me there—I suppose about seventy-five or eighty yards, and that is where they would bring the colored men that they would capture. Every time they would come in General Butler would yell, "Good boys! God damn it! turn your hounds loose, and bring the last one in." That was General M. C. Butler, and also Pick. Butler. They were together most of the time, and they would ask, "God damn it! can't you find that Dock Adams? We want to get him," (that was myself;) and some asked what kind of a man I was, and some would try and agree what sort of a man I was—"a man with side-wiskers and moustache"—and some would roll up their sleeves and write it on their cuffs. One man wrote down my description on the bosom of his shirt, and said, "We'll have him before day;" and I was standing right there, looking at him. I was looking through the blinds, where, I reckon, there was about a half-dozen slabs broke out right at the end, and I could stand there and look at them. I could move back where they could not see me, and it was dark anyhow. So I staid right there till day. I guess that was about between two and three o'clock. So finally time commenced running out, and they said, "Well, we had better go to work and kill all the niggers we have got. We won't be able to find that son of a bitch."

Q. Could you distinguish who said that?—A. Well, I don't think I could tell who it was that made use of the expression. It was made in the crowd. Some said, "We had better kill all," and some would say, "We had better find out." From what I heard men say, General Butler had moved men around to the corner house, on Main street, in the rear of the building, and had made that his headquarters. Some would say, "We will go around to 'Davis's store and there we will find General Butler," and then he says, "We will do just whatever he says." Some of the men would say, "We had better kill all, because, if we don't, they will give testimony against us some day to come." So they had quite a wrangle among themselves at one time, because some of them did not want to kill all. They wanted to pick out certain men, and some wanted to kill all, and they got up quite a fuss, and talked about shooting among themselves about it. Finally, there was a man from Augusta—I know the man well, but I can't think of his name now, to save my life; he has a kind of a curious name, and I have been trying to think of his name ever since I have been here; but anyhow he told them that they had better have a court-martial of twenty men, and whatever that court-martial decided on, then do it. So they agreed to that; they went off, and when they came back they had the men's names that they intended to kill down on paper, and called them out one by one and would carry them off across the South Carolina Railroad, by that corn-field, and stand them up there and shoot them. I saw M. C. Butler. He came around there once, about the time the court-martial was decided, and was telling them what men to kill and what men he wanted to be killed; and I heard him call Attaway's name distinctly, and another by the name of Dave Phillips. The other names I could not hear. They wanted to kill some who got away.

Q. You heard Butler call those names as the names of the persons who were to be killed?—A. Yes, sir; I did. The men seemed to be very much dissatisfied, and they said that General Butler ought to kill the last one of them. They wanted to kill all of them, and they were sort of dissatisfied about it. Some said they would go off home, because they would not kill all.

By Mr. Christiancy:

Q. What did this Georgia man do?—A. He said there ought to be a court-martial; he was not in favor of killing all. There was one or two men taken out of the ring that they wanted to kill, and carried-over in Georgia by some one or two of the Georgians. They got a man by the name of Spencer Harris, who was in the dead-ring, and they slipped him off; also Gilbert Miller; and they carried another young man by the name of Frank Robinson across the river to save his life. A man by the name of Pompey Curry, he was to be killed. They called him, and when they called him he answered to his name, and then jumped and run at the same time. They shot him down, but he got up and got away at last, he lingered a good while, but he is up there now. He has never been able to be out much since.

By Mr. Cameron:

Q. What time of the day were these last men that you have mentioned shot?—A. They were shot, I guess, about 3 or 4 o'clock in the morning.

Q. Was it daylight?—A. No, sir; it wasn't quite daylight; the moon was shining very bright—about as bright as ever you seem it shine. It appeared to me that the moon shone brighter than it ever did before.

By Mr. Christiancy:
Q. You did not want it to shine half so brightly?—A. No, sir.

By Mr. Cameron:
Q. How many were shot at that time?—A. There was four men killed out of that dead-ring.
Q. Give the names of those who were killed.—A. The first was A. T. Ataway, the first lieutenant; the next was David Phillips.
Q. Was he a member of your company?—A. He was; he was the armorer. The third one was Alfred Minyon.
Q. Was he member of your company?—A. Yes, sir; he was. There was another one—I can't think of his first name, but his last name was Stephens; but he was not a member of the company. . . .
Q. How long did you remain in the house?—A. I remained in the house until the main crowd had dispersed, except some few stragglers. I remained there until you could just discover day. I came down then out of the building from where I was and went out of the back lot and looked at Jimmy Cook, the town marshal, that was killed by Getsen and Morgan; and afterward I went right on out through the back way down and got on the South Carolina Railroad, and I then came to Aiken.
Q. How far is that from Hamburgh?—A. Seventeen miles from Hamburgh. We had a good many in this dead ring. I suppose some twenty-five or thirty. They just went into their houses and took them out of their houses—men who had taken refuge in their own houses to save themselves, and had nothing to do with the affair.
Q. They did not kill them?—A. No, sir, only Stephens; they took him out of his house and killed him. I heard—I am not able to say who the men were, there was such a crowd—but right near where I was standing they expressed their reasons why Minyon and Stephens were killed. A man by the name of Lamar, (I forget his other name—I am sorry I can't recollect it,) but it was from some previous falling out that they had had at some sale prior to that, and he wanted him killed on that account; that was expressed in my hearing by some of the men. Also Stephens was another man that some man had a grudge against him; but these others were killed down there simply because they were leading republicans, and also belonged to that company. . . .

Q. During the night while that crowd of armed men were around there, and when they were killing these colored men, was anything said about politics?—A. Yes, sir; that was the whole talk all the time. You could just hear it all the time: "By God! we will carry South Carolina now; about the time we kill four or five hundred more we will scare the rest." You could hear them say, "This is only the beginning of it. We have got to have South Carolina; we have got to go through; the State has got to be democratic; the white man has got to rule; this is a white man's government!" Politics was used all night long, all the time; even in the evening, before it begun, you could hear, "We are going to redeem South Carolina today!" You could hear them singing it on the streets, "This is the beginning of the redemption of South Carolina." And they allowed there was no court in South Carolina that would try them; that every hundred years the law run out, and there was no law now. They tell it constantly up about Hamburgh that they ain't begun to kill out what they are going to kill. They, most all of them around there, say they intend to kill me, if I am the last man on earth; and I have received from time to time, I reckon, a dozen notes. I have got some now, and I wish I had known I would be called in and I should have presented them.
Q. Do you think it safe for you to return to Hamburgh?—A. No, sir; it is not safe for me to be there, but I am compelled to be there; when I am elsewhere I am on expenses; I haven't been able to make five cents since that time; I am afraid to work.

By Mr. Cameron:
Q. What is your business?—A. I am a boss-carpenter by trade.
Q. Have you heard threats made to colored people since the Hamburgh riot, or at any time during the summer?—A. Every day.
Q. State generally what the nature of these threats was?—A. Well, even up to the election and since the election, it has been usually expressed that they were going to kill out all the radicals, and all those that didn't vote the democratic ticket they would kill. They said there would be clubs after the election until the next election, and every colored man that didn't join the clubs they were going to kill, if they lived in South Carolina. . . .

Frederick Douglass Protests the Supreme Court Decision in the Civil Rights Cases

Frederick Douglass

Friends and Fellow-Citizens:

I have only a very few words to say to you this evening, and in order that those few words shall be well-chosen, and not liable to be misunderstood, distorted, or misrepresented, I have been at the pains of writing them out in full. It may be, after all, that the hour calls more loudly for silence than for speech. Later on in this discussion, when we shall have the full text of the recent decision of the Supreme Court before us, and the dissenting opinion of Judge Harlan, who must have weighty reasons for separating from all his associates, and incurring thereby, as he must, an amount of criticism from which even the bravest man might shrink, we may be in better frame of mind, better supplied with facts, and better prepared to speak calmly, correctly, and wisely, than now. The temptation at this time, is of course, to speak more from feeling than reason, more from impulse than reflection.

We have been, as a class, grievously wounded, wounded in the house of our friends, and this wound is too deep and too painful for ordinary measured speech.

"When a deed is done for Freedom,
Through the broad earth's aching breast
Runs a thrill of joy prophetic,
Trembling on from east to west."

But when a deed is done from slavery, caste and oppression, and a blow is struck at

human progress, whether so intended or not, the heart of humanity sickens in sorrow and writhes in pain. It makes us feel as if some one were stamping upon the graves of our mothers, or desecrating our sacred temples of worship. Only base men and oppressors can rejoice in a triumph of injustice over the weak and defenceless, for weakness ought itself to protect from assaults of pride, prejudice and power.

The cause which has brought us here tonight is neither common nor trivial. Few events in our national history have surpassed it in magnitude, importance and significance. It has swept over the land like a moral cyclone, leaving moral desolation in its track.

We feel it, as we felt the furious attempt, years ago, to force the accursed system of slavery upon the soil of Kansas, the enactment of the Fugitive Slave Bill, the repeal of the Missouri Compromise, the Dred Scott decision. I look upon it as one more shocking development of that moral weakness in high places which has attended the conflict between the spirit of liberty and the spirit of slavery from the beginning, and I venture to predict that it will be so regarded by after-coming generations.

Far down the ages, when men shall wish to inform themselves as the real state of liberty, law, religion and civilization in the United States at this juncture of our history, they will overhaul the proceedings of the Supreme Court, and read the decision declaring the Civil Rights Bill unconstitutional and void.

From this they will learn more than from many volumes, how far we have advanced, in this year of grace, from barbarism toward civilization.

Source: Frederick Douglass Protests the Supreme Court Decision in the Civil Rights Cases. From *Proceedings of the Civil Rights Mass-meeting, Held at Lincoln Hall [Washington], October 22, 1883* (Washington, 1883).

Fellow-citizens: Among the great evils which now stalk abroad in our land, the one, I think, which most threatens to undermine and destroy the foundations of our free institutions, is the great and apparently increasing want of respect entertained for those to whom are committed the responsibility and the duty of administering our government. On this point, I think all good men must agree, and against this evil I trust you feel, and we feel, the deepest repugnance, and that we will, neither here nor elsewhere, give it the least breath of sympathy or encouragement. We should never forget, that, whatever may be the incidental mistakes or misconduct of rulers, government is better than anarchy, and patient reform is better than violent revolution.

But while I would increase this feeling, and give it the emphasis of a voice from heaven, it must not be allowed to interfere with free speech, honest expression, and fair criticism. To give up this would be to give up liberty, to give up progress, and to consign the nation to moral stagnation, putrefaction, and death.

In the matter of respect for dignitaries, it should never be forgotten, however, that duties are reciprocal, and while the people should frown down every manifestation of levity and contempt for those in power, it is the duty of the possessors of power so to use it as to deserve and to insure respect and reverence.

To come a little nearer to the case now before us. The Supreme Court of the United States, in the exercise of its high and vast constitutional power, has suddenly and unexpectedly decided that the law intended to secure to colored people the civil rights guaranteed to them by the following provision of the Constitution of the United States, is unconstitutional and void. Here it is:

"No State," says the 14th Amendment, "shall make or enforce any law which shall abridge the privileges or immunities of citizens of the United States; nor shall any State deprive any person of life, liberty, or property without due process of law; nor deny any person within its jurisdiction the equal protection of the laws."

Now, when a bill has been discussed for weeks and months, and even years, in the press and on the platform, in Congress and out of Congress; when it has been calmly debated by the clearest heads, and the most skillful and learned lawyers in the land; when every argument against it has been over and over again carefully considered and fairly answered; when its constitutionality has been especially discussed, pro and con; when it has passed the United States House of Representatives, and has been solemnly enacted by the United States Senate, perhaps the most imposing legislative body in the world; when such a bill has been submitted to the Cabinet of the Nation, composed of the ablest men in the land; when it has passed under the scrutinizing eye of the Attorney-General of the United States; when the Executive of the Nation has given to it his name and formal approval; when it has taken its place upon the statute-book, and has remained there for nearly a decade, and the country has largely assented to it, you will agree with me that the reasons for declaring such a law unconstitutional and void, should be strong, irresistible and absolutely conclusive.

Inasmuch as the law in question is a law in favor of liberty and justice, it ought to have had the benefit of any doubt which could arise as to its strict constitutionality. This, I believe, will be the view taken of it, not only by laymen like myself, but by eminent lawyers as well.

All men who have given any thought to the machinery, the structure, and practical operation of our Government, must have recognized the importance of absolute harmony between its various departments of powers and duties. They must have seen clearly the mischievous tendency and danger to the body politic of any antagonisms between its various branches. To feel the force of this thought, we have only to remember the administration of President

Johnson, and the conflict which then took place between the National Executive and the National Congress, when the will of the people was again and again met by the Executive veto, and when the country seemed upon the verge of another revolution. No patriot, however bold, can wish for his country a repetition of those gloomy days.

Now let me say here, before I go on a step further in this discussion, if any man has come here to-night with his breast heaving with passion, his heart flooded with acrimony, wishing and expecting to hear violent denunciation of the Supreme Court, on account of this decision, he has mistaken the object of this meeting, and the character of the men by whom it is called.

We neither come to bury Caesar, nor to praise him. The Supreme Court is the autocratic point in our National Government. No monarch in Europe has a power more absolute over the laws, lives and liberties of his people, than that Court has over our laws, lives, and liberties. Its Judges live, and ought to live, an eagle's flight beyond the reach of fear or favor, praise or blame, profit or loss. No vulgar prejudice should touch the members of that Court, anywhere. Their decisions should come down to us like the calm, clear light of Infinite justice. We should be able to think of them and to speak of them with profoundest respect for their wisdom, and deepest reverence for their virtue; for what His Holiness, the Pope, is to the Roman Catholic church, the Supreme Court is to the American State. Its members are men, to be sure, and may not claim infallibility, like the Pope, but they are the Supreme power of the Nation, and their decisions are law.

What will be said here to-night, will be spoken, I trust, more in sorrow than in anger, more in a tone of regret than of bitterness.

We cannot, however, overlook the fact that though not so intended, this decision has inflicted a heavy calamity upon seven millions of the people of this country, and left them naked and defenceless against the action of a malignant, vulgar, and pitiless prejudice.

It presents the United States before the world as a Nation utterly destitute of power to protect the rights of its own citizens upon its own soil.

It can claim service and allegiance, loyalty and life, of them, but it cannot protect them against the most palpable violation of the rights of human nature, rights to secure which, governments are established. It can tax their bread and tax their blood, but has no protecting power for their persons. Its National power extends only to the District of Columbia, and the Territories—where the people have no votes—and where the land has no people. All else is subject to the States. In the name of common sense, I ask, what right have we to call ourselves a Nation, in view of this decision, and this utter destitution of power?

In humiliating the colored people of this country, this decision has humbled the Nation. It gives to a South Carolina, or a Mississippi, Railroad Conductor, more power than it gives to the National Government. He may order the wife of the Chief Justice of the United States into a smoking-car, full of hirsute men and compel her to go and listen to the coarse jests of a vulgar crowd. It gives to a hotel-keeper who may, from a prejudice born of the rebellion, wish to turn her out at midnight into the darkness of the storm, power to compel her to go. In such a case, according to this decision of the Supreme Court, the National Government has no right to interfere. She must take her claim for protection and redress, not to the Nation, but to the State, and when the State, as I understand it, declares there is upon its Statute book, no law for her protection, the function and power of the National Government is exhausted, and she is utterly without redress.

Bad, therefore, as our case is under this decision, the evil principle affirmed by the court is not wholly confined to or spent upon persons of color. The wife of Chief Justice Waite—I speak of respectfully—is protected to-day, not by law, but solely by the accident of her color. So far as the law of the land is concerned, she is in the same condition as that of the humblest colored woman in the Republic. The difference between colored and white, here, is, that the one, by reason of color, needs legal protection, and the other, by reason of color, does not need protection. It is nevertheless true, that manhood is insulted, in both cases. No man can put a chain about the ankle of his fellow man, without at last finding the other end of it fastened about his own neck.

The lesson of all the ages on this point is, that a wrong done to one man, is a wrong done to all men. It may not be felt at the moment, and the evil day may be long delayed, but so sure as there is a moral government of the universe, so sure will the harvest of evil come.

Color prejudice is not the only prejudice against which a Republic like ours should guard. The spirit of caste is dangerous everywhere. There is the prejudice of the rich against the poor, the pride and prejudice of the idle dandy against the hard handed working man. There is, worst of all, religious prejudice; a prejudice which has stained a whole continent with blood. It is, in fact, a spirit infernal, against which every enlightened man should wage perpetual war. Perhaps no class of our fellow citizens has carried this prejudice against color to a point more extreme and dangerous than have our Catholic Irish fellow citizens, and yet no people on the face of the earth have been more relentlessly persecuted and oppressed on account of race and religion, than the Irish people.

But in Ireland, persecution has at last reached a point where it reacts terribly upon her persecutors. England to-day is reaping the bitter consequences of her injustice and oppression. Ask any man of intelligence to-day, "What is the chief source of England's weakness?" "What has reduced her to the rank of a second-class power?" and the answer will be *"Ireland!"* Poor, ragged, hungry, starving and oppressed as she is, she is strong enough to be a standing menace to the power and glory of England.

Fellow-citizens! We want no black Ireland in America. We want no aggrieved class in America. Strong as we are without the Negro, we are stronger with him than without him. The power and friendship of seven millions of people scattered all over the country, however humble, are not to be despised.

To-day, our Republic sits as a Queen among the nations of the earth. Peace is within her walls of plenteousness within her palaces, but he is a bolder and a far more hopeful man than I am, who will affirm that this peace and prosperity will always last. History repeats itself. What has happened once may happen again.

The Negro, in the Revolution, fought for us and with us. In the war of 1812 Gen. Jackson, at New Orleans, found it necessary to call upon the colored people to assist in its defence against England. Abraham Lincoln found it necessary to call upon the Negro to defend the Union against rebellion, and the Negro responded gallantly in all cases.

Our legislators, our Presidents, and our judges should have a care, lest, by forcing these people outside of law, they destroy that love of country which is needful to the Nation's defense in the day of trouble.

I am not here, in this presence, to discuss the constitutionality or unconstitutionality of this decision of the Supreme Court. The decision may or may not be constitutional. That is a question for lawyers, and not for laymen, and there are lawyers on this platform as learned, able, and eloquent as any who have appeared in this case before the Supreme Court, or is any in the land. To these I leave the exposition of the Constitution; but I claim the right to remark upon a strange and glaring inconsistency with former decisions, in the action of the court on this Civil Rights Bill. It is a new departure, entirely out of the line of the precedents and decisions of the Supreme Court at other times and in other directions where the rights of colored men were concerned. It has utterly ignored and rejected the force and application of object and intention as a rule of interpretation. It has construed the Constitution in defiant disregard of what was the object and intention of the adoption of the Fourteenth Amendment. It has made no account whatever of the intention and purpose of Congress and the President in putting the Civil Rights Bill upon the Statute Book of the Nation. It has seen fit in this case, affecting a weak and much persecuted people, to be guided by the narrowest and most restricted rules of legal interpretation. It has viewed both the Constitution and the law with a strict regard to their letter, but without any generous recognition of their broad and liberal spirit. Upon those narrow principles the decision is logical and legal, of course. But what I complain of, and what every lover of liberty in the United States has a right to complain of, is this sudden and causeless reversal of all the great rules of legal interpretation by which this Court was governed in other days, in the construction of the Constitution and of laws respecting colored people.

In the dark days of slavery, this Court, on all occasions, gave the greatest importance to *intention* as a guide to interpretation. The object and *intention* of the law, it was said, must prevail. Everything in favor of slavery and against the Negro was settled by this object and *intention*. The Constitution was construed according to its *intention*. We were over and over again referred to what the framers *meant*, and plain language was sacrificed that the so affirmed *intention* of these framers might be positively asserted. When we said in behalf of the Negro that the Constitution of the United States was intended to establish justice and to secure the blessings of liberty to ourselves and our posterity, we were told that the words said so but that that was obviously not its *intention*; that it was intended to apply only to white people, and that the *intention* must govern.

When we came to that clause of the Constitution which declares that the immigration or importation of such persons as any of the States may see fit to admit shall not be prohibited, and the friends of liberty declared that that provision of the Constitution did not describe the slave-trade, they were told that while its language applied not to slaves, but to persons, still the object and *intention* of that clause of the Constitution was plainly to protect the slave-trade, and that that *intention* was the law. When we came to that clause of the Constitution which declares that "No person held to service or labor in one State, under the laws thereof, escaping into another, shall in consequence of any law or regulation therein be discharged from such service or labor, but shall be delivered up on claim of the party to whom such service or labor may be due," we insisted that it neither described nor applied to slaves; that it applied only to persons owing service and labor; that slaves did not and could not owe service and labor; that this clause of the Constitution said nothing of slaves or the masters of slaves; that it was silent as to slave States or free States; that it was simply a provision to enforce a contract; to discharge an obligation between two persons capable of making a contract, and not to force any man into slavery, for the slave could not owe service or make a contract.

We affirmed that it gave no warrant for what was called the "Fugitive Slave Bill," and we contended that that bill was therefore unconstitutional; but our arguments were laughed to scorn by that Court. We were told that the *intention* of the Constitution was to enable masters to recapture their slaves, and that the law of Ninety-three and the Fugitive Slave law of 1850 were constitutional.

Fellow-citizens! While slavery was the base line of American society, while it ruled the church and the state, while it was the interpreter of our law and the exponent of our religion, it admitted no quibbling, no narrow rules of legal or scriptural interpretations of

Bible or Constitution. It sternly demanded its pound of flesh, no matter how much blood was shed in the taking of it. It was enough for it to be able to show the *intention* to get all it asked in the Courts or out of the Courts. But now slavery is abolished. Its reign was long, dark and bloody. Liberty *now,* is the base line of the Republic. Liberty has supplanted slavery, but I fear it has not supplanted the spirit or power of slavery. Where slavery was strong, liberty is now weak.

O for a Supreme Court of the United States which shall be as true to the claims of humanity as the Supreme Court formerly was to the demands of slavery! When that day comes, as come it will, a Civil Rights Bill will not be declared unconstitutional and void, in utter and flagrant disregard of the objects and *intentions* of the National legislature by which it was enacted, and of the rights plainly secured by the Constitution.

This decision of the Supreme Court admits that the Fourteenth Amendment is a prohibition on the States. It admits that a State shall not abridge the privileges or immunities of citizens of the United States, but commits the seeming absurdity of allowing the people of a State to do what it prohibits the State itself from doing.

It used to be thought that the whole was more than a part; that the greater included the less, and that what was unconstitutional for a State to do was equally unconstitutional for an individual member of a State to do. What is a State, in the absence of the people who compose it? Land, air and water. That is all. As individuals, the people of the State of South Carolina may stamp out the rights of the Negro wherever they please, so long as they do not do so as a State. All the parts can violate the Constitution, but the whole cannot. It is not the act itself, according to this decision, that is unconstitutional. The unconstitutionality of the case depends wholly upon the party committing the act. If the State commits it, it is wrong, if the citizen of the State commits it, it is right.

O consistency, thou art indeed a jewel! What does it matter to a colored citizen that a State may not insult and outrage him, if a citizen of a State may? The effect upon him is the same, and it was just this effect that the framers of the Fourteenth Amendment plainly intended by that article to prevent.

It was the act, not the instrument, which was prohibited. It meant to protect the newly enfranchised citizen from injustice and wrong, not merely from a State, but from the individual members of a State. It meant to give him the protection to which his citizenship, his loyalty, his allegiance, and his services entitled him, and this meaning, and this purpose, and this intention, is now declared unconstitutional and void, by the Supreme Court of the United States.

I say again, fellow-citizens, O for a Supreme Court which shall be as true, as vigilant, as active, and exacting in maintaining laws enacted for the protection of human rights as in other days was that Court for the destruction of human rights!

It is said that this decision will make no difference in the treatment of colored people; that the Civil Rights Bill was a dead letter, and could not be enforced. There is some truth in all this, but it is not the whole truth. That bill, like all advance legislation, was a banner on the outer wall of American liberty, a noble moral standard, uplifted for the education of the American people. There are tongues in trees, books, in the running brooks,—sermons in stones. This law, though dead, did speak. It expressed the sentiment of justice and fair play, common to every honest heart. Its voice was against popular prejudice and meanness. It appealed to all the noble and patriotic instincts of the American people. It told the American people that they were all equal before the law; that they belonged to a common country and were equal citizens. The Supreme Court has hauled down this flag of liberty in open day, and before all the people, and has thereby given joy to the heart of every man in the land who wishes to deny to others what he claims for himself. It is a concession to race pride, selfishness and meanness, and will be received with joy by every upholder of caste in the land, and for this I deplore and denounce that decision.

It is a frequent and favorite device of an indefensible cause to misstate and pervert the views of those who advocate a good cause, and I have never seen this device more generally resorted to than in the case of the late decision on the Civil Rights Bill. When we dissent from the opinion of the Supreme Court, and give the reasons why we think that opinion unsound, we are straightway charged in the papers with denouncing the Court itself, and thus put in the attitude of bad citizens. Now, I utterly deny that there has ever been any denunciation of the Supreme Court on this platform, and I defy any man to point out one sentence or one syllable of any speech of mine in denunciation of that Court.

Another illustration of this tendency to put opponents in a false position, is seen in the persistent effort to stigmatize the "Civil Rights Bill" as a "Social Rights Bill." Now, nowhere under the whole heavens, outside of the United States, could any such perversion of truth have any chance of success. No man in Europe would ever dream that because he has a right to ride on a railway, or stop at a hotel, he therefore has the right to enter into social relations with anybody. No one has a right to speak to another without that other's permission. Social equality and civil equality rest upon an entirely different basis, and well enough the American people know it; yet to inflame a popular prejudice, respectable papers like the New York *Times* and the Chicago *Tribune*, persist in describing the Civil Rights Bill as a Social Rights Bill.

When a colored man is in the same room or in the same carriage with white people, as a servant, there is no talk of social equality, but if he is there as a man and a gentleman, he is an offence. What makes the difference? It is not color, for his color is unchanged. The whole essence of the thing is a studied purpose to degrade and stamp out the liberties of a race. It is the old spirit of slavery, and nothing else. To say that because a man rides in the same car with another, he is therefore socially equal, is one of the wildest absurdities.

When I was in England, some years ago, I rode upon highways, byways, steamboats, stage coaches, omnibuses; I was in the House of Commons, in the House of Lords, in the British Museum, in the Coliseum, in the National Gallery, everywhere; sleeping sometimes in rooms where lords and dukes had slept; sitting at tables where lords and dukes were sitting; but I never thought that those circumstances made me socially the equal of lords and dukes. I hardly think that some of our Democratic friends would be regarded among those lords as their equals. If riding in the same car makes one equal, I think that the little poodle I saw sitting in the lap of a lady was made equal by riding in the same car. Equality, social equality, is a matter between individuals. It is a reciprocal understanding. I don't think when I ride with an educated polished rascal, that he is thereby made my equal, or when I ride with a numbskull that it makes me his equal, or makes him my equal. Social equality does not necessarily follow from civil equality, and yet for the purpose of a hell black and damning prejudice, our papers still insist that the Civil Rights Bill is a Bill to establish social equality.

If it is a Bill for social equality, so is the Declaration of Independence, which declares that all men have equal rights; so is the Sermon on the Mount, so is the Golden Rule, that commands us to do to others as we would that others should do to us; so is the Apostolic teaching, that of one blood God has made all nations to dwell on all the face of the earth; so is the Constitution of the United States, and so are the laws and customs of every civilized country in the world; for no where, outside of the United States is any man denied civil rights on account of his color.

Colored Women of America

Francis Ellen Watkins Harper

The women as a class are quite equal to the men in energy and executive ability. In fact I find by close observation, that the mothers are the levers which move in education. The men talk about it, especially about election time, if they want an office for self or their candidate, but the women work most for it. They labour in many ways to support the family, while the children attend school. They make great sacrifices to spare their own children during school hours. I know of girls from sixteen to twenty-two who iron till midnight that they may come to school in the day. Some of our scholars, aged about nineteen, living about thirty miles off, rented land, ploughed, planted, and then sold their cotton, in order to come to us. A woman near me, urged her husband to go in debt 500 dollars for a home, as the titles to the land they built on were insecure, and she said to me, "We have five years to pay it in, and I shall begin to-day to do it, if life is spared. I will make a hundred dollars at washing, for I have done it." Yet they have seven little children to feed, clothe, and educate. In the field the women receive the same wages as the men, and are often preferred, clearing land, hoeing, or picking cotton, with equal ability.

In different departments of business, coloured women have not only been enabled to keep the wolf from the door, but also to acquire property, and in some cases the coloured woman is the mainstay of the family, and when work fails the men in large cities, the money which the wife can obtain by washing, ironing, and other services,

often keeps pauperism at bay. I do not suppose, considering the state of her industrial lore and her limited advantages, that there is among the poorer classes a more helpful woman than the coloured woman as a labourer. When I was in Mississippi, I stopped with Mr. Montgomery, a former slave of Jefferson Davis's brother. His wife was a woman capable of taking on her hands 130 acres of land, and raising one hundred and seven bales of cotton by the force which she could organise. Since then I have received a very interesting letter from her daughter, who for years has held the position of Assistant Post-mistress. In her letter she says: "There are many women around me who would serve as models of executiveness anywhere. They do double duty, a man's share in the field, and a woman's part at home. They do any kind of field work, even ploughing, and at home the cooking, washing, milking, and gardening. But these have husbands; let me tell you of some widows and unaided women:—

"1st. Mrs. Hill, a widow, has rented, cultivated, and solely managed a farm of five acres for five years. She makes her garden, raises poultry, and cultivates enough corn and cotton to live comfortably, and keep a surplus in the bank. She saves something every year, and this is much, considering the low price of cotton and unfavourable seasons.

"2nd. Another woman, whose husband died in the service during the war, cultivated one acre, making vegetables for sale, besides a little cotton. She raises poultry, spins thread, and knits hose for a living. She supports herself comfortably, never having to ask credit or to borrow.

"[3rd.] Mrs. Jane Brown and Mrs. Halsey formed a partnership about ten years ago,

Source: Francis Ellen Watkins Harper, "Colored Women of America," Englishwoman's Review (January 15, 1878).

leased nine acres and a horse, and have cultivated the land all that time, just the same as men would have done. They have saved considerable money from year to year, and are living independently. They have never had any expenses for labour, making and gathering the crops themselves.

"4th. Mrs. Henry, by farming and peddling cakes, has the last seven years laid up seven hundred dollars. She is an invalid, and unable to work at all times. Since then she has been engaged in planting sweet potatoes and raising poultry and hogs. Last year she succeeded in raising 250 hogs, but lost two-thirds by disease. She furnished eggs and chickens enough for family use, and sold a surplus of chickens, say fifty dozen chickens. On nine acres she made 600 bushels of sweet potatoes. The present year she has planted ten acres of potatoes. She has 100 hogs, thirty dozen chickens, a small lot of ducks and turkeys, and also a few sheep and goats. She has also a large garden under her supervision, which is planted in cabbages. She has two women and a boy to assist. Miss Montgomery, a coloured lady, says: 'I have constantly been engaged in bookkeeping for eight years, and for ten years as assistant post-mistress, doing all the work of the office. Now, instead of bookkeeping, I manage a school of 133 pupils, and I have an assistant, and I am still attending to the post-office." Of her sister she says, she is a better and swifter worker than herself; that she generally sews, but that last year she made 100 dozen jars of preserved fruit for sale. An acquaintance of mine, who lives in South Carolina, and has been engaged in mission work, reports that, in supporting the family, women are the mainstay; that two-thirds of the truck gardening is done by them in South Carolina; that in the city they are more industrious than the men; that when the men lose their work through their political affiliations, the women stand by them, and say, 'stand by your principles.' And I have been informed by the same person that a number of women have homes of their own,

bought by their hard earnings since freedom. Mr. Stewart, who was employed in the Freedmen's bank, says he has seen scores of coloured women in the South working and managing plantations of from twenty to 100 acres. They and their boys and girls doing all the labour, and marketing in the fall from ten to fifty bales of cotton. He speaks of a mulatto woman who rented land, which she and her children worked until they had made enough to purchase a farm of 130 acres. She then lived alone upon it, hiring help and working it herself, making a comfortable living, and assisting her sons in the purchase of land. The best sugar maker, he observes, he ever saw was a stupid looking coloured woman, apparently twenty-five years old. With a score or more of labourers, she was the 'boss,' and it was her eye which detected the exact consistency to which the syrup had boiled, and while tossing it in the air, she told with certainty the point of granulation."

In higher walks of life too, the coloured women have made progress. The principal of the Coloured High School in Philadelphia was born a slave in the District of Columbia; but in early life she was taken North, and she resolved to get knowledge. When about fifteen years old, she obtained a situation as a house servant, with the privilege of going every other day to receive instruction. Poverty was in her way, but instead of making it a stumbling block, she converted it into a stepping stone. She lived in one place about six years, and received seven dollars a month. A coloured lady presented her a scholarship, and she entered Oberlin as a pupil. When she was sufficiently advanced, Oberlin was brave enough to accord her a place as a teacher in the preparatory department of the college, a position she has held for several years, graduating almost every year a number of pupils, a part of whom are scattered abroad as teachers in different parts of the country. Nearly all the coloured teachers in Washington are girls and women, a large percentage of whom were educated in the district of Columbia. Nor is it only in the ranks of teachers that coloured women are content to remain. Some years since, two coloured women were studying in the Law School of Howard University. One of them, Miss Charlotte Ray, a member of this body, has since graduated, being, I believe, the first coloured woman in the country who has ever gained the distinction of being a graduated lawyer. Others have gone into medicine and have been practising in different States of the Union. In the Woman's Medical College of Pennsylvania, two coloured women were last year pursuing their studies as Matriculants, while a young woman, the daughter of a former fugitive slave, has held the position of an assistant resident physician in one of the hospitals. Miss Cole, of Philadelphia, held for some time the position of physician in the State Orphan Asylum in South Carolina.

In literature and art we have not accomplished much, although we have a few among us who have tried literature. Miss Foster has written for the *Atlantic Monthly*, and Mrs. Mary Shadd Cary for years edited a paper called the *Provincial Freeman*, and another coloured woman has written several stories, poems, and sketches, which have appeared in different periodicals. In art, we have Miss Edmonia Lewis, who is, I believe, allied on one side to the negro race. She exhibited several pieces of statuary, among which is Cleopatra, at the Centennial.

The coloured women have not been backward in promoting charities for their own sex and race. One of the most efficient helpers is Mrs. Madison, who although living in a humble and unpretending home, had succeeded in getting up a home for aged coloured women. By organized effort, coloured women have been enabled to help each other in sickness, and provide respectable funerals for the dead. They have institutions under different names; one of the oldest, perhaps the oldest in the country, has been in existence, as I have been informed, about fifty years, and has been officered and managed almost solely by women for about half a century. There are also, in several States, homes for aged coloured women: the largest I know of being in Philadelphia. This home was in a measure built by Stephen and Harriet Smith, coloured citizens of the State of Pennsylvania. Into this home men are also admitted. The city of Philadelphia has also another home for the homeless, which, besides giving them a temporary shelter, provides a permanent home for a number of aged coloured women. In looking over the statistics of miscellaneous charities, out of a list of fifty-seven charitable institutions, I see only nine in which there is any record of coloured inmates. Out of twenty-six Industrial Schools, I counted four. Out of a list of one hundred and fifty-seven orphan asylums, miscellaneous charities, and industrial schools, I find fifteen asylums in which there is some mention of coloured inmates. More than half the reform schools in 1874, had admitted coloured girls. The coloured women of Philadelphia have formed a Christian Relief Association, which has opened sewing schools for coloured girls, and which has been enabled, year after year, to lend a hand to some of the more needy of their race, and it also has, I understand, sustained an employment office for some time.

Memorial from Negroes of Indian Territory

James Ladd, Richard Brashears, and N. C. Coleman

To the Senate and House of Representatives in Congress assembled: The undersigned, a committee on behalf of the colored people of the Choctaw and Cherokee tribes of Indians, appointed at a convention held by said colored people near Scullyville, Indian Territory, on the 15th of January, 1870, would respectfully represent to your honorable bodies—

That, although freed from slavery by the result of the late war, we enjoy few, if any, of the benefits of freedom.

Being deprived as yet of every political right, we are still wholly in the power of our late masters, who were almost a unit on the side of the rebellion against the government, and who, from having been compelled to relinquish their ownership in us, regard our presence among them with no favorable eye.

That we, under these circumstances and in our helpless condition, have suffered, and still do suffer, many ills and outrages, even to the loss of many a life, may be readily surmised, and is a notorious fact.

By the treaty held at Fort Smith, Ark., in September, 1865, the following stipulations were enacted in our behalf, viz:

Art. 3. The Choctaws and Chickasaws, in consideration of the sum of $300,000, hereby cede to the United States the territory west of the 98° west longitude, known as the leased district, provided that the said sum shall be invested and held by the United States, at an interest not less than 5%, in trust for said nations, until the legislatures of the Choctaw and Chickasaw nations respectively shall have made such laws, rules, and regulations as may be necessary to give all persons of African descent, resident in

the said nations at the date of the treaty of Fort Smith, and their descendants, heretofore held in slavery among said nations, all the rights, privileges, and immunities, including the right of suffrage, of citizens of said nations, except in the annuities, moneys, and public domain claimed by, or belonging to, said nations respectfully; and also to give to such persons who were residents as aforesaid, and their descendants, 40 acres each of the land of said nations on the same terms as the Choctaws and Chickasaws, to be selected on the survey of said land, after the Choctaws and Chickasaws and Kansas Indians have made their selections as herein provided; and immediately on the enactment of such laws, rules, and regulations, the said sum of $300,000 shall be paid to the said Choctaw and Chickasaw nations in the proportion of 3/4 to the former and 1/4 to the latter, less such sum, at the rate of $100 *per capita*, as shall be sufficient to pay such persons of African descent before referred to as within 90 days after the passage of such laws, rules, and regulations shall elect to remove from the said nations respectively. And should the said laws, rules, and regulations not be made by the legislatures of the said nations respectively within two years from the ratification of this treaty, then the said sum of $300,000 shall cease to be held in trust for the said Choctaw and Chickasaw nations, and be held for the use and benefit of such of said persons of African descent as the United States shall remove from the said territory in such manner as the United States shall deem proper, the United States agreeing, within 90 days from the expiration of the said two years, to remove from said nations all such persons of African descent as may be willing to remove; those remaining or returning after having been removed from said nations to have no benefit of said sum of $300,000, or any part thereof, but shall be upon the same footing as other citizens of the United States in the said nations.

Art. 4. The said nations further agree that all Negroes, not otherwise disqualified or disabled, shall be competent witnesses in all civil

Source: Memorial from Negroes of Indian Territory. *Senate Miscellaneous Documents No. 106,* 41st Cong., 2nd Sess., (1870).

and criminal suits and proceedings in the Choctaw and Chickasaw courts, any law to the contrary notwithstanding; and they fully recognize the right of the freedmen to a fair remuneration on reasonable and equitable contracts for their labor, which the law should aid them to enforce. And they agree, on the part of their respective nations, that all laws shall be equal in their operation upon Choctaws, Chickasaws, and Negroes, and that no distinction affecting the latter shall at any time be made, and that they shall be treated with kindness and be protected against injury; and they further agree, that while the said freedmen now in the Choctaw and Chickasaw nations remain in said nations, respectively, they shall be entitled to as much land as they may cultivate for the support of themselves and families, in cases where they do not support themselves and families by hiring, not interfering with existing improvements without the consent of the occupant, it being understood that in the event of the making of the laws, rules, and regulations aforesaid, the 40 acres aforesaid shall stand in place of the land cultivated as last aforesaid.

But thus far none of the conditions contained in the above articles has been fulfilled, and the time set for their fulfillment has long since expired.

We sought to bring our grievances to the notice of your honorable bodies at the last session of Congress, and for this purpose held a mass meeting on the 16th of February, 1869, but before we could perfect arrangements to send our petition by a trusty messenger, Congress had adjourned.

On the 25th of September, 1869, the colored people residing in the eastern portion of the Choctaw and Chickasaw country held a convention at Scullyville, near the western boundary of Arkansas, to take in consideration of their condition, and there passed the following resolutions:

Whereas, the Choctaws and Chickasaws utterly failed and wilfully neglected to fulfill the stipulations of the treaty made with the government of the United States, and approved July, 1866, in regard to the colored people of said nations: therefore be it

Resolved, That we do no longer consider those stipulations in relation to us as of any force whatever.

Resolved, That we consider ourselves full citizens of those nations, and fully entitled to all the rights, privileges, and benefits as such, the same as any citizen of Indian extraction.

Resolved, That as we can claim no other country as ours except this Territory, we desire to continue to live in it in peace and harmony with all others living therein.

Resolved, That we are in favor of having this Indian country sectionized and a certain amount of land allotted to each inhabitant as his own.

Resolved, That we are in favor of opening this territory to white immigration, and of selling to them, for the benefit of the whole people of these nations, our surplus lands.

Resolved, That this convention elect three trusty men to act for us as delegates, whenever our interest demands it.

A convention to be held by the colored people of the western portion of the Territory, to take similar action in relation to their condition, was frustrated by the Indians, who threatened the life of any colored man attempting to meet at the appointed place and time, tore down and destroyed the printed posters giving notice of the proposed convention, and had a leading colored man, on his way to the place of meeting, arrested through the United States agent.

Upon this, another meeting of the colored people was held on the 15th of January last, at Scullyville, Indian Territory, at which they reaffirmed the resolutions of September 26, 1869, and passed the following additional resolutions, viz:

Whereas, the colored people of the Choctaw and Chickasaw nations were, by force, intimidation and threats against their lives, prevented from holding a peaceable convention in which to deliberate upon an amelioration of their deplorable condition, and bring it to the notice of the government;

Resolved, That we regard the action of those engaged in preventing us from exercising the right of assemblying peaceably as unwarranted, unjust and tyrannical.

Resolved, That we regard the arrest of Richard Brashears, while on his way to the proposed Armstrong Academy convention, at the instigation of the United States agent and by the United States marshal, as a most outrageous and flagrant violation of our rights as freemen, and a disgrace to the government.

Resolved, That we are less than ever inclined to leave our native country, and more than ever claim protection from the government, equal rights with the Indians, and a speedy throwing open of the Territory to white settlement.

And whereas not a single stipulation of the treaty of Fort Smith concerning us has been kept by our late masters; and whereas, by a most insidious clause in said treaty, a large number of our brethren, who at the time were either still in the Union army or had not ventured to return to their country, are debarred from again becoming residents of their native country;

Resolved, That we earnestly entreat the national government not to permit so cruel an outrage to be inflicted on its own defenders, and not to allow rebels to punish loyal men for their loyalty;

Resolved, That James Ladd, Richard Brashears, and N. C. Coleman be, and are hereby, authorized to act as delegates for us, the colored people of the Choctaw and Chickasaws nations, to lay this our petition for relief before Congress, and in case they are unable to proceed thither, to authorize Hon. V. Dell, of Fort Smith, Ark., to be our representative at Washington.

Believing, as we do, that your honorable bodies have the power and the will to redress our grievances as well as the *right,* notwithstanding all "treaties," so called, of which so much only is kept by our late masters as suits their convenience, we trustfully turn to you to afford us the desired relief, and to secure to us those rights to which we claim to be entitled as men, as citizens of these United States, and as natives of the Indian Territory. And as in duty bound we will ever pray,

James Ladd
Richard Brashears
N. C. Coleman
Committee on the part of the Colored People of
the Choctaw and Chickasaw Nations

Speech on Indian Policy

Blanche K. Bruce

Mr. President, I shall support the pending bill, and without attempting a discussion of the specific features of the measure, I desire to submit a few remarks upon the general subject suggested by it.

Our Indian policy and administration seem to me to have been inspired and controlled by a stern selfishness, with a few

Source: Blanche K. Bruce, Speech on Indian policy, April 7, 1880 in Congressional Record, 46th Congress, 2nd Session, Part 3, pp. 2195–96.

honorable exceptions. Indian treaties have generally been made as the condition and instrument of acquiring the valuable territory occupied by the several Indian nations and have been changed and revised from time to time as it became desirable that the steadily growing, irrepressible white races should secure more room for their growth and more lands for their occupancy; and wars, bounties and beads have been used as auxiliaries for the purpose of temporary peace and security for the whites, and as the preliminary to further aggressions upon the red man's lands, with the ultimate view of his expulsion and extinction from the continent.

No set purpose has been evinced in adequate, sufficient measure to build him up, to civilize him, and to make him part of the great community of states. Whatever of occasional and spasmodic effort has been made for his redemption from savagery and his perpetuity as a race, has been only sufficient to supply that class of exceptions to the rule necessary to prove the selfishness of the policy that we allege to have been practiced toward him.

The political or governmental idea underlying the Indian policy is to maintain the paramount authority of the United States over the Indian Territory and over the Indian tribes, yet recognizing tribal independence and autonomy and a local government, un-American in structure and having no reference to the Constitution or laws of the United States, so far as the tribal governments affect the persons, lives and rights of the members of the tribe alone. Currently with the maintenance of a policy thus based, under treaty obligations, the government of the United States contributes to the support, equipments and comforts of these Indians, not only by making appropriations for food and raiment but by sustaining blacksmiths, mechanics, farmers, millers and schools in the midst of the Indian reservations. This government also, in its treaties and its enforcement thereof, encourages and facilitates the missionary enterprises of the different churches which look to the Christianization and education of the Indians distributed throughout the public domain. The effort, under these circumstances, to preserve peace among the Indian tribes in their relations to each other and in their relations to the citizens of the United States becomes a very onerous and difficult endeavor, and has not heretofore produced results that have either satisfied the expectations and public sentiment of the country, vindicated the wisdom of the policy practiced toward this people, or honored the Christian institutions and civilizations of our great country.

We have in the effort to realize a somewhat intangible ideal—to wit, the preservation of Indian liberty and the administration and exercise of national authority—complicated an essentially difficult problem by surrounding it with needless and equivocal adjuncts; we have rendered a questionable policy more difficult of successful execution by basing it upon a political theory which is un-American in character, and which, in its very structure, breeds and perpetuates the difficulties sought to be avoided and overcome.

Our system of government is complex in that it recognizes a general and local jurisdiction, and seeks to subserve and protect the rights of the individual and of the different political communities and the great aggregates of society making up the nation, by a division of authority distributed among general and local agencies, which are required like "the wheels within wheels" of Ezekiel's vision, to so move in their several appropriate spheres as shall not only prevent attrition and collision, but as shall secure unity in the system, in its fullest integrity, currently with the enjoyment of the largest liberty by the citizen.

Our system, I repeat, is complex, but it is nevertheless homogeneous. It is not incongruous; the general and local organisms belong to the same great class; they are both American, and they are moved by and respond to the same great impulse—the popular will of the American people.

Now, the political system that underlies our Indian policy is not only complex but it is incongruous, and one of the governments embraced in the system, ostensibly to secure the largest license and independence to the red race affected by the subject of this nondescript policy, is foreign in its character; the individuals and the system of laws are neither American. All the contradictions, the absurdities, and impossibilities developed and cropping out on the surface of our administration of Indian affairs are referable to this singular philosophy upon which, as a political theory, the Indian policy of the United States rests.

Now, sir, there must be a change in the Indian policy if beneficent practical results are expected, and any change that gives promise of solving this red-race problem must be a change based upon an idea in harmony, and not at war, with our free institutions. If the Indian is expected and required to respond to federal authority; if this people are expected to grow up into organized and well-ordered society; if they are to be civilized, in that the best elements of their natures are to be developed in the exercise of their best functions, so as to produce individual character and social groups characteristic of enlightened people; if this is to be done under our system, its ultimate realization requires an adoption of a political philosophy that shall make the Indians, as an individual and as a tribe, subjects of American law and beneficiaries of American institutions, by making them first American citizens, and clothing them, as rapidly as their advancement and location will permit, with the protective and ennobling prerogatives of such citizenship.

I favor the measure pending, because it is a step in the direction that I have indicated. You propose to give the Indian not temporary but permanent residence as a tribe, and not tribal location, but by a division of lands in severalty you secure to him the individual property rights which, utilized, will sustain life for himself and family better than his nomadic career. By this location you lay the foundation for that love of country essential to the patriotism and growth of a people, and by the distribution of lands to the individual, in severalty, you appeal to and develop that essential constitutional quality of humanity, the disposition to accumulate, upon which, when healthily and justly developed, depends the wealth, the growth, the power, the comfort, the refinement and the glory of the nations of the earth.

The measure also, with less directness, but as a necessary sequence to the provisions that I have just characterized, proposes, as preliminary to bringing the red race under the operation of our laws, to present the best phases of civilized life. Having given the red man a habitat, having identified the individual as well as the tribe with his new home, by securing his individual interests and rights therein, having placed these people where law can reach them, govern them and protect them, you purpose a system of administration that shall bring them in contact not with the adventurer of the border, not a speculative Indian agent, not an armed blue-coated soldier, but with the American people, in the guise and fashion in which trade, commerce, arts—useful and attractive—in the panoply that loving peace supplies, and with the plenty and comforts that follow in the footsteps of peace, and for the first time in the Indian's history, he will see the industrial, commercial, comfortable side of the character of the American people, will find his contact and form his associations with the citizens of the great Republic, and not simply and exclusively its armed men—its instruments of justice and destruction. So much this measure, if it should be a type of the new policy, will do for the Indian; and the Indian problem—heretofore rendered difficult of solution because of the false philosophy underlying it and the unjust administration too frequently based upon it, a policy that has kept the Indian a fugitive and a vagabond, that has bred discontent, suspicion and hatred in the mind of the red man—will be settled, not immediately, in a day or a year, but it will be put in course of settlement, and the question will be placed where a successful issue will be secured beyond a peradventure.

Mr. President, the red race are not a numerous people in our land, not equaling probably a half million souls, but they are the remnants of a great and multitudinous nation, and their hapless fortunes heretofore not only appeal to sympathy and to justice in any measures that we may take affecting them, but the vigor, energy, bravery and integrity of this remnant entitle them to consideration on the merits of the question.

Our age has been signalized by the grand scientific and mechanical discoveries and inventions which have multiplied the productive forces of the world. The power of nature has been harnessed to do the work of man, and every hour some new discovery contributes to swell the volume of the physical energies and its utilization, human ingenuity and thought have already been directed to the conservation, to the economy against the waste, of the physical forces. The man is considered a public benefactor who can utilize waste fuel, who can convert to some practical end some physical energy still lost, to a percent at least, through the imperfection of the machinery employed.

Now, sir, the Indian is a physical force; a half million vigorous, physical, intellectual agents ready for the plastic hand of Christian civilization, living in a country possessing empires of untilled and uninhabited lands. The Indian tribes, viewed from this utilitarian standpoint, are worth preservation, conservation, utilization and civilization, and I believe that we have reached a period when the public sentiment of the country demands such a modification in the Indian policy, in its purposes and in its methods, as shall save and not destroy these people.

There is nothing in the matter of obstructions, as suggested by the opponents of this measure, to convince me that the new policy is either impracticable or visionary. As a people, our history is full of surmounted obstacles; we have been solving difficult problems for more than a hundred years; we have been settling material, moral and great political questions that, before our era, had been unsolved, and the possible solution of which, even among the timid in our midst, was questioned.

The Indian is human, and no matter what his traditions or his habits, if you will locate him and put him in contact, and hold him in contact, with the forces of our civilization, his fresh, rugged nature will respond, and the fruit of his endeavor, in his civilization and development, will be the more permanent and enduring because his nature is so strong and obdurate. When you have no longer made it necessary for him to be a vagabond and fugitive; when you have allowed him to see the lovable and attractive side of our civilization as well as the stern military phase; when you have made the law apply to him as it does to others, so that the ministers of the law shall not only be the executors of its penalties but the administrators of its saving, shielding, protecting provisions, he will become trustful and reliable; and when he is placed in position in which not only to become an industrial force—to multiply his comforts and those of his people—but the honest, full sharer of the things he produces, savage life will lose its attractions, and the hunter will become the herdsman, the herdsman in his turn the farmer, and the farmer the mechanic, and out of the industries and growth of the Indian homes will spring up commercial interests and men competent to foster and handle them.

The American people are beginning to reach the conscientious conviction that redemption and civilization are due to the Indian tribes of the United States, and the present popular purpose is not to exterminate them but to perpetuate them on this continent.

The Indian policy has never attracted so much attention as at the present time, and the public sentiment demands that the new departure on this question shall ultimate in measures, toward the wild tribes of America, that shall be Christian and righteous in their character. The destruction of this vigorous race, rather than their preservation and development, is coming to be considered not only an outrage against Christian civilization, but an economic wrong to the people of the United States; and the people of America demand that the measures and administration of government relative to these people shall proceed upon the wise and equitable principles that regulate the conduct of public affairs relative to every other race in the Republic, and when rightful conceptions obtain in the treatment of the red race, the Indian question, with its cost, anxieties and wars, will disappear.

Address to the United States House of Representatives

George E. White

Mr. Chairman: I want to enter a plea for the colored man, the colored woman, the colored boy, and the colored girl of this country. I would not thus digress from the question at issue and detain the House in a discussion of the interests of this particular people at this time but for the constant and the persistent efforts of certain gentlemen upon this floor to mold and rivet public sentiment against us as a people, and to lose no opportunity to hold up the unfortunate few, who commit crimes and depredations and lead lives of infamy and shame, as other races do, as fair specimens of representatives of the entire colored race. And at no time, perhaps, during the 56th Congress were these charges and countercharges, containing, as they do, slanderous statements, more persistently magnified and pressed upon the attention of the nation than during the consideration of the recent reapportionment bill, which is now a law. As stated some days ago on this floor by me, I then sought diligently to obtain an opportunity to answer some of the statements made by gentlemen from different states, but the privilege was denied me; and I therefore must embrace this opportunity to say, out of season perhaps, that which I was not permitted to say in season.

I would like to advance the statement that the musty records of 1868, filed away in the archives of Southern capitols, as to what the Negro was thirty years ago, is not a proper standard by which the Negro living on the threshold of the twentieth century should be measured. Since that time we have reduced the illiteracy of the race at least 45 percent. We have written and published nearly five hundred books. We have nearly eight hundred newspapers, three of which are dailies. We have now in practice over two thousand lawyers, and a corresponding number of doctors. We have accumulated over $12,000,000 worth of school property and about $40,000,000 worth of church property. We have about 140,000 farms and homes, valued in the neighborhood of $750,000,000, and personal property valued about $170,000,000. We have raised about $11,000,000 for educational purposes, and the property per capita for every colored man, woman and child in the United States is estimated at $75.

We are operating successfully several banks, commercial enterprises among our people in the Southland, including one silk mill and one cotton factory. We have 32,000 teachers in the schools of the country; we have built, with the aid of our friends about 20,000 churches, and support seven colleges, seventeen academies, fifty high schools, five law schools, five medical schools and twenty-five theological seminaries. We have over 600,000 acres of land in the South alone. The cotton produced, mainly by black labor, has increased from 4,669,770 bales in 1860 to 11,235,000 in 1899. All this was done under the most adverse circumstances. We have done it in the face of lynching, burning at the stake, with the humiliation of Jim Crow cars, the disfranchisement of our male citizens, slander and degradation of our women, with the factories closed against us, no Negro permitted to be conductor on the railway cars, whether run through the streets of our cities or across the prairies of our great country, no Negro permitted to run as engineer on a locomotive, most of the mines closed against us.

Source: George E. White, "Address to the United States House of Representatives," on January 29, 1901. In Congressional Record, 56th Congress, 2nd Session, 1634–1638.

Labor unions—carpenters, painters, brick masons, machinists, hackmen and those supplying nearly every conceivable avocation for livelihood—have banded themselves together to better their condition, but, with few exceptions, the black man has been left out. The Negroes are seldom employed in our mercantile stores. At this we do not wonder. Some day we hope to have them employed in our own stores. With all these odds against us we are forging our way ahead, slowly perhaps, but surely. You may tie us and then taunt us for a lack of bravery, but some day we will break the bonds. You may use our labor for two and a half centuries and then taunt us for poverty, but let me remind you we will not always remain poor. You may withhold even the knowledge of how to read God's word and learn the way from earth to glory and then taunt us for our ignorance, but we will remind you that there is plenty of room at the top, and we are climbing.

After enforced debauchery with many kindred horrors incident to slavery, it comes with ill grace from the perpetrators of these deeds to hold up the shortcomings of some of our race to ridicule and scorn.

The new man, the slave who has grown out of the ashes of thirty-five years ago, is inducted into the political and social system, cast into the arena of manhood, where he constitutes a new element and becomes a competitor for all its emoluments. He is put upon trial to test his ability to be counted worthy of freedom, worthy of the elective franchise; and after thirty-five years of struggling against almost insurmountable odds, under conditions but little removed from slavery itself, he makes a fair and just judgment, not of those whose prejudice has endeavored to forestall, to frustrate, his every forward movement, rather those who have lent a helping hand, that he might demonstrate the truth of the "fatherhood of God and the brotherhood of man."

Now, Mr. Chairman, before concluding my remarks I want to submit a brief recipe for the solution of the so-called American Negro problem. He asks no special favors, but simply demands that he be given the same chance for existence, for earning a livelihood, for raising himself in the scales of manhood and womanhood, that are accorded to kindred nationalities. Treat him as a man; go into his home and learn of his social conditions; learn of his cares, his troubles and his hope for the future; gain his confidence; open the doors of industry to him; let the word "Negro," "colored," and "black" be stricken from all the organizations enumerated in the Federation of Labor.

Help him to overcome his weaknesses, punish the crime-committing class by the courts of the land, measure the standard of the race by its best material, cease to mold prejudicial and unjust public sentiment against him, and—my word for it—he will learn to support, hold up the hands of, and join in with that political party, that institution, whether secular or religious, in every community where he lives, which is destined to do the greatest good for the greatest number. Obliterate race hatred, party prejudice, and help us to achieve nobler ends, greater results and become satisfactory citizens to our brother in white.

This, Mr. Chairman, is perhaps the Negro's temporary fare-well to the American Congress; but let me say, phoenixlike he will rise up some day and come again. These parting words are in behalf of an outraged, heartbroken, bruised and bleeding, but God-fearing, people, faithful, industrious, loyal people, rising people, full of potential force.

Mr. Chairman, in the trial of Lord Bacon, when the court disturbed the counsel for the defendants, Sir Walter Raleigh raised himself up to his full height and addressing the court, said, "Sir, I am pleading for the life of a human being."

The only apology that I have to make for the earnestness with which I have spoken is that I am pleading for the life, the liberty, the future happiness, and manhood suffrage for one eighth of the entire population of the United States.

SUGGESTED READINGS

James Anderson, *The Education of Blacks in the South, 1860–1935* (Chapel Hill, N. C., 1988)

Stephen Ward Angell, *Bishop Henry McNeal Turner and African American Religion in the South* (Knoxville, Tenn., 1992)

Melba Joyce Boyd, *Discarded Legacy: Politics and Poetics in the Life of Francis E. W. Harper, 1825–1911* (Detroit, 1994)

W. E. B. Du Bois, *Black Reconstruction in America: An Essay toward a History of the Part which Black Folk Played in an Attempt to Reconstruct Democracy in America, 1860–1880* (New York, 1935)

Laura Edwards, *Gendered Strife and Confusion: The Political Culture of Reconstruction* (Urbana, Ill., 1997)

Eric Foner, *Reconstruction: America's Unfinished Revolution, 1863–1877* (New York, 1988)

Thomas C. Holt, *Black Over White: Negro Political Leadership in South Carolina During Reconstruction* (Urbana, Ill., 1977)

Gerald David Jaynes, *Branches Without Roots: Genesis of the Black Working Class in the American South, 1862–1882* (New York, 1986)

Jacqueline Jones, *Labor of Love, Labor of Sorrow: Black Women, Work, and the Family from Slavery to the Present* (New York, 1985)

Edward Magdol, *A Right to the Land: Essays on the Freedmen's Community* (Westport, Conn., 1977)

Robert C. Morris, *Reading, 'Riting, and Reconstruction: The Education of Freedmen in the South, 1861–1870* (Chicago, 1981)

Claude F. Oubre, *Forty Acres and a Mule: The Freedmen's Bureau and Black Landownership* (Baton Rouge, La., 1978)

Nell Irvin Painter, *Exodusters: Black Migration to Kansas After Reconstruction* (New York, 1976)

Howard N. Rabinowitz, ed., *Southern Black Leaders of the Reconstruction Era* (Urbana 1982)

Peter J. Rachleff, *Black Labor in the South: Richmond, Virginia, 1865–1890* (Philadelphia, 1984)

Roger L. Ransom and Richard Sutch, *One Kind of Freedom: The Economic Consequences of Emancipation* (Cambridge, England, 1977)

Wille Lee Rose, *Rehearsal for Reconstruction: The Port Royal Experiment* (Indianapolis, 1964)

Julie Saville, *The Work of Reconstruction: From Slave to Wage Laborer in South Carolina, 1860–1870* (Cambridge, England, 1994)

Leslie A. Schwalm, *A Hard Fight for We: Women's Transition from Slavery to Freedom in South Carolina* (Urbana, Ill., 1997)

Amy Dru Stanley, *From Bondage to Contract: Wage Labor, Marriage and the Market in the Age of Slave Emancipation* (Cambridge, England, 1998)

Allen W. Trelease, *White Terror: The Ku Klux Klan Conspiracy and Southern Reconstruction* (New York, 1971)

Clarence Earl Walker, *A Rock in a Weary Land: The African Methodist Episcopal Church during Civil War and Reconstruction* (Baton Rouge, La., 1982)

Colored school in Monticello, Arkansas, 1906. (*Source:* Bracey Family Archives.)

Chapter

7

The Onset of Jim Crow

The period from 1880 to the First World War is generally known as the "nadir" in black history, a term coined by the historian Rayford Logan, to describe the rapidly deteriorating conditions of African Americans in the south. The selection from T. Thomas Fortune describes these circumstances and the triumph of white supremacy. Through escalating violence, fraud, complicated laws, and—starting from the 1890s—the rewriting of state constitutions, southern states systematically disfranchised African Americans. A majority of black people labored as sharecroppers in the plantations of the rural south, where they were grossly exploited by white landowners and merchants. The new plantation regimen is illustrated by documents on sharecropping, debt peonage, and descriptions of southern agricultural practices. By law and custom, southern states inaugurated a system of segregation in schools, public accommodations, and transportation. The "racial etiquette" of Jim Crow included arbitrary and demeaning provisions on how black people should behave in public, how one addressed whites as individuals, and the general range of acceptable behavior toward whites. The 1896 Supreme Court decision in the case of Plessy v. Ferguson, included in this chapter, provided the ultimate legal sanction for segregation. Finally, African Americans were subject to brutal vio-

lence epitomized by the horror of lynching. In 1892 alone, 161 black men and women were lynched. Ida B. Wells's famous pamphlet documents the extent of lynching in the United States and her efforts to bring international attention to it.

Within this world of segregation, African Americans continued to build institutions and organizations based on racial loyalty and solidarity in order to survive and to control as much of their lives as possible. National black organizations such as the National Negro Business League, Booker T. Washington's brainchild, and the National Association of Colored Women, headed by Mary Church Terrell, were founded during this period. Two documents in this chapter illustrate the philosophy and the work of such organizations. Despite the dismal conditions of black life, African American leaders and intellectuals were engaged in rich political debate over how to address the problem of race in the United States. From 1895, Washington established the dominant tone of gradualism and accommodation to southern conditions. In the document included here, Washington expresses his views on industrial education. Since his public remarks were ambiguous, whites mistook his strategy for his ultimate goals. Secretly, he spent large amounts of money fighting segregation and disfranchisement. *Washington's most prominent black critic was W. E. B. Du Bois, who helped found the Niagara movement in 1905 and the NAACP in 1909. Both organizations were devoted to winning political rights for African Americans and removing racial discrimination from American society. Du Bois' criticism of* Washington is included in this chapter. The last document, "Lift Ev'ry Voice and Sing," which was adopted as the "Negro National Anthem," expresses the stubborn optimism and deep faith in the ultimate achievement of social justice that have informed the lives and struggles of African Americans in the twentieth century.

Proceedings of the National Conference of the Colored Men of the United States

THIRD DAY

The National Colored Conference reassembled at 9 o'clock, President J. R. Lynch in the chair.

C. O. H. Thomas said he had remarked on the evening previous that he desired the following morning to answer pertinently the reflections cast upon him by Governor Pinchback, but as the Governor was not present he would postpone his remarks.

The following resolutions were offered and referred:

By B. A. J. Nixon:

To the honorable and august body of Colored Men in Conference assembled:
  We, the people of Giles county, Tennessee, send greeting to your honorable body, and earnestly ask that you, after having carefully considered the various subjects announced by the Executive Committee, to present to us and the colored people all over these United States some remedy for the untold injustices which

our people have endured and are enduring. We of Giles county can very easily enumerate the evils under which we have been laboring for more than a decade of years, but our best judgment and most extended research have been baffled when attempting to devise a remedy. It has been said, and wisely, we think, that in counsel there is much wisdom. Therefore, we ask your body to promulgate to the colored people of the United States some remedy for the innumerable injuries we are suffering.

  Whereas the colored people of the Southern States are being stirred up on the subject of emigration; therefore
  Resolved, That a committee be appointed by this Conference, be known as the National Emigration Committee, consisting of one gentleman from each State, whose duty it shall be to organize similar committees in each of the Southern States.

By J. Henri Burch, of Louisiana:

  Whereas there is now going on, and has been for some time past an exodus of the colored people of certain Southern States to the state of Kansas and other Northern States; and
  Whereas, while said exodus has on the one side attracted the attention sympathies, and efforts of all lovers of universal equality before the law, it has on the other given rise to various harsh criticisms on the part of those opposed to emigration, who are using the silence of the Negro as a race to declare that it is put

Source: From *Proceedings of the National Conference of the Colored Men of the United States, Held in the State Capitol at Nashville, Tennessee, May 6, 7, 8, 9, 1879* (Washington, D.C.: Rufus H. Darby, 1879), pp. 22–28, 83–86, 100–105.

into operation solely for political purposes; that the Negro is happy and contented in the South, and that he has no real cause for emigrating, and other specious arguments calculated to place the emigrationists in a false position; and

Whereas the purpose of dealing with this question as colored men and from a national standpoint;

Resolved, That the Committee on Emigration, when appointed, be requested to take under consideration, and report back to this Convention, the following subjects pertaining to said exodus:

1. What are the causes that have given rise to the exodus movement among the colored people?

2. If there is any truth in the report that the scheme was gotten up to irate the North against the South?

3. What are the remedies to be pursued to stop the movement? Would the colored people accept concessions if made to them; and, if so, of what nature?

4. Are the colored people pursuing the wisest course of migration?

5. How is this movement likely to affect the two political parties in their respective States and nationally?

6. Any other observations that may occur to the committee.

By T. W. Lott:

Whereas there is an unsettled state of affairs in the Southern States, resulting in the exodus of a large number of colored people from that section of the country; and

Whereas this state of unrest is pervading the entire colored community, creating almost uncontrollable anxiety on their part as to the final result; and

Whereas it is not the desire of the people, nor the sense of this Conference that the migration of said people continue without an adequate cause to the evident and irreparable loss to both the colored and the white; and

Whereas it is expected that this Conference take into serious consideration this matter in all its various aspects; be it therefore

Resolved, That it is due to the colored race, especially to those of our suffering brethren of the South, that this body do give a dispassion-

ate, searching, and positive expression as to the existing causes, whether political or otherwise, with a view to the incitement of a more earnest endeavor looking to their removal and immediate restoration to confidence and prosperity in said States, and that, should said causes be traced to the unjust discrimination toward the colored man on account of race, color, or previous condition of servitude as to the real, proper, and unmistakable source, that we, in the name of the oppressed race of, which this body is a part, deprecate in unmeasured terms, as shocking to the highest sensibilities of an enlightened civilization, such discrimination, being an unmerited return for the noble achievements of the Negro, the blessings of which the white race are the favored recipients.

Resolved, That in the discussion of this momentous and all-absorbing question we indulge in no language which justly and impartially interpreted will cast any reflection upon the white man or reflect discredit upon this body.

By C. O. H. Thomas:

Resolved, That this Conference of representative colored men of the United States of America are pledged by the sacred bond of kindred blood and of a common humanity, to devote their best efforts for the establishment of civil and political rights;

Resolved, That the rights of the freedmen are inseparable from the condition of freedom. Therefore, being free and invested with that potent talisman of liberty, the ballot, which will enable us to maintain our rights, we here declare that we wish to possess and exercise, as prudent, law-abiding citizens, all the rights possessed in common by other citizens of the United States. We furthermore avow our earnest hope that the noble men and women of our country who are seeking to lift up their sisters to a higher plane of womanhood by giving them a larger scope in the activities and responsibilities of life by means of the ballot, may succeed in consummating their great purpose, for it would be a wretched commentary upon our liberty-loving profession if we proved not our faith by our works in refusing to aid in the complete freedom and exaltation of women.

Resolved, That the right to labor and to receive wages commensurate with the labor performed are sacred principles underlying the primal foundation of human society. It is, therefore, as much treason against God and humanity to close up an avenue of labor by which people gain a living as to steal the sweat of their brows by paying them wages inadequate to the work performed. The party in power, if it would continue to be the shepherd of the people, must not waver from the steadfast adherence to the principles which gave it its present glory.

Resolved, That the vast body of the working men of this country white or colored, require a policy which shall elevate labor, giving them higher wages and better homes in the South, and throw open to them the avenues of industry and emolument to race.

Resolved, That we behold with feelings of deep mortification and regret the widespread demoralization of the almost utter advancement of earnest efforts for self-culture and intellectual development by our young men and women. We call upon our ministers and others to whose care is committed the moral and mental training of the young to strive with all their might to reclaim those who are walking down the broad road that leads to moral and physical death.

Resolved, We also deplore the existence of a fact equally bad. Among our so-called leading men there is no general spirit of public enterprise nor of laudable ambition to place within the hands of their race the means of their self-elevation; no building associations; no industrial avenue through which a knowledge of the various mechanical arts can be obtained. The work-shops, the counting-rooms, clerkships in stores, and employment in the busy commercial marts of our cities and towns are closed to us as a rule, and we have yet to learn the sad lesson that the spirit of caste and of prejudice will continue to prevail just so long as we are poor and needy.

Resolved, That on the subject of migration we will give it our special unbiased and unprejudiced consideration, and will so act as to redound to the good and benefit of all concerned—to both rulers and the ruled.

By L. A. Roberts, of Grand Junction, Tenn.:

Whereas there is at the present time a spirit of emigration existing among the colored people of the South, especially in the valley of the Mississippi, caused by oppression and otherwise, and non-protection in their rights as American citizens in the several Southern States, with no prospect existing of a change for the better; therefore

Resolved, By this, the National Convention of colored citizens: First that it is expedient and wise for all who can to emigrate to some parts of the United States where they can enjoy all the rights and immunities granted them under the Constitution and laws of the United States, without fear or molestation; second, that in order to carry out the project of emigration systematically and advantageously, an emigration society be organized, whose duty shall be to assist those who desire to leave their homes in the South in so doing, and to reach their destination in any of the Northwestern States or Territories, to establish bureaus and agencies at one or more points on the Mississippi, Tennessee, Cumberland, Ohio and Missouri rivers, connected with the principal railroads leading West and Northwest, to look after the welfare and interest of the emigrants at the several places of embarking, and change of cars and disembarking; third, that as the boats on the Mississippi river have refused to carry colored emigrants, steps be taken to charter one or more boats for that purpose, and if possible bring suit against those who have refused; fourth, this society shall be known as the "North American Colored Emigration Society," and shall in all respects be officered and managed as other societies of the same character which are best adapted to the wants and interests of those whom it seeks to benefit.

Referred to the Committee on Migration.

By James D. Kennedy, of Louisiana:

Resolved, That the Committee on Permanent Organization be instructed to inquire into the practicability of holding a conference every year, and report the result of labor at the earliest moment.

Referred.

By W. F. Yardley:

Resolved, That it is the sense of this Conference that colored people should migrate to those States and Territories where they can enjoy all the rights which are guaranteed by the laws and Constitution of the United States, and enforced by the Executive departments of such States and Territories, and we ask of Congress of the United States an appropriation of $500,000 to aid in the removal of our people from the South.

By G. W. Darden, of Kentucky:

Whereas the colored people of the South are so cruelly treated in the South, being slain by rifle clubs and lynch law; and

Whereas in the South slavery is not dead, but sleeping; and

Whereas in the South election day is a day of terror with the colored man; and

Whereas the Southern Negro is not as well treated as the Southern dog by the white man, who rightly claims that this is a white man's Government; and

Whereas the colored man is not recognized here as human, but, as Tom Paine asserted, as a species of the monkey; and

Whereas the ex-Confederate President seems to indorse Tom Paine by saying that the idea of educating the Negro is a piece of nonsense; therefore be it

Resolved, That the colored man of the South save his dollars and cents in order to emigrate.

Resolved, That we pay no heed to such men as Fred. Douglass and his accomplices, for the simple reason that they are well-to-do Northern men who will not travel out of their way to benefit the suffering Southern Negro, and who care not for the interests of their race.

By J. M. Smith, of Tennessee:

Whereas there is great excitement among our race of people that is causing great suffering: We therefore ask of this Conference to use their best influence in pacifying the minds of their countrymen. We ignore the practice that is played upon the colored man in this country. We therefore ask this honorable Conference to give some aid if possible to their countrymen. The real cause is the reduction of wages and the shameful manner in which we are treated in traveling over the great thoroughfares of the country. We also clamor for our rights as free citizens in the country, which are denied us. This excitement is causing an exodus which is causing much suffering. They are leaving the houses

of their childhood, trusting their fortune to an experiment. It is an experiment which, if it fails, will ruin us forever. We therefore ask that this matter be carefully considered and the minds of the people pacified. Thousands have left their homes penniless, not knowing when nor where it will end. We therefore demand all of our rights as citizens, and unless we do receive our just rights, we resolve to emigrate to the North or Northwest. We pledge ourselves to come together in all parts of the country as free citizens and demand our rights. We know the color line has been struck, and unless it be withdrawn, we will immediately seek for our suffrage, which, if it cannot be obtained here, we will remove from among them where we can enjoy our free privileges. We therefore ask this honorable Conference to use their best influence in our behalf.

By J. C. Napier:

Whereas the civil and political rights of the Negro, from the Ohio river to the Gulf of Mexico, are abridged and curtailed in every conceivable manner, he being denied almost every privilege that is calculated to elevate him in his moral, intellectual and political status; as compared with the public school privileges of the white man, his are a mere mockery; in the courts, as compared to that justice which is meted out to white men, his is entirely farcical, he seldom or never enjoying that right which the Constitution of our country guarantees to every citizen, namely, the right to be tried by a jury of his peers; and

Whereas it appears there is no disposition on the part of a great majority of the Southern people to grant to the Negro those rights which the word citizenship should carry with it, or to relinquish any of their old customs and prejudices; therefore,

Resolved, That it is the sense of this conference that the great current of migrations which has, within the past few weeks, taken thousands of our people from our midst, and which is daily carrying hundreds from the extreme Southern States, should be encouraged and kept in motion until those who are left are awarded every right and privilege to which the Constitution and laws of our country entitle us; or, until we are all in a land where our rights are in no respect questioned.

By B. F. Williams: Setting apart June 19 as a national holiday for the colored people as the anniversary of the emancipation of the race.

The introducer was called on to "explain" this resolution. He said the people of Texas were in the last stage of creation, and that the colored people were freed on that day. It was not freedom until all were free, and therefore he had selected that day as the anniversary.

Rev. G. H. Shaffer moved to amend by inserting the "22d of September," instead of "June 19."

W. H. Council moved to amend by inserting "January 1," as a more suitable day.

J. W. Cromwell moved to fix upon the 30th of March, when the fifteenth amendment was passed.

The vice-president thought January 1 the best day.

A member in the rear said they were not free yet. They were still killed in the South.

Mr. Williams. Yes, and they kill them in the North as well as in the South. [Laughter.]

Colonel Robert Harlan moved to lay the subject on the table.

A motion to adjourn prevailed and a recess was taken until 2 p. m. . . .

RACE UNITY—ITS IMPORTANCE AND NECESSITY—CAUSES WHICH RETARD ITS DEVELOPMENT—HOW IT MAY BE SECURED—OUR PLAIN DUTY

By Ferdinand L. Barnett, of Illinois.

Mr. Chairman and Gentlemen of the Conference: The subject assigned is one of great importance. The axioms which teach us of the strength in unity and the certain destruction following close upon the heels of strife and dissension, need not be here repeated. Race elevation can be attained only through race unity. Pious precepts, business integrity, and moral stamina of the most exalted stamp, may win the admiration for a noble few, but unless the moral code, by the grandeur of its teachings, actuates every individual and incites us as a race to nobler as-

pirations and quickens us to the realization of our moral shortcomings, the distinction accorded to the few will avail us nothing. The wealth of the Indies may crown the efforts of fortune's few favored ones. They may receive all the homage wealth invariably brings, but unless we as a race check the spirit of pomp and display, and by patiently practicing the most rigid economy, secure homes for ourselves and children, the preferment won by a few wealthy ones will prove short-lived and unsatisfactory. We may have our educational lights here and there, and by the brilliancy of their achievements they may be living witnesses to the falsity of the doctrine of our inherited inferiority, but this alone will not suffice. It is a general enlightenment of the race which must engage our noblest powers. One vicious, ignorant Negro is readily conceded to be a type of all the rest, but a Negro educated and refined is said to be an exception. We must labor to reverse this rule; education and moral excellence must become general and characteristic, with ignorance and depravity for the exception.

Seeing, then, the necessity of united action and universal worth rather than individual brilliancy, we sorrowfully admit that race unity with us is a blessing not yet enjoyed, but to be possessed. We are united only in the conditions which degrade, and actions which paralyze the efforts of the worthy, who labor for the benefit of the multitude. We are a race of leaders, every one presuming that his neighbor and not himself was decreed to be a follower. To-day, if any one of you should go home and announce yourself candidate for a certain position, the following day would find a dozen men in the field, each well prepared to prove that he alone is capable of obtaining and filling the position. Failing to convince the people, he would drop out the race entirely or do all in his power to jeopardize the interest of a more successful brother.

Why this non-fraternal feeling? Why such a spirit of dissension? We attribute it, first, to lessons taught in by-gone days by those whose security rested in our disunion. If the same spirit of race unity had actuated the Negro which has always characterized the Indian, this Government would have trembled under the blow of that immortal hero, John Brown, and the first drop of fratricidal blood would have been shed, not at Fort Sumter, but at Harper's Ferry. Another cause may be found in our partial enlightenment. The ignorant man is always narrow-minded in politics, business or religion. Unfold to him a plan, and if he cannot see some interest resulting to self, however great the resulting good to the multitude, it meets only his partial approbation and fails entirely to secure his active co-operation. A third reason applies, not to the unlearned, but to the learned. Too many of our learned men are afflicted with a mental and moral aberration, termed in common parlance "big-headed." Having reached a commendable degree of eminence, they seem to stand and say, "Lord, we thank Thee we are not as other men are." They view with perfect unconcern the struggles of a worthy brother; they proffer him no aid, but deem it presumption in him to expect it. They may see a needed step but fail to take it. Others may see the necessity, take steps to meet it, and call them to aid. But, no; they did not lead; they will not follow, and half of their influence for good is sacrificed by an insane jealousy that is a consuming fire in every bosom wherein it finds lodgment.

A few of the prominent causes which retard race unity having been noticed, let us look for the remedy. First, our natural jealousy must be overcome. The task is no easy one. We must look for fruits of our labor in the next generation. With us our faults are confirmed. An old slave once lay dying, friends and relatives were gathered around. The minister sat at the bedside endeavoring to prepare the soul for the great change. The old man was willing to forgive every one except a certain particularly obstreperous African who had caused him much injury. But being over-persuaded he yielded and said: "Well, if I dies I forgives him, but if I lives—dat darkey better take care." It is

much the same with us; when we die our natures will change, but while we live our neighbors must take care. Upon the young generation our instruction may be effective. They must be taught that in helping one another they help themselves; and that in the race of life, when a favored one excels and leads the rest, their powers must be employed, not in retarding his progress, but in urging him on and inciting others to emulate his example.

We must dissipate the gloom of ignorance which hangs like a pall over us. In former days we were trained in ignorance, and many of my distinquished hearers will remember when they dare not be caught cultivating an intimate acquaintance with the spelling-book. But the time is passed when the seeker-after-knowledge is reviled and persecuted. Thoughout the country the public school system largely obtains; books without number and papers without price lend their enlightenment; while high schools, colleges and universities all over our broad domain throw open their inviting doors and say, "Whosoever will may come."

We must not fail to notice any dereliction of our educated people. They must learn that their duty is to elevate their less favored brethren, and this cannot be done while pride and conceit prevent them from entering heartily into the work. A spirit of missionary zeal must actuate them to go down among the lowly, and by word and action say: "Come with me and I will do you good."

We must help one another. Our industries must be patronized, and our laborers encouraged. There seems to be a natural disinclination on our part to patronize our own workmen. We are easily pleased with the labor of the white hands, but when the same is known to be the product of our own skill and energy, we become extremely exacting and hard to please. From colored men we expect better work, we pay them less, and usually take our own good time for payment. We will patronize a colored merchant as long as he will credit us, but when, on the verge of bankruptcy he is obliged to stop the credit system, we pass by him and pay our money to the white rival. For these reasons our industries are rarely remunerative. We must lay aside these "besetting sins" and become united in our appreciation and practical encouragement of our own laborers.

Our societies should wield their influence to secure colored apprentices and mechanics. By a judicious disposition of their custom, they might place colored apprentices in vocations at present entirely unpracticed by us. Our labor is generally menial. We have hitherto had a monopoly of America's menial occupations, but thanks to a progressive Caucasian element, we no longer *suffer* from that monopoly. The white man enters the vocations hitherto exclusively ours, and we must enter and become proficient in professions hitherto exclusively practiced by him.

Our communities must be united. By concerted action great results can be accomplished. We must not only act upon the defensive, but when necessary we should take the offensive. We should jealously guard our every interest, public and private. Let us here speak of our schools. They furnish the surest and swiftest means in our power of obtaining knowledge, confidence and respect. There is no satisfactory reason why all children who seek instruction should not have full and equal privileges, but law has been so perverted in many places, North and South, that sanction is given to separate schools; a pernicious system of discrimination which invariably operates to the disadvantage of the colored race. If we are separate, let it be from "turret to foundation stone." It is unjust to draw the color line in schools, and our communities should resent the added insult of forcing the colored pupils to receive instructions from the refuse material of white educational institutions. White teachers take colored schools from necessity, not from choice. We except of course those who act from a missionary spirit.

White teachers in colored schools are nearly always mentally, morally, or financially bankrupts, and no colored community should tolerate the imposition. High schools and colleges are sending learned colored teachers in the field constantly, and it is manifestly unjust to make them stand idle and see their people taught by those whose only interest lies in securing their monthly compensation in dollars and cents. Again, colored schools thrive better under colored teachers. The St. Louis schools furnish an excellent example. According to the report of Superintendent Harris, during the past two years the schools have increased under colored teachers more than fifty per cent, and similar results always follow the introduction of colored teachers. In cases of mixed schools our teachers should be eligible to positions. They invariably prove equal to their requirements. In Detroit and Chicago they have been admitted and proved themselves unquestionably capable. In Chicago their white pupils outnumber the colored ten to one, and yet they have met with decided success. Such gratifying results must be won by enertic, united action on the part of the interested communities. White people grant us few privileges voluntarily. We must wage continued warfare for our rights, or they will be disregarded and abridged.

Mr. President, we might begin to enumerate the rich results of race unity at sunrise and continue to sunset and half would not be told. In behalf of the people we are here to represent, we ask for some intelligent action of this Conference; some organized movement whereby concerted action may be had by our race all over the land. Let us decide upon some intelligent, united system of operation, and go home and engage the time and talent of our constituents in prosperous labor. We are laboring for race elevation, and race unity is the all-important factor in the work. It must be secured at whatever cost. Individual action, however insignificant, becomes powerful when united and exerted in a common channel. Many thousand years ago, a tiny coral began a reef upon the ocean's bed. Years passed and others came. Their fortunes were united and the structure grew. Generations came and went, and corals by the million came, lived, and died, each adding his mite to the work, till at last the waters of the grand old ocean broke in ripples around their tireless heads, and now, as the traveler gazes upon the reef, hundreds of miles in extent, he can faintly realize what great results will follow united action. So we must labor, with the full assurance that we will reap our reward in due season. Though deeply submerged by the wave of popular opinion, which deems natural inferiority inseparably associated with a black skin, though weighted down by an accursed prejudice that seeks every opportunity to crush us, still we must labor and despair not—patiently, ceaselessly, and unitedly. The time will come when our heads will rise above the troubled waters. Though generations come and go, the result of our labors will yet be manifest, and an impartial world will accord us that rank among other races which all may aspire to, but only the worthy can win. . . .

REPORT OF THE COMMITTEE ON MIGRATION

To the honorable the Chairman and the Members of the Colored Men's National Conference: Your committee appointed to take under consideration the subject relative to the present migration of the colored people from certain Southern States to certain Northern States, having had the same under consideration, by leave do respectfully report as follows:

Taking into consideration the self-evident fact that oppression, intimidation and violence of lawless men have and do now exist—men who continue to outrage the rights and privileges granted said colored people by the Constitution of the United States, and render it almost, if not quite so, impossible for colored men to exercise with any degree of safety any of the rights, privileges, or immunities of American citizens, your committee is of the opinion that this exodus owes its origin to this fact more than any other. Your committee would further re-

port that they have carefully examined the resolutions and papers referred to this committee, and after mature deliberation have concluded to report to your honorable body in accordance with the resolution, adopted by you in Thursday's session to wit, dividing the subject under various headings.

First—*The Causes.* The causes that have given rise to the migration among the colored people of the South are so generally known, and so numerous, that neither time nor space is at the command of your committee to enumerate them here. These are, however, some of the most potent causes which can be easily produced, and which will not occupy much time and space.

1. This migration movement is based on a determined and irrepressible desire, on the part of the colored people of the South, to go anywhere where they can escape the cruel treatment and continued threats of the dominant race in the South.

They are now told, and in addition thereto made to feel, the full force of this declaration: That this is a white man's government, and that none but white men shall govern it, rule in it, or dominate it. This declaration, in the opinion of every thinking man, is but Southern exemplification and revivication of the infamous partisan-accepted decision of the late Judge Taney, "that a Negro has no rights which a white man is bound to respect." Reason, sense, and justice have stamped this unrighteous verdict out from the statutes of our land; but it has found an abiding place in the South, and it is to-day one of their most cherished and faithfully-executed dogmas. Following up this pernicious creed, false as it is, those who insist on a white man's government will not stop short of any means to practically disfranchise all who are not white men, on the grounds that all white men have equal-rights, and that all other colors have just such rights as the whites may please to accord them.

As citizens of the States in the South and of the United States, the colored people of the South, invested with the rights, prerogatives, and high privileges of citizenship by the national Congress, do dispute the title of the white man to the sole government of this country, whether he is situated in South Carolina or Massachusetts, Louisiana or Kansas.

It is also a well-known fact that during the past two years the Democratic party in the South has had entire control of all their respective State governments, until the South has, under such control, passed into the proverb, "the solid South." They have, in plain words, their own local self-governments, and in every instance it has resulted in handing over every Southern State to Democratic rule, whether they were entitled to it or not. The colored people of the South have closely watched events that have transpired under this new order of things. They have felt keenly the policy which transferred them from a National and Republican protection—so far as their lives and rights were concerned—to a solid Democratic South, against which the Southern Negro had so determinedly and persistently voted since he possessed the right to vote.

But even then we did not hear of any extended migration movement on the part of the colored people so transferred. No, not even because Democracy and the champions and defendents of a white man's government had obtained complete control of their votes, their rights—aye, even their lives. It is only now, after two years' experience of the true inwardness of Democratic rule from a Southern standpoint, that the colored people are fleeing from what they justly consider the inadequateness, unwillingness, or downright refusal and failure—call it what you will—of the Democratic party to protect them in their civil, religious, and political rights.

2. Another and important cause is the almost, if not the total, failure on the part of any Democratic State administration in the South to faithfully carry out and perform their promises made to the colored people when said Democracy assumed control of their respective State governments.

The whole country knows what those Democratic promises were—made in some instances through Democratic orators, newspapers, conventions, but more notably, and in many instances, through legislative enactments. They were telegraphed all over the country, and published in nearly every newspaper in the land. We were to have no more political proscription; no more murders for political or color causes. The courts were to protect their black as well as their white citizens. The white lion and the black lamb were to lie down together, and a local democratic self-government was to lead them toward a new era of peace, prosperity, and good will to all men in the Southern States. Need we ask, have these legislative promises been kept? True, Democracy has "led" the colored man; but it has led him to believe that any place is better for him than his present home.

In the short space of two years the Democratic party of the South has fully satisfied the colored people here that they are not the safe custodians of their political and civil rights. They also find that the political prejudices of the Democratic party are paramount to all promises heretofore made by the representatives of said party; for, be it remembered, these promises were not made to the colored people alone, but to the Federal Government and the people of the United States; and the colored man naturally argues that if the Democratic party of the South proves false to promises made to such high authorities, he certainly has no hope for their being carried out with him. He has been made to feel, very sensibly, that the more vigorously he remonstrates against Democratic rule by the ballot, the greater the disfavor in which he stands, and the larger the measure of the local denial of his constitutional rights.

Finally, as to the causes: The colored people of the Southern States have become thoroughly alarmed at the constant attacks on their political and civil rights, not only by legislative enactments and verdicts of courts, but more especially through and by the medium of State constitutional conventions. These conventions have been called in nearly every State once ruled by Republicans, but now under the rule of the Democratic party. In every instance the openly-avowed object for the holding of these constitutional conventions by Democrats is to overturn and repeal all laws passed by Republican conventions or legislatures looking toward the protection of colored people in all of their political, civil, and educational rights. In nearly every instance whenever these conventions have been held by Democrats, restrictions upon the rights of colored people have been enacted and passed to the statute-books of the State. These Democratic enactments have made the colored people the target for so-called vagrant laws, unjust poll-taxes, and curtailed educational advantages, and all legislation has been toward enfeebling them in all that Republican legislation strengthened and protected them.

The colored people of the South have no way of judging what Democracy in that section of the country will do in the future, only by what they are now doing and have done in the past; and, judging by that, they have come to the conclusion that it is better to fly to evils (if any there be) they know not of, rather than to continue under the present evils, to which they have fallen heir through a Democratic bequest.

Second.—Is there any truth in the report, that it is a scheme gotten up to irate the North against the South?

Your committe thinks it unjust to attribute this exodus or migration of colored people from the South to any such motives. It might as well be charged that such alone were the motives of the early abolitionist who demanded liberty for the slaves, and who perished in his demands until slavery was abolished. His scheme was founded on righteousness, justice, and right; and if at this time certain men of the North are to-day demanding civil, religious, and political rights for the freedmen of the South at home if possible, elsewhere if necessary; they are but making a grand finale of the original human undertaking of their predecessors who labored so faithfully that slavery should be abolished from our land. There may be, in some instances, those who would exult over the depopulation of the South, of her laboring classes, but such is not the great underlying principle of this exodus. This emigration scheme is not a spurt or sudden impulse, but the culmination of events which have been in an embryo condition since the war.

You will, doubtless, remember that near the close of the late war an effort was made to remove the colored people of the Southern States to Liberia, and for that purpose money was contributed by individuals, and the scheme started. It did not, however, succeed, owing to a disinclination of any great number of colored people to avail themselves of an opportunity to leave the United States. Another Liberian emigration scheme was started last year in South Carolina, but did not accomplish much. But these two instances differ materially from the present migration; while the colored people have always exhibited a disinclination to leave the South for any foreign country, they have never exhibited a disinclination to leave any Southern State, where, under Democratic rule, their rights have been curtailed or threatened. Notably is this the case in South Carolina, Georgia and Alabama. A steady stream of colored people from these States has been pouring into Mississippi and Louisiana for the past four or five years, solely on account of the unjust laws enacted by Democratic constitutional conventions and legislatures, whose principal achievements were the repeal of nearly every law passed by Republicans for their protection. They came into Louisiana and Mississippi because these States were under Republican rule, and they left Alabama, Georgia, and other Southern States because they were under Southern Democratic rule. Surely, if they left those States because of the evils in operation against them there, it is but natural that they should leave Mississippi and Louisiana, for they are experiencing the same there. There are no other Southern

States for them to go to, consequently they will take Horace Greeley's advice, and go West.

For these and many other reasons which your committee could adduce, if time and space permitted, your committee is clearly of the opinion that the migration of the Southern colored people to Kansas and other Northern States is not for the purpose of irritating the North against the South.

Third.—What are the remedies to be pursued to stop the movement? Would the colored people accept concessions if made to them; and if so, of what nature?

This proposition, like the first one, is of such moment that your committee could not find time or space at this time to enter into an extended argument on this subject.

There is no desire on the part of the colored people of the South to deny the fact that they are thoroughly attached to their homes in the South, and would prefer remaining there than going anywhere else on earth. Indeed, so great is their love for the South that no ordinary consideration would induce them to abandon it. This declaration is amply proven by the fact that, although their former masters went into the rebellion to continue and strengthen their system of slavery, the slaves remained quietly at home and tilled the soil and cared for the families of the absent Confederate soldiers. When they were called into the service of the United States as soldiers, they served; but when they were discharged they returned to their former plantations, even as the Confederate soldier returned to his home. When Abraham Lincoln proclaimed them free, they did not abandon their homes, except in some instances to follow the American flag as a protection to them in their new found freedom; and here they have attempted to stay, under all manner of iniquities, outrages and wrong; but as these were perpetrated on him during the time that Republican laws were in the ascendency, he stayed, hoping in the final triumph of right over might. But to-day all this is changed. The Democracy rule; their promises to the colored people have not been kept; legislation, capital and one class of people are against them; he has been subjected to greater outrages under Democratic rule than ever before under Republican rule; and even now their rights are further threatened.

There must be no uncertain powerful public sentiment in the country at large, and a returning sense of justice in the disturbed localities. To start with this course will be to suggest and apply correctives to the abuses which have brought about this migration, and the dominant class, convinced not only of the wickedness but the folly of their proscription, may so enforce the law as to secure to all citizens the enjoyment, practically, of equality of rights.

In this event the migration would be undoubtedly checked, and even if it was persevered in, but comparatively few would avail themselves of this dernier resort. However, it cannot successfully be denied that proscription and outrage against the colored people have obtained in certain localities to such an extent as to breed profound discontent and prevalent restlessness in many communities, and which must be absolutely and unmistakably allayed in order to estop this flight of the colored people out from their modern Egypt.

We affirm that only by the equal justice of laws grouping together the common interests of all her citizens, regardless of race or parties; the strength of the united energies, minds and sinews of her whole people; the experience and maturity of the intellect and wisdom of her true sons; and the willing, eager thirst after protection in all their rights here at home, by her unfortunate colored citizens—freedom from persecution, violence and bloodshed—by only these just results can a remedy be found which will surely induce these people to remain.

Fourth.— Have colored people pursued the wisest course by migrating?

Your committee simply answer this question by referring to the history of those who

The Onset of Jim Crow

have in the past left their homes, firesides and fortunes, and sought perfect freedom from persecution, proscription and might triumphing over right, and gone forth among strangers, in strange lands, seeking for that which they were denied at home.

Fifth.—Question. How is the movement likely to affect the two political parties in the next canvass, both State and national?

Answer. The political effect of this migration is afar off, and in our opinion, considerably removed from the next campaign. If, under the existing state of affairs, they all stay, the South is hopelessly Democratic, although there are more Republicans in the Southern States than Democrats. If they are compelled to leave—why, the Southern States are Democratic still. So much for the State. Nationally it will be some time before the Southern States would be made to feel the loss of her colored voters, probably not until after the next United States census is taken, when each Southern State may find herself minus one or more Congressmen, and this loss added to the representation of some Northern State.

But the Negro of the South does not desire to predicate his right to free suffrage on the score of controlling the offices in the gift of his party alone: he believes that his duty as a voter is that he may assist in perpetuating this Union against those who may, in the future, attempt, as they did in the past, to destroy it, or even separate it. The Negro voter of the South believes, and takes pride in that belief, that their votes are necessary to support, sustain and perpetuate the great principles of the Republican party, and further the scheme of universal suffrage, a united country and a prosperous, happy future for all her citizens, irrespective of race, color, nationality or party.

In the South especially has the Negro been led to believe that his vote was necessary to keep the Southern States within the Union, and to assist in reorganizing these States in keeping with the Constitution of our land. How well he has performed his

duty, with what fidelity and faithfulness, and at what sacrifices he has carried his sacred responsibilities, need not be repeated here.

What the Negro voter of the South demands politically is not the mere vote. What he demands is that it shall be as safe to deposit a colored Republican vote in Alabama, Georgia, Mississippi or Louisiana, as it is to cast a white Republican vote in New York, Pennsylvania or Massachusetts. He demands that Republicanism in the South, whether successful or otherwise, shall be as safe and free from terrorism as it is in the North. Nothing short of this will satisfy the colored voter of the South, and if he cannot enjoy these natural privileges in the South, he will be pretty apt to seek some other place within the United States where he can exercise them without fear or hindrance.

Question. Any other remarks or observations that may occur to you?
Answer. We have already said so much on the subject that it is hardly necessary for us to add any more in the shape of remarks or observations.

The colored people, by their involuntary pilgrimage hence for some spot in this country where they can live as freemen, free to vote and act in all that belong to American citizens, sweep away the oft-repeated declaration of Democratic orators, Congressmen and newspapers, that under Democratic rule the Negro of the South was better off, better contented, and better protected than he was under Republican rule. Southern Democratic orators in Congress may assert that the Negro is quiet and contented under the government. They are quickly and decisively answered by the fact that they are leaving their sunny Southern homes for Northern climes and the fullest liberty. This exodus is an argument against the declaration of their content, and an argument that can neither be gainsaid nor successfully denied.

We beg leave to submit the following resolutions:

Whereas the political and civil rights of the colored people from the Ohio River to the Gulf of Mexico are abridged and curtailed in every conceivable manner:

Whereas there seems to be no disposition on the part of the great majority of Southern whites to better this condition of affairs, or to grant the colored people their full rights of citizenship; and

Whereas a further submission to the wrongs imposed, and a further acquiescence in the abrogation of our rights and privileges would prove us unfit for citizenship, devoid of manhood, and unworthy the respect of men; therefore

Resolved, That it is the sense of this Conference that the great current of migration, which has, for the past few months, taken so many of our people from their homes in the South, and which is still carrying hundreds to the free and fertile West, should be encouraged and kept in motion until those who remain are accorded every right and privilege guaranteed by the Constitution and laws.

Resolved, That we recommend great care on the part of those who migrate. They should leave home well prepared with certain knowledge of localities to which they intend to move; money enough to pay their passage and enable them to begin life in their new homes with prospect of ultimate success.

Resolved, That this Conference indorse the Windom Committee as the permanent National Executive Committee on migration.

Resolved, That the American Protective Society, organized by this Conference, be, and are hereby, authorized and ordered to co-operate with the said committee in the earnest endeavor to secure homes in the West for those of our race who are denied the full enjoyment of American citizenship.

We also recommend the adoption of the following resolution:

Resolved, That this Conference recommend that the National Executive Committee, of which Senator Windom is chairman, appoint a committee of three to visit the Western States and Territories, and report not later than the 1st of November upon the health, climate, and productions of said States and Territories.

Hon. J. T. Rapier, Alabama; George N. Perkins, Arkansas; J. C. Napier, Tennessee; R. W. Fitzhugh, Mississippi; G. W. Gentry, Kentucky; Hon. J. H. Burch, Louisiana; W. R. Lawton, Missouri; W. B. Higginbotham, Georgia; John Averett, Virginia; J. H. S. Parker, District of Columbia; B. F. Williams, Texas; D. Jones, Oregon; John D. Lewis, Pennsylvania; F. L. Barnett, Illinois; Colonel Robert Harlan, Ohio; H. G. Newsom, Nebraska; Hon. J. H. Rainey, South Carolina; S. E. Hardy, Minnesota; G. L. Knox, Indiana—*Committee.*

Black and White: Land, Labor and Politics in the South

T. Thomas Fortune

THE NEGRO AND THE NATION

The war of the Rebellion settled only one question: It forever settled the question of chattel slavery in this country. It forever

Source: From T. Thomas Fortune, *Black and White: Land, Labor and Politics in the South* (New York: Forde, Howard and Hulbert, 1884), pp. 27–51, 95–99, 109–11.

choked the life out of the infamy of the Constitutional right of one man to rob another, by purchase of his person, or of his honest share of the produce of his own labor. But this was the only question permanently and irrevocably settled. Nor was this *the* all-absorbing question involved. The right of a State to secede from the so-called *Union* remains where it was when the treasonable shot upon Fort Sumter aroused the people to all the horrors of internecine war. And the measure of protection which the National government owes the individual members of States, a right imposed upon it by the adoption of the XIVth Amendment to the Constitution, remains still to be affirmed.

It was not sufficient that the Federal government should expend its blood and treasure to unfetter the limbs of four millions of people. There can be a slavery more odious, more galling, than mere chattel slavery. It has been declared to be an act of charity to enforce ignorance upon the slave, since to inform his intelligence would simply be to make his unnatural lot all the more unbearable. Instance the miserable existence of Æsop, the great black moralist. But this is just what the manumission of the black people of this country has accomplished. They are more absolutely under the control of the Southern whites; they are more systematically robbed of their labor; they are more poorly housed, clothed and fed, than under the slave régime; and they enjoy, practically, less of the protection of the laws of the State or of the Federal government. When they appeal to the Federal government they are told by the Supreme Court to go to the State authorities—as if they would have appealed to the one had the other given them that protection to which their sovereign citizenship entitles them!

Practically, there is no law in the United States which extends its protecting arm over the black man and his rights. He is, like the Irishman in Ireland, an alien in his native land. There is no central or auxiliary authority to which he can appeal for protection. Wherever he turns he finds the strong arm of constituted authority powerless to protect him. The farmer and the merchant rob him with absolute immunity, and irresponsible ruffians murder him without fear of punishment, undeterred by the law, or by public opinion—which connives at, if it does not inspire, the deeds of lawless violence. Legislatures of States have framed a code of laws which is more cruel and unjust than any enforced by a former slave State.

The right of franchise has been practically annulled in every one of the former slave States, in not one of which, to-day, can a man

vote, think or act as he pleases. He must conform his views to the views of the men who have usurped every function of government—who, at the point of the dagger, and with shotgun, have made themselves masters in defiance of every law or precedent in our history as a government. They have usurped government with the weapons of the coward and assassin, and they maintain themselves in power by the most approved practices of the most odious of tyrants. These men have shed as much innocent blood as the bloody triumvirate of Rome. To-day, red-handed murderers and assassins sit in the high places of power, and bask in the smiles of innocence and beauty.

The newspapers of the country, voicing the sentiments of the people, literally hiss into silence any man who has the courage to protest against the prevailing tendency to lawlessness* and bare-faced usurpation; while par-

---

*While I write these lines, the daily newspapers furnish the following paragraph. It is but one of the *waifs* that are to be found in the newspapers day by day. There is always some *circumstance* which justifies the murder and exculpates the murderer. The black always deserves his fate. I give the paragraph:

"Spear, Mitchell Co., N.C., March 19, 1884.— Col. J. M. English, a farmer and prominent citizen living at Plumtree, Mitchell County, N.C., shot and killed a mulatto named Jack Mathis at that place Saturday, March 1. There had been difficulty between them for several months.

"Mathis last summer worked in one of Col. English's mica mines. Evidence pointed to him as being implicated in the systematic stealing of mica from the mine. Still it was not direct enough to convict him, but he was discharged by English. Mathis was also a tenant of one of English's houses and lots. In resentment he damaged the property by destroying fences, tearing off weather boards from the house, and injuring the fruit trees. For this Col. English prosecuted the Negro, and on Feb. 9, before a local Justice, ex-Sheriff Wiseman, he got a judgment for $100. On the date stated, during a casual meeting, hot words grew into an altercation, and Col. English shot the Negro. Mathis was a powerful man. English is a cripple, being lame in a leg from a wound received in the Mexican war.

ties have ceased to deal with the question for other than purposes of political capital. Even this fruitful mine is well-nigh exhausted. A few more years, and the usurper and the man of violence will be left in undisputed possession of his blood-stained inheritance. No man will attempt to deter him from sowing broadcast the seeds of revolution and death. Brave men are powerless to combat this organized brigandage, complaint of which, in derision, has been termed "waving the bloody shirt."

Men organize themselves into society for mutual protection. Government justly derives its just powers from the consent of the governed. But what shall we say of that society which is incapable of extending the protection which is inherent in it? What shall we say of that government which has not power or inclination to insure the exercise of those solemn rights and immunities which it guarantees? To declare a man to be free, and equal with his fellow, and then to refrain from enacting laws powerful to insure him in such freedom and equality, is to trifle with the most sacred of all the functions of sovereignty. Have not the United States done this very thing? Have they not conferred freedom and the ballot, which are necessary the one to the other? And have they not signally failed to make omnipotent the one and practicable the other? The questions hardly require an answer. The measure of freedom

"A trial was had before a preliminary court recently, Col. S. C. Vance appearing for Col. English. After a hearing of all the testimony the court reached a decision of justifiable homicide and English was released. The locality of the shooting is in the mountains of western North Carolina, and not far from the Flat Rock mica mine, the scene of the brutal midnight murder, Feb. 17, of Burleson, Miller, and Horton by Rae and Anderson, two revenue officers, who took this means to gain possession of the mica mine."

My knowledge of such affairs in the South is, that the black and the white have an altercation over some trivial thing, and the white to end the argument shoots the black man down. The Negro is always a *"powerful fellow"* and the white man a "weak sickly man." The law and public opinion always side with the white man.

the black man enjoys can be gauged by the power he has to vote. He has, practically, no voice in the government under which he lives. His property is taxed and his life is jeopardized, by states on the one hand and inefficient police regulations on the other, and no question is asked or expected of him. When he protests, when he cries out against this flagrant nullification of the very first principles of a republican form of government, the insolent question is asked: "What are you going to do about it?" And here lies the danger.

You may rob and maltreat a slave and ask him what he is going to do about it, and he can make no reply. He is bound hand and foot; he is effectually gagged. Despair is his only refuge. He knows it is useless to appeal from tyranny unto the designers and apologists of tyranny. Ignominious death alone can bring him relief. This was the case of thousands of men doomed by the institution of slavery. *But such is not the case with free men.* You cannot oppress and murder freemen as you would slaves: you cannot so insult them with the question, "What are you going to do about it?" When you ask free men that question you appeal to men who, though sunk to the verge of despair, yet are capable of uprising and ripping hip and thigh those who deemed them incapable of so rising above their condition. The history of mankind is fruitful of such uprising of races and classes reduced to a condition of absolute despair. The American Negro is no better and no worse than the Haytian revolutionists headed by Toussaint l'Overture, Christophe and the bloody Dessalaines.

I do not indulge in the luxury of prophecy when I declare that the American people are fostering in their bosoms a spirit of rebellion which will yet shake the pillars of popular government as they have never before been shaken, unless a wiser policy is inaugurated and honestly enforced. All the indications point to the fulfillment of such declaration.

The Czar of Russia squirms upon his throne, not because he is necessarily a bad man, but because he is the head and center of a condition of things which squeezes the life out of the people. His subjects hurl infernal machines at the tyrant because he represents the system which oppresses them. But the evil is far deeper than the throne, and cannot be remedied by striking the occupant of it—*the throne itself must be rooted out and demolished.* So the Irish question has a more powerful motive to foment agitation and murder than the landlord and landlordism. The landlord simply stands out as the representative of the real grievance. To remove *him* would not remove the evil; agitation would not cease; murder would still stalk abroad at noonday. *The real grievance is the false system which makes the landlord possible.* The appropriation of the fertile acres of the soil of Ireland, which created and maintains a privileged class, a class that while performing no labor, wrings from the toiler, in the shape of rents, so much of the produce of his labor that he cannot on the residue support himself and those dependent upon him aggravates the situation. It is this system which constitutes the real grievance and makes the landlord an odious loafer with abundant cash and the laborer a constant toiler always upon the verge of starvation. Evidently, therefore, to remove the landlord and leave the system of land monopoly would not remove the evil. Destroy the latter and the former would be compelled to go.

Herein lies the great social wrong which has turned the beautiful roses of freedom into thorns to prick the hands of the black men of the South; which made slavery a blessing, paradoxical as it may appear, and freedom a curse. It is this great wrong which has crowded the cities of the South with an ignorant pauper population, making desolate fields that once bloomed "as fair as a garden of the Lord," where now the towering oak and pine-tree flourish, instead of the corn and cotton which gladdened the heart and filled the purse. It was this gigantic iniquity which created that arrogant class who have exhausted the catalogue of violence to obtain power and the lexicon of sophistry for arguments to extenuate the exceeding heinousness of crime. How could it be otherwise? To tell a man he is free when he has neither money nor the opportunity to make it, is simply to mock him. To tell him he has no master when he cannot live except by permission of the man who, under favorable conditions, monopolizes all the land, is to deal in the most tantalizing contradiction of terms. But this is just what the United States did for the black man. And yet because he had not grown learned and wealthy in twenty years, because he does not own broad acres and a large bank account, people are not wanting who declare he has no capacity, that he is improvident by nature and mendacious from inclination.

THE TRIUMPH OF THE VANQUISHED

There are those throughout the length and breadth of our great country who make a fair living by traducing better men than themselves; by continually crying out that the black man is incapable of being civilized; that he is born with the elements of barbarity, improvidence and untruthfulness so woven into his very nature that no amount of opportunity, labor, love, or sacrifice can ever lift him out of the condition, the "sphere God designed him to occupy"—as if the great Common Parent took any more pains in the making of one man than another. But those who utter such blasphemy, who call in the assistance of the Almighty to fight the battles of the devil, are the very persons who do most by precept and example to make possible the verification of their blasphemy. They carry their lamentations into the pulpit, grave convocations, newspapers, and even into halls of legislation, State and Federal. They are the false prophets who blind the eye of reason and blunt the sympathies of honest, well-meaning men. They are the Jonases on board the ship of progress. They belong to that class of men who would pick flaws in the finest work of art. They find fault with the great mass of ignorance around them, contending that the poor victims have only themselves to blame for their destitute and painful condition, and, therefore, are not entitled to the sympathy or charity of their more fortunate brethren—unmindful that the great Master, judging by the false laws of men, declared that "the poor ye have always with you;" while the very rich are held up as monsters of selfishness, rapactiy and the most loathsome of social vices. It is, therefore, hardly to be expected that this class of persons would find anything good in the nature of the lately enslaved black man, or any improvement in his condition since a generous Government had made him an ignorant voter and a confirmed pauper—the victim of his former master, to be robbed outright by designing and unscrupulous harpies of trade, and to be defrauded of his franchise by blatant demagogues or by outlaws, to whom I will not apply the term "assassins" for fear of using bad English.

When the American Government conferred upon the black man the boon of freedom and the burden of the franchise, it added four million men to the already vast army of men who appear to be specially created to labor for the enrichment of vast corporations, which have no souls, and for individuals, whom our government have made a privileged class, by permitting them to usurp or monopolize, through the accepted channel of barter and trade, the soil, from which the masses, the laboring masses, must obtain a subsistence, and without the privilege of cultivating which they must faint and die.* It also added four millions of souls to what have been termed, in the refinement of sarcasm, "the dangerous classes"*—meaning by which the vast army of men and women who, while willing and anxious to make an honest living by the labor of their hands, and who—when speculators cry "over-production," "glutted market," and other claptrap—threaten to take by force from society that which society prevents them from making honestly.

When a society fosters as much crime and destitution as ours, with ample resources to meet the actual necessities of every one, there must be something radically wrong, not in the society but in the foundation upon which society is reared. Where is this ulcer located? Is it to be found in the dead-weight of illiteracy which we carry? The masses of few countries are more intelligent than ours. Is it to be found in burdensome taxation or ill-adjusted tariff regulations? Few countries are burdened with less debt, and many have

---

*We of the United States take credit for having abolished slavery. Passing the question of how much credit the majority of us are entitled to for the abolition of Negro slavery, it remains true that we have only abolished one form of slavery—and that a primitive form which had been abolished in the greater portion of the country by social development, and that, notwithstanding its race character gave it peculiar tenacity, would in time have been abolished in the same way in other parts of the country. We have not really abolished slavery; we have retained it in its most insidious and widespread form—in a form which applies to whites as to blacks. So far from having abolished slavery, it is extending and intensifying, and we made no scruple of setting into it our own children—the citizens of the Republic yet to be. For what else are we doing in selling the land on which future citizens must live, if they are to live at all.—Henry George, *Social Problems*, p. 209.

*Although for the present there is a lull in the conflict of races at the South, it is a full which comes only from the breathing-spells of a great secular contention, and not from any permanent pacification founded on a resolution of the race problem presented by the Negro question in its present aspects. So long as the existing mass of our crude and unassimilated colored population holds its present place in the body politic we must expect that civilization and political rights will oscillate between alternate perils—the peril that comes from the white man when he places civilization or sometimes his travesty of it, higher than the Negro's political rights, and the peril that comes from the black man when his political rights are placed by himself or others higher than civilization—President James C. Willing, on "Race Education" in *The North American Review,* April, 1883.

far worse tariff laws than curse our country. Is it to be found in an unjust pension list? We hardly miss the small compensation which we grant to the men (or their heirs) who, in the hour of National peril, gave their lives freely to perpetuate the Union of our States. Where, then, is secreted the parasite which is eating away the energies of the people, making paupers and criminals in the midst of plenty and the grandest of civilizations? Is it not to be found in the powerful monopolies we have created? Monopoly in land, in railroads, telegraphs, fostered manufactures, etc.,—the gigantic forces in our civilization which are, in their very nature, agents of public convenience, comfort and absolute necessity? Society, in the modern sense, could not exist without these forces; they are part and parcel of our civilization. Naturally, therefore, society should control them, or submit to the humiliation of being ruled by them. And this latter is largely the case at the present time. Having evolved those forces out of its necessities, made them strong and permanent, society failed to impose such conditions as wise policy should have dictated, and now suffers the calamitous consequences. The tail wags the dog, instead of the dog wagging the tail.

No government can afford, with any degree of safety, to make four million of citizens out of so many slaves. And when it is remembered that our slaves were turned loose upon their former masters—lifted by one stroke of the pen, as it were, from the most degraded condition to the very pinnacle of sovereign manhood—the equals in unrestricted manhood, with the privileges and immunities of citizens who had been born to rule, apparently, instead of being ruled—it will be seen readily how critical was the situation.

But the condition having once been created by the strong arm of the Federal Government, based upon a bloody and costly war and in open defiance of the Constitution as designed by the compromising Fathers of the Republic; the slave once made a free man the same as his former master, and given the ballot, the highest privilege of government a man can

exercise;—the Government having once gone so far, there was absolutely nothing for it to do but to interpose its omnipotent authority between the haughty and arrogant free man on the one hand and the crouching and fearful freed man on the other—the lion and the lamb. To do less would be more than cruel, it would be murderous;—the agency which created the condition was bound by all law and precedent to see that those conditions were maintained in their entirety. It could not evade the issue except at the expense of dignity, consistency and humanity. There was but one honorable course to pursue. Any other would be a horrible abandonment of principle. If it were powerful to create, to make free men and citizens, it must, manifestly, be powerful to insure the enjoyment of the freedom conferred, and protect the inviolability of the franchise granted. Any other conclusion would make government a byword and a scoffing to the nations; any other conclusion would make its conferring of freedom and citizenship absurd in the extreme, a mere trick of the demagogue to ease the popular conscience. To do such a thing would sink a decent government lower in the estimation of the world than the miserable apology of government represented by the Khedive of Egypt.

No patriotic American would admit to himself, or to a foreigner that the United States Government, through its accredited representatives in Congress, possessed constitutional power to confer a benefit and did not possess power to make that benefit available; to contract an obligation, pecuniary or other, which it had not inherent power to liquidate. The validity of a contract, as a matter of fact, depends upon the ability of the parties to enter into it, for no court can enforce a contract when it is shown that the principals to it had not legal right to make it or to fulfill the conditions of it. It is accepted as a surety of power to observe the conditions when a sovereign government makes itself a party to a contract. The people are bound by their agents, to whom they delegate authority. Nothing is regarded in a more obnoxious light than the repudiation of their honest debts by sovereign States. It is regarded in financial circles as the crime of all crimes the blackest. The credit of the State is reduced to a song, and moneyed men shun it as they would a rattlesnake. The State and its people are held up as monsters of depravity. It matters not how unjust the debt, how poor the people; the mere fact that they repudiate an obligation which they entered into in good faith is sufficient to destroy their credit in New York or London and make them the target of every virtuous newspaper which voices the sentiment of the class that deals in "futures" and "corners." As an illustration, take the State of Virginia. The people of that State contracted large debts to aid and abet the cause of the so-called Confederate Government, a thing which crystallized around the question: "Have the Sovereign States absolute, undivided authority to regulate their own internal concerns, slave and other, or is this authority vested in the Federal or National Government?" When the people of Virginia contracted those large debts, drawing upon her future resources, and placing burdens upon men yet unborn, to propagate theories at variance with sound doctrines of government, and to perpetuate an institution too vile to be mentioned with respect, in 1860, and immediately subsequent thereto, when the State of Virginia contracted the debts in question for the perpetuation of slavery, she had a population of 1,047,299; 65.6 per cent. of which was white (free), and 34.4 per cent. was colored (slave). Virginia, therefore, in contracting debts in 1860, did not calculate that twenty-two years thereafter the obligations would be repudiated, and the credit of the State depreciated, by the assistance of the very class of persons to bind whom to a cruel and barbarous servitude those debts were contracted. It is one of the most striking instances of retributive justice that I ever knew. Nothing was more natural, when the question came up for final settlement a few years ago, than that the black voters of Virginia should take sides with those who opposed the full settlement of the indebtedness. It is too much to expect of sensible men that they will assent, in a state of sovereign citizenship, to cancel debts contracted when they had no voice in the matter, and when, as a matter of fact, the debts were contracted to rivet upon them the chains of death. And yet for the part the black men of Virginia took upon the settlement of her infamous debt, they have been abused and maligned from one end of the country to the other. Because they refused to vote to tax themselves to pay money borrowed without their consent, and applied to purposes of death and slaughter, no man has been found to commend them or to accept as sufficiently extenuating, the peculiar circumstances surrounding the question. Shylock must have his pound of flesh, though the unlucky victim bleed his life away. But there are laws "higher" than any framed in the interest of tyrannical capital. In my opinion, the man who deliberately invests his money to perpetuate so vile an institution as slavery deserves not only to lose the interest upon his investment but the principal as well. I therefore have not a grain of sympathy for the greedy cormorants who invested their money in the so-called Confederate Government. Neither have I any sympathy for the people of the South who, having invested all their money in human flesh, found themselves at the close of the Rebellion paupers in more senses than one—being bankrupt in purse and unused to make an honest living by honest labor—too proud to work and too poor to loaf.

In a question of this kind, no one disputes the power of Virginia to contract debts to propagate opinions, erroneous or other, but it is a question whether the people of one generation have the right to tax—that is, enslave—the people of generations yet unborn. The creation of public debts is pernicious in practice, productive of more harm than good. What right have I to create debts for my grandson or granddaughter? I have no right even to presume that I will have a grandson, certainly none that he will be able to meet his own debts in addition to those I entail upon him. The character of the people called upon to settle the debt of Virginia, contracted in 1860, before or immediately after, differed radically from the character of the people who were called upon to tax themselves to cancel that debt. Not only had the character of the people undergone a radical change; the whole social and industrial mechanism of the state had undergone a wonderful, almost an unrecognizable, metamorphosis. The haughty aristocrat, with his magnificent plantation, his army of slaves, and his "cattle on a thousand hills," who eagerly contracted the debt, had been transformed into a sour pauper when called upon to honor his note; while the magnificent plantation had been in many instances cut into a thousand bits to make homes for the former slaves, now freemen and citizens, the equals of "my lord," while "his cattle on a thousand hills" had dwindled down to a stubborn jackass and a worn out milch cow. True, the white man possessed, largely the soil; but he was, immediately after the war, utterly incapable of wringing from it the bounty of Nature; he had first to be re-educated.

But, when the bloody rebellion was over, the country, in its sovereign capacity, and by individual States, was called upon to deal with grave questions growing out of the conflict. Mr. Lincoln, by a stroke of the pen,* transferred the battle from the field to the halls of legislation. In view of the "Emancipation proclamation" as issued by Mr. Lincoln, and the invaluable service rendered by black

*By virtue of the power and for the purposes aforesaid, I do ordain and declare that all persons held as slaves within said designated States and parts of States, are and henceforth shall be free; and that the Executive Government of the United States, including the military and naval authorities thereof, will recognize and maintain the freedom of said persons.—Abraham Lincoln's *"Emancipation Proclamation."*

troops* in the rebellion, legislation upon the status of the former slave could not be avoided. The issue could not be evaded; like Banquo's ghost, it would not down. There were not wanting men, even when the war had ended and the question of chattel slavery had been forever relegated to the limbo of "things that were," who were willing still to toy with half-way measures, to cater to the caprices of that treacherous yet brave power—the South. They had not yet learned that Southern sentiment was fundamentally revolutionary, dynamitic in the extreme, and could not be toyed with as with a doll-baby. So the statesmen proceeded to manufacture the "Reconstruction policy"—a policy more fatuous, more replete with fatal concessions and far more fatal omissions than any ever before adopted for the acceptance and governance of a rebellious people on the one hand and a newlymade, supremely helpless people on the other. It is not easy to regard with equanimity the blunders of the "Reconstruction policy" and the manifold infamies which have followed fast upon its adoption.

The South scornfully rejected and successfully nullified the legislative will of the victors.

*From William's *"History of the Negro Race in America"* I construct the following table showing the number of colored troops employed by the Federal Government during the war of the Rebellion:

Colored Troops Furnished 1861–'65	
Total of New England States	7,916
Total of Middle States,	13,922
Total, Western States and Territories,	12,711
Total, Border States,	45,184
Total, Southern States,	63,571
Grand Total of States,	143,304
At Large,	733
Not accounted for,	5,083
Officers,	7,122
Grand Total	156,242

This gives colored troops enlisted in the States in Rebellion; besides this, there were 92,576 colored troops (included with the white soldiers) in the quotas of the several States.

Judge Albion W. Tourgee says of this policy in his book called *"A Fool's Errand:"* "It was a magnificent sentiment that underlay it all,—an unfaltering determination, an invincible defiance to all that had the seeming of compulsion or tyranny. One cannot but regard with pride and sympathy the indomitable men, who, being conquered in war, yet resisted every effort of the conqueror to change their laws, their customs, or even the *personnel* of their ruling class; and this, too, not only with unyielding stubbornness, but with sucess. One cannot but admire the arrogant boldness with which they charged the nation which had overpowered them—even in the teeth of her legislators—with perfidy, malice, and a spirit of unworthy and contemptible revenge. How they laughed to scorn the Reconstruction Acts of which the wise men boasted! How boldly they declared the conflict to be irrepressible, and that white and black could not and should not live together as co-ordinate ruling elements! How lightly they told the tales of blood—of the Masked Night-Riders, of the Invisible Empire of Rifle clubs and Saber clubs (all organized for peaceful purposes), of warnings and whippings and slaughter! Ah, it is wonderful! * * * Bloody as the reign of Mary, barbarous as the chronicles of the Comanche!"

HOW NOT TO DO IT

. . . There is no error which has been productive of more disaster and death than the stupid plan adopted by the Federal government in what is known as the "Reconstruction policy." This *policy,* born out of expediency and nurtured in selfishness, was, in its inception, instinct with the elements of failure and of death. Perhaps no piece of legislation, no policy, was ever more fatuous in every detail. How could it be otherwise? How could the men who devised it expect for it anything more than a speedy, ignominious collapse? All the past history of the Southern states unmistakably pointed to the utter failure of any policy in which the whites were not made the masters; unless, indeed, they were subjected to that severe governmental control which their treason merited, until such time as the people were prepared for self-government by education, the oblivion of issues out of which the war grew, the passing away by death of the old spirits, and the complete metamorphosis of the peculiar conditions predicated upon and fostered by the unnatural state of slavery.

At the close of the Rebellion, in 1865, the United States government completely transformed the social fabric of the Southern state governments; and, without resorting to the slow process of educating the people; without even preparing them by proper warnings; without taking into consideration the peculiar relations of the subject and dominant classes—the slave class and the master class—instantly, as it were, the lamb and the lion were commanded to lie down together. The master class, fresh from the fields of a bloody war, with his musket strapped to his shoulder and the sharp thorn of ignominious defeat penetrating his breast; the master class, educated for two hundred years to dominate in his home, in the councils of municipal, state and Federal government; the master class, who had been taught that slavery was a divine institution and that the black man, the unfortunate progeny of Ham, was his lawful slave and property; and the slave class, born to a state of slavery and obedience, educated in the school of improvidence, mendacity and the lowest vices:—these two classes of people, born to such widely dissimilar stations in life and educated in the most extreme schools, were declared to be *free, and equal before the law,* with the right to vote; to testify in courts of law; to sit upon jury and in the halls of legislation, municipal and other; to sue and be sued; to buy and to sell; to marry and give in marriage. In short, these two classes of people were made co-equal citizens, entitled alike to the protection of the laws and the benefits of government.

I know of no instance in the various history of mankind which equals in absurdity the presumption of the originators of our "Reconstruction policy" that the master class would accept cordially the conditions forced upon them, or that the enfranchised class would prove equal to the burden so unceremoniously forced upon them. On the one hand, a proud and haughty people, who had stubbornly contested the right of the government to interfere with the extension of slavery, not to say confiscation of slave property—a people rich in lands, in mental resources, in courage; on the other, a poor, despised people, without lands, without money, without mental resources, without moral character,—these peoples *equal,* indeed! These peoples go peaceably to the ballot-box together to decide upon the destiny of government! These peoples melt into an harmonious citizenry! These peoples have and exercise mutual confidence, esteem and appreciation of their common rights! These peoples *dissolve into one people!* The bare statement of the case condemns it as impracticable, illusory, in the extreme. And, yet, these two peoples, so different in character, in education and material condition, were turned loose to enjoy the same benefits in common—to be one! And the *wise men* of the nation—as, Tourgee's *Fool* ironically names them—thought they were legislating for the best; thought they were doing their duty. And, so, having made the people free, and equal before the law, and given them the ballot with which to settle their disputes, the *"wise men"* left the people to live in peace if they could, and to cut each other's throats if they could not. That they should have proceeded to cut each other's throats was as natural as it is for day to follow night.

I do not desire to be understood as inveighing against the manumission of the slave or the enfranchisement of the new-made free man. To do so, would be most paradoxical on my part, who was born a slave and spent the first nine years of my life in that most unnatural condition. What I do inveigh against, is the unequal manner in which the colored people were pitted against the white people; the placing of these helpless people absolutely in the power of this hereditary foeman—more absolutely in their power, at their mercy, than under the merciless system of slavery, when sordid interest dictated a modicum of humanity and care in treatment. And I arraign the "Reconstruction policy" as one of the hollowest pieces of perfidy ever perpetrated upon an innocent, helpless people; and in the treatment of the issues growing out of that policy, I arraign the dominant party of the time for base ingratitude, subterfuge and hypocrisy to its black partisan allies. With the whole power of the government at its back, and with a Constitution so amended as to extend the amplest protection to the new-made citizen, it left him to the inhuman mercy of men whose uncurbed passions, whose deeds of lawlessness and defiance, pale into virtues the ferocity of Cossack warfare. And, for this treachery, for leaving this people alone and single-handed, to fight an enemy born in the lap of self-confidence, and rocked in the cradle of arrogance and cruelty, the "party of great moral ideas" must go down to history amid the hisses and the execrations of honest ment in spite of its good deeds. There is not one extenuating circumstance to temper the indignation of him who believes in justice and humanity. . . .

THE NATION SURRENDERS

. . . In each of the late rebellious states the ballot-box has been closed against the black man. To reach it he is compelled to brave the muzzles of a thousand rifles in the hands of silent sentinels who esteem a human life as no more sacred than the serpent that drags his tortuous length among the grasses of the field, and whose head mankind is enjoined to crush.

The thirteenth, fourteenth and fifteenth amendments to the Federal constitution which grew out of the public sentiment created by thirty long years of agitation of the abolitionists and of the "emancipation proclamation"—issued as a war measure by

President Lincoln—are no longer regarded as fundamental by the South. The beneficiaries of those amendments have failed in every instance to enjoy the benefits that were, presumably, intended to be conferred.

These laws—having passed both branches of the Federal legislature, having received the approval and signature of the Chief Executive of the nation, and having been ratified by a majority of the states composing the sisterhood of states—these laws are no longer binding upon the people of the South, who fought long and desperately to prevent the possibility of their enactment; and they no longer benefit, if they ever did, the people in whose interest they were incorporated in the *Magna Charta* of American liberty; *while the Central authority which originated them, has, through the Supreme Court, declared nugatory, null and void all supplementary legislation based upon those laws, as far as the government of the United States is concerned!* The whole question has been remanded to the legislatures of the several states! The Federal Union has left to the usurped governments of the South the adjudication of rights which the South fought four years in honorable warfare to make impossible, and which it has since the war exhausted the catalogue of infamy and lawlessness to make of no force or effect. The fate of the lamb has been left to the mercy of the lion and the tiger.

The "party of great moral ideas," having emancipated the slave, and enfranchised disorganized ignorance and poverty, finally finished its mission, relinquished its right to the respect and confidence of mankind when, in 1876, it abandoned all effort to enforce the provisions of the war amendments. That party stands to-day for organized corruption, while its opponent stands for organized brigandage. The black man, who was betrayed by his party and murdered by the opponents of his party, is absolved from all allegiance which *gratitude* may have dictated, and is to-day free to make conditions the best possible with any faction which will insure him in his right to "life, liberty and the pursuit of happiness."

The black men of the United States are, to-day, free to form whatever alliances wisdom dictates, to make sure their position in the social and civil system of which, in the wise providence of a just God, they are a factor, for better or for worse.

Southern Horrors: Lynch Law in All Its Phases

Ida B. Wells

THE OFFENSE

Wednesday evening May 24th, 1892, the city of Memphis was filled with excitement. Editorials in the daily papers of that date caused a meeting to be held in the Cotton Exchange

Source: From Ida B. Wells, *Southern Horrors: Lynch Law in All Its Phases* (New York, 1892).

Building; a committee was sent for the editors of the "Free Speech" an Afro-American journal published in that city, and the only reason the open threats of lynching that were made were not carried out was because they could not be found. The cause of all this commotion was the following editorial published in the "Free Speech" May 21st, 1892, the Saturday previous.

"Eight Negroes lynched since last issue of the "Free Speech" one at Little Rock, Ark., last

Saturday morning where the citizens broke (?) into the penitentiary and got their man; three near Anniston, Ala., one near New Orleans; and three at Clarksville, Ga., the last three for killing a white man, and five on the same old racket—the new alarm about raping white women. The same programme of hanging, then shooting bullets into the lifeless bodies was carried out to the letter.

Nobody in this section of the country believes the old thread bare lie that Negro men rape white women. If Southern white men are not careful, they will over-reach themselves and public sentiment will have a reaction; a conclusion will then be reached which will be very damaging to the moral reputation of their women."

"The Daily Commercial" of Wednesday following, May 25th, contained the following leader:

> Those Negroes who are attempting to make the lynching of individuals of their race a means for arousing the worst passions of their kind are playing with a dangerous sentiment. The Negroes may as well understand that there is no mercy for the Negro rapist and little patience with his defenders. A Negro organ printed in this city, in a recent issue publishes the following atrocious paragraph: "Nobody in this section of the country believes the old thread-bare lie that Negro men rape white women. If Southern white men are not careful they will overreach themselves, and public sentiment will have a reaction; and a conclusion will be reached which will be very damaging to the moral reputation of their women."
>
> The fact that a black scoundrel is allowed to live and utter such loathsome and repulsive calumnies is a volume of evidence as to the wonderful patience of Southern whites. But we have had enough of it.
>
> There are some things that the Southern white man will not tolerate, and the obscene intimations of the foregoing have brought the writer to the very outermost limit of public patience. We hope we have said enough.

The "Evening Scimitar" of same date, copied the "Commercial's" editorial with these words of comment: "Patience under such circumstances is not a virtue. If the Negroes themselves do not apply the remedy without delay it will be the duty of those whom he has attacked to tie the wretch who utters these calumnies to a stake at the intersection of Main and Madison Sts., brand him in the forehead with a hot iron and perform upon him a surgical operation with a pair of tailor's shears."

Acting upon this advice, the leading citizens met in the Cotton Exchange Building the same evening, and threats of lynching were freely indulged, not by the lawless element upon which the deviltry of the South is usually saddled—but by the leading business men, in their leading business centre. Mr. Fleming, the business manager and owning a half interest the Free Speech, had to leave town to escape the mob, and was afterwards ordered not to return; letters and telegrams sent me in New York where I was spending my vacation advised me that bodily harm awaited my return. Creditors took possession of the office and sold the outfit, and the "Free Speech" was as if it had never been.

The editorial in question was prompted by the many inhuman and fiendish lynchings of Afro-Americans which have recently taken place and was meant as a warning. Eight lynched in one week and five of them charged with rape! The thinking public will not easily believe freedom and education more brutalizing than slavery, and the world knows that the crime of rape was unknown during four years of civil war, when the white women of the South were at the mercy of the race which is all at once charged with being a bestial one.

Since my business has been destroyed and I am an exile from home because of that editorial, the issue has been forced, and as the writer of it I feel that the race and the public generally should have a statement of the facts as they exist. They will serve at the same time as a defense for the Afro-Americans Sampsons who suffer themselves to be betrayed by white Delilahs.

The whites of Montgomery, Ala., knew J. C. Duke sounded the keynote of the situation—which they would gladly hide from the world, when he said in his paper, "The Herald," five years ago: "Why is it that white women attract Negro men now more than in former days? There was a time when such a thing was unheard of. There is a secret to this thing, and we greatly suspect it is the growing appreciation of white Juliets for colored Romeos." Mr. Duke, like the "Free Speech" proprietors, was forced to leave the city for reflecting on the "honor" of white women and his paper suppressed; but the truth remains that Afro-American men do not always rape (?) white women without their consent.

Mr. Duke, before leaving Montgomery, signed a card disclaiming any intention of slandering Southern white women. The editor of the "Free Speech" has no disclaimer to enter, but asserts instead that there are many white women in the South who would marry colored men if such an act would not place them at once beyond the pale of society and within the clutches of the law. The miscegnation laws of the South only operate against the legitimate union of the races; they leave the white man free to seduce all the colored girls he can, but it is death to the colored man who yields to the force and advances of a similar attraction in white women. White men lynch the offending Afro-American, not because he is a despoiler of virtue, but because he succumbs to the smiles of white women.

THE BLACK AND WHITE OF IT

The "Cleveland Gazette" of January 16, 1892, publishes a case in point. Mrs. J. S. Underwood, the wife of a minister of Elyria, Ohio, accused an Afro-American of rape. She told her husband that during his absence in 1888, stumping the State for the Prohibition Party, the man came to the kitchen door, forced his way in the house and insulted her. She tried to drive him out with a heavy poker, but he overpowered and chloroformed her, and when she revived her clothing was torn and she was in a horrible condition. She did not know the man but could identify him. She pointed out William Offett, a married man, who was arrested and, being in Ohio, was granted a trial.

The prisoner vehemently denied the charge of rape, but confessed he went to Mrs. Underwood's residence at her invitation and was criminally intimate with her at her request. This availed him nothing against the sworn testimony of a minister's wife, a lady of the highest respectability. He was found guilty, and entered the penitentiary, December 14, 1888, for fifteen years. Some time afterwards the woman's remorse led her to confess to her husband that the man was innocent.

These are her words: "I met Offett at the Post Office. It was raining. He was polite to me, and as I had several bundles in my arms he offered to carry them home for me, which he did. He had a strange fascination for me, and I invited him to call on me. He called, bringing chestnuts and candy for the children. By this means we got them to leave us alone in the room. Then I sat on his lap. He made a proposal to me and I readily consented. Why I did so, I do not know, but that I did is true. He visited me several times after that and each time I was indiscreet. I did not care after the first time. In fact I could not have resisted, and had no desire to resist."

When asked by her husband why she told him she had been outraged, she said: "I had several reasons for telling you. One was the neighbors saw the fellows here, another was, I was afraid I had contracted a loathsome disease, and still another was that I feared I might give birth to a Negro baby. I hoped to save my reputation by telling you a deliberate lie." Her husband horrified by the confession had Offett, who had already served four years, released and secured a divorce.

There are thousands of such cases throughout the South, with the difference that the Southern white men in insatiate fury wreak their vengeance without intervention of law upon the Afro-Americans who consort with their women. A few instances to substantiate the assertion that some white women love the company of the Afro-American will not be out of place. Most of these cases were reported by the daily papers of the South.

In the winter of 1885–6 the wife of a practicing physician in Memphis, in good social standing whose name has escaped me, left home, husband and children, and ran away with her black coachman. She was with him a month before her husband found and brought her home. The coachman could not be found. The doctor moved his family away from Memphis, and is living in another city under an assumed name.

In the same city last year a white girl in the dusk of evening screamed at the approach of some parties that a Negro had assaulted her on the street. He was captured, tried by a white judge and jury, that acquitted him of the charge. It is needless to add if there had been a scrap of evidence on which to convict him of so grave a charge he would have been convicted.

Sarah Clark of Memphis loved a black man and lived openly with him. When she was indicted last spring for miscegenation, she swore in court that she was *not* a white woman. This she did to escape the penitentiary and continued her illicit relation undisturbed. That she is of the lower class of whites, does not disturb the fact that she is a white woman. "The leading citizens" of Memphis are defending the "honor" of *all* white women, *demi-monde* included.

Since the manager of the "Free Speech" has been run away from Memphis by the guardians of the honor of Southern white women, a young girl living on Poplar St., who was discovered in intimate relations with a handsome mulatto young colored man, Will Morgan by name, stole her father's money to send the young fellow away from that father's wrath. She has since joined him in Chicago.

The Memphis "Ledger" for June 8th has the following; "If Lillie Bailey, a rather pretty white girl seventeen years of age, who is now at the City Hospital, would be somewhat less reserved about her disgrace there would be some very nauseating details in the story of her life. She is the mother of a little coon. The truth might reveal fearful depravity or it might reveal the evidence of a rank outrage. She will not divulge the name of the man who has left such black evidence of her disgrace, and, in fact, says it is a matter in which there can be no interest to the outside world. She came to Memphis nearly three months ago and was taken in at the Woman's Refuge in the southern part of the city. She remained there until a few weeks ago, when the child was born. The ladies in charge of the Refuge were horified. The girl was at once sent to the City Hospital, where she has been since May 30th. She is a country girl. She came to Memphis from her father's farm, a short distance from Hernando, Miss. Just when she left there she would not say. In fact she says she came to Memphis from Arkansas, and says her home is in that State. She is rather good looking, has blue eyes, a low forehead and dark red hair. The ladies at the Woman's Refuge do not know anything about the girl further than what they learned when she was an inmate of the institution; and she would not tell much. When the child was born an attempt was made to get the girl to reveal the name of the Negro who had disgraced her, she obstinately refused and it was impossible to elicit any information from her on the subject."

Note the wording. "The truth might reveal fearful depravity or rank outrage." If it had been a white child or Lillie Bailey had told a pitiful story of Negro outrage, it would have been a case of woman's weakness or assault and she could have remained at the Woman's Refuge. But a Negro child and to withhold its father's name and thus prevent the killing of another Negro "rapist." A case of "fearful depravity."

The very week the "leading citizens" of Memphis were making a spectacle of themselves in defense of all white women of every kind, an Afro-American, M. Stricklin, was found in a white woman's room in that city. Although she made no outcry of rape, he was jailed and would have been lynched, but the woman stated she bought curtains of him (he was a furniture dealer) and his business in her room that night was to put them up. A white woman's word was taken as absolutely in this case as when the cry of rape is made, and he was freed.

What is true of Memphis is true of the entire South. The daily papers last year reported a farmer's wife in Alabama had given birth to a Negro child. When the Negro farm hand who was plowing in the field heard it he took the mule from the plow and fled. The dispatches also told of a woman in South Carolina who gave birth to a Negro child and charged three men with being its father, *everyone of whom has since disappeared.* In Tuscumbia, Ala., the colored boy who was lynched there last year for assaulting a white girl told her before his accusers that he had met her there in the woods often before.

Frank Weems of Chattanooga who was not lynched in May only because the prominent citizens became his body guard until the doors of the penitentiary closed on him, had letters in his pocket from the white woman in the case, making the appointment with him. Edward Coy who was burned alive in Texarkana, January 1, 1892, died protesting his innocence. Investigation since as given by the Bystander in the Chicago Inter-Ocean, October 1, proves:

1. The woman who was paraded as a victim of violence was of bad character; her husband was a drunkard and a gambler.
2. She was publicly reported and generally known to have been criminally intimate with Coy for more than a year previous.
3. She was compelled by threats, if not by violence, to make the charge against the victim.
4. When she came to apply the match Coy asked her if she would burn him after they had "been sweethearting" so long.

5. A large majority of the "superior" white men prominent in the affair are the reputed fathers of mulatto children.

These are not pleasant facts, but they are illustrative of the vital phase of the so-called "race question," which should properly be designated an earnest inquiry as to the best methods by which religion, science, law and political power may be employed to excuse injustice, barbarity and crime done to a people because of race and color. There can be no possible belief that these people were inspired by any consuming zeal to vindicate God's law against miscegnationists of the most practical sort. The woman was a willing partner in the victim's guilt, and being of the "superior" race must naturally have been more guilty.

In Natchez, Miss., Mrs. Marshall, one of the *creme de la creme* of the city, created a tremendous sensation several years ago. She has a black coachman who was married, and had been in her employ several years. During this time she gave birth to a child whose color was remarked, but traced to some brunette ancestor, and one of the fashionable dames of the city was its godmother. Mrs. Marshall's social position was unquestioned, and wealth showered every dainty on this child which was idolized with its brothers and sisters by its white papa. In course of time another child appeared on the scene, but it was unmistakably dark. All were alarmed, and "rush of blood, strangulation" were the conjectures, but the doctor, when asked the cause, grimly told them it was a Negro child. There was a family conclave, the coachman heard of it and leaving his own family went West, and has never returned. As soon as Mrs. Marshall was able to travel she was sent away in deep disgrace. Her husband died within the year of a broken heart.

Ebenzer Fowler, the wealthiest colored man in Issaquena County, Miss., was shot down on the street in Mayersville, January 30, 1885, just before dark by an armed body of white men who filled his body with bullets. They charged him with writing a note to a white woman of the place, which they intercepted and which proved there was an intimacy existing between them.

Hundreds of such cases might be cited, but enough have been given to prove the assertion that there are white women in the South who love the Afro-American's company even as there are white men notorious for their preference for Afro-American women.

There is hardly a town in the South which has not an instance of the kind which is well-known; and hence the assertion is reiterated that "nobody in the South believes the old thread bare lie that Negro men rape white women." Hence there is a growing demand among Afro-Americans that the guilt or innocence of parties accused of rape be fully established. They know the men of the section of the country who refuse this are not so desirous of punishing rapists as they pretend. The utterances of the leading white men show that with them it is not the crime but the *class*. Bishop Fitzgerald has become apologist for lynchers of the rapists of *white* women only. Governor Tillman, of South Carolina, in the month of June, standing under the tree in Barnwell, S.C., on which eight Afro-Americans were hung last year, declared that he would lead a mob to lynch a *Negro* who raped a *white* woman." So say the pulpits, officials and newspapers of the South. But when the victim is a colored woman it is different.

Last winter in Baltimore, Md., three white ruffians assaulted a Miss Camphor, a young Afro-American girl, while out walking with a young man of her own race. They held her escort and outraged the girl. It was a deed dastardly enough to arouse Southern blood, which gives its horror of rape as excuse for lawlessness, but she was an Afro-American. The case went to the courts, an Afro-American lawyer defended the men and they were acquitted.

In Nashville, Tenn., there is a white man, Pat Hanifan, who outraged a little Afro-American girl, and, from the physical injuries received, she has been ruined for life.

He was jailed for six months, discharged, and is now a detective in that city. In the same city, last May, a white man outraged an Afro-American girl in a drug store. He was arrested, and released on bail at the trial. It was rumored that five hundred Afro-Americans had organized to lynch him. Two hundred and fifty white citizens armed themselves with Winchesters and guarded him. A cannon was placed in front of his home, and the Buchanan Rifles (State Militia) ordered to the scene for his protection. The Afro-American mob did not materialize. Only two weeks before Eph. Grizzard, who had only been *charged* with rape upon a white woman, had been taken from the jail, with Governor Buchanan and the police and militia standing by, dragged through the streets in broad daylight, knives plunged into him at every step, and with every fiendish cruelty a frenzied mob could devise, he was at last swung out on the bridge with hands cut to pieces as he tried to climb up the stanchions. A naked, bloody example of the blood-thirstiness of the nineteenth century civilization of the Athens of the South! No cannon or military was called out in his defense. He dared to visit a white woman.

At the very moment these civilized whites were announcing their determination "to protect their wives and daughters," by murdering Grizzard, a white man was in the same jail for raping eight-year-old Maggie Reese, an Afro-American girl. He was not harmed. The "honor" of grown women who were glad enough to be supported by the Grizzard boys and Ed Coy, as long as the liasion was not known, needed protection; they were white. The outrage upon helpless childhood needed no avenging in this case; she was black.

A white man in Guthrie, Oklahoma Territory, two months ago inflicted such injuries upon another Afro-American child that she died. He was not punished, but an attempt was made in the same town in the month of June to lynch an Afro-American who visited a white woman.

In Memphis, Tenn., in the month of June, Ellerton L. Dorr, who is the husband of Russell Hancock's widow, was arrested for attempted rape on Mattie Cole, a neighbor's cook; he was only prevented from accomplishing his purpose, by the appearance of Mattie's employer. Dorr's friends say he was drunk and not responsible for his actions. The grand jury refused to indict him and he was discharged.

THE NEW CRY

The appeal of Southern whites to Northern sympathy and sanction, the adroit, insiduous plea made by Bishop Fitzgerald for suspension of judgment because those "who condemn lynching express no sympathy for the *white* woman in the case," falls to the ground in the light of the foregoing.

From this exposition of the race issue in lynch law, the whole matter is explained by the well-known opposition growing out of slavery to the progress of the race. This is crystalized in the oft-repeated slogan: "This is a white man's country and the white man must rule." The South resented giving the Afro-American his freedom, the ballot box and the Civil Rights Law. The raids of the Ku-Klux and White Liners to subvert reconstruction government, the Hamburg and Ellerton, S.C., the Copiah County Miss., and the Layfayette Parish, La., massacres were excused as the natural resentment of intelligence against government by ignorance.

Honest white men practically conceded the necessity of intelligence murdering ignorance to correct the mistake of the general government, and the race was left to the tender mercies of the solid South. Thoughtful Afro-Americans with the strong arm of the government withdrawn and with the hope to stop such wholesale massacres urged the race to sacrifice its political rights for sake of peace. They honestly believed the race should fit itself for government, and when that should be done, the objection to race participation in politics would be removed.

But the sacrifice did not remove the trouble, nor move the South to justice. One by one the Southern States have legally (?) disfranchised the Afro-American, and since the repeal of the Civil Rights Bill nearly every Southern State has passed separate car laws with a penalty against their infringement. The race regardless of advancement is penned into filthy, stifling partitions cut off from smoking cars. All this while, although the political cause has been removed, the butcheries of black men at Barnwell, S.C., Carrolton, Miss., Waycross, Ga., and Memphis, Tenn., have gone on; also the flaying alive of a man in Kentucky, the burning of one in Arkansas, the hanging of a fifteen year old girl in Louisiana, a woman in Jackson, Tenn., and one in Hollendale, Miss., until the dark and bloody record of the South shows 728 Afro-Americans lynched during the past 8 years. Not 50 of these were for political causes; the rest were for all manner of accusations from that of rape of white women, to the case of the boy Will Lewis who was hanged at Tullahoma, Tenn., last year for being drunk and "sassy" to white folks.

These statistics compiled by the Chicago "Tribune" were given the first of this year (1892). Since then, not less than one hundred and fifty have been known to have met violent death at the hands of cruel bloodthirsty mobs during the past nine months.

To palliate this record (which grows worse as the Afro-American becomes intelligent) and excuse some of the most heinous crimes that ever stained the history of a country, the South is shielding itself behind the plausible screen of defending the honor of its women. This, too, in the face of the fact that only *one-third* of the 728 victims to mobs have been *charged* with rape, to say nothing of those of that one-third who were innocent of the charge. A white correspondent of the Baltimore Sun declares that the Afro-American who was lynched in Chestertown, Md., in May for assault on a white girl was innocent; that the deed was done by a white man who had since disappeared. The girl herself maintained that her assailant was a white man. When that poor Afro-American was murdered, the whites excused their refusal of a trial on the ground that they wished to spare the white girl the mortification of having to testify in court.

This cry has had its effect. It has closed the heart, stifled the conscience, warped the judgment and hushed the voice of press and pulpit on the subject of lynch law throughout this "land of liberty." Men who stand high in the esteem of the public for christian character, for moral and physical courage, for devotion to the principles of equal and exact justice to all, and for great sagacity, stand as cowards who fear to open their mouths before this great outrage. They do not see that by their tacit encouragement, their silent acquiescence, the black shadow of lawlessness in the form of lynch law is spreading its wings over the whole country.

Men who, like Governor Tillman, start the ball of lynch law rolling for a certain crime, are powerless to stop it when drunken or criminal white toughs feel like hanging an Afro-American on any pretext.

Even to the better class of Afro-Americans the crime of rape is so revolting they have too often taken the white man's word and given lynch law neither the investigation nor condemnation it deserved.

They forget that a concession of the right to lynch a man for a certain crime, not only concedes the right to lynch any person for any crime, but (so frequently is the cry of rape now raised) it is in a fair way to stamp us a race of rapists and desperadoes. They have gone on hoping and believing that general education and financial strength would solve the difficulty, and are devoting their energies to the accumulation of both.

The mob spirit has grown with the increasing intelligence of the Afro-American. It has left the out-of-the-way places where ignorance prevails, has thrown off the mask and with this new cry stalks in broad daylight in large cities, the centres of civilization, and is encouraged by the "leading citizens" and the press.

THE MALICIOUS AND UNTRUTHFUL WHITE PRESS

The "Daily Commercial" and "Evening Scimitar" of Memphis, Tenn., are owned by leading business men of that city, and yet, in spite of the fact that there had been no white woman in Memphis outraged by an Afro-American, and that Memphis possessed a thrifty law-abiding, property owning class of Afro-Americans the "Commercial" of May 17th, under the head of "More Rapes, More Lynchings" gave utterance to the following:

The lynching of three Negro scoundrels reported in our dispatches from Anniston, Ala., for a brutal outrage committed upon a white woman will be a text for much comment on "Southern barbarism" by Northern newspapers; but we fancy it will hardly prove effective for campaign purposes among intelligent people. The frequency of these lynchings calls attention to the frequency of the crimes which causes lynching. The "Southern barbarism" which deserves the serious attention of all people North and South, is the barbarism which preys upon weak and defenseless women. Nothing but the most prompt, speedy and extreme punishment can hold in check the horrible and beastial propensities of the Negro race. There is a strange similarity about a number of cases of this character which have lately occurred.

In each case the crime was deliberately planned and perpetrated by several Negroes. They watched for an opportunity when the women were left without a protector. It was not a sudden yielding to a fit of passion, but the consummation of a devilish purpose which has been seeking and waiting for the opportunity. This feature of the crime not only makes it the most fiendishly brutal, but it adds to the terror of the situation in the thinly settled country communities. No man can leave his family at night without the dread that some roving Negro ruffian is watching and waiting for this opportunity. The swift punishment which invariably follows these horrible crimes doubtless acts as a deterring effect upon the Negroes in that immediate neighborhood for a short time. But the lesson is not widely learned nor long remembered. Then such crimes, equally atrocious, have happened in quick succession, one in Tennessee, one in Arkansas, and one in Alabama. The facts of the crime appear to appeal more to the Negro's lustful imagination than the facts of the punishment do to his fears. He sets aside all fear of death in any form when opportunity is found for the gratification of his bestial desires.

There is small reason to hope for any change for the better. The commission of this crime grows more frequent every year. The generation of Negroes which have grown up since the war have lost in large measure the traditional and wholesome awe of the white race which kept the Negroes in subjection, even when their masters were in the army, and their families left unprotected except by the slaves themselves. There is no longer a restraint upon the brute passion of the Negro.

What is to be done? The crime of rape is always horrible, but the Southern man there is nothing which so fills the soul with horror, loathing and fury as the outraging of a white woman by a Negro. It is the race question in the ugliest, vilest, most dangerous aspect. The Negro as a political factor can be controlled. But neither laws nor lynchings can subdue his lusts. Sooner or later it will force a crisis. We do not know in what form it will come.

In its issue of June 4th, the Memphis "Evening Scimitar" gives the following excuse for lynch law:

Aside from the violation of white women by Negroes, which is the outcropping of a bestial perversion of instinct, the chief cause of trouble between the races in the South is the Negro's lack of manners. In the state of slavery he learned politeness from association with white people, who took pains to teach him. Since the emancipation came and the tie of mutual interest and regard between master and servant was broken, the Negro has drifted away into a state which is neither freedom nor bondage. Lacking the proper inspiration of the one and the restraining force of the other he has taken up the idea that boorish insolence is independence, and the exercise of a decent degree of breeding toward white people is identical with servile submission. In consequence of the prevalence of this notion there are many

Negroes who use every opportunity to make themselves offensive, particularly when they think it can be done with impunity.

We have had too many instances right here in Memphis to doubt this, and our experience is not exceptional. *The white people won't stand this sort of thing, and whether they be insulted as individuals or as a race, the response will be prompt and effectual.* The bloody riot of 1866, in which so many Negroes perished, was brought on principally by the outrageous conduct of the blacks toward the whites on the streets. It is also a remarkable and discouraging fact that the majority of such scoundrels are Negroes who have received educational advantages at the hands of the white taxpayers. They have got just enough of learning to make them realize how hopelessly their race is behind the other in everything that makes a great people, and they attempt to "get even" by insolence, which is ever the resentment of inferiors. The are well-bred Negroes among us, and it is truly unfortunate that they should have to pay, even in part, the penalty of the offenses committed by the baser sort, but this is the way of the world. The innocent must suffer for the guilty. If the Negroes as a people possessed a hundredth part of the self-respect which is evidenced by the courteous bearing of some that the "Scimitar" could name, the friction between the races would be reduced to a minimum. It will not do to beg the question by pleading that many white men are also stirring up strife. The Caucasian blackguard simply obeys the promptings of a depraved disposition, and he is seldom deliberately rough or offensive toward strangers or unprotected women.

The Negro tough, on the contrary, is given to just that kind of offending, and he almost invariably singles out white people as he victims.

On March 9th, 1892, there were lynched in this same city three of the best specimens of young since-the-war Afro-American manhood. They were peaceful, law-abiding citizens and energetic business men.

They believed the problem was to be solved by eschewing politics and putting money in the purse. They owned a flourishing grocery business in a thickly populated suburb of Memphis, and a white man named Barrett had one on the opposite corner. After a personal difficulty which Barrett sought by going into the "People's Grocery" drawing a pistol and was thrashed by Calvin McDowell, he (Barrett) threatened to "clean them out." These men were a mile beyond the city limits and police protection; hearing that Barrett's crowd was coming to attack them Saturday night, they mustered forces and prepared to defend themselves against the attack.

When Barrett came he led a *posse* of officers, twelve in number, who afterward claimed to be hunting a man for whom they had a warrant. That twelve men in citizen's clothes should think it necessary to go in the night to hunt one man who had never before been arrested, or made any record as a criminal has never been explained. When they entered the back door the young men thought the threatened attack was on, and fired into them. Three of the officers were wounded, and when the *defending* party found it was officers of the law upon whom they had fired, they ceased and got away.

Thirty-one men were arrested and thrown in jail as "conspirators," although they all declared more than once they did not know they were firing on officers. Excitement was at fever heat until the morning papers, two days after, announced that the wounded deputy sheriffs were out of danger. This hindered rather than helped the plans of the whites. There was no law on the statute books which would execute an Afro-American for wounding a white man, but the "unwritten law" did. Three of these men, the president, the manager and clerk of the grocery—"the leaders of the conspiracy"—were secretly taken from jail and lynched in a shockingly brutal manner. "The Negroes are getting too independent," they say, "we must teach them a lesson."

"What lesson? The lesson of subordination. "Kill the leaders and it will cow the Negro who dares to shoot a white man, even in self-defense."

Although the race was wild over the outrage, the mockery of law and justice which disarmed men and locked them up in jails where they could be easily and safely reached by the mob—the Afro-American ministers, newspapers and leaders counselled obedience to the law which did not protect them.

Their counsel was heeded and not a hand was uplifted to resent the outrage; following the advice of the "Free Speech," people left the city in great numbers.

The dailies and associated press reports heralded these men to the county as "toughs," and "Negro desperadoes who kept a low dive." This same press service printed that the Negro who was lynched at Indianola, Miss., in May, had outraged the sheriff's eight-year-old daughter. The girl was more than eighteen years old, and was found by her father in this man's room, who was a servant on the place.

Not content with misrepresenting the race, the mob-spirit was not to be satisfied until the paper which was doing all it could to counteract this impression was silenced. The colored people were resenting their bad treatment in a way to make itself felt, yet gave the mob no excuse for further murder, until the appearance of the editorial which is construed as a reflection on the "honor" of the Southern white women. It is not half so libelous as that of the "Commercial" which appeared four days before, and which has been given in these pages. They would have lynched the manager of the "Free Speech" for exercising the right of free speech if they had found him as quickly as they would have hung a rapist, and glad of the excuse to do so. The owners were ordered not to return, "The Free Speech" was suspended with as little compunction as the business of the "People's Grocery" broken up and the proprietors murdered.

THE SOUTH'S POSITION

Henry W. Grady in his well-remembered speeches in New England and New York pictured the Afro-American as incapable of self-government. Through him and other leading men the cry of the South to the country has been "Hands off! Leave us to solve our problem." To the Afro-American the South says, "the white man must and will rule." There is little difference between the Ante-bellum South and the New South.

Her white citizens are wedded to any method however revolting, any measure however extreme, for the subjugation of the young manhood of the race. They have cheated him out of his ballot, deprived him of civil rights or redress therefor in the civil courts, robbed him of the fruits of his labor, and are still murdering, burning and lynching him.

The result is a growing disregard of human life. Lynch law has spread its insidious influence till men in New York State, Pennsylvania and on the free Western plains feel they can take the law in their own hands with impunity, especially where an Afro-American is concerned. The South is brutalized to a degree not realized by its own inhabitants, and the very foundation of government, law and order, are imperilled.

Public sentiment has had a slight "reaction" though not sufficient to stop the crusade of lawlessness and lynching. The spirit of christianity of the great M. E. Church was aroused to the frequent and revolting crimes against a weak people, enough to pass strong condemnatory resolutions at its General Conference in Omaha last May. The spirit of justice of the grand old party asserted itself sufficiently to secure a denunciation of the wrongs, and a feeble declaration of the belief in human rights in the Republican platform at Minneapolis, June 7th. Some of the great dailies and weeklies have swung into line declaring that lynch law must go. The President of the United States issued a proclamation that it be not tolerated in the territories over which he has jurisdiction. Governor Northern and Chief Justice Bleckley of Georgia have proclaimed against it. The citizens of Chattanooga, Tenn., have set a worthy example in that they not only condemn lynch law, but her public men demanded a trial for Weems, the

accused rapist, and guarded him while the trial was in progress. The trial only lasted ten minutes, and Weems chose to plead guilty and accept twenty-one years sentence, than invite the certain death which awaited him outside that cordon of police if he had told the truth and shown the letters he had from the white woman in the case.

Col. A. S. Colyar, of Nashville, Tenn., is so overcome with the horrible state of affairs that he addressed the following earnest letter to the Nashville "American." "Nothing since I have been a reading man has so impressed me with the decay of manhood among the people of Tennessee as the dastardly submission to the mob reign. We have reached the unprecedented low level; the awful criminal depravity of substituting the mob for the court and jury, of giving up the jail keys to the mob whenever they are demanded. We do it in the largest cities and in the country towns; we do it in midday; we do it after full, not to say formal, notice, and so thoroughly and generally is it acquiesced in that the murderers have discarded the formula of masks. They go into the town where everybody knows them, sometimes under the gaze of the governor, in the presence of the courts, in the presence of the sheriff and his deputies, in the presence of the entire police force, take out the prisoner, take his life, often with fiendish glee, and often with acts of cruelty and barbarism which impress the reader with a degeneracy rapidly approaching savage life. That the State is disgraced but faintly expresses the humiliation which has settled upon the once proud people of Tennessee. The State, in its majesty, through its organized life, for which the people pay liberally, makes but one record, but one note, and that a criminal falsehood, 'was hung by persons to the jury unknown.' The murder at Shelbyville is only a verification of what every intelligent man knew would come, because with a mob a rumor is as good as a proof."

These efforts brought forth apologies and a short halt, but the lynching mania was raged again through the past three months with unabated fury.

The strong arm of the law must be brought to bear upon lynchers in severe punishment, but this cannot and will not be done unless a healthy public sentiment demands and sustains such action.

The men and women in the South who disapprove of lynching and remain silent on the perpetration of such outrages, are particeps criminis, accomplices, accessories before and after the fact, equally guilty with the actual law-breakers who would not persist if they did not know that neither the law nor militia would be employed against them.

SELF HELP

In the creation of this healthier public sentiment, the Afro-American can do for himself what no one else can do for him. The world looks on with wonder that we have conceded so much and remain law-abiding under such great outrage and provocation.

To Northern capital and Afro-American labor the South owes its rehabilitation. If labor is withdrawn capital will not remain. The Afro-American is thus the backbone of the South. A thorough knowledge and judicious exercise of this power in lynching localities could many times effect a blood less revolution. The white man's dollar is his god, and to stop this will be to stop outrages in many localities.

The Afro-Americans of Memphis denounced the lynching of three of their best citizens, and urged and waited for the authorities to act in the matter and bring the lynchers to justice. No attempt was made to do so, and the black men left the city by thousands, bringing about great stagnation in every branch of business. Those who remained so injured the business of the street car company by staying off the cars, that the superintendent, manager and treasurer called personally on the editor of the "Free Speech," asked them to urge our people to give them their patronage again. Other business men became alarmed over the situation and the "Free Speech" was run away that the colored people might be more easily controlled. A meeting of white citizens in June, three months after the lynching, passed resolutions for the first time, condemning it. *But they did not punish the lynchers.* Every one of them was known by name, because they had been selected to do the dirty work, by some of the very citizens who passed these resolutions. Memphis is fast losing her black population, who proclaim as they go that there is no protection for the life and property of any Afro-American citizen in Memphis who is not a slave.

The Afro-American citizens of Kentucky, whose intellectual and financial improvement has been phenomenal, have never had a separate car law until now. Delegations and petitions poured into the Legislature against it, yet the bill passed and the Jim Crow Car of Kentucky is a legalized institution. Will the great mass of Negroes continue to patronize the railroad? A special from Covington, Ky., says:

Covington, June 13th.—The railroads of the State are beginning to feel very markedly, the effects of the separate coach bill recently passed by the Legislature. No class of people in the State have so many and so largely attended excursions as the blacks. All these have been abandoned, and regular travel is reduced to a minimum. A competent authority says the loss to the various roads will reach $1,000,000 this year.

A call to a State Conference in Lexington, Ky., last June had delegates from every county in the State. Those delegates, the ministers, teachers, heads of secret and others orders, and the head of every family should pass the word around for every member of the race in Kentucky to stay off railroads unless obliged to ride. If they did so, and their advice was followed persistently the convention would not need to petition the Legislature to repeal the law or raise money to file a suit. The railroad corporations would be so effected they would in self-defense lobby to have the separate car law repealed. On the other hand, as long as the railroads can get Afro-American excursions they will always have plenty of money to fight all the suits brought against them. They will be aided in so doing by the same partisan public sentiment which passed the law. White men passed the law, and white judges and juries would pass upon the suits against the law, and render judgment in line with their prejudices and in deference to the greater financial power.

The appeal to the white man's pocket has ever been more effectual than all the appeals ever made to his conscience. Nothing, absolutely nothing, is to be gained by a further sacrifice of manhood and self-respect. By the right exercise of his power as the industrial factor of the South, the Afro-American can demand and secure his rights, the punishment of lynchers, and a fair trial for accused rapists.

Of the many inhuman outrages of this present year, the only case where the proposed lynching did *not* occur, was where the men armed themselves in Jacksonville, Fla., and Paducah, Ky., and prevented it. The only times an Afro-American who was assaulted got away has been when he had a gun and used it in self-defense.

The lesson this teaches and which every Afro-American should pondor well, is that a Winchester rifle should have a place of honor in every black home, and it should be used for that protection which the law refuses to give. When the white man who is always the aggressor knows he runs as great risk of biting the dust every time his Afro-American victim does, he will have greater respect for Afro-American life. The more the Afro-American yields and cringes and begs, the more he has to do so, the more he is insulted, outraged and lynched.

The assertion has been substantiated throughout these pages that the press contains unreliable and doctored reports of lynchings, and one of the most necessary things for the race to do is to get these facts before the public. The people must know before they can act, and there is no educator to compare with the press.

The Afro-American papers are the only ones which will print the truth, and they lack means to employ agents and detectives to get at the facts. The race must rally a mighty host to the support of their journals, and thus enable them to do much in the way of investigation.

A lynching occurred at Port Jarvis, N.Y., the first week in June. A white and colored man were implicated in the assault upon a white girl. It was charged that the white man paid the colored boy to make the assault, which he did on the public highway in broad day time, and was lynched. This, too, was done by "parties unknown." The white man in the case still lives. He was imprisoned and promises to fight the case on trial. At the preliminary examination, it developed that he had been a suitor of the girl's. She had repulsed and refused him, yet had given him money, and he had sent threatening letters demanding more.

The day before this examination she was so wrought up, she left home and wandered miles away. When found she said she did so because she was afraid of the man's testimony. Why should she be afraid of the prisoner? Why should she yield to his demands for money if not to prevent him exposing something he knew? It seems explainable only on the hypothesis that a *liason* existed between the colored boy and the girl, and the white man knew of it. The press is singularly silent. Has it a motive? We owe it to ourselves to find out.

The story comes from Larned, Kansas, Oct. 1st, that a young white lady held at bay until daylight, without alarming any one in the house, "a burly Negro" who entered her room and bed. The "burly Negro" was promptly lynched without investigation or examination of inconsistant stories.

A house was found burned down near Montgomery, Ala., in Monroe County, Oct. 13th, a few weeks ago; also the burned bodies of the owners and melted piles of gold and silver.

These discoveries led to the conclusion that the awful crime was not prompted by motives of robbery. The suggestion of the whites was that "brutal lust was the incentive, and as there are nearly 200 Negroes living within a radius of five miles of the place the conclusion was inevitable that some of them were the perpetrators."

Upon this "suggestion" probably made by the real criminal, the mob acted upon the "conclusion" and arrested ten Afro-Americans, four of whom, they tell the world, confessed to the deed of murdering Richard L. Johnson and outraging his daughter, Jeanette. These four men, Berrell Jones, Moses Johnson, Jim and John Packer, none of them 25 years of age, upon this conclusion, were taken from jail, hanged, shot, and burned while yet alive the night of Oct. 12th. The same report says Mr. Johnson was on the best of terms with his Negro tenants.

The race thus outraged must find out the facts of this awful hurling of men into eternity on supposition, and give them to the indifferent and apathetic country. We feel this to be a garbled report, but how can we prove it?

Near Vicksburg, Miss., a murder was committed by a gang of burglars. Of course it must have been done by Negroes, and Negroes were arrested for it. It is believed that 2 men, Smith Tooley and John Adams belonged to a gang controlled by white men and, fearing exposure, on the night of July 4th, they were hanged in the Court House yard by those interested in silencing them. Robberies since committed in the same vicinity have been known to be by white men who had their faces blackened. We strongly believe in the innocence of these murdered men, but we have no proof. No other news goes out to the world save that which stamps us as a race of cut-throats, robbers and lustful wild beasts. So great is Southern hate and prejudice, they legally (?) hung poor little thirteen year old Mildrey Brown at Columbia, S.C., Oct. 7th, on the circumstantial evidence that she poisoned a white infant. If her guilt had been proven unmistakably, had she been white, Mildrey Brown would never have been hung.

The country would have been aroused and South Carolina disgraced forever for such a crime. The Afro American himself did not know as he should have known as his journals should be in a position to have him know and act.

Nothing is more definitely settled than he must act for himself. I have shown how he may employ the boycott, emigration and the press, and I feel that by a combination of all these agencies can be effectually stamped out lynch law, that last relic of barbarism and slavery. "The gods help those who help themselves."

Shadow of the Plantation

Charles S. Johnson

The Damascus Baptist Church stands at a far junction of the dusty and tortuous road leading out from Hardaway, with no other build-

Source: Charles S. Johnson, *Shadow of the Plantation* pp. 153–162. Copyright 1934 University of Chicago Press. Used with permission.

ing within sight, or in fact within miles, save an old and sagging school building close by it. The church is a small, painfully conventional boxlike structure with gabled roof and a small bell tower over the entrance. It has once or twice been whitewashed but is now gray under the long assault of time and the elements. Two giant oaks at the rear, dripping with a Spanish trailing moss, give shelter for the horses and mules of the communicants. Back of the schoolhouse with its broken windows and sagging shutters is a small cemetery with boards and short tombstones jutting up at odd angles to mark the mounds of departed members. Twelve mules and a horse are hitched to the oak trees, and farm wagons, still holding empty chairs and baskets, are scattered about the green. Besides these conveyances are fully a dozen Ford automobiles, worn and plastered with dry mud, and, lounging in these cars, engaged in conversation are men, young and old, carefree and serious. The principal cluster of women and small children is around a pump which stands midway between the church and the school. They are drinking with an easy leisure.

Inside the church there are three rows of plain wooden benches. The walls of the interior are of white, painted, horizontal boards, and the ceiling, as far up as could be reached, is painted a vivid green. At the end of the room is a very cluttered rostrum. The inclined pedestal has the center; the pastor's seat is directly behind. Then there are three small benches for the choir, two hat racks, and an old clock which is out of order. On the wall back of the rostrum is a large calendar with a picture of Lincoln, an even larger placard announcing a "drive" for. $225,000 on behalf of Selma University in 1927, a framed crayon portrait of a former pastor, a placard warning in red letters of the danger of malaria, and two framed certificates. Beside the rostrum is a coal stove.

There is a cheerful bustling among the two hundred and fifty or more persons in the building as they fan themselves and accommodate their natural flow of conversation and gossip to the novelty of church clothes. From one corner of the room a voice is heard above the hum of conversation, trailing tentatively into a longmeter hymn. It is the beginning of the preparation for the mood of worship. The noise of the congregation dies down as the voice gains in volume and certainty, and others take up the lines.

Finally, the congregation is singing lustily. A deacon of the church rises and in loud supplication raises a prayer:

> Lord our Father who art in Heaven, let your will be done on earth as it is in Heaven. Give us this day our daily bread and forgive our debts as we forgive those who debt against us, for thine is the Kingdom. Heavenly Father, we feel thankful this morning and ask you to send the Holy Ghost for Jesus' sake. Bless these our sisters and brethren, O Lord, our Heavenly Father, and we want dying men and women to know that besides you there is no other God before you, and they must know that they got to give account of all the deeds done in this body.

The audience has been only politely restrained during this part of his prayer, and the younger members are frankly whispering and continuing their greetings. There is need of more warmth in his address to God, and he forsakes the repetition of one set of stereotypes drawn from lines of scripture for another which has a more certain response value:

> I'm talking about that same God who bled and was crucified and died on Calvary's hill; [almost angrily] talking about that same God John saw.

There were scattered "Amens."

> Behold the Lamb of God who take away the sins of the world. Have mercy on us, Lord.

(More "Amens.")

> Father, bless the church, bless the sick and 'flicted; remember the minister, remember the members, and when we done going up and down the road be with us and stand by us and the praise will be "Thanks for Christ our Redeemer's sake. Amen."

Before his voice is still a song is raised, a formal hymn:

My soul be on thy guard, ten thousand foes
　arise
The hosts of sin are pressing
To draw thee from the skies.

Another member, who has stood up in readiness during the last verses of the hymn, intones:

Lord, our Father, some have gone to the left and some have gone to the right; O Lord, bless those who stick close to the cross; throw around them your strong arm of protection; help our dark days, O Lord. You know you said you would protect us and stand by us. Bless the sick; bless the Pastor; bless the Deacon Board; help them to lead us and guide us. Heavenly Father, help us to grow stronger in the faith; be with us and stand by us. You said a long time ago that if I pray and pray hard you would hear me again. Bless my sister's children; bless my mother who has gone before me. If I don't ever meet her in this world let me meet her when we have done done with this old world. Amen.

There is now a more fitting mood for the minister. During the singing and praying he has been detached, sometimes rapt in abstraction, sometimes leaning over to whisper matters of practical concern over the business of the church. He is a stocky, dark, elderly man, well aware of his rank as a preacher. Now he is all attention, and with a heavy solemnity he approaches the pedestal.

My friends, we are very glad to meet you here this morning. [Don't talk, don't talk.] Everybody ought to be happy today. I am going to ask Deacon Brown to take all these baskets and carry them right back yonder, out of the way. Some of us could be in our sick rooms, and some of us could be in our liquish graves, but we are here, and we wants to ask you for your prayers. 'Tis good to pray. Prayers of the righteous prevaileth much. Sisters and brothers, God done set time to make things known to us, and I'm not satisfied unless I'm preaching the word of God.

He is reminding his audience of his obligation to preach, of the unquenchable instinct to evangelism on which a large part of his authority rests.

The Gospel is the bread of life and it must be preached throughout the world. One morning this week I felt like preaching. I was jest thirsty ter preach. You know if you is praying and someone slips up on you, you gits shame, so I choosed my wife and told her ter watch, and I stood before the mirrow till my soul was satisfied, and one time I heard her tipping round by the side of the house ter hear me. Her soul was hungry too, sisters and brothers. These words were spoken by Paul. Paul was a great man, you know.

He is a minister who has not lived always in the community, and he has some basis in his experience for a comparison of his people with others. He can hold out a light. This is one of the social functions of the church.

Paul studied education; he didn't mind going to school. Lots of our boys and girls don't lak ter go ter school. We laks' ter play hookie. We turn our back on learnings, but Paul wan't lak that, and after he educated he turned himself as who we call a sheriff terday. You know, sisters and brothers, after you get an education there is a chance fer you, you can git a position. You know Paul didn't know anything 'bout Jesus. He ain't come in contact wid Jesus yet. The other day a lady was coming through the community. Dr. C———and I was passing down the highway, and she greeted us wid a smile, and as far down the road as I saw her I could see the intelligence in her, and later when I talked wid her, I got acquainted wid her through her smile. That's the way wid Jesus.

Paul was lak you and I. He was choosen among one hundred and one thousand men and told "As you go, go and preach the Gospel." Before we seek our soul salvation we could go ter the dancing room, and after the dungeon shuk and chains fell off, we could have a vision wid God.

Instruction is not, however, the main function of the sermon. There must be enthusiasm, even ecstasy, and the minister who is incapable of stimulating this is soon out. The reference to education is brief, but it is possible to wax eloquent over the horrible sin of dancing. This is a part of the dogma of the church which affects only the younger members, but which is clung to tenaciously as an element of the respectability of church membership. Other more serious forms of social behavior prevailing in the community are not often touched upon, or if referred to at all it is done in a spirit of great daring.

> Paul ain't no Christian now; ever'where he would hear the Gospel preached he would go and bring the news back ter Jerusalem. Sisters and brothers, you know ever'where the Gospel is preached the devil is there to 'sturb the souls of Christians; ain't many been really borned again, you know. Them's that done been borned again is a few. Ananias done been down ter Damascus, and he said, "I'll go down ter Damascus," oh, yes, my sisters and brothers, he said, "I'll go down and preach until they come off the dancing floor and till the dancing mistress pulls off her dancing shoes; till she change her soul and seeing Jesus is near ter my soul." I can see Ananias preaching. He was afraid of Paul. I can see Paul, oh, yes, I can see him when he got the news that Paul was down in Damascus, and the devil tuk the British soil, and Paul decided he would put a stumblingblock in this preacher's way. Then I can see him when he went ter Jerusalem ter git his letter and saying, "I want ter go down ter Damascus where Ananias is preaching, and find him and bring him back ter Jerusalem." I can see when the devil began ter write the letter. Then I kin see him when he went ter the brothers ter go on their wicked journey.

The words of the minister are not so impressive as the manner in which he intones them, in an excited singsong. Once well launched, the audience gives encouragement in their responses: "Amen"; "Yes, Lord"; "Preach it, boy"; "Uh huh!"; "Have mercy, Jesus"; "Come, Holy Spirit, we need you now"; "Jesus comes by." The imagery, which is most effective, is that which is en-shrouded in the most impenetrable cloud of mystery.

> Sisters and brothers, you know God is so high you can't go over him, and so wide you can't go 'round him, and so low you can't go under him. Jesus says yer got ter come in by the door. Jesus went down ter Damascus and saw the people shaking and shouting in glory. He told Ananias that Paul was riding. Ain't nobody never heard no voice lak dat before. Brothers, help me, help me preach this Gospel now.

A point of enthusiastic departure is that of some great conflict of the soul. This can be made more realistic by sudden allusions to well-known experiences.

> When Paul got 'way down the road on his journey he fell down prostrate on the ground three days. *Hallelujah!* No doubt the birds was singing sweet gongs. He got hungry; hungry for bread; thirsty fer water. "Stay, stay there," God said; "lay right there three days." Finally God tempted him wid his Godlike power. O Paul, O Paul, O, O Paul, did the Gospel call you one morning wid his still voice? Oh, yes, sisters and brothers, and he said, "Saul, Saul," and Paul answered, "Here am I, Lord. I know I been against thy work; what wilt thou have me ter do?" He looked at his hands and his hands looked new; looked at his feet and his feet looked new; and, O sisters and brothers, he said, "Git on your journey, Saul, and keep on down ter Damascus. Don't go back ter Jerusalem." Oh, no, I'm not afraid of praying. I can see Jesus going down ter Damascus. The people was sick and he opened the door and said ter Ananias, "Don't be afraid of Paul. Paul is coming in the morning. If you get tired of setting, go right in the house of Judea." God done told Paul that Ananias would meet him, and he tell one that the child of God done tuk his feet out of the miry clay and waited for Ananias. I'm talking wid my God, sisters and brothers, and that makes everything all right, and soon that morning Ananias made an address ter Paul; the greatest ever been made in the world. Paul go on back ter Jerusalem. God done purged Paul wid the Holy Ghost on high. Paul said, "I'm gonna preach from on high." Brothers and sisters, they was standing

on the highway. I can see them now. The world was waiting. I can see the children bound by the hands of the devil standing by the wayside. Look at him; jest listen how he preached. *Hallelujah!* He jest wanted ter join Christ's men. The people done heard so much bout Paul some of them was so 'fraid, some started to murder him. But somebody tuk him from the mob crowd by the wall. Sisters and brothers, that was the Holy Ghost. Chillen, if you pray the world can't do you no harm. The first morning Paul went out he 'sulted wid God. He met my friend, O God! Preached until men believed. When Paul started on his second missionary journey he said, "O God, who must I git ter go wid me?" and Jesus said, "Go on the outskirts of the city of Philippi. Believe I am the son of God. A woman stays there; she is a po' woman, but she will give you room in her home. You stay there." I can see, brothers—I can see, brothers—he began preaching the Gospel. I believe that Jesus Christ is the Son of God. People begin ter git on easy, but he preached on and on till they began ter believe and thirst for the word of God. But soon they tuk Paul and Silas and bound 'em in the jail.

The dramatization of incidents of the New Testament constitutes a large part of the sermon, but the experiences are so related as to make it possible for his people to identify themselves with the characters in this great struggle. All that God asks either of ancient and eminent Saul or of modern and humble Susie Keys is faith and prayer.

I can see when they began ter put them in the Philippi jail. Children, have you prayed? I done prayed. Silas asked, "What will we do?" Paul said, "I want ter have a little talk wid God." Chillen, I tell you a child of God has a hard time in this world.

Preacher sits down, still speaking:

Night come and the roosters didn't crow. Birds wan't singing no sweet songs. Cows wan't chewing no cuds. Way, way in the night—chillen, do you ever pray in the night? I heard old Saul singing, "Amazin' grace, how sweet

the sound that saved a wretch like me." 'Bout that time old Paul said, "Lord, O Lord, you promised good ter me. You is my sword and shield, and you got my portion due." Then Paul said, "Jesus, I am your child." Then Jesus told his angel to "git two wings ter cover your head, two ter cover your feet, go down ter Jerusalem and shake jail, and buckle loose the jail and let my chillen free." "Take this key of gold." Looka yonder, looka yonder, chillen.

[Getting up.] 'Fore day Paul on one side an Silas on the other. Silas said, "Lord, Lord, what will you have me ter do?" He said ter him, "Stand right there; don't move a step."

The shouting has begun with sudden sharp groans of spiritual torture, then screams of exultation. Three or four persons are expressing themselves with shouts accompanied by a variety of physical demonstrations, while most of the audience responds in low accents. There is a phase of worship referred to as "helpin' out" the preacher, in which a line will be repeated several times by the minister or even a leader from the floor, and the audience joins in with a low moan. "The mountains so high, but I'm coming on"; "Lord, I done started and I can't turn back"; "Lord, I didn't come here for to do no harm"; "Trouble done been here, calling us a long ways"; "Well, you talk about Jesus; he's a friend of mine"; "Well, it's all night long I'm on my knees"; "I jest come here, Lord, for to sing and pray"; "Well, I feel like moaning. . . ." The preacher continues:

When the clouds swing high over your head say, "World, World, O World, I done fought a good fight. Sometimes my heart was bleeding, sometimes runned over and called ever'thing 'cept a child God." Sisters, is you on the right track? Is all your tickets been signed and your chains fell off? Did you tell ever'body, the white, the colored, the po', the sick? Is you got a letter written in your heart? Makes your heart burn, makes you cry, makes you laugh. Is you done told ever'body? Oh, yes, ever'body! Amen, Amen.

Song: "Long Ago."

I think somebody oughta get 'quainted wid Jesus. We gonna sing while the doors of the church be open.

> My soul, be on thy guard,
> Ten thousand foes arise.
> The hosts of sin are pressing hard
> To draw me from the skies.

Someone wid de spirit please come ter the alter and pray.

An old man arises and grips the bench ahead, with heavy, gnarled hands:

O my Heavenly Father, hit is again I done bowed on my knees ter give thanks fer thy holy name. Nothing we feel worthy ter offer Thee but a sinful heart fer your judgment. We bow not fer show ter the world, and not ter be well spoke of but because we know we got ter die. You done lent us this life and, Heavenly Father, we got a duty ter perform. We come first thanking Thee for this guidance. Help us ter rastle wid the combats of the world. Don't let us get weak on the way. In acts of confusion guide us and we will follow. Lord, lead us we ask Thee. We thank Thee that we is working for a Kingdom not made wid hands. We are following you, Captain Jesus, 'cause you said your Kingdom last always. Sometimes, Jesus, you know the devil gits us by the hand, but we want you ter catch us by the hand and lead us out. Amen.

The song which follows is one of humble triumph:

My Lord done been here, blessed my soul, and
    gone away.
I wouldn't be a sinner, I'll tell you the reason
    why—
If my Lord God would come here I wouldn't
    be ready to die.
My Lord done been here, blessed my soul, and
    gone away.
I wouldn't be a gambler, I'll tell you the reason
    why—
If my good Lord would come here I wouldn't
    be ready to die.

The preacher has done his duty in arousing the audience. He turns again to the problem of behavior.

My friends, we done sung the songs of Zion; done broke ter you the bread of life; done opened ter you de doors of de church; and done prayed these 'firmed prayers; and still there's more. You know I thinks 'bout the people in the community; how can you dance when there's a starvin' family over there? When you been dancing all Saturday night you ain't a fit subject fer the Lord. You gotta cut the dancing out. If you go up there ter the graveyard you'll see just as many short graves as long un's. You oughta quit dancing. You say you is a Christian; if you is a Christian you better show some signs. If you don't quit you're on the road to hell; talkin' 'bout you 'blige ter dance and you can't help it. 'Member in Noah's time, when the world was 'stroyed? Last night me and my wife was settin' outside the house and we heard singing and dancing, and here starvation is in your meal barrel. The old folks talking 'bout chillen young gotta have some fun, but they just stumblingblocks in their way. I laks ball games well as you, but I don't lak ter hear my members down there cussin'. Then you don't 'speck your pastor when you see him in all places. Me and my wife sets out ever' Saturday instead and reads God's word. You ought not ter do things 'gainst the plans of salvation. You ought ter show some signs of Christians down there. If you can act it at the church and on the roads and in the fields you can act it down there. Chillen, you better quit dancing. Now next month when the convention meets in Birmingham, I wants you sisters and brothers ter git around and git your pastor a seersucker suit, some socks, and some shirts. And I need shoes too. I gotta go down there and represent you, and I wanta do hit right.

The collection is lifted. Four young men stand before the pulpit and begin to sing, while two deacons stand by the table and persuade the members to come up and contribute.

Forced Labor in the New South

Warren S. Reese
S. D. Redmond

A. 1903: A U.S. ATTORNEY'S REPORT TO THE ATTORNEY GENERAL

DEPARTMENT OF JUSTICE,
OFFICE OF THE UNITED STATES ATTORNEY,
  MIDDLE DISTRICT OF ALABAMA
              Montgomery, June 15, 1903.
The Attorney General,
Washington, D.C.

Sir:-

Your favor of June 12, 1903, initialled M.D.P.–5280–1903, directing me to make a full report relative to the investigation of the peonage cases recently had before the Grand Jury of this District, has been received and given very careful consideration.

In compliance with your request I have to report that this Grand Jury up to and within a few days ago, has confined its investigations to violations of the peonage, kidnapping and conspiracy statutes of the United States occurring in the two counties of Coosa and Tallapoosa. These investigations have developed that there have been flagrant abuses and violations of these laws on the part of wealthy and influential men in these counties. These violations have not been confined to one or two periodical and independent instances, but it has developed into a miserable business and custom to catch up ignorant and helpless Negro men and women upon the flimsiest and the most baseless charges and carry them before a jus-

tice of the peace who is usually a paid hireling of these wealthy dealers. The form of a trial is sometimes gone through, but usually that even is dispensed with. The victim is found guilty and a fine is assessed which, in the beginning, cannot be paid by the victim, and then it is that one of these slave dealers steps up, pretends to be the friend of the Negro, and has a short conference with him telling him he will pay him out if he will sign a contract to work for him on his farm, to which the Negro readily agrees rather than go to the mines, as he is informed he will have to do, his fine is paid, the contract is signed, and the Negro is taken to the farm or mine or mill or quarry of the employer. At once he is placed into a condition of involuntary servitude, he is locked up at nights in a cell, worked under guards during the day from 3 o'clock in the morning until 7 or 8 o'clock at night, whipped in a most cruel manner, is insufficiently fed and poorly clad—in fact the evidence in nearly all of the cases investigated reveals that the Negro men are worked nearly naked, while the women are worked in an equally disgraceful manner. Brutal things have transpired, and sometimes death has resulted in the infliction of corporal punishment upon these unfortunates. When the time of a good working Negro is nearing an end, he is rearrested upon some trumped up charge and again carried before some bribed justice and resentenced to an additional time. In this way Negroes have been known to have worked on these places in this situation for years and years. They can get no word to friends, nor is word allowed to reach them from the outside world. If they write letters they go through the hands of a visor, and if letters are directed to them they are visored,

Source: Forced Labor in the New South. Warren S. Reese to the Attorney General, June 15, 1903. Folded file 5280–03, Department of Justice, National Archives. Record Group 60. These copies were kindly supplied by Pete Daniel.

and thus it is they are held in abject slavery without any knowledge of what goes on in the outside world. If they run away the dogs are placed upon their track, and they are invariably retaken and subjected to more cruel treatment. This gives an idea of the conditions.

The prosecutions already instituted are for violations of Section: 5508, 5525 and 5526 of the Revised Statutes, viz, for conspiracy to injure and oppress a citizen in the enjoyment of a right and privilege guaranteed to him by the Constitution and laws of the United States; for kidnapping any person with the intent that he shall be delivered into slavery; and for holding any person to a condition of peonage. The indictments so far found are based upon some twenty-five Negro men and women who have been the subjects of these violations. These are some of the most severe instances, but it has been discovered that there are hundreds of other cases covering several years time. The men who are responsible for these conditions consist of three or four classes: First, those who are known as the proprietors of the plantations, mills, mines or quarries; second, those men who go out and catch up these Negroes, such as the constables and the pretended prosecutor; third, the Justices of the Peace before whom these Negroes are tried; and, fourth, the guards, overseers and boss men who actually with knowledge held these unfortunates in a condition of peonage and involuntary servitude. All of these men can be held under Section 5508 of the Revised Statutes of the United States, that is conspiring to injure and oppress citizens of the United States in the full exercise and enjoyment of a right and privilege guaranteed to them under the Constitution and laws of the United States.

As to the first class of men, the Grand Jury has found true bills based upon the three separate statutes named against John W. Pace, a wealthy farmer, land owner and mill man; J. F. Turner, a wealthy farmer and land owner; George D. Cosby, B. F. Cosby and W. D. Cosby, large land owners, in Tallapoosa county. These are not all of the proprietors involved in these transactions, but they are some of the main ones. . . .

The Grand Jury has found in all 80 indictments against the parties named above [twenty-one men in all, from all four "classes"] for violations of the Statutes indicated. Bonds have been required in all of these cases, except three, returnable to the May term, 1903, of the District Court of the United States. In short, the cases are to be tried as speedily as practicable consistent with our ability to get them in shape for presentation. Notices have been served upon each and every one of the defendants to be and appear in the District Court of the United States on June 22, 1903, when this office will move the court to have these cases set down for trial for some day during the remaining portion of this term. It is the object of this office to mete out justice speedily.

The Grand Jury has now under investigation matters of the same nature arising in Lowndes county, in the heart of the black belt of the State. This county is really the center where it is charged these practices are more freely indulged than anywhere else. This county, it is claimed, is honey-combed with slavery. The investigations now being had before the Grand Jury involve such men as the Sheriff of that county who is a large land owner. One of the most severe cases which the evidence reveals, is that of Dillard Freeman, who after being convicted before the Justice upon some flimsy charge, was fined, and the Sheriff of the county paid his fine. His name is J. W. Dixon. Dillard Freeman thereupon entered into a labor contract to work out the fine and costs so paid. This boy asked to be allowed to go to see his sick brother some four or five miles away, and his request was not granted. He was compelled to work by force, and had to ask for permission to leave before he could get away from the plantation. He tried to get permission several times, and it was refused. He finally one Sunday walked over to his mother's, and while there Mr. Dixon drove up with one of his men and beat the boy in the presence of his mother unmercifully with a pistol until he was bloody. Then the boy was tied around the neck, just as you tie an animal, his hands were handcuffed behind him, and the other end of the rope was placed in the hands of one of his men who was on a mule, and the boy was compelled to run afoot for six or seven miles behind this mule, while Mr. Dixon himself followed horseback whipping him whenever he would lag behind. Exhausted the boy reached the farm place of Mr. Dixon, where he was at once whipped with a piece of gin belt attached to a wooden handle. Four men were required to hold him off the ground while Mr. Dixon himself administered the punishment. When Mr. Dixon became tired, another man was made to do the whipping. In this way the boy was whipped nigh unto death. He cannot tell how many licks he was hit, nor can he tell how long he was whipped. The best evidence of the severity of this whipping is the boy's back, which is one mass of scars from his thighs to his neck. After being whipped the boy was chained to the floor at the foot of the bed of Mr. Dixon near the bed of Mr. Folmer, Mr. Dixon's overseer. He was chained every night and handcuffed. He was required to work two days after being whipped, his back was in such a condition that it had to be greased so that he could go to work. No doctor was called, and the boy suffered tortures. One of the Dixons followed the boy to the grand jury room, and it was impossible to get anything out of him because of his fear of death with which they had threatened him if he told anything in the grand jury room about his treatment—so the boy stated. He now tells the entire truth upon the assurance that he will not be made to go back to Lowndes county.

One of the grand jurors, who is a very intelligent colored man, unassuming and unpretentious, who lives in Lowndes county, went home last Saturday, and while there with his wife, this office is informed, five Dixon brothers rode up on their horses at 12 o'clock Saturday night, got down and demanded to know what was going on in Montgomery. Upon being told that he did not know, they said to him that he had to live in Lowndes county, and if he did not

stand up for his own people he knew what to expect. In short, it was a plain attempt to intimidate a grand juror in the faithful discharge of his sworn duty. These Dixons are men of the highest political and financial influence not only in Lowndes county but in the State of Alabama. They are large planters and control a great deal of labor. J. W. Dixon is Sheriff of Lowndes County. They are said to be dangerous men. They are said to have killed several men. It is believed that witnesses who come here and who expect to return to Lowndes county, are practically compelled to perjure their souls because they fear their lives. So that if an end is to be put to the outrages that have been transpiring there, some provision will have to be made for the protection of these witnesses, as well as their preservation after they have given up the truth at Montgomery.

This office is daily receiving letters from other counties where these practices are said to be indulged, such as Wilcox, Sumter, Chambers and Coffee Counties. Unquestionably there are hundreds of these people in this district who are held in abject slavery.

What is commonly known as the "contract labor law" in this State is recognized by reputable lawyers as being an unconstitutional law. It undertakes to regulate farm labor in such a way as to constitute class legislation and is violative, not only of the constitution of the State of Alabama, but of the United States as well. Judge Thos. G. Jones, of the District Court of the United States in response to an inquiry made by this Grand Jury regarding this very law, has rendered an elaborate and well considered opinion today declaring that law to be unconstitutional. This, in effect, amounts to an actual and not a theoretical emancipation of the Negro, and it is now necessary that this office make an effort to rescue these people from their condition by and through habeas corpus proceedings, and in order to effectively put an end to these criminal violations and this involuntary servitude as well as to institute these habeas corpus proceedings, it is suggested as being necessary that this office be furnished with a special secret service man as well as a special assistant out of this office to go from county to county to make the proper investigations. The special assistant should be a man well acquainted with the situation, people and the conditions. The financial condition of these people is such that unless the government will take steps to bring these habeas corpus proceedings that they will not be much benefited by these investigations unless the government of the United States intervene in their behalf.

Since writing you the above, I have just received your wire directing me to report to you at Washington, and in reply thereto I have wired you this day as follows: "Telegram of fifteenth received. I will report to you at ten o'clock morning of seventeenth."

Your respectfully,
W. S. Reese,
U.S. Attorney

B. 1927: A NEGRO LAWYER'S COMPLAINT TO THE ATTORNEY-GENERAL

July 5th, 1927

Hon. John Sargent,
U.S. Att'y Gen'l,
Washington, D.C.

My Dear General Sargent:

Some several days ago a Mr. Nunan, special agent of the Department of Justice, called to see me relative to a letter I wrote President Coolidge several weeks ago, concerning the handling of flood sufferers in Mississippi.

My reason for writing you is that, in view of the fact that Mr. Nunan did not seem to possess an open mind on the matters stated

Source: S. D. Redmond to Attorney General. July 5, 1927. File 50–637. Department of Justice, National Archives, Record Group RG 60.

in my letter to the President, I do not feel that his report on the matter can possibly be such a report as one would have made who viewed the situation purely from an unbiassed standpoint, which I feel was wholly impossible in Mr. Nunan's case, from the way he expressed himself to me.

In talking with me, Mr. Nunan impressed me more as one who came to defend the planters and to disprove everything I said, than otherwise.

As I told him, most statements I made in that letter were taken from newspaper reports but if he wanted to verify my statement on this point he might do so by perusing the Jackson *Daily News* and the Memphis *Commercial Appeal,* say from April 1st to May 15th, and visit the various camps in this state, Arkansas, and Louisiana, and see for himself. Yet, I feel that in view of the general complaints that had been made prior to his interview with me the situation was generally better at the time of Mr. Nunan's visit to the camp.

Now, relative to the holding of people in camps contrary to their will, I do not feel that there is any doubt whatever but that this was true in many, many instances, and that practically all Negro refugees were held non communicado to the outside world, is common knowledge.

And you can very readily see how very easily many of the labor contractors would get into such a thing and how easily thousands of laborers would be made to feel that they were being legally held, since there is an old Mississippi statute which makes it unlawful for an employee to leave his employer when indebted to him.

Of course, this statute has been declared unconstitutional several times by the Supreme Court of Mississippi but never repealed, and you can very readily see how few of the rural people residing in the remote districts would know this, especially when most of them are illiterate. Again, you can very readily appreciate the natural maneuverings of land-holders with probably a hundred or more tenants being carried a hundred or more miles from their plantations to places of safety, practically all of them at least theoretically indebted to the landlord, as is generally the custom of that section.

That many of these landlords would connive and conspire to keep these tenants and laborers under surveillance, could hardly be questioned, under the custom of arresting people for debt and placing them in jail for attempting to leave the creditor; and especially since most of the guards were from that same locality, and were doubtless, in many instances of many planters' way of thinking; to say nothing of the fact that it was generally announced through the press that these refugees would be kept from all "labor agents" and all outsiders were, therefore, looked upon by the guards it seems, as "labor agents".

In the first place, the entire guard feature of it was an unlawful proposition on its face, as I know you will agree.

These guards, U. S. soldiers, with rifles on their shoulders, were stationed only a few feet apart around all Negro camps in this state. This was not true around the white camps.

I had been chairman of relief work here in my town among colored people for about six weeks, had raised money for the flood sufferers and corralled much bedding and clothing, and having heard so much about camp life at Vicksburg and other places, I took it upon myself one afternoon to motor over to Vicksburg with several friends and see the situation for ourselves.

Upon arriving at the Negro camps there, we found, as I have said guards standing every few feet apart, all along the driveway on which the Negro camp abutted, with rifles in hand, and upon stopping our car in the roadway in front of the camps, we were immediately ordered to "move on' by the guard, with gun uplifted, and were told "You can't stop there." We went on down a short distance further and received the same orders from another guard with rifle in hand.

We then meandered and got over behind the camp and when out of sight of the guards, we stopped within about five feet of the tents and talked with many of the inmates, who told us that they were not allowed to leave camp without a special permit and that outsiders were not allowed to come into the camps, nor to talk with them without special permission.

We saw that there were many, many people *sleeping on the ground without cots*; that the tents were not ditched around; that they were billetted on hillsides and that very naturally the water would run down under them at night as they slept on the ground.

Since writing my letter to President Coolidge I was appointed a member of a committee whose duty it was to visit all of the camps of the flood-ridden area, and I take the liberty to enclose herewith a newspaper clipping which will give you, in a general way, a brief synopsis of this committee's report, a committee which was made up of some of those most conservative men of the country.

Trusting that you will pardon me for writing you so much at length, I am

Very truly yours,
S. D. Redmond

Plessy v. Ferguson

Henry Billings Brown
John Marshall Harlan

Mr. Justice Brown, after stating the case, delivered the opinion of the court. This case turns upon the constitutionality of an act of the General Assembly of the State of Louisiana, passed in 1890, providing for separate railway carriages for the white and colored races. Acts 1890, No. 111, p. 152.

The first section of the statute enacts "that all railway companies carrying passengers in their coaches in this State, shall provide equal but separate accommodations for the white, and colored races, by providing two or more passenger coaches for each passenger train, or by dividing the passenger coaches by a partition so as to secure separate accommodations: *Provided,* That this section shall not be construed to apply to street railroads. No person or persons, shall be admitted to occupy seats in coaches, other than, the ones, assigned, to them on account of the race they belong to."

By the second section it was enacted "that the officers of such passenger trains shall have power and are hereby required to assign each passenger to the coach or compartment used for the race to which such passenger belongs; any passenger insisting on going into a coach or compartment to which by race he does not belong, shall be liable to a fine of twenty-five dollars, or in lieu thereof to imprisonment for a period of not more than twenty days in the parish prison, and any officer of any railroad insisting on assigning a passenger to a coach or compartment other than the one set aside for the race to which said passenger belongs, shall be liable to a fine of twenty-five dollars, or in lieu thereof to

imprisonment for a period of not more than twenty days in the parish prison; and should any passenger refuse to occupy the coach or compartment to which he or she is assigned by the officer of such railway, said officer shall have power to refuse to carry such passenger on his train, and for such refusal neither he nor the railway company which he represents shall be liable for damages in any of the courts of this State."

The third section provides penalties for the refusal or neglect of the officers, directors, conductors, and employés of railway companies to comply with the act, with a proviso that "nothing in this act shall be construed as applying to nurses attending children of the other race." The fourth section is immaterial.

The information filed in the criminal District Court charged in substance that Plessy, being a passenger between two stations within the State of Louisiana, was assigned by officers of the company to the coach used for the race to which he belonged, but he insisted upon going into a coach used by the race to which he did not belong. Neither in the information nor plea was his particular race or color averred.

The petition for the writ of prohibition averred that petitioner was seven eighths Caucasian and one eighth African blood; that the mixture of colored blood was not discernible in him, and that he was entitled to every right, privilege and immunity secured to citizens of the United States of the white race; and that, upon such theory, he took possession of a vacant seat in a coach where passengers of the white race were accommodated, and was ordered by the conductor to vacate said coach and take a seat in another assigned to persons of the colored race, and having refused to comply with such demand he was forcibly ejected with

Source: Plessy v. Ferguson (May 18, 1896), Majority Opinion by Justice Henry Billings Brown and Dissenting Opinion by Justice John Marshall Harlan.

the aid of a police officer, and imprisoned in the parish jail to answer a charge of having violated the above act.

The constitutionality of this act is attacked upon the ground that it conflicts both with the Thirteenth Amendment of the Constitution, abolishing slavery, and the Fourteenth Amendment, which prohibits certain restrictive legislation on the part of the States.

1. That it does not conflict with the Thirteenth Amendment, which abolished slavery and involuntary servitude, except as a punishment for crime, is too clear for argument. Slavery implies involuntary servitude—a state of bondage; the ownership of mankind as a chattel, or at least the control of the labor and services of one man for the benefit of another, and the absence of a legal right to the disposal of his own person, property and services. This amendment was said in the *Slaughter-house cases,* 16 Wall. 36, to have been intended primarily to abolish slavery, as it had been previously known in this country, and that it equally forbade Mexican peonage or the Chinese coolie trade, when they amounted to slavery or involuntary servitude, and that the use of the word "servitude" was intended to prohibit the use of all forms of involuntary slavery, of whatever class or name. It was intimated, however, in that case that this amendment was regarded by the statesmen of that day as insufficient to protect the colored race from certain laws which had been enacted in the Southern States, imposing upon the colored race onerous disabilities and burdens, and curtailing their rights in the pursuit of life, liberty and property to such an extent that their freedom was of little value; and that the Fourteenth Amendment was devised to meet this exigency.

So, too, in the *Civil Rights cases,* 109 U. S. 3, 24, it was said that the act of a mere individual, the owner of an inn, a public conveyance or place of amusement, refusing accommodations to colored people, cannot be justly regarded as imposing any badge of slavery or servitude upon the applicant, but only as involving an ordinary civil injury,

properly cognizable by the laws of the State, and presumably subject to redress by those laws until the contrary appears. "It would be running the slavery argument into the ground," said Mr. Justice Bradley, "to make it apply to every act of discrimination which a person may see fit to make as to the guests he will entertain, or as to the people he will take into his coach or cab or car, or admit to his concert or theatre, or deal with in other matters of intercourse or business."

A statute which implies merely a legal distinction between the white and colored races—a distinction which is founded in the color of the two races, and which must always exist so long as white men are distinguished from the other race by color—has no tendency to destroy the legal equality of the two races, or reëstablish a state of involuntary servitude. Indeed, we do not understand that the Thirteenth Amendment is strenuously relied upon by the plaintiff in error in this connection.

2. By the Fourteenth Amendment, all persons born or naturalized in the United States, and subject to the jurisdiction thereof, are made citizens of the United States and of the State wherein they reside; and the States are forbidden from making or enforcing any law which shall abridge the privileges or immunities of citizens of the United States, or shall deprive any person of life, liberty or property without due process of law, or deny to any person within their jurisdiction the equal protection of the laws.

The proper construction of this amendment was first called to the attention of this court in the *Slaughter-house cases,* 16 Wall. 36, which involved, however, not a question of race, but one of exclusive privileges. The case did not call for any expression of opinion as to the exact rights it was intended to secure to the colored race, but it was said generally that its main purpose was to establish the citizenship of the negro; to give definitions of citizenship of the United States and of the States, and to protect from the hostile legislation of the States the privileges and immunities of citizens of the United

States, as distinguished from those of citizens of the States.

The object of the amendment was undoubtedly to enforce the absolute equality of the two races before the law, but in the nature of things it could not have been intended to abolish distinctions based upon color, or to enforce social, as distinguished from political equality, or a commingling of the two races upon terms unsatisfactory to either. Laws permitting, and even requiring, their separation in places where they are liable to be brought into contact do not necessarily imply the inferiority of either race to the other, and have been generally, if not universally, recognized as within the competency of the state legislatures in the exercise of their police power. The most common instance of this is connected with the establishment of separate schools for white and colored children, which has been held to be a valid exercise of the legislative power even by courts of States where the political rights of the colored race have been longest and most earnestly enforced.

One of the earliest of these cases is that of *Roberts* v. *City of Boston*, 5 Cush. 198, in which the Supreme Judicial Court of Massachusetts held that the general school committee of Boston had power to make provision for the instruction of colored children in separate schools established exclusively for them, and to prohibit their attendance upon the other schools. "The great principle," said Chief Justice Shaw, p. 206, "advanced by the learned and eloquent advocate for the plaintiff," (Mr. Charles Sumner,) "is, that by the constitution and laws of Massachusetts, all persons without distinction of age or sex, birth or color, origin or condition, are equal before the law. . . . But, when this great principle comes to be applied to the actual and various conditions of persons in society, it will not warrant the assertion, that men and women are legally clothed with the same civil and political powers, and that children and adults are legally to have the same functions and be subject to the same treatment; but only that the rights of all, as they are settled and regulated by law, are

equally entitled to the paternal consideration and protection of the law for their maintenance and security." It was held that the powers of the committee extended to the establishment of separate schools for children of different ages, sexes, and colors, and that they might also establish special schools for poor and neglected children, who have become too old to attend the primary school, and yet have not acquired the rudiments of learning, to enable them to enter the ordinary schools. Similar laws have been enacted by Congress under its general power of legislation over the District of Columbia, Rev. Stat. D. C. § § 281, 282, 283, 310, 319, as well as by the legislatures of many of the States, and have been generally, if not uniformly, sustained by the courts. *State* v. *McCann*, 21 Ohio St. 198; *Lehew* v. *Brummell*, 15 S. W. Rep. 765; *Ward* v. *Flood*, 48 California, 36; *Bertonneau* v. *School Directors*, 3 Woods, 177; *People* v. *Gallagher*, 93 N. Y. 438; *Cory* v. *Carter*, 48 Indiana, 327; *Dawson* v. *Lee*, 83 Kentucky, 49.

Laws forbidding the intermarriage of the two races may be said in a technical sense to interfere with the freedom of contract, and yet have been universally recognized as within the police power of the State. *State* v. *Gibson*, 36 Indiana, 389.

The distinction between laws interfering with the political equality of the negro and those requiring the separation of the two races in schools, theatres and railway carriages has been frequently drawn by this court. Thus in *Strauder* v. *West Virginia*, 100 U. S. 303, it was held that a law of West Virginia limiting to white male persons, 21 years of age and citizens of the State, the right to sit upon juries, was a discrimination which implied a legal inferiority in civil society, which lessened the security of the right of the colored race, and was a step toward reducing them to a condition of servility. Indeed, the right of a colored man that, in the selection of jurors to pass upon his life, liberty and property, there shall be no exclusion of his race, and no discrimination against them because of color, has been asserted in a number of cases. *Virginia* v. *Rives*, 100 U. S. 313; *Neal* v. *Delaware*, 103 U. S. 370; *Bush* v. *Kentucky*, 107 U. S. 110; *Gibson* v. *Mississippi*, 162 U. S. 565. So, where the laws of a particular locality or the charter of a particular railway corporation has provided that no person shall be excluded from the cars on account of color, we have held that this meant that persons of color should travel in the same car as white ones, and that the enactment was not satisfied by the company's providing cars assigned exclusively to people of color, though they were as good as those which they assigned exclusively to white persons. *Railroad Company* v. *Brown*, 17 Wall. 445.

Upon the other hand, where a statute of Louisiana required those engaged in the transportation of passengers among the States to give to all persons travelling within that State, upon vessels employed in that business, equal rights and privileges in all parts of the vessel, without distinction on account of race or color, and subjected to an action for damages the owner of such a vessel, who excluded colored passengers on account of their color from the cabin set aside by him for the use of whites, it was held to be so far as it applied to interstate commerce, unconstitutional and void. *Hall* v. *De Cuir*. 95 U. S. 485. The court in this case, however, expressly disclaimed that it had anything whatever to do with the statute as a regulation of internal commerce, or affecting anything else than commerce among the States.

In the *Civil Rights case[s]*, 109 U. S. 3, it was held that an act of Congress, entitling all persons within the jurisdiction of the United States to the full and equal enjoyment of the accommodations, advantages, facilities and privileges of inns, public conveyances, on land or water, theatres and other places of public amusement, and made applicable to citizens of every race and color, regardless of any previous condition of servitude, was unconstitutional and void, upon the ground that the Fourteenth Amendment was pro-

hibitory upon the States only, and the legislation authorized to be adopted by Congress for enforcing it was not direct legislation on matters respecting which the States were prohibited from making or enforcing certain laws, or doing certain acts, but was corrective legislation, such as might be necessary or proper for counteracting and redressing the effect of such laws or acts. In delivering the opinion of the court Mr. Justice Bradley observed that the Fourteenth Amendment "does not invest Congress with power to legislate upon subjects that are within the domain of state legislation; but to provide modes of relief against state legislation, or state action, of the kind referred to. It does not authorize Congress to create a code of municipal law for the regulation of private rights; but to provide modes of redress against the operation of state laws, and the action of state officers, executive or judicial, when these are subversive of the fundamental rights specified in the amendment. Positive rights and privileges are undoubtedly secured by the Fourteenth Amendment; but they are secured by way of prohibition against state laws and state proceedings affecting those rights and privileges, and by power given to Congress to legislate for the purpose of carrying such prohibition into effect; and such legislation must necessarily be predicated upon such supposed state laws or state proceedings, and be directed to the correction of their operation and effect."

Much nearer, and, indeed, almost directly in point, is the case of the *Louisville, New Orleans &c. Railway* v. *Mississippi*, 133 U. S. 587, wherein the railway company was indicted for a violation of a statute of Mississippi, enacting that all railroads carrying passengers should provide equal, but separate, accommodations for the white and colored races, by providing two or more passenger cars for each passenger train, or by dividing the passenger cars by a partition, so as to secure separate accommodations. The case was presented in a different aspect from the one under consideration, inasmuch as it was an indictment against the railway company for failing to provide the separate accommodations, but the question considered was the constitutionality of the law. In that case, the Supreme Court of Mississippi, 66 Mississippi, 662, had held that the statute applied solely to commerce within the State, and, that being the construction of the state statute by its highest court, was accepted as conclusive. "If it be a matter," said the court, p. 591, "respecting commerce wholly within a State, and not interfering with commerce between the States, then, obviously, there is no violation of the commerce clause of the Federal Constitution. . . . No question arises under this section, as to the power of the State to separate in different compartments interstate passengers, or affect, in any manner, the privileges and rights of such passengers. All that we can consider is, whether the State has the power to require that railroad trains within her limits shall have separate accommodations for the two races; that affecting only commerce within the State is no invasion of the power given to Congress by the commerce clause."

A like course of reasoning applies to the case under consideration, since the Supreme Court of Louisiana in the case of the *State ex rel. Abbott v. Hicks, Judge, et al.,* 44 La. Ann. 770, held that the statute in question did not apply to interstate passengers, but was confined in its application to passengers travelling exclusively within the borders of the State. The case was decided largely upon the authority of *Railway Co. v. State,* 66 Mississippi, 662, and affirmed by this court in 133 U. S. 587. In the present case no question of interference with interstate commerce can possibly arise, since the East Louisiana Railway appears to have been purely a local line, with both its termini within the State of Louisiana. . . .

While we think the enforced separation of the races, as applied to the internal commerce of the State, neither abridges the privileges or immunities of the colored man, deprives him of his property without due process of law, nor denies him the equal protection of the laws, within the meaning of the Fourteenth Amendment, we are not prepared to say that the conductor, in assigning passengers to the coaches according to their race, does not act at his peril, or that the provision of the second section of the act, that denies to the passenger compensation in damages for a refusal to receive him into the coach in which he properly belongs, is a valid exercise of the legislative power. Indeed, we understand it to be conceded by the State's attorney, that such part of the act as exempts from liability the railway company and its officers is unconstitutional. The power to assign to a particular coach obviously implies the power to determine to which race the passenger belongs, as well as the power to determine who, under the laws of the particular State, is to be deemed a white, and who a colored person. This question, though indicated in the brief of the plaintiff in error, does not properly arise upon the record in this case, since the only issue made is as to the unconstitutionality of the act, so far as it requires the railway to provide separate accommodations, and the conductor to assign passengers according to their race.

It is claimed by the plaintiff in error that, in any mixed community, the reputation of belonging to the dominant race, in this instance the white race, is *property*, in the same sense that a right of action, or of inheritance, is property. Conceding this to be so, for the purposes of this case, we are unable to see how this statute deprives him of, or in any way affects his right to, such property. If he be a white man and assigned to a colored coach, he may have his action for damages against the company for being deprived of his so called property. Upon the other hand, if he be a colored man and be so assigned, he has been deprived of no property, since he is not lawfully entitled to the reputation of being a white man.

In this connection, it is also suggested by the learned counsel for the plaintiff in error that the same argument that will justify the state legislature in requiring railways to provide separate accommodations for the two races will also authorize them to require separate cars to be provided for people whose hair is of a certain color, or who are aliens, or who belong to certain nationalities, or to enact laws requiring colored people to walk upon one side of the street, and white people upon the other, or requiring white men's houses to be painted white, and colored men's black, or their vehicles or business signs to be of different colors, upon the theory that one side of the street is as good as the other, or that a house or vehicle of one color is as good as one of another color. The reply to all this is that every exercise of the police power must be reasonable, and extend only to such laws as are enacted in good faith for the promotion for the public good, and not for the annoyance or oppression of a particular class. Thus in *Yick Wo v. Hopkins,* 118 U. S. 356, it was held by this court that a municipal ordinance of the city of San Francisco, to regulate the carrying on of public laundries within the limits of the municipality, violated the provisions of the Constitution of the United States, if it conferred upon the municipal authorities arbitrary power, at their own will, and without regard to discretion, in the legal sense of the term, to give or withhold consent as to persons or places, without regard to the competency of the persons applying, or the propriety of the places selected for the carrying on of the business. It was held to be a covert attempt on the part of the municipality to make an arbitrary and unjust discrimination against the Chinese race. While this was the case of a municipal ordinance, a like principle has been held to apply to acts of a state legislature passed in the exercise of the police power....

So far, then, as a conflict with the Fourteenth Amendment is concerned, the case reduces itself to the question whether the statute of Louisiana is a reasonable regulation, and with respect to this there must necessarily be a large discretion on the part of the legislature. In determining the question of reasonableness it is at liberty to act with reference to the established usages, customs and traditions of the people, and with a view to the promotion of their comfort, and the preservation of the public peace and good order. Gauged by this standard, we cannot say that a law which authorizes or even requires the separation of the two races in public conveyances is unreasonable, or more obnoxious to the Fourteenth Amendment than the acts of Congress requiring separate schools for colored children in the District of Columbia, the constitutionality of which does not seem to have been questioned, or the corresponding acts of state legislatures.

We consider the underlying fallacy of the plaintiff's argument to consist in the assumption that the enforced separation of the two races stamps the colored race with a badge of inferiority. If this be so, it is not by reason of anything found in the act, but solely because the colored race chooses to put that construction upon it: The argument necessarily assumes that if, as has been more than once the case, and is not unlikely to be so again, the colored race should become the dominant power in the state legislature, and should enact a law in precisely similar terms, it would thereby relegate the white race to an inferior position. We imagine that the white race, at least, would not acquiesce in this assumption. The argument also assumes that social prejudices may be overcome by legislation, and that equal rights cannot be secured to the negro except by an enforced commingling of the two races. We cannot accept this proposition. If the two races are to meet upon terms of social equality, it must be the result of natural affinities, a mutual appreciation of each other's merits and a voluntary consent of individuals. As was said by the Court of Appeals of New York in *People v. Gallagher,* 93 N. Y. 438, 448, "this end can neither be accomplished nor promoted by laws which conflict with the general sentiment of the community upon whom they are designed to operate. When the government, therefore, has secured to each of its citizens equal rights before the law and equal opportunities for improvement and progress, it has accomplished the end for which it was organized and performed all of the functions respecting social advantages with which it is endowed." Legislation is powerless to eradicate racial instincts or to abolish distinctions based upon physical differences, and the attempt to do so can only result in accentuating the difficulties of the present situation. If the civil and political rights of both races be equal one cannot be inferior to the other civilly or politically. If one race be inferior to the other socially, the Constitution of the United States cannot put them upon the same plane.

It is true that the question of the proportion of colored blood necessary to constitute a colored person, as distinguished from a white person, is one upon which there is a difference of opinion in the different States, some holding that any visible admixture of black blood stamps the person as belonging to the colored race, (*State* v. *Chavers*, 5 Jones, [N. C.] 1, p. 11); others that it depends upon the preponderance of blood, (*Gray* v. *State*, 4 Ohio, 354; *Monroe* v. *Collins*, 17 Ohio St. 665); and still others that the predominance of white blood must only be in the proportion of three fourths. (*People* v. *Dean*, 14 Michigan, 406; *Jones* v. *Commonwealth*, 80 Virginia, 538.) But these are questions to be determined under the laws of each State and are not properly put in issue in this case. Under the allegations of his petition it may undoubtedly become a question of importance whether, under the laws of Louisiana, the petitioner belongs to the white or colored race.

The judgment of the court below is, therefore,

Affirmed.

Mr. Justice Harlan dissenting. By the Louisiana statute, the validity of which is here involved, all railway companies (other than street railroad companies) carrying passengers in that State are required to have separate but equal accommodations for white and colored persons, "by providing two or more passenger coaches for each pas-

senger train, *or* by dividing the passenger coaches by a *partition* so as to secure separate accommodations." Under this statute, no colored person is permitted to occupy a seat in a coach assigned to white persons; nor any white person, to occupy a seat in a coach assigned to colored persons. The managers of the railroad are not allowed to exercise any discretion in the premises, but are required to assign each passenger to some coach or compartment set apart for the exclusive use of his race. If a passenger insists upon going into a coach or compartment not set apart for persons of his race, he is subject to be fined, or to be imprisoned in the parish jail. Penalties are prescribed for the refusal or neglect of the officers, directors, conductors and employés of railroad companies to comply with the provisions of the act.

Only "nurses attending children of the other race" are excepted from the operation of the statute. No exception is made of colored attendants travelling with adults. A white man is not permitted to have his colored servant with him in the same coach, even if his condition of health requires the constant, personal assistance of such servant. If a colored maid insists upon riding in the same coach with a white woman whom she has been employed to serve, and who may need her personal attention while travelling, she is subject to be fined or imprisoned for such an exhibition of zeal in the discharge of duty.

While there may be in Louisiana persons of different races who are not citizens of the United States, the words in the act, "white and colored races," necessarily include all citizens of the United States of both races residing in that State. So that we have before us a state enactment that compels, under penalties, the separation of the two races in railroad passenger coaches, and makes it a crime for a citizen of either race to enter a coach that has been assigned to citizens of the other race.

Thus the State regulates the use of a public highway by citizens of the United States solely upon the basis of race.

However apparent the injustice of such legislation may be, we have only to consider whether it is consistent with the Constitution of the United States.

That a railroad is a public highway, and that the corporation which owns or operates it is in the exercise of public functions, is not, at this day, to be disputed. Mr. Justice Nelson, speaking for this court in *New Jersey Steam Navigation Co. v. Merchants' Bank,* 6 How. 344, 382, said that a common carrier was in the exercise "of a sort of public office, and has public duties to perform, from which he should not be permitted to exonerate himself without the assent of the parties concerned." Mr. Justice Strong, delivering the judgment of this court in *Olcott v. The Supervisors,* 16 Wall. 678, 694, said: "That railroads, though constructed by private corporations and owned by them, are public highways, has been the doctrine of nearly all the courts ever since such conveniences for passage and transportation have had any existence. Very early the question arose whether a State's right of eminent domain could be exercised by a private corporation created for the purpose of constructing a railroad. Clearly it could not, unless taking land for such a purpose by such an agency is taking land for public use. The right of eminent domain nowhere justifies taking property for a private use. Yet it is a doctrine universally accepted that a state legislature may authorize a private corporation to take land for the construction of such a road, making compensation to the owner. What else does this doctrine mean if not that building a railroad, though it be built by a private corporation, is an act done for a public use?" So, in *Township of Pine Grove v. Talcott,* 19 Wall. 666, 676: "Though the corporation [a railroad company] was private, its work was public, as much so as if it were to be constructed by the State." So, in *Inhabitants of Worcester v. Western Railroad Corporation,* 4 Met. 564: "The establishment of that great thoroughfare is regarded as a public work, established by public authority, intended for the public use and benefit, the use of which is secured to the whole community, and constitutes, therefore, like a canal, turnpike or highway, a public easement." It is true that the real and personal property, necessary to the establishment and management of the railroad, is vested in the corporation; but it is in trust for the public."

In respect of civil rights, common to all citizens, the Constitution of the United States does not, I think, permit any public authority to know the race of those entitled to be protected in the enjoyment of such rights. Every true man has pride of race, and under appropriate circumstances when the rights of others, his equals before the law, are not to be affected, it is his privilege to express such pride and to take such action based upon it as to him seems proper. But I deny that any legislative body or judicial tribunal may have regard to the race of citizens when the civil rights of those citizens are involved. Indeed, such legislation, as that here in question, is inconsistent not only with that equality of rights which pertains to citizenship, National and State, but with the personal liberty enjoyed by every one within the United States.

The Thirteenth Amendment does not permit the withholding or the deprivation of any right necessarily inhering in freedom. It not only struck down the institution of slavery as previously existing in the United States, but it prevents the imposition of any burdens or disabilities that constitute badges of slavery or servitude. It decreed universal civil freedom in this country. This court has so adjudged. But that amendment having been found inadequate to the protection of the rights of those who had been in slavery, it was followed by the Fourteenth Amendment, which added greatly to the dignity and glory of American citizenship, and to the security of personal liberty, by declaring that "all persons born or naturalized in the United States, and subject to the jurisdiction thereof, are citizens of the United States and of the State wherein they reside," and that "no State shall make or enforce any law which shall abridge the privileges or immunities of citizens of the United States; nor shall any State deprive any person of life, liberty or property without due process of law, nor deny to any person within its jurisdiction the equal protection of the laws." These two amendments, if enforced according to their true intent and meaning, will protect all the civil rights that pertain to freedom and citizenship. Finally, and to the end that no citizen should be denied, on account of his race, the privilege of participating in the political control of his country, it was declared by the Fifteenth Amendment that "the right of citizens of the United States to vote shall not be denied or abridged by the United States or by any State on account of race, color or previous condition of servitude."

These notable additions to the fundamental law were welcomed by the friends of liberty throughout the world. They removed the race line from our governmental systems. They had, as this court has said, a common purpose, namely, to secure "to a race recently emancipated, a race that through many generations have been held in slavery, all the civil rights that the superior race enjoy." They declared, in legal effect, this court has further said, "that the law in the States shall be the same for the black as for the white; that all persons, whether colored or white, shall stand equal before the laws of the States, and, in regard to the colored race, for whose protection the amendment was primarily designed, that no discrimination shall be made against them by law because of their color." We also said: "The words of the amendment, it is true, are prohibitory, but they contain a necessary implication of a positive immunity, or right, most valuable to the colored race—the right to exemption from unfriendly legislation against them distinctively as colored—exemption from legal discriminations, implying inferiority in civil society, lessening the security of their enjoyment of the rights which others enjoy, and discriminations which are steps toward reducing them to the condition of a subject race." It was, consequently, adjudged that a state law that excluded citizens of the colored race from juries, because of their race and however well qualified in other re-

spects to discharge the duties of jurymen, was repugnant to the Fourteenth Amendment. . . .

At the present term, referring to the previous adjudications, this court declared that "underlying all of those decisions is the principle that the Constitution of the United States, in its present form, forbids, so far as civil and political rights are concerned, discrimination by the General Government or the States against any citizen because of his race. All citizens are equal before the law." *Gibson* v. *Mississippi*, 162 U. S. 565.

The decisions referred to show the scope of the recent amendments of the Constitution. They also show that it is not within the power of a State to prohibit colored citizens, because of their race, from participating as jurors in the administration of justice.

It was said in argument that the statute of Louisiana does not discriminate against either race, but prescribes a rule applicable alike to white and colored citizens. But this argument does not meet the difficulty. Every one knows that the statute in question had its origin in the purpose, not so much to exclude white persons from railroad cars occupied by blacks, as to exclude colored people from coaches occupied by or assigned to white persons. Railroad corporations of Louisiana did not make discrimination among whites in the matter of accommodation for travellers. The thing to accomplish was, under the guise of giving equal accommodation for whites and blacks, to compel the latter to keep to themselves while travelling in railroad passenger coaches. No one would be so wanting in candor as to assert the contrary. The fundamental objection, therefore, to the statute is that it interferes with the personal freedom of citizens. "Personal liberty," it has been well said, "consists in the power of locomotion, of changing situation, or removing one's person to whatsoever places one's own inclination may direct, without imprisonment or restraint, unless by due course of law." 1 Bl. Com. *134. If a white man and a black man choose to occupy the same public conveyance on a public highway, it is their right to do so, and no government, proceeding alone on grounds of race, can prevent it without infringing the personal liberty of each.

It is one thing for railroad carriers to furnish, or to be required by law to furnish, equal accommodations for all whom they are under a legal duty to carry. It is quite another thing for government to forbid citizens of the white and black races from travelling in the same public conveyance, and to punish officers of railroad companies for permitting persons of the two races to occupy the same passenger coach. If a State can prescribe, as a rule of civil conduct, that whites and blacks shall not travel as passengers in the same railroad coach, why may it not so regulate the use of the streets of its cities and towns as to compel white citizens to keep on one side of a street and black citizens to keep on the other? Why may it not, upon like grounds, punish whites and blacks who ride together in street cars or in open vehicles on a public road or street? Why may it not require sheriffs to assign whites to one side of a court-room and blacks to the other? And why may it not also prohibit the commingling of the two races in the galleries of legislative halls or in public assemblages convened for the consideration of the political questions of the day? Further, if this statute of Louisiana is consistent with the personal liberty of citizens, why may not the State require the separation in railroad coaches of native and naturalized citizens of the United States, or of Protestants and Roman Catholics?

The answer given at the argument to these questions was that regulations of the kind they suggest would be unreasonable, and could not, therefore, stand before the law. Is it meant that the determination of questions of legislative power depends upon the inquiry whether the statute whose validity is questioned is, in the judgment of the courts, a reasonable one, taking all the circumstances into consideration? A statute may be unreasonable merely because a sound public policy forbade its enactment. But I do not understand that the courts have anything to do with the policy or expediency of legislation. A statute may be valid, and yet, upon grounds of public policy, may well be characterized as unreasonable. Mr. Sedgwick correctly states the rule when he says that the legislative intention being clearly ascertained, "the courts have no other duty to perform than to execute the legislative will, without any regard to their views as to the wisdom or justice of the particular enactment." Stat. & Const. Constr. 324. There is a dangerous tendency in these latter days to enlarge the functions of the courts, by means of judicial interference with the will of the people as expressed by the legislature. Our institutions have the distinguishing characteristic that the three departments of government are coördinate and separate. Each must keep within the limits defined by the Constitution. And the courts best discharge their duty by executing the will of the law-making power, constitutionally expressed, leaving the results of legislation to be dealt with by the people through their representatives. Statutes must always have a reasonable construction. Sometimes they are to be construed strictly; sometimes, liberally, in order to carry out the legislative will. But however construed, the intent of the legislature is to be respected, if the particular statute in question is valid, although the courts, looking at the public interests, may conceive the statute to be both unreasonable and impolitic. If the power exists to enact a statute, that ends the matter so far as the courts are concerned. The adjudged cases in which statutes have been held to be void, because unreasonable, are those in which the means employed by the legislature were not at all germane to the end to which the legislature was competent.

The white race deems itself to be the dominant race in this country. And so it is, in prestige, in achievements, in education, in wealth and in power. So, I doubt not, it will continue to be for all time, if it remains true to its great heritage and holds fast to the principles of constitutional liberty. But in view of the Constitution, in the eye of the law, there is in this country no superior, dominant, ruling class of citizens. There is no caste here. Our

Constitution is color-blind, and neither knows nor tolerates classes among citizens. In respect of civil rights, all citizens are equal before the law. The humblest is the peer of the most powerful. The law regards man as man, and takes no account of his surroundings or of his color when his civil rights as guaranteed by the supreme law of the land are involved. It is, therefore, to be regretted that this high tribunal, the final expositor of the fundamental law of the land, has reached the conclusion that it is competent for a State to regulate the enjoyment by citizens of their civil rights solely upon the basis of race.

In my opinion, the judgment this day rendered will, in time, prove to be quite as pernicious as the decision made by this tribunal in the *Dred Scott case*. It was adjudged in that case that the descendants of Africans who were imported into this country and sold as slaves were not included nor intended to be included under the word "citizens" in the Constitution, and could not claim any of the rights and privileges which that instrument provided for and secured to the citizens of the United States; that at the time of the adoption of the Constitution they were "considered as a subordinate and inferior class of beings, who had been subjugated by the dominant race, and, whether emancipated or not, yet remained subject to their authority, and had no rights or privileges but such as those who held the power and the government might choose to grant them." 19 How. 393, 404. The recent amendments of the Constitution, it was supposed, had eradicated these principles from our institutions. But it seems that we have yet, in some of the States, a dominant race—a superior class of citizens, which assumes to regulate the enjoyment of civil rights, common to all citizens, upon the basis of race. The present decision, it may well be apprehended, will not only stimulate aggressions, more or less brutal and irritating, upon the admitted rights of colored citizens, but will encourage the belief that it is possible, by means of state enactments, to defeat the beneficient purposes which the people of the United States had in view when they adopted the recent amendments of the Constitution, by one of which the blacks of this country were made citizens of the United States and of the States in which they respectively reside, and whose privileges and immunities, as citizens, the States are forbidden to abridge. Sixty millions of whites are in no danger from the presence here of eight millions of blacks. The destinies of the two races, in this country, are indissolubly linked together, and the interests of both require that the common government of all shall not permit the seeds of race hate to be planted under the sanction of law. What can more certainly arouse race hate, what more certainly create and perpetuate a feeling of distrust between these races, than state enactments, which, in fact, proceed on the ground that colored citizens are so inferior and degraded that they cannot be allowed to sit in public coaches occupied by white citizens? That, as all will admit, is the real meaning of such legislation as was enacted in Louisiana.

The sure guarantee of the peace and security of each race is the clear, distinct, unconditional recognition by our governments, National and State, of every right that inheres in civil freedom, and of the equality before the law of all citizens of the United States without regard to race. State enactments, regulating the enjoyment of civil rights, upon the basis of race, and cunningly devised to defeat legitimate results of the war, under the pretence of recognizing equality of rights, can have no other result than to render permanent peace impossible, and to keep alive a conflict of races, the continuance of which must do harm to all concerned. This question is not met by the suggestion that social equality cannot exist between the white and black races in this country. That argument, if it can be properly regarded as one, is scarcely worthy of consideration; for social equality no more exists between two races when travelling in a passenger coach or a public highway than when members of the same races sit by each other in a street car or in the jury box, or stand or sit with each other in a political assembly, or when they use in common the streets of a city or town, or when they are in the same room for the purpose of having their names placed on the registry of voters, or when they approach the ballot-box in order to exercise the high privilege of voting.

There is a race so different from our own that we do not permit those belonging to it to become citizens of the United States. Persons belonging to it are, with few exceptions, absolutely excluded from our country. I allude to the Chinese race. But by the statute in question, a Chinaman can ride in the same passenger coach with white citizens of the United States, while citizens of the black race in Louisiana, many of whom, perhaps, risked their lives for the preservation of the Union, who are entitled, by law, to participate in the political control of the State and nation, who are not excluded, by law or by reason of their race, from public stations of any kind, and who have all the legal rights that belong to white citizens, are yet declared to be criminals, liable to imprisonment, if they ride in a public coach occupied by citizens of the white race. It is scarcely just to say that a colored citizen should not object to occupying a public coach assigned to his own race. He does not object, nor, perhaps, would he object to separate coaches for his race, if his rights under the law were recognized. But he objects, and ought never to cease objecting to the proposition, that citizens of the white and black races can be adjudged criminals because they sit, or claim the right to sit, in the same public coach on a public highway.

The arbitrary separation of citizens, on the basis of race, while they are on a public highway, is a badge of servitude wholly inconsistent with the civil freedom and the equality before the law established by the Constitution. It cannot be justified upon any legal grounds.

If evils will result from the commingling of the two races upon public highways established for the benefit of all, they will be infinitely less than those that will surely come from state legislation regulating the enjoyment of civil rights upon the basis of race. We boast of the freedom enjoyed by our people above all other peoples. But it is difficult to reconcile that boast with a state of the law which, practically, puts the brand of servitude and degradation upon a large class of our fellow-citizens, our equals before the law. The thin disguise of "equal" accommodations for passengers in railroad coaches will not mislead any one, nor atone for the wrong this day done.

The result of the whole matter is, that while this court has frequently adjudged, and at the present term has recognized the doctrine, that a State cannot, consistently with the Constitution of the United States, prevent white and black citizens, having the required qualifications for jury service, from sitting in the same jury box, it is now solemnly held that a State may prohibit white and black citizens from sitting in the same passenger coach on a public highway, or may require that they be separated by a "partition," when in the same passenger coach. May it not now be reasonably expected that astute men of the dominant race, who affect to be disturbed at the possibility that the integrity of the white race may be corrupted, or that its supremacy will be imperilled, by contact on public highways with black people, will endeavor to procure statutes requiring white and black jurors to be separated in the jury box by a "partition," and that, upon retiring from the court room to consult as to their verdict, such partition, if it be a moveable one, shall be taken to their consultation room, and set up in such a way as to prevent black jurors from coming too close to their brother jurors of the white race. If the "partition" used in the court room happens to be stationary, provision could be made for screens with openings through which jurors of the two races could confer as to their verdict without coming into personal contact with each other. I cannot see but that, according to the principles this day announced, such state legislation, although conceived in hostility to, and enacted for the purpose of humiliating citizens of the United States of a particular race, would be held to be consistent with the Constitution.

I do not deem it necessary to review the decisions of state courts to which reference was made in argument. Some, and the most important, of them are wholly inapplicable, because rendered prior to the adoption of the last amendments of the Constitution, when colored people had very few rights which the dominant race felt obliged to respect. Others were made at a time when public opinion, in many localities, was dominated by the institution of slavery; when it would not have been safe to do justice to the black man; and when, so far as the rights of blacks were concerned, race prejudice was, practically, the supreme law of the land. Those decisions cannot be guides in the era introduced by the recent amendments of the supreme law, which established universal civil freedom, gave citizenship to all born or naturalized in the United States and residing here, obliterated the race line from our systems of governments, National and State, and placed our free institutions upon the broad and sure foundation of the equality of all men before the law.

I am of opinion that the statute of Louisiana is inconsistent with the personal liberty of citizens, white and black, in that State, and hostile to both the spirit and letter of the Constitution of the United States. If laws of like character should be enacted in the several States of the Union, the effect would be in the highest degree mischievous. Slavery, as an institution tolerated by law would, it is true, have disappeared from our country, but there would remain a power in the States, by sinister legislation, to interfere with the full enjoyment of the blessings of freedom; to regulate civil rights, common to all citizens, upon the basis of race; and to place in a condition of legal inferiority a large body of American citizens, now constituting a part of the political community called the People of the United States, for whom, and by whom through representatives, our government is administered. Such a system is inconsistent with the guarantee given by the Constitution to each State of a republican form of government, and may be stricken down by Congressional action, or by the courts in the discharge of their solemn duty to maintain the supreme law of the land, anything in the constitution or laws of any State to the contrary notwithstanding.

For the reasons stated, I am constrained to withhold my assent from the opinion and judgment of the majority.

Industrial Education for the Negro

Booker T. Washington

One of the most fundamental and far-reaching deeds that has been accomplished during the last quarter of a century has been that by which the Negro has been helped to

Source: Booker T. Washington, "Industrial Education for the Negro." *The Negro Problem: A Series of Articles by Representative American Negroes of Today* (New York: James Pott and Company, 1903), pp. 7–30.

find himself and to learn the secrets of civilization—to learn that there are a few simple, cardinal principles upon which a race must start its upward course, unless it would fail, and its last estate be worse than its first.

It has been necessary for the Negro to learn the difference between being worked and working—to learn that being worked meant degradation, while working means civilization; that all forms of labor are honorable, and all forms of idleness disgraceful. It has been necessary for him to learn that all races that have got upon their feet have done so largely by laying an economic foundation, and, in general, by beginning in a proper cultivation and ownership of the soil.

Forty years ago my race emerged from slavery into freedom. If, in too many cases, the Negro race began development at the wrong end, it was largely because neither white nor black properly understood the case. Nor is it any wonder that this was so, for never before in the history of the world had just such a problem been presented as that of the two races at the coming of freedom in this country.

For two hundred and fifty years, I believe the way for the redemption of the Negro was being prepared through industrial development. Through all those years the Southern white man did business with the Negro in a way that no one else has done business with him. In most cases if a Southern white man wanted a house built he consulted a Negro mechanic about the plan and about the actual building of the structure. If he wanted a suit of clothes made he went to a Negro tailor, and for shoes he went to a shoemaker of the same race. In a certain way every slave plantation in the South was an industrial school. On these plantations young colored men and women were constantly being trained not only as farmers but as carpenters, blacksmiths, wheel-wrights, brick masons, engineers, cooks, laundresses, sewing women and housekeepers.

I do not mean in any way to apologize for the curse of slavery, which was a curse to both races, but in what I say about industrial training in slavery I am simply stating facts. This training was crude, and was given for selfish purposes. It did not answer the highest ends, because there was an absence of mental training in connection with the training of the hand. To a large degree, though, this business contact with the Southern white man, and the industrial training on the plantations, left the Negro at the close of the war in possession of nearly all the com-

mon and skilled labor in the South. The industries that gave the South its power, prominence and wealth prior to the Civil War were mainly the raising of cotton, sugar cane, rice and tobacco. Before the way could be prepared for the proper growing and marketing of these crops forests had to be cleared, houses to be built, public roads and railroads constructed. In all these works the Negro did most of the heavy work. In the planting, cultivating and marketing of the crops not only was the Negro the chief dependence, but in the manufacture of tobacco he became a skilled and proficient workman, and in this, up to the present time, in the South, holds the lead in the large tobacco manufactories.

In most of the industries, though, what happened? For nearly twenty years after the war, except in a few instances, the value of the industrial training given by the plantations was overlooked. Negro men and women were educated in literature, in mathematics and in the sciences, with little thought of what had been taking place during the preceding two hundred and fifty years, except, perhaps, as something to be escaped, to be got as far away from as possible. As a generation began to pass, those who had been trained as mechanics in slavery began to disappear by death, and gradually it began to be realized that there were few to take their places. There were young men educated in foreign tongues, but few in carpentry or in mechanical or architectural drawing. Many were trained in Latin, but few as engineers and blacksmiths. Too many were taken from the farm and educated, but educated in everything but farming. For this reason they had no interest in farming and did not return to it. And yet eighty-five per cent. of the Negro population of the Southern states lives and for a considerable time will continue to live in the country districts. The charge is often brought against the members of my race—and too often justly, I confess—that they are found leaving the country districts and flocking into the great cities where temptations are more frequent and harder to resist, and where the Negro people too often become demoralized. Think, though, how frequently it is the case that from the first day that a pupil begins to go to school his books teach him much about the cities of the world and city life, and almost nothing about the country. How natural it is, then, that when he has the ordering of his life he wants to live it in the city.

Only a short time before his death the late Mr. C. P. Huntington, to whose memory a magnificent library has just been given by his widow to the Hampton Institute for Negroes, in Virginia, said in a public address some words which seem to me so wise that I want to quote them here:

"Our schools teach everybody a little of almost everything, but, in my opinion, they teach very few children just what they ought to know in order to make their way successfully in life. They do not put into their hands the tools they are best fitted to use, and hence so many failures. Many a mother and sister have worked and slaved, living upon scanty food, in order to give a son and brother a "liberal education," and in doing this have built up a barrier between the boy and the work he was fitted to do. Let me say to you that all honest work is honorable work. If the labor is manual, and seems common, you will have all the more chance to be thinking of other things, or of work that is higher and brings better pay, and to work out in your minds better and higher duties and responsibilities for yourselves, and for thinking of ways by which you can help others as well as yourselves, and bring them up to your own higher level."

Some years ago, when we decided to make tailoring a part of our training at the Tuskegee Institute, I was amazed to find that it was almost impossible to find in the whole country an educated colored man who could teach the making of clothing. We could find numbers of them who could teach astronomy, theology, Latin or grammar, but almost none who could instruct in the making of clothing, something that has to be used by every one of us every day in the year. How

often have I been discouraged as I have gone through the South, and into the homes of the people of my race, and have found women who could converse intelligently upon abstruse subjects, and yet could not tell how to improve the condition of the poorly cooked and still more poorly served bread and meat which they and their families were eating three times a day. It is discouraging to find a girl who can tell you the geographical location of any country on the globe and who does not know where to place the dishes upon a common dinner table. It is discouraging to find a woman who knows much about theoretical chemistry, and who cannot properly wash and iron a shirt.

In what I say here I would not by any means have it understood that I would limit or circumscribe the mental development of the Negro student. No race can be lifted until its mind is awakened and strengthened. By the side of industrial training should always go mental and moral training, but the pushing of mere abstract knowledge into the head means little. We want more than the mere performance of mental gymnastics. Our knowledge must be harnessed to the things of real life. I would encourage the Negro to secure all the mental strength, all the mental culture—whether gleaned from science, mathematics, history, language or literature that his circumstances will allow, but I believe most earnestly that for years to come the education of the people of my race should be so directed that the greatest proportion of the mental strength of the masses will be brought to bear upon the every-day practical things of life, upon something that is needed to be done, and something which they will be permitted to do in the community in which they reside. And just the same with the professional class which the race needs and must have, I would say give the men and women of that class, too, the training which will best fit them to perform in the most successful manner the service which the race demands.

I would not confine the race to industrial life, not even to agriculture, for example, although I believe that by far the greater part of the Negro race is best off in the country districts and must and should continue to live there, but I would teach the race that in industry the foundation must be laid—that the very best service which any one can render to what is called the higher education is to teach the present generation to provide a material or industrial foundation. On such a foundation as this will grow habits of thrift, a love of work, economy, ownership of property, bank accounts. Out of it in the future will grow practical education, professional education, positions of public responsibility. Out of it will grow moral and religious strength. Out of it will grow wealth from which alone can come leisure and the opportunity for the enjoyment of literature and the fine arts.

In the words of the late beloved Frederick Douglass: "Every blow of the sledge hammer wielded by a sable arm is a powerful blow in support of our cause. Every colored mechanic is by virtue of circumstances an elevator of his race. Every house built by a black man is a strong tower against the allied hosts of prejudice. It is impossible for us to attach too much importance to this aspect of the subject. Without industrial development there can be no wealth; without wealth there can be no leisure; without leisure no opportunity for thoughtful reflection and the cultivation of the higher arts."

I would set no limits to the attainments of the Negro in arts, in letters or statesmanship, but I believe the surest way to reach those ends is by laying the foundation in the little things of life that lie immediately about one's door. I plead for industrial education and development for the Negro not because I want to cramp him, but because I want to free him. I want to see him enter the all-powerful business and commercial world.

It was such combined mental, moral and industrial education which the late General Armstrong set out to give at the Hampton Institute when he established that school thirty years ago. The Hampton Institute has continued along the lines laid down by its great founder, and now each year an increasing number of similar schools are being established in the South, for the people of both races.

Early in the history of the Tuskegee Institute we began to combine industrial training with mental and moral culture. Our first efforts were in the direction of agriculture, and we began teaching this with no appliances except one hoe and a blind mule. From this small beginning we have grown until now the Institute owns two thousand acres of land, eight hundred of which are cultivated each year by the young men of the school. We began teaching wheelwrighting and blacksmithing in a small way to the men, and laundry work, cooking and sewing and housekeeping to the young women. The fourteen hundred and over young men and women who attended the school during the last school year received instruction—in addition to academic and religious training—in thirty-three trades and industries, including carpentry, blacksmithing, printing, wheelwrighting, harnessmaking, painting, machinery, founding, shoemaking, brickmasonry and brickmaking, plastering, sawmilling, tinsmithing, tailoring, mechanical and architectural drawing, electrical and steam engineering, canning, sewing, dressmaking, millinery, cooking, laundering, housekeeping, mattress making, basketry, nursing, agriculture, dairying and stock raising, horticulture.

Not only do the students receive instruction in these trades, but they do actual work, by means of which more than half of them pay some part or all of their expenses while remaining at the school. Of the sixty buildings belonging to the school all but four were almost wholly erected by the students as a part of their industrial education. Even the bricks which go into the walls are made by students in the school's brick yard, in which, last year, they manufactured two million bricks.

When we first began this work at Tuskegee, and the idea got spread among the people of my race that the students who came to the Tuskegee school were to be taught industries in connection with their academic studies, were, in other words, to be taught to work, I received a great many verbal messages and letters from parents informing me that they wanted their children taught books, but not how to work. This protest went on for three or four years, but I am glad to be able to say now that our people have very generally been educated to a point where they see their own needs and conditions so clearly that it has been several years since we have had a single protest from parents against the teaching of industries, and there is now a positive enthusiasm for it. In fact, public sentiment among the students at Tuskegee is now so strong for industrial training that it would hardly permit a student to remain on the grounds who was unwilling to labor.

It seems to me that too often mere book education leaves the Negro young man or woman in a weak position. For example, I have seen a Negro girl taught by her mother to help her in doing laundry work at home. Later, when this same girl was graduated from the public schools or a high school and returned home she finds herself educated out of sympathy with laundry work, and yet not able to find anything to do which seems in keeping with the cost and character of her education. Under these circumstances we cannot be surprised if she does not fulfill the expectations made for her. What should have been done for her, it seems to me, was to give her along with her academic education thorough training in the latest and best methods of laundry work, so that she could have put so much skill and intelligence into it that the work would have been lifted out from the plane of drudggery. The home which she would then have been able to found by the results of her work would have enabled her to help her children to take a still more responsible position in life.

Almost from the first Tuskegee has kept in mind—and this I think should be the policy of all industrial schools—fitting students for occupations which would be open to them in their home communities. Some years ago we

noted the fact that there was beginning to be a demand in the South for men to operate dairies in a skillful, modern manner. We opened a dairy department in connection with the school, where a number of young men could have instruction in the latest and most scientific methods of dairy work. At present we have calls—mainly from Southern white men—for twice as many dairymen as we are able to supply. What is equally satisfactory, the reports which come to us indicate that our young men are giving the highest satisfaction and are fast changing and improving the dairy product in the communities into which they go. I use the dairy here as an example. What I have said of this is equally true of many of the other industries which we teach. Aside from the economic value of this work I cannot but believe, and my observation confirms me in my belief, that as we continue to place Negro men and women of intelligence, religion, modesty, conscience and skill in every community in the South, who will prove by actual results their value to the community, I cannot but believe, I say, that this will constitute a solution to many of the present political and social difficulties.

Many seem to think that industrial education is meant to make the Negro work as he worked in the days of slavery. This is far from my conception of industrial education. If this training is worth anything to the Negro, it consists in teaching him how not to work, but how to make the forces of nature—air, steam, water, horse-power and electricity—work for him. If it has any value it is in lifting labor up out of toil and drudgery into the plane of the dignified and the beautiful. The Negro in the South works and works hard; but too often his ignorance and lack of skill causes him to do his work in the most costly and shiftless manner, and this keeps him near the bottom of the ladder in the economic world.

I have not emphasized particularly in these pages the great need of training the Negro in agriculture, but I believe that this branch of industrial education does need very great emphasis. In this connection I want to quote some words which Mr. Edgar Gardner Murphy, of Montgomery, Alabama, has recently written upon this subject:

"We must incorporate into our public school system a larger recognition of the practical and industrial elements in educational training. Ours is an agricultural population. The school must be brought more closely to the soil. The teaching of history, for example, is all very well, but nobody can really know anything of history unless he has been taught to see things grow—has so seen things not only with the outward eye, but with the eyes of his intelligence and conscience. The actual things of the present are more important, however, than the institutions of the past. Even to young children can be shown the simpler conditions and processes of growth—how corn is put into the ground—how cotton and potatoes should be planted—how to choose the soil best adapted to a particular plant, how to improve that soil, how to care for the plant while it grows, how to get the most value out of it, how to use the elements of waste for the fertilization of other crops; how, through the alternation of crops, the land may be made to increase the annual value of its products—these things, upon their elementary side are absolutely vital to the worth and success of hundreds of thousands of these people of the Negro race, and yet our whole educational system has practically ignored them.

* * * * * *

"Such work will mean not only an education in agriculture, but an education through agriculture and education, through natural symbols and practical forms, which will ed-ucate as deeply, as broadly and as truly as any other system which the world has known. Such changes will bring far larger results than the mere improvement of our Negroes. They will give us an agricultural class, a class of tenants or small land owners, trained not away from the soil, but in relation to the soil and in intelligent dependence upon its resources."

I close, then, as I began, by saying that as a slave the Negro was worked, and that as a freeman he must learn to work. There is still doubt in many quarters as to the ability of the Negro unguided, unsupported, to hew his own path and put into visible, tangible, indisputable form, products and signs of civilization. This doubt cannot be much affected by abstract arguments, no matter how delicately and convincingly woven together. Patiently, quietly, doggedly, persistently, through summer and winter, sunshine and shadow, by self-sacrifice, by foresight, by honesty and industry, we must re-enforce argument with results. One farm bought, one house built, one home sweetly and intelligently kept, one man who is the largest tax payer or has the largest bank account, one school or church maintained, one factory running successfully, one truck garden profitably cultivated, one patient cured by a Negro doctor, one sermon well preached, one office well filled, one life cleanly lived—these will tell more in our favor than all the abstract eloquence that can be summoned to plead our cause. Our pathway must be up through the soil, up through swamps, up through forests, up through the streams, the rocks, up through commerce, education and religion!

Organizing Local Business League

Fred R. Moore

The way to organize is to *organize*. Where there is a will there is always a way. If an individual or individuals are anxious to see results and believe in the advancement of the race and of individuals in their communities, they will use every effort to get the people together in an organization. Some say that those engaged in business should get together; this is quite true. My contention is, however, that business men and those who believe in giving them support should get together. Your local leagues will be stronger when you bring into them all the citizens of character who believe in race effort. I would require every person who joins a local league to pledge himself to support all worthy enterprises managed by men and women of the race, and when I found him doing otherwise, unless for good reason, I would fire him out of the local organization. When a prescription is to be filled or medicine purchased, the drug store kept by a member of the race should have the filling of the same. The doctor of your race when in need of medical attention, the lawyer of your race when in need of legal advice or having legal papers drawn. When in need of literature subscribe to those periodicals published by members of the race. All business enterprises should be supported, how else can we expect to be respected by the world at large and be representative of something if we do not begin to practice what a great many of us preach? How can we otherwise succeed? Some would say that this was drawing the color line. I do not believe it. Jews support Jews; Germans support Germans; Italians support Italians, until they get strong enough to complete with their brothers in the professions and trades; and Negroes should now begin to support Negroes. Don't delay this, but begin today. The preacher says: "To-day is the day of salvation; harden not your hearts, for to-morow ye may die."

I say to-day is the time to organize, and this should be your slogan. Organize, organize and don't delay.

When the white race sees us organized in support of one another they will have greater respect for us. I lose respect for the individual who doubts the capacity of his people to do; that we cannot do as well as the whites. How can we ever prove that we have the ability to compete unless supported by our people. I believe that we can do anything the white man does, if only given the chance. We are constantly appealing to the whites to hold open the door of opportunity, but we are not doing it for ourselves as we should. We must begin to recognize the true principle and we should educate the race up to it; and that principle is—believe in your race and practice it by giving them proper support in all proper undertakings. What a mighty power we shall be when we begin to do this, and we shall never be a mighty people until we do begin.

WHAT A LOCAL LEAGUE SHOULD STAND FOR TO MAKE IT EFFECTIVE

It should have direct oversight over the interests of the people; in fact, it should be the Chamber of Commerce; guarding, and, as far as possible, protecting the people against

Source: From Fred R. Moore, "Organizing Local Business League," *Report of the Fifth Annual Convention of the National Negro Business League, . . .* 1904 (Pensacola, Fla.: M. M. Lewey, n.d.), pp. 42–48.

unwise investments, and exposing fake companies organized to take advantage of the ignorant by promising large profits. The local league should seek constantly to better the business engaged in by individuals, by suggesting improvements; insist on business methods, fair prices and cleanliness in appearance; guard against failures by advocating loyal support, and a good supply of common sense. A local business league should control the employment of labor and bestow it where it will do the most good.

A local business league to be effective, must hold regular monthly meetings, and where our people are in large numbers and are not thoroughly organized, the meetings should be held weekly. A general interchange of ideas as to the conduct of business with experienced persons to discuss the question, or read a paper on business effort, would be most helpful. There should be charged a fee for joining of not more than twenty-five cents, and monthly dues of ten cents to cover cost of necessary stationery and meeting place. With a good corps of officers and a very active secretary, the wisdom and the helpfulness of such an organization would soon be apparent, and would be appreciated by the people.

As to the individual who is always advocating the support of enterprises with his mouth. Watch the man who believes in supporting all of the enterprises instituted by members of the race with his mouth, but has never been known to go down in his pocket and give tangible evidence of his sympathy and support; he is a "fakir." The one way to demonstrate is to produce the goods.

The dreamers who believe that everything comes to him who waits and are constant critics of the doers, are usually lost in the shuffle. You must get together in support of the individual or individuals, learn to concentrate your monies and make a success of one thing at a time. Learn to value money and study thoroughly the plan of investment. Don't always be governed by sentiment; let it be business all the way through, all other things being equal.

The power of organization is in what is accomplished. It is not necessary to wait for large numbers, but get together four or five active men in your community and have your plans well thought out and put them into immediate operation. Hold weekly meetings, constantly adding to your membership. Do not be discouraged if you should be unsuccessful at the start, but persevere. It is the determined individual who succeeds, and to succeed you must be willing to make sacrifices.

The National Organization had its being by and through this very idea. Its object is to give encouragement to the people to stand together, to build up individuals in various communities, and show to the world the capabilities and possibilities of the race along all lines if given a chance; and to demonstrate to the race that largely our success is with ourselves. Let me, therefore urge upon you the great importance of keeping together. Do not argue for organization here and when you return to your homes lose sight of putting it in actual operation. Have the same interest in the race at home that some of you have when away from home. Be as big a man at home as you seek to be away from home. Advocate the value of a local league in your community as strongly as you do when absent. Urge the people to stand together; assist them in bettering their condition by showing them how to be helpful to one another. All of this can be done, if you will but make the effort.

Of Mr. Booker T. Washington and Others

W. E. B. Du Bois

Easily the most striking thing in the history of the American Negro since 1876 is the ascendancy of Mr. Booker T. Washington. It began at the time when war memories and ideals were rapidly passing; a day of astonishing commercial development was dawning; a sense of doubt and hesitation overtook the freedmen's sons,—then it was that his leading began. Mr. Washington came, with a single definite programme, at the psychological moment when the nation was a little ashamed of having bestowed so much sentiment on Negroes, and was concentrating its energies on Dollars. His programme of industrial education, conciliation of the South, and submission and silence as to civil and political rights, was not wholly original; the Free Negroes from 1830 up to war-time had striven to build industrial schools, and the American Missionary Association had from the first taught various trades; and Price and others had sought a way of honorable alliance with the best of the Southerners. But Mr. Washington first indissolubly linked these things; he put enthusiasm, unlimited energy, and perfect faith into this programme, and changed it from a by-path into a veritable Way of Life. And the tale of the methods by which he did this is a fascinating study of human life.

It startled the nation to hear a Negro advocating such a programme after many decades of bitter complaint; it startled and won the applause of the South, it interested and won the admiration of the North; and after a confused murmur of protest, it silenced if it did not convert the Negroes themselves.

To gain the sympathy and coöperation of the various elements comprising the white South was Mr. Washington's first task; and this, at the time Tuskegee was founded, seemed, for a black man, well-nigh impossible. And yet ten years later it was done in the word spoken at Atlanta: "In all things purely social we can be as separate as the five fingers, and yet one as the hand in all things essential to mutual progress." This "Atlanta Compromise" is by all odds the most notable thing in Mr. Washington's career. The South interpreted it in different ways: the radicals received it as a complete surrender of the demand for civil and political equality; the conservatives, as a generously conceived working basis for mutual understanding. So both approved it, and to-day its author is certainly the most distinguished Southerner since Jefferson Davis, and the one with the largest personal following.

Next to this achievement comes Mr. Washington's work in gaining place and consideration in the North. Others less shrewd and tactful had formerly essayed to sit on these two stools and had fallen between them; but as Mr. Washington knew the heart of the South from birth and training, so by singular insight he intuitively grasped the spirit of the age which was dominating the North. And so thoroughly did he learn the speech and thought of triumphant commercialism, and the ideals of material prosperity, that the picture of a lone black boy poring over a French grammar amid the weeds and dirt of a neglected home soon seemed to him the acme of absurdities. One wonders what Socrates and St. Francis of Assisi would say to this.

Source: W. E. B. Du Bois, "Of Mr. Booker T. Washington and Others," in Du Bois, *Souls of Black Folk* (Chicago: A. C. McClurg, 1903), pp. 42–54.

And yet this very singleness of vision and thorough oneness with his age is a mark of the successful man. It is as though Nature must needs make men narrow in order to give them force. So Mr. Washington's cult has gained unquestioning followers, his work has wonderfully prospered, his friends are legion, and his enemies are confounded. To-day he stands as the one recognized spokesman of his ten million fellows, and one of the most notable figures in a nation of seventy millions. One hesitates, therefore, to criticise a life which, beginning with so little, has done so much. And yet the time is come when one may speak in all sincerity and utter courtesy of the mistakes and shortcomings of Mr. Washington's career, as well as of his triumphs, without being thought captious or envious, and without forgetting that it is easier to do ill than well in the world.

The criticism that has hitherto met Mr. Washington has not always been of this broad character. In the South especially has he had to walk warily to avoid the harshest judgments,—and naturally so, for he is dealing with the one subject of deepest sensitiveness to that section. Twice—once when at the Chicago celebration of the Spanish-American War he alluded to the color-prejudice that is "eating away the vitals of the South," and once when he dined with President Roosevelt—has the resulting Southern criticism been violent enough to threaten seriously his popularity. In the North the feeling has several times forced itself into words, that Mr. Washington's counsels of submission overlooked certain elements of true manhood, and that his educational programme was unnecessarily narrow. Usually, however, such criticism has not found open expression, although, too, the spiritual sons of the Abolitionists have not been prepared to acknowledge that the schools founded before Tuskegee, by men of broad ideals and self-sacrificing spirit, were wholly failures or worthy of ridicule. While, then, criticism has not failed to follow Mr. Washington, yet the prevailing public opinion of the and has

been but too willing to deliver the solution of a wearisome problem into his hands, and say, "If that is all you and your race ask, take it."

Among his own people, however, Mr. Washington has encountered the strongest and most lasting opposition, amounting at times to bitterness, and even to-day continuing strong and insistent even though largely silenced in outward expression by the public opinion of the nation. Some of this opposition is, of course, mere envy; the disappointment of displaced demagogues and the spite of narrow minds. But aside from this, there is among educated and thoughtful colored men in all parts of the land a feeling of deep regret, sorrow, and apprehension at the wide currency and ascendancy which some of Mr. Washington's theories have gained. These same men admire his sincerity of purpose, and are willing to forgive much to honest endeavor which is doing something worth the doing. They coöperate with Mr. Washington as far as they conscientiously can; and, indeed, it is no ordinary tribute to this man's tact and power that, steering as he must between so many diverse interests and opinions, he so largely retains the respect of all.

But the hushing of the criticism of honest opponents is a dangerous thing. It leads some of the best of the critics to unfortunate silence and paralysis of effort, and others to burst into speech so passionately and intemperately as to lose listeners. Honest and earnest criticism from those whose interests are most nearly touched,—criticism of writers by readers, of government by those governed, of leaders by those led,—this is the soul of democracy and the safeguard of modern society. If the best of the American Negroes receive by outer pressure a leader whom they had not recognized before, manifestly there is here a certain palpable gain. Yet there is also irreparable loss,—a loss of that peculiarly valuable education which a group receives when by search and criticism it finds and commissions its own leaders.

The way in which this is done is at once the most elementary and the nicest problem of social growth. History is but the record of such group-leadership; and yet how infinitely changeful is its type and character! And of all types and kinds, what can be more instructive than the leadership of a group within a group?—that curious double movement where real progress may be negative and actual advance be relative retrogression. All this is the social student's inspiration and despair.

Now in the past the American Negro has had instructive experience in the choosing of group leaders, founding thus a peculiar dynasty which in the light of present conditions is worth while studying. When sticks and stones and beasts form the sole environment of a people, their attitude is largely one of determined opposition to and conquest of natural forces. But when to earth and brute is added an environment of men and ideas, then the attitude of the imprisoned group may take three main forms,—a feeling of revolt and revenge; an attempt to adjust all thought and action to the will of the greater group; or, finally, a determined effort at self-realization and self-development despite environing opinion. The influence of all of these attitudes at various times can be traced in the history of the American Negro, and in the evolution of his successive leaders.

Before 1750, while the fire of American freedom still burned in the veins of the slaves, there was in all leadership or attempted leadership but the one motive of revolt and revenge,—typified in the terrible Maroons, the Danish blacks, and Cato of Stono, and veiling all the Americas in fear of insurrection. The liberalizing tendencies of the latter half of the eighteenth century brought, along with kindlier relations between black and white, thoughts of ultimate adjustment and assimilation. Such aspiration was especially voiced in the earnest songs of Phyllis, in the martyrdom of Attucks, the fighting of Salem and Poor, the intellectual accomplishments of Banneker and

Derham, and the political demands of the Cuffes.

Stern financial and social stress after the war cooled much of the previous humanitarian ardor. The disappointment and impatience of the Negroes at the persistence of slavery and serfdom voiced itself in two movements. The slaves in the South, aroused undoubtedly by vague rumors of the Haytian revolt, made three fierce attempts at insurrection,—in 1800 under Gabriel in Virginia, in 1822 under Vesey in Carolina, and in 1831 again in Virginia under the terrible Nat Turner. In the Free States, on the other hand, a new and curious attempt at self-development was made. In Philadelphia and New York color-prescription led to a withdrawal of Negro communicants from white churches and the formation of a peculiar socio-religious institution among the Negroes known as the African Church,—an organization still living and controlling in its various branches over a million of men.

Walker's wild appeal against the trend of the times showed how the world was changing after the coming of the cotton-gin. By 1830 slavery seemed hopelessly fastened on the South, and the slaves thoroughly cowed into submission. The free Negroes of the North, inspired by the mulatto immigrants from the West Indies, began to change the basis of their demands; they recognized the slavery of slaves, but insisted that they themselves were freemen, and sought assimilation and amalgamation with the nation on the same terms with other men. Thus, Forten and Purvis of Philadelphia, Shad of Wilmington, Du Bois of New Haven, Barbadoes of Boston, and others, strove singly and together as men, they said, not as slaves; as "people of color," not as "Negroes." The trend of the times, however, refused them recognition save in individual and exceptional cases, considered them as one with all the despised blacks, and they soon found themselves striving to keep even the rights they formerly had of voting and working and moving as freemen. Schemes of migration and colonization arose among them; but these they refused to entertain, and they eventually turned to the Abolition movement as a final refuge.

Here, led by Remond, Nell, Wells-Brown, and Douglass, a new period of self-assertion and self-development dawned. To be sure, ultimate freedom and assimilation was the ideal before the leaders, but the assertion of the manhood rights of the Negro by himself was the main reliance, and John Brown's raid was the extreme of its logic. After the war and emancipation, the great form of Frederick Douglass, the greatest of American Negro leaders, still led the host. Self-assertion, especially in political lines, was the main programme, and behind Douglass came Elliot, Bruce, and Langston, and the Reconstruction politicians, and, less conspicuous but of greater social significance Alexander Crummell and Bishop Daniel Payne.

Then came the Revolution of 1876, the suppression of the Negro votes, the changing and shifting of ideals, and the seeking of new lights in the great night. Douglass, in his old age, still bravely stood for the ideals of his early manhood,—ultimate assimilation *through* self-assertion, and on no other terms. For a time Price arose as a new leader, destined, it seemed, not to give up, but to restate the old ideals in a form less repugnant to the white South. But he passed away in his prime. Then came the new leader. Nearly all the former ones had become leaders by the silent suffrage of their fellows, had sought to lead their own people alone, and were usually, save Douglass, little known outside their race. But Booker T. Washington arose as essentially the leader not of one race but of two,—a compromiser between the South, the North, and the Negro. Naturally the Negroes resented, at first bitterly, signs of compromise which surrendered their civil and political rights, even though this was to be exchanged for larger chances of economic development. The rich and dominating North, however, was not only weary of the race problem, but was investing largely in Southern enterprises, and welcomed any method of peaceful coöperation. Thus, by national opinion, the Negroes began to recognize Mr. Washington's leadership; and the voice of criticism was hushed.

Mr. Washington represents in Negro thought the old attitude of adjustment and submission; but adjustment at such a peculiar time as to make his programme unique. This is an age of unusual economic development, and Mr. Washington's programme naturally takes an economic cast, becoming a gospel of Work and Money to such an extent as apparently almost completely to overshadow the higher aims of life. Moreover, this is an age when the more advanced races are coming in closer contact with the less developed races, and the race-feeling is therefore intensified; and Mr. Washington's programme practically accepts the alleged inferiority of the Negro races. Again, in our own land, the reaction from the sentiment of war time has given impetus to race-prejudice against Negroes, and Mr. Washington withdraws many of the high demands of Negroes as men and American citizens. In other periods of intensified prejudice all the Negro's tendency to self-assertion has been called forth; at this period a policy of submission is advocated. In the history of nearly all other races and peoples the doctrine preached at such crises has been that manly self-respect is worth more than lands and houses, and that a people who voluntarily surrender such respect, or cease striving for it, are not worth civilizing.

In answer to this, it has been claimed that the Negro can survive only through submission. Mr. Washington distinctly asks that black people give up, at least for the present, three things,—

First, political power,

Second, insistence on civil rights,

Third, higher education of Negro youth,—

and concentrate all their energies on industrial education, the accumulation of wealth, and the conciliation of the South. This policy has been courageously and insistently advocated for over fifteen years, and has been triumphant for perhaps ten years. As a result of this tender of the palm-branch, what has been the return? In these years there have occurred:

1. The disfranchisement of the Negro.
2. The legal creation of a distinct status of civil inferiority for the Negro.
3. The steady withdrawal of aid from institutions for the higher training of the Negro.

These movements are not, to be sure, direct results of Mr. Washington's teachings; but his propaganda has, without a shadow of doubt, helped their speedier accomplishment. The question then comes: Is it possible, and probable, that nine millions of men can make effective progress in economic lines if they are deprived of political rights, made a servile caste, and allowed only the most meagre chance for developing their exceptional men? If history and reason give any distinct answer to these questions, it is an emphatic *No*. And Mr. Washington thus faces the triple paradox of his career:

1. He is striving nobly to make Negro artisans business men and property-owners; but it is utterly impossible, under modern competitive methods, for workingmen and property-owners to defend their rights and exist without the right of suffrage.
2. He insists on thrift and self-respect, but at the same time counsels a silent submission to civic inferiority such as is bound to sap the manhood of any race in the long run.
3. He advocates common-school and industrial training, and depreciates institutions of higher learning; but neither the Negro common-schools, nor Tuskegee itself, could remain open a day were it not for teachers trained in Negro colleges, or trained by their graduates.

This triple paradox in Mr. Washington's position is the object of criticism by two classes of colored Americans. One class is spiritually descended from Toussaint the Savior, through Gabriel, Vesey, and Turner, and they represent the attitude of revolt and revenge; they hate the white South blindly and distrust the white race generally, and so far as they agree on definite action, think that the Negro's only hope lies in emigration beyond the borders of the United States. And yet, by the irony of fate, nothing has more effectually made this programme seem hopeless than the recent course of the United States toward weaker and darker peoples in the West Indies, Hawaii, and the Philippines,—for where in the world may we go and be safe from lying and brute force?

The other class of Negroes who cannot agree with Mr. Washington has hitherto said little aloud. They deprecate the sight of scattered counsels, of internal disagreement; and especially they dislike making their just criticism of a useful and earnest man an excuse for a general discharge of venom from small-minded opponents. Nevertheless, the questions involved are so fundamental and serious that it is difficult to see how men like the Grimkes, Kelly Miller, J. W. E. Bowen, and other representatives of this group, can much longer be silent. Such men feel in conscience bound to ask of this nation three things:

1. The right to vote.
2. Civic equality.
3. The education of youth according to ability.

They acknowledge Mr. Washington's invaluable service in counselling patience and courtesy in such demands; they do not ask that ignorant black men vote when ignorant whites are debarred, or that any reasonable restrictions in the suffrage should not be applied; they know that the low social level of the mass of the race is responsible for much discrimination against it, but they also know, and the nation knows, that relentless color-prejudice is more often a cause than a result of the Negro's degradation; they seek the abatement of this relic of barbarism, and not its systematic encouragement and pampering by all agencies of social power from the

Associated Press to the Church of Christ. They advocate, with Mr. Washington, a broad system of Negro common schools supplemented by thorough industrial training; but they are surprised that a man of Mr. Washington's insight cannot see that no such educational system ever has rested or can rest on any other basis than that of the well-equipped college and university, and they insist that there is a demand for a few such institutions throughout the South to train the best of the Negro youth as teachers, professional men, and leaders.

This group of men honor Mr. Washington for his attitude of conciliation toward the white South; they accept the "Atlanta Compromise" in its broadest interpretation; they recognize, with him, many signs of promise, many men of high purpose and fair judgment, in this section; they know that no easy task has been laid upon a region already tottering under heavy burdens. But, nevertheless, they insist that the way to truth and right lies in straightforward honesty, not in indiscriminate flattery; in praising those of the South who do well and criticising uncompromisingly those who do ill; in taking advantage of the opportunities at hand and urging their fellows to do the same, but at the same time in remembering that only a firm adherence to their higher ideals and aspirations will ever keep those ideals within the realm of possibility. They do not expect that the free right to vote, to enjoy civic rights, and to be educated, will come in a moment; they do not expect to see the bias and prejudices of years disappear at the blast of a trumpet; but they are absolutely certain that the way for a people to gain their reasonable rights is not by voluntarily throwing them away and insisting that they do not want them; that the way for a people to gain respect is not by continually belittling and ridiculing themselves; that, on the contrary, Negroes must insist continually, in season and out of season, that voting is necessary to modern manhood, that color discrimination is barbarism, and that black boys need education as well as white boys.

In failing thus to state plainly and unequivocally the legitimate demands of their people, even at the cost of opposing an honored leader, the thinking classes of American Negroes would shirk a heavy responsibility,—a responsibility to themselves, a responsibility to the struggling masses, a responsibility to the darker races of men whose future depends so largely on this American experiment, but especially a responsibility to this nation,—this common Fatherland. It is wrong to encourage a man or a people in evildoing; it is wrong to aid and abet a national crime simply because it is unpopular not to do so. The growing spirit of kindliness and reconciliation between the North and South after the frightful difference of a generation ago ought to be a source of deep congratulation to all, and especially to those whose mistreatment caused the war; but if that reconciliation is to be marked by the industrial slavery and civic death of those same black men, with permanent legislation into a position of inferiority, then those black men, if they are really men, are called upon by every consideration of patriotism and loyalty to oppose such a course by all civilized methods, even though such opposition involves disagreement with Mr. Booker T. Washington. We have no right to sit silently by while the inevitable seeds are sown for a harvest of disaster to our children, black and white.

First, it is the duty of black men to judge the South discriminatingly. The present generation of Southerners are not responsible for the past, and they should not be blindly hated or blamed for it. Furthermore, to no class is the indiscriminate endorsement of the recent course of the South toward Negroes more nauseating than to the best thought of the South. The South is not "solid"; it is a land in the ferment of social change, wherein forces of all kinds are fighting for supremacy; and to praise the ill the South is to-day perpetrating is just as wrong as to condemn the good. Discriminating and broad-minded criticism is what the South needs,—needs it for the sake of her own white sons and daughters, and for the insurance or robust, healthy mental and moral development.

To-day even the attitude of the Southern whites toward the blacks is not, as so many assume, in all cases the same; the ignorant Southerner hates the Negro, the working-men fear his competition, the money-makers wish to use him as a laborer, some of the educated see a menace in his upward development, while others—usually the sons of the masters—wish to help him to rise. National opinion has enabled this last class to maintain the Negro common schools, and to protect the Negro partially in property, life, and limb. Through the pressure of the money-makers, the Negro is in danger of being reduced to semi-slavery, especially in the country districts; the workingmen, and those of the educated who fear the Negro, have united to disfranchise him, and some have urged his deportation; while the passions of the ignorant are easily aroused to lynch and abuse any black man. To praise this intricate whirl of thought and prejudice is nonsense; to inveigh indiscriminately against "the South" is unjust; but to use the same breath in praising Governor Aycock, exposing Senator Morgan, arguing with Mr. Thomas Nelson Page, and denouncing Senator Ben Tillman, is not only sane, but the imperative duty of thinking black men.

It would be unjust to Mr. Washington not to acknowledge that in several instances he has opposed movements in the South which were unjust to the Negro; he sent memorials to the Louisiana and Alabama constitutional conventions, he has spoken against lynching, and in other ways has openly or silently set his influence against sinister schemes and unfortunate happenings. Notwithstanding this, it is equally true to assert that on the whole the distinct impression left by Mr. Washington's propaganda is, first, that the South is justified in its present attitude toward the Negro because of the Negro's degradation; secondly, that the prime cause of the Negro's failure to rise more quickly is his wrong education in the past; and, thirdly,

that his future rise depends primarily on his own efforts. Each of these propositions is a dangerous halftruth. The supplementary truths must never be lost sight of: first, slavery and race-prejudice are potent if not sufficient causes of the Negro's position; second, industrial and common-school training were necessarily slow in planting because they had to await the black teachers trained by higher institutions,—it being extremely doubtful if any essentially different development was possible, and certainly a Tuskegee was unthinkable before 1880; and, third, while it is a great truth to say that the Negro must strive and strive mightily to help himself, it is equally true that unless his striving be not simply seconded, but rather aroused and encouraged, by the initiative of the richer and wiser environing group, he cannot hope for great success.

In his failure to realize and impress this last point, Mr. Washington is especially to be criticised. His doctrine has tended to make the whites, North and South, shift the burden of the Negro problem to the Negro's shoulders and stand aside as critical and rather pessimistic spectators; when in fact the burden belongs to the nation, and the hands of none of us are clean if we bend not our energies to righting these great wrongs.

The South ought to be led, by candid and honest criticism, to assert her better self and do her full duty to the race she has cruelly wronged and is still wronging. The North— her co-partner in guilt—cannot salve her conscience by plastering it with gold. We cannot settle this problem by diplomacy and suaveness, by "policy" alone. If worse come to worst, can the moral fibre of this country survive the slow throttling and murder of nine millions of men?

The black men of America have a duty to perform, a duty stern and delicate,—a forward movement to oppose a part of the work of their greatest leader. So far as Mr. Washington preaches Thrift, Patience, and Industrial Training for the masses, we must hold up his hands and strive with him, rejoicing in his honors and glorying in the strength of this Joshua called of God and of man to lead the headless host. But so far as Mr. Washington apologizes for injustice, North or South, does not rightly value the privilege and duty of voting, belittles the emasculating effects of caste distinctions, and opposes the higher training and ambition of our brighter minds,—so far as he, the South, or the Nation, does this,—we must unceasingly and firmly oppose them. By every civilized and peaceful method we must strive for the rights which the world accords to men, clinging unwaveringly to those great words which the sons of the Fathers would fain forget: "We hold these truths to be self-evident: That all men are created equal; that they are endowed by their Creator with certain unalienable rights; that among these are life, liberty, and the pursuit of happiness."

Club Work of Colored Women

Mary Church Terrell

Should anyone ask me what special phase of the Negro's development makes me most hopeful of his ultimate triumph over present obstacles, I should answer unhesitatingly, it is the magnificent work the women are doing to regenerate and uplife the race. Though there are many things in the Negro's present condition to discourage him, he has some blessings for which to be thankful: not the least of these is the progress of our women in everything which makes for the culture of the individual and the elevation of the race.

For years, either banding themselves into small companies or struggling alone, colored women have worked with might and main to improve the condition of their people. The necessity of systematizing their efforts and working on a larger scale became apparent not many years ago, and they decided to unite their forces. Thus it happened that in the summer of 1896 the National Association of Colored Women was formed by the union of two large organizations, from which the advantage of concerted action had been learned. From its birth till the present time its growth has been steady. Interest in the purposes and plans of the National Association has spread so rapidly that it has already been represented in twenty-six states. Handicapped though its members have been, because they lacked both money and experience, their efforts have for the most part been crowned with success.

Kindergartens have been established by some of its organizations, from which encouraging reports have come. A sanitarium with a training school for nurses has been set on such a firm foundation by the Phyllis Wheatley Club of New Orleans, Louisiana, and has proved itself to be such a blessing to the entire community, that the municipal government of that Southern city has voted it an annual appropriation of several hundred dollars. By the members of the Tuskegee branch of the association the work of bringing the light of knowledge and the gospel of cleanliness to their poor benighted sisters on the plantations in Alabama has been conducted with signal success. Their efforts have thus far been confined to four estates, comprising thousands of acres of

Source: Mary Church Terrell, "Club Work of Colored Women," *Southern Workman,* XXX (August, 1901), pp. 435–38.

land, on which live hundreds of colored people yet in the darkness of ignorance and in the grip of sin, and living miles away from churches and schools.

Plans for aiding the indigent orphaned and aged have been projected, and in some instances have been carried into successful execution. One club in Memphis, Tenn., has purchased a large tract of land on which it intends to erect an Old Folks' Home, part of the money for which has already been raised. Splendid service has been rendered by the Illinois Federation of Colored Women's Clubs, through whose instrumentality schools have been visited, truant children looked after, parents and teachers urged to cooperate with each other, rescue and reform work engaged in, so as to reclaim unfortunate women and tempted girls, public institutions investigated and garments cut, made and distributed to the needy poor.

Questions affecting our legal status as a race are sometimes agitated by our women. In Tennessee and Louisiana colored women have several times petitioned the legislature of their respective states to repeal the obnoxious Jim-Crow car laws. In every way possible we are calling attention to the barbarity of the convict lease system, of which Negroes, and especially the female prisoners, are the principal victims, with the hope that the conscience of the country may soon be touched, and this stain upon its escutcheon be forever wiped away.

Against the one-room cabin we have inaugurated a vigorous crusade. When families of eight or ten men, women and children are all huddled promiscuously together in a single apartment, a condition common among our poor all over the land, there is little hope of inculcating morality and modesty. And yet, in spite of the fateful heritage of slavery, in spite of the manifold pitfalls and peculiar temptations to which our girls are subjected, and though the safeguards usually thrown around maidenly youth and innocence are in some sections entirely withheld from colored girls, statistics compiled by men not inclined to falsify in *favor* of the Negro, show that immorality among colored women is not so great as among women who are equally ignorant and poor in some foreign countries.

Believing that it is only through the home that a people can become really good and truly great, the National Association has entered that sacred domain. Homes, more homes, better homes, purer homes, is the text upon which our sermons have been and will be preached. There has been a determined effort to have heart-to-heart talks with our women, that we may strike at the root of evils, many of which lie at the fireside. If the women of the dominant race, with all the centuries of education, culture and refinement back of them, with all the wealth of opportunity ever present with them, feel the need of a Mothers' Congress, that they may be enlightened upon the best methods of rearing their children and conducting their homes, how much more do our women, for whom shackles were stricken but yesterday, need information on the same vital subjects! And so the Association is working vigorously to establish mothers' congresses on a small scale, wherever our women can be reached.

From this brief and meagre account of the work which has been and is still being accomplished by colored women through the medium of clubs, it is easy to observe how earnest and effective have been our efforts to elevate the race. No people need ever despair whose women are fully aroused to the duties which rest upon them, and are willing to shoulder responsibilities which they alone can successfully assume. The scope of our endeavors is constantly widening. Into the various channels of generosity and beneficence the National Association is entering more and more every day.

Some of our women are urging their clubs to establish day nurseries, a charity of which there is an imperative need. The infants of wage-earning mothers are frequently locked alone in a room from the time the mother leaves in the morning until she returns at night. Not long ago I read in a Southern newspaper that an infant thus locked alone in the room all day had cried itself to death. When one reflects on the slaughter of the innocents which is occurring with pitiless persistency every day, and thinks of the multitudes who are maimed for life or are rendered imbecile, because of the treatment received during their helpless infancy, it is evident that by establishing day nurseries colored women will render one of the greatest services possible to humanity and to the race.

Through our clubs we are studying the labor question and are calling the attention of our women to the alarming rapidity with which the Negro is losing ground in the world of labor. We are preaching in season and out that it is the duty of every wage-earning colored woman to become thoroughly proficient in whatever work she engages, so that she may render the best service of which she is capable and thus do her part toward establishing a reputation for excellent workmanship among colored women. Our clubs all over the country are being urged to establish schools of domestic science as soon as their means will permit. It is believed that by founding schools in which colored girls could be trained to be skilled domestics, we should do more to solve the labor problem, so far as it affects our women, than by using any other means it is in our power to employ.

We believe that our organization can do much to purify the social atmosphere by showing the enormity of the double standard of morals, which teaches that we should turn the cold shoulder upon a fallen sister, but greet her destroyer with open arms and a gracious smile. False accusations and malicious slanders are circulated against us by the press and also at times by the direct descendants of those who, in years past, were responsible for the moral degradation of their female slaves. The National Association insists that is members can do much to prove the falsity of these accusations by refusing in their social life to compromise with what is questionable or countenance what is wrong.

Finally, nothing lies nearer the heart of colored women than the cause of the children. We feel keenly the need of kindergartens, and are putting forth earnest efforts to honeycomb this country with them from one extreme to the other. The more unfavorable the environments of children the more necessary is it that steps be taken to counteract baleful influences upon innocent victims. How imperative is it then, that, as colored women, we inculcate correct principles and set good examples for our own youth, whose little feet will have so many thorny paths of prejudice, temptation and injustice to tread. The colored youth is vicious, we are told. Statistics showing the large number of our boys and girls who crowd the penitentiaries and fill the jails appall and dishearten us. But side by side with these facts and figures of crime, I would have pictured and presented the miserable hovels from which these youthful criminals come. Make a tour of the settlements of colored people, who in many cities are crowded into the most noisome sections permitted by the municipal government, and behold the mites of humanity who infest them. Here are our little ones, the future representatives of the race, fairly drinking in the pernicious example of their elders, coming in contact with nothing but ignorance and vice till, at the age of four, evil habits are formed which no amount of civilizing or Christianizing will ever completely break. The National Association of Colored Women is listening to the cry of the children. So keenly alive is it to the necessity of rescuing the little ones, whose evil nature alone is encouraged to develop and whose noble qualities are deadened and dwarfed by the very atmosphere which they breathe, that its officers are trying to raise money with which to send out a kindergarten organizer, whose duty it shall be to arouse the conscience of our women and to establish kindergartens wherever means therefor can be secured.

And so, lifting as we climb, onward and upward we go, struggling, striving and hoping that the buds and blossoms of our desires will burst into glorious fruition ere long. With courage born of success achieved in the past, we look forward to a future large with promise and hope. Seeking no favors because of our color, nor patronage because of our needs, we knock at the bar of Justice and ask for an equal chance.

Lift Ev'ry Voice and Sing

James Weldon Johnson
J. Rosamond Johnson

Lift ev'ry voice and sing,
Till earth and heaven ring,
Ring with the harmonies of liberty;
Let our rejoicing rise,
High as the list'ning skies,
Let it resound loud as the rolling sea.
Sing a song full of the faith that the dark past has taught us,
Sing a song full of hope that the present has brought us,
Facing the rising sun,
Of our new day begun,
Let us march on till victory is won.

Stony the road we trod,
Bitter the chast'ning rod,
Felt in the days when hope unborn had died;
Yet with a steady beat,
Have not our weary feet
Come to the place for which our fathers sighed?
We have come over a way that with tears has been watered,
We have come, treading our path thro' the blood of the slaughtered,
Out from the gloomy past,
Till now we stand at last
Where the white gleam of our bright star is cast.

God of our weary years,
God of our silent tears,
Thou who has brought us thus far on our way,
Thou who has by Thy might
Let us into the light,
Keep us forever in the path, we pray;
Lest our feet stray from the places, our God, where we met Thee,
Lest, our hearts drunk with the wine of the world, we forget Thee;
Shadowed beneath Thy hand,
May we forever stand,
True to our God, True to our native land.

Source: James Weldon Johnson and J. Rosamond Johnson, Lift Ev'ry Voice and Sing (New York: Edward B. Marks Music Corporation, 1900).

SUGGESTED READINGS

Eric Arnesen, *Waterfront Workers of New Orleans: Race, Class, and Politics, 1863–1923* (New York, 1991)

Gail Bederman, *Manliness and Civilization: A Cultural History of Gender and Race in the United States, 1880–1917* (Chicago, 1995)

W. Fitzhugh Brundage, *Lynching in the New South: Georgia and Virginia, 1880–1930* (Urbana, 1993)

William Cohen, *At Freedom's Edge: Black Mobility and the Southern White Quest for Racial Control, 1861–1915* (Baton Rouge, 1991)

Pete Daniel, *The Shadow of Slavery: Peonage in the South, 1901–1969* (New York, 1972)

Philip Dray, *At the Hands of Persons Unknown: The Lynching of Black America* (New York, 2002)

Glenda Elizabeth Gilmore, *Gender and Jim Crow: Women and the Politics of White Supremacy in North Carolina, 1890–1920* (Chapel Hill, N.C., 1996)

Louis Harlan, *Booker T. Washington: The Making of a Leader, 1856–1901* (New York, 1972)

Louis Harlan, *Booker T. Washington: The Wizard of Tuskegee, 1901–1915* (New York, 1983)

Evelyn Brooks Higginbotham, *Righteous Discontent: The Women's Movement in the Black Baptist Church, 1880–1920* (Cambridge, Mass., 1993)

Tera W. Hunter, *To 'Joy My Freedom: Southern Black Women's Lives and Labors after the Civil War* (Cambridge, Mass., 1997)

J. Morgan Kousser, *The Shaping of Southern Politics: Suffrage Restriction and the Establishment of the One-Party System, 1880–1910* (New Haven, 1974)

David Levering Lewis, *W. E. B. DuBois: Biography of a Race, 1868–1919* (New York, 1993)

Alex Lichtenstein, *Twice the Work of Free Labor: The Political Economy of Convict Labor in the New South* (New York, 1996)

Leon Litwack, *Trouble in Mind: Black Southerners in the Age of Jim Crow* (New York, 1998)

August Meier, *Negro Thought in America, 1880–1915: Racial Ideologies in the Age of Booker T. Washington* (Ann Arbor, Mich., 1963)

Stephanie J. Shaw, *What a Woman Ought to Be and to Do: Black Professional Women Workers During the Jim Crow Era* (Chicago, 1996)

Emma Lou Thornbrough, *T. Thomas Fortune: Militant Journalist* (Chicago, 1972)

Country agricultural agent supervising loading of crops. Helena, Arkansas, early 1930s. (*Source:* Bracey Family Archives.)

Chapter 8

The Age of Migrations

In addition to racism, the external processes of industrialization, urbanization, expansion of capitalism, and war worked to define the social parameters within which blacks as individuals and as a group had to live and make decisions. During the period of the Great Migration, African Americans started to move from the southern countryside into southern and northern cities. The extreme conditions of racial oppression in the south acted as "push" factors, and growing job opportunities in the north, especially during World War I, acted as "pull" factors in this migration. The first four documents in this chapter detail the conditions in the Jim Crow south, including the ubiquity of lynching and racial violence that black people sought to escape. The black population of northern cities mushroomed. For instance, in Chicago it more than doubled from 44,000 in 1910 to 109,000 in 1920, with the bulk of the increase coming after 1916. The document containing letters of black migrants reveal that many of these immigrants to the urban north were not just displaced peasants but black workers with skills seeking better wages and a better life. The selection from Horace Cayton's book reveals the reaction of one unusual black migrant to the emergence of the "urban ghetto." Black migrants, however, faced exclusion from jobs, schools, and housing, and faced poverty and racism at every turn. The end of the First World War was marked by a number of race riots generally provoked by white distaste for the actions of black veterans or fear of blacks moving into all-white neighborhoods. The description of the 1919 Chicago race riot illustrates this phenomena.

In the face of racial repression in the urban north, African Americans continued to struggle for political and civil rights. This was evident in the growth of interracial organizations such as NAACP and the National Urban League. The latter was specifically formed to address the problems of black urbanization and poverty. The next two documents illustrate the work of these two organizations. Their attempts to acculturate black migrants to middle class norms of behavior to ease the transition from the rural south to the urban north is evident in the document on the NAACP guidelines on rules of behavior for the migrants. The article by E. Franklin Frazier, a black sociologist, reveals the growth of the new black middle class.

The postwar era also saw the rise of nationalist sentiments that had been building in black communities since the 1880s. When Marcus Garvey came to the United States and began his Universal Negro Improvement Association in 1916, he found a receptive audience among the new urban migrants and West Indian immigrants. The UNIA rejected the assimilationist orientation of contemporary civil rights organizations and had the largest following among black masses at this time. Garvey hoped to liberate Africa from European colonialism and black Americans from their oppressors by the migration of African Americans to Africa. He was ultimately arrested and, after serving a brief time in jail, was deported. Two selections from Garvey's speech in 1921 and his letter from the Atlanta federal penitentiary document the rise and fall of Garveyism.

Finally, the last four documents in this chapter reveal some of the contours of black social and cultural life in the urban north: the age of the New Negro (Alice Dunbar-Nelson, Carter G. Woodson, and Alain Locke) and the flowering of the "Harlem Rennaissance" (James Weldon Johnson). Black music, dance, art, literature, and theater distinguished this era as the age when the Negro was in vogue.

Tenancy

Carter G. Woodson

In spite of improvements here and there, agriculture in the South is handicapped by the peculiar turn which it took immediately after the Civil War when a readjustment in the economic system became necessary. Nominal slavery at least had passed away, but the dependence of the poor freedmen upon their former masters remained to continue the institution in another form. It was naturally expected that the planters would adopt the wage system of paying the laborer a definite amount in money for his service by the day, month, or year; and as a matter of fact some of these landlords did so, as was and is the custom among most of the farmers of other sections of the country. In the majority of cases in the area devastated by the sectional conflict, however, the owners of large plantations thought that their interest could be better taken care of in their impecunious condition by adopting a system which has become known as "tenancy." The freed-

men had little choice in the matter. They were dependents who had to take whatever was offered them or drift into vagabondage.[*]

History has shown, however, that although there might have been some good intentions which prompted land owners in this direction, it has proved to be the worst evil from which the South has to suffer. Thinking people who can see future consequences from an error of the past and present commonly refer to "tenancy" as an evil much worse than illiteracy, intemperance, or lynching, about which we daily hear so much from the rostrum and the press. In fact, "tenancy" is in a large measure the cause of these other evils in the South. The system has given rise to a transitory, migratory class which has no permanent attachment to and no abiding interest in the communities in which they sojourn. "Tenancy" supplants the idea of home owner-

---

[*]This has been discussed in *The Journal of Negro History,* IX, 241–364, 381–569; XI, 243–415, 425–537.

ship, and thus prevents the building of a desirable rural civilization as is the case with absentee ownership. The agencies like the school and church under such circumstances cannot carry out any constructive program where there is no permanent home life. This class of mentally and spiritually undeveloped people, then, whether whites or blacks, necessarily show evidences of evil habits, irreligion, and lawlessness.

What then is tenancy? Ordinarily we refer to tenants as persons paying for the use of property, but otherwise just as independent in their transactions as the owners of the property themselves. In the case of farm operators in the South, however, the significance is more far reaching. In the first place, there are many different kinds of tenants, each one enjoying more or less independence or exercising more or less liberty in proportion as he finds himself closer to or farther removed from the owner of the land. The persons thus occupied are generally spoken of as tenants, renters, or croppers. All of these operate only rented land. Yet for a better understanding of their situation the United States Bureau of the Census divides them into five classes: share tenants who pay a certain share of the crop for the use of the land but furnish their work animals; croppers whose work animals are furnished by the planters; share-cash tenants who pay the rent partly in cash and partly in products; cash tenants who pay cash altogether for the use of the land; and standing renters who pay a stated amount of farm products for the use of the farm land.* The croppers and standing renters are the most dependent of all classes of tenants. Almost everything is furnished them by the owners of the land, and consequently they receive less of the returns from their labor. Being so dependent, they are allowed such a little liberty that

Negro Population in the United States, 1790 to 1915, pp. 459 to 464; and *United States Census of Agriculture,* 1925, pp. 14 and 15.

their will is subject almost altogether to that of the landlords to whom they are attached.

These relations are usually determined by conference with the tenants about the beginning or end of the year. They agree then to sign a contract which may be enforced at law. Inasmuch as these illiterate people have little or no knowledge of law, they sign away their own rights and liberties, not knowing what they are doing. Most of these contracts are decidedly unfavorable to the tenant, but in addition to this disadvantage the interpretation of the agreement is altogether in the hands of the planter assisted by the officers of the law whom he can always summon to his assistance and make the contract mean whatever he desires it to be. So far as the Negro tenants are concerned they have no law to which they can appeal. For them law is the will of the particular planter with whom they may be dealing. To question his word or to invoke aid against the carrying out of his wishes would be a disastrous procedure for the tenants. A tenant, therefore, easily becomes a peon or slave, about whose condition we shall hear in the next chapter.

This low status is well reflected in the contracts very much like the following lease which tenants have had to sign:

Said tenant further agrees that if he violates the contract, or neglects, or abandons or fails (or in the owner's judgment violates this contract or fails) to properly work or cultivate the land early or at proper times, or in case he should become physically or legally incapacitated from working said lands or should die during the term of his lease, or fails to gather or save the crops when made, or fails to pay the rents or advances made by the owner, when due, then in case of full possession of said premises, crops and improvements, in which event this contract may become void and cancelled at the owner's option, and all indebtedness by the tenant for advances or rent shall at once become due and payable to the owner who may treat them as due and payable without further notice to the tenant; and the tenant hereby agrees to surrender the quiet and peaceable possession of said premises to the owner at said time, in which event the owner is hereby authorized to transfer, sell or dispose of all property thereon the tenant has any interest in, and in order to entitle the owner to do so, it shall not be necessary to give any notice of any failure or violation of this contract by the tenant, the execution of this lease being sufficient notice of defalcation on the part of the tenant, and shall be so construed between the parties hereto, any law, usage or custom to the contrary notwithstanding.*

The routine of the work of these laborers will enable us better to understand the status of these tenants. After the cropper has agreed to become a tenant he comes under the supervision of the landlord who sends out his rider, a man employed to supervise all work on the plantation. This white boss apportions the acreage for cultivation, decides the amount of fertilizer each family must use on its parcel of land, when the crop should be planted, and on what particular spot. The cropper is obligated to rise as early as there is sufficient light to work, about four o'clock on long summer days, and he must toil until dark. There is a bell or some other signal informing the croppers when to start and when they may stop work. If his wife and children work in the fields, either she or some nearly grown girl is permitted to stop about eleven to prepare dinner. On some plantations the dinner intermission is two hours on very hot days; but on others only one hour can be spared. If the planter happens to be liberal he allows the cropper and his associates to cease work on Saturday afternoons.[†]

When the crop is harvested by the tenant the planter deducts therefrom his stipulated share and takes out also the value of clothing, food, and supplies which the planter has furnished the cropper during the year. If there is anything left the planter usually buys the cropper's residue, for the latter is not in a position to hold the crop for a better price, and few planters would permit such an exercise of foresight or business acumen even if the cropper so desired to do so.

Throughout the year both the landlord and the cropper have each tried to give the least and get the most out of an impossible situation. Inasmuch as the landlord has the advantage of owning the stock, the implements, the land, and sometimes by an unwritten law the cropper himself, the landlord usually has whatever apparent profit results from the transaction. Sometimes, however, the landlord sees that he is not making any headway at such an unprofitable task, and he disposes of the land to Negroes. In this way there has been some increase in the number of Negro farmers. This, however, does not happen so often as exploiters of philanthropists would have the public believe.

The extent to which tenancy exists in the South, therefore, will be further enlightening as to the Negro's condition in that section. In the South there are about 40,000 plantations with an average of about five tenants each. The history of tenancy, however, shows that with respect to the Negro it is slowly decreasing, although it still has a strong foothold in most of the Lower South. Tenancy on the strictly renting basis which obtains largely in the North and West is its first step toward the breakup of large land estates and the development of the small farming class. A large planter has more land than he can properly cultivate, and he rents out a part of it. If he finds this unprofitable he sells it. Farms in this country, therefore, have decreased in size; but at the same time they have increased in number, although farm land has increased very little since the Civil War. In some parts the farmers have brought a larger acreage under cultivation, but this

---

*American Statistical Association, *Quarterly Publications*, XIII, pp. 82 to 83.

[†]For a general discussion of these advantages and disadvantages see "The Rural Life of the South," by John Lee Coulter in the *South Atlantic Quarterly*, XII, pp. 60–71; and American Statistical Association, *Quarterly Publications*, XIII, pp. 45–58.

may mean either one of two things, an increase in owners or an increase in tenants. Often, too, an increase in tenants means an increase of the share croppers who are only one stage removed from the wage hands. Almost half, more than one-third of Negro farmers, are share tenants. A small farming class is most desirable, but if the land tenure leads to a condition of the dependency of the tenant upon the landlord, which approaches serfdom, it becomes undesirable.

This is just what has happened in the South. While some plantations have been apparently divided into small farms operated by renters, they are hardly more than debased hired laborers whose plans of work are drawn up altogether by the owners of the land or managers employed by them. This was the fatal mistake in the economic reconstruction of the Southern States. More than half of the states of the Lower South have their farms thus worked and between 25 and 40 per cent of those in other parts of the South adhere to the same plan. Hardly one-third of the farmers in the Southern States employ labor. They prefer to buy it.

The present status is most nearly presented by the statistics of 1925.* According to this data there had been a slight decrease in tenancy but not enough to show any appreciable change in the status of the Negroes on the plantations. In 1910 there were 678,118 tenants; 714,441 in 1920; and 636,248 in the South alone in 1925. Other tenants of color are included in the figure for 1925 as in the cases of 1910 and 1920; and the 1925 report does not give the number of Negro farmers outside of the South. In 1925 these tenants were divided as 78,760 cash tenants, 344,322 croppers, and 213,166 other tenants. All croppers of both races operated 22,985,660 acres in 1925 and harvested 16,093,431 acres in 1924. The value of the land thus operated in 1925 was $1,133,205,380 and the implements used were considered as worth $39,871,615.

This shows the large area of the soil of the South on which are stationed thousands of operators who have not much more of a future than that of slaves. Persons have included this area and these values in estimates to show what progress Negroes have made. That the Negroes are thus situated is no fault of theirs, but the fact is one for lamentation rather than a cause for the rejoicing so frequently indulged in by misinformants of the public. It may require a stronger force than those now operative to disrupt the present system and hasten the dawn of a new day. Practically all of the plantations which have broken up into small farms have done so because of being hard pressed or because the owner found farming unprofitable. Few have been moved by the doctrine of the desirability of the small farming class.*

In view of these things some have advocated the breakup of the plantation. In defence of the system against peasant proprietorship, however, there have been advanced various theories. It is said that the small farm cannot be operated as economically as a large plantation. The small investment and the work required would not permit an outlay for improved machinery, the introduction of the best stock, and the scientific preservation of dairy products, foods, and vegetables. As a matter of fact, however, the large planter does not always introduce modern appliances as soon as they appear. Industrial history shows that the large employer usually holds wages down to have his work done as long as he can by cheap labor to obviate the necessity for the outlay involved in the introduction of modern machinery. Experience has shown, moreover, that what the small farmer loses in being unable to practice economies of the large plantation the small farmer gains by coöperation with his fellows. If properly conducted, coöperative associations among the peasant proprietors may

---

United States Census of Agriculture, 1925.

*W. M. Brewer, "The Plantation," in the Georgia Historical Quarterly, XI, 254.

enable them to produce their staple just as economically as the large planters. The efforts of the agents of the United States Department of Agriculture and of the State Departments of Agriculture, assisted by workers from Land Grant Colleges and privately endowed industrial schools like Hampton and Tuskegee, have shown how this can be done wherever a sufficiently large number of such farmers can be induced to support community efforts of this sort. Such agents, however, are sometimes opposed by the planters because their efforts are considered prejudicial to the interests of the landed aristocracy.*

Investigators assert, too, that the rise of the small farm will be impossible as long as there is the absence of the instinct of land ownership. American native whites have become so accustomed to the abundance of free land that they do not generally aspire to ownership so rapidly as foreigners, who, coming from a country where land is scarce, quickly acquire it here. Only about a fourth of the Negro farmers are actual owners, but, as stated above, they are acquiring land much faster than the native whites. In the passing of the free arable land of the West and the concentration of people in cities requiring larger food supplies, land ownership is becoming more of an attraction and the idea is taking root in the tenancy area in the South. With respect to the Negroes, however, there are some whites who do not encourage their becoming owners of land and actually refuse to sell it to them. Some of those who believe that the Negroes should become owners, moreover, would restrict them to certain areas, carrying out the iniquitous principle of segregation which is now being

*This was the report of John McKinley from South Carolina from several places where this obtained; also that of a worker still active in Louisiana. The writer himself learned of such conditions in the backward parts of Florida and Alabama, which he surveyed.

worked out in cities. Here, then, is a social problem which the unwisdom of Americans has permitted to interfere with the solution of an economic problem which is doing so much to hold the rural South back.

Others advocate the hired labor system as the easiest solution of the problem of tenancy. Pay the laborer, they say, a fixed stipend, and then assume full supervision of his work. Every phase of the work could be so directed as to make it an harmonious operation. The whole plantation would then be developed according to the program of the planter only. This would make it much easier to introduce the latest farming methods, to rotate crops, introduce machinery, and fertilize the soil. The hired labor system would do just as much to increase production, to improve the breed of stocks and products, to increase the income of the owners, and to enhance the value of the land. Under this system, too, the laborers would have ample opportunity to learn scientific farming.

The whole system would be educational, the laborer learning from the employer. Such hired laborers would learn to save sufficient money to improve their situation by becoming owners themselves. The principles of frugality and foresight not found in the shifting tenants would develop in the hired laborers. The hired laborers might first use their savings to become long time lessees and with the income accruing from their efforts they might purchase the very land which they rent. Production throughout the agricultural area would be systematized and agricultural resources would be preserved. The whole country would profit by this economic readjustment of a large producing area of the modern world.

To cure the evils of tenancy one finds here and there those who advocate long time leases as the first step toward peasant proprietorship. It is believed that both lords and tenants can be more easily induced to try out such a plan than they could be prevailed upon to dispose of the large plantations to small farmers. In support of this proposal its advocates argue that long time leases will change the attitude of the tenants toward the land which they cultivate. Instead of trying to get the most out of it by putting the least into it, they will cultivate the soil better, keep up its fertility, improve the buildings, devote some time to shrubbery and gardening, repair the country roads, manifest interest in education, and promote religion. Long time lease tenants will also show interest in coöperative organizations for the common good, pay more promptly their obligations to the local merchant or banker, invest their surplus capital in local enterprises, all of which will build up rather than bleed the community. In the case of long time leases, too, it is said that the relation between the landlord and the tenant will improve. The principles of equity and justice will prevail in their transactions. The long lease tenant will have more with which to buy land and become an independent farmer when he ceases to spend money annually moving from place to place seeking a better opportunity which he never finds.

The large plantation and tenant system are still with us, however, and good fortune resulting from the prevalence of the small farm, then, never reaches this area. The system prevents a diffusion of population by keeping permanently settled families far apart. This interferes with transportation because there are not sufficient progressive farmers along the way to build and repair roads and the large farmers may not construct them except for their own convenience. In such a scattered state telephones are not extended to the area, and if found there the connection is more expensive because of the few subscribers. A little contact means little diffusion of new ideas and a consequent running behind the forces of progress. Tenant farmers in such a situation do not know what is going on in their particular sphere and even if they did they would not have sufficient knowledge to make use of advanced information.

And shifting is what makes the situation worse. As most tenants toil from year to year without seeing any material change in their status or one cubit added unto their economic stature, they easily migrate. Hoping to better their miserable condition, they move from one plantation to another at the close of their contracts at the end of the year. According to the statistics of the United States Government nearly half of the Southern tenants move each year. If this tenancy could be rendered stable, the operators remaining on the same land from year to year, there would be less disaster in the system, but up to the present the problem has remained a troublesome one. The aspect of the areas thus afflicted, then, is that of worn out land, short crops, bad roads, rotten bridges, weather beaten houses, and littered yards.

It is almost impossible, also, to interest this landless, homeless, illiterate class in other forces for the common good of the country, so deeply implanted is selfishness or shortsightedness. To make the country attractive there must be labor saving devices, comfortable homes, modern schools, and live churches. The tenant class of people will never demand these things; and, if superimposed, it will be difficult to extract the cost from the returns of these victims. Philanthropy which has been active in other spheres is just beginning to manifest interest in these things.

The reformer, however, meets with obstacles in promoting the various schemes of coöperation which have meant so much in the development of other rural areas. Tenants do not easily take an interest in coöperative stores, warehouses, creameries, cheese factories, marketing societies, purchasing societies, and breeding associations which have remade other rural communities in transforming the people into thrifty, progressive, and intelligent citizenry. Shifting tenants do not stay in one place long enough so to become acquainted with other neighbors as to learn to coöperate in such a serious effort as the business partnership which these measures imply. And even when such efforts are attempted in a modified manner in the light of conditions obtaining, the results have usually been too meager to warrant the outlay in time and energy. Tenancy, then, is the case of a man dying by his own hands and by his own error, brought on by a hardened sense or seared conscience which makes him believe that the cause is remote when it is within.*

People thus situated never advance far in education. Their children do not attend school regularly. They leave one school before they have reached proper grading and pass on to another where they do not stay long enough to be readjusted. In thus moving from place to place they lose what they have acquired from year to year; and, therefore, do not reach any definite stage of mental development. In the absence of a properly graded school system in the South where the teachers are underpaid and consequently inefficient, too, the schools under the most favorable circumstances would not avail much in the uplift of these people. As there is no compulsory school law enforced among Negroes in these parts, the children of these peasants leave school as soon as they are able to do work on the farms. Illiteracy among them runs rather high, and those who obtain some smattering of education can seldom do more than read and write incorrectly.

The rural church suffers also in the same way from the evils of tenancy. The pastor must face a new congregation each year. If he has started with a program requiring time for execution he must abandon it or try it out anew before he has had a chance to put it to a test on those who have gone like birds of passage after tarrying only twelve months. It likewise becomes increasingly difficult to keep up the interest of the shifting tenants in serious matters like things of the spirit. As they have no fixed abode they restrict their interest largely to the immediate necessities of life.

*Most of these views are advanced in the *South Atlantic Quarterly,* in Volume XII, pp. 60–71.

The preacher to such a class, too, is not the best prepared of his group. Only an intelligent man of the greatest spirit of sacrifice could be expected to spend his life in such an uninviting field. Those ministers who are not wanted elsewhere drift into this service; and it becomes worse when the landlord builds the church and actually chooses the minister for the Negroes. Only the preacher who knows how to safeguard the interests of the planter is allowed to function in the premises. His sermons are censored, and if he is found saying or doing anything that might cause dissatisfaction with things as they are, he will have to leave forthwith and anon.*

The banker, the merchant, and the professional man suffer from tenancy along with the teacher and preacher. Credit extended this class may mean ruin to the business man. The tenant has nothing but his labor to sell, and if that is peripatetic the lender is left in a precarious position. To make up for such losses money must be loaned at a rather high rate of interest and goods must be sold at high prices to squeeze out of the honest tenants the amount necessary to make up for the loss of the few who are not honest enough to take care of their obligations promptly. Most of such tenants, however, have credit only in the commissaries of their landlords, and they dare not purchase their necessities elsewhere. In case of professional services rendered the creditor has a better chance when his fees are collected through the landlord; but here again comes the double cost in that the landlord must increase the amount sufficiently to reimburse him against any loss he may sustain in assuming such a responsibility.

The whole system, then, suffers from an unsuccessful effort to hedge in persons and

*This statement is based on facts obtained by several field workers on the staff making this survey. In several places in Louisiana and Mississippi the planters or their representatives were found listening through the windows of churches to find out what Negro ministers said to their congregations.

force them to do what they are supposed to do, and at the same time it afflicts the unoffending class with the burdens resulting from the failings of others. The procession along the circuitous route has begun, however, and must go on although a few see the error of their ways. But what does a knowledge of these things avail since one element in the equation cannot be eliminated without loss to all? When one moves all must go in the same direction. To stop the procession would be tantamount to a revolution, for it would destroy the present economic system at an apparent loss to all concerned.

That this condition of tenancy obtains is not to the discredit of the Negro, and he must not be misunderstood in the discussion of these undesirable conditions. The Negro has tended to rise from tenancy to ownership in spite of the difficulties involved. Negro farmers in the first place have been increasing at a faster rate than white farmers. This increase, too, has been not only in farms operated but in those actually owned. While the white rural population tended to be drawn off to the industrial plants in the South a generation ago, the Negro tended to remain on the farms. This obtained until the upheaval of the World War which carried the Negroes also from the rural communities to the cities. This migration, however, has gradually stabilized itself.

I Investigate Lynchings

Walter F. White

Nothing contributes so much to the continued life of an investigator of lynchings and his tranquil possession of all his limbs as the obtuseness of the lynchers themselves. Like most boastful people who practice direct action when it involves no personal risk, they just can't help talk about their deeds to any person who manifests even the slightest interest in them.

Most lynchings take place in small towns and rural regions where the natives know practically nothing of what is going on outside their own immediate neighborhoods. Newspapers, books, magazines, theatres, visitors and other vehicles for the transmission of information and ideas are usually as strange among them as dry-point etchings. But those who live in so sterile an atmosphere usually esteem their own perspicacity in about the same degree as they are isolated from the world of ideas. They gabble on *ad infinitum*, apparently unable to keep from talking.

In any American village, North or South, East or West, there is no problem which cannot be solved in half an hour by the morons who lounge about the village store. World peace, or the lack of it, the tariff, sex, religion, the settlement of the war debts, short skirts, Prohibition, the carryings-on of the younger generation, the superior moral rectitude of country people over city dwellers (with a wistful eye on urban sins)—all these controversial subjects are disposed of quickly and finally by the bucolic wise men. When to their isolation is added an emotional fixation, such as the rural South has on the Negro, one can

Source: Walter F. White, "I Investigate Lynchings," in V. F. Calverton, ed., *Anthology of American Negro Literature.* Published by The Modern Library, 1929.

sense the atmosphere from which spring the Heflins, the Ku Kluxers, the two-gun Bible-beaters, the lynchers and the anti-evolution-ists. And one can see why no great amount of cleverness or courage is needed to acquire information in such a forlorn place about the latest lynching.

Professor Earle Fiske Young of the University of Southern California recently analyzed the lynching returns from fourteen Southern States for thirty years. He found that in counties of less than 10,000 people there was a lynching rate of 3.2 per 100,000 of population; that in those of from 10,000 to 20,000 the rate dropped to 2.4; that in those of from 20,000 to 30,000, it was 2.1 per cent; that in those of from 30,000 to 40,000, it was 1.7, and that thereafter it kept on going down until in counties with from 300,000 to 800,000 population it was only 0.05.

Of the forty-one lynchings and eight race riots I have investigated for the National Association for the Advancement of Colored People during the past ten years, all of the lynchings and seven of the riots occurred in rural or semi-rural communities. The towns ranged in population from around one hundred to ten thousand or so. The lynchings were not difficult to inquire into because of the fact already noted that those who perpetrated them were in nearly every instance simple-minded and easily fooled individuals. On but three occasions were suspicions aroused by my too definite questions or by informers who had seen me in other places. These three times I found it rather desirable to disappear slightly in advance of reception committees imbued with the desire to make an addition to the lynching record. One other time the possession of a light skin and blue eyes (though I consider myself a colored man) almost cost me my life when (it was during the Chicago race riots in 1919) a Negro shot at me, thinking me to be a white man.

In 1918 a Negro woman, about to give birth to a child, was lynched with almost unmentionable brutality along with ten men in Georgia. I reached the scene shortly after the butchery and while excitement yet ran high. It was a prosperous community. Forests of pine trees gave rich returns in turpentine, tar and pitch. The small towns where the farmers and turpentine hands traded were fat and rich. The main streets of the largest of these towns were well paved and lighted. The stores were well stocked. The white inhabitants belonged to the class of Georgia crackers—lanky, slow of movement and of speech, long-necked, with small eyes set close together, and skin tanned by the hot sun to a reddish-yellow hue.

As I was born in Georgia and spent twenty years of my life there, my accent is sufficiently Southern to enable me to talk with Southerners and not arouse their suspicion that I am an outsider. (In the rural South hatred of Yankees is not much less than hatred of Negroes.) On the morning of my arrival in the town I casually dropped into the store of one of the general merchants who, I had been informed, had been one of the leaders of the mob. After making a small purchase I engaged the merchant in conversation. There was, at the time, no other customer in the store. We spoke of the weather, the possibility of good crops in the fall, the political situation, the latest news from the war in Europe. As his manner became more and more friendly I ventured to mention guardedly the recent lynchings.

Instantly he became cautious—until I hinted that I had great admiration for the manly spirit the men of the town had exhibited. I mentioned the newspaper accounts I had read and confessed that I had never been so fortunate as to see a lynching. My words or tone seemed to disarm his suspicions. He offered me a box on which to sit, drew up another one for himself, and gave me a bottle of Coca-Cola.

"You'll pardon me, Mister," he began, "for seeming suspicious but we have to be careful. In ordinary times we wouldn't have anything to worry about, but with the war there's been some talk of the Federal government looking into lynchings. It seems there's some sort of law during wartime making it treason to lower the man power of the country."

"In that case I don't blame you for being careful," I assured him. "But couldn't the Federal government do something if it wanted to when a lynching takes place, even if no war is going on at the moment?"

"Naw," he said, confidently, obviously proud of the opportunity of displaying his store of information to one who he assumed knew nothing whatever about the subject. "There's no such law, in spite of all the agitation by a lot of fools who don't know the niggers as we do. States' rights won't permit Congress to meddle in lynching in peace time."

"But what about your State government—your Governor, your sheriff, your police officers?"

"Humph! Them? We elected them to office, didn't we? And the niggers, we've got them disfranchised, ain't we? Sheriffs and police and Governors and prosecuting attorneys have got too much sense to mix in lynching-bees. If they do they know they might as well give up all idea of running for office any more—if something worse don't happen to them—" This last with a tightening of the lips and a hard look in the eyes.

I sought to lead the conversation into less dangerous channels. "Who was the white man who was killed—whose killing caused the lynchings?" I asked.

"Oh, he was a hard one, all right. Never paid his debts to white men or niggers and wasn't liked much around here. He was a mean 'un all right, all right."

"Why, then, did you lynch the niggers for killing such a man?"

"It's a matter of safety—we gotta show niggers that they mustn't touch a white man, no matter how low-down and ornery he is."

Little by little he revealed the whole story. When he told of the manner in which the pregnant woman had been killed he chuckled and slapped his thigh and declared it to be "the best show, Mister, I ever did see. You ought to have heard the wench howl when we strung her up."

Covering the nausea the story caused me as best I could, I slowly gained the whole story, with the names of the other participants. Among them were prosperous farmers, business men, bankers, newspaper reporters and editors, and several law-enforcement officers.

My several days of discreet inquiry began to arouse suspicions in the town. On the third day of my stay I went once more into the store of the man with whom I had first talked. He asked me to wait until he had finished serving the sole customer. When she had gone he came from behind the counter and with secretive manner and lowered voice he asked, "You're a government man, ain't you?" (An agent of the Federal Department of Justice was what he meant.)

"Who said so?" I countered.

"Never mind who told me; I know one when I see him," he replied, with a shrewd harshness in his face and voice.

Ignorant of what might have taken place since last I had talked with him, I thought it wise to learn all I could and say nothing which might commit me. "Don't you tell anyone I am a government man; if I *am* one, you're the only one in town who knows it," I told him cryptically. I knew that within an hour everybody in town would share this "information."

An hour or so later I went at nightfall to the little but not uncomfortable hotel where I was staying. As I was about to enter a Negro approached me and, with an air of great mystery, told me that he had just heard a group of white men discussing me and declaring that if I remained in the town overnight "something would happen" to me.

The thought raced through my mind before I replied that it was hardly likely that, following so terrible a series of lynchings, a Negro would voluntarily approach a supposedly white man whom he did not know and deliver such a message. He had been sent, and no doubt the persons who sent him were white and for some reason did not dare tackle me themselves. Had they dared there would have been no warning in advance—

simply an attack. Though I had no weapon with me, it occurred to me that there was no reason why two should not play at the game of bluffing. I looked straight into my informant's eyes and said: "You go back to the ones who sent you and tell them this: that I have a damned good automatic and I know how to use it. If anybody attempts to molest me tonight or any other time, somebody is going to get hurt."

That night I did not take off my clothes nor did I sleep. Ordinarily in such small Southern towns everyone is snoring by nine o'clock. That night, however, there was much passing and re-passing of the hotel. I learned afterward that the merchant had, as I expected, told generally that I was an agent of the Department of Justice, and my empty threat had served to reinforce his assertion. The Negro had been sent to me in the hope that I might be frightened enough to leave before I had secured evidence against the members of the mob. I remained in the town two more days. My every movement was watched, but I was not molested. But when, later, it became known that not only was I not an agent of the Department of Justice but a Negro, the fury of the inhabitants of the region was unlimited—particularly when it was found that evidence I gathered had been placed in the hands of the Governor of Georgia. It happened that he was a man genuinely eager to stop lynching—but restrictive laws against which he had appealed in vain effectively prevented him from acting upon the evidence. And the Federal government declared itself unable to proceed against the lynchers.

An amusing tale is connected with the charge of passing. Many years ago a bill was introduced in the Legislature of that State defining legally as a Negro any person who had one drop or more of Negro blood. Acrimonious debate in the lower house did not prevent passage of the measure, and the same result seemed likely in the State Senate. One of the Senators, a man destined eventually to go to the United States Senate on a campaign of vilification of the Negro, rose at a strategic point to speak on the bill.

As the story goes, his climax was: "If you go on with this bill you will bathe every county in blood before nightfall. And, what's more, there won't be enough white people left in the State to pass it."

When the sheriff threatened me with an indictment for passing as white, a white man in the State with whom I had talked wrote me a long letter asking me if it were true that I had Negro blood. "You did not tell me nor any one else in my presence," he wrote, "that you were white except as to your name. I had on amber-colored glasses and did not take the trouble to scrutinize your color, but I really did take you for a white man and, according to the laws of ——, you may be." My informant urged me to sit down and figure out mathematically the exact percentage of Negro blood that I possessed and, if it proved to be less than one-eighth, to sue for libel those who had charged me with passing.

This man wrote of the frantic efforts of the whites of his State to keep themselves thought of as white. He quoted an old law to the effect that "it was not slander to call one a Negro because everybody could see that he was not; but it was slanderous to call him a mulatto."

On another occasion a serious race riot occurred in Tulsa, Oklahoma, a bustling town of 100,000 inhabitants. In the early days Tulsa had been a lifeless and unimportant village of not more than five thousand people, and its Negro residents had been forced to live in what was considered the least desirable section of the village, down near the railroad. Then oil was discovered nearby and almost overnight the village grew into a prosperous town. The Negroes prospered along with the whites, and began to erect comfortable homes, business establishments, a hotel, two cinemas and other enterprises, all of these springing up in the section to which they had been relegated. This was, as I have said, down near the railroad tracks. The swift growth of the town made this hitherto disregarded land of great value for business purposes. Efforts to purchase the land from the Negro owners at prices far below its value were unavailing. Having built up the neighborhood and knowing its value, the owners refused to be victimized.

One afternoon in 1921 a Negro messenger boy went to deliver a package in an office building on the main street of Tulsa. His errand done, he rang the bell for the elevator in order that he might descend. The operator, a young white girl, on finding that she had been summoned by a Negro, opened the door of the car ungraciously. Two versions there are of what happened then. The boy declared that she started the car on its downward plunge when he was only halfway in, and that to save himself from being killed he had to throw himself into the car, stepping on the girl's foot in doing so. The girl, on the other hand, asserted that the boy attempted to rape her in the elevator. The latter story, at best, seemed highly dubious—that an attempted criminal assault would be made by any person in an open elevator of a crowded office building on the main street of a town of 100,000 inhabitants—and in open daylight!

Whatever the truth, the local press, with scant investigation, published lurid accounts of the alleged assault. That night a mob started to the jail to lynch the Negro boy. A group of Negroes offered their services to the jailer and sheriff in protecting the prisoner. The offer was declined, and when the Negroes started to leave the sheriff's office a clash occurred between them and the mob. Instantly the mob swung into action.

The Negroes, outnumbered, were forced back to their own neighborhood. Rapidly the news spread of the clash and the numbers of mobbers grew hourly. By daybreak of the following day the mob numbered around five thousand, and was armed with machine-guns, dynamite, rifles, revolvers and shotguns, cans of gasoline and kerosene, and—such are the blessings of invention!—airplanes. Surrounding the Negro section, it attacked, led by men who had been officers in the American army in France. Out-numbered and out-equipped, the plight of the Negroes was a hopeless one from the beginning. Driven further and further back, many of them were killed or wounded, among them an aged man and his wife, who were slain as they knelt at prayer for deliverance. Forty-four blocks of property were burned after homes and stores had been pillaged.

I arrived in Tulsa while the excitement was at its peak. Within a few hours I met a commercial photographer who had worked for five years on a New York newspaper and he welcomed me with open arms when he found that I represented a New York paper. From him I learned that special deputy sheriffs were being sworn in to guard the town from a rumored counter attack by the Negroes. It occurred to me that I could get myself sworn in as one of these deputies.

It was even easier to do this than I had expected. That evening in the City Hall I had to answer only three questions—name, age, and address. I might have been a thug, a murderer, an escaped convict, a member of the mob itself which had laid waste a large area of the city—none of these mattered; my skin was apparently white, and that was enough. After we—some fifty or sixty of us—had been sworn in, solemnly declaring we would do our utmost to uphold the laws and constitutions of the United States and the State of Oklahoma, a villainous-looking man next to me turned and remarked casually, even with a note of happiness in his voice: "Now you can go out and shoot any nigger you see and the law'll be behind you."

As we stood in the wide marble corridor of the not unimposing City Hall waiting to be assigned to automobiles which were to patrol the city during the night, I noticed a man, clad in the uniform of a captain of the United States Army, watching me closely. I imagined I saw in his very swarthy face (he was much darker than I, but was classed as a white man while I am deemed a Negro) mingled inquiry and hostility. I kept my eye on him without appearing to do so. Tulsa would not have been a very healthy place for me that night had my race or my previous investigations of other race riots been known there. At last the man seemed certain he knew me and started toward me.

He drew me aside into a deserted corner on the excuse that he had something he wished to ask me, and I noticed that four other men, with whom he had been talking, detached themselves from the crowd and followed us.

Without further introduction or apology my dark-skinned, newly made acquaintance, putting his face close to mine and looking into my eyes with a steely, unfriendly glance, demanded challengingly:

"You say that your name is White?"

I answered affirmatively.

"You say you're a newspaper man?"

"Yes, I represent the New York ——. Would you care to see my credentials?"

"No, but I want to tell you something. There's an organization in the South that doesn't love niggers. It has branches everywhere. You needn't ask me the name—I can't tell you. But it has come back into existence to fight this damned nigger Advancement Association. We watch every movement of the officers of this nigger society and we're out to get them for putting notions of equality into the heads of our niggers down South here."

There could be no question that he referred to the Ku Klux Klan on the one hand and the National Association for the Advancement of Colored People on the other. As coolly as I could, the circumstances being what they were, I took a cigarette from my case and lighted it, trying to keep my hand from betraying my nervousness. When he finished speaking I asked him:

"All this is very interesting, but what, if anything, has it to do with the story of the race riot here which I've come to get?"

For a full minute we looked straight into each other's eyes, his four companions meanwhile crowding close about us. At length his eyes fell. With a shrug of his shoulders and a half-apologetic smile, he replied as he turned away, "Oh, nothing, except I wanted you to know what's back of the trouble here."

It is hardly necessary to add that all that night, assigned to the same car with this man

and his four companions, I maintained a considerable vigilance. When the news stories I wrote about the riot (the boy accused of attempted assault was acquitted in the magistrate's court after nearly one million dollars of property and a number of lives had been destroyed) revealed my identity—that I was a Negro and an officer of the Advancement Society—more than a hundred anonymous letters threatening my life came to me. I was also threatened with a suit for criminal libel by a local paper, but nothing came of it after my willingness to defend it was indicated.

A narrow escape came during an investigation of an alleged plot by Negroes in Arkansas to "massacre" all the white people of the State. It later developed that the Negroes had simply organized a coöperative society to combat their economic exploitation by landlords, merchants, and bankers, many of whom openly practiced peonage. I went as a representative of a Chicago newspaper to get the facts. Going first to the capital of the State, Little Rock, I interviewed the Governor and other officials and then proceeded to the scene of the trouble, Phillips county, in the heart of the cotton-raising area, close to the Mississippi.

As I stepped from the train at Elaine, the county seat, I was closely watched by a crowd of men. Within half an hour of my arrival I had been asked by two shopkeepers, a restaurant waiter, and a ticket agent why I had come to Elaine, what my business was, and what I thought of the recent riot. The tension relaxed somewhat when I implied I was in sympathy with the mob. Little by little suspicion was lessened and then, the people being eager to have a metropolitan newspaper give their side of the story, I was shown "evidence" that the story of the massacre plot was well-founded, and not very clever attempts were made to guide me away from the truth.

Suspicion was given new birth when I pressed my inquiries too insistently concerning the share-cropping and tenant-farming system, which works somewhat as follows: Negro farmers enter into agreements to till specified plots of land, they to receive usually half of the crop for their labor. Should they be too poor to buy food, seed, clothing and other supplies, they are supplied these commodities by their landlords at designated stores. When the crop is gathered the landowner takes it and sells it. By declaring that he has sold it at a figure far below the market price and by refusing to give itemized accounts of the supplies purchased during the year by the tenant, a landlord can (and in that region almost always does) so arrange it that the bill for supplies always exceeds the tenant's share of the crop. Individual Negroes who had protested against such thievery had been lynched. The new organization was simply a union to secure relief through the courts, which relief those who profited from the system meant to prevent. Thus the story of a "massacre" plot.

Suspicion of me took definite form when word was sent to Phillips county from Little Rock that it had been discovered that I was a Negro, though I knew nothing about the message at the time. I walked down West Cherry Street, the main thoroughfare of Elaine, one day on my way to the jail, where I had an appointment with the sheriff, who was going to permit me to interview some of the Negro prisoners who were charged with being im-

plicated in the alleged plot. A tall, heavy-set Negro passed me and, *sotto voce,* told me as he passed that he had something important to tell me, and that I should turn to the right at the next corner and follow him. Some inner sense bade me obey. When we had got out of sight of other persons the Negro told me not to go to the jail, that there was great hostility in the town against me and that they planned harming me. In the man's manner there was something which made me certain he was telling the truth. Making my way to the railroad station, since my interview with the prisoners (the sheriff and jailer being present), was unlikely to add anything to my story, I was able to board one of the two trains a day out of Elaine. When I explained to the conductor—he looked at me so inquiringly—that I had no ticket because delays in Elaine had given me no time to purchase one, he exclaimed, "Why, Mister, you're leaving just when the fun is going to start! There's a damned yaller nigger down here passing for white and the boys are going to have some fun with him."

I asked him the nature of the fun.

"Wal, when they get through with him," he explained grimly, "he won't pass for white no more."

Letters of Black Migrants

Carter G. Woodson, Editor

Mobile, Ala., 4–26–17

Dear Sir Bro.: I take great pane in droping you a few lines hopeing that this will find you enjoying the best of health as it leave me at this time present. Dear sir I seen in the Defender where you was helping us a long in se-

curing a posission as brickmason plaster cementers stone mason. I am writing to you for advice about comeing north. I am a brickmason an I can do cement work an stone work. I written to a firm in Birmingham an they sent me a blank stateing $2.00 would get me a ticket an pay 10 per ct of my salary for the 1st month and $24.92c would be paid after I reach Detorit and went to work where they sent me to work. I had to stay there until I pay them

---

Source: Letters of Black Migrants. In Carter G. Woodson Collection, Library of Congress.

the sum of $24.92c so I want to leave Mobile for there. if there nothing there for me to make a support for my self and family. My wife is seamstress. We want to get away the 15 or 20 of May so please give this matter your earnest consideration an let me hear from you by return mail as my bro. in law want to get away to. He is a carpenter by trade. so please help us as we are in need of your help as we wanted to go to Detroit but if you says no we go where ever you sends us until we can get to Detroit. We expect to do whatever you says. There is nothing here for the colored man but a hard time wich these southern crackers gives us. We has not had any work to do in 4 wks. and every thing is high to the colored man so please let me hear from you by return mail. Please do this for your brother.

Greenville, S.C., April 29, 1917

Dear Sir: I would like for you to write me and tell me how is time up there and jobs is to get. I would like for you to get me a job and my wife. She is a no. 1 cook, maid, nurse job I am a fireing boiler, steame fitter and experiences mechencs helpe and will do laboring work if you can not get me one off those jobs above that i can do. I have work in a foundry as a molder helper and has lots of experense at that. I am 27 yrs of age. If you can get me job I would like for you to do so please and let me no and will pay for trouble. looking to hear from you wright away please if you new off any firm that needs a man give them my address please I wont to get out of the south where I can demand something for my work. I will close.

Houston, Tex., 4–29–17

Dear Sir: I am a constant reader of the "Chicago Defender" and in your last issue I saw a want ad that appealed to me. I am a Negro, age 37, and am an all round foundry man. I am a core maker by trade having had about 10 years experience at the business, and hold good references from several shops, in which I have been employed. I have worked at various shops and I have always been able to make good. It is hard for a black man to hold a job here, as prejudice is very strong. I have never been discharged on account of dissatisfaction with my work, but I have been "let out" on account of my color. I am a good brassmelter but i prefer core making as it is my trade. I have a family and am anxious to leave here, but have not the means, and as wages are not much here, it is very hard to save enough to get away with. If you know of any firms that are in need of a core maker and whom you think would send me transportation, I would be pleased to be put in touch with them and I assure you that effort would be appreciated. I am a core maker but I am willing to do any honest work. All I want is to get away from here. I am writing you and I believe you can and will help me. If any one will send transportation, I will arrange or agree to have it taken out of my salary untill full amount of fare is paid. I also know of several good fdry. men here who would leave in a minute, if there only was a way arranged for them to leave, and they are men whom I know personally to be experienced men. I hope that you will give this your immediate attention as I am anxious to get busy and be on my way. I am ready to start at any time, and would be pleased to hear something favorable.

Mobile, Ala., April 30, 1917

Dear Sir: I was reading in the Chicago defender where They wanted so many men to work. I am very anxious to work. I can do most any kind of work I have been out of a job ever since January. will you please try and get me in Chicago, so that I can be able to get one of those jobs. please get me a job. I have a wife and we can hardly live in this place. I am a machinist by trade. I am a Schauffer also. I can repair an auto to. please send for me at once, as I am in need of work.

My age is 25 years and my wife 21 years. My name is ——.

Grabow, Louisiana, 5/9/17

My dear Sir: your letter to me togeather with information was received and noted carefully from the same I find that work in and about Chicago is not plentiful as agents are makeing out as I know for myself that I have been talked to hard to leave at once for Chicago. I am a carpenter by trade tho I have 10 years experience in the shop. I were under the empression that one would have to join the carpenter's union or machinist union on order to obtain work. Tho I know joining a union would put a stress om me as my straight life policy exemps me from such. Your letter being wrote in paragraphs I Parag 5) you are advising men who knows the molders trade or wanting to learn the machinist trade which are those 4 or 5 cities? Should chances in the same better I would not get as far as Chicago. I am a man of family and contemplated that with my Hudson could drive to Chicago by land in 8 days, but as you advise leaving my family I consider you knows best, tho at present I dont see any enducements at all. $3.00 per day is carpenter wedge in this part of Louisiana for 10 hours and $4.00 machinest. But our chances are so slim. Causes me to be disgusted at the south. Our poll tax paid, state and parish taxes yet with donations we cannot get schools. What do you think of conditions here? Thanking you for your past and in advance for your future information I am verry truly yours.

New Orleans, La., 5–20–17

Dear Sir: I am sure your time is precious, for being as you an editor of a newspaper such as the race has never owned and for which it must proudly bost of as being the peer in the pereoidical world. am confident that yours is a force of busy men. I also feel sure that you will spare a small amount of your time to give some needed information to one who wishes to relieve himselfe of the burden of the south. I indeed wish very much to come north anywhere in Ill. will do since I am away from the Lynchman's noose and torchman's fire. Myself and a friend wish to come but not without information regarding work and general suroundings. Now hon sir if for any reason you are not in position to furnish us with the information desired. please do the act of kindness of placing us in tuch with the organization who's business it is I am told to furnish said information. we are firemen machinist helpers practical painters and general laborers. And most of all, ministers of the gospel who are not afraid of labor for it put us where we are. Please le me hear from you.

Long Old Road

Horace Cayton

When I got off the train I didn't know what to expect. I told a cab driver to take me to the best Negro hotel, and he looked at me quizzically, then drove me to a hotel on Oakwood Boulevard. It was neat and clean but not nearly as large or pretentious as I had expected. Besides, there were girls in the lobby whom I suspected were prostitutes. Vastly disappointed, still I was excited about being in Chicago.

Never had I seen so many Negroes: it came almost as a shock to see so many dark faces. In Seattle I had seen perhaps a hundred or more together at some special affair, but I was unprepared for this sea of black, olive, and brown faces everywhere. On a narrow tongue of land seven miles long and a mile and a half wide were packed more then 300,000 Negroes.

Seemingly, only the variety of colored faces distinguished this section from any other area in the city, but beneath the surface were patterns of life and thought, attitudes, and customs which made it a unique and distinctive community. Understand Chicago's black belt and I would understand the black belts of a dozen other large American cities. To do this became an immediate challenge.

It had first appeared upon the urban checkerboard well over a century ago. Its population grew, but before long it was unable either to expand or to scatter. The section persisted as a city within a city, reflecting in itself the crosscurrents of life in a midwestern metropolis but remaining isolated from the mainstream. As a community it was the end result of a hundred and fifty years of intense competition among native whites, Negroes, and the foreign-born for living space, economic goods, and prestige.

Looking around, I found that the lives of the people were as varied as their faces. There were Negro policemen, Negro restaurants, and hundreds of Negro churches—small churches, large churches, churches of countless denominations. Besides the many orthodox denominations there were many less conventional—the Hebrew Baptist Church, Baptized Believers Holiness Church, a Universal Union Independent Church of Love and Faith, and many others.

In Seattle there had been one colored undertaking establishment; here there were hundreds—large, small, shabby, pretentious. It seemed as if these hundreds of thousands of people of different colors either died or prayed most of the time: along with various beauticians' services, these two activities afforded Negroes their limited possibilities of making big money. I visited the George Cleveland Hall Library, staffed with Negro librarians; and the Provident Hospital with its colored doctors, nurses, and orderlies.

Even the business office of the hospital, which handled the money, was manned by Negroes. And I saw Washington Park, where only Negroes played ball, strolled in pairs, or sat on the grass.

As I walked through other neighborhoods I saw rickety frame dwellings that sprawled along the railroad tracks, bespeaking a way of life at the opposite pole from that of the quiet and well groomed middle-class neighborhoods. I observed still stately old mansions, long since abandoned by Chicago's wealthy whites, impressive at first, but, I was to learn later, concealing interiors that were foul and decayed.

Even more impressive than the faces on the street was the uninhibited spirit of life which surged through the people. This was a city apart from the rest of Chicago, bounded by chains invisible but impenetrable, a city of poverty and overcrowding. But the vigor with which these people lived belied the obvious fact that it was a poverty-stricken ghetto. Negroes were at home here in a way that they never could have been on the streets of downtown Chicago. Here they were away from white folks and they were making the best of it. There was loud talk and the taking of to me unfamiliar and tabooed oaths; friend greeted friend in boisterous, vulgar phrases not meant for white ears.

All this was both familiar and strange. The language and the establishments—such as the churches—were American, but there were subtle differences. These differences came from the concentration of Negroes, which made more spectacular and intense the nature of the fabric of their existence in America. The content of speech and other behavior patterns sprang out of the Negro's American experience—the adjustment to his isolation from the broader aspects of American life, which produced a self-consciousness and an exaggeration of certain national traits. I felt I was finally entering the mainstream of Negro life. There was much that was similar, as well as many things in contrast, to the Mississippi from which my parents had escaped.

One question haunted me: could I feel at home in this fantastic city as crowded as Calcutta, as bizarre as Baghdad? Would I be satisfied within the boundaries of the black belt, this ghetto of the outcast and under-privileged? And what about Bonnie, who would soon join me; what about Bonnie?

This was Chicago in the fall of 1931. The depression had struck this midwestern city a particularly paralyzing blow. People were out of work; many had been ejected from their homes. I did not realize how desperate the situation was until one day, as I sat eating in a small restaurant in the heart of the black belt, I chanced to look out of the window. A number of Negroes were marching by, three abreast, in a long uninterrupted line. What impressed me were their serious and determined faces and their extreme poverty. Not that it was unusual to see poorer Negroes, but this orderly, silent procession, minus the usual loud laughter and good-natured horseplay, this was different. This needed looking into. I decided to join this group of determined men and see what they were up to.

I fell into line and turning to the man marching next to me I asked where we were headed and what we were going to do once we got there. He looked surprised and said that they were going to put back a family who had been evicted for not paying their rent. He said they were going to put an end to people being treated in such fashion.

When we got to the dingy, ill-kept street of houses we found that those who had arrived ahead of us had already put back into the house the few miserable belongings of the woman who had been evicted. She was standing surrounded by the group, intermittently crying and loudly thanking God. Her audience was equally as responsive; they seemed about to break into song. It reminded me of a revival meeting.

Then a roar went up—there was another family on the next street over who were about to be put out. We started off again, and this time I found myself near the head of the procession. We were met at the corner by

two squad cars of police, who asked where we were going. The crowd swarmed around the police cars like bees. The cops jumped out of their cars and ordered the crowd to disperse. No one moved, they simply stood and stared. A policeman lost his head and drew his gun, leveling it at the crowd.

A young Negro stepped out of the crowd. "You can't shoot all of us so you might as well shoot me. I'd as soon die now as any time. All we want is to see that these people get back into their homes. We have no money, no jobs, sometimes no food. We've got to live some place."

The officer stared at the young man, then at the crowd, and the crowd stared back. No threats, no murmurs, no disorder; they just looked at him. There he stood, surrounded by a crowd of dirty, ragged Negroes, a sea of dark eyes watching him. He replaced his gun in its holster.

At the back of the crowd someone got up on a soapbox and began to speak, an old, wild-eyed, haglike woman. The crowd turned to listen as she harangued them about bread, and jobs, and places to sleep. It was as if I had awakened from a pleasant dream to find myself suddenly face to face with hard cold reality.

These people had migrated a few years ago from the South—in wagons, in cars, by train, some even walking. They had left their homes with happy songs and hymns on their lips, full of prayers to the Almighty for their deliverance, and in the North they had been welcomed, for this great pool of un-skilled labor was needed to win the war. But soon the war was over, and before long the good times and prosperity it had brought were over, too. Now hard times had brought real poverty, and they were virtually starving to death.

The crowd stood silently and listened. It had grown larger, and now a few white faces were visible. There was nobody there, white or black, who did not in some degree face the same problem. Even the policemen paid more or less respectful attention. Someone in the crowd asked if they didn't think it was a shame to put someone out in the street. One of the cops answered that it was tough, and that what they were doing didn't make any difference to him so long as they didn't start any trouble.

And then a siren sounded, a far-off whisper at first, then an ugly rising scream.

"Hold your places!" shouted the old woman who was making the speech. "Act like men!"

Most of the spectators melted away, and the active participants formed a small nucleus around the speaker, a solid black ring of people as the riot squad turned in to the street, four prowl cars full of blue-coated police and a paddy wagon. Cops jumped out before the cars had even come to a stop and charged into the crowd, night sticks playing a tatoo on black heads.

"Hold your places!" screamed the old woman on the soapbox.

The crowd stood like dumb beasts—no one ran, no one fought back or offered any resistance. They just stood, an immovable black mass. The police broke through and started to pull the speaker off her box. Clubs came down in a sickening rain of blows on the head of one of the boys who was guarding her. Blood spurted from his mouth and nose, and finally the woman was down. A tremor of nervousness ran through the crowd.

Then someone turned and ran, and in a minute the whole mob was running for cover. One of the police fired two shots in the air; the orator struggled helplessly in the arms of two husky policemen. It was all over in a minute, and all that was left was the soapbox and the struggling black woman. I turned and left.

This was my first encounter with what were later to be called the Unemployed Councils, which were eventually taken over by the Communists. But at this time they were spontaneous uprisings of hungry, desperate people. From them I learned what hunger and desperation could do to men; how it could give them dignity and courage. I had never seen hungry people before. Cruelty and brutality I had experienced, but

never anything like what I came to know in the early days of the depression in Chicago.

All the city suffered from the depression, but the black belt suffered more and differently. The first reaction was panic and a deep sense of frustration, followed by spontaneous, unorganized demonstrations, such as the one I had witnessed. Finally the community began to form some semblance of an organization to meet the impending crisis. A movement was directed against white men who did business in the black belt and hired only white help, and one could see groups of ragged pickets walking in front of chain stores, the beginning of a movement which stirred the community as nothing had since the race riot. A Negro newspaper, risking reprisal from white advertisers, politicians, and mortgage holders, became the aggressive spokesman for the "Spend Your Money Where You Can Work" campaign, a boycott against all white businesses in the black belt which would not employ Negroes.

The movement had some minor success; the Woolworth stores, which for a time stubbornly resisted the pressure, finally hired twenty-one Negro girls, later raising the proportion of colored employees in all stores in Negro neighborhoods to twenty-five per cent. But of these feeble efforts to meet mass unemployment the Communists, who were becoming more active and vocal:

> The triviality of this proposal [Spend Your Money Where You Can Work] is obvious on the face of it. It is indeed possible on occasion to kick up a row big enough to force a Woolworth store in Chicago to make a promise. But what has this to do with hundreds of thousands of Negro workers in the coal, iron, steel, oil, automobile and packing industries?

For many this was a hard argument to counter, yet the Spend Your Money campaign had a strong emotional appeal and was actively supported by many churches. It did open up a few hundred white-collar jobs, though it did not solve the problem of the unemployed thousands. Negroes watched white artisans coming into their neighborhood to work or white maintenance workers repairing streets and streetcar tracks in the black belt, and their resentment deepened.

On one occasion this antagonism exploded with dramatic violence. A mob of unemployed Negroes attacked a group of white laborers who were laying a streetcar track and chased them from the site. The Negroes then refused to leave until the mayor, our colored congressman, and several traction officials assured them that colored laborers would get their share of work. There were reports that this demonstration was the work of the Communists, but most people realized that it was a truly spontaneous expression of resentment.

The Communists became still more active, and the Unemployed Councils, which they by then dominated, began to demand more adequate relief. Violence increased, and on one occasion several thousand people marched to a house in a poverty-stricken neighborhood to forestall an eviction. By the time the police arrived there were at least five thousand people on hand, and they refused to be dispersed. There was scuffling, guns blazed, and three Negroes lay dead on the pavement. By nightfall fifty thousand leaflets had been distributed throughout the black belt—DEMAND THE DEATH PENALTY FOR THE MURDERS OF THE WORKERS! There followed a massive funeral demonstration in which both whites and Negroes participated.

Chicago was frightened. If it had been a race riot it would have been understandable; Chicago had had them before. But the funeral and the mass meetings that followed were attended by both Negroes and whites. A race riot, or worse, a Communist-led revolution, seemed imminent, the city officials decided. The Renters' Court immediately suspended all evictions, and both city and state began to make comprehensive plans for a relief program. By demonstrating their discontent, Negroes had set in motion a chain of events that was to benefit the entire city.

Then came Roosevelt, and the chaotic turbulence of the early Thirties began to subside. Various New Deal measures went into effect; relief and work projects helped stabilize the Negro community. The Communists continued to attract large crowds at their meetings, but their behavior became more disciplined; it was limited to protests against relief cuts and demands for social security, an end to all discrimination, and for more federal housing projects. More important were the happenings in the labor movement, where John L. Lewis withdrew from the A.F.L. to found the C.I.O. and organize the mass-production industries, realistically including Negroes as union members.

Negroes continued to flock to Chicago from the Deep South, and the conditions of poverty, bad housing, poor health, and crime continued. But there were some definite changes as a result of the depression. For one thing, Negroes left the Republican party in large numbers. The Negro South Side became a solid New Deal town, and Negroes were firmly established in the labor movement. But more important, black citizens of Chicago discovered new ways of letting the city know that they were restive about the conditions under which they were forced to live. The black belt would never, and could never, be quite the same again.

Meanwhile, Bonnie had joined me, and I had begun work at the University of Chicago. My work in the Social Science Division was exciting, especially the sociology department, which was using the city as a laboratory to study urban life. As a result of its many studies more became known about the sprawling metropolis of Chicago—how it was run, how it loved, stole, helped, gave, cheated, and even killed—than perhaps any city in the world. In no other place had social scientists studied a locality so intensively. Under the direction of Robert E. Park and Ernest Burgess, the statistics of economic organization, social stratification, and the dynamics of population movement were compiled and charted in a manner which has never been equaled.

There also began to emerge a new Chicago school of writers. Its forerunners were Carl Sandburg, Sherwood Anderson, Edgar Lee Masters, Floyd Dell, Ben Hecht, and Theodore Dreiser. These writers were investigating the city much as the sociologists were doing. James T. Farrell wrote realistically of Chicago's Irish population; Albert Halper depicted the Jewish citizens' attempts to be taken into the mainstream of the city's culture; and Nelson Algren produced a sensitive and penetrating analysis of the Poles in the city jungles of the near North Side. But it was Richard Wright's *Native Son,* the study of a black boy who couldn't adjust to the white world's impossible demands, that made the greatest impact of all.

Stimulated by this atmosphere of investigation, I was determined to learn all there was to know about the Negro community. The huge South Side black belt fascinated, frightened, and haunted me with its crime, disease, local color, and vitality; I eagerly, responded to its jazz and rocking gospel music. No one really knew the whys and wherefores of this isolated island of color where people died from tuberculosis seven times faster than did whites, a seat of grinding poverty which still had a verve and vitality that white people secretly envied.

My first research job was to study, under the direction of Dr. Harold Gossnell, the Negro politician; my special assignment, to interview Negro policemen. This took me to police precinct stations and into the homes of black policemen from the rank of patrolman to lieutenant. It also made me aware for the first time of the ramifications of the numbers rackets, which reached out beyond the black belt to the offices of the mayor, the governor, and perhaps even beyond.

I knew policemen, through my law enforcement experience in Seattle, and I was comfortable in my work. I sat in the kitchens of honest and efficient Negro officers and in the luxurious apartments of corrupt Negro cops who were stashing away fortunes from "policy" and the other forms of graft permitted and even encouraged by the Kelly-Nash political machine.

I was most fascinated by the older officers who had been on the force for many years, for they had come as refugees from the South like my father. Some had succeeded and were retired, living comfortable lives in middle-class neighborhoods. Others had failed to adjust to city life, though they were in the minority, and it was to them that I was drawn, for in their lives one saw clearly the stresses and strains which accompany a change from peasant life in the South to urban existence in this jungle of concrete and steel.

We enjoyed a pleasant social life around the university, and had found a cheap but pleasant apartment. At the University of Washington, where I was one of three Negro students, I had been completely isolated. It was different at Chicago. I had a great many friends, most of them in the graduate school. My marriage to Bonnie was no handicap. But Bonnie and I soon began to move in different circles. She had gotten a job as a social worker with the United Charities and had formed friendships among her fellow workers. I thought of myself as a "pure scientist" and looked down on social workers, associating mostly with the university crowd, with whom Bonnie felt intellectually insecure. . . .

The Negro in Chicago: A Study of Race Relations and a Race Riot

Chicago Commission on Race Relations

BACKGROUND

In July, 1919, a race riot involving whites and Negroes occurred in Chicago. For some time thoughtful citizens, white and Negro, had sensed increasing tension, but, having no local precedent of riot and wholesale bloodshed, had neither prepared themselves for it nor taken steps to prevent it. The collecting of arms by members of both races was known to the authorities, and it was evident that this was in preparation for aggression as well as for self-defense.

Several minor clashes preceded the riot. On July 3, 1917, a white saloon-keeper who, according to the coroner's physician, died of heart trouble, was incorrectly reported in the press to have been killed by a Negro. That evening a party of young white men riding in an automobile fired upon a group of Negroes at Fifty-third and Federal streets. In July and August of the same year recruits from the Great Lakes Naval Training Station clashed frequently with Negroes, each side accusing the other of being the aggressor.

Gangs of white "toughs," made up largely of the membership of so-called athletic clubs from the neighborhood between Roosevelt Road and Sixty-third Street, Wentworth Avenue and the city limits—a district contiguous to the neighborhood of the largest Negro settlement—were a constant menace to Negroes who traversed sections of the territory going to and returning from work. The activities of these gangs and athletic clubs became bolder in the spring of 1919, and on the night of June 21, five weeks before the riot, two wanton murders of Negroes occurred, those of Sanford Harris and Joseph Robinson. Harris, returning to his home on Dearborn Street at about 11:30 at night, passed a group of young white men. They threatened him and he ran. He had gone but a short distance when one of the group shot him. He died soon afterward. Policemen who came on the scene made no arrests, even when the assailant was pointed out by a white woman witness of the murder. On the same evening Robinson, a Negro laborer, forty-seven years of age, was attacked while returning from work by a gang of white "toughs" at Fifty-fifth Street and Princeton Avenue, apparently without provocation, and stabbed to death.

Negroes were greatly incensed over these murders, but their leaders, joined by many friendly whites, tried to allay their fears and counseled patience.

After the killing of Harris and Robinson, notices were conspicuously posted on the South Side that an effort would be made to "get all the niggers on July 4th" The notices called for help from sympathizers. Negroes, in turn, whispered around the warning to prepare for a riot; and they did prepare.

Since the riot in East St. Louis, July 4, 1917, there had been others in different parts of the country which evidenced a widespread lack of restraint in mutual antipathies and suggested further resorts to lawlessness. Riots and race clashes occurred in Chester, Pennsylvania; Longview, Texas; Coatesville, Pennsylvania; Washington, D. C.; and Norfolk, Virginia, before the Chicago riot.

Source: From *The Chicago Commission on Race Relations*, The Negro in Chicago: A Study of Race Relations and a Race Riot (Chicago: University of Chicago Press 1922).

Aside from general lawlessness and disastrous riots that preceded the riot here discussed, there were other factors which may be mentioned briefly here. In Chicago considerable unrest had been occasioned in industry by increasing competition between white and Negro laborers following a sudden increase in the Negro population due to the migration of Negroes from the South. This increase developed a housing crisis. The Negroes overran the hitherto recognized area of Negro residence, and when they took houses in adjoining neighborhoods friction ensued. In the two years just preceding the riot, twenty-seven Negro dwellings were wrecked by bombs thrown by unidentified persons.

STORY OF THE RIOT

Sunday afternoon, July 27, 1919, hundreds of white and Negro bathers crowded the lakefront beaches at Twenty-sixth and Twenty-ninth streets. This is the eastern boundary of the thickest Negro residence area. At Twenty-sixth Street Negroes were in great majority; at Twenty-ninth Street there were more whites. An imaginary line in the water separating the two beaches had been generally observed by the two races. Under the prevailing relations, aided by wild rumors and reports, this line served virtually as a challenge to either side to cross it. Four Negroes who attempted to enter the water from the "white" side were driven away by the whites. They returned with more Negroes, and there followed a series of attacks with stones, first one side gaining the advantage, then the other.

Eugene Williams, a Negro boy of seventeen, entered the water from the side used by Negroes and drifted across the line supported by a railroad tie. He was observed by the crowd on the beach and promptly became a target for stones. He suddenly released the tie, went down and was drowned. Guilt was immediately placed on Stauber, a young white man, by Negro witnesses who declared that he threw the fatal stone.*

White and Negro men dived for the boy without result. Negroes demanded that the policeman present arrest Stauber. He refused; and at this crucial moment arrested a Negro on a white man's complaint. Negroes then attacked the officer. These two facts, the drowning and the refusal of the policeman to arrest Stauber, together marked the beginning of the riot.

Two hours after the drowning, a Negro, James Crawford, fired into a group of officers summoned by the policeman at the beach and was killed by a Negro policeman. Reports and rumors circulated rapidly, and new crowds began to gather. Five white men were injured in clashes near the beach. As darkness came, Negroes in white districts to the west suffered severely. Between 9:00 P.M. and 3:00 A.M. twenty-seven Negroes were beaten, seven stabbed, and four shot. Monday morning was quiet, and Negroes went to work as usual.

Returning from work in the afternoon, many Negroes were attacked by white ruffians. Streetcar routes, especially at transfer points, were the centers of lawlessness. Trolleys were pulled from the wires, and Negro passengers were dragged into the street, beaten, stabbed, and shot. The police were powerless to cope with these numerous assaults. During Monday, four Negro men and one white assailant were killed, and thirty Negroes were severely beaten in streetcar clashes. Four white men were killed, six stabbed, five shot, and nine severely beaten. It was rumored that the white occupants of the Angelus Building at Thirty-fifth Street and Wabash Avenue had shot a Negro. Negroes gathered about the building. The white tenants sought police protection, and one hundred policemen, mounted and on

---

*The coroner's jury found that Williams had drowned from fear of stone-throwing which kept him from the shore.

foot, responded. In a clash with the mob, the police killed four Negroes and injured many.

Raids into the Negro residence area then began. Automobiles sped through the streets, the occupants shooting at random. Negroes retaliated by "sniping" from ambush. At midnight surface and elevated car service was discontinued because of a strike for wage increases, and thousands of employees were cut off from work.

On Tuesday, July 29, Negro men en route on foot to their jobs through hostile territory were killed. White soldiers and sailors in uniform, aided by civilians, raided the "Loop" business section, killing two Negroes and beating and robbing several others. Negroes living among white neighbors in Englewood, far to the south, were driven from their homes, their household goods were stolen, and their houses were burned or wrecked. On the West Side an Italian mob, excited by a false rumor that an Italian girl had been shot by a Negro, killed Joseph Lovings, a Negro.

Wednesday night at 10:30 Mayor Thompson yielded to pressure and asked the help of the three regiments of militia which had been stationed in nearby armories during the most severe rioting, awaiting the call. They immediately took up positions throughout the South Side. A rainfall Wednesday night and Thursday kept many people in their homes, and by Friday the rioting had abated. On Saturday incendiary fires burned forty-nine houses in the immigrant neighborhood west of the Stock Yards. Nine hundred and forty-eight people, mostly Lithuanians, were made homeless, and the property loss was about $250,000. Responsibility for the fires was never fixed.

The total casualties of this reign of terror were thirty-eight deaths—fifteen white, twenty-three Negro—and 537 people injured. Forty-one per cent of the reported clashes occurred in the white neighborhood near the Stock Yards between the south branch of the Chicago River and Fifty-fifth Street, Wentworth Avenue and the city limits, and 34 per cent in the "Black Belt" between Twenty-second and Thirty-ninth streets, Wentworth Avenue and Lake Michigan. Others were scattered.

Responsibility for many attacks was definitely placed by many witnesses upon the "athletic clubs," including "Ragen's Colts," the "Hamburgers," "Aylwards," "Our Flag," the "Standard," the "Sparklers," and several others. The mobs were made up for the most part of boys between fifteen and twenty-two. Older persons participated but the youth of the rioters was conspicuous in every clash. Little children witnessed the brutalities and frequently pointed out the injured when the police arrived.

RUMORS AND THE RIOT

Wild rumors were in circulation by word of mouth and in the press throughout the riot and provoked many clashes. These included stories of atrocities committed by one race against the other. Reports of the numbers of white and Negro dead tended to produce a feeling that the score must be kept even. Newspaper reports, for example, showed 6 per cent more whites injured than Negroes. As a matter of fact, there were 28 per cent more Negroes injured than whites. The *Chicago Tribune* on July 29 reported twenty persons killed, of whom thirteen were white and seven colored. The true figures were exactly the opposite.

Among the rumors provoking fear were numerous references to the arming of Negroes. In the *Daily News* of July 30, for example, appeared the subheadline: "Alderman Jos. McDonough tells how he was shot at on South Side visit. Says enough ammunition in section to last for years of guerrilla warfare." In the article following, the reference to ammunition was repeated but not elaborated or explained.

The alderman was quoted as saying that the mayor contemplated opening up Thirty-fifth and Forty-seventh streets in order that colored people might get to their work. He thought this would be most unwise for, he stated, "They are armed and white people are not. We must defend ourselves if the city authorities won't protect us." Continuing his story, he described bombs going off: "I saw white men and women running through the streets dragging children by the hands and carrying babies in their arms. Frightened white men told me the police captains had just rushed through the district crying, 'For God's sake, arm; they are coming; we cannot hold them.'"

Whether or not the alderman was correctly quoted, the effect of such statements on the public was the same. There is no record in any of the riot testimony in the coroner's office or state's attorney's office of any bombs going off during the riot, nor of police captains warning the white people to arm, nor of any fear by whites of a Negro invasion. In the Berger Odman case before a coroner's jury, there was a statement to the effect that a sergeant of police warned the Negroes of Ogden Park to arm and to shoot at the feet of rioters if they attempted to invade the few blocks marked off for Negroes by the police. Negroes were warned, not whites.

CONDUCT OF THE POLICE

Chief of Police John J. Garrity, in explaining the inability of the police to curb the rioters, said that there was not a sufficient force to police one-third of the city. Aside from this, Negroes distrusted the white police officers, and it was implied by the chief and stated by State's Attorney Hoyne, that many of the police were "grossly unfair in making arrests." There were instances of actual police participation in the rioting as well as neglect of duty. Of 229 persons arrested and accused of various criminal activities during the riot, 154 were Negroes and seventy-five were whites. Of those indicted, eighty-one were Negroes and forty-seven were whites. Although this, on its face, would indicate great riot activity on the part of Negroes, further

reports of clashes show that of 520 persons injured. 342 were Negroes and 178 were whites. The fact that twice as many Negroes appeared as defendants and twice as many Negroes as whites were injured leads to the conclusion that whites were not apprehended as readily as Negroes.

Many of the depredations outside the "Black Belt" were encouraged by the absence of policemen. Out of a force of 3,000 police, 2,800 were massed in the "Black Belt" during the height of the rioting. In the "Loop" district, where two Negroes were killed and several others wounded, there were only three policemen and one sergeant. The Stock Yards district, where the greatest number of injuries occurred, was also weakly protected.

THE MILITIA

Although Governor Lowden had ordered the militia into the city promptly and they were on hand on the second day of the rioting, their services were not requested by the mayor and chief of police until the evening of the fourth day. The reason expressed by the chief for this delay was a belief that inexperienced militiamen would add to the deaths and disorder. But the troops, when called, proved to be clearly of high character, and their discipline was good, not a case of breach of discipline being reported during their occupation. They were distributed more proportionately through all the riotous areas than the police and, although they reported some hostility from members of "athletic clubs," the rioting soon ceased.

RESTORATION OF ORDER

Throughout the rioting, various social organizations and many citizens were at work trying to hold hostilities in check and to restore order. The Chicago Urban League, Wabash Avenue Y.M.C.A., American Red Cross, and various other social organizations and the churches of the Negro community gave attention to caring for stranded Negroes, advising them of dangers, keeping them off the streets and, in such ways as were possible, co-operating with the police. The packing companies took their pay to Negro employees, and various banks made loans. Local newspapers in their editorial columns insistently condemned the disorder and counseled calmness.

THE AFTERMATH

Of the thirty-eight persons killed in the riot:

Fifteen met death at the hands of mobs. Coroner's juries recommended that the members of the unknown mobs be apprehended. They were never found.

Six were killed in circumstances fixing no criminal responsibility: three white men were killed by Negroes in self-defense, and three Negroes were shot by policemen in the discharge of their duty.

Four Negroes were killed in the Angelus riot. The coroner made no recommendations, and the cases were not carried farther.

Four cases, two Negro and two white, resulted in recommendations from coroner's juries for further investigation of certain persons. Sufficient evidence was lacking for indictments against them.

Nine cases led to indictments. Of this number four cases resulted in convictions.

Thus in only four cases of death was criminal responsibility fixed and punishment meted out.

Indictments and convictions, divided according to the race of the persons criminally involved, were as follows:

	Negro		White	
	Cases	Persons	Cases	Persons
Indictments	6	17	3	4
Convictions	2	3	2	2

Despite the community's failure to deal firmly with those who disturbed its peace and contributed to the reign of lawlessness that shamed Chicago before the world, there is evidence that the riot aroused many citizens of both races to a quickened sense of the suffering and disgrace which had come and might again come to the city, and developed a determination to prevent a recurrence of so disastrous an outbreak of race hatred. This was manifest on at least three occasions in 1920 when, confronted suddenly with events out of which serious riots might easily have grown, people of both races acted with such courage and promptness as to end the trouble early. One of these was the murder of two innocent white men and the wounding of a Negro policeman by a band of Negro fanatics who styled themselves "Abyssinians"; another was the killing of a white man by a Negro whom he had attacked while returning from work; and still another was the riotous attacks of sailors from the Great Lakes Naval Training Station on Negroes in Waukegan, Illinois.

OUTSTANDING FEATURES OF THE RIOT

This study of the facts of the riot of 1919, the events as they happened hour by hour, the neighborhoods involved, the movements of mobs, the part played by rumors, and the handling of the emergency by the various authorities, shows certain outstanding features which may be listed as follows:

a. The riot violence was not continuous hour by hour, but was intermittent.

b. The greatest number of injuries occurred in the district west and inclusive of Wentworth Avenue, and south of the south branch of the Chicago River to Fifty-fifth Street, or in the Stock Yards district. The next greatest number occurred in the so-called Black Belt: Twenty-second to Thirty-ninth streets, inclusive, and Wentworth Avenue to the lake, exclusive of Wentworth Avenue; Thirty-ninth to Fifty-fifth streets, inclusive, and Clark Street to Michigan Avenue, exclusive of Michigan Avenue.

c. Organized raids occurred only after a period of sporadic clashes and spontaneous mob outbreaks.

d. Main thoroughfares witnessed 76 per cent of the injuries on the South Side. The streets which suffered most severely were State, Halsted, Thirty-first, Thirty-fifth, and Forty-seventh. Transfer corners were always centers of disturbances.

e. Most of the rioting occurred after work hours among idle crowds on the streets. This was particularly true after the streetcar strike began.

f. Gangs, particularly of young whites, formed definite nuclei for crowd and mob formation. "Athletic clubs" supplied the leaders of many gangs.

g. Crowds and mobs engaged in rioting were generally composed of a small nucleus of leaders and an acquiescing mass of spectators. The leaders were mostly young men, usually between the ages of sixteen and twenty-one. Dispersal was most effectively accomplished by sudden, unexpected gun fire.

h. Rumor kept the crowds in an excited, potential mob state. The press was responsible for giving wide dissemination to much of the inflammatory matter in spoken rumors, though editorials calculated to allay race hatred and help the forces of order were factors in the restoration of peace.

i. The police lacked sufficient forces for handling the riot; they were hampered by the Negroes' distrust of them; routing orders and records were not handled with proper care; certain officers were undoubtedly unsuited to police or riot duty.

j. The militiamen employed in this riot were of an unusually high type. This unquestionably accounts for the confidence placed in them by both races. Riot training, definite orders, and good staff work contributed to their efficiency.

k. There was a lack of energetic co-operation between the police department and the state's attorney's office in the discovery and conviction of rioters.

The riot was merely a symptom of serious and profound disorders lying beneath the surface of race relations in Chicago. The study of the riot, therefore, as to its interlocking provocations and causes, required a study of general race relations that made possible so serious and sudden an outbreak. Thus to understand the riot and guard against another, the Commission probed systematically into the principal phases of race contact and sought accurate information on matters which in the past have been influenced by dangerous speculation; and on the basis of its discoveries certain suggestions to the community are made.

Activities of the NAACP

MEMBERSHIP GROWTH

December 31, 1917, 80 Branches, 9,282 Members.

December 31, 1918, 165 Branches, 43,994 Members.

Nearly 35,000 New Members

It is in no boasting spirit that the National Association for the Advancement of Colored People alludes to the year's increase in the number of its branches and in membership, but with a deepening and sobering sense of opportunity and responsibility.

On January 1, 1918, the records of the National Association showed a membership of 9,282, distributed among 80 branches and 846 members at large. On December 31st there were 165 branches and approximately 44,000 (43,994) members, 1,272 of whom are members at large, and 42,722 branch members.

Distributed by geographical divisions, according to the classification adopted by the Bureau of the Census, the number of branches and branch members in each of the several divisions is as follows.

In the three divisions containing the Southern States, it is interesting to note that there are 69 Branches and 11,858 members. Adding to these the membership of the District of Columbia Branch, the Association shows a membership in the South and near South of 18,701, or more than twice that of the whole membership one year ago.

Divisions	Branches	Members
New England States	6	4,978
Middle Atlantic States	20	4,701
East North Central	36	8,021
West North Central	14	3,257
South Atlantic	44	5,661
District of Columbia	1	6,843
East South Central	6	2,591
West South Central	19	3,606
Mountain	5	717
Pacific	11	2,142
Outside U.S.	3	206

Increase in Size of Branches

Notable, too, is the increase in the size of the branches themselves. There are 126 branches with memberships of 50 and over; 73 with memberships of 100 and over; 42 with more than 200 members; 33 have 300 or more; 32 have more than 500, while 9 branches exceed 1,000 in number and 2 have more than 2,500 members.

In percentages, 20 per cent of the branches have more than 300 members each; 25 per cent more than 200 each and 44 per cent of the branches count 100 members or more on their membership rolls. One-seventh of them have more than 500 members, while less than one-fourth fall below 50 members. Some of these latter, the majority in fact, are on probation, so to speak, awaiting an increase to at least 50 members before they are eligible for formal chartering. . . .

The total increase for the year was 85 new branches and 34,712 members, which, expressed in percentages, is equivalent to an increase of 375 per cent in membership and over 100 per cent in the number of branches.

Significance of Membership Growth

That so many new branches and members have enlisted under the banner of the National

Source: "Activities of the NACCP." From Report of the National Association for the Advancement of Colored People for the Years 1917 and 1918. Eighth and Ninth Annual Reports (New York: NAACP, 1919), Ninth Annual Report, pp. 17–23, 25–36, 44–49, 61–68.

Association for the Advancement of Colored People during a year when the nation was straining its resources to the utmost to defeat the purposes of threatening autocracy, and when colored people from their smaller resources were doing their full share in subscribing to Liberty Loan, Red Cross and War Relief funds, is, indeed, a matter for congratulation. The colored people of the nation, stirred as they have never been before by the idealism of an appeal to "make the world safe for democracy," have responded to the nation's call for service and sacrifice in such high spirit of devotion, their sons have fought Liberty's battles on the shell-swept plains of France in such unflinching fashion, as to have earned them the spontaneous tributes of the press and the peoples of America and the Allied countries. Had colored men never fought before, their fame as soldiers would have been securely established by the exploits of individuals like Needham Roberts and Henry Johnson and of regiments like the 369th (the old New York 15th) and the 367th, and other Negro units whose members received the honor of the French croix de guerre as a testimony to the bravery of the whole personnel of both regiments!

Comment by the Way

An increased executive and clerical staff has permitted the Association to devote more time and thought to its Anti-Lynching work and to conduct a more energetic campaign for legal trial of Negro alleged offenders, than in any previous year of the Association's history. Lynching is rapidly becoming a national issue. Under the stress of war time, mob violence has menaced communities heretofore relatively immune. Four white men were lynched in 1918. And yet, when all the facts are summed up, and we would be the last to minimize the evil of mob violence or to excuse it in the least degree, *the lynching of Negroes by whites* is the outstanding fact in the situation.

Sixty-three Negroes are known to have died at the hands of white mobs during 1918, as we point out in succeeding pages. These lynchings might well be regarded as evidences of civil war were it not that *up to this time* the Negroes have not retaliated in kind. In the absence of combined action by Negroes forcibly to protect members of their race, the lynching of black men and women by white men for all causes and no cause, so far as crimes are concerned, can only be compared, although in lesser degree, to Russian pogroms against Jews under the Tzarist regime, or to Turkish attack upon the Armenians.

We would deeply deplore the forcible defense of Negroes by other Negroes, since it would perhaps lead to sanguinary conflicts between the lower element of whites and the Negroes, but no sane observer can fail to reflect that either white men, who make and enforce the laws, must stop mob attacks upon black men, no matter what reason may be given for the attacks, or confess themselves unable to maintain law and order and protect *all* citizens from unlawful attack. No class of citizens can be denied the protection of the law with impunity.

The National Association for the Advancement of Colored People fights this evil, as others in its program, with spiritual and legal weapons. Its appeal is to the heart, the mind, the conscience of America. It insists upon "ordered law and humane justice," to quote a phrase used by President Wilson in his appeal to the country against lynching. It has hoped that the better South would rouse itself and wipe out this terrible blot upon its honor. But the wait has been a long one. Can the Negro depend upon securing *his day in court* so long as he has no say as to who sits upon the bench, in the jury box, or who becomes the sheriff or chief of police? Think it over in the light of experience, ye voters and students of history and politics!

Extent of the Lynching Evil*

Previous to 1918. The records show that from 1885 to 1917, both inclusive, approxi-

*The Association has in preparation a pamplet, which will appear in April, 1919, entitled, "Thirty Years of Lynching in the United States, 1889–1918," which can be secured from the secretary.

mately 3,740 lynchings have occurred in the United States. Two thousand seven hundred and forty-three (2,743) of this number have had colored persons as victims and nine hundred and ninety-seven (997) have been white. The relative percentages of white and colored victims for the 33 years covered is 26 per cent, white; 74 per cent, colored.

Assuming that the record for the earlier years is less accurate than for the later period, because of many factors (all lynching figures are probably minimum), the figures for the 18 years, 1900 to 1917, both inclusive, are given. Fourteen hundred and twenty-seven (1,427) lynchings are recorded for the period named. Twelve hundred and forty-one (1,241) of these (86.7 per cent) were Negroes; 186 (13.3 per cent) were white. The relative decrease of white victims is marked.

The victims of the East St. Louis mob riots of July, 1917, are excluded, as are those of the mob riot at Chester, Pa. The number of victims at East St. Louis has been estimated at as many as 175. In the report of the Congressional Investigating Committee (House Document No. 1,231, 65th Congress, 2nd Session) the Committee says that "at least 39 Negroes and 8 white people were killed outright, and hundreds of Negroes were wounded and maimed."*

During 1918. During 1918, 63 Negroes and 4 white persons were lynched, as established by well authenticated evidence.[†] The Executive Office has been advised of a probable increase of this figure by 12 cases of which it is said that confirmation of lynching can be obtained, but, as the Executive Office has been unable to investigate these cases, they have, of course, been excluded from our figures.

An Association staff member, while in the South studying special problems, was informed by reliable colored people in Georgia that twelve unreported cases (in the press or elsewhere) have occurred since the Association investigated the Brooks and Lowndes Counties, Georgia, lynching orgy of May, 1918, and that the only apparent effect in Georgia of the President's lynching pronouncement of July 26th last, has been an apparently concerted agreement on the part of press and authorities to keep all news regarding lynchings out of the Georgia press. Lending some color to this charge, is the fact that, so far as we are aware, no Georgia daily has at any time since May, 1918, published any account of the investigation made by the Association or of the fact that 17 names of mob leaders were put in the hands of Governor Dorsey, despite the considerable press comment in the press of other states.

One of our Texas branches (Houston) reported the case of one alleged victim of a mob who was buried secretly and no publicity given to the facts. The branch's president had written to the acting-governor requesting an investigation of the circumstances.* Finally, some lynchings which do not get into the press, are not carried beyond the immediate neighborhood, sometimes a very small one, unless there is some unusual feature to distinguish the event.

Distribution of the 1918 Lynchings

During 1918 lynchings have occurred in the following states:[†]

---

*"The bodies of the dead Negroes," testified an eye-witness, "were thrown into a morgue like so many dead hogs." Ibid., page 4.
[†]See "Lynching Record for 1917 and 1918," Appendix III, page 89, for chronological list of name, place, date and alleged cause of lynchings for 1917 and 1918.

*Nothing came of this request in the way of legal action.
[†]Four of the lynched victims were white men (one each in Arkansas, California, Illinois and Texas), 63 were Negroes and 5 of the latter women.

Alabama	3
Arkansas	3
California	1
Florida	2
Georgia	19
Kentucky	1
Louisana	9
Illinois	1
Mississippi	7
North Carolina	2
Oklahoma	1
South Carolina	1
Tennessee	4
Texas	11*
Virginia	1
Wyoming	1
	67

Special Features of Lynching

Five of the Negro victims have been women. Two colored men were burned at the stake before death; four Negroes were burned after death; three Negroes, aside from those burned at the stake, were tortured before death; in one case the victim's dead body was carried into town on the running board of an automobile and thrown into a public park where "it was viewed by thousands;" one Negro victim was captured and handed to the officers of the law by Negroes themselves. A mother and her five children were lynched by a Texas mob, the mother having been shot as she was attempting to drag the bodies of her four dead sons from their burning home at daybreak, the house (only a cabin) having been fired by the mob. The crime in this case was "alleged

*In *The Crisis* for February, 1919, page 181, this total is given at 12. The case of George Cabiness, whose mother and four brothers and sister were lynched, for alleged threats to avenge the killing of George, has been eliminated from the lynching record as the latter was alleged to have been killed resisting arrest.

conspiracy to avenge" the killing of another son by officers who had come to arrest him for "evading the draft law." This latter case has not been classified as a lynching.

Offenses Charged Against the 1918 Victims*

Negroes

"Attacks on white women"	13
"Attacks on colored women"	1
"Living with white woman"	1
"Too revolting to publish"	2
"Shooting and killing officer of law"	10
"Murder of civilian"	14
"Shooting and wounding"	4
"Conspiracy to avenge killing of relative"	6
"Accomplice in murder"	3
"Aiding mob victim in attempt to escape"	1
"Intent to rob and kidnap"	1
"Quarrel with employer"	1
"Creating disturbance"	1
"Stealing hogs"	3
"Unknown"	2
	63

Whites

"Disloyal utterances"	2
"Murder"	2
	4

Most atrocious of all, so far as the community was concerned, was the five days' orgy in Brooks and Lowndes Counties, which has been made the occasion for special publicity and special efforts by the Association, . . . In that case the particularly vicious brutality of the mob went beyond what one is prepared to expect from Georgia mobs—and one expects a good deal in the way of "cruel and unusual punishments" from them. The horrible cruelties visited upon Mary Turner, an eight month's preg-

*According to press accounts, except in a very few cases in which the victim was actually tried before a court and later taken from the jail and lynched.

nant woman, are recited in the investigation published of our investigator's findings.*

In two cases the lynchings were carried out in the court house yard and in one of these picture post card photos were sold on the streets at 25 cents each.

Taken from Peace Officers and Jails

Our records show the following number of cases of lynchings of Negroes in which the victim was taken from officers or jails:

Alabama	2
Georgia	4
Louisana	2
Mississippi	1
North Carolina	1
Oklahoma	1
South Carolina	1
Tennessee	1
	13

Innocence Admitted Publicly

In three cases of which we have record the press has spoken of the innocence of victims; one of these involved three persons, another the ten victims of Brooks and Lowndes Counties mobs (aside from the one person who shot the white farmer which was the incentive to the lynchings). In another case it is the common belief in the community in which a Negro was lynched for "killing a white woman" that the husband of the woman was himself the murderer. No charge has been brought against him, however, by the authorities. In such cases, Negroes are usually too fearful of danger and too hopeless of anything being done, to initiate legal action. In an additional case a bank cashier declared in an interview in an Alabama paper, that a certain lynching victim had committed no offense, that there had been a mistake made in the man the mob was after.

Legal Action Taken by Public Officials

Governor Thomas W. Bickett of North Carolina ordered the sheriff to investigate one case, but the sheriff reported that the "guilty parties could not be ascertained." The Governor in another case personally appealed to a mob at midnight and prevented the lynching of a man who was later hanged. The same Governor in November appealed to the Federal authorities and secured the support of a tank corps of 250 Federal army men to assist the authorities of Winston-Salem, North Carolina, in holding the local jail against a mob which was attempting to get a Negro prisoner to lynch him.

The Mayor and "Home Guards" of Winston-Salem, aided by the Federal soldiers alluded to, protected the aforementioned prisoner at the cost of the lives of some of the "Home Guards," for which public service, so unusual where Negro-hunting mobs are concerned, they should receive the tributes of all good citizens. (The Association's appreciation was made known to all concerned by a public commendation).*

Governor Richard I. Manning of South Carolina ordered a sheriff to arrest 17 prominent farmers who had participated in a lynching. Bail was fixed at a total of $97,500, in February. From the Judge who placed the men under bail we learn that no indictments were found by the grand jury. "Lack of evidence," is given as the reason.

Governor Charles Henderson of Alamaba, in November, actively supported the attorney general of the state, who, at the instance of the

---

*Published in *The Crisis* for September, 1918 *The Work of a Mob,* and reprinted by the Association under the title, *"The Lynchings of May, 1918, in Brooks and Lowndes Counties, Georgia,"* September, 1918, 6 p.

*As we go to press, information has come that Judge B. F. Long has sentenced 15 men involved in the attempt to storm the Winston-Salem jail to prison terms ranging from fourteen months to six years. This is indeed a rarity and an occasion for rejoicing.

Governor, personally took charge of an investigation of two lynchings which occurred in that state on the 10th and 12th of that month.

When a regular grand jury then in session failed to indict, a prominent detective agency was engaged and upon the evidence secured by them, a special grand jury, headed by a local clergyman, brought in 24 indictments. Seventeen men were lodged in jail without bail.*

Special investigations by a member of the staff have been made of lynchings at Fayetteville, Ga., Brooks and Lowndes Counties, Ga., Estill Springs, Tenn., Blackshear, Ga., and of race riots and disturbances at Camp Merritt, N. J., Brooklyn, N. Y. and Philadelphia, Pa.†

Memoranda were prepared and sent to the President of the United States, to the Attorney General of the United States and to the executive committees of the American Bar Association, on the general subject of lynching, but with reference to immediate practical action desired by the Association. Letters requesting editorial interest in the fight against lynching were addressed to the leading papers of the country on several occasions and matter has been prepared for specific use by individual papers.

Publicity in the press was secured for the memorandum to the President and to the Attorney General. Mr. Storey's address to the Wisconsin Bar Association, June, 1918, on "The Negro Question," which contains much reference to lynching, was sent to all the members of the Cabinet and of the Congress, to Governors of all the states, mayors of cities, to newspapers, periodicals, and to leading citizens and will be given wider circulation during the early part of 1919.*

The members of the executive staff have made reference to lynching in addresses in many cities to both white and colored audiences. Certain of Field Secretary Johnson's addresses before white audiences have met with notable responses.†

The offer of the publishers of the *San Antonio Express*, San Antonio, Texas, made in April, to pay rewards of $1,000, for each conviction and punishment of the lynchers of a Negro (and $500, if white), has been given wide publicity among the branches and the colored press. (No one has claimed a reward from this fund as yet, however.)

Illustration of Results Following the Association's Publicity Work

The following examples of results following publicity sent out by the Association and telegrams addressed to Governors and Chambers of Commerce are reviewed:

On November 9, telegrams of inquiry and appeal for legal action in the case of the lynching of George Taylor at Rolesville, near Raleigh, N. C., were sent to Governor Bickett of North Carolina, to the County Solicitor of Wake County and to the Chamber of Commerce of Raleigh, of which that to the Governor was acknowledged. The Governor said that he agreed with the points made in the

---

*At the trial of the two alleged ringleaders of the mobs, which was held at Tuscumbia, Alabama, on February 3 and 4, 1919, the jury, assembled from neighborhood, found a verdict of not guilty. The secretary of the Association was in attendance at the trial and has written a report of it which has been published as a special pamphlet Dispensing With Justice in Alabama—a Report of the Trial of Frank Dillard, Alleged Lyncher, at Tuscumbia, Alabama, February 3 and 4, 1919, by John R. Shillady, Secretary, National Association for the Advancement of Colored People.

†Of these investigations, the following have been published and may be obtained upon application to the National Secretary: Brooks and Lowndes Counties, Georgia; Estill Springs, Tenn. (See *The Crisis* for May, 1918, pages 16–20); Philadelphia Race Riots of July 26 to July 31, 1918, 8 p.

*Printed by the National Association for the Advancement of Colored People as "The Negro Question" (with resolutions adopted by the Bar Association following the delivery of the address), 30 pages, ten cents per copy.

telegram and would back the County Solicitor in efforts to fix the blame for the affair. The Solicitor carried on an investigation for two weeks, examining 21 white and 9 colored witnesses. The coroner's jury ran true to form, finding that the victim came to his death at the hands of "parties unknown" to the jury.

The two leading Raleigh newspapers, one of them owned by Secretary of the Navy Daniels, carried strong editorial comment against the lynching and criticized the dereliction of the officers in allowing their prisoner to be taken from them. One of them commented directly and favorably on the Association's telegrams to the Governor.

Ten days later, as has been mentioned on a preceding page of this report, the same Governor appealed successfully to an adjacent army camp for help to support the mayor and "home guards" of Winston-Salem in holding the local jail against a mob which was attempting to seize a Negro prisoner to lynch him.

The Chambers of Commerce of Montgomery and Birmingham, Alabama, acknowledged telegrams and letters of the Association sent during November, saying that they supported our view (that the lynchers of Will Byrd and Henry Whiteside should be ascertained and legal action against them taken) and that the Governor had ordered the action referred to on a previous page of this report, that of instructing the attorney general of the state to push an investigation of the lynchings at Sheffield and Tuscumbia, Alabama.

Space forbids the citation of further examples. In many cases, however, no direct effect was produced by the Association's long distance efforts. It would be a mistake, however, to assume that no beneficial results can be credited to such of the Association's forty telegraphic inquiries (accompanied by newspaper publicity) as had occasioned no immediate action. Correspondents have written and callers at the National Headquarters have assured the National Officers of the value of this publicity work. In some cases

local leaders among the white citizens have called upon colored people to assure them of their concern for the well being and protection of the *good* Negro and incidentally, we are told, to advise them against allying themselves with "northern agitators."

That the pressure of national opinion is felt and feared, even in the center of the lynching area, is evidenced by such editorials as that following a protest against a Louisiana lynching, in which a local editor devoted a column of matter to "lambasting" the National Secretary under the caption "No Outside Scolds Needed." It was asked why this "Association with the long name" was endeavoring to hold Louisiana up to the *scorn of the country*, etc., *ad lib.* . . .

FIGHTING THE COLOR LINE

Employment. Despite the greatly increased opportunities for employment, the Executive Office has continued to receive considerable numbers of complaints of employment discriminations, largely on work conducted for or by the government and in federal departments. Many of these concerned the departments at Washington. The District of Columbia Branch is the Association's most effective means of dealing with complaints affecting federal departments at Washington, although in some cases such matters have been handled directly by the Executive Office.*

It is the belief of the District of Columbia Branch, based upon experience and upon proof, that it is the settled policy at present of many of the heads of federal departments to discriminate against colored people wherever possible. The policy of the civil service

---

*Special acknowledgment is due Mr. Archibald H. Grimké, President of that Branch for unfailing attention to numerous matters sent him for attention, many of which were complaints and inquiries from individuals and branches in various parts of the country.

commission in requiring photographs of applicants permits of color discrimination in an easy way and is so used by many of the Departments. A number of cases could be cited where persons who had successfully passed civil service examinations had been directed, often by telegraph, to report for duty, only to be informed, when they did appear, that an error had been made and that there were no vacancies. That errors in such cases had been made, the Association is convinced, but the "errors" were on the part of clerks in the office of the appointing power, who had failed to learn that the persons so urgently needed to "win the war" were colored, and, therefore, not so urgently needed as had been supposed when it was believed they were white.

A few cases are cited to illustrate the results of the Association's efforts in fighting employment discriminations.*

An Airplane Plant

Complaint that the Curtiss Airplane Company of Buffalo, New York, was discriminating against colored girls was made by the Buffalo Branch. After much negotiation with the Department of Labor, principally through the new Bureau of Negro Economics, this discrimination was abolished.

Railroad Color Line Fought

An order issued in November by Regional Director of Railroads (for the North Western District) Aishton, advising the heads of operating companies to refrain from employing colored men as switchmen, firemen, hostlers, etc., or in any positions in which they had not theretofore been employed, was protested to Director General McAdoo and through press publicity, with the result that this order was withdrawn. The occasion for its issuance in

the first instance was said to be the refusal of white union employees to work with colored men. As the railroad unions in the operating branch of the service do not admit colored men to membership, it is evident that the refusal to work with colored men may be attributed to race, and not to mere anti-union, discrimination.

Union Discrimination

In a case involving five colored bricklayers, members of a trade union, hired through a United States employment bureau at Cleveland, Ohio, and sent to Sheffield, Alabama, where their fellow unionists refused to work with them, because of their color, the Association succeeded only in establishing the facts and getting comprehensive statements from all concerned. The case was presented to the employers, to the International union affected, through the Executive Council of the American Federation of Labor and to the United States Department of Labor. This complaint was presented to the Executive Office by the Cleveland Branch, which also endeavored to press the matter locally.

Hospital Care Secured—Intimidation Checked

Illustrations of successful efforts to overcome discrimination against colored people in fields other than employment, are shown in the following two cases: the first of successful efforts to secure the admission of colored people to the State Tuberculosis Sanatorium of Wisconsin, after the superintendent had given an unsatisfactory reason for their exclusion; the second that of the Treasury Department's action in correcting the bad habits of intimidation of a Louisiana War Savings Stamp Committee, whose Chairman had threatened "to use force to make Negroes buy more War Savings Stamps." In both cases press publicity was resorted to to secure results. In the latter state, and in the immediate district of the offending committee's activities, a colored

---

*The Association's activities and experience in this field of effort, and in regard to color discrimination generally, would fill many pages of text, if recited in detail.

man (David H. Raines of Vivian, La.) was the largest individual buyer in the Fourth Liberty Loan, having purchased $100,000 worth of bonds, the purchase having been called to the personal attention of President Wilson by the local Liberty Loan Chairman.

Incidental to the tuberculosis sanatorium case, the interest of the National Tuberculosis Association was enlisted to the extent that they have undertaken a survey of the provisions for the care of colored tuberculosis patients throughout the United States, a project which has been under way for some time and the results of which, we expect, will before long be available.

Attempts to Secure Redress—Efforts Failed

Typical of instances in which the Association's efforts have borne no fruit, although the case is an extremely outrageous one, is the case of an estimable Negro physician of Vicksburg, Mississippi, upon whom a demand was made in June by the local and State War Savings Committees to purchase $1,000 worth of war savings stamps, and in which case, after the physician's refusal, on the ground that he could not afford so large a purchase, he was at first arrested, "to protect him," it was said, and afterwards tarred and feathered and driven from the city, the tarring and feathering being done, it was claimed, and evidence submitted to substantiate the claim, at the order of leading citizens and officials of the city.

Two other prominent colored men of the city were driven out at the same time, the real offense of these men being, it was contended in their behalf, that they had been leaders in efforts made by the colored people of the city to prevent two notorious colored women, mistresses of politicians, from being appointed as teachers in the colored schools. Added to this was the further fact that they had endeavored to protect some of the first colored soldiers to appear on the streets of Vicksburg from having their uniforms torn from their backs, as was threatened.

The Association's efforts in these cases extended to appeals to the mayor, to the United States Attorney General, and to the Department of the Treasury. In the case of the latter, the reply of a Treasury official to our inquiry concerning the first-mentioned victim, was that they had inquired of the State Chairman of the War Stamp Savings Committee (one of those complained of, by the way) and he had assured them that there was no ground for complaint, the Treasury official adding that Mr. McAdoo had full confidence in the above-mentioned chairman. Our readers may be left to their own conclusions.

In the case of one of the men, a druggist, he was compelled to sell his property at what he said was one-fourth of its value, whereupon he was transferred by the local draft board from class four to class one and immediately inducted into military service upon the ground, that, having disposed of his business, there was sufficient money in his possession from the proceeds to maintain his wife and child during the period of the war. The War Department's reply to the druggist when he protested at the action of the draft board, was that *"the fact that registrant had some difficulty with a few people at Vicksburg has no bearing upon the case in so far as the selective service officials are concerned."* The Executive Office did not pursue this matter further with the War Department because the armistice was signed at about the time it could have been handled.

Campaign Against the "Birth of a Nation"

The National Office and the branches have been active at various times throughout the year in efforts to prevent the vicious motion picture play, "The Birth of a Nation" from being shown. Objected to, and suppressed on occasion in one place or another, this menace to harmonious relations between the races would bob up every week or two in a new place. In October the National Office addressed letters to the Governors of all the states and to the state Councils of Defense, asking that they use the power of their offices to prevent the play being shown. Its thoroughly vicious character was pointed out as strongly and as truthfully as the National Office could phrase its opinion of the film's harmful effects on national morale. This national campaign against the picture play was featured in the *Branch Bulletin* for November and the cooperation of the branches solicited. A press story on the matter was sent out widely.

Governor James M. Cox of Ohio had secured the film's withdrawal from Ohio during the war. After the armistice was signed, when it again appeared, the National Office, at the request of certain Ohio branches, induced Governor Cox to act in the same manner as before. The film was once more withdrawn from Ohio. The West Virginia Council of Defence suppressed it in that state. It was suppressed in Kansas. Similar action was taken, in some cases by voluntary action, and more often on account of legal action, in California, North Carolina, Kentucky and Alaska. Favorable replies were received from other governors and Councils of Defense, promising action should the film appear in their states.

WORK OF THE ASSOCIATION'S BRANCHES

Meeting monthly in many cases, the rapidly increasing number of Association branches have maintained a keen local, as well as national, interest in the movement to which the Association is dedicated. The officers of the branches, all volunteers, receive no compensation for their efforts, and devote themselves to the work in such leisure time as can be spared from bread-winning.

That so much is given in such splendid spirit speaks well for the ultimate success of the cause of justice to the colored race. We summarize topically below the principal activities of the branches. In addition to the achievements specified, many of the branches carried out an educational program dealing with public questions of special interest to colored people. All of them enlist in the work of adding to the Association's membership and support, of which fact this year's growth bears conclusive testimony.

Labor

With the cessation of immigration, incident upon the European War, hundreds of thousands of colored men and women entered upon new employment. This was not accomplished without many a battle. In Charleston, S. C., the Navy Yard needed women workers, but did not want to employ colored. The Branch, aided by the President of the District of Columbia Branch, succeeded in getting about 250 colored women into the Yard, in jobs which they have held satisfactorily. At San Antonio, Texas, the Branch, under its able executive, secured employment for three hundred colored women at the Reclamation Station. At Memphis and Louisville, colored women were put at over-rough, disgusting tasks by the military authorities. The Branch had them removed and better work assigned them. The Buffalo, N. Y., Branch itself fought locally and through its Congressman the refusal of an air-plane plant to employ colored girls, to the successful conclusion of which allusion has already been made.

Cleveland and Detroit were confronted with a great influx of southern labor into workshops and factories, and their Branches investigated conditions and did much to improve them. The colored workers have had their bouts with union labor. National headquarters has handled more than one case. At Charleston, W. Va., the Branch acting alone, successfully reinstated two colored plumbers with whom the white workmen refused to work.

The Boston, Mass., Branch championed the cause of a young colored girl who was being mistreated by her employers, succeeded in removing her from them, despite threats of legal action, and placing her in satisfactory employment elsewhere.

Combating civil service discriminations, the Detroit Branch succeeded in getting a colored woman postal clerk into the position to which her examinations entitled her. Danville, Va., saw to it that a Negro who had five times successfully passed his examination as letter carrier secured his position. But the bulk of this civil service work falls on the District of Columbia Branch. Washington is the center for government jobs. One time it is the case of a colored typist who is refused a registration card. The Branch sees that she is registered. Again a stenographer, summoned from a distant state, appears at the appointed place and because she is colored is told that she is not wanted. The Branch has her receive her appointment. All cases do not turn out so favorably as these, but the President of the Branch and his able Executive Committee (a committee that meets every Saturday afternoon throughout the year) see to it that cases are protested and that discrimination does not pass unchallenged.

Our Southern Branches have been confronted with a new reading of the "work or fight" order making it applicable to anyone whom an employer wants to keep or to get at a low wage! A hairdresser must drop her trade and do her white neighbor's washing. This is reported by the Montgomery, Ala., Branch to the State Council of Defense and the fine is remitted. A woman, in Augusta, Ga., is arrested for leaving domestic service to go into a better job, but when she comes before the court her case is dismissed, since the judge sees the room filled with influential, respected colored N.A.A.C.P. members. Little Rock, Ark., reports and gets action against the efforts of the cotton planters to keep women at a low wage in the fields. And the Atlanta, Ga., Branch after a vigorous fight, keeps the newly enacted compulsory work law from being applied in its state to women.

Education

For thirty-two years the anomalous situation has existed at Charleston, S. C., of colored children, not permitted to associate at school with white children, and yet taught by white teachers—teachers who never failed to let the children know they felt themselves their superiors. The Charleston colored people have long protested against this, and the Branch backed by the Branch at Columbia, the state capital, was especially active this year. In consequence, the March *Crisis* carried the news that the white teachers are to go out and the colored teachers to come into the colored schools.

Charleston, W. Va., the capital of the state, has the immense advantage of having three colored men in the state legislature. Through their influence, with the active, energetic support of the Branch, much more money than formerly has been appropriated for colored state schools, and especially, provision has been made for an adequate building for the colored deaf and dumb children. In the District of Columbia, the Branch, under the chairman of the education committee, expects to secure a fairer distribution of the city's funds than formerly.

There are many branches that find they must be on the alert to prevent some form of segregation in the public schools. This reached even as far north as Hartford, Conn., where the Branch came into existence in a spirited and successful protest against the placing of colored children recently arrived from the South in classes by themselves. The same is true of Moline, Ill. Ypsilanti, Mich., wakes up to find that it has a separate school, forms a branch and has an injunction issued to see that the school is closed.

Legislation

The next few years should see considerable legislation favorable to the Negro. The recent coming together of the Texas branches, all only a few months old, to petition the governor to push an Anti-Lynching bill for the state is a sign of the power the Negro will wield. Not the power that works for personal, political gain, but the strength of united public opinion. Where the Negro has the vote we are beginning to have colored members of the legislature. Our Branch on the Isthmus of Panama reports to us that a Negro has been reappointed judge in the Canal Zone. Houston, Texas, secured the right of colored women to register in the primaries.

Jim-Crowing

In our northern and western cities, where the Negro is a voter, he must nevertheless be on the alert lest his rights be curtailed by those white people whose superiority consists in making other people uncomfortable. From Ohio, through its Cleveland, Toledo and Lorain branches, we learn that signs proclaiming that colored people will not be admitted to certain restaurants have been removed. The same news comes from Lincoln, Neb., Mercer County, Pa., Philadelphia (where theatres are also convinced it is best to stop segregation), Moline, Ill., and Santa Monica Bay, Cal. The Wilmington, Del., Branch is working against segregation in the court-room, while Denver has objectionable signs removed from the city's tennis courts. San Antonio, Texas, reports that it has secured better accommodations for the traveling colored public on the railroads in and out of its city; and Columbus, Ohio, is investigating the occasional Jim-Crowing of passengers between that city and Cincinnati.

A most important Jim-Crow case has been tried and reported by the Baltimore Branch. Dr. Julia B. Coleman, a colored woman physician, brought suit against the W. B. and A. Railway Company for attempting to segregate her. The case was tried by Mr. W. Ashbie Hawkins and a judgment of one cent damages and cost was rendered. The case was appealed and the judge assessed the damages at twenty dollars. Mr. Hawkins writes: "I think the road is not enforcing the

regulation now *except with such persons as it feels will not give trouble."*

Criminal Cases

To report the branch cases where colored men or women have been beaten up, or killed, by policemen; where they have been convicted of crime on what has seemed to the unprejudiced onlooker insufficient and prejudiced evidence would take many pages. Cases have come to us from Lynchburg, Va., Oklahoma, Raleigh, N. C., Newark, N. J., Fort Worth, Texas, Kansas City, Kan., Bakersfield, Cal. The dramatic criminal N.A.A.C.P. case of 1918, ably handled by the Boston Branch, was that of John Johnson, accused of a crime in West Virginia, who fled to Boston. Governor McCall refused to send him back to West Virginia, on the grounds that he would not get a fair trial in his state. Witnesses were brought from Charleston, W. Va., and after a trial that lasted eighteen days extradition was refused.

San Antonio, Texas, reported a case where damages were secured from a white man who struck a colored woman; and again a colored man whipped a white man for insulting his daughter, and was protected by the sheriff. Too often, however, where the white man is guilty, the justice meted out is similar to that of a case reported from Charleston, S. C., where a father appeared against a white man charged with raping his ten-year-old daughter. The grand jury did not even examine all the witnesses, but at once brought in a bill of "No case."

"The Birth of a Nation"*

The activity of the Branches has prevented the performance of this photoplay at Louisville, Ky., at Gary, Ind., and has again stopped it when a performance was at-

*General reference to the nation-wide efforts against this photoplay have been made in an earlier part of this report.

tempted in Ohio. At Lincoln, Neb., and Springfield, Mo., objectionable features were removed. The Governor of the State of Pennsylvania in a letter to the Harrisburg Branch, which with Philadelphia, Washington and Newcastle, has worked to have the film stopped throughout the state, says that he considers the play an outrage against one of Pennsylvania's greatest statesmen, Thaddeus Stevens.

Another photo-play, "Free and Equal," had an objectionable Negro feature and owing to the energy of the branches at Los Angeles and Washington, Pa., that part was eliminated.

The Army—Social Service

The Ohio Branches acted energetically in the attempted Student Training Corps discrimination, of which mention has been made heretofore. At Ohio State University when the students were drawn up for drill, an order came for the Negroes to fall out. It was then explained to them by their Major that they would have to go to colored colleges for their training. The Cleveland, Columbus, Cincinnati and Oberlin, Ohio, Branches made immediate protest on the ground and to Washington, reporting the circumstances to National Headquarters. Something of the same sort happened at Nebraska, where the Lincoln Branch was active. The Philadelphia Branch through its president worked assiduously to prevent segregation at mess among the white and colored workers at the shipyards at Hog and League Islands. Branch members were very active in the Y.M.C.A., Red Cross work, and gave generously to the Liberty Loans and the several allied drives. The Boston, Mass., Branch collected money for a Soldiers' Rest House, open to both races, reported by the War Department to be one of the best in the country. This Branch was represented on the Massachusetts Committee on Public Safety by its secretary, who was also Executive Chairman of the Commonwealth Fourth Liberty Loan Committee (among colored people), chairman of a board of draft appeal agents, serving during the war, a member of the executive committees "to welcome home returning soldiers and sailors" and of the Federal Board of Management for Returning Soldiers and Sailors. The President of the San Antonio, Texas, Branch gave $5,000 for a Rest House. The Boston Branch secured redress for a soldier who was abused by a superior officer, the case resulting in a general order prohibiting epithets. It also secured an army order allowing five physicians who were inducted into the service as privates to be given the choice of commissions and details to training camps or to be returned at once to civil life.

Apart from war work we hear of the Hartford, Conn., Branch starting classes for the children of southern immigrants; of Toledo planning a field day for the colored children of the city, and Christmas festivities for those who without their help would have had none; and of Atlanta, Ga., turning to its civic tasks and rooting out dives and "blind tigers."

Censoring the Press

The branches keep up a steady censorship of the press. Objectionable articles are not allowed to pass unchallenged; news letters insulting the colored man are answered. The Branches are insisting that the word *Negro,* as long as it is to be used at all, shall be used as the name of a race and, therefore, capitalized. And while the press is censored, the Association's organ is brought before the people. Many public libraries have been presented by their N.A.A.C.P. Branches with *The Crisis*. New Orleans, La., boasts a weekly newssheet published by the Branch.

NAACP Bulletins

DETROIT BRANCH
National Association For the Advancement of Colored People

BULLITEN NUMBER ONE   SEP. 13. 1920
Office, 465 Beaubien St.   Cherry 8099

ON OUR SCHOOL SITUATION

School time is here again The Detroit Branch realizes that everything in our power must be done to prevent the increase of prejudice and to secure justice for our people.

It urges, therefore, that all our people carefully read the suggestions outlined below and pass it on. These suggestions are made after careful study has proven their need. They are made with the knowledge that hundreds of parents do all they ask and more. There are, however, hundreds who do not carry them out.

TO PARENTS AND GUARDIANS

1. See that your children's faces, necks and hands are washed clean; that their hair is combed, their shoes shined and their clothes whole and clean when they go to school.

Dirty faces and hands, ragged and dirty clothes create prejudice and discrimination. Soap and water needle and thread are available to the poorest. Patches are honorable, but holes and tatters are not.

2. Don't arrange your child's hair in "corn rows." It makes her a laughing stock and an object of ridicule. See that hair ribbons are clean and not gaudy. Choose quiet colors.

3. Have your child to school on time. See that he attends every day.

4. See that he does not neglect his school lessons and that he behaves in school. By him a race is being judged.

5. Keep your child in school if possible until he finishes High School. An education is more valuable than anything he can earn. Don't follow his wishes in this. He does not know.

6. Pastors are urged to form "Parents' Associations in each church to visit regularly the schools and to observe the treatment of the children.

7. ATTEND NIGHT SCHOOL. Find out from your pastor what courses are available, when and where. Everyone has a chance to get an education here, free, if he will. Avail yourself of this chance.

DETROIT BRANCH
National Association For The Advancement Of Colored People

BULLETIN NO. 2   APRIL 22, 1921
Office 2323 St. Antoine St. PhoneMain 1824

TO WHOM IT MAY CONCERN:

The Educational Committee of the National Association for the Advancement of Colored People, after visiting some of the schools in the eastern section of the city and finding the Homes about the schools, and the Children in the Schools in such untidy conditions, are asking you to assist us in trying to improve these conditions.

1. See that your windows are clean and hung with clean neat curtains.

2. When persons are sitting on your front porch see that they appear neat and clean.

3. If you have roomers do not permit them to put their feet on the porch railing or on your window sills.

4. If you have a place of business do not permit the grounds outside your door and in

Source: NAACP Bulletins, Detroit Branch, September 13, 1920 and April 22, 1921.

front of your show windows to be used as a Rest Room.

5. When we are grouped on corners, in stores, or any public place, let us not be boisterous in our manner; let us cultivate refinement. Let us stand erect on our feet and talk to those concerned and not to all in the block.

6. If you see a child pass your home going to school with holes in its clothing and hair that has not been combed or an unwashed face; you put yourself in the place of that poor mother who had to leave for work in the early morning, and could not get her child ready for school, and ask that child to step in your home and clean up a bit. We feel sure that the mother will thank you very much.

Let Our Motto Be:

"All For Each and Each For All"

Thanking you for all that you may do to help us in the uplift of our children, we remain,

Yours,
DETROIT BRANCH N. A. A. C. P.

La Bourgeoisie Noire

E. Franklin Frazier

Radicals are constantly asking the question: Why does the Negro, the man farthest down in the economic as well as social scale, steadily refuse to ally himself with the radical groups in America? On the other hand, his failure so far to show sympathy to any extent with the class which *a priori* would appear to be his natural allies has brought praise from certain quarters. Southern white papers when inclined to indulge in sentimental encomiums about the Negro cite his immunity to radical doctrines as one of his most praiseworthy characteristics. Negro orators and, until lately, Negro publications, in pleading for the Negro's claim to equitable treatment, have never failed to boast of the Negro's undying devotion to the present

economic order. Those whites who are always attempting to explain the Negro's social behavior in terms of hereditary qualities have declared that the Negro's temperament is hostile to radical doctrines. But the answer to what is a seeming anomaly to many is to be found in the whole social background of the Negro. One need not attribute it to any peculiar virtue (according as one regards virtue) or seek an explanation in such an incalculable factor as racial temperament.

The first mistake of those who think that the Negro of all groups in America should be in revolt against the present system is that they regard the Negro group as homogeneous. As a matter of fact, the Negro group is highly differentiated, with about the same range of interests as the whites. It is very well for white and black radicals to quote statistics to show that ninety-eight percent of the Negroes are workers and should seek release from their economic slavery; but as a matter of fact ninety-eight per cent of the Negroes do not regard themselves as in

Source: E. Franklin Frazier, "La Bourgeoisie Noire." In V. F. Calverton, ed., *Anthology of American Negro Literature*. Published by The Modern Library, 1929.

economic slavery. Class differentiation among Negroes is reflected in their church organizations, educational institutions, private clubs, and the whole range of social life. Although these class distinctions may rest upon what would seem to outsiders flimsy and inconsequential matters, they are the social realities of Negro life, and no amount of reasoning can rid his mind of them. Recently we were informed in Dr. Herskovits' book on the Negro that color is the basis of social distinctions. To an outsider or a superficial observer, this would seem true; but when one probes the tissue of the Negro's social life he finds that the Negro reacts to the same illusions that feed the vanity of white men.

What are some of the marks of distinction which make it impossible to treat the Negro group as a homogeneous mass? They are chiefly property, education, and blood or family. If those possessing these marks of distinction are generally mulattoes, it is because the free Negro class who first acquired these things as well as a family tradition were of mixed blood. The church in Charleston, South Carolina, which was reputed not to admit blacks did not open its doors to nameless mulatto nobodies. Not only has the distinction of blood given certain Negro groups a feeling of superiority over other Negroes, but it has made them feel superior to "poor whites." The Negro's feeling of superiority to "poor whites" who do not bear in their veins "aristocratic" blood has always created a barrier to any real sympathy between the two classes. Race consciousness to be sure has constantly effaced class feeling among Negroes. Therefore we hear on every hand Negro capitalists supporting the right of the Negro worker to organize—against white capitalists, of course. Nevertheless class consciousness has never been absent.

The Negro's attitude towards economic values has been determined by his economic position in American life. First of all, in the plantation system the Negro has found his adjustment to our economic system. The plantation system is based essentially upon enforced labor. Since emancipation the Negro has been a landless peasant without the tradition of the European peasant which binds the latter to the soil. Landownership remained relatively stationary from 1910 to 1920; while the number of landless workers increased. If this class of black workers were to espouse doctrines which aimed to change their economic status, they would be the most revolutionary group in America. From ignorant peasants who are ignorant in a fundamental sense in that they have no body of traditions even, we cannot expect revolutionary doctrines. They will continue a mobile group; while the white landlords through peonage and other forms of force will continue to hold them to the land.

Another factor of consequence in the Negro's economic life is the fact of the large number of Negroes in domestic service. One psychologist has sought to attribute this fact to the strength of the "instinct of submission" in the Negro. But it has represented an adjustment to the American environment. Nevertheless, it has left its mark on the Negro's character. To this is due the fact that he has taken over many values which have made him appear ridiculous and at the same time have robbed him of self-respect and self-reliance. This group is no more to be expected to embrace radical doctrines than the same class was expected to join slave insurrections, concerning which Denmark Vesey warned his followers: "Don't mention it to those waiting men who receive presents of old coats, etc., from their masters, or they'll betray us."

Even this brief consideration of the social situation which has determined the Negro's attitudes towards values in American life will afford a background for our discussion of the seeming anomaly which he presents to many spectators. We shall attempt to show that, while to most observers the Negro shows an apparent indifference to changing his status, this is in fact a very real and insistent stimulus to his struggles. The

Negro can only envisage those things which have meaning for him. *The radical doctrines appeal chiefly to the industrial workers, and the Negro has only begun to enter industry.* For Negroes to enter industries which are usually in the cities and escape the confinement of the plantation, they have realized a dream that is as far beyond their former condition as the New Economic Order is beyond the present condition of the wage earner. It has often been observed that the Negro subscribes to all the canons of consumption as the owning class in the present system. Even here we find the same struggle to realize a status that he can envisage and has a meaning for him. Once the Negro struggled for a literary education because he regarded it as the earmark of freedom. The relatively segregated life which the Negro lives makes him struggle to realize the values which give status within his group. An automobile, a home, a position as a teacher, or membership in a fraternity may confer a distinction in removing the possessor from an inferior social status, that could never be appreciated by one who is a stranger to Negro life. Outsiders may wonder why a downtrodden, poor, despised people seem so indifferent about entering a struggle that is aimed to give all men an equal status. But if they could enter the minds of Negroes they would find that in the world in which they live they are not downtrodden and despised, but enjoy various forms of distinction.

An interesting episode in the life of the Negro which shows to what extent he is wedded to bourgeois ideals is the present attempt of the Pullman porters to organize. Some people have very superficially regarded this movement as a gesture in the direction of economic radicalism. But anyone who is intimately acquainted with the psychology of the Negro group, especially the porters, knows that this is far from true. One who is connected with the white labor movement showed a better insight through his remark to the writer that the porters showed little working class psychology and

showed a disposition to use their organization to enjoy the amenities of bourgeois social life. The Pullman porters do not show any disposition to overthrow bourgeois values. In fact, for years this group was better situated economically than most Negroes and carried over into their lives as far as possible the behavior patterns which are current in the middle class. In some places they regarded themselves as a sort of aristocracy, and as a colored woman said in one of their meetings recently, "Only an educated gentleman with culture could be a Pullman porter." The advent of a large and consequential professional and business class among Negroes has relegated the Pullman porters to a lower status economically as well as otherwise. Collective bargaining will help them to continue in a role in the colored group which is more in harmony with their conception of their relative status in their group. It is far from the idea of the Pullman porters to tear down the present economic order, and hardly any of them would confess any spiritual kinship with the "poor whites." The Pullman porters are emerging, on the other hand, as an aristocratic laboring group just as the Railroad Brother-hoods have done.

The Negro's lack of sympathy with the white working class is based on more than the feeling of superiority. In the South, especially, the caste system which is based on color, determines the behavior of the white working class. If the Negro has fatuously claimed spiritual kinship with the white bourgeois, the white working class has taken over the tradition of the slave-holding aristocracy. When white labor in the South attempts to treat with black labor, the inferior status of the latter must be conceded in practice and in theory. Moreover, white labor in the South not only has used every form of trickery to drive the Negro out of the ranks of skilled labor, but it has resorted to legislation to accomplish its aims. Experience, dating from before the Civil War, with the white group, has helped to form the attitude of

Negro towards white labor as well as traditional prejudices.*

In the February number of the *Southern Workman* there appears an article in which the psychology of the Negro is portrayed as follows. The discovery is made by a white business man in Chicago:

> The average working-class Negro in Chicago earns $22 a week. His wife sends her children to the Day Nursery or leaves them with relatives or friends, and she supplements the family income by from $10 to $15 or more per week. The average white man of the same class earns $33 per week and keeps his wife at home. This colored man will rent a $65 per month apartment and buy a $50 suit of clothes while the white man will occupy a $30 per month apartment and buy a $25 suit of clothes. This average white man will come into our store to buy furniture and about $300 will be the limit of his estimated purchase, while the colored man will undertake a thousand dollar purchase without the least thought about meeting the payments from his small income.

To the writer of the article the company's new policy in using colored salesmen is a wonderful opportunity for colored men to learn the furniture business. The furniture company is going to make Negroes better citizens, according to the author of the article, by encouraging them to have better homes. This situation represents not only the extent to which the average Negro has swallowed middle-class standards but the attitude of the upper-class Negro towards the same values.

There is much talk at the present time about the New Negro. He is generally thought of as the creative artist who is giving expression to all the stored-up æsthetic emotion of the race. Negro in Art Week has come to take its place beside, above, or below the other three hundred and fifty-two weeks in the American year. But the public is little aware of the Negro business man who regards himself as a new phenomenon. While the New Negro who is expressing himself in art promises in the words of one of his chief exponents not to compete with the white man either politically or economically, the Negro business man seeks the salvation of the race in economic enterprise. In the former case there is either an acceptance of the present system or an ignoring of the economic realities of life. In the case of the latter there is an acceptance of the gospel of economic success. Sometimes the New Negro of the artistic type calls the New Negro business man a Babbitt, while the latter calls the former a mystic. But the Negro business man is winning out, for he is dealing with economic realities. He can boast of the fact that he is independent of white support, while the Negro artist still seeks it. One Negro insurance company in a rather cynical acceptance of the charge of Babbittry begins a large advertisement in a Negro magazine in the words of George F. Babbitt.

A perusal of Negro newspapers will convince anyone that the Negro group does not regard itself as outcasts without status. One cannot appeal to them by telling them that they have nothing to lose but their chains. The chains which Negroes have known in the South were not figurative. Negro newspapers are a good index of the extent to which middle-class ideals have captured the imagination of Negroes. In one newspaper there is a column devoted to What Society Is Wearing. In this column the apparel of those who are socially prominent is described in detail. The parties, the cars, the homes, and the jewelry of the élite find a place in all of these papers. In fact, there is no demand on the part of Negro leaders to tear down social distinctions and create a society of equals. As the writer heard a colored editor tell a white man recently, "the white people draw the line at the wrong point and put all of us in the same class."

*E. Franklin Frazier, *The Negro in the Industrial South*, *The Nation*. Vol. 125, No. 3238.

Negro schools in the South furnish an example of the influence of middle-class ideals which make Negroes appear in a ridiculous light. These schools give annually a public performance. Instead of giving plays such as Paul Green's folk plays of Negro life, they give fashion shows which have been popularized to boost sales. Negro students appear in all kinds of gorgeous costumes which are worn by the leisured middle class. One more often gets the impression that he has seen a Mardi Gras rather than an exhibition of correct apparel.

Even the most ardent radical cannot expect the Negro to hold himself aloof from the struggle for economic competence and only dream of his escape from his subordinate economic status in the overthrow of the present system. A Negro business man who gets out of the white man's kitchen or dining room rightly regards himself as escaping from economic slavery. Probably he will maintain himself by exploiting the Negro who remains in the kitchen, but he can always find consolation in the feeling, that if he did not exploit him a white man would. But in seeking escape from economic subordination, the Negro has generally envisaged himself as a captain of industry. In regard to group efficiency he has shown no concern. For example, a group isolated to the extent of the Negro in America could have developed cooperative enterprises. There has been no attempt in schools or otherwise to teach or encourage this type of economic organization. The idea of the rich man has been held up to him. More than one Negro business has been wrecked because of this predatory view of economic activity.

Many of those who criticize the Negro for selecting certain values out of American life overlook the fact that the primary struggle on his part has been to acquire a culture. In spite of the efforts of those who would have him dig up his African past, the Negro is a stranger to African culture. The manner in which he has taken over the American culture has never been studied in intimate

enough detail to make it comprehensible. The educated class among Negroes has been the forerunners in this process. Except, perhaps, through the church, the economic basis of the civilized classes among Negroes has not been within the group. Although today the growing professional and business classes are finding support among Negroes, the upper classes are subsidized chiefly from without. To some outsiders such a situation makes the Negro intellectual appear as merely an employee of the white group. At times the emasculating effect of Negro men appearing in the role of mere entertainers for the whites has appeared in all its tragic reality. But the creation of this educated class of Negroes has made possible the civilization of the Negro. It may seem conceivable to some that the Negro could have contended on the ground of abstract right for unlimited participation in American life on the basis of individual efficiency; but the Negro had to deal with realities. It is strange that today one expects this very class which represents the most civilized group to be in revolt against the system by which it was created, rather than the group of leaders who have sprung from the soil of Negro culture.

Here we are brought face to face with a fundamental dilemma of Negro life. Dean Miller at Howard University once expressed this dilemma aphoristically, namely, that the Negro pays for what he wants and begs for what he needs. The Negro pays, on the whole, for his church, his lodges and fraternities, and his automobile, but he begs for his education. Even the radical movement which had vogue a few years back was subsidized by the white radical group. It did not spring out of any general movement among Negroes towards radical doctrines. Moreover, black radicals theorized about the small number of Negroes who had entered industry from the security of New York City; but none ever undertook to enter the South and teach the landless peasants any type of self-help. What began as the organ of the struggling working masses became the mouthpiece of Negro capitalists.

The New Negro group which has shown a new orientation towards Negro life and the values which are supposed to spring from Negro life has restricted itself to the purely cultural in the narrow sense.

In his article the writer has attempted to set forth the social forces which have caused the Negro to have his present attitude towards the values in American life. From even this cursory glance at Negro life we are able to see to what extent bourgeois ideals are implanted in the Negro's mind. We are able to see that the Negro group is a highly differentiated group with various interests, and that it is far from sound to view the group as a homogeneous group of outcasts. There has come upon the stage a group which represents a nationalistic movement. This movement is divorced from any program of economic reconstruction. It is unlike the Garvey movement in that Garvey, through schemes—fantastic to be sure—united his nationalistic aims with an economic program. This new movement differs from the program of Booker Washington, which sought to place the culture of the Negro upon a sound basis by making him an efficient industrial worker. Nor does it openly ally itself with those leaders who condemn the organization of the Pullman porters and advise Negroes to pursue an opportunistic course with capitalism. It looks askance at the new rising class of black capitalism while it basks in the sun of white capitalism. It enjoys the congenial company of white radicals while shunning association with black radicals. The New Negro Movement functions in the third dimension of culture; but so far it knows nothing of the other two dimensions—Work and Wealth.

Speech Delivered at Liberty Hall, N. Y. C., During Second International Convention of Negroes

Marcus Garvey

Four years ago, realizing the oppression and the hardships from which we suffered, we organized ourselves into an organization for the purpose of bettering our condition, and founding a government of our own. The four years of organization have brought good results, in that from an obscure, de-

Source: Marcus Garvey, Speech Delivered at Liberty Hall, N. Y. C., During Second International Convention of Negroes, August 1921. From Amy Jacques-Garvey, ed., *Philosophy and Opinions of Marcus Garvey* (New York; Universal Publishing House, 1923, 1925), Volume I, pp. 93–97, 237–39.

spised race we have grown into a mighty power, a mighty force whose influence is being felt throughout the length and breadth of the world. The Universal Negro Improvement Association existed but in name four years ago, today it is known as the greatest moving force among Negroes. We have accomplished this through unity of effort and unity of purpose, it is a fair demonstration of what we will be able to accomplish in the very near future, when the millions who are outside the pale of the Universal Negro Improvement Association will have linked themselves up with us.

By our success of the last four years we will be able to estimate the grander success of a free and redeemed Africa. In climbing the heights to where we are today, we have had to surmount difficulties, we have had to climb over obstacles, but the obstacles were stepping stones to the future greatness of this Cause we represent. Day by day we are writing a new history, recording new deeds of valor performed by this race of ours. It is true that the world has not yet valued us at our true worth but we are climbing up so fast and with such force that every day the world is changing its attitude towards us. Wheresoever you turn your eyes to-day you will find the moving influence of the Universal Negro Improvement Association among Negroes from all corners of the globe. We hear among Negroes the cry of "Africa for the Africans". This cry has become a positive, determined one. It is a cry that is raised simultaneously the world over because of the universal oppression that affects the Negro. You who are congregated here tonight as Delegates representing the hundreds of branches of the Universal Negro Improvement Association in different parts of the world will realize that we in New York are positive in this great desire of a free and redeemed Africa. We have established this Liberty Hall as the centre from which we send out the sparks of liberty to the four corners of the globe, and if you have caught the spark in your section, we want you to keep it a-burning for the great Cause we represent.

There is a mad rush among races everywhere towards national independence. Everywhere we hear the cry of liberty of freedom, and a demand for democracy. In our corner of the world we are raising the cry for liberty, freedom and democracy. Men who have raised the cry for freedom and liberty in ages past have always made up their minds to die for the realization of the dream. We who are assembled in this Convention as Delegates representing the Negroes of the world give out the same spirit that the fathers of liberty in this country gave out over one hundred years ago. We give out a spirit that knows no compromise, a spirit that re-

fuses to turn back, a spirit that says "Liberty or Death", and in prosecution of this great ideal—the ideal of a free and redeemed Africa, men may scorn, men may spurn us, and may say that we are on the wrong side of life, but let me tell you that way in which you are travelling is just the way all peoples who are free have travelled in the past. If you want Liberty you yourselves must strike the blow. If you must be free you must become so through your own effort, through your own initiative. Those who have discouraged you in the past are those who have enslaved you for centuries and it is not expected that they will admit that you have a right to strike out at this late hour for freedom, liberty and democracy.

At no time in the history of the world, for the last five hundred years, was there ever a serious attempt made to free Negroes. We have been camouflaged into believing that we were made free by Abraham Lincoln. That we were made free by Victoria of England, but up to now we are still slaves, we are industrial slaves, we are social slaves, we are political slaves, and the new Negro desires a freedom that has no boundary, no limit. We desire a freedom that will lift us to the common standard of all men, whether they be white men of Europe or yellow men of Asia, therefore, in our desire to lift ourselves to that standard we shall stop at nothing until there is a free and redeemed Africa.

I understand that just at this time while we are endeavoring to create public opinion and public sentiment in favor of a free Africa, that others of our race are being subsidized to turn the attention of the world toward a different desire on the part of Negroes, but let me tell you that we who make up this Organization know no turning back, we have pledged ourselves even unto the last drop of our sacred blood that Africa must be free. The enemy may argue with you to show you the impossibility of a free and redeemed Africa, but I want you to take as your argument the thirteen colonies of America, that once owed their sovereignity to great Britain, that soverignity has been destroyed to make a United States of America. George Washington was not God Almighty. He was a man like any Negro in this building, and if he and his associates were able to make a free America, we too can make a free Africa. Hampden, Gladstone, Pitt and Disraeli were not the representatives of God in the person of Jesus Christ. They were but men, but in their time they worked for the expansion of the British Empire, and today they boast of a British Empire upon which "the sun never sets." As Pitt and Gladstone were able to work for the expansion of the British Empire, so you and I can work for the expansion of a great African Empire. Voltaire and Mirabeau were not Jesus Christs, they were but men like ourselves. They worked and overturned the French Monarchy. They worked for the Democracy which France now enjoys, and if they were able to do that, we are able to work for a democracy in Africa. Lenine and Trotzky were not Jesus Christs, but they were able to overthrow the despotism of Russia, and today they have given to the world a Social Republic, the first of its kind. If Lenine and Trotzky were able to do that for Russia, you and I can do that for Africa. Therefore, let no man, let no power on earth, turn you from this sacred cause of liberty. I prefer to die at this moment rather than not to work for the freedom of Africa. If liberty is good for certain sets of humanity it is good for all. Black men, Colored men, Negroes have as much right to be free as any other race that God Almighty ever created, and we desire freedom that is unfettered, freedom that is unlimited, freedom that will give us a chance and opportunity to rise to the fullest of our ambition and that we cannot get in countries where other men rule and dominate.

We have reached the time when every minute, every second must count for something done, something achieved in the cause of Africa. We need the freedom of Africa now, therefore, we desire the kind of leadership that will give it to us as quickly as possible. You will realize that not only individuals, but governments are using their influence against us. But what do we care about the unrighteous influence of any government? Our cause is based upon righteousness. And anything that is not righteous we have no respect for, because God Almighty is our leader and Jesus Christ our standard bearer. We rely on them for that kind of leadership that will make us free, for it is the same God who inspired the Psalmist to write "Princes shall come out of Egypt and Ethiopia shall stretch out her hands unto God". At this moment methinks I see Ethiopia stretching forth her hands unto God and methinks I see the Angel of God taking up the standard of the Red, the Black and the Green, and saying "Men of the Negro Race, Men of Ethiopia, follow me". Tonight we are following. We are following 400,000,000 strong. We are following with a determination that we must be free before the wreck of matter, before the crash of worlds.

It falls to our lot to tear off the shackles that bind Mother Africa. Can you do it? You did it in the Revolutionary War. You did it in the Civil War; You did it at the Battles of the Marne and Verdun; You did it in Mesopotamia. You can do it marching up the battle heights of Africa. Let the world know that 400,000,000 Negroes are prepared to die or live as free men. Despise us as much as you care. Ignore us as much as you care. We are coming 400,000,000 strong. We are coming with our woes behind us, with the memory of suffering behind us—woes and suffering of three hundred years—they shall be our inspiration. My bulwark of strength in the conflict for freedom in Africa, will be the three hundred years of persecution and hardship left behind in this Western Hemisphere. The more I remember the suffering of my fore-fathers, the more I remember the lynchings and burnings in the Southern States of America, the more I will fight on even though the battle seems doubtful. Tell me that I must turn back, and I laugh you to scorn. Go on! Go on! Climb ye the heights of liberty and cease not in well doing until you have planted the banner of the Red, the Black and the Green on the hill-tops of Africa.

FIRST MESSAGE TO THE NEGROES OF THE WORLD FROM ATLANTA PRISON

February 10, 1925.

Fellow Men of the Negro Race, Greeting: I am delighted to inform you, that your humble servant is as happy in suffering for you and our cause as is possible under the circumstances of being viciously outraged by a group of plotters who have connived to do their worst to humiliate you through me, in the fight for real emancipation and African Redemption.

I do trust that you have given no credence to the vicious lies of white and enemy newspapers and those who have spoken in reference to my surrender. The liars plotted in every way to make it appear that I was willing to surrender to the court. My attorney advised me that no mandate would have been handed down for ten or fourteen days, as is the custom of the courts, and that would have given me time to keep speaking engagements I had in Detroit, Cincinnati and Cleveland. I hadn't left the city for ten hours when the liars flashed the news that I was a fugitive. That was good news to circulate all over the world to demoralize the millions of Negroes in America, Africa, Asia, the West Indies and Central America, but the idiots ought to know by now that they can't fool all the Negroes at the same time.

I do not want at this time to write anything that would make it difficult for you to meet the opposition of the enemy without my assistance. Suffice it to say that the history of the outrage shall form a splendid chapter in the history of Africa redeemed, when black men will no longer be under the heels of others, but have a civilization and country of their own.

The whole affair is a disgrace, and the whole black world knows it. We shall not forget. Our day may be fifty, a hundred or two hundred years ahead, but let us watch, work and pray, for the civilization of injustice is bound to crumble and bring destruction down upon the heads of the unjust.

The idiots thought that they could humiliate me personally, but in that they are mistaken. The minutes of suffering are counted, and when God and Africa come back and measure out retribution these minutes may multiply by thousands for the sinners. Our Arab and Riffian friends will be ever vigilant, as the rest of Africa and ourselves shall be. Be assured that I planted well the seed of Negro or black nationalism which cannot be destroyed even by the foul play that has been meted out to me.

Continue to pray for me and I shall ever be true to my trust. I want you, the black peoples of the world, to know that W. E. B. Du Bois and that vicious Negro-hating organization known as the Association for the Advancement of "Colored" People are the greatest enemies the black people have in the world. I have so much to do in the few minutes at my disposal that I cannot write exhaustively on this or any other matter, but be warned against these two enemies. Don't allow them to fool you with fine sounding press releases, speeches and books; they are the vipers who have planned with others the extinction of the "black" race.

My work is just begun, and when the history of my suffering is complete, then future generations of Negroes will have in their hands the guide by which they shall know the "sins" of the twentieth century. I, and I know you, too, believe in time, and we shall wait patiently for two hundred years, if need be, to face our enemies through our posterity.

You will cheer me much if you will now do even more for the organization than when I was among you. Hold up the hands of those who are carrying on. Help them to make good, so that the work may continue to spread from pole to pole.

I am also making a last minute appeal for support to the Black Cross Navigation and Trading Company. Please send in and make your loans so as to enable the directors to successfully carry on the work.

All I have I have given to you. I have sacrificed my home and my loving wife for you. I entrust her to your charge, to protect and defend her in my absence. She is the bravest little woman I know. She has suffered and sacrificed with me for you; therefore, please do not desert her at this dismal hour, when she stands alone. I have left her penniless and helpless to face the world, because I gave you all, but her courage is great, and I know she will hold up for you and me.

After my enemies are satisfied, in life or death I shall come back to you to serve even as I have served before. In life I shall be the same; in death I shall be a terror to the foes of Negro liberty. If death has power, then count on me in death to be the real Marcus Garvey I would like to be. If I may come in an earthquake, or a cyclone, or plague, or pestilence, or as God would have me, then be assured that I shall never desert you and make your enemies triumph over you. Would I not go to hell a million times for you? Would I not like Macbeth's ghost, walk the earth forever for you? Would I not lose the whole world and eternity for you? Would I not cry forever before the footstool of the Lord Omnipotent for you? Would I not die a million deaths for you? Then, why be sad? Cheer up, and be assured that if it takes a million years the sins of our enemies shall visit the millionth generation of those that hinder and oppress us.

Remember that I have sworn by you and my God to serve to the end of all time, the wreck of matter and the crash of worlds. The enemies think that I am defeated. Did the Germans defeat the French in 1870? Did Napolean really conquer Europe? If so, then I am defeated, but I tell you the world shall hear from my principles even two thousand years hence. I am willing to wait on time for my satisfaction and the retribution of my enemies. Observe my enemies and their children and posterity, and one day you shall see retribution settling around them.

If I die in Atlanta my work shall then only begin, but I shall live, in the physical or spiritual to see the day of Africa's glory. When I am dead wrap the mantle of the Red, Black and Green around me, for in the new life I shall rise with God's grace and blessing to lead the millions up the heights of triumph with the colors that you well know. Look for me in the whirlwind or the storm, look for me all around you, for, with God's grace, I shall come and bring with me countless millions of black slaves who have died in America and the West Indies and the millions in Africa to aid you in the fight for Liberty, Freedom and Life.

The civilization of today is gone drunk and crazy with its power and by such it seeks through injustice, fraud and lies to crush the unfortunate. But if I am apparently crushed by the system of influence and misdirected power, my cause shall rise again to plague the conscience of the corrupt. For this I am satisfied, and for you, I repeat, I am glad to suffer and even die. Again, I say, cheer up, for better days are ahead. I shall write the history that will inspire the millions that are coming and leave the posterity of our enemies to reckon with the hosts for the deeds of their fathers.

With God's dearest blessings, I leave you for awhile.

Black Manhattan

James Weldon Johnson

Williams and Walker came from out of the West. They came singing one of the catchiest songs of the day, "Dora Dean," which they themselves had written after the quite adequate inspiration of a sight of Miss Dora Dean, one of the famed beauties of the *Creole Show.* They reached New York in 1896. They had been together as a team for several years, undergoing all the special vicissitudes of a coloured vaudeville team of the period, when they were engaged to appear in *The Gold Bug,* produced at the Casino Theatre by Canary and Lederer. *The Gold Bug* did not quite catch Broadway's fancy, but Williams and Walker did; and after the failure of the Casino show they were engaged for the famous Koster and Bial's, where they played a record run of forty weeks. It was during this engagement that Williams and Walker made the cake-walk not only popular, but fashionable. They were assisted by two girls; one of them, Stella Wiley, was the cleverest coloured soubrette of the day. Cake-walk pictures posed for by the quartet were reproduced in colours and widely distributed as advertisements by one of the big cigarette concerns. And the execution of cake-walk steps was taken up by society. Cake-walking became such a society fad that on Sunday morning, January 16, 1898, Williams and Walker, dressed just a point or two above the height of fashion, dared, as a publicity stunt, to call at the home of William K. Vanderbilt and leave the following letter:

To Mr. William K. Vanderbilt
Corner of Fifty-second Street
and Fifth Avenue
New York

Dear Sir:
In view of the fact that you have made a success as a cake-walker, having appeared in a semi-public exhibition and having posed as an expert in that capacity, we, the undersigned world-renowned cake-walkers, believing that the attention of the public has been distracted from us on account of the tremendous hit which you have made, hereby challenge you to compete with us in a cake-walking match, which will decide which of us shall deserve the title of champion cake-walker of the world.

As a guarantee of good faith we have this day deposited at the office of the New York *World* the sum of $50. If you purpose proving to the public that you really are an expert cake-walker we shall be pleased to have you cover that amount and name the day on which it will be convenient for you to try odds against us.

Yours very truly,
Williams and Walker.

Regarding the size of the stakes, Williams, who habitually left all business matters to Walker, is reported as saying: "It's a shame to take the money, so make the stakes small, George."

The two comedians next tried the London music-halls, but the English appeared not to be able to understand or appreciate their particular brand of humour; so they came back to New York and went out at the head of a mediocre show, *A Senegambian Carnival,* which promptly stranded. They followed with *4—11—44,* afterwards changed to *The*

Source: From James Weldon Johnson, *Black Manhattan.* Published by Viking 1930.

Policy Players. This was also a failure. In 1900 they brought out *The Sons of Ham,* and in this humorous-pathetic musical farce they struck their stride. In 1902 they produced *In Dahomey* and made Negro theatrical history by opening at the very centre of theatredom, at the New York Theatre in Times Square. In the spring of 1903 *In Dahomey* was taken to London. The two principals, remembering their reception in the London music-halls, were somewhat apprehensive about the venture; but the show was a success and ran for seven months at the Shaftesbury Theatre, afterwards touring the provinces. The unquestioned stamp of approval was put on it when at the end of the first month the company received a royal command for a performance at Buckingham Palace, on June 23. The performance was part of the celebration in honour of the ninth birthday of the present Prince of Wales and was given on a stage erected on the lawn. *In Dahomey* made the cake-walk a social fad in England and France. In 1906 Williams and Walker opened with *In Abyssinia* at the Majestic Theatre in Columbus Circle, New York. This was followed by *Bandana Land* in 1907.

Bandana Land was the last play in which Williams and Walker appeared together; during its run George Walker's health broke and he never again stepped on the stage. The Williams and Walker company was, all in all, the strongest Negro theatrical combination that has yet been assembled. In addition to Williams and Walker there were Jesse Shipp, Alex Rogers, Will Marion Cook, and Ada Overton. Mr. Shipp had had long theatrical experience, beginning with minstrelsy, and he it was who worked out the details of the construction of the plays, after the idea had been discussed and adopted by the above-named heads. Mr. Rogers was the lyricist and the author of the words to many of the most popular of the Williams and Walker songs; among them: "Why Adam Sinned," "I May Be Crazy, but I Ain't No Fool," "The Jonah Man," "Bon Bon Buddy, the Chocolate Drop," and "Nobody." He also contributed much of the droll humour and many of the ludicrous situations for which these plays were noted. Mr. Cook, of whom we have already spoken, was the composer-in-chief. Ada Overton (Mrs. George Walker) was beyond comparison the brightest star among women on the Negro stage of the period; and it is a question whether or not she has since been surpassed. She was an attraction in the company not many degrees less than the two principals. And there was also one of the best singing choruses ever heard on a musical-comedy stage. Of course the main strength of the combination centered in the two comedians; George Walker as the sleek, smiling, prancing dandy, and Bert Williams as the slow-witted, good-natured, shuffling darky. Together they achieved something beyond mere fun; they often achieved the truest comedy through the ability they had to keep the tears close up under the loudest laughter.

Bert Williams went out alone in 1909 in *Mr. Lode of Kole,* which had little success and was the last Negro show in which he ever appeared. The next year he was engaged for the Ziegfeld *Follies* and remained a member of the cast for practically ten seasons. In 1920 he was the star in *Broadway Brevities,* and in 1922 the star in *The Pink Slip,* which after a tryout was rewritten and called *Under the Bamboo Tree.* He was a sick man when he went out with this last play; and after it had been on the road but a few weeks, he had to be brought back to New York. He died March 11, 1922, not yet forty-seven years old. Bert Williams goes down as one of America's great comedians. He has had few equals in the art of pantomime—a judgment with which those who saw him in his poker scene will agree. In the singing of a plaintive Negro song he was beyond approach. His singing of "Nobody" was perfection.

After three seasons with Cole and Johnson's *A Trip to Coontown* Bob Cole, in 1901, formed a partnership with another Johnson, this time J. Rosamond Johnson, the musician and singer, and the new Cole and Johnson became head-liners in big-time vaudeville.

They sang their own songs and were a success in this country and in Europe. In the mean time they collaborated on the writing of white musical plays, and through this some of their songs gained worldwide popularity. In 1906 Cole and Johnson wrote and appeared in a musical play called *The Shoofly Regiment*, which played in New York at the Bijou Theatre on Broadway. In 1908 they came out in another play of their own, *The Red Moon*. Each of these plays was a true operetta with a well-constructed book and a tuneful, well-written score. On these two points no Negro musical play has equalled *The Red Moon*. The Cole and Johnson combination lacked any such fun-makers as were Williams and Walker, but in some other respects they excelled their great rivals; their plays, on the whole, were better written, and they carried a younger, sprightlier, and prettier chorus, which, though it could not sing so powerfully, could outdance the heavier chorus of the other company by a wide margin.

The break in health that ended the careers of Bob Cole and George Walker, and the defection of Bert Williams to the white stage, all happening within a brief period of time, put a sudden stop to what had been a steady development and climb of the Negro in the theatre. In this first decade of the century plays headed by Ernest Hogan and Smart and Williams, and S. H. Dudley, and some other performers, were produced, but all these shows, though organized in New York, were road shows and of secondary merit. The Hogan shows, *Rufus Rastus* and *The Oyster Man*, were the most important of them. Hogan might have carried on, because he was a splendid comedian and had a New York reputation; but he died a short while before George Walker's retirement.

There came an interval, and the efforts of the Negro in New York in the theatre were for a while transferred to Harlem.

Towards the close of the minstrel era and during the middle theatrical period the Negro in New York gained an important place among the makers of the nation's songs. For a century or more the Negro in America had been a folk-song maker. Blackface minstrelsy, in its beginnings, depended for its songs almost entirely on the Negro plantation jingles. In the earliest attempts to write songs for the minstrel stage there was merely slavish imitation or outright appropriation of this folk-material. It is plain that even so great a song-writer as Stephen Foster, who wrote his best songs when he lived in Cincinnati, just across the river from Kentucky, was greatly indebted to the enormous supply of Negro folk-song material at hand. But quite early the Negro emerged as an individual song-maker. Foster, America's first real song-writer, was at his height in the fifties; and in 1855 there appeared a song which became as popular and remains as lasting as any song he wrote, with the exception, perhaps, of "My Old Kentucky Home," "Old Folks at Home," and "Old Black Joe." In Philadelphia there lived a coloured barber named Richard Milburn, who worked in his father's shop on Lombard Street near Sixth. He was a guitar-player and a marvellous whistler, and it was he who originated the melody and at least the title of "Listen to the Mocking-Bird." Credit for this song is given to Septimus Winner (or to Alice Hawthorne, which was his mother's name, under which he published some of his compositions), but the truth is that Winner only set down the melody and arranged it after it had been played and whistled and sung over to him by Milburn. Winner or someone else may have furnished most or all of the words, but the life of the song springs from the melody. Old coloured residents of Philadelphia used to relate that before the song was ever published, Milburn played and whistled it at several gatherings, notably at a concert that was given at St. Thomas's Church, the coloured Episcopal church in Philadelphia. But the incontrovertible proof of Milburn's part in the making of the song is shown by its title-page as originally published by Winner and Shuster, under the copyright date of

1855, which reads: "Sentimental Ethiopian Ballad—*Listen To The Mocking Bird*—Melody by Richard Milburn—Written and arranged by Alice Hawthorne." The title-page of the song as published by Lee and Walker, under the copyright date of 1856, reads: "*Listen to the Mocking Bird*—As sung by Rose Merrifield—Written and arranged by Alice Hawthorne." Richard Milburn's name has not since appeared on the song.

One of the most popular of the minstrel songs of the seventies was "Carve dat 'Possum," written by Sam Lucas. Then from the ranks of the Negro minstrels there rose a really great song-writer in James Bland, who has already been mentioned. Bland wrote a long list of songs, of which four, at least, possess the qualities that entitle him to a place in the front rank of American song-writers. They are: "Carry Me Back to Old Virginny." "Oh, dem Golden Slippers," "In the Morning by the Brightlight," and "In the Evening by the Moonlight." Where is there the close-harmony quartet that has not revelled in the possibilities for barber-shop chords furnished by "In the Evening by the Moonlight"? Frequently upon occasions "Carry Me Back to Old Virginny" is used in lieu of a state song. The bust of Patrick Henry was unveiled at the Hall of Fame May 8, 1930; the Governor of Virginia delivered the address of dedication, and immediately after the unveiling the trumpeters played "Carry Me Back to Old Virginny." All of Bland's songs hark back to the South—a South of tenderness and beauty. Following him came Gussie L. Davis, a typical New York writer, whose songs have not the slightest relation to the South or even to the Negro. Davis was a writer of popular ballads and as such had no superior, as anyone familiar with the songs of a generation ago will agree. Among many other songs he wrote: "Down in Poverty Row," "The Fatal Wedding," "In a Lighthouse by the Sea," "We Sat Beneath the Maple on the Hill," "Send Back the Picture and the Wedding Ring," and "The Baggage Coach Ahead."

The close of the nineties and the following decade was the high-water-mark period of the coloured writers of popular songs in New York. Some were writers of only one or perhaps two songs that caught the public, and others wrote long lists of hits. Let those with an interest in the old songs muse for a moment over the following bit of cataloguing: Ernest Hogan wrote one song that swept this and other countries, a song which he, later in life, expressed regret at ever having written; it was "All Coons Look Alike to Me." The melody of the song was beautiful and the words quite innocuous, but the little became a byword and an epithet of derision. Another writer of a single hit with a title that became a catch phrase was Al Johns, who wrote "Go 'Way Back and Sit Down." He wrote a number of other songs, some of them beautiful love-ballads, but it was this musical oddity that brought him his moment of fame. Will Accoe wrote "My Samoan Beauty." Chris Smith, with R. C. McPherson doing the words, wrote "Good Morning, Carrie," a song with a melody that sang itself. Tim Brymn, with R. C. McPherson, wrote "Please Go 'Way and Let Me Sleep" and "Josephine, My Jo." Sheppard Edmonds wrote "I'm Goin' to Live Anyhow until I Die." Irving Jones, a happy-go-lucky philosopher in song, wrote "I'm Living Easy" and "Take Your Clothes and Go." Williams and Walker had everybody singing "Dora Dean," "Why Don't You Get a Lady of Your Own," "I Don't Like No Cheap Man," "When It's All Goin' Out and Nothin' Comin' In," and other songs besides. The Cole and Johnson combination, through their collaboration on Broadway musical plays, wrote a string of popular hits. Among them were: "Under the Bamboo Tree," "The Congo Love Song," "The Maiden with the Dreamy Eyes," "Nobody's Looking but the Owl and the Moon," "Lazy Moon," "My Castle on the Nile," "I've Got Troubles of My Own," "Tell Me, Dusky Maiden," "I Must have been A-Dreaming," and "Oh, Didn't He Ramble?" The Cole and Johnson songs were sung by the most popular musical-comedy stars of the day: May Irwin, Marie Cahill, Fay Templeton, Lillian Russell, Anna Held, Virginia Earle, Marie George, Mabelle Gilman. Will Marion Cook wrote "Exhortation," "Rain Song," and "Bon Bon Buddy, the Chocolate Drop"—with words by Alex Rogers. Bert Williams, with Rogers, wrote "Jonah Man," "I May be Crazy but I Ain't No Fool," "Nobody," and "Why Adam Sinned"—better known, perhaps, as "Adam Never had no Mammy." There were also several writers of popular instrumental music, the outstanding one being Will Tyers, who wrote "La Trocha," "La Mariposa," and "Maori." This list of writers could be extended, as could the lists of songs by the several writers; but here is enough to indicate how important the Negro in New York came to be in the making of popular songs for the American people. There are at present a score or so of coloured writers of popular songs in New York actively at work in that profession. Outstanding among them are Jimmy Johnson, Spencer Williams, Andy Razaf and Thomas (Fats) Waller, who together wrote "My Fate is in Your Hands," which is now very popular, and Maceo Pinkard, who wrote "Mammy," a song made famous by Al Jolson. Eight or ten Negro writers are members of the American Society of Composers, Authors and Publishers, where they are received on an equal footing with others. This organization has for its purpose the collecting of royalty for the performance of music written by its members that may be performed in the theatres, broadcasting stations, hotels, restaurants, cabarets, and such places. There are similar societies in other countries, but the American society is the strongest in the world; last year it distributed among its members nearly a million and a half dollars.

In the mean time Harry T. Burleigh was writing songs which were to give him his place among American composers. In the work of writing the more musicianly songs J. Rosamond Johnson and Will Marion Cook also took part. These three men, unlike the other song-writers named, are thoroughly trained musicians. Mr. Burleigh was a stu-dent at the National Conservatory of Music in New York while Anton Dvorák was director. He studied harmony with Rubin Goldmark and counterpoint with Max Spicker. He not only studied with Dvorák, but spent a good deal of time with him at his home. It was he who called to the attention of the great Bohemian composer the Negro Spirituals and is therefore in that degree responsible for the part they play in the "New World" Symphony. In 1894 he had the unique distinction of being made baritone soloist at St. George's Church. Regarding this revolutionary innovation, Dr. William S. Rainsford, then rector of St. George's, says in his autobiography: "I broke the news to them [the St. George's choir] that I was going to have for soloist a Negro, Harry Burleigh. Then division, consternation, confusion, and protest reigned for a time. I never knew how the troubled waters settled down. Indeed, I carefully avoided knowing who was for and who against my revolutionary arrangement. Nothing like it had even been known in the church's musical history. The thing was arranged and I gave no opportunity for its discussion." The troubled waters did settle down, and Mr. Burleigh has held his position for now thirty-six years. In 1900 he became a member of the choir of Temple Emanu-El, at Fifth Avenue and Forty-third Street, and at the end of his twenty-fifth year was given an engrossed testimonial expressing the appreciation of the congregation for his services. He has written more than a hundred songs besides his arrangements of the Spirituals. Among them are "Jean," "Little Mother of Mine," "Just You" "The Young Warrior," and "The Glory of the Day was in Her Face."

Mr. Johnson received his training at the New England Conservatory of Music, Boston. Mr. Cook studied at the Hochschule in Berlin, and the violin under Joachim. These two men have worked in both the popular and the more classical field, but their reputations have been gained chiefly in the former. Mr. Burleigh, on the other hand, has consistently stuck to the latter. Mr. John-son has had a varied musical career and has shown great versatility. He has written the music for Negro musical comedies; he has written scores for white Broadway musical comedies; he was the Supervisor of Music at the London Opera House, Oscar Hammer-stein's venture in the English metropolis; and when Messrs. Harris and Lasky at-tempted to give New York something more Parisian than anything in the French capital in *Hello Paris* at the Folies Bergére (now the Fulton Theatre), he wrote the music for that spicy revue, trained the members of the company, and conducted the orchestra, this being, it seems, the only time a Negro has conducted a white orchestra in a New York Theatre for a play with a white cast. He has written songs of every description, from a Mississippi roust-about frolic like "Roll dem Cotton Bales" to a delicate love-song like "Three Questions." The best-known of his more ambitious songs are: "Sence You Went Away," "Lit'l Gal," and "The Awakening." He has arranged some hundred and fifty Negro Spirituals. But his most widely sung composition is "Lift Ev'ry Voice and Sing," a song that is used as a national hymn in coloured schools and churches and at Negro gatherings all over the country.

In the midst of the period we are now considering, another shift in the Negro pop-ulation took place; and by 1900 there was a new centre established in West Fifty-third Street. In this new centre there sprang up a new phase of life among coloured New Yorkers. Two well-appointed hotels, the Marshall and the Maceo, run by coloured men, were opened in the street and became the centres of a fashionable sort of life that hitherto had not existed. These hotels served dinner to music and attracted crowds of well-dressed people. On Sunday evenings the crowd became a crush; and to be sure of service one had to book a table in advance. This new centre also brought about a revolu-tionary change in Negro artistic life. Those engaged in artistic effort deserted almost

completely the old clubs farther downtown, and the Marshall, run by Jimmie Marshall, an accomplished Boniface, became famous as the headquarters of Negro talent. There gathered the actors, the musicians, the com-posers, the writers, and the better-paid vaudevillians; and there one went to get a close-up of Cole and Johnson, Williams and Walker, Ernest Hogan, Will Marion Cook, Jim Europe, Ada Overton, Abbie Mitchell, Al Johns, Theodore Drury, Will Dixon, and Ford Dabney. Paul Laurence Dunbar was often there. A good many white actors and musi-cians also frequented the Marshall, and it was no unusual thing for some among the biggest Broadway stars to run up there for an evening. So there were always present numbers of those who love to be in the light reflected from celebrities. Indeed, the Mar-shall for nearly ten years was one of the sights of New York, for it was gay, entertain-ing, and interesting. To be a visitor there, without at the same time being a rank out-sider, was a distinction. The Maceo run by Benjamin F. Thomas had the more staid clientele.

In the brightest days of the Marshall the temporary blight had not yet fallen on the Negro in the theatre. Williams and Walker and Cole and Johnson were at their height; there were several good Negro road compa-nies touring the country, and a considerable number of coloured performers were on the big time in vaudeville. In the early 1900's there came to the Marshall two young fel-lows, Ford Dabney and James Reese Europe, both of them from Washington, who were to play an important part in the artistic devel-opment of the Negro in a field that was, in a sense, new. It was they who first formed the coloured New York entertainers who played instruments into trained, organized bands, and thereby became not only the daddies of the Negro jazz orchestras, but the grand-daddies of the unnumbered jazz orchestras that have followed. Ford Dabney organized and directed a jazz orchestra which for a number of years was a feature of Florenz

Ziegfeld's roof-garden shows. Jim Europe organized the Clef Club. Joe Jordan also became an important factor in the development of Negro bands.

How long Negro jazz bands throughout the country had been playing jazz at dances and in honky-tonks cannot be precisely stated, but the first modern jazz band ever heard on a New York stage, and probably on any other stage, was organized at the Marshall and made its début at Proctor's Twenty-third Street Theatre in the early spring of 1905. It was a playing-singing-dancing orchestra, making dominant use of banjos, mandolins, guitars, saxophones, and drums in combination, and was called the Memphis Students—a very good name, overlooking the fact that the performers were not students and were not from Memphis. There was also a violin, a couple of brass instruments, and a double-bass. The band was made up of about twenty of the best performers on the instruments mentioned above that could be got together in New York. They had all been musicians and entertainers for private parties, and as such had played together in groups varying in size, according to the amount the employing host wished to spend. Will Marion Cook gave a hand in whipping them into shape for their opening. They scored an immediate success. After the Proctor engagement they went to Hammerstein's Victoria, playing on the vaudeville bill in the day, and on the roof-garden at night. In the latter part of the same year they opened at Olympia in Paris; from Paris they went to the Palace Theatre in London, and then to the Schumann Circus in Berlin. They played all the important cities of Europe and were abroad a year.

At the opening in New York the performers who were being counted on to carry the stellar honours were: Ernest Hogan, comedian; Abbie Mitchell, soprano; and Ida Forsyne, dancer; but while they made good, the band proved to be the thing. The instrumentalists were the novelty. There was one thing they did quite unconsciously; which,

however, caused musicians who heard them to marvel at the feat. When the band played and sang, there were men who played one part while singing another. That is, for example, some of them while playing the lead, sang bass, and some while playing an alto part sang tenor; and so on, in accordance with the instrument each man played and his natural voice. The Memphis Students deserve the credit that should go to pioneers. They were the beginners of several things that still persist as jazzband features. They introduced the dancing conductor. Will Dixon, himself a composer of some note, conducted the band here and on its European tour. All through a number he would keep his men together by dancing out the rhythm, generally in graceful, sometimes in grotesque, steps. Often an easy shuffle would take him across the whole front of the band. This style of directing not only got the fullest possible response from the men, but kept them in just the right humour for the sort of music they were playing. Another innovation they introduced was the trick trap-drummer. "Buddy" Gilmore was the drummer with the band, and it is doubtful if he has been surpassed as a performer of juggling and acrobatic stunts while manipulating a dozen noise-making devices aside from the drums. He made this style of drumming so popular that not only was it adopted by white professionals, but many white amateurs undertook to learn it as a social accomplishment, just as they might learn to do card tricks. The whole band, with the exception, of course, of the players on wind-instruments, was a singing band; and it seems safe to say that they introduced the singing band—that is, a band singing in four-part harmony and playing at the same time.

One of the original members of the Memphis Students was Jim Europe. Afterwards he went for a season or two as the musical director with the Cole and Johnson shows; and then in the same capacity with Bert William's *Mr. Lode of Kole.* In 1910 he carried out an idea he had, an idea that had a business as well as an artistic reason behind it, and organized the

Clef Club. He gathered all the coloured professional instrumental musicians into a chartered organization and systematized the whole business of "entertaining." The organization purchased a house in West Fifty-third Street and fitted it up as a club, and also as booking-offices. Bands of from three to thirty men could be furnished at any time, day or night. The Clef Club for quite a while held a monopoly of the business of "entertaining" private parties and furnishing music for the dance craze, which was then just beginning to sweep the country. One year the amount of business done amounted to $120,000.

The crowning artistic achievement of the Clef Club was a concert given at Carnegie Hall in May 1912. The orchestra for the occasion consisted of one hundred and twenty-five performers. It was an unorthodox combination—as is every true jazz orchestra. There were a few strings proper, the most of them being 'cellos and double-basses; the few wind-instruments consisted of cornets, saxophones, clarinets, and trombones; there was a battery of drums; but the main part of the orchestra was composed of banjos, mandolins, and guitars. On this night all these instruments were massed against a background of ten upright pianos. In certain parts the instrumentation was augmented by the voices. New York had not yet become accustomed to jazz; so when the Clef Club opened its concert with a syncopated march, playing it with a biting attack and an infectious rhythm, and on the finale bursting into singing, the effect can be imagined. The applause became a tumult. It is possible that such a band as that could produce a similar effect even today.

Later Jim Europe with his orchestra helped to make Vernon and Irene Castle famous. When the World War came, he assembled the men for the band of the Fifteenth, New York's noted Negro regiment. He was with this band giving a concert in a Boston theatre, after their return from the War, when he met his tragic end.

1912 was also the year in which there came up out of the South an entirely new genre of Negro songs, one that was to make an immediate and lasting effect upon American popular music; namely, the blues. These songs are as truly folk-songs as the Spirituals, or as the original plantation songs, levee songs, and rag-time songs that had already been made the foundation of our national popular music. The blues were first set down and published by William C. Handy, a coloured composer and for a while a bandleader in Memphis, Tennessee. He put out the famous "Memphis Blues" and the still more famous "St. Louis Blues" and followed them by blues of many localities and kinds. It was not long before the New York songwriters were turning out blues of every variety and every shade. Handy followed the blues to New York and has been a Harlemite ever since, where he is known as the "Father of the Blues." It is from the blues that all that may be called *American music* derives its most distinctive characteristic.

It was during the period we have just been discussing that the earliest attempt at rendering opera was made by Negroes in New York. Beginning in the first half of the decade 1900–10 and continuing for four or five years, the Theodore Drury Opera Company gave annually one night of grand opera at the Lexington Opera House. Among the operas sung were *Carmen*, *Aida*, and *Faust*. These nights of grand opera were, at least, great social affairs and were looked forward to months ahead. In September 1928 H. Lawrence Freeman, a Negro musician and the composer of six grand operas, produced his opera *Voodoo* at the Fifty-second Street Theatre. Mr. Freeman's operas are *The Martyr*, *The Prophecy*, *The Octoroon*, *Plantation*, *Vendetta*, and *Voodoo*. In the spring of the present year he presented scenes from various of his works in Steinway Hall. He was the winner of the 1929 Harmon Award and Medal for musical composition.

Some Things Negroes Need to Do*

Carter G. Woodson

There are certain things the Negroes in this country must do if they hope to enjoy the blessings of real democracy, if it ever comes.

In the first place, we need to attain economic independence. You may talk about rights and all that sort of thing. The people who own this country will rule this country. They always have done so and they always will. The people who control the coal and iron, the banks, the stock markets, and all that sort of thing, those are the people who will dictate exactly what shall be done for every group in this land. More than that, liberty is to come to the Negro, not as a bequest, but as a conquest. When I speak of it as a conquest, I mean that the Negro must contribute something to the good of his race, something to the good of his country, and something to the honor and glory of God. Economic independence is the first step in that direction.

I was in Washington the other day and a man told me that the colored people were about to have a new bank there—"and they have two already," he said. I answered, "They should have had ten banks forty years ago." Two banks among a hundred thousand Negroes! We must learn to take these things more seriously.

I was speaking to a gentleman the other day about the organization of an insurance company, and he was telling of the wonderful things we have done in the way of insurance. After he had summarized the receipts of the various companies now organized among Negroes it was just a little modicum, so to speak, compared with the great achievements in insurance on the part of members of the white race. Here we are, rejoicing over these little things, and we have hardly begun to make a beginning.

Then we must have educational independence. If the Negro is not going to become an educational factor among his own people, then education is not the leverage to lift him, in the sense it has lifted other people; for a man is educated when he can do without a teacher, when he can and will develop and grow without the stimulus of instruction. So must it be with a race. If we are not going to reach that point some day in our lives when we shall be able to go out and establish schools and become persons well rounded in philosophy and science and history and what-not, and be able to help one another; if we are not going to prepare ourselves here, three generations from slavery, to do that work for ourselves, then we cannot say that education has done for our group what it has done for others.

Then the Negro needs to develop a press. Some of us never read a Negro newspaper— and some are not worth reading. A few, however, tell the story of the Negro in a cool, calm way. They tell of the strivings of the Negro in such a way as to be an inspiration to youth. Every Negro ought to read the publications of his own race.

I was impressed in California to find that, although there are only ten thousand Japanese in San Francisco, they have two daily papers—only ten thousand, but they have two daily papers of eight pages each. We have over ten million in the United States and we have not yet developed a real daily newspaper. We should not complain if the white papers do not tell our own story. We complain because they publish our crimes and tell of

Source: Carter G. Woodson, "Some Things Negroes Need to Do." *The Southern Workman,* Vol. LI, No. 1 (January, 1922), pp. 33–36.

*Excerpts from an address at Hampton Institute, November 5, 1921.

the evils that we do but do not say anything of our achievements in those lines that tend to stamp us as people of the world. We must learn to tell the story ourselves. It is our duty to develop a press.

We should also develop a literature. Negroes should read some things written by their own people that they may be inspired thereby. You will never be a George Washington or a Thomas Jefferson—you will never be a white man—but you will be a Negro, and we must realize that there are certain things in the Negro race worth developing. Those things may be worth as much to the world as the things of the white race when they are properly developed. We must cease trying to straighten our hair and bleach our faces, and be Negroes—and be good ones.

In this literature you will get the inspiration you need to be like Frederick Douglass, Booker Washington, S. Coleridge-Taylor, or Paul Laurence Dunbar. If you can contribute to the world what those men have you will have no reason to regret that you cannot be a George Washington or a Thomas Jefferson, because you will still be identified with some of the greatest men who have ever appeared in the history of the world.

The Negro must learn to preserve his own records. He must learn the value of tradition. I was speaking to a teacher the other day. I wanted to get some information as to his people. I asked him who his grandfather was. "I am not sure," he said, "what my grandfather's name was." It may be that some of you do not know your grandfathers. You have not thought they were worth while. Although they perhaps could not read and write, they contributed much to the making of the race. They made it possible for you to be where you are to-day. They bore the burden and heat of the day. Some of them achieved a great deal more than some of us could have achieved.

If you should go to Cincinnati and speak with some of the old citizens—those who lived there before the Civil War—they would tell you that the Negroes of Cincinnati achieved more prior to the Civil War than they have since. There was a man who had patented a cord-bed which became popular throughout the United States, just as the spring-bed is popular to-day. In the exploitation of that patent he built up a large business and employed scores of white men and Negroes. He was worth thousands of dollars.

There was a Negro who went from this State—a Negro from Richmond, Va., who had worked in a blacksmith shop. His master permitted him to sell the slack of the coal. He accumulated a large sum of money, about $15,000, and he went to his master and purchased himself. He then went North and settled finally in Cincinnati. He knew the coal business and entered that business there. The people thought they would run him out of business and they said, "We coal dealers will get together and lower the price of coal to such an extent that he will be ruined." This Negro was wise. He sent mulattoes around to fill all his orders at the white coal yard, so that his supply would be kept on hand. The white coal dealers exhausted their supply and there came a great freezing. No coal could get through up the river and the railroads had not been constructed. This Negro had all his coal on hand. Nobody else could get any, and he sold out at a handsome profit. He then had so much money to enlarge his business that they never thought of combining against him again. That was in 1869. That Negro was worth something like $60,000. There isn't a Negro in Cincinnati to-day worth $60,000.

We have a wonderful history behind us. We of the *Journal of Negro History* shall have going the rounds soon a lecture on the antebellum period, setting forth the stories of Negroes who did so much to inspire us. It reads like the history of people in an heroic age. We expect to send out from time to time books written for the express purpose of showing you that you have a history, a record, behind you. If you are unable to demonstrate to the world that you have this record, the world will say to you, "You are not worthy to enjoy the blessings of democracy or anything else." They will say to you, "Who are you, anyway? Your ancestors have never controlled empires or kingdoms and most of your race have contributed little or nothing to science and philosophy and mathematics." So far as you know, they have not; but if you will read the history of Africa, the history of your ancestors—people of whom you should feel proud—you will realize that they have a history that is worth while. They have traditions that have value of which you can boast and upon which you can base a claim for a right to a share in the blessings of democracy.

Let us, then, study this history, and study it with the understanding that we are not, after all, an inferior people, but simply a people who have been set back, a people whose progress has been impeded. We are going back to that beautiful history and it is going to inspire us to greater achievements. It is not going to be long before we can so sing the story to the outside world as to convince it of the value of our history and our traditions, and then we are going to be recognized as men.

Enter the New Negro

Alain Locke

In the last decade something beyond the watch and guard of statistics has happened in the life of the American Negro and the three norns who have traditionally presided over the Negro problem have a changeling in their laps. The Sociologist, The Philanthropist, the Race-leader are not unaware of the New Negro, but they are at a loss to account for him. He simply cannot be swathed in their formulae. For the younger generation is vibrant with a new psychology; the new spirit is awake in the masses, and under the very eyes of the professional observers is transforming what has been a perennial problem into the progressive phases of contemporary Negro life.

Could such a metamorphosis have taken place as suddenly as it has appeared to? The answer is no; not because the New Negro is not here, but because the Old Negro had long become more of a myth than a man. The Old Negro, we must remember, was a creature of moral debate and historical controversy. His has been a stock figure perpetuated as an historical fiction partly in innocent sentimentalism, partly in deliberate reactionism. The Negro himself has contributed his share to this through a sort of protective social mimicry forced upon him by the adverse circumstances of dependence. So for generations in the mind of America, the Negro has been more of a formula than a human being—a something to be argued about, condemned or defended, to be "kept down," or "in his place," or "helped up," to be worried with or worried over, harassed or patronized, a social bogey or a social burden. The thinking Negro even has been induced to share this same general attitude, to focus his attention on controversial issues, to see himself in the distorted

Source: Alain Locke, "Enter the New Negro." *Survey,* LIII (March 1, 1925), pp. 631–634.

perspective of a social problem. His shadow, so to speak, has been more real to him than his personality. Through having had to appeal from the unjust stereotypes of his oppressors and traducers to those of his liberators, friends and benefactors he has subscribed to the traditional positions from which his case has been viewed. Little true social or self-understanding has or could come from such a situation.

But while the minds of most of us, black and white, have thus burrowed in the trenches of the Civil War and Reconstruction, the actual march of development has simply flanked these positions, necessitating a sudden reorientation of view. We have not been watching in the right direction; get North and South on a sectional axis, we have not noticed the East till the sun has us blinking.

Recall how suddenly the Negro spirituals revealed themselves; suppressed for generations under the stereotypes of Wesleyan hymn harmony, secretive, half-ashamed, until the courage of being natural brought them out—and behold, there was folk-music. Similarly the mind of the Negro seems suddenly to have slipped from under the tyranny of social intimidation and to be shaking off the psychology of imitation and implied inferiority. By shedding the old chrysalis of the Negro problem we are achieving something like a spiritual emancipation. Until recently, lacking self-understanding, we have been almost as much of a problem to ourselves as we still are to others. But the decade that found us with a problem has left us with only a task. The multitude perhaps feels as yet only a strange relief and a new vague urge, but the thinking few know that in the reaction the vital inner grip of prejudice has been broken.

With this renewed self-respect and self-dependence, the life of the Negro community is bound to enter a new dynamic phase, the buoyancy from within compensating for whatever pressure there may be of conditions from without. The migrant masses, shifting from countryside to city, hurdle several generations of experience at a leap, but

more important, the same thing happens spiritually in the life-attitudes and self-expression of the Young Negro, in his poetry, his art, his education and his new outlook, with the additional advantage, of course, of the poise and greater certainty of knowing what it is all about. From this comes the promise and warrant of a new leadership. As one of them has discerningly put it:

> We have tomorrow
> Bright before us
> Like a flame.
> Yesterday, a night-gone thing
> A sun-down name.
> And dawn today
> Broad arch above the road we came.
> We march!

This is what, even more than any "most creditable record of fifty years of freedom," requires that the Negro of today be seen through other than the dusty spectacles of past controversy. The day of "aunties," "uncles" and "mammies" is equally gone. Uncle Tom and Sambo have passed on, and even the "Colonel" and "George" play barnstorm roles from which they escape with relief when the public spotlight is off. The popular melodrama has about played itself out, and it is time to scrap the fictions, garret the bogeys and settle down to a realistic facing of facts.

First we must observe some of the changes which since the traditional lines of opinion were drawn have rendered these quite obsolete. A main change has been, of course, that shifting of the Negro population which has made the Negro problem no longer exclusively or even predominantly Southern. Why should our minds remain sectionalized, when the problem itself no longer is? Then the trend of migration has not only been toward the North and the Central Midwest, but city-ward and to the great centers of industry—the problems of adjustment are new, practical, local and not peculiarly racial. Rather they are an integral part of the large industrial and social problems of our present-day democracy. And finally, with the Negro rapidly in process of class differentiation, if it ever was warrantable to regard and treat the Negro en masse it is becoming with every day less possible, more unjust and more ridiculous.

The Negro too, for his part, has idols of the tribe to smash. If on the one hand the white man has erred in making the Negro appear to be that which would excuse or extenuate his treatment of him, the Negro, in turn, has too often unnecessarily excused himself because of the way he has been treated. The intelligent Negro of today is resolved not to make discrimination an extenuation for his short-comings in performance, individual or collective; he is trying to hold himself at par, neither inflated by sentimental allowances nor depreciated by current social discounts. For this he must know himself and be known for precisely what he is, and for that reason he welcomes the new scientific rather than the old sentimental interest. Sentimental interest in the Negro has ebbed. We used to lament this as the falling off of our friends; now we rejoice and pray to be delivered both from self-pity and condescension. The mind of each racial group has had a bitter weaning, apathy or hatred on one side matching disillusionment or resentment on the other; but they face each other today with the possibility at least of entirely new mutual attitudes.

It does not follow that if the Negro were better known, he would be better liked or better treated. But mutual understanding is basic for any subsequent cooperation and adjustment. The effort toward this will at least have the effect of remedying in large part what has been the most unsatisfactory feature of our present stage of race relationships in America, namely the fact that the more intelligent and representative elements of the two race groups have at so many points got quite out of vital touch with one another.

The fiction is that the life of the races is separate, and increasingly so. The fact is that they have touched too closely at the unfavorable and too lightly at the favorable levels.

While inter-racial councils have sprung up in the South, drawing on forward elements of both races, in the Northern cities manual laborers may brush elbows in their everyday work, but the community and business leaders have experienced no such interplay or far too little of it. These segments must achieve contact or the race situation in America becomes desperate. Fortunately this is happening. There is a growing realization that in social effort the cooperative basis must supplant long-distance philanthropy, and that the only safeguard for mass relations in the future must be provided in the carefully maintained contacts of the enlightened minorities of both race groups. In the intellectual realm a renewed and keen curiosity is replacing the recent apathy; the Negro is being carefully studied, not just talked about and discussed. In art and letters, instead of being wholly caricatured, he is being seriously portrayed and painted.

To all of this the New Negro is keenly responsive as an augury of a new democracy in American culture. He is contributing his share to the new social understanding. But the desire to be understood would never in itself have been sufficient to have opened so completely the protectively closed portals of the thinking Negro's mind. There is still too much possibility of being snubbed or patronized for that. It was rather the necessity for fuller, truer self-expression, the realization of the unwisdom of allowing social discrimination to segregate him mentally, and a counter-attitude to cramp and fetter his own living—and so the "spite-wall" that the intellectuals built over the "color-line" has happily been taken down. Much of this reopening of intellectual contacts has centered in New York and has been richly fruitful not merely in the enlarging of personal experience but in the definite enrichment of American art and letters and in the clarifying of our common vision of the social tasks ahead.

The particular significance in the reestablishment of contact between the more advanced and representative classes is that it promises to offset some of the unfavorable reaction of the past, or at least to re-surface race contacts somewhat for the future. Subtly the conditions that are moulding a New Negro are moulding a new American attitude.

However, this new phase of things is delicate; it will call for less charity but more justice; less help, but infinitely closer understanding. This is indeed a critical stage of race relationships because of the likelihood, if the new temper is not understood, of engendering sharp group antagonism and a second crop of more calculated prejudice. In some quarters, it has already done so. Having weaned the Negro, public opinion cannot continue to paternalize. The Negro today is inevitably moving forward under the control largely of his own objectives. What are these objectives? Those of his outer life are happily already well and finally formulated, for they are none other than the ideals of American institutions and democracy. Those of his inner life are now in process of formation, for the new psychology at present is more of a consensus of feeling than of opinion, of attitude rather than of program. Still some points seem to have crystallized.

Up to the present one may adequately describe the Negro's "inner objectives" as an attempt to repair a damaged group psychology and reshape a warped social perspective. Their realization has required a new mentality for the American Negro. And as it matures we begin to see its effects; at first, negative, iconoclastic, and then positive and constructive. In this new group psychology we note the lapse of sentimental appeal, then the development of a more positive self-respect and self-reliance; the repudiation of social dependence, and then the gradual recovery from hyper-sensitiveness and "touchy" nerves, the repudiation of the double standard of judgment with its special philanthropic allowances and then the sturdier desire to objective and scientific appraisal; and finally the rise from social disillusionment to race pride, from the sense of social debt to the responsibilities of social contribution, and of setting the necessary working and commonsense acceptance of restricted conditions, the belief in ultimate esteem and recognition. Therefore the Negro today wishes to be known for what he is, even in his faults and shortcomings, and scorns a craven and precarious survival at the price of seeming to be what he is not. He resents being spoken for as a social ward or minor, even by his own, and to being regarded a chronic patient for the sociological clinic, the sick man of American Democracy. For the same reasons, he himself is through with those social nostrums and panaceas, the so-called "solutions" of his "problem," with which he and the country have been so liberally dosed in the past. Religion, freedom, education, money—in turn, he has ardently hoped for and peculiarly trusted these things; he still believes in them, but not in blind trust that they all will solve his life-problem.

Each generation, however, will have its creed, and that of the present is the belief in the efficacy of collective effort in race cooperation. This deep feeling of race is at present the mainspring of Negro life. It seems to be the outcome of the reaction to proscription and prejudice; an attempt, fairly successful on the whole, to convert a defensive into an offensive position, a handicap into an incentive. It is radical in tone, but not in purpose and only the most stupid forms of opposition, misunderstanding or persecution could make it otherwise. Of course, the thinking Negro has shifted a little toward the left with the world-trend, and there is an increasing group who affiliate with radical and liberal movements. But fundamentally for the present the Negro is radical on race matters, conservative on others, in other words, a "forced radical," a social protestant rather than a genuine radical. Yet under further pressure and injustice iconoclastic thought and motives will inevitably increase. Harlem's quixotic radicalisms call for their ounce of democracy today lest tomorrow they be beyond cure.

The Negro mind reaches out as yet to nothing but American wants, American ideas. But this forced attempt to build his Americanism on race values is a unique social experiment, and its ultimate success is impossible except through the fullest sharing of American culture and institutions. There should be no delusion about this. American nerves in sections unstrung with race hysteria are often fed the opiate that the trend of Negro advance is wholly separatist, and that the effect of its operation will be to encyst the Negro as a benign foreign body in the body politic. This cannot be—even if it were desirable. The racialism of the Negro has no limitation or reservation with respect to American life; it is only a constructive effort to build the obstructions in the stream of his progress into an efficient dam of social energy and power. Democracy itself is obstructed and stagnated to the extent that any of its channels are closed. Indeed they cannot be selectively closed. So the choice is not between one way for the Negro and another way for the rest, but between American institutions frustrated on the one hand and American ideals progressively fulfilled and realized on the other.

There is, of course, a warrantably comfortable feeling in being on the right side of the country's professed ideals. We realize that we cannot be undone without America's undoing. It is within the gamut of this attitude that the thinking Negro faces America, but the variations of mood in connection with it are if anything more significant than the attitude itself. Sometimes we have it taken with the defiant ironic challenge of McKay:

Mine is the future grinding down today
Like a great landslip moving to the sea,
Bearing its freight of debris far away
Where the green hungry waters restlessly
Heave mammoth pyramids and break and
  roar
Their eerie challenge to the crumbling shore.

Sometimes, perhaps more frequently as yet, in the fervent and almost filial appeal and counsel of Weldon Johnson's:

O Southland, dear Southland!
Then why do you still cling
To an idle age and a musty page,
To a dead and useless thing.

But between defiance and appeal, midway almost between cynicism and hope, the prevailing mind stands in the mood of the same author's To America, an attitude of sober query and stoical challenge:

How would you have us, as we are?
Or sinking 'neath the load we bear,
Our eyes fixed forward on a star,
Or gazing empty at despair?

Rising or falling? Men or things?
With dragging pace or footsteps fleet?
Strong, willing sinews in your wings,
Or tightening chains about your feet?

More and more, however, an intelligent realization of the great discrepancy between the American social creed and the American social practice forces upon the Negro the taking of the moral advantage that is his. Only the steadying and sobering effect of a truly characteristic gentleness of spirit prevents the rapid rise of a definite cynicism and counter-hate and a defiant superiority feeling. Human as this reaction would be, the majority still deprecate its advent, and would gladly see it forestalled by the speedy amelioration of its causes. We wish our race pride to be a healthier, more positive achievement than a feeling based upon a realization of the shortcomings of others. But all paths toward the attainment of a sound social attitude have been difficult; only a relatively few enlightened minds have been able as the phrase puts it "to rise above" prejudice. The ordinary man has had until recently only a hard choice between the alternatives of supine and humiliating submission and stimulating but hurtful counter-prejudice. Fortunately from some inner, desperate resourcefulness has recently sprung up the simple expedient of fighting prejudice by mental passive resistance, in other words by trying to ignore it. For the few, this manna may perhaps be effective, but the masses cannot thrive on it.

Fortunately there are constructive channels opening out into which the balked social feelings of the American Negro can flow freely.

Without them there would be much more pressure and danger than there is. These compensating interests are racial but in a new and enlarged way. One is the consciousness of acting as the advanceguard of the African peoples in their contact with Twentieth Century civilization; the other, the sense of a mission of rehabilitating the race in world esteem from that loss of prestige for which the fate and conditions of slavery have so largely been responsible. Harlem, as we shall see, is the center of both these movements; she is the home of the Negro's "Zionism." The pulse of the Negro world has begun to beat in Harlem. A Negro newspaper carrying news material in English, French and Spanish, gathered from all quarters of America, the West Indies and Africa, has maintained itself in Harlem for over five years. Two important magazines, both edited from New York, maintain their news and circulation consistently on a cosmopolitan scale. Under American auspices and backing, three pan-African congresses have been held abroad for the discussion of common interests, colonial questions and the future cooperative development of Africa. In terms of the race question as a world problem, the Negro mind has leapt, so to speak, upon the parapets of prejudice and extended its cramped horizons. In so doing it has linked up with the growing group consciousness of the dark-peoples and is gradually learning their common interests. As one of our writers has recently put it: "It is imperative that we understand the white world in its relations to the non-white world." As with the Jew, persecution is making the Negro international.

As a world phenomenon this wider race consciousness is a different thing from the much asserted rising tide of color. Its in-evitable causes are not of our making. The consequences are not necessarily damaging to the best interests of civilization. Whether it actually brings into being new Armadas of conflict or argosies of cultural exchange and enlightenment can only be decided by the attitude of the dominant races in an era of critical change. With the American Negro his new internationalism is primarily an effort to recapture contact with the scattered peoples of African derivation. Garveyism may be a transient, if spectacular, phenomenon, but the possible role of the American Negro in the future development of Africa is one of the most constructive and universally helpful missions that any modern people can lay claim to.

Constructive participation in such causes cannot help giving the Negro valuable group incentives, as well as increased prestige at home and abroad. Our greatest rehabilitation may possibly come through such channels, but for the present, more immediate hope rests in the revaluation by white and black alike of the Negro in terms of his artistic endowments and cultural contributions, past and prospective. It may be increasingly recognized that the Negro has aleady made very substantial contributions, not only in his folk-art, music especially, which has always found appreciation, but in larger, though humbler and less acknowledged ways. For generations the Negro has been the peasant matrix of that section of America which has most undervalued him, and here he has contributed not only materially in labor and in social patience, but spiritually as well. The South has unconsciously absorbed the gift of his folk-temperament. In less than half a generation it will be easier to recognize this, but the fact remains that a leaven of humor, sentiment, imagination and tropic nonchalance has gone into the making of the South from a humble, unacknowledged source. A second crop of the Negro's gifts promises still more largely. He now becomes a conscious contributor and lays aside the status of a beneficiary and ward for that of a collaborator and participant in American civilization. The great social gain in this is the releasing of our talented group from the arid fields of controversy and debate to the productive fields of creative expression. The especially cultural recognition they win should in turn prove the key to that revaluation of the Negro which must precede or accompany any considerable further betterment of race relationships. But whatever the general effect, the present generation will have added the motives of self-expression and spiritual development to the old and still unfinished task of making material headway and progress. No one who understandingly faces the situation with its substantial accomplishment or views the new scene with its still more abundant promise can be entirely without hope. And certainly, if in our lifetime the Negro should not be able to celebrate his full initiation into American democracy, he can at least, on the warrant of these things, celebrate the attainment of a significant and satisfying new phase of group development, and with it a spiritual Coming of Age.

The Negro Looks at an Outworn Tradition

Alice Dunbar Nelson

The New Negro—that altogether fascinating and partially mythical creature, conceived by Dr. Alain Locke, and adopted by most of the United States—is living up to the reputation given him by his progenitor. In addition to the usual shibboleths of "seeing life whole," "facing the sun," "expressing himself," he is beginning to think, weigh, consider, analyze. Particularly is he gravely analyzing the dividing line between myth and history, religion and superstition, tradition and fact. He is beginning to learn that much of what he has accepted as Gospel for centuries is nothing but stale and outworn creeds, dogmas, catch-words, slogans, dripping with falsity, and mouldy with senility, not inherent in himself either as a race or as an individual, but foisted upon him by a Caucasian world apprehensive of destruction, and bolstering its supremacy by mental subjugation of the underling.

Source: Alice Dunbar Nelson, "The Negro Looks at an Outworn Tradition." *The Southern Workman,* Vol. LVII, No. 5, (May, 1928), pp. 195–200.

The Negro has begun to study his own history. Like most of the movements, which we call Renaissance, this study is nothing absolutely new. Since emancipation and the "Auto-biography of Frederick Douglass" there have been sporadic books, histories of the Negro, histories of the Negro in war, more or less authentic, more or less written with regard for conventional English, descending to biographical sketches or certain obscure individuals who had contributed to the publication of these volumes.

But this Renaissance has dealt more with historical background. Hardly any other Renaissance has paid so much attention to history. The Negro has learned about his African backgrounds, his African tradition, his African culture. He has learned about his contribution to the culture of this continent. He knows what gifts he has brought to America. He is racially conscious as never before.

But this movement, as with all movements in which the Negro is a component part, is one with a confused objective. He has acquired all the Caucasian's traditions, superstitions, ideas, inhibitions, narrowness.

Centuries of slavery had wiped clean the slate of his past. He had nothing of his own. He took on the language, religion, customs of his owners.

Therefore, it is no wonder that he has the white man's idea of history—a chronicle of wars, murders, plots and counterplots, obscure kinglets, stupid rulers, foolish ceremonies. As Voltaire caustically puts it, "History is nothing more than a picture of crimes and misfortunes * * * much like reading the history of highway robbers." So his earlier books chronicle the Negro in war, battles, regiments. It was a generation before the progress of the race meant anything but the story of valor on the battlefield.

This is the one objective. The other is the Negro's own ideal. His definition of contribution to the nation is that of the arts of peace. He is prone to tell you proudly of the first blood shed in the War for Independence. But his pride in that is merely a reflex of the traditions of Massachusetts and the Boston Tea Party. He is actually more proud of Phillis Wheatley's poem to George Washington, of Banneker's Almanac and his friendship with Thomas Jefferson, of the bar sinister on Alexander Hamilton's escutcheon. When he discusses the French and Indian War, because the white American has taught in the histories that that bloody conflict was a moral procedure on account of European conditions, the Negro will boast of the sporadic groups of free and enslaved of his race who helped win the wilderness from France; but in the next breath, he will declaim proudly of the forests he felled, the bridges he built, the streams he dammed, the protection he gave to his owners.

It is a significant fact that the splendid work of Dr. Carter Woodson reflects something of this ideal of a peaceful contribution to the nation. Volume after volume tells of economic progress, scientific strivings, literary ambitions. Dr. W. E. B. DuBois spends a volume to tell of the "Gift of Black Folk" and he is far more interested in the story of the granulation of sugar, of the life of Dr. John Derham, the first Negro physician, and such

chronicles, than in the war record of the black man, even at New Orleans with Andrew Jackson.

This confused objective, this dual outlook, is one of the tragedies of the life of the Negro. Like any other people thrown into an alien civilization with no memories of his own that could have survived his introduction to this continent, he must of necessity, chameleon-like, take on the coloring of his surroundings. When militarism is rampant, he is a militarist. He boasts that the old flag never touched the ground, and hates Indians, Germans, Mexicans, Chinese, anyone who threatens the supremacy of the white American with a fine disregard for personal interests or truth. He has taken on this civilization and he swears by it, even though it destroys his racial life and makes of him a mere adjunct to the pomp and circumstance of his oppressor. He worships a white God, with Nordic angels, and once accepted the Biblical interpretation of the necessity of slavery, even as a certain civilization in an earlier day accepted the Old Testament pronouncement on polygamy. The Negro had taken his ideals of dress, manners, customs, everything from the white man. His superstitions, later research has proved, are not altogether the remnants of African voodoo and *obeah*. The witches of Salem, the "hex" doctors of Pennsylvania, the backwoods rites of the South filtered to the Negro, rather than the Negro giving his rites to the white man.

Nothing is more illustrative of the white man's inhibitions caught and held by the Negro than his attitude on the question of votes for women. He had heard through generations of slavery the Southern ideal of false chivalry, of woman's place in the home, of her constitution too tender and delicate to be exposed to the ruthless gaze of the ballot box. And he gravely advanced like arguments against his own women voting, regardless of the fact that the Negro woman had always had to work, had never had the privilege of staying at home and nursing her delicateness, was pretty strong and capable, and had probably made a more practical contribution to the race than like numbers of males.

Small wonder, then, that the Negro found himself caught in the whirlwind of war. Small wonder, then, that he was confused, floundering; that two ideals presented themselves for his consideration, and that he hesitated to choose, and so hesitating, was all but lost.

For the Negro is by nature a lover of peace. By his own nature, by his deep-seated religious fervor, by his love of home and family, by his gentle and kindly spirit, by the tenderness of his native sympathies, by his centuries of patience and gentleness and forbearance, by his horror of violence and the deeds of violence, he is opposed to war. He will contend and hold on and be stubborn in his moral fight for his rights, privileges, children, religion, racial integrity—but organized warfare is a thing he enters only under the tutelage of the white man. In short, the Negro is brave, but he is not a mass murderer. If rage and hate and the lust of killing make him mad, he kills alone—but he does not lynch the helpless with a mob.

He believes in Christianity. If it were not for the black man in this country, the Christian religion would be at a low point on the graph. And he takes the teaching of the Master literally. If Christianity means the cessation of strife among nations, and he is a Christian, then he believes in his soul that war is wrong.

The New Negro—he who has come of age since 1918—is more firmly convinced even than his elder brother who went overseas, his father who charged up San Juan Hill, or his grandfather who wore the blue in the sixties, that it is all a holocaust of unnecessary carnage. He is weighing skeptically the struggles of that father or uncle who for all his uniform suffered martyrdom in Brownsville and Leavenworth; of that elder brother, who for all his sacrifice in Flanders to make a world safe for democracy, who, in spite of his glorious uniform and medals pinned on his breast for valor, yet has been barred from some of the chapters of the American Legion, and sternly rejected from the coveted "Forty and Eight."

Someone has wittily said that "Old men make wars, young men fight them, women and children suffer from them." A nation is militarized because older men have greed. Grasping for iron and coal and oil, they invent insults, and the flower of the youth of the countries goes forth to avenge fancied wrongs. The Negro is an integral part of whatever nation wherein he happens to be born, and he takes on the customs, languages, wrongs, insults, superstitions, traditions, loyalties, ideals of that land. Therefore the flower of his race, too, went forth for cannon fodder. What it was all about he did not know, did not ask, any more than any other youth. He was fighting the white man's battles, to avenge insults to the white man, given by other white men. And when it was all over, he came home to be kicked around by these same white men. The glorious exception, of course, was the Civil War. There has been no occasion since for the Negro to fight for his own cause. On the other occasions, it seems as if his reward has been a thrill that ceased when the last note of the drum beat had died away.

An age of skepticism toward conventions, a break-down of traditions, has brought with it an attitude of analysis of the clinging to outworn traditions. Just why should the Negro continue in his allegiance toward certain traditional beliefs? Just why shall he accept certain ready-made convictions, slogans, Babbitries? Why send him to school for sixty years, and spend billions upon his education if it were not to develop within him the faculty of reasoning, of weighing, considering, judging for himself? So he turns the white light of his focus upon the vital questions touching life: Religion, Society, Politics, War. And in this last he finds matter for profound consideration. Peace against War. Christ against cannon. Lincoln, Sherman, and Grant against Bismarck. Kant and the great philosophers against Nietsche and Hearst and the jingoes. With the Quaker in Voltaire's

"Dictionaire Philosophique" he says, "Our God, who has bidden us love our enemies and suffer evil without complaint, assuredly has no mind that we should cross the sea to go and cut the throats of our brothers because murderers in red clothes and hats two feet high enlist citizens by making a noise with two sticks on an ass's skin."

The Negro has been misunderstood so much himself that he sympathizes most deeply with those who are misunderstood. He therefore can look most deeply into the causes of war. He can clearly visualize it as the result of misunderstanding, noncomprehension of the essentials of *meum* and *teum*. Rather than murder in cold blood the robber of his hen roost or wood yard, he would apprehend the intruder, and hale him before a court of law there to be given a punishment to fit the crime. Then there is no murder on his soul, no widow to call down curses upon his hasty temper, no orphans whose lives are changed from opportunity to bitterness.

This does not mean that the Negro, whose thoughts are turning to the peaceful solution of the world's maladjustments, is disloyal to his country and his flag. There is no group in this land more passionately loyal or patri-

otic. The favorite boast of the race is that in its hands "the old flag never touched the ground." The favorite peroration of the Negro spell-binder, and one which always evokes the most sustained applause is the recital of his patriotic devotion to the nation in time of war, his readiness when the country calls. He is none the less ready. But he does not want the land of his birth to plunge itself into unnecessary and avertable conflicts.

But looking around him, the Negro is aghast at the implications and perhaps imprecations hurled upon the simple believer in the teachings of Christ, the clear thinker who sees the futility of carnage to settle disputes, the member of a race who believes with Washington that it were better to keep free of entangling alliances. "Pacifist" is a term of contempt in time of peace, of opprobrium in time of war. And there are some organizations of peace and amity and goodwill in which a Negro is not wanted any more than in some war organizations. Small wonder then, if the Negro sadly concludes that peace is ofttimes a white man's peace, as war is ofttimes a white man's war—until time of dire emergency.

SUGGESTED READINGS

Jacqueline Goggin, *Carter G. Woodson: A Life in Black History* (Baton Rouge, La., 1993)

Peter Gottlieb, *Making Their Own Way: Southern Blacks' Migration to Pittsburgh, 1916–1930* (Urbana, Ill., 1997)

Farah Jasmine Griffin, *"Who Set You Flowin'?": The African-American Migration Narrative* (New York, 1995)

James R. Grossman, *Land of Hope: Chicago, Black Southerners, and the Great Migration* (Chicago, 1989)

Nathan Huggins, *Harlem Renaissance* (New York, 1971)

Winston James, *Holding Aloft the Banner of Ethiopia: Caribbean Radicalism in Early Twentieth Century America* (London, 1998)

David Katzman, *Before the Ghetto: Black Detroit in the Nineteenth Century* (Urbana, Ill., 1973)

Kenneth L. Kusmer, *A Ghetto Takes Shape: Black Cleveland, 1870–1930* (Urbana, Ill., 1976)

David Levering Lewis, *W. E. B. DuBois: The Fight for Equality in the American Century, 1919–1963* (New York, 2000)

David Levering Lewis, *When Harlem Was in Vogue* (New York, 1982)

Carole Marks, *Farewell—We're Good and Gone: The Great Black Migration* (Bloomington, Ind., 1989)

Kimberley L. Phillips, *Alabama North: African-American Migrants, Community, and Working-Class Activism in Cleveland, 1919–1945* (Urbana, Ill., 1999)

Arnold Rampersad, *The Life of Langston Hughes*, 2 volumes (New York, 1986–88)

Milton C. Sernett, *Bound for the Promised Land: African American Religion and the Great Migration* (Durham, N.C., 1997)

James E. Smethurst, *The New Red Negro: The Literary Left & African American Poetry, 1930–1946* (New York, 1999)

Steven C. Tracy, *Langston Hughes and The Blues* (Urbana, Ill., 1988)

Joe William Trotter, Jr., *Black Milwaukee: The Making of an Industrial Proletariat, 1919–1945* (Urbana, Ill., 1985)

William M. Tuttle, Jr., *Race Riot: Chicago in the Red Summer of 1919* (New York, 1970)

Nancy J. Weiss, *The National Urban League, 1910–1940* (New York, 1974)

Deborah Gray White, *Too Heavy a Load: Black Women in Defense of Themselves, 1894–1994* (New York, 1999)

Lillian Serece Williams, *Strangers in the Land of Paradise: The Creation of an African American Community, Buffalo, NY, 1900–1940* (Bloomington, Ind., 1999)

Mary McLeod Bethune visiting Sanford, Florida, 1936. (*Source:* Bracey Family Archives.)

Chapter 9

A New Deal for Blacks

The Great Depression had serious consequences for the political and economic development of Black America. The gains made in black employment were largely wiped out, and the black unemployment rate grew to be twice that of whites. The establishment of black businesses that peaked in the 1920s came to an abrupt end. Black tenants and sharecroppers were pushed off the land in the south largely as a result of the discriminatory implementation of New Deal agricultural policies. African Americans also did not reap the benefits of such New Deal programs as social security that failed to extend coverage to agricultural and domestic labor. On the whole, however, the New Deal marked a shift in black political loyalties from the party of Lincoln and Frederick Douglass, the Republican party, to the Democratic party and towards an alliance with white liberals and trade unionists. Urban political machines in the north made black voters (nearly half of the black population now resided in the north) an integral part of the New Deal coalition. During the 1930s, the Communist Party, because of its policy favoring interracial organizing both in its own ranks and in the new industrial and tenant farmer unions, and its championship of cases such as Scottsboro, attracted some blacks to its ranks. With the coming of the Second World War, African Americans, who fought in segregated units and faced severe discrimination in the home front, fought for a "Double V," victory against fascism abroad and racism at home. Growing black frustration at the slow pace of change during and after the war would form the backdrop to the rise of one of the largest mass movements in U.S. history, the Civil Rights movement.

The documents presented here illustrate this transition in African American history. The documents on conditions in Harlem before the outbreak of the race riot of 1935 and female domestic workers reveal the economic plight of African Americans during the depression. The resolutions of the Second Amenia Conference indicate the black response to the problems posed by the Great Depression. Roi Ottley's description of the "Black Cabinet," a group of leading African American men and women who sought to influence public policy, reveal black reactions to the New Deal. Attempts to ease black unemployment through "Don't Buy Where You Can't Work" campaigns and to combat discrimination against African Americans in the defense industries led to A. Phillip Randolph's call for a March on Washington for jobs. The proposed march pushed President Franklin D. Roosevelt to issue an Executive Order mandating fair employment practices, the first federal intervention to prevent racial discrimination since Reconstruction. Both documents are included in this chapter.

233

Selections by Ulysses Lee and Mattie Tread-well illustrate the extent of racism in the still-segregated U.S. Army during the Second World War. President Truman, who desegregated the army in 1948, made civil rights a part of the Democratic party agenda when he formed the President's Commission on Civil Rights, whose report is given below. Kenesaw Landis's description of segregation in Washington, D.C., and the sym-posium on the fate of all-black colleges in the era of integration set the stage for the debates over integration in the Civil Rights era. The chapter ends with vivid portraits of two prominent African Americans from the interwar years: Carter G. Woodson, the great black historian, and Mary McLeod Bethune, an activist in the cause of education and her race.

Resolutions of the Second Amenia Conference, August 18–21, 1933

This conference was called to make a critical appraisal of the Negro's existing situation in American society and to consider underlying principles for future action. Such criticism at this stage does not involve the offering of concrete program for any organization for administrative guidance.

There has been no attempt to disparage the older type of leadership. We appreciate its importance and contributions, but we feel that in a period in which economic, political, and social values are rapidly shifting, and the very structure of organized society is being revamped, the leadership which is necessary is that which will integrate the special problems of the Negro within the larger issues facing the nation.

The primary problem is economic. Individual ownership expressing itself through the control and exploitation of natural resources and industrial machinery has failed

Source: "Resolutions of the Second Amenia Conference, August 18–21, 1933," NAACP Papers. Copyright 1933 NAACP. The author wishes to thank the National Association for the Advancement of Colored People for authorizing the use of this work.

in the past to equalize consumption with production.

As a result of this failure the whole system of private property and private profit is being called into question. The government is being forced to attempt an economic reorganization based upon a "co-partnership" between capital, labor and government itself. The government is attempting to augment consumptive power by increasing wages, shortening hours and controlling the labor and commodity markets. As a consumer the Negro has always had a low purchasing power as a result of his low wages coming from his inferior and restricted position in the labor market. If the government program fails to make full and equal provision for the Negro, it cannot be effective in restoring economic stability.

In the past there has been a greater exploitation of Negro labor than of any other section of the working class, manifesting itself particularly in lower wages, longer hours, excessive use of child labor and a higher proportion of women at work. Furthermore, there has been slight recognition by Negro labor or Negro leaders of the significance of this exploitation in the economic order. No technique or philosophy has been developed to change the historic status of Negro labor. Hence in the present governmental set-up there is grave danger that this historic status will be perpetuated. As a result the lower wages on the one hand will reduce the purchasing power of Negro labor and on the other be a constant threat to the standards and security of white labor.

The question then arises how far existing agencies working among and for Negroes are theoretically and structurally prepared to cope with this situation. It is the opinion of the conference that the welfare of white and black labor are one and inseparable and that the existing agencies working among and for Negroes have conspicuously failed in facing a necessary alignment of black and white labor.

It is impossible to make any permanent improvement in the status and the security of white labor without making an identical improvement in the status and the security of Negro labor. The Negro worker must be made conscious of his relation to white labor and the white worker must be made conscious that the purposes of labor, immediate or ultimate cannot be achieved, without full participation by the Negro worker.

The traditional labor movement, based upon craft autonomy and separatism, which is non-political in outlook and which centers its attention upon the control of jobs and wages for the minority of skilled white workers, is an ineffective agency for aligning white and black labor for the larger labor objectives.

These objectives can only be attained through a new labor movement. This movement must direct its immediate attention to the organizing of the great mass of workers both skilled and unskilled, white and black. Its activities must be political as well as economic for the purpose of effecting such social legislation as old age pensions, unemployment insurance, the regulation of child and female labor, etc. These social reforms may go to the extent of change in the form of government itself. The conference sees three possibilities:

1. Fascism
2. Communism
3. Reformed Democracy

The conference is opposed to Fascism because it would crystalize the Negro's position at the bottom of the social structure. Communism is impossible without a fundamental transformation in the psychology and the attitude of white workers on the race question and a change in the Negro's conception of himself as a worker. A Democracy that is attempting to reform itself is a fact which has to be reckoned with. In the process of reform, the interests of the Negro cannot be adequately safeguarded by white paternalism in government. It is absolutely indispensable that in this attempt of the government to control agriculture and industry, there be adequate Negro representations on all boards and field staffs.

While the accomplishment of these larger aims cannot be achieved except through the cooperation of white and black, the primary responsibility for the initiation, development and execution of this program rests upon the Negro himself. This is predicated upon the increased economic independence of the Negro. No matter what articifical class difference may seem to exist within the Negro group it must be recognized that all elements of the race must weld themselves together for the common welfare. This point of view must be indoctrinated through the churches, educational institutions and other agencies working in behalf of the Negro. The first steps toward the rapproachement between the educated Negro and the Negro mass must be taken by the educated Negro himself.

The Findings Committee recommends that the practical implications of this program be referred to a committee on continuation to be appointed by and at this conference.

The Negro in Harlem: A Report on Social and Economic Conditions Responsible for the Outbreak of March 19, 1935

Mayor's Commission on Conditions in Harlem

THE PROBLEM OF MAKING A LIVING

The Negro Community in Harlem

In the Harlem community, which for the purposes of this report includes the area bounded on the North and South by 181st and 99th Streets and on the east by the East and Harlem Rivers and on the West by the Hudson River, there are over 200,000 Negroes.* According to a survey by the New York City Housing Authority in 1934, the Negro population in this area comprised 56,157 family groups. While these Negro families represented 31.1 per cent of all families in the area, the Negro population is concentrated near the center of the area and is surrounded, with the exception of the Puerto Ricans on the South, by whites, about a third of whom are foreign born. In spite of its poverty and the fact that the majority of its population is from the rural South or the West Indies, the Negro community is not a slum area but constitutes in many respects a city in itself. In the area between Eighth and Lenox Avenues and 134th and 135th Streets, there are to be found the same population characteristics, the same types of institutions, and the same manifestations of behavior as distinguish the centers of most modern urban communities. Here the smallest proportion of children in the Negro population are to be found in conjunction with the largest proportion of single men and women in the community. In this same area we find Negro businesses and places of amusement concentrated, and the greatest amount of mobility represented in the movement of people and the dissemination of news. From this center, which includes the location of the first Negro residents in the area, the Negro community spreads out in all directions.

The rapid growth of the Negro community in Harlem is recorded in the Federal Census figures and other sources of information on this area. Between 1910 and 1920 the Negro population grew from 28,690 to 83,597, which represented an increase of 191.3 per cent. During the next decade the rate of increase was 144.0 per cent, the Negro population being 204,318 in 1930. Since 1930 the Negro population has seemingly become almost stationary, for according to the New York City Housing Authority there were 204,510 Negroes in this area in 1934. In considering the numerical growth of the Negro population in this area, it should be kept in mind that this population is composed mainly of adults. As far back as 1910, about 72 per cent of the population was twenty years of age or over; and since then, because of migration, the proportion has increased so that at the present time three-fourths of population is made up of persons twenty or over. In this connection another feature of the population also deserves attention. In

Source: From The Mayor's Commission on Conditions in Harlem, *The Negro in Harlem: A Report on Social and Economic Conditions Responsible for the Outbreak of March 19, 1935* (New York, 1935; typescript, Fiorello H. LaGuardia Papers, Municipal Archives of New York City, pp. 19–34, 67–80.

*The 1930 Federal Census statistics for this area were as follows: Native whites of native parentage: 124,669; native whites of foreign or mixed parentage: 187, 724; foreign born whites: 187,713; Negro 204,318.

the Harlem area, the percentage of Negro women in the population exceeds that of men by five per cent.

While these figures show the rapid growth of the Negro Population and something of its general character, they give no indication of the social and economic problems that have attended the incursion during the last fifteen years of 120,000 people, representing a different racial group and without experience in urban life, into the heart of an already fairly densely populated community. The fact that the sudden expansion of the Negro community has not resulted in any serious friction with other racial groups in the area has tended to obscure the seriousness and extent of the problems of the Negro community. Yet the Negro in Harlem has been confronted at all times with the problem of securing suitable homes and free access to the institutions which were intended to serve the needs of the community. Although, strange as it might seem, the presence of this large Negro community in Harlem is due primarily to economic forces, particularly the labor demands growing out of the feverish industrial activity during the World War, the problem of primary importance to the Harlem Negro has been that of securing employment.

How Negro Harlem Makes a Living

While there are no available statistics on the occupations of, Negroes in the Harlem area, we can get a fairly accurate picture of the situation from the census figures for the Borough of Manhattan as a whole. From the table below, it appears that Negro men have since 1910 shifted from domestic and personal service to manufacturing and mechanical industries and transportation. While a similar shift is noticeable for Negro women, they have drifted back to domestic and personal services. Both men and women, the women more so than the men, have shown gains in professional services and clerical occupations. However, these figures should not be taken at their face value as indications of the upward movement of the Negro in the economic structure. A closer analysis of the figures on occupations show that while the proportion of Negro men and women in manufacturing and mechanical industries has doubled since 1910, they are still in the lowest paid and unskilled occupations. For example, a third of the Negro men in manufacturing and mechanical industries are common laborers and about another third are unskilled workers. The same is true of Negroes classified under transportation where about a third

TABLE I   Percentage of Negro Men and Women Employed in Major Occupational Divisions in the Borough of Manhattan, New York City: 1910–1930.

	1910		1920		1930	
Occupations	*Male*	*Female*	*Male*	*Female*	*Male*	*Female*
Manufacturing and Mechanical Industries	11.8	9.7	20.6	24.4	22.1	17.2
Transportation	13.1	0.1	19.9	1.0	17.5	0.4
Trade	8.8	0.4	6.9	0.7	8.7	1.0
Public Service	1.3	—	2.2	—	1.4	—
Professional Service	3.2	1.8	2.9	2.0	4.3	3.7
Domestic and Personal Service	54.1	55.4	40.9	70.1	39.8	76.1
Clerical	4.3	0.8	6.3	1.2	6.1	1.7
Total	96.5	98.2	99.7	99.4	99.1	100.0

are working as common laborers and a fourth as stevedores and dock hands. While it is recognized that a large proportion of Negroes who have had little experience in industry and trade would naturally be found in the lowest paid and unskilled occupations because of forces inherent in our competitive economic system, yet, as we shall see below, discrimination and non-economic factors are responsible to a large extent for the present state of affairs.

The Harlem Negro endeavors to make a living not only by offering his labor for sale but also through setting up business enterprises of his own. A survey of 52 of the 78 census tracts in the Harlem area which . . . was Negro showed that Negroes conduct 1,928 or 18.6 per cent of the 10,319 businesses. The main types of businesses conducted by Negroes differ considerably from the chief businesses in which whites are engaged. More than a third—36.5 per cent—of the Negro businesses provide personal services such as barber shops, beauty parlors and cleaning and pressing shops where little capital is needed. On the other hand, the same percentage—36.3—of the business conducted by whites provide the basic needs of the community. These businesses include grocery stores, meat markets, bakeries, coal and ice companies, restaurants, clothing, department and furniture stores. Only 18.4 of the Negro businesses in the community provide such basic needs. Moreover, a closer inspection of the types of businesses in this general class shows that the majority of Negro businesses are restaurants. Viewing Negro business as a whole, our survey shows that a half of such enterprises provide personal and professional services to the Negro community.

Even this cursory view of the occupational status of the Negro in Harlem as well as the analysis of the character and extent of his business enterprises shows that he must depend mainly upon the industries, trading establishments, and other economic institutions of the larger New York community for a living. Therefore, the policies and practices of these economic institutions of the City of New York in regard to the employment of Negroes determine in the final analysis the economic wellbeing of the Negro citizens of Harlem. We shall now turn our attention to this phase of the problem.

Discrimination in Employment

Public Utilities. We shall consider first the public utilities which have maintained a caste system in regard to the employment of Negroes. The Fifth Avenue Coach Company is so fixed in its policy of the exclusion of Negroes from employment that it refused even to discuss the question. While the officials in the other public utilities will give a polite ear to the question, their records indicate that they have systematically excluded Negro workers or restricted them to a relatively few menial jobs. The Consolidated Gas Company has only 213 Negroes among its 10,000 employees. Practically all of these Negro workers are employed either as hallmen or porters. Likewise among the approximately 10,000 employees of the New York Edison Company there are even fewer Negroes employed. This company employs only 65 Negroes, all of whom are confined to such menial jobs as porters, cleaners and hallmen. The same situation was found to exist in the case of the New York Telephone Company which employs only a small number of Negroes as laborers; and in the case of the New York Railways Company which employs about twenty-five Negroes, most of them in menial positions, out of a total of around 1700 employees. Among the 16,000 employees of the Interborough Rapid Transit Company we found that there were about 550 Negroes employed as messengers, porters and cleaners; while the Brooklyn Manhattan Transportation Company has a contingent of about 200 Negroes in similar positions. In regard to the 244 Negroes among the 2800 employees of the Independent Subway System, we shall have more to say below. The status of the Negro in the Western Union Telegraph Company has been modified to some extent during recent years through the employment of two clerks and two operators in the Harlem office; but outside of this office the Negroes employed by this corporation occupy the same menial positions as colored employees in the other public utilities.

An investigation of the reasons offered by those in charge of the public utilities for discrimination against Negro workers revealed that they are the same as the excuses which have been used for nearly a century to prevent the Negro from competing on an equal basis with the whites. First, the excuse is offered by the officials of these companies that tradition and custom have restricted the employment of Negroes in positions symbolic of their inferior status in American civilization. For example, Mr. R. H. Boggs, Vice-President in charge of personnel of the New York Telephone Company did not regard the exclusion of Negroes from all positions, except a few jobs as laborers, as discrimination but only as a customary practice. The same excuse was given by an official in the New York Railways Company. A second reason put forward for the exclusion of Negroes from the higher positions was that they were less efficient than white workers in similar positions. This was the reason offered by officials in both the Consolidated Gas Company and the New York Edison Company which had, according to their statements, employed Negro collectors at one time in Harlem. A third reason given by officials of some companies for the failure to employ Negroes was that whites and Negroes could not work in harmony. This type of excuse is represented by the statement of an official of the New York Telephone Company who thought that the training of colored operators would require a separate school and that friction between white and colored employees would slow up the service.

The reasons offered by the officials of the public utilities are on the whole merely rationalizations of policies and practices which have no basis in reason or fact. Undoubtedly, tradition and custom have played a part in the almost total exclusion of the Negro from all but the most menial positions. But in a large cosmopolitan community like New York City where all races of the globe are engaged in its competitive life, custom and tradition do not present insuperable obstacles to the employment of Negroes as they would in a small community. Negroes, contrary to traditional and customary ideas regarding their economic status, occupy positions of authority requiring intelligence and character in federal, state and municipal agencies. What peculiar circumstances, one may ask, exist in the public utilities which make it necessary to exclude the Negro or keep him in menial jobs. Moreover, in regard to the argument that Negroes and whites can not work together harmoniously, one need only cite the public school system where white and colored teachers work together harmoniously in various parts of the city. The argument that Negro collectors are less competent than whites is unsound because it is a type of generalization concerning the moral and intellectual character of Negroes that can not be sustained by facts. Individual Negroes may be dishonest and incompetent but this is no reason for the exclusion of the entire race from employment.

The refusal on the part of the public utilities to employ Negroes except in a few menial occupations makes them in the eyes of the people of Harlem chiefly agencies for exploiting the Negro. The Negro has no choice but to avail himself of the services of the public utilities which autocratically deny him all opportunity to share in the employment which he helps to provide other workers. While it is neither socially nor economically sound to employ Negroes or any other racial group in proportion to their importance as consumers or in areas in which they predominate, nevertheless, it may help to emphasize the injustice against the Negro worker by calling attention to the fact of the extent to which the Negro figures as a consumer of the services of some of these public utilities. Even on a conservative estimate, the 50,157 Negro families in Harlem spend annually around two million dollars with the gas and electric companies and three-fourths of a million dollars with the telephone company. Yet none of the public utilities give employment to more than a few hundred Negroes who are restricted to the lowest and least remunerative forms of employment. Increasingly, the Negroes of Harlem are becoming conscious of the discrimination practiced in regard to employment on the part of the public utilities. Throughout the public hearings conducted by the Commission there were protests against the policy of these corporations which were held up as the chief obstacles to the economic advancement of the Negro.

Discrimination against Negro workers on the part of the public utilities is at present beyond municipal control; for in spite of their public character, the practices of these corporations represent the acts of private individuals. But these limitations do not exist in the case of the Independent Subway System which comes definitely under the jurisdiction of the municipal government. From the beginning, the Independent Subway System attempted to restrict the Negro to employment in those positions which have been traditionally regarded as Negro jobs. From evidence given before the hearings conducted by the Sub-Committees, it appears that it was the established practice to refuse to give Negroes application blanks for any position but that of porter. Although after the Independent Subway System was placed under the Civil Service, this policy was modified, Negroes are still serving chiefly as porters. The relatively few Negroes who have been employed as platform men or in the booths have been restricted to the Harlem area or other areas where Negroes predominate.

In addition to these general discriminatory practices, it was brought to the attention of the Commission during the course of its hearings that Negro workers who fill the so-called "Negro job" or porter are forced to suffer unnecessary hardships both in respect to pay and the conditions under which they are compelled to work. According to the schedule of pay, as far as one was able to learn from testimony given at the hearings, no porters are paid the maximum figure. The rate of pay for

this position, occupied exclusively by Negroes, is less than that paid trackmen whose work requires no additional skill and incurs no greater danger. Moreover, it was also brought out in the hearings that the porters are forced to work even during the winter months in wet clothing without a room in which they might warm themselves. In fact, no place is provided for these men to change from street to work clothes. There is no choice left them but to come to and from work in their work clothes. When the porters have complained about the lack of adequate quarters, their protests have been ignored or dismissed as frivolous. At the same time, they have been forbidden the use of the dressing rooms which are reserved for the white conductors and motormen. The complaints of the porters against these hardships cannot be dismissed on the grounds that they are inherent in the nature of their work. The hardships which the porters are compelled to endure are tantamount to discriminations against a racial group inasmuch as these discriminations are practiced against a race that is restricted to employment of this occupational level, a level which is considered proper in accordance with its general status as a race.

Private Enterprises. Discrimination against Negro workers on the part of private enterprises is shown either in the restriction of the Negro to certain menial jobs or in his total exclusion from all types of occupations. While the Negro accepted this discrimination outside of Harlem with resignation, he has gradually developed a determination to fight it within the area which he regards as his own community. As the economic crisis became more acute, various groups began agitation for jobs in the different enterprises that drew their support from Negroes. The demand on the part of these various groups was not simply for the menial jobs which have been traditionally given to Negroes but for the so-called white collar jobs and other positions where intelligence and a high degree of responsibility were required. The outburst on March nineteenth expressed the pent up resentment of the Negro against exclusion from all but the most menial jobs in the establishments which he supported to a large extent.

A survey of eleven of the census tracts in which 75 to 85 per cent of the population is composed of Negroes showed that 2,173 or 45.7 per cent of the 4,750 employees regularly employed in businesses were Negroes. However, since 848 or 39 percent of the Negro employees were in businesses conducted by Negroes, only 1,325 or a third of the employees in the businesses conducted by whites were Negroes. Since, as we have pointed out above, the whites conduct the most substantial and important businesses, only three out five of the Negro employees in the businesses of this area share the fruits of the most profitable enterprises in the area. Moreover, it should be borne in mind that the vast majority of these Negro employees are employed either in menial positions or in small white grocery stores and shops which have adopted this policy in order to avoid the hostility of their Negro patrons. The larger white businesses have either ignored the agitation on the part of the Negro or have adopted subterfuges. The Kress store on 125th Street where the outburst started adopted the subterfuge of employing Negro girls at the lunch counter claiming that it had thereby placed Negro girls on the sales force. The Negroes in Harlem readily saw through this subterfuge, as they recognized that it was strictly in keeping with tradition for Negroes to serve food, and they have continued their agitation.

Outside of Harlem the Negro is very often excluded from the very jobs in which he has traditionally found employment. Let us take first the case of the Terminal Barber Shops, a corporation which operates barbershops in various large hotels and transportation centers in Manhattan. The man in charge of the personnel work thought that it would be most extraordinary to see a Negro in a white barbershop in any capacity and confessed that he would be embarrassed if a Negro applied for a job. This man, evidently of foreign birth and therefore never having heard

that a Southern gentleman would never permit a poor white man to shave him, gave as his opinion that white people preferred white barbers and added that the workers would object to Negro barbers. It is needless to comment on such rationalizations which were used to exclude the Negro from employment. The exclusion of Negro waiters, cooks and other classes of employees from the hotels would probably be supported by similar types of reasoning. Our survey of 393 hotels of all types in the Borough of Manhattan showed that 238 or 61 per cent had no Negro employees. Thus the Negro worker, for no other reason than because of the arbitrary practice or prejudice of hotel managers, is denied employment in a field in which he once found a steady source of income.

On the whole, the stores and other types of business enterprises outside of Harlem may be divided into two classes in regard to the employment of Negroes: Those that employ Negroes in menial positions and those that employ no Negroes at all. For example a representative of the first class is Macy's, which has employed Negroes for many years, with Negroes serving as elevator starters, escalator attendants, and in the cafeteria and tea rooms. On the other hand, there is Gimbel's which excludes Negroes from any type of employment. Most of the Negroes employed downtown occupy jobs as elevator operators, porters and to a less extent as messengers. While some of the business establishments excluding Negroes from employment in their downtown establishments seemingly attempt to compensate for their discrimination by employing them in Harlem, the insurance companies with thousands of policy holders in Harlem are adamant in their policy of refusing to employ Negro agents even in Harlem. First among such companies is the Metropolitan Life Insurance Company with over a hundred thousand policy holders among the Negroes in Harlem. This company attempts to excuse its policy on the ground that white agents produce better results. But the experience of Negro companies, which depend solely upon Negro agents, refutes this charge. The same is true of the Workingmen's Cooperative Association of the United Insurance League of New York, of whose 13,620 policy holders (as of December 31, 1935) about 95 per cent are Negroes, 5,000 being in Harlem. The Secretary-Treasurer of the company gave as his excuse for not employing Negro agents that, since the average Negro family consulted the insurance agent on matters other than insurance, they preferred white agents! The president of the Golden Eagle Life and Accident Association with headquarters in Brooklyn offered a similar excuse for not employing Negro agents. Between eight and nine per cent of the policy holders in this company are Negroes and about half of them live in Harlem.

The Labor Unions. No Study of discrimination against Negroes in employment could be complete without consideration of the discriminatory practices of the labor unions. In spite of the repeated resolutions by the American Federation of Labor at its annual meetings to the effect that it discountenanced racial discrimination, its pious pronouncements have had little effect upon the practices of its constitutent national and international unions. Although only a few of these national and international unions which limit the employment of Harlem Negroes have constitutional or ritual provisions excluding Negro workers, the actual practices of these unions are as effective as constitutional restrictions. For example, an apprenticeship requirement for admission to a union may very effectively exclude Negro members. Take for example the International Brotherhood of Electrical Workers, Local Union No. 3, with a membership of 6,000, none of whom are Negroes. Although this union has no provisions concerning Negro membership, the seven years' apprenticeship requirement excludes Negroes as members as effectively as the constitutional provision in the charter of the Commercial Telegraphers' Union which states that only

white persons may become members. Sometimes the unions excuse the absence of Negro members on the grounds that no Negroes were in the particular trade or occupation which they represent. For example, the Railway Express Employees, Local 808, of the International Brotherhood of Teamsters and Chauffeurs does not have a single Negro among its 2,000 members for the reason, they claim, that the Railway Express Agency does not employ Negroes as chauffeurs, helpers or stablemen. The same reason was offered by the President of the New York Newspaper Printing Pressmen and Assistant's Union of North America, for the fact that not one of the union's 2,600 members was a Negro.

As a matter of fact, some of the unions attempt to limit their membership, especially during periods of unemployment, and this applies to the white worker as well as the Negro. The International Alliance of Bill Posters and Billers of America, Local No. 2, with a membership of 300, accomplishes this end through the high initiation fee. Since this fee is $500, one can readily understand why no Negro is a member although it was stated that they would accept a Negro if he applied for membership. Bartenders' Union, Local No. 3, with 1,100 members, according to the secretary, had never thought of organizing Negro bartenders, since they are so few, *into a separate local.* So far as taking them into Local No. 3, he did not know whether the men would like it and such a step would call "for a lot of other considerations." It is quite unnecessary to catalogue the various unions. The available figures on the membership of Negroes in the various locals in New York City are probably the best indication of the policies of the different unions.

In the various locals representing the building trades, there are less than 1,000 Negroes in a membership close to 40,000. In the Clothing and Textile Industries about 6,704 Negroes are to be found among a membership of over 150,000 in the various unions. Almost all of these Negro union members are in the International Ladies' Garment Workers'

Union. Negro members are excluded entirely from the clerical unions. With the exception of the Association of Workers in Public Relief Agencies, the Postal Workers locals, and Sanitary Chauffeurs, Negroes are practically excluded from the unions representing public service. We find practically the same situation in regard to the field of amusements and the professions, if we exclude the American Federation of Musicians, Local 802, which has over 85 per cent of the Negro union members in this general field.

The general policy of many of these unions was probably unconsciously expressed by the representative of one when he said that, since there had been no strikes, his union had not thought of organizing Negro workers. This statement taken together with that above of the secretary of the bartenders' union sums up the situation which we see illustrated in the case of the Motion Picture Operators' Union, Local 306. When the Negro motion picture operators organized and applied to this local for membership, they were offered a limited membership, that is, they were to pay the regular dues and be subject to the same rules as other members of the union, but they had no vote and were not to attend the meetings. The Negro operators naturally refused. When they were later admitted to full membership, the membership proved simply a means of controlling the Negro worker. He was assigned only to work in the theaters in the Negro section of Harlem. When work became slack during the present depression, other forms of discrimination were practiced. The white members of the union are given a chance to earn a regular week's pay at least twice a month at a salary around fifty-one dollars per week while the colored operators are given only one week's work at a theatre in Harlem and are paid the $18 weekly unemployment benefit out of union funds for the remainder of the time.

This extraordinary record of discrimination against the Harlem Negro in the matter of employment accounts to a large extent for the continuous impoverishment of the more than 200,000 citizens of this area of New York City. It represents a denial of the fundamental rights of a people to a livelihood. No amount of charity, good will, social privileges, or political freedom can compensate for the enforced idleness and poverty of the citizens of this community. The low economic status of the Negro in Harlem is basic to every other problem in the community. It is idle to reflect upon the large numbers of Negroes unemployed or their poor housing conditions, or their petty thefts, while the right to work at lawful occupations is denied them. The social costs of such a policy may not be apparent but, nevertheless, they are a constant drain on the economic resources of the larger community. Moreover, in times of stress when relief fails to compensate for systematic exclusion from legitimate work, we have such occurrences as the outbreak of March nineteenth.

THE PROBLEM OF EDUCATION AND RECREATION

Probably the greatest boon which a city like New York offers the Negro at present is an opportunity for his children to receive an education comparable to that given the white child. Since many of the children themselves received a part of their education in the schools of the South, New York City affords them their first experience in adequately equipped and manned schools. Naturally there arise problems of adjustment which tax the patience and administrative capacity of school authorities and teachers. However, these problems are not essentially different from those arising as the result of the presence of large numbers of children of foreign-born parentage. In fact, the schools of New York City have been the one institution in which democratic principles have tended to break down racial and national differences. Except for the West Indian element, the American Negro population is native-born and the West Indians themselves are an English speaking people. Therefore, except for the fact of color the entire Negro population—West Indian as well as the American-born—would be more easily assimilated into the school system than most children of foreign-born parentage. On the whole, Negro parents have taken advantage of the educational opportunities offered and the Negro child has become adjusted to the educational system of New York City. On the other hand, the school authorities have shown a disposition to maintain the democratic ideals of the school system by assigning Negro teachers to various sections of the city. Nevertheless, the Negro in Harlem has made serious complaints against the schools of his community on the grounds that they are old, poorly equipped and overcrowded and constitute fire hazards, in addition to the fact that, in the administration of these schools, the welfare of the children is neglected and racial discrimination is practiced.

Physical Aspects of the Schools

In the entire Harlem community there are twenty-one elementary schools, five junior high schools, one senior high school, an annex of the Straubemuller Textile High School and the Manhattan Industrial Trade School for Boys. All of these school buildings except four, two of which were leased, are brick and stone structures, the remaining being constructed of brick. According to the Annual Financial and Statistical Report of the Board of Education for 1933, seventeen of these buildings are fire proof, nine partly fire proof, and one of the type erected before 1892. Eleven of these buildings were erected before 1900, although eight of them have had subsequent additions, in most cases, however, before 1900. While thirteen of the school buildings were constructed in 1900 or later, only five of these thirteen have been erected since 1910. If we consider only these schools in the area in which Negroes are concentrated, we find no elementary school has been erected during the past ten years. The last school to be built in the Negro area was the junior high school at 135th Street and Edgecombe Avenue, which was erected in 1925.

In order to get a real picture of the schools which the vast majority of the Negro children attend, one must go behind the above figures concerning their age, the material of which they are constructed, and their classification relative to fire risks. One needs only to enter one of these schools to be made aware of its age which is reflected in its shabbiness, its unsanitary condition, and its antiquated architecture. Let us take a look at, perhaps, the worst of these schools, P. S. 89, at the corner of 135th Street and Lenox Avenue, which was built in 1889 and had an addition made to it in 1895. This school contains in an extreme degree all the bad features of the schools of Harlem. First of all, within a radius of two blocks of this school, there are eighteen beer gardens, six liquor saloons, four moving picture houses and two hotels alleged to be disreputable, besides one solid block of rooming houses which are known to be the center of vice and the hide-outs of vendors of narcotics and other criminals. If one attempts to enter the building, one must be careful to step between or walk around unemployed men seated on the steps of the entrance. After entering the school building, an offensive odor greets one as he passes up the stairs leading to the principal's office and the classrooms. On the day that one of our investigators visited this building, the first thing that attracted his attention in the principal's office was a pile of old shoes strung across the floor and a pile of old clothes stacked in one corner. The principal's office was equipped with an old dilapidated desk and two chairs, one of which was broken.

The physical appearance of the principal's office was typical of the building as a whole. While this school has classes from the kindergarten to the sixth grade, the seats are of the type suited to kindergarten children. These seats are naturally uncomfortable for the majority of the children in the school who are over eight years of age. The classrooms are dark and stuffy; the blackboards are old and defective; and the wooden floors are dirty and offensive. At the time the visit was made to this school, ten of the forty-five rooms were out of use because of a recent fire. This school, which is classified as a partially fireproof building had had six fires during the past four years. This school, like other schools in the Negro area, is overcrowded and therefore must run two sessions. However, the school has no gymnasium or library and is generally lacking in the educational equipment which is deemed necessary.

While this is probably the worst school in the Negro section of Harlem, the majority of the other schools show similar characteristics in varying degrees. Since most of them were built from twenty-five to forty years ago, they show many of the same characteristics relative to construction, lack of equipment, and, in some cases, fire hazards. One principal excused the school's bad odor, which he tried to have overcome by spreading carbolic acid about, on the ground that students not caring to go to the lavatories outside used the stairs for toilets. In another school, where there had been a fire five years ago and the fire department had made recommendations, none of them had been followed. In many of the other schools, one finds the same problem of overcrowding. That this overcrowding affects chiefly the schools in which Negro children represent the majority of the pupils is shown by the figures on schools having more than one session. Of the nine schools in this area, only one school with practically 100 per cent Negro attendance has a single session. In five of these schools in which Negro children constitute from 85 to 100 per cent of the pupils, there are three sessions in three schools and double sessions in the other two. The remaining three schools in which Negro children constitute from 10 to 20 per cent of the pupils have only single sessions. In addition to two and three sessions in at least half of the elementary schools, there are between forty and fifty pupils per class.

Administrative and Educational Problems

Overcrowding under any circumstances would tend to make more difficult the prob-lem of discipline. Therefore, it is not surprising to find that in these schools discipline presents a serious problem. However, there are other factors that are responsible for the situation. In regard to what extent each factor is responsible for the general lack of discipline in these schools, one may indicate in what way each contributes to the present condition. We shall consider, first, the teaching staff in these schools, not however because they are primarily responsible, for we believe that there are more fundamental factors. It seems that many of the white teachers appointed to the schools of Harlem regard the appointment as a sort of punishment. They look upon their appointment in Harlem in this way, not only because they are to teach Negroes, but also because of the conditions under which they teach. At any rate, there appears to be a great deal of turnover in the white personnel of these schools. It is quite natural that teachers who regard their work in this light certainly will not have a sympathetic attitude towards the children who present many behavior problems in the Harlem schools. In the second place, it appears from observation of the schools, and some principals have substantiated the observation, that a disproportionate number of older white teachers are to be found in the Harlem schools. It has been claimed that these teachers have asserted their right to remain in the schools in which they have served a long time although the influx of Negroes has brought new problems, or they have been appointed to serve in Harlem until they were eligible for retirement. These older teachers are naturally impatient and unsympathetic towards the children. Moreover, the problems presented in these schools often require the physical vigor and energy which only young men and women are able to exert. These statements in regard to white teachers in Harlem are not criticisms directed at white teachers as a group for many of them exhibit an intelligent and sympathetic understanding of Negro children which some Negro teachers in these schools do not possess.

No one should expect teachers, either white or colored, to overcome the deficiencies in training which result from broken homes, poverty, a vicious environment, retardation, and ill-health. Yet the general lack of discipline which the teachers have to deal with are due in part to all of these factors. About 25 per cent of the Negro families of Harlem are broken families; i. e., families with only a woman as head. According to the principal of one of the schools of Harlem, in 699 of 1,600 families represented by the children, the father was either dead or had deserted his family. That delinquency among the school children seemed to be tied up with broken homes appeared in the report of another principal who found that 75 per cent of delinquent children in his school had come from broken homes. The facts governing the family background of a large percentage of the school children of Harlem are indicative of some of the social and cultural factors which must be taken into consideration in relation to the lack of discipline. They call attention to the vicious neighborhoods in which these children are forced to live as well as the vicious neighborhoods surrounding these schools. One principal, in denying that there was a sex problem in his school, admitted that men and older boys who did not attend the school often chased girl students into the school and there are instances when these girls have been attacked. It is not surprising that this happens since it appears that the principals are powerless to exert any pressure on the police to prevent such occurrences or to close the vicious resorts which are allowed to operate in the neighborhood of the schools. It is difficult to say to what extent the vicious behavior exhibited by the students in their practice of carrying weapons or in their homosexual relations is a direct reflection of the vicious environment about the schools.

Since poverty . . . is the problem of primary importance to the Negro in Harlem, it is responsible for many of the problems of the schools in the community. Many of the children stay away from school because of the lack of food and especially clothing.

Many come to school hungry and are listless or complain because of the lack of food. In one school alone, 1000 free lunches were served daily. The lack of nourishment is responsible for low vitality and makes the children susceptible to disease. In a junior high school, between January 4th and June 20th, 1935, there were 139 cases of malnutrition and 8 cases of tuberculosis brought to the attention of the school authorities.

Along with the delinquency, truancy, and ill health, retardation constitutes one of the major problems of the schools of Harlem. Like these other problems, it cannot be considered in isolation from the other social problems of the schools or the social and economic problems of the community. Overaged pupils in the classes create problems of discipline and are responsible for delinquency and truancy. Some of the retardation is due to the fact that these children received part of their education in the schools of the South. But one can not discount the general environment from which these children come to the city of New York. In some of the schools, twenty-five per cent or more of the children are retarded. While special classes to deal with this problem are found in some of the schools, on the whole, personnel and equipment are lacking.

In fact, one of the most serious charges that must be brought against the schools in Harlem is that they lack the personnel and the equipment which modern schools have at their disposal for handling intelligently and efficiently the social problems of the pupils, as distinguished from the educational problems in the traditional sense of the term. Recreational facilities are lacking in most of the schools. Children are forced to use the streets for playgrounds and thereby are thrown in contact with the vicious elements in the community. Very few schools have the services of a visiting teacher. Harlem is the only section of the city without nursery schools, although no section needs them more than this area of broken homes and with a large proportion of mothers who must work. Moreover, if a Negro child is on the verge of delinquency, the school principals do not have the assistance of psychologists and psychiatrists. Usually the child is dismissed from school without any further provisions. The New York Training School for Boys at Warwick, New York, is the only corrective institution in the state where Negro delinquents are admitted. It is worth while to note that this school must serve the entire state. . . . In regard to the health of the school children, the same situation prevails. There is no program for dealing systematically with the health problems of children in this area. Moreover, welfare agencies cooperating with the schools have not made the same provisions for sending Negro children to camp and the seashore as they have done in the case of the whites.

Discriminatory Practices

Although the public schools of New York City are supposed to be free from racial discrimination and we have already commented upon the extent to which they have lived up to democratic ideals, our study of the school system in Harlem has brought out many forms of discrimination which are racial in character. First, "the grossly unfair, discriminatory and prejudiced treatment of the Negro child appears from the fact that the Board of Education in asking funds from the federal government for 168 new school buildings in New York asked for but one annex in Harlem." In spite of the conditions which we have described above, of the $120,747,000 asked, only $400,000 was earmarked for schools attended by the vast majority of colored children. Although this program has been abandoned, it indicates the general attitude of the school authorities towards the educational needs of the Harlem community.

Moreover, our investigations enable us to point to types of discrimination which have become established practices in the Harlem schools so far as Negro pupils are concerned. In this connection, we turn our attention first to the Wadleigh High School where most of the Negro girls in the Harlem area are required to do their senior high school work. The main building of this school is located on 114th Street between 7th and 8th Avenues and has two annexes, one on 102nd Street and the other on 135th Street and Convent Avenue. About thirty per cent of the student body is Negro, the remainder being divided as follows: white American and Jewish, 25 per cent each; Italian, 15 per cent; and Spanish, 5 per cent. All of these racial groups are represented on the teaching staff but for some reason the name of the Negro teacher who has been at the school three years does not appear as a member of the teaching staff in the school's handbook. Most of the Negro girls—about seventy-five percent—attending this school are pursuing courses in dressmaking, domestic science, and other vocational courses which are given in the main building. Only ten per cent of the pupils in the 102nd Street annex where the commercial courses are given are Negro. In the 135th Street annex where the academic work, preparing pupils for entrance to institutions of collegiate standing, is given, only fifteen per cent of the pupils are Negro. But in the special courses which prepare girls for the outstanding women's colleges not a single Negro girl was enrolled for the term of 1935. A comparatively large number of these Negro girls, about twelve per cent, are dropped from the academic department because of deficiencies.

In seeking the cause for the concentration of Negro girls in certain types of courses, one is naturally interested to know whether it is due to their peculiar aspirations, intelligence and general social background or to some selective and directing influence exercised by the school authorities. In the first place, the relatively small number of Negro girls who go from the junior to the senior high school is due to the fact they are selected on the basis of their attainments in the junior high schools. Many of these girls are deficient in their training, not because of any fault of their own, but because the poorly equipped and crowded junior high schools of Harlem do not give them adequate preparation for entrance to a senior high school. While this accounts in part for the small number entering the senior high school and their concentration in the vocational courses, it is not the whole story. The selection is due in the main to the policy of the educational advisers. These advisers, often reflecting the traditional belief concerning the capacity of the Negro for purely academic pursuits, direct these girls into vocational courses. These educational advisers discourage Negro girls from taking the commercial courses on the ground that opportunities are not open to Negro girls in the commercial field.

The problem of giving vocational guidance to the Negro children of Harlem is an especially difficult one even for the fair-minded educational adviser. As one seemingly conscientious and intelligent adviser put the problem: Should she direct Negro children into lines of occupations according to their intelligence and interest, although it was known that Negroes were not employed in such occupations; or should she, taking into consideration this fact, direct them into fields in which they would be likely to find employment. While it is true that a conscientious adviser may be conscious of the problem involved, as a matter of fact, it requires more than conscientiousness. Some of these advisers have no knowledge of the occupations in which Negroes have been able to enter in spite of traditional notions and prejudices nor are they concerned with the Negro's struggle to break down the color barrier in industry. Vocational counsellors who are charged with mapping out the future careers of Negro children in Harlem should only be such persons as possess a broad knowledge and understanding of the Negro's economic problems and who are in sympathy with his aspirations. No one who is dominated by traditional beliefs concerning the Negro's capacity for intellectual culture or his proper place in society is fit to counsel him in his choice of a career.

While it is naturally difficult to gauge the extent of racial discrimination in the schools of Harlem there is enough authentic evidence to justify this charge on the part of the citizens of Harlem. One need go no further

than Wadleigh High School, which we have been considering. Discrimination becomes evident especially in the social relations of the students. This has been excused on the grounds that southern white teachers in the school object to the mingling of white and Negro children in purely social affairs. Each year the school gives a boat ride to Indian Point where there is a swimming pool. The Negro girls are barred from the swimming pool at this resort on the grounds that the owner has a provision in the lease that Negroes are not to use the pool. It is rumored that this restriction has not been objected to on the part of the school authorities because it offers a means of discouraging Negro girls from going on the outing. In either case, if the owner of the resort insists upon including such a provision against Negroes, it is clearly the duty of the school authorities to refuse to lease his resort. Neither the racial prejudices of southern white teachers nor the prejudice of the owner of a pleasure resort should be of greater consideration than the insult that is offered to Negro children and the consequent damage that is done to the personality of young people by making them feel that they are unfit for association with other human beings.

Other cases of racial discrimination could be cited. But more important, though less well defined, practices of the school authorities in regard to the Negro need to be considered. For example, was it a mere accident that a visitor to one of the elementary schools saw the white girls dressed in nurses' uniforms directing visitors about while the Negro girls were dressed as waitresses and served the visiting teachers. Most of the white teachers and principals of Harlem deny that there is any racial discrimination and generally back up their statement by emphasizing the lack of overt acts of discrimination against the Negro. This often is true, for the discrimination is subtle to the extent that the Negro is ignored or regarded as non-existent. This becomes obvious when one attends the public functions of the schools. On these occasions when the community is requested to participate in the life of the school, one would think that there were no Negroes in the world or at least capable of appearing as its representatives. Of course, often the Negro is not thought of simply because many of the teachers know nothing of Negroes except in the role of servants, clowns, or criminals. This has furnished the basis for the contention on the part of the citizens of Harlem that courses in Negro history should be given in the schools and that the teachers in these schools should know something of the Negro's attainments in American civilization.

Vocational education for the Negro in Harlem deserves separate consideration. The situation in regard to this whole question presents a strange paradox. On the one hand, it is thought proper that Negro children should have industrial training, but, when it comes to giving them real vocational training, it is said that they are not prepared for such training. So what do we find. Let us consider the Harlem annex of the Straubemuller Textile High School, which seemingly has become a dumping ground for the dull or problem children in the area from which it draws the majority of its pupils. This school has practically no equipment to carry on the work it is supposed to do. That is, of course, no fault of the principal in charge of the school. There are no facilities to give the work of the dressmaking department in which practically all the pupils are Negro. The shop in which electricity is taught is equipped with two dynamos supplied by the instructor himself since the Board of Education has never put any equipment in the shop. The same is true in respect to the courses in biology, chemistry and physics. Since it is obviously impossible to give courses in this annex in any way comparable to those given in the main building, it appears that students are kept there until they reach the age limit for compulsory school attendance.

At the Manhattan Trade School for Boys where real vocational training is given, we find relatively few Negro boys getting the advantage of the training which this school offers. Although this school is located in the heart of Harlem, nearly three-fourths of the day students come from the Bronx. The majority of the students in the evening school are Negroes. The fact that relatively few Negro students attend the day classes has been blamed partly on the principals who make the selection and partly on the American Federation of Labor's policies in regard to the Negro in certain trades. At any rate, it appears that if the educational authorities were serious in their avowed intentions to give the Negro child vocational training this school in the Harlem community should be utilized for the vocational needs of the Negro. This same observation applies to the vocational needs of the Negro girls who comprise about 14 per cent of the students in the Manhattan Industrial School for Girls. It is claimed that Negro girls do not measure up to the standards set by this school. So here again appears the strange paradox; Negro girls should take vocational education instead of academic work but they are not prepared to take it. Therefore Negro girls are directed to the vocational courses given in the junior and senior high school or sent to the Harlem annex of the Textile High School. In regard to the vocational and trade schools, attention should be called to the fact that no Negro teachers are employed in them since it appears that they must have some years of experience in addition to their educational preparation and this experience is denied them by the unions.

This last observation brings us back to the observation which was made at the beginning of our survey of the schools in Harlem. The school situation is related to the other problems—economic, health, and housing—of the Negro. Discrimination in one field has its ramifications in all other fields of Negro life. The problem of education is the same as all other problems; namely, to make the same educational provisions for the school children of Harlem as are made for children in other sections of New York City and to see that Negro teachers are admitted to all branches of the teaching staff as other races.

The Black Cabinet

Roi Ottley

A little-known force in the drive to bring democracy to the Negro community is the "Black Cabinet"—a corps of highly intelligent Negroes who hold key positions in Washington. As a liaison group, sometimes called the "Black Brain Trust," it functions as racial adviser to the government heads, and as such is one of the realities of government today. It is, as well, an integral part of the organized movement to end color distinctions. The men and women who form this influential body are determined, one of them told me, "to secure for Negroes *all* the rights, privileges, and benefits now enjoyed by whites."

This group, which forms the Washington arm of the national Negro leadership, is opposed to anything that smacks of race separatism—they are aggressively for integration. Indicative of this is the vigor with which it opposed the creation of a "Super-Negro Bureau," which was a plan being considered by the Washington administration to deal with all problems affecting Negroes. Members of the Black Cabinet fought the whole idea because they felt that such an agency would tend to make the Negro a ward of the government, and thus would subtly extend and perpetuate segregation.

Alert to trends, the Black Cabinet has managed to make definite strides in advancing the Negro's cause—always with the formidable aid of the mass-organization leaders—and Negroes count carefully the gains made.

The Black Cabinet has trained its heaviest guns on the employment of Negroes in government and war industries. I was frankly surprised when I was in Washington recently to see the thousands of Negroes who were working for the government and to see the variety of jobs they were doing—jobs hitherto beyond wishful thinking. Many held positions of authority and influence, and others were patiently solving technical problems as economists, lawyers, chemists, and consultants of various sorts. Hundreds were operating office machines and a few worked as secretaries to both white and Negro officials.

The number of Negro employees of the federal government jumped in recent years by more than one hundred thousand—with others being added daily. Negroes frankly say that a large factor in the Negro's integration in government service has been due lately to the vigorous way the Civil Service Commission kicked the bucket of tradition—photographs have been banned, designation of race on applications has been abolished, and the rule permitting a selection of one out of three eligible people—which once allowed discriminations—has been shelved. Working conditions also have improved. Today, many of the government cafeterias have been opened to Negro workers, separate rest-room accommodations eliminated, and in offices Negroes and whites work at adjoining desks.

These are the trends. . . .

Much remains to be accomplished.

The delicate task of negotiating further gains is the business before the Black Cabinet. But the very limitations of their roles as "advisers" is a clear impediment. Though their abilities are unquestioned, they deal only with "Negro" problems. This fact caused George S. Schuyler, the *Courier's* columnist, to call the group "Porkbarrelensis Africanus." He held that, "While they are appointed as advisers, they actually give little or no advice

Source: Roi Ottley, *New World A-Coming,* pp. 254–267, copyright 1943 Roi Ottley.

at all and have no part in shaping policy. What advice they give is usually when outraged Negroes squawk against some particularly unpalatable discrimination." Some Negroes are unkind enough to say that the Black Cabineteers are salesmen for the New Deal. But in the summer of 1942, the Washington *Tribune,* a Negro newspaper, proudly published a long list of Negro federal employees, detailing their duties, with this head: "These Represent Special Race Consideration."

To some people the idea of a Black Cabinet may have a curious ring. In reality, it is one of the Negro's methods of exercising his "right to petition" the government. As a matter of fact, similar groups have been an anonymous feature of American life since Booker T. Washington took the pulse of the Negro, hurried to the White House to report, and returned with reassuring antidotes. He headed a group called the "Kitchen Cabinet," which more or less functioned as adviser to the government. Its members held three jobs mainly—which came to be known as "Negro jobs"—Register of the Treasury, Auditor of the Navy, and Recorder of Deeds. Lack of accomplishment by this and similar groups was due mostly to the fact that their members were largely political hacks, who had been put on the government payroll for services rendered the Republican Party, and they had little influence in the Negro community or within the government. Its modern counterpart—the Black Cabinet—which rode to power on the smooth pavement of the New Deal, is a streamlined edition, but with vastly different objectives, and with vastly more influence.

The group's immediate objectives include (1) an increase in the number of Negroes in government service, at least as many as they are entitled to by population percentage; (2) the giving of jobs to Negroes according to their ability and training, and not confining most of them to work as char-women and to messenger and janitorial service; (3) appointment of Negroes to policy-making positions and to the diplomatic and consular service; and (4) to secure jobs for Negroes in private industry to forward the war effort.

The Black Cabinet is a product of economic compulsions. . .

In the early days of the Roosevelt administration, intelligent and well-educated young Negroes just out of school were meeting tremendous hardships in getting private employment. Naturally they turned to government service for jobs, but again found barriers. A long series of protests by Negroes and liberal whites against discrimination in the government, which they said gave comfort to private employers with discriminatory policies, brought about the appointment of Negro racial advisers to secure better treatment for Negroes. No mere window-dressing, they almost immediately sought equality of employment for their people.

Help came from unexpected sources. Without much publicity, their aspirations received warm support from President and Mrs. Roosevelt, and almost overnight things began to happen. Heading a régime committed to change, the President issued orders against discrimination by government—later to reaffirm this policy with his historic Executive Order 8802, which strongly urged both government administrators and private employers "to examine their employment and training policies to determine whether or not these policies make ample provision for the full utilization of available and competent Negro workers." Meanwhile, Mrs. Roosevelt, beloved by Negroes, championed the Negro's cause, kept in touch with Negro thought, and by her own acts encouraged the acceptance of Negroes. . . . This attitude was implemented through the office of Harold L. Ickes. Secretary of the Interior; Wayne Coy, the President's Liaison with department heads: and Doctor Will W. Alexander, W.P.B. consultant on minority groups.

The Negro racial advisers who form the Black Cabinet are young men who have been trained as analysts, economists, educators, professors, labor organizers, newspapermen, and research and social workers. Many of them have been educated at the finest universities both here and abroad. Yet they do not regard themselves as an educated élite, but rather as "intellectual workers." Permeated with the bold thinking of the New Deal, slanted to meet the peculiar needs of the Negro, they help to unravel the knotty problems of racial relations in the government which crop up from time to time.

By and large they are cut from the same college-bred cloth, and although temperamentally, sharply vivid differences exist among them, as to objectives they are as close as white on rice. They do their thinking and talking together. Studies are initiated by them. Negro sentiment tested frequently, abstractions harnessed, and eventually mature programs formulated. Much constructive work thus has been accomplished. The effectiveness of the group stems from the fact that it usually operates as a cohesive unit, with well-defined objectives unencumbered by rigid party lines. In collaboration with liberal white government officials and Negro leaders, they advance the Negro's cause.

Late in the summer of 1940, with war threatening, A. Philip Randolph, president of the Brotherhood of Sleeping Car Porters; Walter White, executive secretary of the National Association for the Advancement of Colored People; and Doctor Channing H. Tobias, Negro Y.M.C.A. executive, among others, conferred with President Roosevelt on the status of the Negro in the armed services and war industries. They presented a memorandum whose intent sought integration of Negroes in the national war program. Sometime later Stephen Early, the President's press secretary, issued an ambiguous White House statement outlining the segregation policy to which the United States Army intended to adhere—"not to intermingle colored and white enlisted personnel"—and, worse, intimated that such a policy had been requested by Negro leaders. The ink had hardly dried on Early's release when Randolph, White, and Doctor Tobias wired the President, "In a written memorandum we submitted we specifically repudiated segregation." The Negro

press rose in all its inflammatory might and denounced the President. Headlines shouted, "WHITE HOUSE BLESSES JIM CROW." Statements of the Negro leaders were quoted in full, accompanied by much critical comment. The Negro communities were incensed by what they termed a "trick."

To top this off, with the 1940 elections only a few days away, Early was charged with kicking a Negro policeman assigned to Pennsylvania Station in New York. The New York *Herald Tribune*, opposing Roosevelt's re-election observed in its story of the encounter that Early was the "son of a Confederate general." Negro press and pulpit denounced the indignity as reflecting the attitude of people close to the President. This threw the White House advisers and Democratic campaign strategists into something of a dither. A hurried call was put through to assemble the racial advisers, to offer views on how to counteract the situation. Some White House advisers thought the President, or a ranking cabinet member, ought to deliver a strong speech on the general Negro question, nicely outlining all that the administration had done for Negroes. The Negro advisers felt differently. "Since the Negro's whole resentment is directed at the Army," they argued, "the situation can only be counteracted by some concrete and favorable development there." Doctor Robert C. Weaver, spokesman for the Black Cabinet, then suggested as a means of stimulating Negro morale, that there be some Negro representation in the military councils of America's expanding war effort. Although the Army officials were opposed to it, the President, a few days before elections, finally took the bull by the horns and elevated Colonel Benjamin O. Davis to brigadier general, appointed Judge William H. Hastie as civilian aide to Secretary of War Stimson, and made Lieutenant Colonel Campbell C. Johnson executive assistant to Brigadier General Lewis B. Hershey.

As it turned out, these appointments proved to be key spots in a developing war program. The two men chosen to perform the civilian tasks have sharply contrasted personalities. Tall, wiry Judge Hastie is the younger man, and today an important figure in the Black Cabinet. Lieutenant Colonel Johnson is a silent, graying veteran of the last war who hardly speaks above a whisper. Though he lacks the scintillation of most members of the Black Cabinet, he nevertheless has a quiet aggressiveness which is much admired by his white colleagues. His sober influence often acts as a check on the more impatient young men. Every inch the soldier—erect, commanding, decisive, and with simple dignity—his concern is primarily in getting Negroes into the Army with a minimum of racial hitches.

Judge Hastie, who recently resigned, was concerned with the morale of the Negro soldiers. What he advised as to their welfare eventually had far-reaching effect upon thousands. His job was made extremely difficult by clashes between Negro soldiers and white civilians—for he not only had to suggest possible solutions, but had to explain to an uneasy Negro public what efforts were being made to correct such conditions.

A typical situation developed at Fort Huachuca, planted smack in the middle of the Arizona Desert near the Mexican border. Except for a couple of squatter villages, the nearest town (Tombstone, population eight hundred), is twenty miles away—and Negroes are none too welcome. Darkness covers Huachuca early, for the camp is situated in the shadow of a high mountain. Almost devoid of recreational facilities, the Negro soldiers stationed here had a hard time finding things to do after nightfall. Once they pooled seven hundred dollars of their wages to bring a Negro name-band from the West Coast. Beyond this there was nothing. The boys were plenty salty about it all—and this situation culminated in clashes with the white townspeople near-by.

When Hastie caught wind of the situation, he swiftly went into action. After conferences with Army officials, a recreational program was put into operation inside and outside the cantonment. Hostesses were brought in, baseball teams were set up, and arrangements were made for regular weekend trips to the big towns. A number of U.S.O. men are now established in the population centers around the camp, preparing programs of civilian-soldier cooperation in entertainment. Today, Camp Huachuca is well on its way to live down its once bad reputation.

Nothing in Hastie's manner suggests the aggressive executive. He is reserved, professorial, even a bit other-worldly, yet he has a crisp, businesslike mind. He has a fascinating coffee-and-cream complexion which shows off strikingly against smooth black hair and a thin, trim mustache. "The Jedge," as he is called off the record, is a graduate of Amherst College (with Phi Beta Kappa honors) and Harvard Law School. Formerly dean of Howard Law School, he came into the government as assistant solicitor of the Interior Department. He is the first Negro to be appointed to a federal judgeship, a post in the Virgin Islands which he resigned because, as he put it, "no one has a right to personal security in these times." Negroes have considerable confidence in him—his zealous integrity being a strong factor.

Early in 1943, Hastie became fed up and resigned his job, charging the War Department with an anti-Negro bias that made his work there a travesty. He held that it was almost impossible to get things done, and, moreover, no one in the department seemed disposed to correct the flagrant Jim Crow policy against Negroes. He particularly flayed the Air Forces for maintaining a discriminatory policy which almost entirely excluded Negroes from the service. His resignation produced a sensation in the Negro community—and indeed elevated him to something of a hero. In his wake followed Truman Gibson, a young Negro lawyer, who is attempting to piece together the remains of the job.

Top man today is handsome Doctor Robert C. Weaver, racial adviser to Paul V. McNutt, chairman of the War Manpower Commission. He has the vastly important job of keeping an alert finger on the pulse of the Negro labor supply. He must devise means and techniques of getting Negroes into war industries—and this, without upsetting the racial apple-cart and thereby retarding production. How to utilize a million Negro workers, with employed or underemployed, was the first big problem he had to wrestle with when he was made chief of the Negro manpower service—now defunct. Negro morale was at a low ebb. Negroes saw, he observed, white neighbors with no better or even poorer qualifications rapidly absorbed in war industries. To meet this problem, he approached factory-owners and persuaded them to consider the employment of Negroes. "It is not enough," he said, "for management to have an *inclination* to use Negro labor; it must have a *conviction,* and transmit this conviction to supervisors, foremen, and workers." Where there was a strong labor organization, he sought the active cooperation of the union. Finally he attempted to work out harmonious relations between labor and management for the easy introduction of the new Negro workers.

Weaver, who wears his clothes with a stylish flare, is of very light complexion—Negroes call him "high yaller." He is possessed of a refined intelligence, but is coolly aloof to acquaintances, and critics have pointed to this as a defect. Nicknamed "Bob," he is not one of the boys in the hail-fellow-well-met sense. Essentially, he is the student, discerning, deliberate, and removed. He is the first Negro to earn a Ph.D. in economics from Harvard University, and he entered the government in the early days of the New Deal—a protégé of Ickes. As racial adviser in the Interior Department, he procured promotions for long-neglected Negro employees, job opportunities for Negro technical men, and other benefits for colored citizens from the programs under the jurisdiction of the Interior Department. Though there has been much rank-and-file criticism scoring his lack of aggressiveness on behalf of Negroes, his associates regard him as a sound and resourceful leader.

The most picturesque member of the Black Cabinet is noisy, flamboyant Ted Poston, racial adviser to Elmer Davis, head of the Office of War Information. As head of the Negro press relations, he provides Negroes with an account of how the war is proceeding and a basis for judging how well or ill the fortunes of Negroes fare. His task is to stimulate the energy of Negroes, through their press, and imbue them with a will to win the war. Beyond his job, he is famed in Negro circles as a master of the tall tale, and wrote that delightful *New Republic* piece, "Revolt of the Evil Fairies," in which he pictured himself as assaulting a Prince Charming! As an active participant in Harlem's *Amsterdam-News* strike during 1935, he helped throw into discard the tradition that Negro workers would not act against Negro bosses. He has an agile mind, and is alert to seize opportunities. His chief facetious boast is that he put his birthplace, Hopkinsville, Kentucky, on the map.

A key man in the Black Cabinet is Frank S. Horne, shrewd, with a sly sense of humor, who is chief of the racial relations office of the Federal Public Housing Administration. He is ever alert to see that Negroes are not overlooked, and has been successful in getting many projects erected for them. Today, with large-scale migration of Negroes to the industrial centers, the importance of his work has expanded considerably. Horne studied at the Northern Illinois College of Opthalmology, attended New York City College and Columbia University, and then taught school. A New Yorker by birth, he smokes innumerable cigarettes and likes an occasional drink. He is a poet of some distinction, but no long-haired intellectual, and is trained to look a problem squarely in the eye.

The women in the Black Cabinet have vastly different backgrounds. Only two figures are prominent. Mrs. Mary McLeod Bethune, director of the Office of Negro Affairs in the National Youth Administration; and Crystal Bird Fauset, racial relations adviser to Dean Landis, head of the Office of Civilian Defense. They are a contrast in early training, previous occupation, and personality. Mrs. Bethune is an educator. Mrs. Fauset is a politician. The former is a very dark woman, who is possessed of extraordinary charm and dignity, with a fine talent for winning friends, both Negro and white. Mrs. Fauset is very light in complexion, wears modish clothes, and is easy-on-the-eye. A consummate politican hailing from Philadelphia, she tiptoed tactfully over the prostrate forms of dancers, athletes, and thespians to survive the early purges of O.C.D. A competent, friendly woman, with exceeding resiliency under pressure, her job is to activize Negroes in the civilian defense programs. She is a rare type to be found in influential government circles today—a Negro politican, and, as such, the only one in the Black Cabinet.

Her colleague, Mrs. Bethune, is the self-taught founder and president of Bethune-Cookman College, which she "prayed up, sung up, and talked up" into an outstanding institution for girls. Today, she is a leading spirit in youth and women's movements, and is president of the National Council of Negro Women, a powerful organization. Ida M. Tarbell once named her as one of the fifty outstanding American women. To her intimates, however, she is simply "Ma Bethune." Despite her advanced age and inclination to take on weight, she moves about with the vigor of a much younger woman. Her influence in the Black Cabinet rests on her link with the past, wide contacts among whites, mature judgment, and a willingness to "go to the front" in critical situations.

An incident which occurred in the summer of 1942 will illustrate her forthright attitude on questions affecting her people. One of the most critical situations the Black Cabinet had to face was the execution of a Negro sharecropper, Odell Waller, who had killed his white landlord in Virginia. The case was brought forward by the Workers' Defense League. Acknowledgeing extenuating circumstances, the liberal opinion of the country had clamored for clemency. Negro leaders had attempted to prevail upon government officials to step in, but had little success.

Finally, Mrs. Bethune made a last appeal . . .

At one o'clock in the morning, a few hours before the scheduled execution, she called the White house by telephone and succeeded in talking with Mrs. Roosevelt—one of her keenest admirers. Mrs. Bethune pleaded fervently for a stay. Mrs. Roosevelt's response was immediate. She awoke the President and stated the case to him. Attorney General Biddle was called and asked his opinion. He closed the affair by saying the federal government had no jurisdiction. Next morning the Negro sharecropper went to his death—but Mrs. Bethune's status as a leader was secure.

The Black Cabinet, to accomplish its ends, often employs much of the positive features of the lobby—it arouses public interest through the press and pulpit, approaches influential white persons, puts the heat under congressmen with large Negro constituencies, and frequently goes directly to the White House. Sometimes it plants ideas in persons whose support would be helpful, and prods key public figures into assuming leadership of new programs, while the Black Cabinet itself does the in-fighting within the government arena. The source of its power and inspiration is undoubtedly the prevalent aggressive temper of the Negro people—to which the Black Cabinet is alertly responsive.

Sharp cognizance was taken of the Black Cabinet on the issue of the Detroit race riot early in 1942—an occurrence which shocked the nation, and also brought the activities of this group into the open. The situation in Detroit seemed clear enough to members of the Black Cabinet. Before the completion of Detroit's Sojourner Truth Homes, a government housing project erected with public funds, the Washington housing authorities notified the Detroit Housing Commission to certify Negroes for occupancy. White people in the area protested, and led by Congressman Tenerowicz of Michigan, the issue was taken to the top officials. Twenty-four hours later the decision was reversed, and the project was opened for whites only.

Members of the Black Cabinet met and decided on a course of action. Before the Washington housing authorities could readily be approached, it was decided that public interest would have to be aroused. Within a short time the Negro press began blasting the housing officials, decrying in particular their weak-kneed policy. Negro organizations—the N.A.A.C.P., the National Urban League, and others—sent representatives to Washington to protest. Housing officials were deluged with telegrams and letters, and a march on Washington was staged by Detroit Negroes, who called on government officials and visited congressmen. No opportunity for publicity was overlooked. Negro demands were kept at a fever pitch by press and pulpit. With the barrage thus laid down, the Black Cabinet presented the demands of a united Negro community, taking the issue to the White House. The order was rescinded again, in favor of Negroes, reportedly upon White House intervention.

White people began a day-and-night vigil before Detroit's City Hall in protest. When the Ku Klux Klan entered the picture, the picket lines were shifted to the project's location—and the racial explosion occurred when Negroes sought to move into the buildings. Without government protection, Negroes were blocked from entering the project for months. Meantime an F.B.I. investigation turned up links with Axis agents among the agitators. Soon a large section of the liberal white public took up the issue and supported the Negroes' right to live in the houses. Pressure by Negroes was again applied to make the Washington officials stand firmly by their decision, and the Sojourner Truth Homes were finally turned over to Negroes.

The Michigan *Chronicle*, a Negro newspaper, afterward declared that "It was clear that the government [Negro] advisers put the welfare of their people above their jobs." This view was expressed somewhat by Congressman Tenerowicz when he rose in the House of Representatives, observed that the affair had "reverberated throughout the country," and demanded to know whether "the membership of the House must consult this new agency, the Black Cabinet, regarding any and all racial questions."

The Negro Woman Worker

Jean Collier

INTRODUCTION

One in every six women workers in America is a Negro, according to the latest census figures—those of 1930. In all, nearly 2,000,000 Negro women were classed as gainful workers at that time. How many of these women

Source: Jean Collier, *The Negro Woman Worker.* (Washington: U.S. Department of Labor, Women's Bureau, 1938).

now have jobs and how many are unemployed; where the employed women are working; how much they earn, and how their wages compare with those of white women workers: these are questions that have a direct bearing on the economic problems of today.

Though women in general have been discriminated against and exploited through limitation of their opportunities for employment, through long hours, low wages, and harmful working conditions, such hardships have fallen upon Negro women with double harshness. As the members of a new and inexperienced group arrive at the doors of industry, the jobs that open up to them ordinarily are those vacated by other workers who move on to more highly paid occupations. Negro women have formed such a new and inexperienced group in wage employment. To their lot, therefore, have fallen the more menial jobs, the lower paid, the more hazardous—in general, the least agreeable and desirable. And one of the tragedies of the depression was the realization that the unsteady foothold Negro women had attained in even these jobs was lost when great numbers of unemployed workers from other fields clamored for employment.

Not very much is actually known about the economic position of Negro women today. The depression caused serious employment displacements that cannot be measured accurately. However, certain work problems of Negro women are outstanding and may be discussed with some measure of authority. To that end it may be well to discuss what is known concerning the general occupational position of Negro women; and further, something of each major occupational group as to numbers of workers, employment opportunities, hours, wages, and working conditions, and any other factors that may be of special importance.

OCCUPATIONAL STATUS

On the whole, most women, white or Negro, work for their living just as do men, not because they want to but because they must. The reason larger proportions of Negro than of white women work lies largely in the low scale of earnings of Negro men. In their pre-Civil War status it was the ability of Negro women to work that governed their market value. At the close of the Civil War a large proportion of all Negro women—married as well as single—were forced to engage in breadwinning activities. In 1930, at the time of the latest census, it was found still true that a larger proportion of Negro women than of white women were gainfully occupied. Practically 2 in 5 Negro women, in contrast to 1 in 5 white women, work for their living.

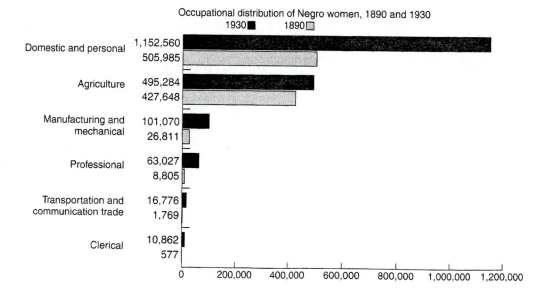

Occupational distribution of Negro women, 1890 and 1930
1930 ■   1890 ▨

Occupation	1930	1890
Domestic and personal	1,152,560	505,985
Agriculture	495,284	427,648
Manufacturing and mechanical	101,070	26,811
Professional	63,027	8,805
Transportation and communication trade	16,776	1,769
Clerical	10,862	577

In pre-Civil War days the employment of the Negro woman was almost completely restricted to two fields where work is largely unskilled and heavy—agriculture and domestic service. Agriculture utilized the large majority of workers. In 1930 about 9 in every 10 Negro women still were engaged in farm work or in domestic and personal service, with more than two-thirds of them in domestic and personal service. The major occupational shift for Negro women has been, therefore, within these two large fields of employment. What occupational progress Negro women have made has been for the most part in connection with their entrance into the better paid, better standardized occupations in domestic and personal service. In addition, increases have been shown in the last 20 years in the professions and in clerical work. From 1910 to 1930 there was an increase of 33,000 Negro women in manufacturing, though a small decrease took place between 1920 and 1930.

DOMESTIC AND PERSONAL SERVICE

Numbers Employed

In 1930, the date of the latest Nation-wide census, 3 in 5 Negro women workers reported their usual occupation as in domestic and personal service. Included in this broad classification were more than 600,000 domestic employees in private homes; over 250,000 laundresses not in laundries; 50,000 laundry and cleaning and dyeing workers; about 18,000 housekeepers and stewards, and practically the same number of waitresses; 16,000 untrained nurses and midwives; almost 13,000 hairdressers and manicurists; more than 11,000 charwomen and cleaners; and over 4,000 elevator tenders. The number of Negro women in domestic and personal service in 1930—1,150,000—represented a gain of nearly 50 percent from 1920 to 1930. Negro women in household employment increased by 81 percent.

Unemployment

Today, 8 years after that census, though there are no complete statistics on unemployment for the whole country, it is certain that the plight of Negro domestics since the beginning of the depression has been an exceedingly serious one. Certain scattered data such as follow are indicative of the situation as a whole.

In a comprehensive study of employment and unemployment in Louisville, Ky., conducted by the State Department of Labor in the spring of 1933, it was found that a little over one-half of the Negro women, in contrast to less than three-tenths of the white women, were without jobs. More than three-fourths of the Negro women wage earners in the survey depended on domestic and personal service for their livelihood, but the depression had thrown 56 percent of these out of work.

In a survey by the Federal Emergency Relief Administration of persons on relief in 40 urban centers as of May 1, 1934, over two-thirds of the approximately 150,000 women who described their usual occupations in terms of servants and allied workers were Negro. For 23 northern and midwestern cities the difference in number between white and Negro women in this classification was not so great—54,000 Negro women as against 37,000 white women; but in the 17 southern cities covered in the F. E. R. A. report there were only 5,000 white women, as against 52,000 Negro women, classed as servants and allied workers.

Household Service

So much for the unemployment of Negro domestic labor. But what about the working conditions of various types of domestic and personal service workers? The largest group, and the one concerning which there is the least definite information as to employment standards, is that of household workers.

From common knowledge, and according to the few recent scattered studies that are available, low wages and long hours are characteristic of household service. In a survey of household employment in Lynchburg, Va., in the spring of 1937, the typical wage of the group covered—largely Negro workers—was $5 or $6 a week. Two cases were reported at $1.50 and one at $10, and there was one report of payment in the form of a house "on the lot" rent-free, and one of payment made only in clothing. The typical hours were 72 a week. There were 16 reports of 80 to 90 hours and there was 1 report of a week of 91 hours.

A compilation of household employment data for the South in 1934, in which some 26 Y. W. C. A. local associations cooperated, showed that the average weekly wage for Negro workers was $6.17 and the average workweek was 66 hours.

During the period of the National Recovery Administration a survey of household employment in 33 northern counties in Mississippi, conducted by the Joint Committee on National Recovery, showed that wages of Negro domestics usually amounted to less than $2 a week.

An informal investigation of household employment was made in the spring of 1937 by a Washington, D.C., committee representing women's organizations, by inquiries of both private and public employment agencies. The study showed that the general minimum weekly wage at which workers were placed was $5, and the average was from $7 to $10. The chief demands were for mothers' helpers at the $5 wage, and for general workers. The large majority of applicants were Negro women. Inadequate living and working conditions on the job were reported for many households. In a number of homes no bathing facilities were provided for the workers; too often the bed was found to consist of a cot in the living room or furnace room. Long hours and heavy work were characteristic of many jobs and the difficulty

of managing children constituted another problem.

Laundresses and Laundry Operatives

The census makes a distinction between women laundresses who are self employed, working in their own or their employers' homes, and operatives employed in commercial laundries. In 1930 there still were about 270,000 Negro women laundresses not in laundries, despite the rapid rise of power laundries in the decade from 1920 to 1930. There were nearly 50,000 Negro women laundry operatives.

Though employment conditions generally are better standardized and more favorable for women in commercial laundries than in private homes, the direct influence of home laundry work on the hour and wage standards set by the commercial laundry can be seen clearly. In a study of laundries by the Women's Bureau in 1935, Bureau agents were told again and again that commercial laundries, especially in the South, were having a terrific struggle to compete with Negro washwomen. The following comments made by laundry employers, employment office officials, and other informed persons illustrate the conditions at that time:

> Since the depression, servants are required to do laundry as well as maid work; most of them get only $3 a week on the average.
> Greatest competition is colored washwomen. Will take a 30-pound bundle for a dollar. Some of them do a week's washing for 50 cents.
> The washwoman charges only 60 to 75 percent of what the laundry charges for the same size bundle.
> The manager knew of a number of washwomen who were glad to get a day's work for carfare, lunch, and an old dress.

Data of much interest concerning employment conditions of Negro women in laundries are found in the Women's Bureau laundry study. Conducted during the N. R. A. period, the study shows a relation between code rates and actual conditions, and indicates what amounted to a race differential in the minimum wages set, as follows: Minimum-wage rates set by the N. R. A. laundry code for a 40-hour week ranged from 14 cents to 30 cents an hour, depending on geographical section and size of city within the section. In the nine southern States, for whose entire area the weekly minimum was set at $5.60, three-fourths of the women laundry workers were Negroes, according to the 1930 census. On the other hand, in 10 States for which the highest minimum was set, 4 in the far West and the others in New England, less than 4 percent of the women laundry workers were Negroes.

Wage data in the study showed average weekly earnings considerably higher in the North than in the South. The average for all men employees—productive labor, office employees, routemen, and other labor—ranged from $27.63 a week in Boston to $16.44 in Savannah. For all women employees the range was from $13.38 in Boston to $5.79 in Charleston.

For white and Negro women on productive work weekly earnings were just about comparable in Atlantic City—$7.99 for the white and $7.64 for the Negro women. Negro women in Chicago had the highest average weekly earnings of any such city group covered by the study, $9.83, but the earnings of the white women averaged $11.14.

Wages of women workers in the South were distressingly low for both white and Negro workers on productive work. The widest differences in average weekly wages was in Memphis, where white women received $9.21 for an average week's work while Negro women found but $5.57 in an average pay envelope. In Jacksonville the earnings were $8.43 for white women and $5.01 for Negro women; in Charlotte they were $8.47 for white and $5.25 for Negro; in Greenville they were respectively $7.84 and $5.45; in Savannah, $7.62 and $5.32. In no southern city covered by the Women's Bu-

reau in the laundry study did the average earnings of Negro women reach the exceedingly low minimum of $5.60 set by the N. R. A. laundry code.

Hotels and Restaurants

Many Negro women have found work in one or another of the branches of public housekeeping, as cooks, waitresses, chambermaids, cafeteria counter girls, and so forth. In 1930, the census reported more than 86,000 Negro women in such occupations. Though hours tend to be shorter and better standardized in public than in private housekeeping, the workweek of the woman in a hotel or restaurant is likely to be much longer than that of the woman in factory, store, or laundry.

Negro women in hotels and restaurants were included in a Women's Bureau survey of the wages and hours of Tennessee women in the winter of 1935–36. In the hotel industry in Tennessee more jobs are open to Negro than to white employees, so the data in the study are of special interest.

In the lodging departments of hotels most of the jobs open to women are those of chambermaids, cleaners, and linen-room attendants. The first two were filled by Negro women and the last by white women. Average week's earnings for Negro chambermaids and general cleaners were $5.65, the most common rate of pay for this work being about $25 a month. About two-fifths of the employees in the lodging departments were given a noon meal or their meals and lodging. For the few hotels with laundries the average week's earnings of the women laundry workers—chiefly Negroes—were only $4.60.

In hotel kitchens Negro women generally were found doing vegetable or pantry work, most of the cooks being men. Meals allowed on duty augmented somewhat the low average week's earnings of $5.50. For the smaller group of white women doing somewhat similar work the week's earnings averaged about $8. Very few Negro waitresses were found in hotel dining rooms.

While the wage scale for women in the kitchens of restaurants not in hotels was somewhat higher than of those in hotels, the average earnings of Negro women in such kitchens were but $8.55. Over 80 percent of the Negro women, many of whom served as the chief cook of the restaurant, had earnings below $10.

Beauty Shops

A relatively new occupation for Negro women workers is that of beauty service. That this occupation is developing rapidly for Negro women is common knowledge, but this fact is proved by the census, which shows that while in 1910 there were only about 3,800 Negro women workers in such employment, in 1930 the number was 3½ times as large, or about 13,000.

Some indication of employment conditions for Negro women in beauty shops may be gained from a Women's Bureau study of such establishments in the winter of 1933–34. In the four cities covered by the survey, 390 white shops employing some 1,300 women, and 75 Negro shops employing 150 women, were covered. Most of the Negro women were serving the needs of their own race, but a few were at work in white beauty shops or barber shops.

Though beauty-shop employment is sometimes considered to offer desirable vocational opportunities for Negro girls and women, earnings reported to Women's Bureau agents were low. The average weekly wage was only $8, or about three-fifths of that of the white women in the industry. Almost two-thirds of the women received less than $10 a week and only about 1 in 16 earned as much as $15. Hours were very long. Three of every five Negro women reported had a schedule longer than 48 hours. More than two-thirds of these women had worked, or been ready for service, more than 54 hours in the week. Closing hours were later and the spread of hours was longer than in the white shops.

AGRICULTURE

Long as may be the hours of the Negro domestic worker, low as may be her earnings and those of the Negro woman in laundry, hotel, or restaurant, in general the economic status of these workers is much more favorable than that of the Negro woman agricultural laborer. For this woman worker there are few aspects of her working life over which she has any real control. Crop conditions, markets, and prices; the employment status of her family, whether as owners, tenant farmers, sharecroppers, or wage workers; the necessity of accepting field work as one of a family group rather than on an individual basis; lack of educational facilities, particularly in the rural South, which would enable her to equip herself for other employment if it were available—these are some of the factors that materially affect her living.

Numbers Employed

In 1930, agriculture absorbed the services of the second largest group of Negro women—about half a million. Roughly seven in eight of these women—about one-fourth of whom were wage workers and three-fifths unpaid family workers—were in the seven southern States of Alabama, Georgia, Louisiana, Mississippi, North Carolina, South Carolina, and Texas. Cotton is, of course, the major crop in these States, and it is on cotton that Negro labor is so largely employed.

Typical Employment Conditions

A marked trend from tenant farmer to the lower status of sharecropper is shown for Negro labor in the South from 1920 to 1935 by United States Department of Agriculture reports—a trend not shared to the same extent by the white agricultural group. Though many stories have appeared recently in periodicals and the press concerning the near-desperate plight of some of these workers, little information is available to define the problem with any exactitude. A brief but vivid description of the Southern sharecropper-system was given by a Negro woman sharecropper at a national economic conference sponsored by the Joint Committee on National Recovery, from which the following is quoted:

And clothing isn't in it. Since they stopped using fertilizer the clothes are very scanty, because we could take fertilizer sacks and make aprons and dresses for the little children. But since they are not using fertilizer very much you just can't hide their nakedness through the winter. Sometimes you find in some of the houses that the little children are barefooted, and the children in some of the houses couldn't go to school in the winter because they did not have clothes to go in. And some of them haven't even got houses to stay in as good as lots of common barns. And some families of 12 or 14 live in houses with maybe one room and kitchen, with maybe three beds where 10 or 12 are sleeping in the three beds, and the kitchen is so open that you can just pass by and look through and see them all sitting in there, and not even have a flue for the stove pipe to go in, and the stove is setting out in the floor. And maybe they have two joints of a stove-pipe, and maybe one piece of elbow, and when you start a fire you will get smoke all over the house until it gets started burning good, and you have to stay outside until it starts burning good because it smokes you out. Families have to put up with all kinds of things like that.

Though data on Negro agricultural workers are difficult to secure, a survey of agricultural labor conditions in Concordia Parish, La., issued by the United States Department of Agriculture in October 1937, throws some light on the status of these workers in a rich cotton section. Both men and women cotton pickers were interviewed by Government agents. Wages were found to be unbelievably low, year's earnings for agricultural work averaging only $41.67 for women, $120.19 for men. The average income for a whole year, including earnings of dependents, relief (both work and direct), and nonagricultural earnings, was only $62.36

for the women; for men it reached $177.53. None of the women who did only farm work had more than 150 days of employment, and most of them had less than 90 days in the year.

After stating that more than half of the Negro women interviewed had less than a fifth-grade education, this Department of Agriculture report concludes by outlining in general the economic status of Negro cotton labor:

In summary, the basis of the labor supply on the plantations of Concordia Parish is this uneducated and racially distinct group of people. Both men and women work in the fields. The combination of low wage rates and intermittent employment means meager annual earnings. Many of the workers, though not employed full time, live in shacks on the plantation the year round; others come from nearby villages or come across the river from Natchez, Miss. Social contact is primarily within the group itself with little or no outside association. Concordia Parish presents a picture of the evolution of the old plantation with its slave labor emerging as a unit operated with cropper or wage labor. The position of its laboring class has not changed materially from that of earlier times.

The future of Southern Agriculture and the Negro Worker

Disheartening as are the present circumstances of Negro agricultural workers in the South, the future seems to hold even more serious threats to their economic security. An article in the Monthly Labor Review for July 1937, by N. A. Tolles of the Bureau of Labor Statistics, discusses among other topics the relocation of displaced farm tenants:

The greatest potential source of future migration in the United States is to be found among the tenant farmers of the southeastern Cotton Belt. The thousands of former tenants now to be found seeking casual jobs in Florida may be only the forerunners of much greater numbers of both white and Negro migrants.

Tenancy in the Old South is the successor to the slave system. Both institutions were, in different ways, devices for holding on the land, on a subsistence basis, sufficient labor to meet the maximum seasonal requirements of agriculture. As a result, the Southeast is now drenched with labor and is therefore especially vulnerable to all forces which may cause the displacement of workers. The depression, followed by the crop-restriction program, has already forced some displacement of tenants. Much greater displacements may be caused in the near future as a result of technical developments. If the mechanical cotton picker is perfected, most of the demand for tenants and wage workers in the eastern Cotton Belt may be eliminated. But apart from the cotton picker, the spread of improved methods already in use is likely to cause considerable displacement. Mechanical equipment and the use of check-row planting are capable of eliminating much of the labor requirement for cotton raising, except in the picking season. It is questionable whether the landowner of the Old South will continue to provide subsistence the year round for workers who are needed only during a brief season. To compete with the rapidly developing areas of the West and of foreign countries, the plantation of the Old South may be forced to adopt its competitors' method of hiring workers only during the season when their labor is required. In that case a large fraction of the 1,000,000 tenants of the old Cotton Belt may be converted into constant migrants from job to job or displaced from agriculture altogether.

MANUFACTURING AND MECHANICAL INDUSTRIES

The industries the census classifies as "manufacturing and mechanical" rank third in giving jobs to Negro women; the number so employed was 101,000 in 1930. The situation with regard to employment opportunities for Negro women in this group of industries differed widely from that of the domestic and personal service occupations in the 10 years between 1920 and 1930. While thousands of new workers found jobs as domestic employees, laundry operatives, or beauty-shop at-

tendants, there was actually a small decrease in the total number of Negro women employed by industry.

Why this decrease took place cannot be explained. One possible cause is that in 1920 there still were many Negro women employed in the jobs they had taken on during the war-time period of labor scarcity, and that by 1930 most of these jobs would have reverted to white men or women. Another explanation concerns the tremendous technological changes in industry, which have been focused largely on the elimination of low-skilled jobs, the jobs on which the majority of Negro women are employed.

Numbers Employed

The tobacco industries employed more than 18,000 Negro women in 1930. Next in rank as employers of Negro women were the clothing industries, with 16,000; food and allied products, with 11,000; textiles, with 6,000; lumber and furniture, with 3,200; iron and steel, with 1,600; and paper, printing, and allied industries, with 1,400. Miscellaneous manufacturing accounted for an additional 10,000 Negro women, and dressmakers not in factories for 20,000.

General Characteristics of Factory Employment for Negro Women

In a compilation by the Women's Bureau of data on Negro women in industry from reports for 15 States secured over a number of years, it was shown that large numbers of these workers were employed in sweeping and cleaning of various kinds. Others worked at tasks that might be classed as general labor. This would include most of the work done in glass factories; in textiles, with the exception of hosiery; in the wood industry; in tobacco rehandling; in meat packing, in which a third of the women reported worked with casings and chitterlings; the washing of cans or dishes in bakeries, canneries, and food establishments; peeling or pitting fruit; cleaning and pressing clothing, done by over half the women reported in clothing establishments; sorting rags in rag and paper factories; and picking out nut meats. Though in some instances Negro women were found in considerable numbers to be operating machines of various kinds, many of these involved only simple operations or repetitive movements, though some required dexterity or a degree of skill. A few Negro women were in supervisory posts or in other positions involving more or less responsibility.

Though current information concerning the work status of Negro women in industry is scattered and not comprehensive, brief summaries from various reports may serve to outline certain economic problems such women must meet.

Tobacco Stemmeries

In 1934 the Women's Bureau made an investigation of the current pay rolls of the stemmery departments in three branches of the tobacco-manufacturing industry in Virginia and North Carolina. An overwhelming majority of the stemmeries' employees were found to be women, largely Negro women, whose work consists of removing the stem from the leaf and of getting the tobacco ready for the various processes of manufacture.

Weekly earnings were very low. Of all employees included, one-tenth earned less than $5 for the week, not far from half earned less than $10, and about 87 percent received less than $12. Over four-fifths of the employees covered by the survey worked full-time hours.

That many workers in the tobacco plants have failed to earn a livelihood and required supplementary aid from relief agencies was evident from the firms' pay-roll data and facts from the emergency relief agencies. In a tobacco manufacturing center the emergency relief administration reported in one month that slightly more than 10 percent of its case load was experienced tobacco-factory workers. In another city over one-sixth

of the cases in one month, and over one-seventh in another month, were families in which one or more members were tobacco workers. In one city, roughly two-thirds of the families were receiving full relief, and relief of tobacco workers in this city was averaging a few thousand dollars a month.

In regard to the ability of the industry to pay a living wage, the Women's Bureau report stated:

> Labor cost is comparatively such a small part of the total production costs that the wage levels could be raised without making an appreciable difference to the industry. One stemmery, with 2,000 employees showing an average weekly wage of $10.82, had produced during the week over 3,000,000 pounds of strips, or enough tobacco for a billion cigarettes. The cost of labor operations was less than a penny a pound of prepared tobacco, or less than a mill per package of 20 cigarettes.

Negro Women in Tennessee Factories

Not far from 1,000 Negro women in factories were included by the Women's Bureau in its State-wide study of women in Tennessee industries in the winter of 1935–36. In the middle Tennessee area the average week's earnings for the 361 women covered were $7.30. Most of the women were employed in tobacco plants and warehouses on jobs such as stemming, stripping, and hanging tobacco leaf.

One large hosiery mill employed women on boarding—that is, pulling damp stockings over heated forms to shape and press them, an operation usually done by men and boys.

Negro women formed a larger proportion (18 percent) of all women employed in manufacturing in the western area of the State, especially in Memphis, than elsewhere. They were working as operatives in one or more establishments in the shelling of nuts; in work on cotton and burlap bags, especially the rehandling of bags; in various jobs in wood-working, caning chairs, and making fruit boxes and baskets; in packing cosmetics and other pharmaceutical products; and in making paper boxes for cosmetics. The average weekly earnings of Negro women in this section were the exceedingly low amount of $4.50. Women worked 4 or 5 days a week picking nut meats for earnings of $2.55. Year's earnings were reported for 62 Negro women in Tennessee factories. For this group the average for the year was only $345.

Negro Women in Chicago Factories

An informal survey by a branch of the Chicago Y. W. C. A. of a relatively small number of Negro women industrial workers in the spring of 1936 provided material of interest. Describing the cotton-garment industry as one of the more important industries employing Negroes, the report states that usually the work is power-machine operating on a straight piece-work basis. During the N. R. A. the minimum rate for experienced workers was $13 a week. Of nine girls experienced in this field, five showed earnings of less than $10 after the N. R. A. ceased to function. One earned less than $5. Other summarized statements from the report follow:

> Another industry in which many Negro girls have had experience is that of dates and nuts. Though employed for only a very short season of the year, earnings are notoriously low. Of 17 applicants who worked in this industry since the N. R. A., all specified their earnings to be less than $10 a week. Six of them were earning between $5 and $7.50. Two of them made less than $5. Though hours of work were not reported, it is known that the industry works full time during the busy season, during which all these girls were employed.
>
> Another industry that employs chiefly Negro workers is the used burlap bag industry. Reports of workers indicate that wages are somewhat higher, or between $10 and $12.50. This is an industry with disagreeable and hazardous conditions. The presence of dust and lint in the air, unless carefully controlled, is a

well-known hazard, and the material is disagreeable to handle and hard on the hands.

> Of 91 girls who had factory experience since May 1935, half earned less than $10 a week, and of the industries represented the lowest paid was the date and nut industry, with an average of $6.72 a week. These figures present a glaring contrast to the general average of $14.97 a week for women workers in Chicago factories in 1935, compiled by the division of statistics and research of the Illinois Department of Labor.

Another study by the same Y. W. C. A. was concerned with employment possibilities of Negro women workers in the Chicago needle trades. The investigation showed that Negro workers were chiefly employed in the cotton goods lines, generally somewhat less skilled. Of the 48 firms about which information was secured, only 13 employed any Negro workers. All but two made house dresses and aprons. Even within this industry, opportunities were distinctly limited. Several of the firms employed Negroes only on pressing, a job that requires unusual strength and endurance, on the ground that "the Negro can stand heat better than a white girl." Comparatively few concerns had both white and Negro workers on power-machine work. The few that did employ many Negro workers employed virtually no white workers.

NEGRO WOMEN AS WHITE-COLLAR WORKERS

Numbers Employed

In 1910 there were only about 30,000 Negro women in professional service; in 1920 there were almost 40,000; in 1930 there were 63,000. These figures represent an increase of more than 100 percent from 1910 to 1930. Clerical workers within the ranks of gainfully employed Negro women numbered only 3,000 in 1910; in 1920 there were 8,000 such workers; and in 1930 there were 11,000. More than 7,000 Negro women worked in stores in 1910;

in 1920 this group had increased to 11,500; and in 1930 the total was 14,500.

In all, Negro women in what may be termed "white-collar occupations"—in transportation and communication, trade, public service, professional service, and clerical occupations—totaled but 91,600 in 1930, or only about 5 percent of the Negro women gainfully occupied. On the other hand, native white women in the same occupations totaled 4,330,000 in the same year, or 56 percent of all gainfully occupied white women of native birth.

Reasons for Small Numbers of Negro White-Collar Workers

Naturally there are many reasons for this disparity in the proportions of Negro and white workers in the better paid, more highly skilled, occupational fields. Educational facilities for Negro workers are notoriously inadequate in some sections of the United States. Negroes have had a relatively short span of years in which to demonstrate their ability in certain fields requiring training and skill. But there is an additional reason of much significance, which is clearly suggested in a recent publication of the Works Progress Administration of Georgia, a State which contains only slightly less than a tenth of all the Negroes in the United States, entitled "Occupational Characteristics of White-Collar and Skilled Negro Workers."

The shift downward in the present [the shift from white-collar to skilled, semiskilled, and unskilled positions] was caused by the depression. White-collar occupations among Negroes depend, for the most part, upon the Negroes themselves. The doctors in the main have only Negro patients; Negro lawyers have Negro clients; and Negro teachers must teach in Negro schools. Negro business has a limited market, as it is confined to the Negro group. During a period of retrenchment, certain phases of white-collar work continue while others disappear. Negro businesses with no reserve disappear during periods of depression, and the clerks, stenographers, and messenger boys hired must find other occupations. Gen-

erally, there is nothing else but to go to lower occupational levels.

With the great bulk of Negro workers, men and women, receiving wages that permit of only the barest subsistence—as has been shown by the data for various occupational groups in the present report—the reasons for the limitations of Negro white-collar opportunities become plain. Unless Negro workers have adequate purchasing power, they are unable to secure needed professional services; to buy from Negro stores; to attend Negro theaters and other places of amusement; to protect themselves through insurance agencies and the like. Increased white-collar employment among Negro workers inevitably will follow a rise in the economic status of all Negro wage earners.

Negro White-Collar Workers in Atlanta

The Georgia Works Progress Administration report, to which reference has been made, contains interesting data concerning Negroes—both men and women—in white-collar jobs, including those of the professions, in Atlanta. This survey, conducted from January to July 1936, covered nearly 5,000 persons. Of 1,500 Negro women white-collar and skilled workers in Atlanta, just half reported their usual occupation as professional in character and nearly one-fourth as clerical. With regard to their jobs at the time the survey was made, however, only 38 percent were employed in the professions and about 19 percent in clerical work. Over a fifth of all the women were unemployed.

The average monthly income for just over 3,300 white-collar and skilled workers in this Atlanta study was $60. The professional workers had the highest income ($72.75), the skilled workers followed ($70), and the clerical workers ranked lowest ($63).

Negro Professional Women

Teachers accounted for nearly three-fourths of Negro professional women in 1930, and trained nurses for nearly one-tenth. In addition, at least 1,000 Negro women were employed as actresses, as college presidents and professors, and as musicians and teachers of music.

Information on the salaries paid to Negro teachers is available in a report prepared by the Office of Education of the United States Department of the Interior issued in 1934. Salaries of rural teachers in 17 States and the District of Columbia averaged $945 for white teachers and $388 for Negro teachers. For teachers in junior and senior high schools in 17 States and the District of Columbia, salaries averaged $1,479 for the white and $926 for the Negro teachers.

Additional information on salaries paid Negro rural teachers in a number of States is available in a 1937 report of the National Education Association. The lowest annual salary for Negro rural teachers was $150 in Mississippi, where white teachers received an average salary of $458, more than three times as high. The highest Negro average for rural teachers was $812 in Maryland, in which State white teachers averaged $1,474.

Negro Women as Clerical Workers

A survey of office workers in seven cities was conducted by the Women's Bureau during 1931 and the early part of 1932. In two of these cities—Atlanta and Chicago—an effort was made to secure information for Negro women employed in the types of office covered. The two races were not employed together in any office visited, but five insurance companies and one publisher in Chicago, and two insurance offices in Atlanta, all controlled and managed by Negro ownership, were found to employ Negroes. In both cities several banks and other types of office employing Negroes were visited, but they had only from one to three women, all combined being too few to form a representative group.

In the 6 Chicago offices 101 Negro women, 90 in insurance and 11 in publishing, were included. Their average monthly salary in insurance was $80, as compared to $94 for the white women in insurance. In Atlanta insurance offices the average monthly salary for Negro women was $55, in contrast to $94 for white women. In Chicago about one-third of the Negro women (including 11 in publishing), and in Atlanta about seven-eighths, were on salaries of less than $75 a month. Four-fifths in Chicago and 98 percent in Atlanta were on salaries of less than $100.

One fact of special interest in this study was that the amount of general schooling and the attendance at business schools were higher for the Negro women than for the study as a whole. In Chicago 50 of the 100 women with education reported had completed high school and 34 had some advanced training. In Atlanta 16 of 56 were high-school graduates and 23 had had some advanced training.

Negro Women in Retail Trade

Through no information is at hand showing wages or working conditions of Negro women in stores, an article in the November 1937 issue of the Monthly Labor Review on "The Negro in Retail Trade" may serve to indicate something of the present status of employment opportunities in this field. The report states that—

Negro proprietors in 1935 were operating 23,490 retail stores in the United States—a decrease of 2,211 stores as compared with 1929. The reduction in the number of such stores in the South was 2,936. In the North and West, however, they increased respectively by 490 and 235.

In 1929 the pay rolls of these stores totaled $8,528,000; in 1935, $5,021,000, a drop of 41.1 percent. For the same years the total value of sales was respectively $101,146,000 and $48,987,000—a decline of 51.6 percent. Within this period, 1929 to 1935, the number of retail stores operated by proprietors of all racial groups expanded by 110,803, although the chain-store units decreased by 19,828, pay rolls dwindled 30.2 percent, and the aggregate value of all sales declined 32.5 percent.

MEASURES FOR IMPROVING THE ECONOMIC STATUS OF NEGRO WOMEN WORKERS

The public must pay heavily for the substandard working and living conditions of many thousands of Negro women workers. When people have no jobs or their wages are too low for adequate support, they still must have food, shelter, and clothing. The presence on relief rolls in 1935—the last date for which there is accurate information—of one in every four Negro women workers, and the fact that two-fifths of these unemployed women were the economic heads of families, constitute a situation that is of grave import to the citizens who must support these women and their families.

Experience has shown further that low living standards are costly in that they breed crime and disease, which affect all citizens. Workers desperate for jobs are the prey of unscrupulous employers, who by using cheap labor are able to undercut employers willing to pay fair wages. At times such workers are available as strikebreakers. When a significant proportion of the population is forced to live at a substandard economic level, all classes—farmers, factory workers, merchants, professional men—are deprived of the benefits resulting from adequate purchasing power in the hands of those who would spend if they could.

Because of the relation of the problems of Negro women to those of other community groups, it may be helpful to discuss certain measures for improving the economic status of Negro women that seem most practicable and realistic at the present time.

Social and Labor Legislation

In general, woman labor has benefited markedly from social and labor legislation during recent years. State hour and minimum-wage laws, workmen's compensation provisions, the joint Federal and State social security program, have served to make more secure and satisfactory woman's economic status.

Unfortunately, Negro women workers have by no means shared equally with white women in the benefits of these provisions. Workers in agriculture and domestic service, largely because of the difficulty of labor-law administration, have been exempted from the coverage of most of the laws; and it has been shown that the great majority of Negro women workers are to be found within these two occupational fields.

Take minimum-wage laws, for example. Such laws to date have been enacted by 25 States, the District of Columbia, and Puerto Rico. In general, minimum-wage legislation has been designed for several purposes: To set a bottom limit below which wage rates cannot fall; to assure to women wages adequate to meet the cost of a healthful standard of living; to end sweatshops and cutthroat competition among employers; to relieve the community of supplementing low wages by public and private relief; and to establish on the part of workers the purchasing power that is necessary to bring about and maintain industrial recovery.

However, rough estimates made in the Women's Bureau indicate that only about 1 in 10 of all Negro women workers are covered potentially by minimum-wage legislation, though about one-fourth of all such workers are to be found in States having minimum-wage laws. Of all women, Negro and white, roughly 4,000,000, or well over one-third of all employed women, are covered by such laws. It is evident that minimum-wage laws thus far have not been an important factor in raising the wages of the bulk of Negro women workers.

On the other hand, one aspect of minimum-wage administration during recent months has been of considerable benefit to large numbers of Negro women. When the States with newly enacted laws have begun to issue individual wage orders covering specific occupations, almost universally they have covered first the service industries where many Negro women are employed. Laundries, hotels and restaurants, and beauty shops have been among the first industries for which wage rates have been set.

Improvement in Educational and Training Facilities

In addition to general schooling, specialized training in an occupational field at some stage of the education process is desirable for all young Americans. It is also very useful for older workers who have not had such opportunities at an earlier period. The worker with no special training whatsoever is at a serious disadvantage in seeking employment in an age that is rapidly becoming more highly specialized.

The present demand for skilled domestic workers, so much greater than the supply, points to an urgent need for better training facilities for such workers. In the spring of 1937, in the neighborhood of 400,000 applicants describing themselves as domestic employees were registered in the active files of the United States Employment Service though a survey conducted by the Employment Service as of January 1, 1937, had indicated that at least 500 cities were facing a shortage of trained household workers, and possible placement in these cities over a year might reach nearly half a million.

An important contribution to household training has been made by the Works Progress Administration in many centers throughout the country. For example, during the year 1936, training projects for domestics were conducted in 184 centers. Of 3,629 persons receiving certificates as domestic trainees, 3,491 were placed through the facilities of the many offices of the United States Employment Service. Other agencies, public and private, offer training facilities for household workers, though the combined efforts of all these groups fall far short of taking care of the existing needs in this regard. Schools are badly needed also for vocational training in other lines, such as beauty culture, millinery, and power-machine operating.

Trade-Union Organization

Recent developments in American trade-unionism have been significant in relation to Negro workers. For instance, one of the most important union contracts affecting women workers in American trade-union history was negotiated in August 1937 between the United Laundry Workers Local 300 of the Amalgamated Clothing Workers of America and a large New York City firm which is in the towel and uniform supply laundry business. The agreement covers drivers and also about 8,000 inside workers, by far the greatest proportion of whom are women. Among the important provisions in the contract are the following: A limitation of hours for women to 45 a week; a minimum wage for inside employees of $15.75 for a 45-hour week, with a guaranteed minimum of $15 a week for 11 months; a raise in wage rates of at least 10 percent, with a minimum raise of $2 unless a greater raise is required to bring the weekly earnings up to $15.75; a week's vacation and 3 days' sick leave with pay for each worker after 1 year's service; and 7 fixed holidays with pay. An additional provision of particular interest which is made a condition of the continuation of the agreement is to the effect that "the union shall make all reasonable, customary, and usual attempts authorized by law to procure contracts with the said competitors of the employer within a reasonable time from the date thereof."

The success of the laundry workers' union in New York City that negotiated this agreement for a section of its membership is attested by a recently estimated membership of 30,000 persons, men and women and white and Negro. While the union has obtained a guaranteed annual wage in the linen-supply division only, union contracts with other firms regularize many important aspects of employment.

But it is far simpler to talk about the economic problems of Negro women workers and to suggest possible remedies than it is to take definite action toward their solution. These problems have taken deep root in the social and economic structure during past decades, and only untiring effort on the part of Negroes themselves, aided by the Nation's socially minded citizens, will succeed in eradicating them.

Call to the March on Washington of 1941

A. Philip Randolph

We call upon you to fight for jobs in National Defense.

We call upon you to struggle for the integration of Negroes in the armed forces, such as the Air Corps, Navy, Army and Marine Corps of the Nation.

We call upon you to demonstrate for the abolition of Jim-Crowism, in all Government departments and defense employment.

This is an hour of crisis. It is a crisis of democracy. It is a crisis of minority groups. It is a crisis of Negro Americans.

What is this crisis?

To American Negroes, it is the denial of jobs in Government defense projects. It is racial discrimination in Government departments. It is wide-spread Jim-Crowism in the armed forces of the Nation.

While billions of the taxpayers' money are being spent for war weapons, Negro workers are being turned away from the gates of factories, mines and mills—being flatly told, "NOTHING DOING." Some employers refuse to give Negroes jobs when they are without "union cards," and some unions refuse Negro workers union cards when they are "without jobs."

What shall we do?

What a dilemma!

What a runaround!

What a disgrace!

What a blow below the belt!

Though dark, doubtful and discouraging, all is not lost, all is not hopeless. Though battered and bruised, we are not beaten, broken or bewildered.

Verily, the Negroes' deepest disappointments and direst defeats, their tragic trials and outrageous oppressions in these dreadful days of destruction and disaster to democracy and freedom, and the rights of minority peoples, and the dignity and independence of the human spirit, is the Negroes' greatest opportunity to rise to the highest heights of struggle for freedom and justice in Government, in industry, in labor unions, education, social service, religion and culture.

With faith and confidence of the Negro people in their own power for self-liberation, Negroes can break down the barriers of discrimination against employment in National Defense. Negroes can kill the deadly serpent of race hatred in the Army, Navy, Air and Marine Corps, and smash through and blast the Government, business and labor-union red tape to win the right to equal opportunity in vocational training and re-training in defense employment.

Most important and vital to all. Negroes, by the mobilization and coordination of their mass power, can cause *President Roosevelt to issue an executive order abolishing discrimination in all government departments, Army, Navy, Air Corps, and National Defense jobs.*

Of course, the task is not easy. In very truth, it is big, tremendous and difficult.

It will cost money.

It will require sacrifice.

It will tax the Negroes' courage, determination and will to struggle. But we can, must and will triumph.

The Negroes' stake in national defense is big. It consists of jobs, thousands of jobs. It may represent millions, yes, hundreds of millions of dollars in wages. It consists of new industrial opportunities and hope. This is worth fighting for.

But to win our stakes, it will require an "all-out," bold and total effort and demonstration of colossal proportions.

Negroes can build a mammoth machine of mass action with a terrific and tremendous

Source: "A. Philip Randolph's March on Washington Call." From *The Black Worker* (May, 1941), p. 4. Copyright 1941 The Black Worker.

driving and striking power that can shatter and crush the evil fortress of race prejudice and hate, if they will only resolve to do so and never stop, until victory comes.

Dear fellow Negro Americans, be not dismayed in these terrible times. You possess power, great power. Our problem is to harness and hitch it up for action on the broadest, daring and most gigantic scale.

In this period of power politics, nothing counts but pressure, more pressure, and still more pressure, through the tactic and strategy of broad, organized, aggressive mass action behind the vital and important issues of the Negro. To this end, we propose that ten thousand Negroes *March on Washington for jobs in National Defense and equal integration in the fighting forces of the United States.*

An "all-out" thundering march on Washington, ending in a monster and huge demonstration at Lincoln's Monument will shake up white America.

It will shake up official Washington.

It will give encouragement to our white friends to fight all the harder by our side, with us, for our righteous cause.

It will gain respect for the Negro people.

It will create a new sense of self-respect among Negroes.

But what of national unity?

We believe in national unity which recognizes equal opportunity of black and white citizens to jobs in national defense and the armed forces, and in all other institutions and endeavors in America. We condemn all dictatorships, Fascist, Nazi and Communist. We are loyal, partiotic Americans, all.

But, if American democracy will not defend its defenders; if American democracy will not protect its protectors; if American democracy will not give jobs to its toilers because of race or color; if American democracy will not insure equality of opportunity, freedom and justice to its citizens, black and white, it is a hollow mockery and belies the principles for which it is supposed to stand.

To the hard, difficult and trying problem of securing equal participation in national defense, we summon all Negro Americans to march on Washington. We summon Negro Americans to form comittees in various cities to recruit and register marchers and raise funds through the sale of buttons and other legitimate means for the expenses of marchers to Washington by buses, train, private automobiles, trucks, and on foot.

We summon Negro Americans to stage marches on their City Halls and Councils in their respective cities and urge them to memorialize the President to issue an executive order to abolish discrimination in the Government and national defense.

However, we sternly counsel against violence and ill-considered and intemperate action and the abuse of power. Mass power, like physical power, when misdirected is more harmful than helpful.

We summon you to mass action that is orderly and lawful, but aggressive and militant, for justice, equality and freedom.

Crispus Attucks marched and died as a martyr for American independence. Nat Turner, Denmark Vesey, Gabriel Prosser, Harriet Tubman and Frederick Douglass fought, bled and died for the emancipation of Negro slaves and the preservation of American democracy.

Abraham Lincoln, in times of the grave emergency of the Civil War, issued the Proclamation of Emancipation for the freedom of Negro slaves and the preservation of American democracy.

Today, we call upon President Roosevelt, a great humanitarian and idealist, to follow in the footsteps of his noble and illustrious predecessor and take the second decisive step in this world and national emergency and free American Negro citizens of the stigma, humiliation and insult of discrimination and Jim-Crowism in Government departments and national defense.

The Federal Government cannot with clear conscience call upon private industry and labor unions to abolish discrimination based upon race and color as long as it practices discrimination itself against Negro Americans.

Executive Order 8802, Fair Employment Practice Commission

Franklin Delano Roosevelt

Reaffirming Policy of Full Participation in the Defense Program by All Persons, Regardless of Race, Creed, Color, or National Origin, and Directing Certain Action in Furtherance of Said Policy *Whereas* it is the policy of the United States to encourage full participation in the national defense program by all citizens of the United States, regardless of race, creed, color, or national origin, in the firm belief that the democratic way of life within the Nation can be defended successfully only with the help and support of all groups within its borders; and

Whereas there is evidence that available and needed workers have been barred from employment in industries engaged in defense production solely because of considerations of race, creed, color, or national origin, to the detriment of workers' morale and of national unity:

Now, therefore, by virtue of the authority vested in me by the Constitution and the statutes, and as a prerequisite to the successful conduct of our national defense production effort, I do hereby reaffirm the policy of the United States that there shall be no discrimination in the employment of workers in defense industries or government because of race, creed, color, or national origin, and I do hereby declare that it is the duty of employers and of labor organizations, in furtherance of said policy and of this order, to provide for the full and equitable participation of all workers in defense industries, without discrimination because of race, creed, color, or national origin;

And it is hereby ordered as follows:

1. All departments and agencies of the Government of the United States concerned with vocational and training programs for defense production shall take special measures appropriate to assure that such programs are administered without discrimination because of race, creed, color, or national origin;
2. All contracting agencies of the Government of the United States shall include in all defense contracts hereafter negotiated by them a provision obligating the contractor not to discriminate against any worker because of race, creed, color, or national origin;
3. There is established in the Office of Production Management a Committee on Fair Employment Practice, which shall consist of a chairman and four other members to be appointed by the President. The Chairman and members of the Committee shall serve as such without compensation but shall be entitled to actual and necessary transportation, subsistence and other expenses incidental to performance of their duties. The Committee shall receive and investigate complaints of discrimination in violation of the provisions of this order and shall take appropriate steps to redress grievances which it finds to be valid. The Committee shall also recommend to the several departments and agencies of the Government of the United States and to the President all measures which may be deemed by it necessary or proper to effectuate the provisions of this order.

FRANKLIN D. ROOSEVELT
THE WHITE HOUSE
June 25, 1941

Source: Executive Order 8802. 6 Fed. Reg. 3109 (June 25, 1941)

Harvest of Disorder

Ulysses Lee

When adequate corrective measures for the low morale of Negro troops were not taken, when adequate leadership was not available, when post–community co-operation could not be secured, and when "incidents" without a positive indication of concern on the part of commanders and higher headquarters continued to occur, the chances for open disturbances involving troops remained many and varied. Despite the large number of racial clashes involving soldiers that did occur, when the opportunities for disturbances are considered the actual rate of serious, generalized outbreaks of racial violence involving Negro troops in World War II was small. Nevertheless, cases of physical racial friction, ranging from minor brawls to serious disturbances, ran into the hundreds. They were a continuing cause for concern within the War Department and in the Army's higher commands. They continued to be a threat to discipline, to relations between Negro and white troops, to relations between the Army and civilians, and to unity in the war effort on the home front. As fodder for propaganda against the Army and, in the hands of the enemy, against the nation, they were unsurpassed.

The concern of the War Department in the area of racial disturbances was constant. Local patterns of violence which strengthened and confirmed its anxiety were set early. The pattern of reactions of troops, commands, and the public was set equally early. Racial friction of one sort of another

continued through the war, with the early summer of 1943 marking the high point both of incidents of violence and of official concern. Relatively few disturbances involved mass violence between white and Negro troops, although a number had their root causes in individual incidents between officers and men of the two races. Sometimes erupting disorder had city, state, or military law enforcement agents as its main protagonists; sometimes it involved civilians; sometimes there was no violence at all, but mass demonstrations and "acts to the prejudice of order and discipline," some of them approaching mutiny. Sometimes the "violence" was only that common to the semi-underworld and tenderloin districts of all big cities, the street brawls or Saturday night party fights given additional significance because one and sometimes all participants were in uniform.

No matter what the nature of the disturbance the reaction was much the same. To higher headquarters, in receipt of numerous reports, complaints, and warnings from the distant field, the fact that Negro troops were located on a given post was enough to indicate the possibility of racial disorder there or in nearby communities. To security agencies each disturbance stressed again the need for constant vigilance, both to head off possible repercussions in the civilian society and to stem subversive influences, either of which might interfere seriously with the war effort. To Negro troops, the threat of disorder that might involve them was omnipresent; at times it was thought of as just one more of the inevitables of military service, or, at the least, of passes into certain nearby towns. Early in the war, the Negro public was convinced that the life of the Negro soldier was one of constant fear and danger while his

Source: Ulysses Lee, "Harvest of Disorder." In *The Employment of Negro Troops.* (Washington, D.C.: Office of the Chief of Military History, U.S. Army, 1966), Chap. XII, pp. 348–379.

unit was still in training. The white public, especially in the towns near heavy troop concentrations, was often certain that the threat of town or post race riots was constant. Enough "incidents" occurred during the war years to lend support to each of these views and to each of their infinite variants.

The major significance of disturbances was seldom in the events themselves but in their potentialities. Overt racial friction, military or civilian, affected, in turn, units and stations elsewhere. The more serious disturbances were carried by the news services into the columns of the nation's press. There they affected civilian attitudes, white and Negro, toward the Army and the prosecution of the war. The cumulative effect of racial disturbances on the War Department was to add another item to the growing list of matters to be considered in planning for the employment of increasing numbers of Negro troops, both in training at home and in deployment overseas. It was generally considered a most important addition to this list.

THE MARCH OF VIOLENCE

In April 1941, shortly after the first Negro selectees began to enter the Army, the first major symbolic event in the long chain of racial violence occurred. In a wooded section of Fort Benning, Georgia, the body of a Negro soldier, Pvt. Felix Hall, his hands tied behind him, was found hanging from a tree. How he got there was uncertain. Negroes concluded that he had been lynched. Post authorities suggested that it might have been suicide, but surrounding circumstances were against this solution. The ensuing investigation did not solve the mystery of Hall's death. Speculation continued, but in the absence of proof of foul play, no considerable agitation took place. A queasy uneasiness among Negro troops and the public lingered.

Later in the same month another kind of incident occurred. On Sunday afternoon, 20 April 1941, white Civilian Conservation Corps (CCC) enrollees and Negro troops of the 48th Quartermaster Regiment became involved in an altercation over the use of a diving platform at the YMCA Lake area at Fort Jackson, South Carolina. Already, in the nearby city of Columbia, ill feeling among troops, Negro civilians, and military police had developed. Between afternoon and evening, stories of the clash spread through Fort Jackson. That night, considerable tension was present in the area of the 48th Quartermaster Regiment. At about 9:30 P.M., the Fort Jackson Military Police Company learned that a disturbance was underway. White soldiers from the 30th Division, some in civilian clothes and some in uniform, were assembling in groups, planning to rush the Negro area. There shots were fired as "unknown individual members" incited the men with "greatly exaggerated versions of incidents occurring during the afternoon." Officers of the post, the field officer of the day, the 8th Division officer of the day, members of the main guard of the 30th Division, and the provost marshal halted the movement and dispersed the groups.

Thereafter, difficulties between Fort Jackson's military police and Negro soldiers and civilians in Columbia continued until well into 1942. Beginning in June 1941, fracases involving military policemen, city policemen, soldiers, and civilians occurred frequently in the Negro business area of the city. The Colored Citizens' Committee of Columbia protested in letters, petitions, and visits to post authorities. "Something must be done," the Citizens' Committee declared in January 1942, "as our Colored Citizens are growing restless, suspicious, and what occurred in Alexandria, La., and Fayetteville, N.C., thus far has been averted, because of our vigilance, and talking to our people, but we cannot always hope to hold them down with so much disregard to 'Citizenship rights.' "

The Alexandria and Fayetteville affairs mentioned by Columbia's committee were two of the major similar disturbances that occurred during 1941–42. These were basically conflicts between troops and military police, involving as well town police, Negro and white citizens, and, at times, all five groups. Arguments, rough handling, fights, and near riots were common in these disturbances. A street brawl in Tampa, Florida, on 15 July 1941, was typical of these fracases. At about 11:20 p.m., a Negro soldier, after an argument with a white military policeman in the presence of other Negro soldiers and civilians, was arrested and sent to the military police headquarters in Tampa. The military policeman and a second MP remained in the area. A second Negro soldier, a sergeant who later admitted that he had been drinking, approached the military policeman who had made the arrest and engaged him in conversation. The sergeant, ostensibly trimming his fingernails with a knife, whispered, according to the MP, that he would cut the policeman's throat. The policeman struck the Negro sergeant with his club and drew his pistol; the sergeant knocked the pistol from his hand and threw the policeman to the ground. The second military policeman and a nearby city policeman came to the aid of the MP; the city policeman shot the Negro sergeant while he was on the ground. A third Negro soldier was shot while attempting to disarm the city policeman. Though the setting was there for a full-scale free-for-all with potentially fatal results, no further violence followed. But trouble between Negro soldiers and military policemen on the streets of Tampa went on through the summer.

The pattern of disturbances, all potentially productive of serious riots, continued to develop. The Fayetteville disturbance, on the night of 5–6 August 1941, was the first of a series of serious bus incidents involving military police and Negro soldiers. A large group of Negro soldiers, following pay-day passes, gathered at a bus stop to await transportation back to Fort Bragg. A number had been drinking. As the waiting crowd grew larger, disorder at the bus stop increased. When a bus arrived, disorderly soldiers threatened unarmed Negro military police-

men, whose duty it was to ride the buses, and prevented them from coming aboard. The driver refused to move without police protection. This delay in departure increased the confusion and disorder, while the crowd outside awaiting the next bus continued to grow. A detachment of white military police reinforcements, attempting to quiet the passengers, boarded the halted bus. They succeeded in stirring up further disorder among the jostling, cursing, busload of men. Attempting to arrest the chief troublemakers, military policemen began to use their night sticks. One soldier on the crowded bus grabbed a military policeman's service revolver from its holster. He discharged its full six shots in the direction of the disarmed MP. Another military policeman shot toward the soldier, and other shots from outside the bus followed. When the confusion subsided, one white military policeman and one Negro soldier were dead, two other white military policemen and three Negro soldiers were wounded. The gun fight in Fayetteville was bad enough, but the aftermath at Fort Bragg, especially as reported in the nation's press, was a serious portent of future difficulties. The post's provost marshal ordered all Negro soldiers, except those already in barracks, collected and brought to the stockade adjacent to the guardhouse, where they were held until morning. Men arriving on later buses were searched and threatened by military policemen. No explanation of what had happened or of the purpose of this roundup was given to the men herded into the stockade. Military policemen, angry and resentful over the death of their comrade, and Negro soldiers, equally resentful of the death of the Negro soldier and the methods used to round them up, created a new tension on the post. For days accounts of the brutality used in the forced checking of men who could not have been involved in the bus disturbance reached the public through the press and through soldiers' letters. The revolvers and ammunition of the military police who had been at the scene were not collected on the spot, confounding the possibility of a definite determination of responsibility for the shooting on the bus and thus lending color to the rumors current that military police activities at the post were based not on good police work, but on elemental anger.

The outbreaks of violence during the summer of 1941 reached a climax during the Second Army maneuvers. These maneuvers were marked by incidents between townsfolk and white as well as Negro troops, and were occasioned both by the lack of military discipline and the resentful attitudes of citizens dwelling within maneuver areas toward the presence of large bodies of troops. Before the maneuvers, Lt. Gen. Ben Lear, commanding the Second Army, cautioned the commanders of both the 5th Division, to which the 94th Engineer Battalion was attached, and of the 2d Cavalry Division, to conduct conditioning lectures for their Negro troops before departing for maneuvers. At Murfreesboro, Tennessee, and at Gurdon, Arkansas, Negro troops on maneuvers ran into armed resistance from citizens and state police. The second incident was the more spectacular, and, in the shadow of Fayetteville, came to national attention through the wire services.

Troops of the 94th Engineer Battalion from Fort Custer, Michigan, became embroiled in a series of incidents in the vicinity of Gurdon. Some of the soldiers felt that their difficulties began at Little Rock, Arkansas, where individuals of the unit and white city police engaged in an altercation in a night club. Others, pointing out that neighboring Negro troops from Camp Shelby, Mississippi, had not been molested, felt that the trouble arose because they were Northern troops with Northern white officers. Only in their persistence and intensity were the incidents at Gurdon different from those occurring in many another Southern small town area.

On 11 August 1941, some two or three hundred soldiers of the Negro engineer battalion visited the town of Gurdon in search of recreation. The town had neither recreation to offer nor the desire to offer it. The appearance of so large a body of Negro soldiers from the Chicago-Detroit area excited adverse comments from the white residents of the small town, but nothing untoward happened except that the soldiers congregated in small groups while white military police attempted to keep them moving. In the meantime a rumor, later proved false, spread among the soldiers that one of their number had been arrested and severely beaten by military police. Excitement and resentment mounted when military police instructions were circulated that the town was to be cleared by 10 o'clock. With no transportation available, the soldiers gathered in groups and, in a crude and noisy formation liberally spiced with profanity and uncomplimentary remarks about the South, proceeded along the main street of the town toward their bivouac area. Many, apparently fearing interference, had armed themselves with clubs and missiles. Though no difficulties between them and civilian authorities of the town of Gurdon occurred that evening, the noisy movement of the group of apparently unorganized soldiers through the town, coupled with seeming insubordination toward the few of their officers who were attempting to control the situation during the four-mile trek from the town to their bivouac, intensified the fears of local citizens. Town authorities and the town marshal, who freely declared his intention to use force of arms in the event of trouble, proceeded to swear in new deputies to augment the town police force. Through the night sensational rumors spread, both among members of the battalion and among citizens of the town. The Commanding General, Seventh Corps Area, declared the town of Gurdon off limits and directed that the battalion move its bivouac several miles distant. These decisions were communicated to town and police authorities on 12 August during the working day.

Nevertheless, on the evening of the 12th at about 10 p.m., Arkansas state police with drawn firearms approached the 94th's bivouac area and ordered the camp guard—armed with rifles but without ammunition—

off the highway at the entrance to the camp, striking several of the sentries in the process. Troops visiting Prescott, another nearby town, were harassed by state police who followed their trucks into town, threatening the men upon arrival. On 14 August elements of the battalion, its men demoralized and its officers uncertain, began to move to their new bivouac area. State police, through misrepresentation, excitement, or misunderstanding, notified the provost marshal of the Second Army that a group of unsupervised and disorderly Negro soldiers was proceeding down the highway. The provost marshal, accepting the report as fact, requested the state authorities to take charge until military police arrived. Fully armed state police and deputies started for the reported scene of disorder. In the meantime, the provost marshal, with an assistant, proceeded to the scene and, upon observing the troops moving along in good order, assumed that the area of difficulty must be farther along the road toward Gurdon. He dropped his assistant and set out toward the town. Following his departure, a sergeant of state police arrived with state troopers and a deputized force. State troopers, using insulting epithets to both the troops and their officers, ordered the marching unit off the road and into a ditch lately filled with rain and into nearby woods, while armed deputies, in civilian clothes and therefore civilians as far as the troops could see, stood by. When one of the officers protested the police actions and epithets, a state policeman removed his glasses and struck the "Yankee nigger lover" in the face. Military police had by now arrived at the scene but, until the white lieutenant was struck, their commander, the provost marshal's assistant left at the scene earlier, made no move to interfere. Some of the Negro soldiers, observing that neither they nor their white officers apparently had police protection in Arkansas, left their battalion and, hitch-hiking or by public transportation, made their way back to Fort Custer. At least one soldier, without money and feeling that moving north or east through the Gurdon area was too dangerous, went

southwest through Texas into California. He picked cotton in Arizona and picked figs and cut grapes in Fresno for money for food; he then hopped trains to Fort Warren, Wyoming, where he intended to give himself up, hoping for transportation back to Fort Custer. On learning through rumor that "fugitives" from Arkansas were to be returned there, he left on a wine tank car for Omaha, rode other trains into Michigan, and eventually reached Detroit on 5 September.

The bewilderment and fear of the troops in the face of the Gurdon incident and its implications for morale and discipline among Negro troops in general were probably of greater import than the incident itself. A soldier's letter on the affair reveals to some extent the disorganization and demoralization it caused:

We are scared almost to death. Yesterday we went on a 10 mile hike alongside of the highway off the concrete. All of a sudden six truck loads of mobsters came sizzling down the highway in the other direction. They jumped out with guns and sub-machine guns and [revolvers] drawn, cursing, slapping and saying unheard of things. Sis it was awful. They took us off the highway into the woods. Daring anyone to say a word, they hit two of our white officers who try to say something back. But the bad part of it all, the military police were among them and against us. The State police passed out ammunition to the civilians. We are now about five miles down in the woods hoping that they don't come down here. No one has pitched a single tent today, nor yesterday, we are afraid to, half of our company has left for Michigan already, hoboing. Few have train fare, others went deeper into the woods.

We had a detail down here in a little town called Guidon [sic] working at the depot, when some of the officers went down there they had been stopped by a mob, threatened their lives if they did not leave town in five minutes—yet they could not go down the highway, the only way they know to go. Our officers are nearly all as afraid as we are. They call them "Yankee Nigger lovers," us black "Yankees."

We have guards, guarding a place and the State police deliberately came off the highway, took his gun (rifle) which was empty and beat Yankee Doodle on his head. These people are crazy, stone crazy. Or I am. Yesterday one of our trucks went to get some eats and they wouldn't let us get any. The officers asked that we all be sent back to Fort Custer. None of us can show our faces except in these woods, we can't be seen on or even near the highway. We are undecided now, we all want to know what we are going to do?

Many troops became certain that there was no protection available for them in the South and little understanding from the Army, especially after six of their number were tried by courts-martial and several of their officers whom the men considered to have aided them were relieved. Despite Hastie's recommendation that, to dispel the notion that the Army had viewed the disturbance with complacency, the War Department should issue a statement summarizing the facts in the case, announce the punitive steps taken toward the military police officers as well as toward members of the battalion, and announce the referral of the record to the Department of Justice for such action as might be proper under federal statutes, it was decided that no useful purpose "so far as the best interests of the Army are concerned" would be served by so doing. Both informal and, later, formal requests for the opinion of the Attorney General in the matter resulted in the decision that, since state troopers interceded at the request of military police, there was no suitable basis for federal action.

Months later the battalion had not regained normal morale and discipline, as evidenced by excessively high rates of company punishment, confinements, and arrests; excessive hospital, sick in quarters, and venereal rates; lax military courtesy; and general deficiencies in appearance and posture.

Other incidents, all indicative of a more or less serious state of affairs, continued to occur during that last peacetime summer: in Galveston, a disturbance between Negro troops from Camp Wallace and Negro city policemen, at Camp Livingston, Louisiana, a disturbance following newspaper publication of photographs of a staff sergeant beaten during an arrest; rumors and reports of murders at Camp Claiborne, Louisiana, and Camp Shelby, Mississippi; brawls between soldiers and military police at Camp Davis, North Carolina; and reports of unrest and a "difficult situation" at Camp Stewart, Georgia.

Through all of these ran the common thread of friction between Negro soldiers and both city and military policemen. Where Negro military policemen were used, generally on a temporary basis in the Negro sections of towns, they were usually unarmed, increasing their difficulties in the control of troops. Most of the disturbances were followed by newspaper publicity, not always accurate—the papers could not always get facts from local or other public relations officers and took what they could find to support what became, in the Negro press, a campaign for armed Negro military police and, at times, in the local white press, a campaign for the removal of Negro military police embracing, in some instances, the removal of all Negro soldiers. Widely publicized incidents were followed by what amounted to avalanches of letters and petitions of protest or suggestions to the War Department, most of them coming from sincere persons and organizations but some of them from antipreparedness, isolationist, far left, anti-Negro, and anti-Army sources.

The War Department dispatched investigators to the scenes of most of these disturbances, while local authorities made their own inquiries. Investigations and resulting recommendations, running into the hundreds, sometimes took months and seldom applied to more than the specific case at hand. They had general corrective application only insofar as they served as precedents for later cases. Nevertheless, it was obvious by 1942 that the relations between Negro soldiers and both military and civilian police had reached so unhealthy a point in many parts of the country that future disorders could be expected unless steps were taken to prevent them.

As yet no major disturbances in which Negro troops were the mass aggressors had occurred. But the events of early 1942 left doubts that Negro troops, with access to ammunition and with increasing tensions growing out of their relations with town and military police, would long remain quiescent. The first of a new series of disturbances occurred on 10 January 1942 in Alexandria, Louisiana, the crowded camp town for Camps Polk, Livingston, Beauregard, and Claiborne and for three airfields: Alexandria, Pollock, and Esler. Alexandria, sometimes used by as many as 30,000 soldiers at the height of the war, was the scene of numerous tension-born incidents. The 1942 trouble reached riot proportions, involving hundreds of soldiers and civilians, after the clubbing of a Negro soldier by a military policeman in front of a theater in the heart of the Negro district. In March, large crowds gathered in Little Rock while military police attempted to arrest a Negro soldier. The soldier was finally shot by a civilian policeman. "I would not be surprised if this is not the Alexandria situation repeated, reason and methods both," the editor of the Kansas City *Call* wired to Judge Hastie. On 1 April, at Tuskegee, Alabama, friction between armed Negro military police from the nearby airfield and townsfolk, brewing since January, came to a head. A Negro military policeman took a soldier from the custody of a white city policeman at gunpoint. City police, reinforced by a deputy sheriff, two Alabama state policemen, and about fifteen white civilians armed with shotguns, took the soldier back from military police in a scuffle, during which a military policeman who had drawn his pistol was beaten and the remainder of the military patrol disarmed. A large group of soldiers and civilians gathered. White officers from the post residing in the town rounded up most of the soldiers and returned them to camp, but not before soldiers on the post had become alarmed at the prospect that armed townsfolk

might attack the airfield. At Fort Dix, New Jersey, on 2 April, a gun battle between white military police and Negro soldiers, developing out of an argument over the use of a telephone booth, resulted in the deaths of one white MP and two Negro soldiers. In May, a fight between two Negro soldiers from Mitchel Field developed into a free-for-all between civilian police and colored civilians in Hempstead, New York. Moreover, inspectors and observers were reporting that smoldering resentments lay just under the surface in many other places, ready to burst forth on provocation.

FIRST CORRECTIVES

After the disturbances of the summer of 1941, the first steps toward needed correctives were taken. Following the Fort Jackson incident, directions to adhere more closely to regulations on the protection of ammunition were issued. After Fort Bragg, closer attention to the selection and training of military policemen and provost marshals was recommended. The organization of temporary detachments of untrained military policemen, the failure to use Negro military policemen in camps and towns with large numbers of Negro soldiers, and the close liaison between civilian and military police in many towns, a condition tending to indoctrinate soldier police with the methods and points of view of local civilians, were all severely criticized. The improper training and conduct of military police as revealed during the summer of 1941 and the lack of a central agency to establish doctrine, provide training, and supervise organization and procurement of personnel for military police units were remedied by the establishment of the Corps of Military Police under the Provost Marshal General on 26 September 1941. With the urging of Judge Hastie and upon the recommendation of Maj. Gen. Allen W. Gullion, the new Provost Marshal General, the use of Negro military policemen by camps with sizable bodies of Negro troops was directed. Some local commanders and the Provost Marshal General resisted certain of the recommendations, especially those which directed that, for psychological reasons, town military police headquarters be divorced from city police stations. Townsfolk sometimes resisted the use of Negro military police, especially in cities where local Negroes had been exerting pressures for appointment of Negro civilian police. The seriousness of the situation was impressed upon local commanders not only by communications from the War Department and service commands but also by recurring incidents of friction.

A continuing problem was the quality of military policemen available for duty. Although personnel officers and the Corps of Military Police tried to obtain high caliber men, the number of poorly qualified men gravitating to it remained large. "I am fully conscious of the importance of the primary war effort and the need for first-class fighting troops and I am willing that the military police units shall have their share of those who are morally and physically crippled," General Gullion protested in March 1942, "but I think I ought not to be required to take them all."

Between station complement and tactical units on the same post tense feelings were often common. With military police detachments a part of station complements this feeling was often heightened when tactical units were Negro. It was sometimes necessary for commanders to make strong remonstrances about the treatment of Negro soldiers by police under post control. In one instance, where a post reported that, since "the force employed by the Military Policeman was not excessive or unwarranted" no disciplinary action for beating a soldier need be taken, the division commander of the soldier involved sharply replied:

1. I do not concur with the conclusions reached by your investigating officer. The use of unwar-ranted force by members of your Military Police Detachment is becoming altogether too prevalent and I feel that some of your Military Police are going out of their way to look for instances.
2. In this particular case it seems to me that the Military Policeman went out of his way to find fault with a soldier who was complying with his orders. He was told to return to the Post and upon turning away to comply with the order he located the tie and put it on. It appears to me that the Military Policeman was beyond his rights in following the soldier and accusing him of lying.
3. I do not understand why it is necessary for two Military Policemen to use their clubs to subdue one man. The use of clubs should be rare indeed, and I feel that too many instances are being reported to this headquarters which are entirely unwarranted and which reveal a tendency on the part of your people to assume a bullying attitude unnecessarily.

Ill feeling between troops and military police, founded on experiences of this type, was not uncommon nor was it confined to Negro troops and white police. At Fort Huachuca, where Negro police were used, it existed to some extent; a Thanksgiving Day 1942 disturbance in Phoenix, Arizona, was between members of a Negro infantry unit and Negro military police. But where both troops and police were of different colors, where both brought their civilian attitudes into the Army with them—the one a distrust of police conditioned by long experience and the other a disregard for Negroes conditioned by an equally long apprenticeship—special care in training, discipline, and supervision was necessary to prevent recurring irritations of old, still unhealed wounds.

In the average command, action designed to prevent physical friction consisted of more or less elaborate precautionary directives on the handling and use of ammunition in Negro units. To officers, the receipt of such precautionary directives often produced a new burden to be added to the many others already required in duty with Negro units. One commander found his headquarters' precautionary orders somewhat baffling:

Colonel H—stated that these secret orders grew out of the great concern of the higher command over the possibility of a negro riot or outbreak. He mentioned an incident with which I was unfamiliar purported to have taken place in 1940 in Brownsville, Texas. He mentioned a 1917 episode at Houston, Texas, and also a quite recent incident near Beaumont, Texas, where a negro soldier was shot by a civilian police officer. This action indicating concern of the higher command was somewhat surprising to me because my observation of my own battalion gave me no indication of the faintest possibility of such an occurrence. In fact those familiar with the newness of this organization and the inexperience of the personnel of this organization have complimented the battalion numerous times on the many different phases of its administration and training.

Thereafter this battalion commander was visited by the executive officer of his training group and the incoming post commander, who personally repeated the instructions. Yet no indications of a tendency on the part of his men, either openly or surreptitiously, to collect ammunition had been noted. The commander explained the excessive caution of his check methods to his men by pointing out the necessity of saving their short supply of ammunition and by the necessity of guaranteeing individual safety.

In many another unit no satisfactory explanation was possible. The detailed searches of barracks areas conducted on some posts, including the use of mine detectors to aid in the location of ammunition presumably buried under barracks, increased the apprehension of soldiers and bulwarked their distrust of headquarters' attitudes toward them. In some areas the unrelieved tenseness of units itself was responsible for incidents which might not have occurred otherwise. Normal precautions in the safeguarding of weapons, where followed in all units, could be productive of good results, but abnormal methods, especially when obviously centered on Negro units, often heightened rather than lessened the possibility of disturbances. . . .

RENEWAL AND REASSESSMENT

In the spring of 1943 serious disorders began again. In the preceding months, though isolated skirmishes and incidents occurred at individual posts, becoming a common occurrence at some, no significant event which could be considered a general outbreak of racial friction had transpired. During these months the slow process of building toward an open flare-up had been aided by a steady downward drop of morale in many Negro units. By early summer, the harvest of racial antagonism was beginning to assume bumper proportions. Serious disorders occurred at Camp Van Dorn, Mississippi; Camp Stewart, Georgia; Lake Charles, Louisiana; March Field and Camp San Luis Obispo, California; Fort Bliss, Texas; Camp Phillips, Kansas; Camp Breckinridge, Kentucky; and Camp Shenango, Pennsylvania. Other camps had lesser disorders and rumors of unrest.

The disorders of 1943 differed from those of preceding years. They involved, for the most part, a larger number of troops. They occurred more frequently in the camps themselves where the possibility of mass conflict between men of Negro and white units was greater. Negro troops were as likely to be the immediate aggressors as white troops and civilians. Two of the disorders, those at Camps Van Dorn and Stewart, were especially serious, both for their potentialities and for their effects on the revision of plans for the general employment of Negro troops. Both incidents involved combat troops of particular units, rather than anonymous groups of soldiers from several units, aided and abetted or provoked by civilians and police in the crowded centers of towns on pay nights. Often disorders symbolized the breaking point both of the patience of the troops involved and of the tolerance of the War Department and its higher commands.

Trouble at Camp Van Dorn in May, involving the 364th Infantry, had its beginnings months before. It was intimately entwined with the previous career of the regiment. The 364th had been activated as the 367th Infantry, one of the new Regular Army units, on 25 March 1941. Much of its training took place at Fort Jackson, South Carolina, during the period of the Columbia friction. Despite the usual low range of AGCT scores and lack of wide civilian experience among its men, it became, in its first year, a relatively well-trained unit. The 367th, less its first battalion, was selected to furnish the 24th Infantry with personnel qualified for foreign service when that regiment became the first Negro infantry unit to move overseas in April 1942. Its 1st Battalion was alerted for duty with the Liberia Task Force in March 1942, separating from the regiment and proceeding to the Charleston port the following month. Not until January 1943 did it sail from New York. In the meantime, the remainder of the regiment, not knowing that its 1st Battalion had been redesignated the 367th Infantry Battalion (Separate), waited either to refill or to rejoin its 1st Battalion. Necessarily, because of the secrecy of wartime movements, it could not be informed of the destination of its 1st Battalion nor of its future relations with it. Requests on the part of the regiment to be allowed to refill its 1st Battalion could not be met, for there was no provision in the troop basis for an additional battalion in a regiment all of whose battalions were already active. Because the 1st Battalion had been shipped, with all equipment marked as belonging to the 367th Infantry, the regiment, minus its 1st Battalion, was finally redesignated the 364th Infantry. A new 1st Battalion was formed, for by now it was clear that the remainder of the regiment would not join the detached battalion. The regiment, by now refilled with a considerable proportion of new men and faced with retraining, was assigned to the Western Defense Command's Southern Land Frontier Sector for protective guard duty.

While stationed in Phoenix, Arizona, the regiment became involved in two serious disturbances. In the first of these about 500 men of the unit refused to disperse when ordered to do so by the regimental commander. In the second, occurring on Thanksgiving night of 1942, approximately 100 men of the regiment engaged in a shooting affray with a detachment of Negro military police in Phoenix, with the result that one officer, one enlisted man, and one civilian were killed and twelve enlisted men were seriously wounded. As a result of this disturbance, sixteen members of the regiment were tried by general court-martial, each receiving a sentence of fifty years. The regiment received a new commander and executive officer. These officers tried to eliminate individuals who might be a source of future difficulties. About fifty men were transferred from the regiment during this process. To overcome some of the basic causes of friction within the regiment, a new camp with improved recreational facilities was provided. The new commander was certain that the regiment had returned to a normal state of discipline. The men of the unit, according to intelligence operatives, were equally certain that they had profited from the changes following the clashes.

The Western Defense Command now began to recommend that the regiment be put to other use, and, specifically, that it be considered for employment overseas since "its long retention at this station is likely to produce a deterioration in its present efficiency." In May 1943 the regiment was ordered to Camp Van Dorn, Mississippi, for retraining by Army Ground Forces, a procedure generally followed for units from the defense commands before shipment overseas.

Camp Van Dorn was not only in Mississippi, a fact which members of the regiment, arriving from Phoenix, viewed as a change distinctly for the worse; it was also one of the more isolated of the larger camps located in that state. The nearest town, Centreville, had a normal population of less than 1,200. The nearest sizable towns, McComb, Baton Rouge, and Natchez, were from forty to fifty miles away. Centreville had little to offer any troops in the way of recreation or entertainment, and the prevailing segregation laws and absence of compensating facilities on the post made the men of the 364th especially resentful. Some viewed the change in location as punishment for their continuing difficulties in Phoenix, which had grown distinctly cooler toward their presence as the months passed.

The 364th arrived at Van Dorn in two groups, the first on 26 May and the second on 28 May. The first group, bragging that they were going to "take over" the camp, the town of Centreville, and, if necessary, the state of Mississippi, began to show their resentment to the area to which they had been transferred the day after their arrival. A number of 364th men, visiting the Negro area service club, refused to obey the rules of the club. They arrived in various states of partial uniform, refused to doff caps, used indecent language to the hostesses, and brought beer into the club from a post exchange in violation of camp rules. An hour after the regular closing time, the hostess and the noncommissioned officers in charge were still attempting to clear men of the unit from the building. The following night, after the arrival of the second contingent of the regiment, an exchange manager closed his building because of the threatening conduct of men who insisted that exchange employees had been rude and uncivil to them. Later, several hundred men, most of them from the 364th, broke into the exchange, rifling the stock and damaging equipment. On the next night, a Saturday, a group of about 75 men from the unit visited Centreville and roamed about the town, reportedly using indecent and profane language. The group was accosted by the town chief of police and a number of deputized townsfolk armed with shotguns. Upon arrival of a military police officer, the group dispersed and returned to camp.

On Sunday evening, 30 May, the incident occurred which, considering the rising temper of the regiment, the town, and the remainder of the camp, could have caused a general outbreak. A private from the regiment was accosted outside the reservation by a military policeman and questioned about his improper uniform and lack of a pass. During a fight which followed, the county sheriff arrived. The soldier, attempting to flee, was shot and killed by the sheriff. The commanding officer of the regiment, informed of his soldier's death, dispatched all officers to their respective units and proceeded, with the regimental staff, to the barracks area of the company to which the soldier belonged. There he found the entire company milling around in an uproar, threatening to break into the supply room for rifles and ammunition. He ordered firing pins removed from all rifles and placed an officer guard over the supply room. While this company was being quieted, men of another company stormed their supply room and obtained a number of rifles. Shortly thereafter a crowd of several hundred soldiers gathered near the regimental exchange. A riot squad, made up of Negro military policemen, fired into the crowd when it attempted to rush them. One soldier was wounded by this volley. The regimental commander and his chaplain arrived at this point. After talking and pleading with the men, the commander quieted the group, assembled his battalions, and marched the regiment to its barracks area where the entire unit was confined. It took several days of constant searching, which itself served to keep tension high, to locate and recover all missing rifles. Citizens of the nearby town and county began to arm themselves and to call for an immediate transfer of the regiment.

When apprised of the situation the commander of Army Ground Forces, General McNair, whose command in the past had been faced frequently with demands for the removal of Negro troops from specific communities, determined that to transfer the 364th Infantry to another station would be the worst possible solution, since it was not only what the local citizens wanted but also a possible motive for the unit's actions. He proposed that the regiment be confined to its own area until it disclosed "its real trouble-makers" and that it be deprived of all its privileges until it "demonstrated its worthiness." He proposed further that the citizens of Centreville and other nearby communities be assured that no member of the unit would be permitted to enter these towns until the citizens themselves asked that the ban be lifted. In the meantime, using extra officers if necessary, a training program would be provided which would keep the regiment too busy to allow time for any further demonstrations.

The Inspector General agreed that the proposed action, though "drastic and yet untried," might be valuable under the circumstances. Citizens of the area would probably protest the retention of the regiment at its station, and Negroes would probably protest the disciplinary action taken, but, nevertheless, except for giving the local citizenry control of the future policy of permitting troops to visit surrounding towns—military authorities should be left to determine, on the basis of future developments, when the regiment should return to a normal status—General Peterson recommended that the action proposed be tried. The War Department approved.

Though restrictive disciplinary measures, plus command efforts, brought an outward calm to the regiment, the resentment and disturbed morale of the unit did not alter significantly. Men of the regiment were now aware that they were to be retained at Camp Van Dorn and that over their unit lay the stigma of unusual punishment. A month after the initial Van Dorn disturbances, the unit became embroiled again in an onpost demonstration of near-riot proportions. On the evening of 3 July 1943, a large number of girls had been brought in from neighboring towns for a dance. To help pay their transportation costs, tickets to the dance were sold to soldiers at fifty cents each. Before the dance could start, soldiers, most of them

from the 364th Infantry, began pouring into the service club where the dance was to be held. Coming through side doors and windows as well as through the main entrance, they overran the club. The club assistants, with the help of a number of first sergeants of the regiment, tried to get the building cleared, but the crowd refused to leave. As fast as a few departed through doors, others poured in through windows. The regimental guard and a detachment of Negro military police were called. The field officer of the day, a lieutenant colonel, arrived and, using the public address system set up for the dance, explained the rules for the dance and directed all soldiers to leave the building. The crowd remained. The officer of the day then called for assistance from an alerted white unit, a battalion of the 99th Infantry Division. This battalion arrived, cleared the hall, and dispersed the crowd, now grown to about 2,000.

With the approach of the departure date of the alerted 99th Division, the retention of the 364th Infantry at Van Dorn as the largest single infantry unit on the post took on new significance. Although no ammunition had been issued the unit and the bolts of all rifles had been removed, The Inspector General felt that, "due to the attitude of civilians in this locality relative to racial matters and to the presence of large numbers of northern Negroes, there exists considerable danger of racial disturbances in the general vicinity of this camp." The inspecting officer recommended that the unit be transferred overseas.

The Third Army, however, was now convinced that the unit would not be ready until 1 March 1944. No active theater required a separate infantry regiment. The Operations Division, requested to prevent further deferment of the regiment beyond 1 March, finally arranged for it to replace a white separate regiment in the Aleutians. There it performed garrison duties for the rest of the war.

Decision on the 364th Infantry was complicated by events of the few days following its initial difficulties at Camp Van Dorn. At Camp Stewart, Georgia, near Savannah, in the first week of June, another and larger disturbance involving units of the Antiaircraft Training Command occurred.

The disturbance at Camp Stewart had been brewing for some time. Adverse conditions on this post and in Savannah had been brought to the attention of the War Department as early as 1941. Savannah was a war-crowded town. In addition to its normal population of about 95,000, there were two shipyards close to the city employing about 15,000 people. Camp Stewart had a normal strength of between forty and fifty thousand men. The Savannah Army Air Base at Hunter Field had approximately 9,000 men. In addition, Marine Corps men from Parris Island and Navy and Coast Guard men on liberty used Savannah for recreation. On Saturday nights, shipyard workers, marines, sailors, air-men, and soldiers all came to town. Camp Stewart sent weekly into the city a convoy of about 100 trucks, carrying between 1,200 and 1,500 men, sometimes 75 percent of them Negroes. Neither city nor military police, neither civilians nor volunteer organizations were able to do a great deal to provide adequately for such an influx. Negro troops had been complaining for months about the treatment they received from white civilians and military personnel in Savannah and at Camp Stewart. In the spring of 1943 the situation grew rapidly worse.

At this time there were fourteen Negro antiaircraft units at Camp Stewart. Some of these were old battalions, recently reorganized from regiments being re-formed as groups: others were newly organized battalions, three of them formed with cadres from the 369th AAA Regiment returned from Hawaii. Another of the units was the 100th AAA Gun Battalion, which had been tactically deployed at Fort Brady, Michigan, as part of the defenses of the Sault Ste. Marie area. Just before the outbreak at Camp Stewart, General Davis and Lt. Col. Davis G. Arnold had completed an investigation arising out of the receipt in the War Department of anonymous letters, petitions from civilian organizations, and others concerning conditions at the camp.

General Davis found that dissatisfaction in the 100th Battalion and in the cadre from the 369th was general. These men, mainly from the North, many of them well educated, and fresh from service in areas where civilian customs were more favorable to them, were joined by other units in objections to the designation of latrines and other facilities by race in violation of War Department orders. They reported the usual difficulties with white military police in entering and leaving camp on pass, dissatisfaction with recreational facilities on post, with bus transportation, with treatment by military and civilian police, and with the lack of overnight lodging and meals at reasonable prices in Savannah in comparison with those available for white soldiers. The enlisted cadremen were considered quite capable—the commanding officer at the training center said, "They have the snappiest gun crews that I have ever seen in this whole place, and I go out everyday." But, in presenting their grievances to General Davis, including complaints that their officers, whom they unabashedly referred to as ninety-day wonders, did not have sufficient experience and training, they spoke so rebelliously and so recklessly that General Davis had to caution them on the demeanor expected from disciplined soldiers.

On the basis of the Davis-Arnold report, General Peterson recommended that attempts be made to improve the recreational situation in Savannah, that pass privileges be staggered to prevent overcrowding of both buses and the available facilities, that more Negro military police be employed at entrucking points, and that closer co-ordination be developed among the proper staff and command agencies to prevent serious consequences from the existing unrest.

Before General Peterson's recommendations could start on their way, violence flared at Camp Stewart. The central unit involved was neither the 100th Battalion nor any of the units with returnee cadres, but a unit which, approaching the end of its training, was alerted for overseas movement.

On the evening of 9 June the rumor spread through the Negro area at Camp Stewart—four of the battalion areas were empty, save for guards, because their units were on a field exercise—that a Negro woman had been raped and murdered by white soldiers after they had killed her husband. One version included military policemen among the murderers. The rumor, which was later determined to have been false, was heightened in effect by actual occurrences of the preceding few days: military policemen in vehicles with machine guns had been used to disperse a crowd gathered outside a service club during a dance, and a Negro soldier, asking for a drink of water at an ice plant in nearby Hinesville, had received a blow on the head with ice tongs instead. At about 8:30 nearly a hundred soldiers, some armed with rifles, gathered in the Negro area. Officers sought to halt the growing mob. A wild shot was fired. Military police and vehicles were ordered to the area. The first crowd moved back and broke up but a second mob, tense with excitement and anger, formed later. Gun racks and supply rooms of several Negro battalions were broken into and ammunition, rifles, and submachine guns were removed. Some troops, bent on revenge, joined the mob; some went into the nearby woods in fear; others remained to "fight it out" and to defend their areas. To add to the confusion of the evening, gas alarms rang out in nearly every battalion area.

At about ten o'clock an approaching military police vehicle was fired on from the area of the 458th Battalion. General firing then started from this and several other battalion areas, continuing for the next two hours. Four military policemen were wounded, one seriously; a civilian bus driver, fired on as he approached the area, was slightly wounded. Shortly before midnight, a military police detail crossing a small parade ground on foot was fired on; one military policeman was killed. At 12:30 members of two white battalions moved into the area in half-tracks. The firing ceased shortly thereafter.

In the aftermath of the riot, which had not involved actual fighting between Negro and white troops, a board of officers appointed at Camp Stewart to investigate determined that the disturbance was essentially an outgrowth of long pent-up emotions and resentments. The majority of the Negro soldiers were convinced that justice and fair treatment were not to be had by them in neighboring communities and that the influence of these communities was strongly reflected in the racial policies of the command at Camp Stewart. Many Negro troops feared for their personal safety. Others, gripped by a feeling of desperation, had determined to fight back against existing abuses without regard to consequences. While frequent rumors circulated rapidly throughout the Negro units, no evidence of an organized campaign fostering discontent was uncovered. The arrival of the men and officers from the 100th Battalion and 369th Regiment may have aroused "latent resentment" existing in the minds of soldiers already stationed at the camp, but the board found no evidence that the men of these units were responsible for the dissatisfaction leading to the disturbances. The one unit with all Negro officers, commanded by Lt. Col. DeMaurice Moses, was called into formation by its commander and his staff after the start of the disturbance and remained calm throughout the period. The board, despite its own findings, nevertheless fell back on older formulas, ascribing the difficulties to the stationing of Northern Negroes in the South and to the "average negro soldier's meager education, superstition, imagination and excitability" which, coupled with regimentation, made him "easily misled" and developed a "mass state of mind." It therefore recommended that charges be placed against any individuals involved against whom concrete evidence of criminal activities existed; that better machinery for getting rid of "deliberate agitators" be supplied; that special training for military police in "handling Negro soldiers" be devised; that an educational program be planned for Negro troops to "teach dangers of rumor mongering, acceptance of rumors as truth, avoidance of 'chip on shoulders' attitude," and attempting to take the law into their own hands; and that the 458th Battalion be disbanded, with its enlisted men distributed to other organizations.

These recommendations did not reach to the heart of the board's own findings. The commanding general of the Antiaircraft Command therefore did not concur with the recommendation that the chief offending unit be disbanded. Any guilty noncommissioned officers could be reduced and punished in due course; new men could be transferred into the unit. Army Ground Forces agreed with the command, saying that "This unit appears to have had an excellent record of accomplishment prior to the riot" and the time, money, and effort invested in it could still be utilized. All necessary disciplinary action was already provided for in Army Regulations; the matter of indoctrinating troops was a local problem that required no sanction from higher headquarters.

In the early summer of 1943 events of a similar nature continued to come to the attention of higher headquarters. Before Camp Stewart, there were disturbances at the Fort Bliss, Texas, Antiaircraft Training Center, followed by another later in June on the local celebration of Texas' Emancipation Day (19 June, "Juneteenth"), both of which were accompanied by "isolated incidents of beating of negro troops, rock throwing, and chasing of negroes (by white troops)." At Lake Charles, Louisiana, in May a pre-embarkation disturbance arose from "last fling" activities of soldiers on pass, the arrest of a Negro soldier by a white military policeman despite the local ground rule that only Negro MP's would arrest Negro soldiers, and a failure of other military police, including officers, to function properly. Angered by rough treatment of their fellows in Starkville on the Fourth of July, about fifteen Negro soldiers from Camp McCain, Mississippi, set out with arms and ammunition on

the next night, heading for Starkville, seventy miles away. At nearby Duck Hill, along the Illinois Central tracks, they stopped and fired into the nearer town in retaliation. At Camp Claiborne, Louisiana, where there were approximately 8,500 Negro and 40,000 white troops, a chain of disturbances indicating low morale and poor discipline occurred during the late spring and summer, including mass raids on exchanges, involving loss of merchandise and damage to equipment; attempts by soldiers to overturn buses; and a near riot in a service club when an angry crowd, protesting the mistreatment of a soldier by a white officer, dispersed only after a tear gas candle was used. At the Shenango (Pennsylvania) Replacement Depot, on the evening of 14 July 1943, an altercation between Negro and white soldiers in a post exchange expanded until it involved large numbers of troops in the exchange area. This first disturbance, brought under control by white and Negro military police, was followed by another when two new prisoners, picked up for a pass violation, spread news of the earlier fracas to men in the guardhouse. Negro prisoners broke out of the guard-house and, joined by other soldiers, seized firearms and ammunition from supply rooms. Military police, again white and Negro, killed one and wounded five other soldiers in quelling the second disturbance.

INDIVIDUAL VIOLENCE

Not all of the violence and disorder in which Negro troops became involved resulted from racial friction or mass grievances. Much of it was of a purely indigenous nature, sometimes growing out of cultural traits and patterns of behavior brought into the Army from civilian life and sometimes growing out of contacts between soldiers and civilians whose lives were enmeshed in the semi-underworld of the honky-tonk sections of many camp towns. Throughout the war these provided backdrop and counterpoint to racial violence sometimes difficult to distinguish from the main action and theme. In the prevailing atmosphere of alertness and sensitivity to potential racial disorders, many a street squabble or local fight, normal in war-crowded towns and camps, received attention out of proportion to its importance, for none could draw the line between a minor disorder and one that might portend a major outbreak of violence.

Sometimes civilian crowds, opposed to law enforcement in any form or conditioned to suspect that Negro soldiers would receive less than fair treatment from police officers, came close to precipitating mass violence. In Louisville, Kentucky, in June 1943, street crowds became disorderly when white and Negro military police arrested Negro soldiers. The crowd, seeing soldiers bleeding— they had been fighting among themselves—and concluding that they had been beaten by arresting police, heaped imprecations upon the military police, calling the Negro MP's "mouth-pieces for the white people." When an arrested soldier refused to enter a police car in Tampa, Florida, a crowd of civilians gathered, urging other soldiers to take him away from military police. Not until an armored car arrived did the crowd disperse. Persons in the upper stories of houses continued to hurl bottles, flowerpots, and other objects into the street and upon the armored car below. In another type of disorder not involving racial friction, a feud between two units over the success of one soldier in dating "a much-sought-after colored girl," erupted into disorder in the Quartermaster service area at Camp Rucker, Alabama, following a beer party in one of the units. General disorder at a USO dance at Fort Dix, New Jersey, resulted in the death of one soldier, the wounding of two others, and the beating of one military policeman after Negro military police were called.

In some units, where a high state of discipline had never been achieved, acts of violence were a commonplace. Soldiers of one battalion, while on a recreation trip to Las Vegas, Nevada, became involved in an alter-

cation with civilian and military police, colored and white, in a bar just a short distance from the truck park where their accompanying officers were asleep. One soldier was killed and three others were injured in the ensuing fight. Within the organization itself, during the training period, several men were shot accidentally or by guards while "kidding around." Shortly before the unit moved to a port of embarkation one of its mess sergeants was hacked to death in his kitchen with a cleaver by a technician fifth grade and two accomplices bent on robbing him. In 1944, after three years of dispersed duty in and around New York City, the 372d Infantry was removed to Camp Breckinridge, Kentucky, for retraining. There, in process of reorganization and swollen to nearly twice its normal size by new men—"infantry volunteers" who were often culls from other units—it became the victim of rapidly deteriorating discipline accompanied by continuing breeches of decorum and by acts of violence. The camp commander, as support for a request for additional military police, listed one general and twenty-five specific examples of disorder and breeches of discipline occurring on the post between 24 May and 16 August 1944. Most of these he attributed to this unit. These were purely disciplinary cases, to be handled as other violations of law and order. But the line between them and racially based violence was often vague, especially in the minds of those involved as participants or as immediately responsible commanders.

CIVILIAN DISORDERS

Complementing and complicating the tenseness and disorder within the military establishment were civilian racial disorders. During the summer of 1943 serious disturbances occurred in Los Angeles, Detroit, Beaumont, and New York. Rumors of riots in the offing appeared in other cities: In Houston for "Juneteenth," in Charleston for the last week in June, in Richmond over the Fourth of July weekend, in Washington on the evening chosen for a mass meeting of Negroes protesting the refusal of the local street car company to employ Negro operators, in Pittsburgh over the weekend of 10 July when 300 Negroes stormed a police station to protest the arrest of two men who refused to "move on" when ordered to do so by the police. That civilian and military disorders had connecting links could not be overlooked. Soldiers and sailors were involved in the Detroit and Los Angeles riots. In the Harlem riot of 1943, the precipitating event involved a Negro soldier and a white city policeman, with the policeman accusing the soldier of attempting to interfere with the arrest of a disorderly Negro woman. The rumor spread quickly that the soldier had been killed by the policeman. Rioting, most of it against property rather than against whites themselves, followed, resulting in at least five deaths and several hundred injured. The possibility of further repercussions from these disturbances within the Army was viewed as a real danger. In Harlem, Negro and white soldiers sent into the area to clear the streets and restore order were greeted with cheers. In Detroit, however, the action of the service command in using 2,000 white soldiers only for riot duty brought immediate repercussions in Negro units. Eighty Negro soldiers at nearby Oscoda Army Air Base, mainly members of the 332d Fighter Group and the 96th Service Group, protested to the President that they, too, should have been called for this duty, charging that white soldiers helped white rioters against Negroes and saying that the handling of the riot brought out in bold relief the helpless physical position of Negro soldiers and civilians. The greater fear arising from these continuing disturbances in both the civilian and military spheres was that, with all their interacting potentialities, they would interfere seriously not only with training but also with war production, handing at the same time free copy to enemy propagandists. With the political campaigns of

1944 approaching, attempts to make political capital of the increasingly serious problem were on the horizon. It would therefore behoove the Army, its legislative experts felt, to "keep its skirts clean in the matter" and avoid involvement in the coming campaign.

Army Service Forces, which had primary responsibility for service commands and, through them, for posts, acquired after the middle of 1943 direct responsibility for increasing percentages of Negro troops. ASF began to place prevention of racial friction high on its list of problems toward the end of 1943. There was still a tendency to place the major blame for disturbances upon inadequate recreational facilities, inadequate command, and outside agitation. A representative of The Inspector General, addressing a conference of commanding generals of service commands in midsummer 1943, summed up the situation and the War Department's view of both its origin and its importance:

> In my opinion the toughest problem confronting service commanders today is the one of preventing disturbances involving colored troops, since it involves some matters which are not under your control. The number of such disturbances has materially increased in the last few months. High officials of the War Department are not so much concerned as to how commanders functioned in quelling the disturbances, but rather what had they done to learn that a riot or disturbance was probable and what action had they taken to prevent it.
>
> General Peterson's information indicates that in too many instances commanding officers are too far removed from their colored troops; they are not sufficiently interested in their day-to-day welfare in providing them with reasonable recreational facilities within the post and in seeing that reasonable transportation is provided to and from recreational areas off the post; they are not enough concerned about the discrimination that may be practiced against Negroes in the surrounding country and in the lack of recreational facilities therein; they permit on their own posts discriminations which are contrary to the War Department policies and instructions; they fail

to maintain appropriate standards of discipline in Negro units; they grudgingly accept Negro officers assigned to their commands and thereafter spend a good deal of time griping about the unfitness of a Negro to be an officer, rather than requiring him to meet officer standards.

In stations where conditions exist as I have just described, there grows up the feeling of unrest and resentment, which is flamed by troublemakers within the organization until it gets to the point that only a spark, which is ordinarily a false rumor, converts an organization into a riotous mob. Some officials in Washington believe that some of the disturbances that have occurred could have been prevented had the commanders concerned functioned appropriately. I do not want to give the impression that disturbances are the fault of the commanders, but by failing to act appropriately, they facilitate the work of groups or individuals who are attempting to create unrest and later riots among Negro troops.

As more and more Negro troops came under its direct control, Army Service Forces and its agencies explored ways and means of improving the control of racial tensions within camps and stations. Early in 1944, the continuing examination of policy concerning Negro troops was placed at the top of Army Service Forces' Classified Checklist of Current Policies, with the director of its Military Personnel Division made responsible for close observation of matters arising under these policies. The Inspector General, from mid-summer 1943 to the end of the year, made a series of comprehensive surveys of conditions in several camps and groups of camps. Nine specific recommendations were forwarded by him for War Department consideration. Many of these had been covered before, but from the findings of inspectors they were considered to be in need of further attention. Moreover, The Inspector General, from past reports and observations, viewed the situation as a complex of many strands which, singly or in combination, led to unrest and eventual disorder. The corrective recommendations included: (1) directives "by appropriate authority" to commanders concerned for the purpose of stressing, in the training programs of Negro troops, the necessity of "their accepting and striving to attain the proper standards of military discipline"; (2) utilization of additional Negro military police to provide more adequate and centralized control; (3) the establishment of an "active, attractive, interesting and fully coordinated recreational and entertainment program, including additional facilities therefor;" (4) the necessity of affording Negro officers "the same privileges and opportunities for advancement as those granted white officers" with the requirement that they "be held to the same high degree of leadership, efficiency, performance of duty and discipline"; (5) a clear statement of War Department policy to correct "an unwillingness of commanding officers to bring offenders to trial when the seriousness of the offense manifestly indicated the need therefor"; (6) attainment of closer co-operation of federal and state authorities toward control of venereal diseases; (7) directives to local public relations officers requiring them to gather information on Negro personnel at posts, camps, and stations, to furnish releases to Negro papers and encouragement to the papers to use such releases "with a view to elimination from their publications of erroneous, distorted or inflammatory articles," failing which "drastic steps" should be taken by appropriate government authorities "in cases of publication of articles which adversely affect the War effort;" (8) recommendations to commanding officers that "when there is reason to believe or suspect that there is racial unrest or that racial disturbance is imminent within their commands, they should exercise, in such situations as may warrant it, the military censorship of postal matter authorized by the provisions of paragraph 3d, War Department Training Circular 15, dated 16 February 1943, using the utmost care and secrecy in so doing;" and (9) bringing to the attention of appropriate agencies, with a view to correction "where practicable," the lack of established eating and lodging facilities for Negro personnel traveling in the South.

All of the matters in this portmanteau recommendation had previously come to the attention of one or another of the agencies concerned. Many of them had reminiscent overtones of the recommendations made by Judge Hastie in his pre-Pearl Harbor survey. Much had been done to carry out certain of them. That they were still unfinished business mid-way of the war was an indication of the difficulty which the War Department had had with them. The degree of relationship which the areas of recommended action bore to the problem of violence and discipline differed considerably; that all were contributing to the general problem of the employment of Negro troops could not be denied.

The Employment of Personnel: Minority Groups

Mattie E. Treadwell

The only sizable racial minority group in the WAC was that of the Negro, although a few women of Puerto Rican, Chinese, Japanese, and American Indian descent were also enlisted. Members of most of these groups, except the Negro, were very rarely recruited, and were not segregated, but scattered through ordinary WAC units according to skills.

One exception was the group of Puerto Rican Wacs, who were enlisted, trained, and assigned as a unit. It had been intended to integrate them into other WAC units, but language difficulties made this step impractical. The women presented no notable problems except that of language, which possibly prevented them from receiving assignments commensurate with their intelligence.

Source: Mattie E. Treadwell, "The Employment of Personnel: Minority Groups." In *The Women's Army Corps: United States Army in World War II* (Washington, D.C.: Office of the Chief of Military History. Department of the Army, 1954), Chap. XXX, pp. 589–601.

Considerable numbers of nisei recruits had been expected when, in 1943, the Army began to admit Americans of Japanese descent. In this hope, the Director's staff went to some pains to publish the necessary waivers on height and to request small-sized uniforms. Some five hundred nisei recruits were wanted for employment as translators, but in spite of visits of WAC recruiters to relocation centers, only thirteen could be obtained in the first six months of enlistment, and negligible numbers thereafter. Parental opposition to military service for women was believed to have been the chief deterrent, as well as the fact that the women were by this time permitted to leave the relocation centers for other employment. Somewhat later, the Military Intelligence Language School was able to locate and enlist a few more women who agreed to enter specifically for service at the school. Four more such women, especially enlisted in Hawaii for the language school, were appropriated by the Office of Strategic Services in Washington. There was sometimes a tendency to expect that all nisei Wacs could be assigned as translators, although in actual fact some of them proved to know no more of the Japanese language than any other American.

NEGRO PERSONNEL

Even before the passage of the first WAAC legislation, the War Department announced that the new Corps would follow Army policy by admitting Negroes to basic and officer candidate training, and that two of the first eight companies sent to the field would be composed of Negroes. Forty of the WAAC's first 440 officer candidate vacancies were allotted to Negro women.

Equality of treatment was also required by the confidential official policy which was formulated and approved shortly afterward and which stated:

> On posts where these companies are stationed it should be fundamental that their reception and treatment should be an exemplification of the rights and privileges accorded officers and soldiers of the United States Army. . . . There will be no discrimination in the type of duties to which Negro women in the WAAC may be assigned. . . . Every effort will be made through intensive recruiting to obtain the class of colored women desired, in order that there may be no lowering of the standard in order to meet ratio requirements.

The WAC, like the Army, was directed to accept 10.6 percent of its strength in Negro recruits. In accordance with the policy for men, it was deemed most desirable for adjustment to assign units to posts where a number of Negro troops were stationed, or where there was a large Negro population in nearby cities. Assignment overseas was also approved, contingent upon the request of the overseas commander.

Reports from the first Negro trainees indicated that these prohibitions against discrimination were being upheld to the satisfaction of national Negro organizations. At the request of Dr. Mary McLeod Bethune of the Federal Security Agency, a Negro lawyer in the city of Des Moines questioned the Negro officer candidates closely to see if they could not recall some evidence of discrimination, and found none:

> *Question:* Are Negro girls made to feel that a special concession is being made to them in permitting them to attend this school?
> *Answer:* Yes. The white girls are made to feel the same.

General Marshall himself watched closely for compliance with these directives, and reported with satisfaction to the War Council that a reporter from the *Pittsburgh Courier* had inspected the Negro candidates and after urging them to make complaints could find none. All Negro Waacs assured the investigators that no school subjects were denied them, or jokes or sly remarks made. Some discrimination was noted in the city of Des Moines, but none among the other women, particularly those from the South, of whom Secretary Walter White of the National Association for the Advancement of Colored People (NAACP) asked, "When is Des Moines in general going to become as democratic as the white Waacs from the South?"

SEGREGATION

While thus approving other provisions, Negro organizations and investigators without exception objected to the segregation of Negro personnel, in which the WAAC had been directed to follow the Army policy. During the Corps' first months, numbers of Negro and white investigators arrived at Des Moines to search for bad results of segregation. The NAACP, after a visit by its representatives, wrote both the Secretary of War and the Director to protest the restriction of Negroes to separate barracks, separate tables in mess halls, and different swimming pool hours. Secretary White of the NAACP also repeatedly called at WAAC Headquarters in person to protest the Corps' action in following the Army policy on segregation. The National Board of the YWCA also investigated and wrote the Director to protest segregation. The Boston Urban League did the same. The Julius Rosenwald Fund sent a committee to Des Moines and concluded that segregation in housing would cause a falling off in Negro applications for enlistment.

This concentrated activity within the space of a few weeks caused considerable concern to the WAAC staff. However, it was finally concluded that any new agency would probably receive similar visits, and that Negro organizations, like almost everyone else, did not realize that the WAAC was not an independent command in policy matters. One adviser reported to the Director:

> The War Department, WAAC included, is gradually being maneuvered into the position of being forced to make decisions relative to racial matters which the government and/or the citizens should have made long ago, by legislation and the establishment of a different policy. . . . The Director is going to be in a better position if she allows the Army to care for the things that they normally do. Housing is one of them and it is the camp commanders' problem.

All requests to the WAAC for independent action were necessarily referred to the War Department for consideration, as part of the Army policy. In November of 1942, officers' housing and messing at Fort Des Moines were merged, and also service club facilities, and officer candidate companies became nonsegregated, there being precedent for these steps at some men's schools. On the average Army station, no change in the Army policy was deemed possible, since there was ordinarily only one WAAC unit on a station and its housing was of course segregated regardless of the race of its members.

In attempting even a limited relaxation of segregation at Des Moines, a women's corps dependent upon voluntary recruiting proved to be in a less advantageous position than the rest of the Army. There was some evidence that WAC recruiting soon suffered by comparison with that of the Navy women's services, which did not at this time accept Negro women. One congressman objected to the situation at Des Moines, stating of a constituent, "This fine girl along with others is now forced to share the same living quarters, bathroom facilities, restrooms, and reception rooms with Negroes." Some Louisiana radio stations refused to aid WAC recruiting because a local woman, while housed on a separate floor of the Chamberlain Hotel in Des Moines, had to eat and do kitchen police with Negro women on the next floors. An Army officer reported:

> I am hearing constant rumors as to a relaxing of segregation of Negroes at Fort Des Moines. Such rumors are horrifying to people in this section and I know are interfering seriously with recruiting.

In any attempts to change the Army policy, a newly established volunteer corps, under orders to attempt an expansion program unsupported by selective service, obviously offered the least promising point for a beginning. Only Director Hobby's personal convictions prevented the wiping out of the steps already taken at Fort Des Moines.

RECRUITING

Most Negro organizations alleged that the policy of segregation would deter the best-qualified Negro women from enlistment, and this possibility was recognized and provided for in the original War Department policy concerning Negro Waacs, which stated:

> There is a definite reluctance on the part of the best qualified colored women to volunteer in the WAAC. This is brought about by an impression on their part that they will not be well received or treated on posts where they may be stationed. This could be overcome by an intensive recruiting campaign with the idea in

view of interesting the desired class of colored women in this project and arriving at a thorough understanding of their rights and privileges while in the service. . . . An eminently qualified person, preferably a Negro recruiter, will be sent out to colored colleges in order to secure the proper class of applicants.

Definite instructions requiring the acceptance of Negro applicants were sent out to recruiting stations. Noncompliance was discovered in only five cities and was corrected by telegraph in the WAAC's first week of recruiting. One of these cases, in Pittsburgh, caused the editor of the *Pittsburgh Courier* to demand that a woman from his staff be assigned to the Director's Office, since "We wouldn't want the public to deceive itself with the notion that what happened in Pittsburgh was due to the fact that the Director of the WAAC is a white woman from Texas." The demand for such an adviser became a nationwide campaign with as many as thirty-five mimeographed letters being received from one small Virginia city. However, the work of checking on such complaints was instead given to one of the first Negro officer candidates, Lt. Harriet West of the Director's staff, a former assistant to Dr. Bethune. Later charges of recruiting discrimination were investigated by Lieutenant West. In most cases records revealed that identical recruiting standards had been used, although rejected Negro applicants sometimes tended to blame discrimination rather than their own failure to pass aptitude or physical tests.

Although Negro WAAC recruiting officers were sent to the field as soon as the first class graduated, Negro recruits from the first months failed to come up to expectations in either quantity or quality. An early check made by the Recruiting Service indicated that there were plenty of Negro applicants but that in some localities as many as 85 percent failed the various tests. Also, skills were scarce, and the whole Second Service Command reported that in several months it had been able to secure only one qualified typist and one clerk against its quota.

During the first months of 1943, when standards for all recruits were unwisely lowered to meet expansion quotas, Negro recruits quickly presented a special problem, in that most of those who met enlistment standards tended to meet only the minimum requirements. As soon as educational standards were restored, in April of 1943, this condition became less common, but meanwhile the assignment problem for Negro women had become acute. A Negro training company in this month contained 225 members of whom 192 had no usable military skill. In the same month, the pool of unassignable women contained 180 whites and 776 Negroes. The only available comparison of test scores showed that, of a May 1943 sample, 66 percent of Negro recruits were in the two lowest AGCT groups, IV and V, as against only 15 percent of white recruits; only 6 percent of Negro Wacs were in the two upper brackets, I and II, as against 43 percent of white Wacs. The WAAC Control Division commented that the problem was one of the Corps' most serious, and would become worse when the women reached the field.

Attempts were made to discharge the most hopeless cases, and it was believed that the higher enrollment standards just adopted would prevent similar future difficulty. As for women who could not be discharged, Capt. Harriet West, after an inspection, recommended that they be formed into companies for unskilled work in hospitals, messes, and salvage depots. However, this could not be done because of the War Department policy that Negroes would be assigned to the same type of units as whites, and because most allotments for such jobs were civilian. To ease the situation at Des Moines, a number of the women were shipped to the Fourth Training Center at Fort Devens for general use about the post and for training in motor transport. After about three months, Fort Devens closed out and they were shipped back to Des Moines.

The situation quickly became highly embarrassing to the War Department. Although white women with equal lack of qualifications were equally unassignable, it frequently appeared to Negro organizations that race rather than ability was the determining factor in Army job assignments for Negro women. Every possible solution appeared tinged with discrimination. The WAAC Table of Organization unit had only seventeen vacancies for unskilled women, so that to form such companies of the Negro women was impossible, yet to devise a different T/O for Negroes, entirely composed of menial workers, would have been actual instead of apparent discrimination. Attempts at specialist training were equally futile. For Negroes only, the requirements for motor transport school were waived, and technical subjects removed from the course, but even with this assistance very few qualified drivers could be produced.

In April of 1943, the Secretary of War's civilian aide, Truman Gibson, sent the War Department a complaint that the failure to give Negro women radio and other specialist training represented manipulation of test scores rather than the women's inaptitude; this was formally denied by training authorities. In May, representatives of the NAACP called on Colonel McCoskrie at Des Moines with the same and other complaints, and were again informed that women's alleged qualifications for radio and other training did not show up on tests.

In September of 1943 the civilian aide to the Secretary of War again complained that Negroes were being sent only to cooks and bakers school instead of to higher technical schools, and that white women were being assigned to field jobs while Negro women were not. The Director replied that Negroes could and did go to every specialist school upon the same basis as other women, and in fact had received more educational attention than white women in an effort to make up their deficiencies and permit their assignment to military jobs. The Secretary of War's civilian aide also objected to the fact that Negro women in the pool of unassignables had been allowed to go home on furlough while assignments for them were being sought; this, he charged,

was also discrimination, in that white women did not get such furloughs.

Especial protests concerned the recruiting situation, in which it was felt that the Army was not making every effort to recruit more Negro women. The basis for such complaints was the fact that, in July of 1943, Negro WAC officers were withdrawn from recruiting duty and returned to training centers in what was announced as a move to provide instructors for unassigned Negro women in order to get them assigned to the field as quickly as possible. Under the circumstances, it appeared to the Negro press that the Negro recruiters were being blamed for the low-grade women admitted, or that the move was a prelude to refusal to admit Negro recruits. In spite of this protest, the Negro recruiters were not returned to duty, since a check revealed that their absence had caused no decline in the numbers of Negro recruits. It was known that the presence of Negro recruiters had caused situations prejudicial to white recruiting; in Sacramento, California, intelligence operatives reported a serious situation caused by Negro WAC recruiters who "appeared in public places giving public speeches."

With the end of the T/O system, it became possible to ship to the field a unit chiefly composed of unskilled personnel, and the pool of unassigned women gradually diminished. The difficulty was, however, merely shifted to Army posts. An Army inspector reported that station commanders were quite at a loss as to how to assign the women without putting them into civilian jobs in laundries and service clubs. For example, one Negro unit in the field complained to an inspector of women's assignments, but it was found that only three women of the 135 were above Grade III on AGCT score, while 108 were in Grades IV and V. Their average civilian salary was $13.16 per week, and in civilian life they had been maids, waitresses, laundresses, and housewives. Nevertheless, they said that recruiters had told them that they would be trained to do skilled jobs and promoted at once to the grade of sergeant. Three in the company were described as "agitators," who threatened the other women for refusing to strike against their jobs.

All attempts to place such low-grade women in Army jobs met with opposition. In 1943 and again in 1944 The Surgeon General's Office refused to accept them even as ward orderlies saying:

> No suitable assignments exist for such personnel upon completion of training and further accumulation of surplus colored WAC enlisted women thus trained would constitute an increasing embarrassment to the service.

At the same time The Surgeon General's Office also refused to accept Grades IV and V white women.

The unassignability of unskilled Negro recruits merely served to reinforce a discovery that hardly needed reinforcement: that the Army had few jobs for unskilled and untrainable women of any race, and that to recruit them was invariably ill-advised. For skilled Negro recruits, the situation was considerably different. Negro women who met the intelligence requirements were successfully given specialist training including that of medical and surgical technicians, as well as laboratory, X-ray, and dental technicians; these women proved able to complete the regular course on the same terms as other Wacs. Army posts and air bases where Negro troops were stationed expressed a consistent eagerness to obtain Negro WAC units containing stenographers, typists, and other office workers.

SKILLED WORK DONE BY NEGRO WACS

Scattered reports from Negro WAC units at Army stations showed successful performance by Negro Wacs of a wide variety of administrative and technical work. At Fort Jackson, a Wac sergeant was medical stenographer to the chief of general surgery. At Fort Bragg, a Wac T/5 taught arts and crafts

to soldiers in the recreational therapy shop. At Fort McClellan, fifteen Wac clerks staffed the locator section of the post office, forwarding wrongly addressed mail and packages and keeping locator card files for the post. At Fort Riley, members served not only as ward orderlies but in the more skilled jobs of physical therapy aids, laboratory technicians, X-ray technicians, and dental technicians. At Fort Sheridan, Illinois, the women worked at graphotype machines, processing soldiers' records. At Camp Knight, California, 105 Negro Wacs performed clerical work in the overseas supply division.

In the Army Air Forces, whole units, such as that at the Walla Walla air base, were reported as succeeding in the same type of clerical and other duties performed by white Wacs. At the Sioux City Army air base, Negro Wacs worked in the technical inspector's office. At Douglas Army Airfield, the women were assigned to aircraft maintenance, the flight line, and laboratory work; one also served as photographer in the post public relations office. In the Air Service Command at Fresno, two women served in map and editing work in the war room.

Other duties noted at different stations were those of teletype operators, motion picture projectionists, parachute packers, drivers, cooks, chaplains' assistants, and librarians. The commanding officer of Fort Huachuca wrote, "These young women are showing marked ability in taking over essential jobs. . . . The performance of the Wacs has been very satisfactory in every respect." The commanding officer of Douglas Army Airfield stated, "I've found them cooperative at all times, and their enthusiasm, industry, attention to duty and conduct make them a real asset to this post." "In several cases," Colonel Bandel reported later, "their efficiency and spirit were highly praised by airbase commanders."

Negro WAC officers served not only as troop officers and instructors but in operational jobs, a number also being graduates of the Army's Quartermaster School at Camp Lee.

With the higher enrollment standards, recruiters experienced increased success in obtaining qualified women. A survey of skills in 1944 showed that about one fourth of Negro recruits had clerical and professional skills, as against one half of white recruits. In addition, about 30 percent of the Negro recruits, as compared to 34 percent of the whites, had experience in skilled or unskilled trades. Although thus not as good as the WAC average, the Negro Wacs appeared to be considerably superior in skills to the average for Negro civilian women workers in the United States. Here, more than 64 percent of civilian women were reported to be in service occupations, as against only 35 percent of Negro Wacs with this background.

In employing higher skill and aptitude standards, recruiters were never able to reach the desired goal of 10 percent of the Corps' strength. The peak strength of Negro WAC troops was reached early in 1945 and totaled approximately 4,000 or about 4 percent of the Corps. These women were assigned to some twenty stations in the Army Service Forces and ten stations in the Army Air Forces. The Army Ground Forces employed no Negro Wacs, since most of its troops trained on stations administered by the Service Forces.

PROBLEMS OF NEGRO UNITS

There was little indication that, with a few exceptions, the problems experienced by these Negro WAC units in the field were greatly different in nature from those of other WAC units, but in some cases the normal difficulties of women in the Army were apparently intensified. Unskilled women of any race had been found harder to assign and harder to discipline. Thus, the Negro company officer frequently faced a more difficult command situation than did the average WAC company commander, in proportion as her unit contained more than the average of such women. The post commander at Fort Huachuca noted that the enlisted women were prone to develop "jealousies and cliques" and "bickerings which seem to date back to school days at Des Moines . . . with various kinds of personal gossip about each other."

Unit members also showed a tendency to complain to inspectors about the education and ability of Negro company commanders, who were in fact as well educated and trained as the average WAC commander. To deal with such units frequently required a skill and a degree of leadership highly taxing to the company officer. Some Negro WAC company commanders were reported to have met the challenge with an ingenuity, energy, and sense of humor seldom equaled among other WAC commanders. On the other hand, some were found to share their women's deficiencies: an intelligence report from Fort Des Moines found that jealousy and rivalry had arisen among Negro WAC officers, resulting in a "heated argument" and "emotional display" in the presence of the commandant.

Negro WAC officers also had an especial problem of loneliness on many stations; the WAC policy was to have Negro company officers for Negro troops, but many male Negro units had white officers, so that the WAC officers were apt to be the only Negro officers on a station.

While all WAC units had at first encountered some degree of skepticism concerning their mission in life, this difficulty was apparently intensified for Negro Wacs. The first requisition from the European theater, rejected by Colonel Hobby at the time of the Corps' formation, had been so plainly for "morale purposes" that the Secretary of War's civilian aide, William H. Hastie, protested that "the assignment of units of the WAAC to afford companionship for soldiers would discredit that organization" and was "contrary to its whole plan and purpose."

The first units at Fort Huachuca encountered an exceptionally difficult situation in this respect during the early weeks. While such impressions on stations of assignment could be remedied only by time and demonstrated military behavior, every effort was made to avoid exposing the women unnecessarily to situations that encouraged the misapprehension. Thus, when the inspector general at Sioux Falls suggested that large groups of Negro Wacs be brought by truck from Des Moines to make up for the recreational deficiencies of Negro men at that air base, Colonel Hobby replied with some emphasis that one of the War Department's invariable policies was that Wacs, regardless of race, would not be removed from their jobs to be "social companions."

Negro WAC units also experienced a special problem outside their control in that in some cases a serious race problem had already arisen in certain areas before their arrival, including what was described as "race riots," "unrest," "inflammatory gossip," and "rumor of a nature to incite the men." Not only did such emotions prove contagious, but the sentiment in neighboring civilian communities was also sometimes anything but favorable toward the women's arrival. When it was planned to send a unit to Gardiner General Hospital in Chicago, where a strained situation already existed, protests were received by the Army from four suburban civic groups, to the effect that stationing the women in a restricted white residential area, near a white bathing beach, might cause "incidents" and race riots. Although the Army ignored these protests and successfully stationed the unit at Gardiner General Hospital, such a community reaction obviously presented an adjustment problem to unit members.

The women's adjustment to the Army situation was also rendered more difficult by well-meaning civilian groups in their constant watchfulness for discrimination. It was not surprising that many of the experiences that had been encountered by white Wacs everywhere, and attributed to their sex, should be interpreted by Negro Wacs as racial discrimination: these included the early malassignments, clothing shortages, malicious gossip, and other common difficulties. Possibly the most serious report investigated was one of "terrorization and mistreatment," which actually proved to be the common experience of many WAC units—a chilly initial reception, rude remarks by civilian employees, lack of enthusiasm about Wacs on the part of USO hostesses, and pranks by soldiers. The unit, except for three complaining members, was actually found to be in good morale, satisfied with its recreational facilities, and satisfactory in its duties.

A similar situation arose when, in the last days of the war, both white and Negro units were recruited for general hospitals. Shortly afterward, Congressman Adam C. Powell informed the War Department that "Trouble is brewing at Fort Oglethorpe." Upon investigation it was found that Negro civilian employees were being given better hospital jobs than Negro Wacs; that Negro Wacs worked in hospitals 12 hours a day and civilians only 8; that Negro Wac orderlies had to take orders from civilian nurses. These were exactly the problems currently reported from white hospital units.

An almost identical and widely publicized case of alleged discrimination concerned the court-martial of four Negro Wacs at Lovell General Hospital in Massachusetts. A summary of their grievances was endorsed by white medical technician recruits everywhere:

> They don't want to scrub. . . . They want a future, i. e., training . . . they don't like the civilians because the civilians are late, lazy, and mean . . . they said they knew they weren't wanted in the beginning . . . they want promised ratings.

The conviction that racial discrimination was involved led a part of this Negro unit to refuse to report for duty even after personal pleas from the WAC staff director, two colonels, a judge advocate, an inspector general, and the commanding general of the service command, which finally caused all but four members to return to work. The court-martial of these four was declared proper even by the NAACP, which issued a statement that "We recognize that there is no right to strike in the Armed Services." Although the commanding general upheld the court-martial proceedings, the conviction was reversed by the Judge Advocate General, and the women restored to duty on the technicality that the court was improperly convened.

NEGRO WACS OVERSEAS

The European theater was the only overseas theater to employ Negro Wacs. ETO policy vacillated. Negroes were requisitioned in 1942 with the declaration that "in time of war it is the privilege of all American citizens regardless of race or sex to serve in and with the Armed Forces." However, when Director Hobby refused to let the women be scattered in uncontrolled small field units near male Negro troops, the theater hastily canceled the requisition and stated that "colored Wacs will not be requisitioned until such time as the War Department announces that their shipment to theaters of operation is a necessity."

Pressure of Negro groups finally forced the War Department to direct the European theater to accept Negro Wacs. As directed, the European theater submitted a requisition for approximately 800 Negro women to set up half of a central postal directory. Declaring that these women would not fill any existing military jobs, the theater asked and expected an additional allotment of grades, but none was received.

The unit, the 6888th Central Postal Battalion, was selected from both the Air Forces and the Service Forces in order to give all women a chance at overseas service, but sufficient volunteers to fill the unit could not be found. One Negro editor had alleged that "they are heartbroken because they cannot serve overseas like their white GI sisters," but this opinion apparently did not accurately reflect the sentiments of all of the women, one of whom suggested to an inspector that they ship the NAACP instead.

The battalion arrived in Europe in February of 1945, under the command of Maj. Charity Adams, later promoted to lieutenant colonel. The unit contained 40 percent unskilled workers, as against 1 percent for white Wacs in this theater, and 40 percent in the two lowest AGCT grades, as against 10 percent for white Wacs.

As a separate T/O unit, the battalion naturally had segregated housing and working quarters, but there was no segregation in the use of Red Cross clubs, leave areas, and schools. No particular difficulties were reported in discipline and administration. The unit was congratulated by the theater on its "exceptionally fine" Special Services program. Its observance of military courtesies was also pronounced exemplary, as were the grooming and appearance of members and the maintenance of quarters.

Unit efficiency was difficult to evaluate. Before the women's arrival, the central directory operated with enlisted men and civilians and reported itself "swamped by mail" and with an undelivered backlog of over three million pieces; it also faced the necessity of a move to France, where English-speaking civilians would be more difficult to find. The Wacs' performance was not entirely satisfactory to inspectors, who stated that "production appeared to be low" and that "the girls relax on their jobs while mail accumulates." The women in turn believed that too much pressure was being brought to bear to increase mail output, and that they had not been awarded a well-deserved unit citation.

Some 11 percent of the detachment also had cause for considering themselves malassigned; about 10 percent were typists, and 1 percent were stenographers, and these were admittedly underutilized in a postal directory. Had not the segregation policy prevented, these could have been scattered through other WAC detachments where their skills could have been employed. The other 89 percent appeared to be properly assigned but, like most newly arrived personnel, had difficulty with respiratory disorders; they also reported considerable fatigue.

Some six months after the end of the war in Europe, with the departure of discharge-eligibles, the battalion had shrunk to about 300 members, and its morale and efficiency were pronounced so "exceptionally low" by a WAC inspector from the War Department that she recommended its immediate return to the United States. The theater preferred not to return the unit under circumstances implying failure, which was believed unwarranted, but eventually, with the reduction in size of the theater, there was little work remaining for the women, and they were returned to the United States as a unit. The theater's conclusion was that the problems experienced by Negro Wacs in the European theater were similar to those experienced by other Negro troops and were not peculiar to women, and that the War Department's eventual solution should apply to both.

As soon as shipment was made to the European theater, Negro groups turned toward efforts to get Negro Wacs sent to the Southwest Pacific Area. Such action was never directed by the War Department, since they were not requisitioned by the theater, and since the end of the war intervened. Also, the difficulties currently being encountered by white Wacs in the Pacific would have been difficult to explain to Negro organizations. In any case, the percentage of Negro Wacs overseas was, on the strength of the European battalion, as high as that of all Wacs, or about 20 percent.

CONCLUSIONS

It proved difficult to evaluate the success of the program of employment of Negro Wacs. The second WAC Director, Colonel Boyce, when asked to comment, replied, "The Negro women in the Army are a part of the WAC. The record of achievement of the Corps cannot be attributed to any individual or to any group but to the whole Corps." Training center authorities were inclined to wonder if the nuisance value of the constant civilian searching parties had not outweighed the military contribution by the women. In the field, comments of post commanders applied to ability rather than race: every skilled Wac was assignable regardless of race, and unskilled ones were never wanted. When the WAVES, near the end of the war, were considering admitting Negroes, a WAC authority advised them,

> To speak very frankly, the problems are fundamental ones—charges of segregation, discrimination, not giving them clerical jobs. . . . Success depends in the main on (1) the caliber of officers . . . (2) intelligent assignment and utilization.

It appeared that in some respects the Navy policy had been more successful than that of the Army. The WAVES had not admitted any Negro women until 1945, by which time the Navy had announced an end of segregation for men. At this time the WAVES accepted only 70 Negro enlisted women and no company officers. By virtue of the small numbers, enlistment was highly selective, and only women of high aptitude and skill and good personal appearance were chosen. For this reason, the WAVES were able to abolish segregation from the beginning, and to incorporate the few skilled specialists into existing units. The approval with which the Navy policy was received by Negro organizations strongly suggested that, had the WAC never set a 10 percent quota, and instead limited Negro enlistment to a few women who met the highest standards, it might not only have avoided the burden of unassignable low-grade personnel, but also have successfully abolished segregation. However, the WAC could hardly have adopted this policy in the absence of a change in Army policy.

There was some indication that, as compared to the relative problems of Negro men in all services, the WAC had experienced lesser problems and been more highly regarded by the Negro civilian population. When asked in a nationwide survey "What are your chances in the different services?" more Negro women answered "Good" concerning the WAC than did Negro men concerning any of the armed services. It appeared that the armed forces' eventual decisions concerning male Negro troops would apply equally well to female troops, with the exception—which applied to women of all races—that higher-grade female personnel would continue to be required in view of the fact that women could not perform combat and heavy service duties.

Executive Order 9808, December 5, 1946

Harry S Truman

Whereas the preservation of civil rights guaranteed by the Constitution is essential to domestic tranquility, national security, the general welfare, and the continued existence of our free institutions; and

Whereas the action of individuals who take the law into their own hands and inflict summary punishment and wreak personal vengeance is subversive of our democratic system of law enforcement and public criminal justice, and gravely threatens our form of government; and

Whereas it is essential that all possible steps be taken to safeguard our civil rights:

Now, therefore, by virtue of the authority vested in me as President of the United States by the Constitution and the statutes of the United States, it is hereby ordered as follows:

1. There is hereby created a committee to be known as the President's Committee on Civil Rights, which shall be composed of the following-named members, who shall serve without compensation:

Mr. C. E. Wilson, chairman; Mrs. Sadie T. Alexander, Mr. James B. Carey, Mr. John S. Dickey, Mr. Morris L. Ernst, Rabbi Roland B. Gittelsohn, Dr. Frank P. Graham, The Most Reverend Francis J. Haas, Mr. Charles Luckman, Mr. Francis P. Matthews, Mr. Franklin D. Roosevelt, Jr., The Right Reverend Henry Knox Sherrill, Mr. Boris Shishkin, Mrs. M. E. Tilly, Mr. Channing H. Tobias.

2. The Committee is authorized on behalf of the President to inquire into and to determine whether and in what respect current law-enforcement measures and the authority and means possessed by Federal, State, and local governments may be strengthened and improved to safeguard the civil rights of the people.

3. All executive departments and agencies of the Federal Government are authorized and directed to cooperate with the Committee in its work, and to furnish the Committee such information or the services of such persons as the Committee may require in the performance of its duties.

4. When requested by the Committee to do so, persons employed in any of the executive departments and agencies of the Federal Government shall testify before the Committee and shall make available for the use of the Committee such documents and other information as the Committee may require.

5. The Committee shall make a report of its studies to the President in writing, and shall in particular make recommendations with respect to the adoption or establishment, by legislation or otherwise, of more adequate and effective means and procedures for the

Source: Executive Order 9808, December 5, 1946, Establishing the President's Committee on Civil Rights. 11 Fed. Reg. 14153 (1946). *To Secure These Rights* (Washington, D.C.: U.S. Government Printing Office, 1947), pp. 139–73.

protection of the civil rights of the people of the United States.

6. Upon rendition of its report to the President, the Committee shall cease to exist, unless otherwise determined by further Executive Order.

HARRY S TRUMAN

The White House
December 5, 1946

A PROGRAM OF ACTION: THE COMMITTEE'S RECOMMENDATIONS

The Time Is Now

Twice before in American history the nation has found it necessary to review the state of its civil rights. The first time was during the 15 years between 1776 and 1791, from the drafting of the Declaration of Independence through the Articles of Confederation experiment to the writing of the Constitution and the Bill of Rights. It was then that the distinctively American heritage was finally distilled from earlier views of liberty. The second time was when the Union was temporarily sundered over the question of whether it could exist "half-slave" and "half-free."

It is our profound conviction that we have come to a time for a third re-examination of the situation, and a sustained drive ahead. Our reasons for believing this are those of conscience, of self-interest, and of survival in a threatening world. Or to put it another way, we have a moral reason, an economic reason, and an international reason for believing that the time for action is now.

The Moral Reason

We have considered the American heritage of freedom at some length. We need no further justification for a broad and immediate program than the need to reaffirm our faith in the traditional American morality. The pervasive gap between our aims and what we actually do is creating a kind of moral dry rot which eats away at the emotional and rational bases of democratic beliefs. There are times when the difference between what we preach about civil rights and what we practice is shockingly illustrated by individual outrages. There are times when the whole structure of our ideology is made ridiculous by individual instances. And there are certain continuing, quiet, omnipresent practices which do irreparable damage to our beliefs.

As examples of "moral erosion" there are the consequences of suffrage limitations in the South. The fact that Negroes and many whites have not been allowed to vote in some states has actually sapped the morality underlying universal suffrage. Many men in public and private life do not believe that those who have been kept from voting are capable of self rule. They finally convince themselves that disfranchised people do not really have the right to vote.

Wartime segregation in the armed forces is another instance of how a social pattern may wreak moral havoc. Practically all white officers and enlisted men in all branches of service saw Negro military personnel performing only the most menial functions. They saw Negroes recruited for the common defense treated as men apart and distinct from themselves. As a result, men who might otherwise have maintained the equalitarian morality of their forebears were given reason to look down on their fellow citizens. This has been sharply illustrated by the Army study discussed previously, in which white servicemen expressed great surprise at the excellent performance of Negroes who joined them in the firing line. Even now, very few people know of the successful experiment with integrated combat units. Yet it is important in explaining why some Negro troops did not do well; it is proof that equal treatment can produce equal performance.

. . . .

It is impossible to decide who suffers the greatest moral damage from our civil rights transgressions, because all of us are hurt.

That is certainly true of those who are victimized. Their belief in the basic truth of the American promise is undermined. But they do have the realization, galling as it sometimes is, of being morally in the right. The damage to those who are responsible for these violations of our moral standards may well be greater. They, too, have been reared to honor the command of "free and equal." And all of us must share in the shame at the growth of hypocrisies like the "automatic" marble champion. All of us must endure the cynicism about democratic values which our failures breed.

The United States can no longer countenance these burdens on its common conscience, these inroads on its moral fiber.

The Economic Reason

One of the principal economic problems facing us and the rest of the world is achieving maximum production and continued prosperity. The loss of a huge, potential market for goods is a direct result of the economic discrimination which is practiced against many of our minority groups. A sort of vicious circle is produced. Discrimination depresses the wages and income of minority groups. As a result, their purchasing power is curtailed and markets are reduced. Reduced markets result in reduced production. This cuts down employment, which of course means lower wages and still fewer job opportunities. Rising fear, prejudice, and insecurity aggravate the very discrimination in employment which sets the vicious circle in motion.

Minority groups are not the sole victims of this economic waste; its impact is inevitably felt by the entire population.

. . . .

Discrimination imposes a direct cost upon our economy through the wasteful duplication of many facilities and services required by the "separate but equal" policy. That the resources of the South are sorely strained by the burden of a double system of schools and other public services has already been indicated. Segregation is also

economically wasteful for private business. Public transportation companies must often provide duplicate facilities to serve majority and minority groups separately. Places of public accommodation and recreation reject business when it comes in the form of unwanted persons. Stores reduce their sales by turning away minority customers. Factories must provide separate locker rooms, pay windows, drinking fountains, and washrooms for the different groups.

. . . .

Similarly, the rates of disease, crime, and fires are disproportionately great in areas which are economically depressed as compared with wealthier areas. Many of the prominent American minorities are confined—by economic discrimination, by law, by restrictive covenants, and by social pressure—to the most dilapidated, undesirable locations. Property in these locations yields a smaller return in taxes, which is seldom sufficient to meet the inordinately high cost of public services in depressed areas. The majority pays a high price in taxes for the low status of minorities.

. . . .

. . . It is not at all surprising that a people relegated to second-class citizenship should behave as second-class citizens. This is true, in varying degrees, of all of our minorities. What we have lost in money, production, invention, citizenship, and leadership as the price for damaged, thwarted personalities—these are beyond estimate.

The United States can no longer afford this heavy drain upon its human wealth, its national competence.

The International Reason

Our position in the postwar world is so vital to the future that our smallest actions have far-reaching effects. We have come to know that our own security in a highly interdependent world is inextricably tied to the security and well-being of all people and all countries. Our foreign policy is designed to make the United States an enormous, positive influence for peace and progress throughout the world. We have tried to let nothing, not even extreme political differences between ourselves and foreign nations, stand in the way of this goal. But our domestic civil rights shortcomings are a serious obstacle.

. . . .

We cannot escape the fact that our civil rights record has been an issue in world politics. The world's press and radio are full of it. This Committee has seen a multitude of samples. We and our friends have been, and are, stressing our achievements. Those with competing philosophies have stressed—and are shamelessly distorting—our shortcomings. They have not only tried to create hostility toward us among specific nations, races, and religious groups. They have tried to prove our democracy an empty fraud, and our nation a consistent oppressor of underprivileged people. This may seem ludicrous to Americans, but it is sufficiently important to worry our friends.

. . . .

. . . Our achievements in building and maintaining a state dedicated to the fundamentals of freedom have already served as a guide for those seeking the best road from chaos to liberty and prosperity. But it is not indelibly written that democracy will encompass the world. We are convinced that our way of life—the free way of life—holds a promise of hope for all people. We have what is perhaps the greatest responsibility ever placed upon a people to keep this promise alive. Only still greater achievements will do it.

The United States is not so strong, the final triumph of the democratic ideal is not so inevitable that we can ignore what the world thinks of us or our record.

In the State of the Union Message on January 7, 1948, I spoke of five great goals toward which* we should strive in our con-

stant effort to strengthen our democracy and improve the welfare of our people. The first of these is to secure fully our essential human rights. I am now presenting to the Congress my recommendations for legislation to carry us forward toward that goal.

This Nation was founded by men and women who sought these shores that they might enjoy greater freedom and greater opportunity than they had known before. The founders of the United States proclaimed to the world the American belief that all men are created equal, and that governments are instituted to secure the inalienable rights with which all men are endowed.

. . . .

We believe that all men are created equal and that they have the right to equal justice under law.

We believe that all men have the right to freedom of thought and of expression and the right to worship as they please.

We believe that all men are entitled to equal opportunities for jobs, for homes, for good health and for education.

We believe that all men should have a voice in their government and that government should protect, not usurp, the rights of the people.

These are the basic civil rights which are the source and the support of our democracy.

Today, the American people enjoy more freedom and opportunity than ever before. Never in our history has there been better reason to hope for the complete realization of the ideals of liberty and equality.

. . . .

The Federal Government has a clear duty to see that Constitutional guarantees of individual liberties and of equal protection under the laws are not denied or abridged anywhere in our Union. That duty is shared by all three branches of the Government, but it can be fulfilled only if the Congress enacts modern, comprehensive civil rights laws, adequate to the needs of the day, and demonstrating our continuing faith in the free way of life.

---

*U.S. House of Representatives, *Civil Rights Program Message from the President of the United States,* 80th Congress, 2nd Session, (House Doc. 516).

I recommend, therefore, that the Congress enact legislation at this session directed toward the following specific objectives:

1. Establishing a permanent Commission on Civil Rights, a Joint Congressional Committee on Civil Rights, and a Civil Rights Division in the Department of Justice.
2. Strengthening existing civil rights statutes.
3. Providing Federal protection against lynching.
4. Protecting more adequately the right to vote.
5. Establishing a Fair Employment Practice Commission to prevent unfair discrimination in employment.
6. Prohibiting discrimination in interstate transportation facilities.
7. Providing home-rule and suffrage in Presidential elections for the residents of the District of Columbia.
8. Providing Statehood for Hawaii and Alaska and a greater measure of self-government for our island possessions.
9. Equalizing the opportunities for residents of the United States to become naturalized citizens.
10. Settling the evacuation claims of Japanese-Americans.

Strengthening the Government Organization

As a first step, we must strengthen the organization of the Federal Government in order to enforce civil rights legislation more adequately and to watch over the state of our traditional liberties.

I recommend that the Congress establish a permanent Commission on Civil Rights reporting to the President. The Commission should continuously review our civil rights policies and practices, study specific problems, and make recommendations to the President at frequent intervals. It should work with other agencies of the Federal Government, with state and local governments, and with private organizations.

I also suggest that the Congress establish a Joint Congressional Committee on Civil Rights. This Committee should make a continuing study of legislative matters relating to civil rights and should consider means of improving respect for and enforcement of those rights.

. . . .

A specific Federal measure is needed to deal with the crime of lynching—against which I cannot speak too strongly. It is a principle of our democracy, written into our Constitution, that every person accused of an offense against the law shall have a fair, orderly trial in an impartial court. We have made great progress toward this end, but I regret to say that lynching has not yet finally disappeared from our land. So long as one person walks in fear of lynching, we shall not have achieved equal justice under law. I call upon the Congress to take decisive action against this crime.

Protecting the Right to Vote

Under the Constitution, the right of all properly qualified citizens to vote is beyond question. Yet the exercise of this right is still subject to interference. Some individuals are prevented from voting by isolated acts of intimidation. Some whole groups are prevented by outmoded policies prevailing in certain states or communities.

We need stronger statutory protection of the right to vote. I urge the Congress to enact legislation forbidding interference by public officers or private persons with the right of qualified citizens to participate in primary, special and general elections in which Federal officers are to be chosen. This legislation should extend to elections for state as well as Federal officers insofar as interference with the right to vote results from discriminatory action by public officers based on race, color, or other unreasonable classification.

Requirements for the payment of poll taxes also interfere with the right to vote. There are still seven states which, by their constitutions, place this barrier between their citizens and the ballot box. The American people would welcome voluntary action on the part of these states to remove this barrier. Nevertheless, I believe the Congress should enact measures insuring that the right to vote in elections for Federal officers shall not be contingent upon the payment of taxes.

I wish to make it clear that the enactment of the measures I have recommended will in no sense result in Federal conduct of elections. They are designed to give qualified citizens Federal protection of their right to vote. The actual conduct of elections, as always, will remain the responsibility of State governments.

Fair Employment Practice Commission

We in the United States believe that all men are entitled to equality of opportunity. Racial, religious and other invidious forms of discrimination deprive the individual of an equal chance to develop and utilize his talents and to enjoy the rewards of his efforts.

Once more I repeat my request that the Congress enact fair employment practice legislation prohibiting discrimination in employment based on race, color, religion or national origin. The legislation should create a Fair Employment Practice Commission with authority to prevent discrimination by employers and labor unions, trade and professional associations, and government agencies and employment bureaus. The degree of effectiveness which the wartime Fair Employment Practice Committee attained shows that it is possible to equalize job opportunity by government action and thus to eliminate the influence of prejudice in employment.

Interstate Transportation

The channels of interstate commerce should be open to all Americans on a basis of complete equality. The Supreme Court has recently declared unconstitutional state laws requiring segregation on public carriers in interstate travel. Company regulations must not be allowed to replace unconstitutional state laws. I urge the Congress to prohibit discrimination and segregation, in the use of interstate transportation facilities, by both public officers and the employees of private companies.

. . . .

The position of the United States in the world today makes it especially urgent that we adopt these measures to secure for all our people their essential rights.

The peoples of the world are faced with the choice of freedom or enslavement, a choice between a form of government which harnesses the state in the service of the individual and a form of government which chains the individual to the needs of the state.

. . . .

We know that our democracy is not perfect. But we do know that it offers a fuller, freer, happier life to our people than any totalitarian nation has ever offered.

If we wish to inspire the peoples of the world whose freedom is in jeopardy, if we wish to restore hope to those who have already lost their civil liberties, if we wish to fulfill the promise that is ours, we must correct the remaining imperfections in our practice of democracy.

We know the way. We need only the will.

Segregation in Washington:
A Report of the National Committee on Segregation
in the Nation's Capital, November 1948

Kenesaw M. Landis

UNCLE SAM'S EXAMPLE

As I visited your government offices . . . I gradually became aware that Negroes were employed there almost solely in menial capacities, mostly as messengers, or very low clerks, and in a few departments were not to be seen at all.

Visitor from Denmark

In spite of all its principles and all its professions, its executive orders and directives, the United States Government is systematically denying the colored citizens of the capital equal opportunity in employment, and is setting an example of racial discrimination to the city and nation.

Beginnings of Segregation

The color bar has not always been honored by the American government. During the last half of the 19th century, Negroes served as Register of the Treasury, Auditor of the Navy, as Consul, Collector of Customs, and in many other responsible posts at home and abroad.

Colored employees were not segregated in the Federal agencies from the time of the Civil War down through the administration of Theodore Roosevelt. During the last term of Grover Cleveland, when southern Democrats held positions of leadership in both houses of Congress, the number of Negro clerical jobs actually increased.

Jim Crow seems to have been first recognized in the administration of William Howard Taft. Twenty years ago, a Negro leader in Washington recalled:

Mr. Taft . . . segregated the census takers in this city in 1910, restricting white workers to white, and black workers to black, often duplicating work, as most blocks had white and black residents. And worst of all, he announced that Negroes should not hold office where white people complained.*

The Blow Was Struck

But segregation did not become general government policy until the presidency of Woodrow Wilson. His election in 1912 brought to power in Washington a new kind of southern congressmen, politicians who had won office on the pledge to maintain and extend "white supremacy". Immediately they set about putting the Negro "in his place" in the capital.

An organization known as the "Democratic Fair Play Association" was formed for this purpose. Among its leaders were Senators Hoke Smith of Georgia, Ben (Pitchfork) Tillman of South Carolina, and James K. Var-

---

Source: From *Segregation in Washington: A Report of the National Committee on Segregation in the Nation's Capital, November 1948*. Text by Kenesaw M. Landis (Chicago, 1948), pp. 60–74.

*Thomas, N., President of the Washington Chapter of the National Association for the Advancement of Colored People, Washington *Eagle*, June 6, 1927.

SHALL THE NEGRO RULE?

All other questions are minimized under the shadow of social equality and preference for Negroes in the employ of the government of the United States.

SENATOR JAMES K. VARDAMAN

And other prominent speakers will address the people at a public meeting to be held under the auspices of the National Democratic Fair Play Association which stands for segregation of the races in government employment, and "reorganization of the civil service" as declared in the National Democratic platform of 1912. At this meeting the policy of appointing Negroes to government positions will be fully and freely discussed.

AT OLD MASONIC TEMPLE
COR. 9TH AND F STS. N.W.
WASHINGTON, D.C.

Wednesday Night, August 6, 1913

ADMIT BEARER   AT 8 O'CLOCK

---

daman of Mississippi. President Wilson was made an honorary member. Meetings were held to stir up the local populace. For example, the following is a reprint of a handbill circulated at the time.*

Segregation Becomes a Policy

In the Bureau of Engraving, Negro and white employees were isolated from each other at lunch time. Separate lavatories were installed in the Treasury Department. In 1914 the Civil Service Commission adopted a rule requiring all job applicants to submit a photograph, and stopped calling Negroes for the higher clerical jobs. Every Negro clerk (with two exceptions) in the Auditor's office of the Post Office was reduced in rank.

*La Follette's 1913.

Bills were introduced in Congress to segregate Negro employees by law, to re-establish Jim Crow transportation in the District, and even to repeal the 14th and 15th Amendments. These measures did not pass, but they indicate the general nature of the assault of Negro rights.

With the government setting the example for the community, Negroes lost what rights they had previously enjoyed in Washington theaters and restaurants, and were systematically segregated in housing and private employment. During this period the city was growing rapidly.

The resulting racial tensions, aggravated by the dislocations of the first World War, culminated in the Washington race riot of 1919. After three days of bloody fighting, the riot was brought to an end by a drenching and prolonged rain.

The Government's Example

The colored people of Washington have never recovered from the blow that struck them in the time of Woodrow Wilson. Although sporadic anti-discrimination measures have been sponsored by succeeding administrations, the example set by the government has been one of exclusion and segregation in menial jobs.*

As late as 1938, 90 per cent of all the government's Negro employees were confined to the lowest custodial-labor status. During the labor shortage of World War II, real gains were made by Negroes in Federal service, and at one time only 40 per cent of them were in the lowest category. Now, however, the percentage is rising again.

Only in time of emergency, when the government can't help itself, is the Negro given much chance to show what he can do in the service of his country.

Anatomy of Discrimination

The Ramspeck Act of 1940, the Civil Service Regulations, and a series of Presidential Executive Orders all forbid racial discrimination in Federal employment. Yet discrimination prevails in all the departments in varying forms, usually as a matter of accepted practice. There are three general types of situation.

First, there is the exclusion pattern. Under it Negroes are hired only for the menial jobs that whites will not accept. It is typified by the State Department, the Justice Department, the Bureau of the Budget, the Federal Trade Commission, the Federal Reserve Board and various other independent agencies.

Second, there is the segregation pattern. It is typified by the government's "factories" which employ many Negroes but keep them in the lowest routine jobs in separate units. The Census Bureau, the Government Printing Office, and the Bureau of Engraving and Printing belong in this group.

Third, there is the integration pattern—where jobs are open to Negroes at all levels on equal terms. It is extremely rare, and was largely a war-time phenomenon. War agencies like the Office of Price Administration and the National War Labor Board made some approaches to this practice.*

All Federal agencies fall into one or more of these general types of employment practice. The examples which follow are not singled out to focus attention upon specific agencies. They illustrate the conditions which exist throughout the government service.†

In most Washington offices, Negroes are excluded from all but the lowest custodial and clerical jobs. The State Department is one example of the kind of chance Negroes have under this racial policy.

STATE DEPARTMENT—EXAMPLE OF EXCLUSION

The existence of discrimination against minority groups in this country has an adverse effect upon our relations with other countries.

Acting Secretary of State, 1946

A Celebrated Messenger

Until 1940, the State Department refused to hire colored people in Washington except as chauffeurs, messengers, or janitors.‡ One

---

*The government employs more than a third of all workers in the District of Columbia, and sets the pattern of employment practices and wages for the entire capital. In 1940, 16 per cent of the city's colored employees had Federal jobs, and 40 per cent of the white employees.

*This is also true of the Public Housing Administration (formerly Federal Public Housing Authority), a non-war agency.
†All incidents reported are documented in the files of the National Committee.
‡Between 1924 and 1940 no Negro was employed in the Department above the custodial level. The number of Negroes in the professional Foreign Service is less than half as large as it was forty years ago.

Negro who came close to breaking this rule was a celebrated messenger in the Office of the Secretary who retired after sixty years' service.

In his sixty years, this Negro saw many Secretaries come and go. He was relied upon for his knowledge of diplomatic ceremonial and protocol, and was taken to the Paris Peace Conference of 1919. While he remained a messenger in rank, he was rewarded with clerk's pay in his old age.

A Slight Improvement

During World War II, a high official of the Department tried with slight success to break the racial barrier at the clerical level. As the agency mushroomed in size, Negroes were hired in the lowest clerical grades at routine jobs, a few messengers were upgraded, and toward the end of the war a colored expert on colonial affairs, who had proved his high ability in a war agency, was brought in as an Associate Division Chief.

But otherwise there was little improvement. At the close of the war, the Department was required to absorb parts of three major war agencies in which Negroes occupied a variety of responsible posts. On several occasions, however, old-line officials of the Department have intervened to prevent the hiring and promotion of Negroes by these newly-added units.*

Psychology of Exclusion

The State Department is one of the most class-conscious of all the old-line government agencies. Its tone has been set by the career men who staff the basic policy-making offices. The explanation given by many people in the Department is summed up by a ranking officer:

*This experience is common where agencies have been taken over by the permanent departments.

The attitude is not southern reactionary or plain Negro-hating, but rather the conservatism you find on the Main Line or in the Back Bay. These people who dominate the Department are people who come from, or have the attitudes characteristic of, what most people regard as High Society . . . I suppose it's a matter of regarding Negroes without any questioning at all as naturally belonging in the servant sort of role. (Document 302)

This class-consciousness permeates down through the ranks. Even in the lowest-rated jobs, where Negroes have the best chance, there is a strong feeling of caste. A high administrative officer reported his trouble in implementing the war-time anti-discrimination objectives:

The results were simply pitiful. We finally got a few colored girls in the mimeograph room. After a great deal more effort, the typing pool finally agreed to take a couple. Two or three days later, I asked the pool supervisor how things were coming, and she replied that she had solved the problem completely, that everything was going beautifully. I asked her what she had done, and she showed me a screen in one corner of the big room—behind which the two colored girls were sitting. I stopped that immediately. (Document 301)

All government agencies hesitate to hire Negroes in fear of "bad public relations." But the State Department is super-sensitive on this point. Moreover, according to a responsible official, "it has a strong tradition and a natural conservatism brought on by the delicate and difficult work it does."

Fighting Russia's Propaganda

The statement of any operating official that he will not hire Negroes is taken as final. In practice, this means that they are excluded from all the "prestige" divisions of the Department.

In recent years the State Department has become concerned over propaganda that

Russia is spreading about racial discrimination in the United States. Asked whether the Department was embarrassed by this propaganda, one officer thought for a moment, and said:

> Well, you know that we put out a magazine called "America", which we send to Russia for distribution there. In almost every issue, that magazine carries pictures of Negroes and whites doing things together, or "a spread" on some famous Negro like George Washington Carver. On the information side, we are fighting their propaganda. (Document 303)

Bugaboo of White Supremacy

However, there are many State Department officials who believe that more Negroes could be employed to advantage, both in the capital and abroad. One of them recently proposed that colored Americans be used on a Far Eastern program of the agency. He reports:

> I got the answer from people who have spent a good deal of time in that part of the world that Negroes would be a good deal more effective than whites in the actual administration of the program, but that they might have some difficulties inside the staff. It is quite generally true that the bugaboo of white supremacy is a great handicap to us in the Far East. (Document 309a)

One Department officer, when asked how he thought the traditional exclusion policy might be overcome, made the following suggestion:

> I would seek out the soft spots in the agency— the ones that are bad but have special reasons for being good. The first place I'd hit would be the political divisions, and my argument would be that the agency is trying to sell democracy all around the world so it had better start practicing some of it. (Document 309b)

But another experienced officer pointed out the similarity between the practices of the State Department and of many other agencies. He concluded:

> If you fight this thing by starting at the bottom, breaking down one barrier at a time and gradually giving Negroes a chance at better jobs, you don't get far . . . Only the President can do this job. My experience has convinced me completely that the top people, starting with the President himself, must make it perfectly clear to their subordinates all the way down the line that they want every American to share equally in the chances to hold a job at any level. (Document 319)

BUREAU "X"—EXAMPLE OF SEGREGATION

A Case Study of Segregation

Instead of excluding Negroes, some agencies segregate them in separate units under supervisors of their own race. This is the practice in most departments which employ Negroes in large numbers, like Bureau "X".

Prior to 1940, Bureau "X" employed only a few Negroes outside the custodial labor category. But thousands of workers were added during the war, and at the height of the labor shortage almost half the personnel was colored. The decision to segregate the races was justified by the argument that it would reduce racial friction, and give Negroes more chance for advancement.

To determine the result, a detailed case study of the Bureau was made in 1947. Employment records were made available on the understanding that the name of the Bureau would be withheld, and that the information would be used to illustrate a general situation.

Whites on Top

The records show that almost all Negroes were employed in the lower brackets. Only 4

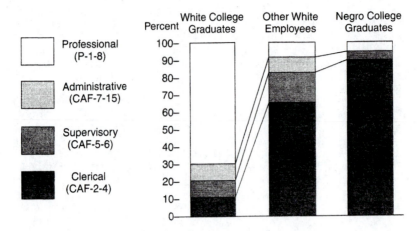

CHART 4   Occupational Distribution of White College Graduate, Other White Employees and Negro College Graduates—Bureau "X," March 22, 1947*

per cent rated higher than clerks, compared to 43 per cent of white employees. Even within the clerical classification, the same pattern appeared. Four-fifths of the lowest-salaried clerks were colored; four-fifths of the highest-salaried clerks were white.

Yet the Bureau attracts many highly trained Negroes who have no opportunity elsewhere. In each of the four major grade groups, the proportion of Negro college graduates was higher than among whites. 12 per cent of the colored clerks and only 3 per cent of the white clerks had college degrees. Nine out of 10 Negro college graduates were employed as clerks. Nine out of 10 white college graduates had better jobs.

Chart 4 shows that white college graduates held better jobs than other white employees, and that the latter held better jobs than Negro college graduates. There was very little difference between the kind of jobs held by highly educated and poorly educated Negroes. Little attempt is made to place Negroes according to their ability and skill.

6 to 1 Odds Against Negroes

To get a closer comparison, a sample grouping was made of forty pairs of white and colored employees who were all hired in the fiscal year 1946, and who matched not only in schooling, but in age, sex, marital status, date hired, division in which hired, job in which hired, and beginning salary. The Bureau considers that all these eight factors have a bearing on work efficiency and chances for promotion.

The records show that the two races had the same average efficiency rating for the beginning months on the job. Three whites in the sample and eight Negroes took and passed in-service training courses—indicating that the colored group had at least as much desire to get ahead. A few more Negroes than whites had the advantage of veterans' status.

*Source of data: Personnel Division, Bureau "X".

But a check in 1947 showed that the forty white employees had received a total of twelve promotions, and the forty colored employees only two promotions. In other words, when background, initial job assignment, and actual work efficiency were roughly equated, whites were promoted six times as frequently as Negroes.*

Negroes Are Held Down

To get the story behind the figures, interviews were conducted at all levels. An Operations Officer told in a few words one reason why it is impossible under a segregated system to promote individuals according to their ability:

> When you have segregation, you make work assignments on a color basis, and the Negro units automatically end up with the simplest operations. This means competent Negroes are held down to these jobs, and the Division does not get the benefit of what they could produce.†

For example, 97 per cent of the Bureau's two hundred card-punch operators (CAF 2) are Negroes. This is low-paying monotonous work, with little future. On the other hand, the great majority of the tabulating machine operators (CAF 3, 4, 5) are white; and all the jobs in the machine division above CAF 4 are held by whites.

An administrative officer explained this situation in terms of the labor market. "The only people we've been able to get," he said, "are Negroes." ‡He agreed that many Negroes hired as card-punch operators are as competent as whites hired at higher levels.

A Ceiling on Promotions

Segregation means that colored people are employed by units in the lowest jobs,

and it imposes an arbitrary ceiling on their individual promotion. This is because any employee who rises above a unit level must usually give orders to both colored and white units. For a colored person to be allowed to have such authority over whites would challenge the segregation principle, which assumes the inferiority of the whole race segregated.

Considerable embarrassment was caused in the Bureau during the war when the sudden expansion of a special project placed a Negro woman supervisor over new white employees. The director of the project wanted the woman kept in charge because she was the only person familiar with the work. But his request was refused, and for two more months she ran the expanded unit without a rating and trained the new white employees, including the incoming white supervisor.

For another six months, she stayed in the background, did all the work-scheduling, kept all the control files, handled all the final reports, and gave advice whenever called upon. Finally, however, she asked to be transferred. "The new supervisor was resenting me," she said, "and the whole situation was quite unpleasant."*

No Competition Allowed

The ceiling affects every colored employee. Whenever there is an office vacancy at a high level, white workers are moved up one notch all along the line. But colored unit supervisors stay where they are, and bottle the ambition of those below.

Instead of producing good racial relations, segregation creates a deep sense of frustration and resentment. In the midst of the war, an altercation between a colored employee of the Bureau and a white employee almost caused a riot in the building.

*Source of data: Personnel Division, Bureau "X".
†Document 16.
‡Documents 3c, 29.

*Document 24.

Most colored employees try to work out philosophies of adjustment, like the unit supervisor who said:

I'm told that I am as high as I can get so I haven't any ambition anymore, and I get used to it. I know it, my boss knows it, and he knows I know it. I'm no radical. I think I understand about these whites, and I make a lot of excuses to my kids for them.*

Yet this same woman expressed regret that segregation was so complete in the Bureau's recreation program. "There isn't even any competition between the white and colored teams," she said. "If they would just have that—it would be something, and you can bet we would put out the best team you ever saw, just to beat them."

O.P.A.—EXAMPLE OF INTEGRATION

A Third Approach

A third approach is possible to the problem of race in employment. This is to hire Negroes like other people on the basis of merit rather than color, and to let them find their place in open competition. Some of the war agencies tried this experiment, and the most successful was the Office of Price Administration.

These war agencies had several things in common. They were new, with no office tradition against Negroes. They were set up in a period of labor shortage, and needed all the qualified help they could get. And the nature of the war itself created a sentiment against master-race doctrines.

At the outset, O.P.A. adopted a firm policy. The anti-discrimination Directives of the President and the Civil Service Commission were declared to be the policy of the agency, and the Administrator warned: "This is not a matter in which the personal views or prejudices of individuals are expected to control."*

No Tradition Against Negroes

An important consideration was O.P.A.'s particular role in the war. The agency was required to deal with problems at the consumer level, and for this reason it attracted an unusually large number of officials who were predisposed to regard Negroes as people, and to deal with them on a man-to-man basis.

Because of the newness of the agency, and the nature of its job, an air of informality prevailed. During the early months of 1942, one of the colored attorneys needed a secretary. A colored girl was certified to him, and he accepted her. Then a white colleague, for whom a white secretary had just been hired, suggested they switch secretaries. This was done, and with no difficulty.

The same spirit of direct action existed at other levels. Early in the life of the agency, union members of both colors walked together into the small cafeteria originally set aside for Negroes so that it became greatly overcrowded. The management thereupon made this cafeteria into an executives' dining-room, leaving the main cafeteria as a place where all office workers could sit as they pleased.

How Negroes Were Accepted

Personnel officials never accepted at face value the refusal of an operating chief to accept Negroes certified to him. But the strategy adopted was one of persuasion and example rather than coercion. Care was taken in filling important vacancies.

---

*Document 23.

*O.P.A. Administrative Order No. 13, Supplement No. 6: Fair Employment Practice, Feb. 16, 1943.

A highly qualified Negro economist was offered to a Division which was desperate to have a long-standing vacancy filled. After some hesitation, the Division accepted him. He made a brilliant record, and a favorable impression on the businessmen who came daily to the office. One of them finally persuaded him to leave O.P.A., and take a high-paying job in private industry.

One O.P.A. official had a job which required him to receive many important visitors, and he protested when a very competent colored girl was certified as his secretary. Although he was a southerner, he insisted he had no personal objection. But he said he was afraid his visitors would object. Finally he agreed to try her out, and to his relief he found no evidence of damaged public relations. Soon he was bragging about his new secretary.

Public objections were fewer than expected. Only two incidents were reported. Once a congressman intervened to secure the transfer of two white constituents who objected to working under a Negro supervisor. Once an O.P.A. District Office in the South protested against the use of a Negro who had been sent there as a field representative for a door-to-door survey.

Union-Management Cooperation

An important factor was the aggressive anti-discrimination policy of the office union. In the winter of 1942–43, the union pressed charges involving racial discrimination against a Branch Chief, and after extended public hearings he was forced to resign. According to the union, this case had a strong influence on all supervisors.

An Administrator can lay down a fair employment policy, and the Personnel Division can implement it, but management doesn't like to bring charges against its own officials. A union, however, is less interested in administrative harmony than in fair working conditions for its members, and for this reason is often in a better position to police discrimination.

At O.P.A., there was a good working relationship between the union and the agency chiefs. Once the union had filed charges, the personnel officer was able to approach the responsible official in a helpful spirit and say: "Look here, I don't know much about this, but the union is raising the devil, and I may be able to help you out."

A Certain Pride Developed

Before long, many grievance cases between white and colored persons were being handled where the question of race was not involved and not even mentioned. As the months passed, the practice of racial equality became a habit and a tradition. A certain pride developed.

A personnel officer stated: "I was as prejudiced as anyone, but that's not the way we do things here." In interview after interview, white employees reported how their own attitudes had changed. Many of them were southerners who had never thought of a Negro "except with a hoe in his hand".

The effect on colored employees was like a tonic. Many said they felt for the first time in their lives like independent, responsible, respected men and women.

Morale Was High

Whatever its faults, O.P.A. came closer than any other government agency to eliminating the problem of race in employment. Out in the open for everyone to see, Negroes worked with whites at all levels from messenger to Assistant General Counsel of the agency.

As in other war agencies, personnel was constantly changing. Yet morale was always high at O.P.A. Even in its death agonies, there was an unmistakable esprit de crops. In the summer of 1946, when for two weeks the agency was without funds of legal authority, employee turnover dropped to the lowest point in months, merely on the basis of an appeal from the Administrator.

What of the Future?

Some exceptions marred O.P.A.'s record of equal opportunity for all, and these exceptions indicate the difficulties ahead for all the agency's colored employees. The exceptions were in the following offices:

1. Two price control divisions, staffed by business-trained executives. These executives handled all their own recruitment and insisted on following the traditional private industry policy of excluding Negroes from white-collar jobs.
2. Another division, whose top personnel came to O.P.A. directly from old-line government agencies. They insisted on following the traditional government policy of segregating Negroes in the lowest jobs.
3. The branch offices of O.P.A. in other cities. They insisted on following the local community custom of excluding Negroes from most good jobs.

The Evil We Fought Against

When the war ended and O.P.A. began to curtail its activities, the prevailing American (or un-American) practice of racial discrimination caused trouble for the agency's outplacement department. In December, 1945, the Administrator reported to the Civil Service Commission that many of the agency's colored employees found it "practically impossible" to secure employment in other government offices. He cited a few examples:

REPORT OF ADMINISTRATOR

Our officer in charge of out-placement . . . found that although the State Department needed several CPC—3 messengers, they must be young, male, white and gentile. In the Weather Bureau, Department of Commerce, he was asked whether the applicants were of light complexion and told that they would not be interested in interviewing any colored applicants. The Naval Research Laboratory indicated that they had no Negro employees and had no facilities for them. The Civil Aeronau-

tics Administration when considering an applicant asked what university she attended. When she replied Howard University, she was informed that they did not anticipate any vacancies for which she might qualify.

This is a matter of serious concern to the Office of Price Administration because of its effect upon morale of our Negro employees . . . They have given the Government their loyal services when it needed them. Both in the armed services and civilian employment, they have contributed their best to win the war. They now feel that to close the doors of economic opportunities to them because of their race, is to succumb to the very evil we all fought against. The merits of their case seem clear.

It is customary to speak of the "Negro problem", and there is such a problem. But there is also a "white problem". To get a complete picture of what segregation means in the Nation's Capital, it may be helpful to see things through the eyes of a colored girl who won an unusual promotion during the war in one of the executive departments of the United States Government. Here is her story in her own words:

A COLORED GIRL'S STORY

In this office, I was the only Negro. You know, all the front offices are white, and people used to walk by our office in the hall, then come back and stare at me in amazement. I was the first Negro they had ever seen in a front office. When my promotion came through, colored girls I had never known would come up to me in the hall and congratulate me, and tell me they were all very happy for me—it must have got around by the grapevine.

At first, of course, I was very green, and I had to ask a lot of questions. Everybody in the office was eager to help me. They were just as nice as they could be about it. But from the day the man from the Civil Service Commission walked in there and talked to me about my promotion, there was tension and they wouldn't help me any more. I had two clerks who worked under me, both of them white.

And I used to have to pet them up—you know, admire their new dresses and talk about their good-looking husbands and so on. They finally realized I was human, too.

I have come to the conclusion that white people are just unbelievably ignorant about Negroes. All the time I was there, the other girls would ask me questions or do things that just seemed silly to me. First, I remember, they wanted to know about my hair. What did I do to it? Did I get a permanent? And so on—and they weren't satisfied until they had touched it. And then they were surprised that is was "so soft".

One girl went to the beach and came back with a nice dark coat of tan. I put my arm beside hers and said: "Now see all the trouble you go through to get your skin the same color as mine?" And one of them piped up "Janet,

can you get sunburned?" I said: "Don't you suppose the sun affects your skin the same as it does mine?" Then, one day a group of us were downtown and we all got weighed. I took a little time on the scale, and one of them said: "Get off that scale, girl, and let me on." And she pulled my arm to get me off. Then she stopped in surprise and said: "Why, your arm is soft!"

After a while, I guess all of us were a little conscious of what was happening. One day when three of us were riding home from work together, one said: "Here's a Catholic, and a Jew, and a Negro, and we like each other. Isn't that terrible!" The questions became less frequent, and we did more things together, and we talked about more ordinary things, the many things we really had in common by then. (Document 21)

Should Negro Colleges Be Perpetuated or Should There Be Integration in Education?

CLARK FOREMAN,

Progressive Party It is hard to see how any one who believes in the American Constitution and democracy as a way of life could possibly stand for the perpetuation of a segregated college system in the South or any other part of this country.

In recent years some notable steps have been taken toward integration in southern colleges. These steps have been uniformly successful with the students. They would never have been undertaken if we had accepted the idea of perpetuating the *status quo*. It is only by understanding that society

is always dynamic, and pressing constantly for a realization of our best principles that we can hope to obtain a free society.

This should, however, not be interpreted as an attack on the Negro colleges which in many cases are doing a competent job against heavy odds. Segregation in education has to be considered as a part of the total picture of segregation. All such arbitrary restrictions to human understanding and association must be fought constantly, but this should not mean that present opportunities for education for Negroes should be destroyed before other opportunities are created.

Organized opposition to segregation must be increased. We must use our strength in the trade unions, at the ballot box and in the courts to see to it that the Constitutional guarantees of justice are put into practice. In that fight we will need the support of as

Source: "Should Negro Colleges Be Perpetuated or Should There Be Integration in Education?" *Harlem Quarterly,* Spring 1950. Copyright 1950 Harlem Quarterly.

many educated Negroes as possible and we should make an effort to prepare them for it in the colleges that now exist. The goal of complete integration on the basis of ability must always be kept before us as the only acceptable American solution.

DR. JOHN HAYNES HOLMES,

Minister Emeritus, Community Church, N. Y. C. I am opposed to segregation wherever it appears, or on whatever line of distinction between blacks and whites.

I feel about colleges in just the same way I feel about churches. We should have no white churches or Negro churches, but just churches, composed of both races, for work and worship together.

Negro colleges have played a great role in history, and have done an heroic service. But has not the time come when, in all our institutions of learning, Negro and white alike, the two races may join hands and hearts in a common pursuit of knowledge?

Now is the time. Let universal brotherhood everywhere prevail.

CHARLES H. HOUSTON,

Legal Counsel, N.A.A.C.P. Last week-end I spent part of the time debating the merits of the United Negro College Fund with a close friend of mine. I supported the Fund; he opposed it.

He is an integrationist, opposed to segregation in any form and makes no compromise. He pointed out the inconsistency of fighting segregation in city hospitals, the armed forces, government services, public accommodations, and strengthening the bonds of segregation in educational institutions.

He argued that the legal efforts to get Southern boys and girls in State universities were dissipated by building up segregated institutions to take the mass pressure off the State universities.

Finally he said that even the reactionary, Southern-infested Army brass had recognized that segregation defeated national ends and was committed to eliminating all segregation in the Army in the next national emergency. He acknowledged we can not eliminate all segregation immediately, but he maintained that this is no reason for voluntarily supporting segregated institutions.

There is no denying his arguments have a punch. Far be it from me to say he is wrong; but in the meantime I still support the United Negro College Fund for the following reasons.

I want integration just as much as he does, but I want to control the terms of integrating. I don't want integration in the sense of merge and disappear.

In my book whoever brings the most attributes and superior qualifications to the market will be able to take the pick of the crop. The world position of colored peoples is improving; politically they are rapidly moving from dependence to independence.

In the United States we are making steady progress both individually and in groups.

Individuals are being integrated today, not at a sacrifice but in recognition of their distinguished personalities and outstanding achievements. But the fact remains that the masses are not integrated; when they are we will no longer be able to speak of them as the masses.

To put integration on a solid basis we must achieve integration for the masses as well as for the favored individuals; and we can not refuse to use any tool which will lift the masses to the point where integration is both possible and desirable.

The individual does not need the colored college in the year 1950, the masses do need it. So I support the United Negro College Fund because it strengthens those colleges which are educating the masses of my people and furnishing them the knowledge and the means by which they themselves will finally blast segregation out of American life.

Finally, I support the United Negro College Fund because ultimately I expect these colleges to improve and survive, not as minority colleges, but as colleges in the over-all plan of American education, with faculty, administration and student body chosen without regard to race.

America can never have too much education, and to my mind these colleges, if they are good enough, will have a place on an entirely integrated basis in the permanent scheme of things.

DR. BENJAMIN E. MAYS,

President, Morehouse College It is not a question of Negro colleges being perpetuated or integration in education. I think any sound-thinking American will agree that all education should be integrated and no colleges should exist primarily for one race. The only question is how best to go about perfecting integration. I do not believe, as some seem to believe, that the way to get it is to destroy every Negro college. To advocate that is to admit that we suffer with a grave inferiority complex. It is tantamount to saying that no Negro college is worth conserving. This would be true of Negro churches, newspapers, insurance companies, banks owned by Negroes, and everything else if we follow that line to its logical conclusion.

Negro colleges should not be abolished to perfect integration any more than the white colleges. As I see it, we should oppose segregation at every point and open Negro colleges to white students and also white colleges to Negro students. In other words integration is not a one way traffic, it is a two way traffic.

DR. FREDERICK D. PATTERSON,

President, Tuskegee Institute A justification for Negro colleges in the South is that with laws against the co-education of the races, they furnish the only opportunity which exists for the masses of Negro youth

to get education above the high school level unless they are sufficiently able to migrate out of the South. It has been shown, of course, that most students attend colleges near their homes because they are unable to do otherwise. For this reason, as long as laws prevent colleges from accepting students on the basis of merit without regard to race, creed, or color, the Negro college must perform a vital and, in fact, indispensable function. I hope the day will come when Negro colleges as such will not be necessary in the sense that they must of necessity enroll only Negro students. I feel, however, that when laws now on the books requiring discrimination in admission no longer exist, that our stronger so-called Negro colleges will continue to be needed as a part of the pattern of higher education for American youth.

Certainly the number of colleges and universities we have are at present inadequate to meet the needs of youth now seeking an education beyond the high school. The President's Commission on Higher Education predicted that enrollment trends would be definitely on the upgrade through 1960, if not beyond. Under these circumstances it is more than apparent that we will need all of the good colleges we can get and the elimination of segregation does not mean the abolition or destruction of the physical plants of colleges which now admit only Negro students. The job before the American people is that of strengthening these institutions so that whether segregated or not, they will give education of comparable quality to that of any other institute and thus hasten the day when education on a segregated basis is no longer required.

W. J. TRENT,

President, Livingstone College, Executive Director, United Negro College Fund, Inc. At the present time there are laws on the statute books of seventeen states requiring separation of educational facilities and services based on race. As a result there are Negro colleges both public and private. Ninety percent of the seventy thousand Negroes who go to college—go to these Negro colleges in the South. It is our belief that it is tremendously important that there be private colleges in the South available to Negro Youth; it would be unfortunate if the entire field of higher education for Negroes were pre-empted by Negro state colleges which have to look to state legislatures for their appropriations.

We believe that Negro colleges, which by law are required to restrict their enrollment to Negro students, ought to be made as strong and efficient as possible for two basic reasons:

1. In order that the young Negro people who attend them can have as fine an educational opportunity as is possible under the circumstances.
2. So that in the future when laws do not separate the races, these colleges can be known as excellent, well administered colleges open to serve all who are qualified.

This last point to me is very important. There are those who see the solution of the problem of segregated education in the South as one which will require the closing up of all Negro colleges and the opening up of all now-white colleges to Negro students. This view to me is extremely dangerous in that there is implicit in it an assumption that just because an institution is manned and operated by Negroes, it is per se inferior. If we accept this view then we are accepting an inferior status for ourselves.

I rather see the solution something like this. Continuous efforts must and will be made to break down the barriers of color in education and other fields. These barriers at present exist in a more rigid form in the South—the section of the country that needs all of the good educational institutions it has—and more. When the barriers are broken. Fisk will enroll white students and Van-

derbilt will enroll Negro students—they both will be interracial. I am certain that there are numerous white students who would welcome an opportunity to study under Ira De A. Reid at Atlanta, or Charles Johnson at Fisk, or to take courses in vocational education at Hampton or Veterinary Science at Tuskegee, etc. Likewise there are a large number of Negro students who would want to take training at Georgia Tech, or Tulane, or the University of North Carolina.

In other words, whether we want to admit it or not, the the quality of work done at a large number of Negro colleges measures up to the quality of work done at white colleges in the South of comparable size and resources. This leaves aside the consideration of the harm done to white boys and girls and Negro boys and girls who by law are not permitted to go to school together. But the harm is in both institutions, not just in Negro institutions.

So we have a choice—either we support these Negro private schools and make them the best ever, or we don't support them and they perish with two results:

1. The higher educational burden will be carried by the state colleges for Negroes with its programs determined pretty largely by state legislatures.
2. And roughly 50 percent of the young people who seek college education will be denied the opportunity to secure one.

I'd rather try to make them as strong and as efficient as possible so that more and better trained Negroes can come along to give a hand in this incessant fight for rights, privileges and responsibilities for Negroes.

A question was raised about whether these colleges would permit their educational facilities to be used to aid in the defense of the "separate but equal" doctrine. I gather that there is some little confusion on this point. It is not the private Negro colleges that are vulnerable on this score — it is the state Negro colleges which must do whatever is required by the legislature in order to provide professional training. But even so, the policy on this must come from the Boards of Trustees of the individual private colleges. They have complete autonomy over the programs of their own institutions. The Fund has no authority to interfere in the policy, operation or administration of the member colleges. We can concern ourselves only with the question of the integrity of the handling of funds and to that end each college files an annual certified audit with us.

I have tried to state what I conceive to be the basic policy of the Fund. I am sure that there are presidents of member colleges of the Fund that are working assiduously in the fight to erase barriers of caste and color. At the recent meeting of the American Association of Colleges in Cincinnati, presidents of three colleges in the Fund led the fight to have the Association adopt a resolution calling for legislation to do away with segregation in higher education.

BY DOXEY A. WILKERSON

Director of Faculty and Curriculum, Jefferson School of Social Science The segregated Negro college should, and must, be abolished. The non-segregated college of predominantly Negro personnel will, and should, continue to develop and flourish for generations to come.

Mandatory school segregation on any level serves the interests of only that small ruling class whose wealth and power rest upon the exploitation of the Negro and white masses of our country. It strenghtens the whole rotten system of Jim Crow oppression, whose sordid effects are seen not only in inferior educational opportunities and other special discriminations against the Negro people, but also in the unduly low living standards and limited political democracy of practically the whole population.

Any requirement that Negroes attend one school and white people another is an abomination which must be destroyed on all educational levels. Those Negro educators whose vested interests lead them to rationalize and defend the segregated school are, thereby, retarding both the liberation of the Negro people from Jim Crow oppression and the building of a secure and democratic society for all Americans.

The ultimate destruction of school segregation will come, of course, only when the people of our country have broken away from domination by the great trusts which are the mainstay of the whole Jim Crow system, when ours is a genuine people's government, truly responsive to the needs and will of the masses of white and Negro Americans. We will yet achieve such a democratic America; and the liberation struggles of the Negro people, linked with those of the progressive working class movement as a whole, will play a decisive role in its attainment.

In this genuinely democratic America, where *all* colleges are open to all who want to attend, there will continue to be an important place for the predominantly Negro college.

The historic forces which have welded Negro Americans together as a distinct people, with strong internal bonds of unity, will continue to operate long after our country has freed itself from the domination of monopoly capitalist rulers. Negroes will, in large measure, continue to develop *as a people*—a free people in a free country—with traditions, culture, problems and organizational forms peculiarly their own. The educational center for this development will continue to be the predominantly Negro (but non-segregated) college.

The coming destruction of the whole system of Jim Crow oppression should carry with it the abolition of scores of second-rate Negro colleges, which will then have no *raison d'etre*. On the other hand, many vital and important centers of Negro higher education—such as Fisk, Howard, Atlanta and others—will only then enter upon their most flourishing period of development.

A Portrait of Carter G. Woodson

W. E. B. Du Bois

Carter Godwin Woodson, who died in Washington on April 3 at the age of seventy-one, illustrates what race prejudice can do to a human soul and also what it is powerless to prevent. Of course, race prejudice is only one particular form of the oppression which human beings have used toward each other throughout the ages. Oppression cramps thought and development, individuality and freedom. Woodson was naturally a big strong man with a good mind; not brilliant, not a genius, but steady, sound and logical in his thinking processes, and capable of great application and concentration in his work. He was a man of normal appetites, who despite extraordinary circumstances carved out a good valuable career. As it happened, he did not have the chance for normal development; he spent his childhood working in a mine and did not get education enough to enter high school until he was twenty; he never married, and one could say almost that he never played; he could laugh and joke on occasion but those occasions did not often arise.

I knew him for forty years and more, and have often wondered what he did for recreation, if anything. He had very little outdoor life, he had few close friends. He cared nothing for baseball or football and did not play cards, smoke or drink. In later years his only indulgence was over-eating so that after fifty he was considerably overweight.

All this arose, in the first place, because like most people on earth he was born poor. But his poverty was the special case of being one of nine children of poor American Ne-

groes who had been born slaves. This meant that from the beginning he was handicapped; it was difficult for him to go regularly to the very poor country school in his neighborhood, and for six years during his youth, when he ought to have been in school, he was working in a coal mine; so that he was grown before he entered high school in Huntington, West Virginia. Once started, however, he went to college at Berca, Kentucky, then to the University of Chicago. He alternated with public school teaching, travel and study in Europe and finally taught ten years, from 1908 to 1918, in the public schools of Washington, D. C.

In 1912, Woodson took his doctorate of philosophy at Harvard in history. It is quite possible that had he been a white man he might have entered a university career, as instructor and eventually as a professor with small but adequate salary; enough for marriage, home and children. But of course, at the time he got his doctorate, there was not the slightest thought that a black man could ever be on the faculty of Harvard or of any other great school. In Washington, he got his main experience of regular teaching work. It was hard and not inspiring. The "Jim-crow" school system of the District of Columbia is perhaps the best of its kind in the United States; but it had the shortcomings of all segregated schools, with special arrangements and peculiar difficulties; they are not the kind of schools which would inspire most men to further study or to an academic career.

After that experience Woodson turned to college work. He served as dean for a year at Howard University and for four years at West Virginia College. He might have ended his career in this way as president of a small Southern colored college. His duties would have been collecting funds and superintending discipline among teachers and students;

Source: W. E. B. Du Bois, "A Portrait of Carter G. Woodson." *Masses & Mainstream,* Vol. 3, June 1950, pp. 19–25. Copyright 1950 W. E. B. Du Bois. Used by permission of David Graham Du Bois.

or if it had been in a state school, he would have cajoled and played up to a set of half-educated Southern whites as trustees, so as to get for Negroes a third or a half of the funds they were legally entitled to. It would have been the kind of executive job which has killed many a man, white and black, either physically or mentally or both; and it was the sort of thing that Woodson was determined not to do.

He had by this time made up his mind that he was going to devote himself to the history of the Negro people as a permanent career. In doing that he knew the difficulties which he would have to face. Study and publication, if at all successful, call for money, and money for any scientific effort for or by a Negro means abject begging; and at begging Woodson was not adept.

It was a time, moreover, when all Negro education was largely charity, not only college education, but elementary and high school training. Groups of Negro and white teachers in Southern schools made regular pilgrimages to the North to collect money from churches and philanthropists in order to support their schools. But the job which Woodson had carved out for himself was not a school; it was a matter of a periodical, with research and publication, and it was to be done in a field not only unpopular but practically unrecognized. Most people, even historians, would have doubted if there was enough of distinctly Negro history in America to call for publication. For thirteen years at Atlanta University we had tried to raise money for research and publication of studies in Negro sociology; five thousand a year, outside my salary. We had to give up the attempt in 1910. But one thing that Woodson's career had done for him was to make him stubborn and single-minded. He had no ties, family or social; he had chosen this life work and he never wavered from it after 1922.

His efforts at raising money for the work had some initial success; for ten years or more Julius Rosenwald, the Jewish philanthropist of Chicago, gave him $400 a year. Woodson organized the Association for the Study of Negro Life and History and already as early as January, 1916, while still teaching, he began publication of *The Journal of Negro History*, a quarterly which is now in its thirty-fourth year of continuous publication.

The Journal was an excellent piece of work and received commendation from high sources. The Carnegie Foundation and afterwards the Spelman Memorial Fund of the Rockefellers gave him $50,000 in installments of $5,000 a year beginning in 1921. But Woodson did not prove the ideal recipient of philanthropy.

He was not a follower of the school of Booker T. Washington and had neither the humility nor the finesse of social uplifters. His independence of thought and action was exaggerated; he went out to meet opposition before it arose, and he was fiercely determined to be master of his own enterprises and final judge of what he wanted to do and say. He pretty soon got the reputation of not being the kind of "trustworthy" Negro to whom help should be given. It was not for a moment intimated that the philanthropists wanted to curb his work or guide it, but if Woodson had anticipated their wishes and conformed to their attitudes, money would have poured in. Only those persons who followed the Washington philosophy and whose attitude toward the South was in accord with the new orientation of the North, could be sure to have encouragement and continued help. After a while it became the settled policy of philanthropic foundations and of academic circles to intimate that Carter Woodson was altogether too self-centered and self-assertive to receive any great encouragement. His work was individual with no guarantee of permanence.

There was just enough truth in this accusation to make the criticism stick. Even his colored friends and admirers encountered refusal to co-operate or take counsel. Twice, alarmed because of his meager income, and his overwork, I ventured to propose alliance and help; I offered to incorporate *The Journal* into the Department of Publications and Research of the N.A.A.C.P., with promise of as much autonomy as was allowed me. He considered, but refused, unless an entirely separate department was set up for him. This the Board refused to consider as I knew it would. Then I suggested incorporation of his work into that of Howard University; but after trial, this also fell through, and his friends concluded that he must be left to carry on his great work without interference in any way from others. Several times he took in assistants and helpers, but never gave them authority or permanent tenure. He was always the lone pioneer and remained this until his death.

It was this very attitude, however, that brought out the iron in Woodson's soul. He was forty-four in 1922 when he began this independent career. He therefore gradually buckled up his belt, gave up most of the things which a man of his age would be looking forward to and put the whole of his energy into his work. As I have said, he never married, he never had a home; he lived in lodgings as a boarder, or ate in restaurants; he schooled himself to small and uncertain income; it is probable that he lived many years on not more than $1000 and probably never as much as $5000.

Deliberately he cut down his wants and that was not difficult in Washington. Washington had no theatre for Negroes; its music was limited; there were art galleries, but they were not particularly attractive until recent years and never catered to black folk. In many cases they refused to exhibit the work of Negro artists. Parks and public recreation had many restrictions; there was little chance at club life or opportunity to meet men of standing, either American or passing foreigners. Woodson did not have enough money to spend much time in New York or abroad. He therefore concentrated his time, his energy, and his little money in building up his enterprise, and especially in organizing a constituency among American Negroes to support his work. That was the most astonishing result of his career.

From subscriptions to his quarterly, from donations made by small groups and organizations, from sale of books, he not only continued to publish his magazine, but he also went into the publishing business and issued a score of books written by himself and by others; and then as the crowning achievement, he established Negro History Week. He literally made this country, which has only the slightest respect for people of color, recognize and celebrate each year, a week in which it studied the effect which the American Negro has upon life, thought and action in the United States. I know of no one man who in a lifetime has, unaided, built up such a national celebration.

Every year in practically every state of the United States, Negro History Week is celebrated; and its celebration was almost forced upon school authorities, on churches and other organizations by the influence of the groups of people who had banded themselves together to help Carter Woodson's Association of Negro Life and History. His chief work, *The Negro in Our History*, went through eight editions, with its nearly eight hundred pages and wealth of illustration, and was used in the Negro public schools of the nation. More lately his monthly *Bulletin* of news had wide circulation and use.

It is a unique and marvelous monument which Carter Woodson has thus left to the people of the United States. But in this and in all his life, he was, and had to be, a cramped soul. There was in him no geniality and very little humor. To him life was hard and cynically logical; his writing was mechanical and unemotional. He never had the opportunity to develop warm sympathy with other human beings; and he did develop a deep-seated dislike, if not hatred, for the white people of the United States and of the world. He never believed in their generosity or good faith. He did not attack them; he did not complain about them, he simply ignored them so far as possible and went on with his work without expecting help or sympathetic cooperation from them.

He did not usually attend meetings of scientists in history; he was not often asked to read papers on such occasions; for the most part so far as the professors in history of this country were concerned he was forgotten and passed over; and yet few men have made so deep an imprint as Carter Woodson on thousands of scholars in historical study and research.

In his death he does not leave many very warm friends; there were few tears shed at his grave. But on the other hand, among American Negroes, and among those whites who knew about his work, and among those who in after years must learn about it, there will be vast respect and thankfulness for the life of this man. He was one who under the hardest conditions of environment kept himself to one great goal, worked at it stubbornly and with unwavering application and died knowing that he had accomplished much if not all that he had planned.

He left unfinished an *Encyclopedia Africana*; it was an idea which I had toyed with in 1909, securing as collaborators Sir Harry Johnston, Flinders-Petrie, Guiseppi Sergi, Albert Hart and Franz Boas. But my project never got beyond the name stage and was forgotten. Later Woodson took up the idea as a by-product of his *Journal*; but few knew of his project at the time. Finally in 1931, the Phelps-Stokes Fund projected an *Encyclopedia of the Negro*, but invited neither Woodson nor me to participate.

However, the group called together, including Moton of Tuskegee and Hope of Atlanta, protested and finally we were both invited. I attended the subsequent meetings but Woodson refused. I and many others talked to him and begged him to come in; but no; there were two reasons: this was, he considered, a white enterprise forced on Negroes; and secondly, he had himself already collected enough data eventually to make an encyclopedia. We demurred, not because we were unwilling to have him work on the encyclopedia; indeed we were eager; but because we knew that one man and especially one man with a rather narrow outlook which had been forced upon him, could not write a scientific encyclopedia of sufficient

breadth to satisfy the world. Eventually this Phelps-Stokes project was unable to collect sufficient funds chiefly, I am sure, because I had been named Editor-in-Chief. So this project closed its effort with the publication of only one thin preliminary volume. But Woodson left the kernel of a great work. It would be a magnificent monument to his memory, if this were to be made the basis of broad rewriting and extension and published as a memorial to his life work.

As a historian, Woodson left something to be desired. He was indefatigable in research: for instance, his collection of photographs of Negroes and abolitionists is invaluable; his *Negro in American History* deserved the wide use which it has had. Some of his works like his *Education of the Negro prior to 1861, A Century of Negro Migration, Negro Orators and their Orations, Free Negro Owners of Slaves in the United States in 1830, Free Negro Heads of Families in the United States, The Mind of the Negro as Reflected in Letters Written During the Crisis, 1800–60*, are solid works of historical research. Others of his books were not of so great value.

Indeed his service to history was not so much his books as his editorship of the *Journal*, which brought into print some of the best scholars in this branch of history. On the other hand, Woodson himself lacked background for broad historical writing; he was almost contemptuous of emotion; he had limited human contacts and sympathies; he had no conception of the place of woman in creation. His book reviews were often pedantic and opinionated. Much of his otherwise excellent research will have to be reinterpreted by scholars of wider reading and better understanding of the social sciences, especially in economics and psychology; for Woodson never read Karl Marx.

The passing of Carter Woodson leaves a vacuum hard to fill. His memory leaves a lesson of determination and sacrifice which all men, young and old, black and white, may emulate to the glory of man and the uplift of his world.

The Legacy of Mary McLeod Bethune

Mary McLeod Bethune

Sometimes as I sit communing in my study I feel that death is not far off. I am aware that it will overtake me before the greatest of my dreams—full equality for the Negro in our time—is realized. Yet I face that reality without tears or regrets. I am resigned to death as all humans must be at the proper time. Death neither alarms nor frightens one who has had a long career of fruitful toil. The knowledge that my work has been helpful to many fills me with joy and great satisfaction.

Since my retirement from an active role in educational work and from the affairs of the National Council of Negro Women, I have been living quietly and working at my desk at my home here in Florida. The years have directed a change of pace for me. I am now 78 years old and my activities are no longer so strenuous as they once were. I feel that I must conserve my strength to finish the work at hand.

Already I have begun working on my autobiography which will record my life-journey in detail, together with the innumerable side trips which have carried me abroad, into every corner of our country, into homes both lowly and luxurious, and even into the White House to confer with Presidents. I have also deeded my home and its contents to the Mary McLeod Bethune Foundation, organized in March, 1953, for research, interracial activity and the sponsorship of wider educational opportunities. . . .

Sometimes I ask myself if I have any other legacy to leave. Truly, my worldly possessions are few. Yet, my experiences have been rich. From them, I have distilled principles and policies in which I believe firmly, for they represent the meaning of my life's work. They are the product of much sweat and sorrow. Perhaps in them there is something of value. So, as my life draws to a close, I will pass them on to Negroes everywhere in the hope that an old woman's philosophy may give them inspiration. Here, then, is my legacy.

I leave you love. Love builds. It is positive and helpful. It is more beneficial than hate. Injuries quickly forgotten quickly pass away. Personally and racially, our enemies must be forgiven. Our aim must be to create a world of fellowship and justice where no man's skin, color or religion, is held against him. "Love thy neighbor" is a precept which could transform the world if it were universally practiced. It connotes brotherhood and, to me, brotherhood of man is the noblest concept in all human relations. Loving your neighbor means being interracial, interreligious and international.

I leave you hope. The Negro's growth will be great in the years to come. Yesterday, our ancestors endured the degradation of slavery, yet they retained their dignity. Today, we direct our economic and political strength toward winning a more abundant and secure life. Tomorrow, a new Negro, unhindered by race taboos and shackles, will benefit from more than 330 years of ceaseless striving and struggle. Theirs will be a better world. This I believe with all my heart.

I leave you the challenge of developing confidence in one another. As long as Negroes are hemmed into racial blocs by prejudice and pressure, it will be necessary for them to band together for economic betterment. Negro banks, insurance companies and other businesses are examples of successful, racial economic enterprises. These institutions were made possible by vision and mutual aid. Confidence was vital in getting them started and keeping them going. Negroes have got to demonstrate still more confidence in each other in business. This kind of confidence will aid the economic rise of the race by bringing together the pennies and dollars of our people and ploughing them into useful channels. Economic separatism cannot be tolerated in this enlightened age, and it is not practicable. We must spread out as far and as fast as we can, but we must also help each other as we go.

I leave you a thirst for education. Knowledge is the prime need of the hour. More and more, Negroes are taking full advantage of hard-won opportunities for learning, and the educational level of the Negro population is at its highest point in history. We are making greater use of the privileges inherent in living in a democracy. If we continue in this trend, we will be able to rear increasing numbers of strong, purposeful men and women, equipped with vision, mental clarity, health and education.

I leave you a respect for the uses of power. We live in a world which respects power above all things. Power, intelligently directed, can lead to more freedom. Unwisely directed, it can be a dreadful, destructive force. During my lifetime I have seen the power of the Negro grow enormously: it has always been my first concern that this power should be placed on the side of human justice.

Now that the barriers are crumbling everywhere, the Negro in America must be ever vigilant lest his forces be marshaled behind wrong causes and undemocratic movements. He must not lend his support to any group that seeks to subvert democracy. That is why we must select leaders who are wise, courageous, and of great moral stature and ability. We have great leaders among us

today: Ralph Bunche, Chaining Tobias, Mordecai Johnson, Walter White, and Mary Church Terrell. (The latter two are now deceased.) We have had other great men and women in the past: Frederick Douglass, Booker T. Washington, Harriet Tubman, Sojourner Truth. We must produce more qualified people like them, who will work not for themselves, but for others.

I leave you faith. Faith is the first factor in a life devoted to service. Without faith, nothing is possible. With it, nothing is impossible. Faith in God is the greatest power, but great, too, is faith in oneself. In 50 years the faith of the American Negro in himself has grown immensely and is still increasing. The measure of our progress as a race is in precise relation to the depth of the faith in our people held by our leaders. Frederick Douglass, genius though he was, was spurred by a deep conviction that his people would heed his counsel and follow him to freedom. Our greatest Negro figures have been imbued with faith. Our forefathers struggled for liberty in conditions far more onerous than those we now face, but they never lost the faith. Their perseverance paid rich dividends. We must never forget their sufferings and their sacrifices, for they were the foundations of the progress of our people.

I leave you racial dignity. I want Negroes to maintain their human dignity at all costs. We, as Negroes, must recognize that we are the custodians as well as the heirs of a great civilization. We have given something to the world as a race and for this we are proud and fully conscious of our place in the total picture of mankind's development. We must learn also to share and mix with all men. We must make an effort to be less race conscious and more conscious of individual and human values. I have never been sensitive about my complexion. My color has never destroyed my self respect nor has it ever caused me to conduct myself in such a manner as to merit the disrespect of any person. I have not let my color handicap me. Despite many crushing burdens and handicaps, I have risen from the cotton fields of South Carolina to found a college, administer it during its years of growth, become a public servant in the government of our country and a leader of women. I would not exchange my color for all the wealth in the world, for had I been born white I might not have been able to do all that I have done or yet hope to do.

I leave you a desire to live harmoniously with your fellow men. The problem of color is world-wide. It is found in Africa and Asia, Europe and South America. I appeal to American Negroes—North, South, East and West—to recognize their common problems and unite to solve them.

I pray that we will learn to live harmoniously with the white race. So often, our difficulties have made us hyper-sensitive and truculent. I want to see my people conduct themselves naturally in all relationships—fully conscious of their manly responsibilities and deeply aware of their heritage. I want them to learn to understand whites and influence them for good, for it is advisable and sensible for us to do so. We are a minority of 15 million living side by side with a white majority. We must learn to deal with these people positively and on an individual basis.

I leave you finally a responsibility to our young people. The world around us really belongs to youth for youth will take over its future management. Our children must never lose their zeal for building a better world. They must not be discouraged from aspiring toward greatness, for they are to be the leaders of tomorrow. Nor must they forget that the masses of our people are still underprivileged, ill-housed, impoverished and victimized by discrimination. We have a powerful potential in our youth, and we must have the courage to change old ideas and practices so that we may direct their power toward good ends.

Faith, courage, brotherhood, dignity, ambition, responsibility—these are needed today as never before. We must cultivate them and use them as tools for our task of completing the establishment of equality for the Negro. We must sharpen these tools in the struggle that faces us and find new ways of using them. The Freedom Gates are half ajar. We must pry them fully open.

If I have a legacy to leave my people, it is my philosophy of living and serving. As I face tomorrow, I am content, for I think I have spent my life well. I pray now that my philosophy may be helpful to those who share my vision of a world of Peace, Progress, Brotherhood and Love.

SUGGESTED READINGS

Jervis Anderson, *A. Philip Randolph: A Biographical Portrait* (New York, 1973)

Dominick J. Capeci, Jr., *The Harlem Riot of 1943* (Philadelphia, 1977)

Dominick J. Capeci, Jr., *Layered Violence: The Detroit Rioters of 1943* (Jackson, Miss., 1991)

Dan T. Carter, *Scottsboro: A Tragedy of the American South* (Baton Rouge, La., 1969)

Melinda Chateauvert, *Marching Together: Women in the Brotherhood of Sleeping Car Porters* (Urbana, Ill., 1998)

Lizabeth Cohen, *Making a New Deal: Industrial Workers in Chicago, 1919–1939* (Cambridge, England 1990)

Elizabeth Clark-Lewis, *Living in Living Out: African American Domestics in Washington D.C., 1910–1940* (Washington, D.C., 1994)

Richard M. Dalfiume, *Desegregation of the U.S. Armed Forces: Fighting on Two Fronts, 1939–1953* (Columbia, Mo., 1969)

Cheryl Lynn Greenberg, *"Or Does It Explode?": Black Harlem in the Great Depression* (New York, 1991)

William Hamilton Harris, *Keeping the Faith: A. Philip Randolph, Milton P. Webster, and the Brotherhood of Sleeping Car Porters, 1925–37* (Urbana, Ill., 1977)

Arnold Hirsch, *Making the Second Ghetto: Race and Housing in Chicago, 1940–1960* (Cambridge, England, 1983)

Robin D. G. Kelley, *Hammer and Hoe: Alabama Communists During the Great Depression* (Chapel Hill, N.C., 1990)

August Meier and Elliot Rudwick, *Black Detroit and the Rise of the UAW* (New York, 1979)

Mark Naison, *Communists in Harlem During the Depression* (Urbana, Ill., 1983)

Bruce Nelson, *Divided We Stand: American Workers and the Struggle for Black Equality* (Princeton, N.J. 2001)

Brenda Gayle Plummer, *Rising Wind: Black Americans and U.S. Foreign Affairs, 1935–1960* (Chapel Hill, N.C., 1996)

Linda Reed, *Simple Decency and Common Sense: The Southern Conference Movement, 1938–1963* (Bloomington, Ind. 1991)

Merl Elwyn Reed, *Seedtime for the Modern Civil Rights Movement: The President's Committee on Fair Employment Practice, 1941–1946* (Baton Rouge, 1991)

William R. Scott, *The Sons of Sheba's Race: African Americans and the Italo-Ethiopian War, 1935–1941* (Bloomington, Ind. 1993)

Harvard Sitkoff, *A New Deal for Blacks: The Emergence of Civil Rights as a National Issue* (New York, 1978)

Patricia Sullivan, *Days of Hope: Race and Democracy in the New Deal Era* (Chapel Hill, N.C., 1996)

Nancy Joan Weiss, *Farewell to the Party of Lincoln: Black Politics in the Age of FDR* (Princeton, N.J., 1983)

Raymond Wolters, *Negroes and the Great Depression: The Problem of Economic Recovery* (Westport, Conn. 1970)

Rosa Parks quietly sits in front of a white man in the front seat of a bus in Montgomery, Alabama, 1955. (*Source:* Corbis-Bettman.)

Chapter 10

Eyes on the Prize

At the close of the Second World War, a number of factors combined to give an impetus to the black struggle for full equality and fight against segregation: the gradual shift in white public opinion, the defeat of fascism that discredited racism, and the effect of the national liberation movements in Asia and Africa. With the onset of the Cold War, the Soviet Union capitalized on the vulnerability of the United States regarding the status of African Americans. The most significant ingredient was the heightened initiative taken by African Americans on their own behalf. White resistance to the legal battles fought and won by the NAACP in the 1940s and 1950s against segregation sparked a decade of mass demonstrations and other forms of nonviolent, direct action by civil rights activists.

The first document contains excerpts from the Supreme Court decision in the famous Brown vs. Board of Education (1954), which declared school segregation unconstitutional and effectively overturned Plessy vs. Ferguson. Segments of the black community, with support from some sympathetic whites, began to try to secure the realization of equality promised by the growing body of Supreme Court decisions and the Civil Rights Acts of 1957 and 1960. In fact, the Congress of Racial Equality had sit-ins and freedom rides challenging segregation as early as the 1940s. However, it was only with the Montgomery bus boycott of 1955–56, which thrust Reverend Martin Luther King, Jr. into national prominence, that the modern Civil Rights movement took off. In 1957, King founded the Southern Christian Leadership Conference (SCLC). The "Negro Revolt" began in earnest when on February 1, 1960, in Greensboro four black students from the North Carolina A & T College refused to leave a Woolworth lunch counter until they were served. In April 1960, representatives of student action groups conducting sit-ins all over the south met in Raleigh, North Carolina, and formed the Student Nonviolent Coordinating Committee (SNCC). In 1961, CORE conducted Freedom Rides challenging segregation in buses. They filled the jails and secured an ICC ruling requiring integration of all interstate buses and terminals. Documents on sit-ins, the founding of SNCC, and the role of women in SNCC are included in this chapter. King conducted a series of nonviolent, direct action campaigns whose high points included the Birmingham demonstrations, the March on Washington in 1963, and the March from Selma to Montgomery, Alabama, in 1965. Black activism in the early 1960s secured the Civil Rights Act of 1964, outlawing segregation, and the Voting Rights Act of 1965, which guaranteed southern blacks' right to vote. The document on the Montgomery movement illustrates King's philosophy and tactics.

In the north, de facto segregation and discrimination in housing, schools, and trade unions were more difficult to tackle. The complexity of the issues involved in combating institutionalized racism can be seen in the King-led "Program of the Chicago Freedom Movement." In the urban ghettoes, Malcolm X, the charismatic Nation of Islam minister, gained a significant following among the youth. The selections from Malcolm X's speeches and writings illustrate his views as a Muslim minister and the subsequent changes in his beliefs after his expulsion from the Nation of Islam and his trip to Mecca. The uprisings in Harlem (1964), Watts (1965), Detroit, Newark, and Chicago (1966–67) radicalized the Civil Rights movement and marked the rise of the black power and black nationalist phase of the movement. In 1967, President Johnson appointed the National Advisory Commission on Civil Disorders headed by Governor Otto Kerner to investigate the riots. The Commission issued the famous Kerner report that blamed white racism for the conditions that led to the riots and suggested some useful social changes that were mostly ignored. However, in most large cities, recommendations for more effective techniques of riot control have been implemented. The speech by Stokely Carmichael, one of the leading advocates of Black Power, illustrates the growing disillusionment of SNCC activists with the strategy of nonviolence and their response to the urban rebellions. Typical of the growing militancy was the formation of groups such as the Black Panther Party founded in 1966 in Oakland, California, by Huey Newton and Bobby Seale. Local law-enforcement officials subjected the Panthers to constant harassment. Included below is the testimony of a Chicago police officer. The article by Roland Snellings and Archie Shepp's interview indicate the impact of the changing political climate on two forms (Jazz and Rhythm and Blues) of African American culture. The final document is an example of the influence of black student militancy on the academy that led to the rise of black studies.

Brown v. Board of Education of Topeka

OPINION ON SEGREGATION LAWS

No. 1. Appeal from the United States District Court for the District of Kansas.*

Mr. Chief Justice Warren delivered the opinion of the Court.

These cases come to us from the States of Kansas, South Carolina, Virginia, and Delaware. They are premised on different facts and different local conditions, but a common legal question justifies their consideration together in this consolidated opinion.

In each of the cases, minors of the Negro race, through their legal representatives, seek the aid of the courts in obtaining admission to the public schools of their community on a non-segregated basis. In each

---

Source: Brown v. *Board of Education of Topeka.* Supreme Court of the United States, 347 U.S. 483 (1954).

*Together with No. 2, *Briggs et al.* v. *Elliott et al.,* on appeal from the United States District Court for the Eastern District of South Carolina, argued December 9–10, 1952, reargued December 7–8, 1953; No. 4, *Davis et al.* v. *County School Board of* *Prince Edward County, Virginia, et al.,* on appeal from the United States District Court for the Eastern District of Virginia, argued December 10, 1952, reargued December 7–8, 1953; and No. 10, *Gebhart et al.* v. *Belton et al.,* on certiorari to the Supreme Court of Delaware, argued December 11, 1952, reargued December 9, 1953.

instance, they have been denied admission to schools attended by white children under laws requiring or permitting segregation according to race. This segregation was alleged to deprive the plaintiffs of the equal protection of the laws under the Fourteenth Amendment. In each of the cases other than the Delaware case, a three-judge federal district court denied relief to the plaintiffs on the so-called "separate but equal" doctrine announced by this Court in *Plessy* v. *Ferguson*, 163 U.S. 537. . . . Under that doctrine, equality of treatment is accorded when the races are provided substantially equal facilities, even though these facilities be separate. In the Delaware case, the Supreme Court of Delaware adhered to that doctrine, but ordered that the plaintiffs be admitted to the white schools because of their superiority to the Negro schools.

The plaintiffs contend that segregated public schools are not "equal" and cannot be made "equal," and that hence they are deprived of the equal protection of the laws. Because of the obvious importance of the question presented, the Court took jurisdiction. Argument was heard in the 1952 Term, and reargument was heard this Term on certain questions propounded by the Court.

Reargument was largely devoted to the circumstances surrounding the adoption of the Fourteenth Amendment in 1868. It covered exhaustively consideration of the Amendment in Congress, ratification by the states, then existing practices in racial segregation, and the views of proponents and opponents of the Amendment. This discussion and our own investigation convince us that, although these sources cast some light, it is not enough to resolve the problem with which we are faced. At best, they are inconclusive. The most avid proponents of the post-War Amendments undoubtedly intended them to remove all legal distinctions among "all persons born or naturalized in the United States." Their opponents, just as certainly, were antagonistic to both the letter and the spirit of the Amendments and wished them to have the most limited effect. What others in Congress and the

state legislatures had in mind cannot be determined with any degree of certainty.

An additional reason for the inconclusive nature of the Amendment's history, with respect to segregated schools, is the status of public education at that time. In the South, the movement toward free common schools, supported by general taxation, had not yet taken hold. Education of white children was largely in the hands of private groups. Education of Negroes was almost nonexistent, and practically all of the race were illiterate. In fact, any education of Negroes was forbidden by law in some states. Today, in contrast, many Negroes have achieved outstanding success in the arts and sciences as well as in the business and professional world. It is true that public school education at the time of the Amendment had advanced further in the North, but the effect of the Amendment on Northern States was generally ignored in the congressional debates. Even in the North, the conditions of public education did not approximate those existing today. The curriculum was usually rudimentary; ungraded schools were common in rural areas; the school term was but three months a year in many states; and compulsory school attendance was virtually unknown. As a consequence, it is not surprising that there should be so little in the history of the Fourteenth Amendment relating to its intended effect on public education.

In the first cases in this Court construing the Fourteenth Amendment, decided shortly after its adoption, the Court interpreted it as proscribing all state-imposed discriminations against the Negro race. The doctrine of "separate but equal" did not make its appearance in this Court until 1896 in the case of *Plessy* v. *Ferguson, supra,* involving not education but transportation. American courts have since labored with the doctrine for over half a century. In this Court, there have been six cases involving the "separate but equal" doctrine in the field of public education. In *Cumming* v. *County Board of Education,* 175 U.S. 528, and *Gong Lum* v. *Rice,* 275 U.S. 78, the validity of the doctrine itself was not challenged. In more recent cases, all on the graduate school level, inequality was found in that specific benefits enjoyed by white students were denied to Negro students of the same educational qualifications. *Missouri ex rel. Gaines* v. *Canada*, 305 U.S. 337; *Sipuel* v. *Oklahoma*, 332 U.S. 631; *Sweatt* v. *Painter*, 339 U.S. 629; *McLaurin* v. *Oklahoma State Regents*, 339 U.S. 637. In none of these cases was it necessary to re-examine the doctrine to grant relief to the Negro plaintiff. And in *Sweatt* v. *Painter*, *supra*, the Court expressly reserved decision on the question whether *Plessy* v. *Ferguson* should be held inapplicable to public education.

In the instant cases, that question is directly presented. Here, unlike *Sweatt* v. *Painter*, there are findings below that the Negro and white schools involved have been equalized, or are being equalized, with respect to buildings, curricula, qualifications and salaries of teachers, and other "tangible" factors. Our decision, therefore, cannot turn on merely a comparison of these tangible factors in the Negro and white schools involved in each of the cases. We must look instead to the effect of segregation itself on public education.

In approaching this problem, we cannot turn the clock back to 1868 when the Amendment was adopted, or even to 1896 when *Plessy* v. *Ferguson* was written. We must consider public education in the light of its full development and its present place in American life throughout the Nation. Only in this way can it be determined if segregation in public schools deprives these plaintiffs of the equal protection of the laws.

Today, education is perhaps the most important function of state and local governments. Compulsory school attendance laws and the great expenditures for education both demonstrate our recognition of the importance of education to our democratic society. It is required in the performance of our most basic public responsibilities, even service in the armed forces. It is the very foundation of good citizenship. Today it is a principal instrument in awakening the child to cultural values, in preparing him for later professional training, and in helping him to adjust normally to his environment. In these days, it is doubtful that any child may reasonably be expected to succeed in life if he is denied the opportunity of an education. Such an opportunity, where the state has undertaken to provide it, is a right which must be made available to all on equal terms.

We come then to the question presented: Does segregation of children in public schools solely on the basis of race, even though the physical facilities and other "tangible" factors may be equal, deprive the children of the minority group of equal education opportunities? We believe that it does.

In *Sweatt* v. *Painter*, *supra*, in finding that a segregated law school for Negroes could not provide them equal educational opportunities, this Court relied in large part on "those qualities which are incapable of objective measurement but which make for greatness in a law school." In *McLaurin* v. *Oklahoma State Regents*, *supra*, the Court, in requiring that a Negro admitted to a white graduate school be treated like all other students, again resorted to intangible considerations: ". . . his ability to study, to engage in discussions and exchange views with other students, and, in general, to learn his profession." Such considerations apply with added force to children in grade and high schools. To separate them from others of similar age and qualifications solely because of their race generates a feeling of inferiority as to their status in the community that may affect their hearts and minds in a way unlikely ever to be undone. The effect of this separation on their educational opportunities was well stated by a finding in the Kansas case by a court which nevertheless felt compelled to rule against the Negro plaintiffs:

Segregation of white and colored children in public schools has a detrimental effect upon the colored children. The impact is greater when it has the sanction of the law; for the policy of separating the races is usually interpreted as denoting the inferiority of the negro group. A sense of inferiority affects the motivation of the child to learn. Segregation with the sanction of law, therefore, has a tendency to [retard] the educational and mental development of negro children and to deprive them of some of the benefits they would receive in a racial[ly] integrated school system.

Whatever may have been the extent of psychological knowledge at the time of *Plessy* v. *Ferguson,* this finding is amply supported by modern authority. Any language in *Plessy* v. *Ferguson* contrary to this finding is rejected.

We conclude that in the field of public education the doctrine of "separate but equal" has no place. Separate educational facilities are inherently unequal. Therefore, we hold that the plaintiffs and others similarly situated for whom the actions have been brought are, by reason of the segregation complained of, deprived of the equal protection of the laws guaranteed by the Fourteenth Amendment. This disposition makes unnecessary any discussion whether such segregation also violates the Due Process Clause of the Fourteenth Amendment.

Because these are class actions, because of the wide applicability of this decision, and because of the great variety of local conditions, the formulation of decrees in these cases presents problems of considerable complexity. On reargument, the consideration of appropriate relief was necessarily subordinated to the primary question—the constitutionality of segregation in public education. We have now announced that such segregation is a denial of the equal protection of the laws. In order that we may have the full assistance of the parties in formulating decrees, the cases will be restored to the docket, and the parties are requested to present further argument on Questions 4 and 5 previously propounded by the Court for the reargument this Term. The Attorney General of the United States is again invited to participate. The Attorneys General of the states requiring or permitting segregation in public education will also be permitted to appear as *amici curiae* upon request to do so by September 15, 1954, and submission of briefs by October 1, 1954.

It is so ordered.

Some Implications of Nonviolence in the Montgomery Resistance Movement

Joffre Stewart*

I want to cover some of the broader implications of the nonviolence invoked in the Montgomery resistance movement. For an atheist like myself it is interesting to see the Negro churches show as much social usefulness as they have in the Montgomery resistance. After hearing so much about churches in Bronzeville being an ignorant and escapist channelization of energy, I would not have expected so much militancy from the churches in the deep South. The local solidarity of the Montgomery resistance is a thing to behold.

We who are assembled here tonight are related to those events as a fragment of the growing country-wide solidarity with that resistance, and I should not be surprised if the world-wide interest grows to movement-like proportions. However, seeing that the present outlook of the resistance is to win less vexing accommodations within the framework of the Alabama segregation laws, I cannot wax overly enthusiastic, since I think that segregation laws or customs are to be broken or ignored or otherwise undone. But, as an anarcho-pacifist, I am committed to nonviolence. Thus, from the standpoint of method, I am very interested in what is coming off in Montgomery, if only because the consequent projection of its methodological beginnings is pregnant with revolutionary meaning and, I hope, possibilities.

Once we begin to think of methods as means we are prepared to think of ends. It is a commonplace to think of means as being consistent with ends. But this has often meant that the means justify the ends—any ends—unquestionably. I assert that we should give more attention to ends being congruent with means. We should take care that the ends are becoming to the means and do not embarrass the means.

Source: Joffre Stewart, "Some Implications of Nonviolence in the Montgomery Resistance Movement." *Balanced Living,* December 1961. Copyright © 1961 Balanced Living.

*Then in his mid-thirties, quiet-mannered Joffre Stewart began his non-cooperation with violence at the age of 18. In 1943, *opposed to* entering military service, he *reluctantly* registered late, *and was a few days jailed for not reporting for induction, before he did so.* During 1944, as a quartermaster *basic trainee* in the U.S. army, he was imprisoned three times for being AWOL. In 1948, he refused military registration. On release from *Washington, D.C. jailing for resisting segregation (1950)* he refused to sign a registration card. The jail clerk appealed to the Justice Dept. and was told, "Put his name on and turn him out." He does not carry this card; has passed out leaflets explaining non-cooperation with the war system and joined CORE in resisting segregation. He has been arrested 18 times in 18 years for these activities *or simply for being. Not reporting for induction* and being AWOL were the only times when laws were broken. Non-cooperation with violence, following the example of Jesus, Tolstoi, Thoreau and Gandhi is known as Civil Disobedience (CD). A very helpful 27-page pamphlet, *Theory and Practice of Civil Disobedience,* can be had for 25¢ from the author, Arthur Harvey, Raymond, N. H.

GANDHI AND NATIONALISM

I think I can best open this problem by making a criticism of Gandhi. This should be pertinent because the name of Gandhi has been so often invoked in this struggle. Gandhi did not see his way clear on means-ends relationships. He was so anxious to get the British out of India that he did not concern himself sufficiently with the kind of sub-continent he wanted or should have wanted as a thoroughgoing champion of nonviolence. Gandhi collaborated with politicians. Today as a result of all the nonviolent patience and travail that the Satyagrahis went through, we have two hostile states—each with their cops, courts, jails and taxes—which would be at war with each other if there was not a truce. There are two states with political frontiers traced with the blood of 8,000,000 Moslems and Hindus and consecrated with the anguish of 14,000,000 displaced persons. Considering the destruction of the economy, the suppression of the intra-Indian minorities and the liberal shootings on crowds of demonstrators, it is hard to imagine that India—both Indias—could be worse off under the British. Such are the fruits of statehoods, of statehoods fought for behind the platitude of "national independence." If Gandhi had chosen ends that would not have embarrassed his means he would have insisted on the dis-establishment of the State. He would have insisted on a copless, courtless, jailless and taxationless India, not merely a Britishless, decolonialized State with new administrators for old. If Gandhi had chosen ends congruent with his means, the movement he influenced would have been just as subversive to the power-seeking aspirations of Congress party politicians—any politicians—as it was to the British Raj.

Superficially this example applies more to Africa than to the U.S.—to Africa where, by means violent or nonviolent, the African blackman is becoming the judge, the jailer, the turnkey and the tax collector. He has proven himself to be just as corruptible by power, just as ruthless in enslaving his fellow countrymen to the impalpable images of productivity and power, and just as able at imbibing the strategy necessary to the Machiavellian conduct of politics as his erstwhile masters and models. These masters and models have retired to the capitols of

Europe laughing at black man cutting the throat of black man under the new management. They thought they were getting freedom when they got rid of the white man, but where there is freedom there is no State, and where there is the State there is no freedom.

FREEDOM FROM WHITES VS. FREEDOM FROM STATE

We can discern the essential similarity between the course which the Zionists, Africans and Asians are taking and the course taken by the Negro if we probe down to some of the psychological mechanisms at work in each case. The colonial finds himself in a subordinate position under the downthrust of authority transmitted through a political hierarchy staffed by European whites. Not only is this a sociological description of his status, but the colonial comes to feel in his psychological being that he is inferior. *But* inferior to the white man instead of understanding his condition in connection with the subordinating mechanism of an impersonal state. So the colonial comes to associate freedom and full manhood with (1) getting rid of the white man, and (2) substituting his brethren of color, with whom he identifies, at the summit of the same impersonal subordinating mechanism. And so he thinks he's free—until he's again beat up and thrown in jail for refusing to pay taxes.

The case of Jews and Zionism is essentially the same. Victimized by the German political authority, they fled as refugees to Palestine. There they carved out the State of Israel and have succeeded in their turn to convert the native-born inhabitants into refugees and second-class citizens. The Zionists learned from Hitler all right, but they only learned to be like Hitler (they did not learn to be unlike Hitler). They did not learn to be anti-political or to anarchize social relationships with nonviolence.

If we translate to the U.S. scene, we get something like this: A *Sun-Times* writer named Bird has noted that for many a white

Southerner, segregation is a religion. Such a Southerner would risk eternal damnation before he would kneel in the same mass with the Negro. Now just as the response of the Zionist and the colonials to oppression is to uncritically accept the coercive instrumentalities of their oppressors for the salvation of their sense of dignity and manhood, just so the Negro responds to the segregationist by adopting an uncritical religion of integration.

And so we are back to ends being congruent with means. That is, if we are to be serious about nonviolence as means, we ought to be discriminating about what we integrate into. I have no quarrel with riding on busses as such. But it is a mistake to mobilize nonviolent pressures to obtain integration in the armed forces. Why be nonviolent in order to improve your opportunity for learning how to kill or to increase your opportunity for getting killed? That issue may be going out of date now that colored boys are fast getting equal chances with white boys to blast whole countries off the map with weapons that can poison the human race. But I insist that if we are serious about nonviolence we can have no interest in raising demands for integration into war jobs or security work. And I do hope that nonviolence is not being used to improve the condition of the Negro only in order to raise his morale that he may become a more avid Chink-killer, Commie-killer, Kike-killer or whomever it is that may be indicated to us at the next turn of the diplomatic game. Such a morale-building stratagem would be the utmost perversion of the spirit of nonviolence.

Let's take a larger view of the problem of integration.

INTEGRATION OR ELIMINATE COERCION?

I think we should think of more than merely solving some of the conditions for the Negro in the U.S. Without changing one basic at-
tribute of the social system it is entirely possible that the Negro can be integrated into all the vices (and otherwise) in the American way of life. But that would not be the end of scape-goating. Already there are bio-cultural groups in the U.S. more depressed than the Negro—the Puerto Ricans, the wetbacks, certain American Indian populations and the Mexican-Americans in the Southwest. For scape-goating is the outcome of any social system which is organized on the basis of subordinating one man to another, whether it is citizen-soldier to president, a worker to his boss, a child to his guardian, a convict to a warden, or a defendant to a judge, to give the most obvious and penetrating examples. If we don't remove this authoritarian feature from our environment, we will merely get new scape-goats for old. Who, in the beginning of June 1950, could have foreseen that in a matter of months the units of the U.S.-led U.N. army would be handing out medals to champion gook-killers in the global civil war that was confined to Korea? And who knows who Mr. Dulles would have us hate tomorrow?

What I like about Montgomery is that people are accomplishing something without casting a ballot; without, as voters, participating in that institution of violence which is the State. In a social order predicated on armed coercion, in a culture devoted to violence, and under social circumstances that alienate man from the best in himself, from responsibility for and control over his work, and above all from his fellowman, non-violent direct action is implicitly and explicitly revolutionary. That is what I like about Montgomery. It is good to be nonviolent, but if you don't have anarchist ends—that is to say, non-authoritarian and anti-authoritarian objectives—you become involved in logical contradictions that make a mockery of both your good means and your good meaning.

And here I would end on a note which, I hope, would inject nonviolence into the mechanics of this meeting. It should be clear that constitutional and legal means, resting as they do on cops, courts, jails and taxes—it should be clear that such means have nothing to do with nonviolence. Consequently I urge that there be two collections, so that persons in accord with this view may have their gifts marked "Not to be used for legal expenses." Let us be equal and worthy of mutual respect simply as human beings, not as citizens under law.

Sit-ins and the NAACP

MEMORANDUM

April 18, 1960

The writer of this memorandum believes that there is a collision of two philosophies in the current efforts to end segregation in the South. This does not mean that one is better than the other. Both can be effective because they appeal to different types of persons.

One of these is the approach of the NAACP. The other is still in the formative stage from an organizational standpoint but some of its exponents come from CORE. It is frequently referred to as a program of nonviolence. It is well known, of course, that the Reverend Martin Luther King and Bayard Rustin are the personalities most often regarded as leaders of this second program to end racial segregation.

In something so enormous as the task of ending racial segregation there is a great deal of room for many workers and many ideas. The problems come only when attempts are made to draw support from the same financial sources and to use the same people for different activities. As an illustration of the conflict on finances, the writer received a call on April 18 that the Omega Psi Phi Fraternity

Source: Clarence Mitchell's Memorandum to Roy Wilkins on Sit-ins, April 18, 1960 and Special Report on Sitdowns: NAACP Staff Activity in the Sitdowns, 1960, NAACP Papers, box III A-289. Copyright © 1960 NAACP. The author wishes to thank The National Association for the Advancement of Colored People for authorizing the use of this material.

had a thousand dollars for the student anti-segregation effort. The question asked was, "where shall we send the money?" This was the answer given:

"The needs of demonstrators are many. There must be funds for transportation, money for sign painters, rental costs for a meeting place, mail, telephone and telegraph costs. There is frequently a heavy cost for bail. This financial burden is now being carried by a number of NAACP branches. If it is desired that the money be used for the foregoing and similar purposes it should be sent to the NAACP at 20 West 40th Street.

"It is obvious that there is and will continue to be a great need for legal services. If those making the contribution want to claim it as an income tax deduction they should send it to the Legal Defense Fund.

"Of course, there are other groups at work in the field of student demonstrations, but some other source should be used for information on their needs."

In discussing the non violent approach to the solution of the South's problem, one is handicapped because there is no standard definition of terms. In order that there will be no misunderstanding of his own concept, the writer states what he believes to be the philosophy of those who sponsor the "nonviolent" movement. It is essentially this. If a man is struck, he will not strike back. If his home is attacked by a mob, he will not defend it. If he is arrested, he is willing to remain in jail rather than obtain release on bail or by paying a fine. A more extensive discussion could be made but this is sufficient for the purpose of this memorandum.

The traditional position of the NAACP is best summed up in this excerpt from the Preamble of the 1959 Convention Resolutions which states:

"We abhor violence. We reject violence as a way to achieve any of the objectives which we and other fair minded people seek for all Americans without regard to race or color. In rejecting violence we do not deny, but reaffirm, the right of individual and collective self defense against unlawful assaults.

"The NAACP has consistently over the years supported this right by defending those who exercised the right of self defense, particularly in the Arkansas Riot Case, the Sweet Case in Detroit, the Columbia, Tennessee, riot cases and the Ingram Case in Georgia."

It is the writer's firm opinion that the NAACP statement is supported by the majority of colored citizens of the United States.

In some of the major urban areas of the South, a demonstrator who begins as a passive resister may, when slapped or kicked, retaliate in kind. There is some chance that he will escape injury at the hands of hoodlums because of prompt police intervention. In Birmingham, Alabama, Jackson, Mississippi, and many other parts of the South even the most faithful of passive resisters may be beaten up or killed with the full approval and participation of the police or other law enforcement officers. The question then arises, should the NAACP sponsor or direct campaigns of non-violent resistence in areas where we know those who participate will be humiliated, beaten and possibly killed outright with no chance for redress under local, state or Federal law? The writer believes that the NAACP must answer this question in the negative. We cannot, at this late date in our history, encourage our people to follow a philosophy which deprives them of the right of self defense. This does not mean that we should oppose the programs of other groups that are willing to make a campaign on the highest level of passive resistence and who are willing to accept death, if necessary, without striking back.

Wherever such persons act we should give them full legal, political, moral and financial support possible, if they will accept it.

With the foregoing in mind, it is suggested that the NAACP sponsored program in this field should be based on the following considerations:

1. The cities or areas selected for demonstrations should be those in which the colored citizens are a significant political factor because they register and vote. There is at least a fair chance of getting some redress in these areas when an attack is unprovoked and the victims resist in self defense.
2. There will be adequate bail money, or the possibility of getting adequate bail money and legal services, when demonstrators are arrested.
3. There will be full time participation and direction by competent NAACP personnel (volunteer or paid) through our regular leadership in the city or area or through persons we recruit and send in from the outside.
4. Where the business places that deny equal treatment are part of national chains, we shall have a systematic program of telling the story and seeking appropriate economic reprisals in all areas where such chain outlets exists. We shall also seek redress through the top offices of such chains.
5. We shall promote an extensive program of public education to show the relationships between the sit-in program and such matters as registration and voting, civil rights legislation in Congress and desegregation of all public facilities, including schools.

Perhaps the most telling illustration of the relationship between the sit-ins and registration and voting is the fact that one of the most vicious police commissioners in the United States now holds office in Birmingham. He would not now be in power if the full potential of colored citizens had registered and voted when he ran for office. In this instance, it cannot be said that the failure of colored citizens to register and vote was due to intimidation. The writer of this memorandum does not even blame that failure on apathy. The Birmingham election turned out as it did because there was not a sufficiently adequate effort on the part of community leaders. This is not said by way of rebuke or criticism. It is said with the hope that those leaders and the leaders in all southern communities will work harder, be given more aid and become successful the next time. A good time to begin preparation for that next time is NOW.

CC: Messrs. Current
　　　　　　Carter
　　　　　　Moon
　　Dr.　　Morsell

ROLE OF THE NAACP IN THE "SIT-INS"

When four students from the North Carolina Agricultural and Technical College at Greensboro sat down on February 1 at a lunch counter in a Woolworth's variety store they little realized that this simple act would set off a southwide protest movement against lunch counter Jim Crowism and rally support for the movement throughout the nation.

The "sit-in" at Greensboro was by no means the first in the country. It was, however, the first time this tactic, involving a group of persons, had been invoked at a lunch counter in any state of the late Confederacy. Eighteen months earlier, in August, 1958, the Oklahoma City NAACP youth council under the leadership of 15-year-old Barbara Posey and with the guidance of the council's adult adviser, Mrs. Clara Luper, conducted carefully planned "sit-in" demonstrations against lunch counters in that city. As a result, Negroes may now be served at some 60 Oklahoma City lunchrooms where service was formerly denied to them.

Even before the Oklahoma City demonstrations, the Association's youth council in Wichita, Kans., had succeeded in breaking the color bar at lunch counters of a chain drug store in that city, the impact of which was extended to certain other communities within the state. Following the success of the

Oklahoma City and Wichita demonstrations, the NAACP through its College and Youth Division called upon its units in other cities to utilize this tactic.

Six months later, in February, 1959, members of the NAACP chapter at Washington University in St. Louis engaged in a "sit-in" designed to end discrimination in off-campus lunchrooms. Four of the young people, including a white student, were arrested and fined for refusing to leave the lunchroom after the Negro students were refused service. Their convictions were later reversed by a higher court.

These three NAACP youth units were honored at the Association's Golden Anniversary Convention in New York City last July. Awards were bestowed upon them at the youth night mass meeting addressed by Dr. Martin Luther King of Montgomery and Dr. Charles Wesley, president of Central State College at Wilberforce, Ohio.

As long ago as the Nineteen-Forties, adult groups sponsored by the NAACP, CORE (Congress of Racial Equality) or other organizations, conducted successful "sit-ins" at restaurants in Chicago, Detroit and Cincinnati. In most of these demonstrations, as at present, there was not only participation by NAACP members but also by local units of the organization which provided guidance, bail money and legal counsel.

After St. Louis, use of the "sit-in" tactic languished until it was revived at Greensboro by four college freshmen, all of them members of the local NAACP youth council. The revived movement spread spontaneously and rapidly to other North Carolina cities and throughout the South until there were anti-segregation demonstrations of one sort or another in every southern state. NAACP members participated in practically all of these, except in Alabama where the organization is banned, and in many instances took the leadership as in Orangeburg and Columbia, S.C.; Durham, N.C.; Norfolk and Richmond, Va.; Chattanooga, Tenn.; St. Joseph, Mo.; and other cities.

In Memphis, the branch raised $4,500, including $3,500 from its own treasury, to pay the bail bonds for the arrested students. Chief counsel for the 150 students arrested in Nashville was Z. Alexander Looby, a member of the NAACP National Board of Directors and of the Nashville City Council. On April 24, Mr. Looby's home was wrecked by a bomb and he and Mrs. Looby narrowly escaped death. He attributed the assassination attempt to resentment because of his role in defense of the students and in other civil rights activities. Nevertheless, he said he would continue. Throughout the region NAACP lawyers have volunteered to defend the students.

Battling now, non-violently, in hardcore segregationist territory, the students have encountered tougher resistance than the young people in the border states of Kansas, Oklahoma and Missouri. Small but significant gains have been made. On May 10, leading department stores in Nashville began serving Negroes seated and unsegregated at their lunch counters. The decision to do so was reached after turbulent demonstrations, the arrest of 150 students, an effective withholding of patronage campaign, and negotiations involving the merchants, city officials and representatives of the students.

Previously, desegregation of lunch counters had been achieved in San Antonio after the NAACP Youth Council had announced plans for "sit-ins" which instigated productive intervention of a bi-racial committee of clergymen and businessmen. Other Texas cities followed suit: Corpus Christi, Galveston and Dallas. In Baltimore, 12 downtown restaurants changed their policy and serve all patrons. Some measure of lunch counter desegregation was achieved in Salisbury, N.C., and in Miami. Elsewhere in the South, the Jim Crow pattern remained intact, although exploratory steps towards settlement of the issue have been initiated in certain cities.

To give additional support to the movement, NAACP Executive Secretary Roy Wilkins on March 16 sent a memorandum to all branches urging them to institute campaigns to withhold patronage from chain stores whose southern outlets denied service to Negroes at their lunch counters. Secretary Wilkins called upon the branches to picket the stores of F.W. Woolworth, S.S. Kresge, S.H. Kress and W.T. Grant, all of which have stores in the South which bar Negroes as lunch counter customers. Money spent in non-southern stores of these chains, he pointed out, helps sustain their Jim Crow policies in the South. Stores of these chains have been picketed in more than 300 cities from New England to California.

Meanwhile, some 1,400 students had been arrested in the South and fined a total of more than $100,000. Some of them refused bail and payment of fines, preferring to serve their sentences as an expression of their resistance to segregation. The legality of the "sit-ins" is yet to be determined definitively. Thurgood Marshall, director-counsel of the NAACP Legal Defense and Educational Fund, Inc., announced on March 19, following a Washington conference of civil rights lawyers from all over the South, that cases to vindicate the legal right of the students would be taken to the Supreme Court, if necessary. The arrests, he said, would be challenged as violations of the Fourteenth Amendment.

Many of the students, however, are far less interested in the legal aspects of their position than in the moral justice of their cause. They seek much more than the right to sit down at a lunch counter for a sandwich and a cup of coffee. They seek demolition of the entire Jim Crow structure and recognition of the dignity of the Negro as a human being entitled to all the rights enjoyed by other persons.

Basically, the "sit-in" movement is a revolt against the caste system which relegates Negroes to an inferior position in American society. The demonstrations dramatize the students' rejection of the outmoded pattern of segregation. They scorn the second-class citizenship which had been forced upon their parents. Their resistance and impatience was born of the conviction that the Negro has already had to wait too long for the constitutional and human rights due him.

This unwavering conviction has given the movement the color of a crusade. The students are prepared to pay whatever price ultimate victory requires—verbal abuse, physical violence, expulsion from college, prison sentences. They reject compromise of moral rights and despise the laws and customs which quarantine Negroes. They are dedicated to the basic principles of democracy and to the tenets of Christianity.

The peaceful non-violent manner in which they have pursued their crusade has rallied wide support to their position. Even in the South, they have won friends for their cause. Northern college students, and some white students in the South, have picketed the chain stores, raised money to aid the aroused Negro students and to provide scholarships for those who have been expelled. Church groups, Jewish organizations, trade unions, and numerous other organizations have backed them up.

The NAACP Youth and College Division has sponsored state and area conferences in North Carolina, South Carolina and Texas for the purpose of coordinating activities of the movement. The Southern Christian Leadership Conference held a conference of students in Raleigh, N.C., to expound the doctrine of passive resistance and to back up the students. CORE has conducted classes instructing students in the methods of passive resistance.

It is noteworthy that the only national figure to condemn the movement has been former President Harry S. Truman who has since back-tracked on his earlier blast against the students in which he declared he would throw anybody out of a place he owned if they refused to leave when requested. He also admitted that he had no proof that the movement was Communist-inspired, as he had charged. In contrast,

President Eisenhower expressed deep sympathy "with efforts of any group to enjoy the rights of equality that they are guaranteed by the Constitution." Vice President Richard M. Nixon, Governors Leroy Collins of Florida and Nelson A. Rockefeller of New York, Mrs. Eleanor Roosevelt, Senators Hubert Humphrey, John Kennedy and Stuart Symington and many others have spoken up in defense of the moral justice of the student effort.

The "sit-ins" have brought forth a new era on the college campus. Suddenly it has become more important to participate in these demonstrations than to win the varsity letter on the athletic field or to be crowned "Queen" of the homecoming game. The jailed student is now more of a hero on the campus than the football star.

Today's demonstrations are taking place in a new South in which Negroes are more assertive of their rights and in which younger and more enlightened white persons are less insistent upon maintaining an inflexible color bar. In large measure this change in attitude and climate of opinion has been the direct result of achievements of the NAACP over a 50-year period. The work of the Association has undermined the legal props to segregation, enlarged the southern Negro's voting strength, contributed to his increased purchasing power through opening up new job opportunities, and sharpened public awareness of the urgency of the human rights issue. All of this laid the groundwork for the present upsurge of Negro youth.

Throughout these demonstrations the NAACP and NAACP members have played vital roles as participants and leaders in the "sit-ins" as sources for bail money and fines, as legal counsel, and as supporters in non-southern areas through their activity in the withholding of patronage from the offending chain stores as set forth in Secretary Wilkins' memorandum of March 16 calling for an "expanded racial defense" program.

May, 1960

N.A.A.C.P. Legal Defense and Educational Fund, Inc.
10 Columbus Circle, New York 19, N. Y.

August 4, 1960

Mr. Marion S. Barry, Jr., Chairman
Student Nonviolent Coordinating
  Committee
208 Auburn Avenue, N.E.
Atlanta 3, Georgia

Dear Mr. Barry:

Your letter of August 1 just reached us and I am sending the information at once with the understanding that we are now in the process of doing a full report on the sit-ins. We have been so busy in the actual defense of these cases that we have not had time to prepare material as accurately as we would wish.

We are now participating in the defense of between 1,500 and 1,750 individuals. In many cases a single individual is actually involved in more than one proceeding. For example, there are some students who have been arrested for sitting-in or demonstrating on several occasions. In other cases the same individual is charged with several different alleged crimes, such as, trespass, conspiracy and violation of fire ordinances. In at least two cities we have had several lawyers tied up in litigation over a period of more than four months on a daily basis.

Although I cannot be certain that the following list is all inclusive, we have cases pending in the following areas:

Arkansas	—Little Rock
Alabama	—Montgomery
Florida	—Tallahassee
Georgia	—Atlanta
Kentucky	—Frankfort
Louisiana	—Baton Rouge
Maryland	—Baltimore
Massachusetts	—Springfield
North Carolina	—Charlotte, Durham, Concord, Greensboro, New Bern, Raleigh, Monroe, Winston-Salem, Statesville
South Carolina	—Charleston, Columbia, Florence, Greenville, Orangeburg, Rock Hill, Sumter
Tennessee	—Memphis, Nashville
Texas	—Marshall
Virginia	—Norfolk, Richmond

If there is any additional information you desire, please feel free to call on us for the information.

Sincerely,

Thurgood Marshall
Director-Counsel

cc: Mr. Roy Wilkins
N.A.A.C.P.
20 W. 40th St.
New York 18, N. Y.

REPORT ON SIT-IN LUNCH COUNTER STRIKES IN NORTH CAROLINA

by
  Charles A. McLean
  Field Secretary

On Monday, February 1, 1960, at 4:30 p.m., four students from A. &. T. College, Greensboro, North Carolina, seated themselves at the lunch counter in the F. W. Woolworth variety store, Greensboro, North Carolina and asked for service. They were not served, but remained seated until the store closed at 5:30 p.m.

Twenty students returned Tuesday, at 10:30 a.m., and occupied seats at the lunch counter until the afternoon, but were not served. White customers continued to sit and get served.

The students organized the Students Executive Committee for Justice, with Franklin McLean and Ezell Blair, Jr. as spokesmen. The group wrote to the president of Woolworth's asking that a firm stand be taken to eliminate discrimination.

The group declared that the movement was student-sponsored, with no backing from the NAACP. They further stated that they expected to count on backing from the NAACP, if such was needed.

By Thursday, February 4, the students had begun occupying seats at Kress's variety store and reinforcements came from other colleges, both white and Negro, in the city. White girls joined in the protest from Women's College of the University of North Carolina and from the following private colleges: Greensboro College, Guilford (a Quaker college)—both white—and Bennett College. On Saturday afternoon, during the demonstration, a bomb scare caused the managers of Woolworth and Kress to close their stores at 1:09 p.m. No bomb was found.

Dr. George Simkins, president of the Greensboro Branch, reported that his first knowledge of the students' plans or actions was when the leaders visited the branch's board meeting at the YMCA the night following the first one-hour sitdown demonstration at Woolworth's to request backing for their movement. The board immediately assured the leaders of NAACP backing.

Mr. Ezell Blair, Sr., Father of A. & T. College student leader, Ezell Blair, Jr., is chairman of the board of the Greensboro Branch. Dr. Simkins told me that he had recently read of the assistance that C.O.R.E. had rendered in a similar strike against W. T. Grant in Baltimore, by negotiating a satisfactory settlement for the Baltimore strikers with the New York office of W. T. Grant. He asked C.O.R.E. official, Gordon Carey, to investigate the possibility of getting Woolworth's officials in New York to order integration of lunch counters in Greensboro. Mr. Carey came to Greensboro to investigate and by the time he arrived, the strikes had spread to other cities. He also visited Durham and Raleigh.

Winston-Salem, N.C.

On Monday afternoon, February 8, Carl Matthews, a recent graduate of Winston-Salem Teachers' College and a member of the Executive Board of the Winston-Salem Branch, occupied a seat at Kress's lunch counter. He was joined by a few others. The Winston-Salem Teachers' College students joined in the sitdown protest spontaneously on Tuesday, Wednesday and Thursday. Many of them were members of the NAACP College Chapter. By that time, the following six lunch counters had closed: Kress; Woolworth; H. L. Green; Walgreen Drug Company—all national chain stores—Bobbitt Drug Store and O'Hanlon Drug Store. Of the six that had closed, two Bobbitt Drug Stores and Walgreen's opened Wednesday without any demonstrations.

On Thursday afternoon, February 11, a spontaneous student rally of about 500 college and high school students occurred on the campus Winston-Salem Teachers' College after the administration had denied the progressive students to hold a meeting in the college chapel. As soon as the rally started, I was called and asked to speak; also Dr. F. W. Jackson, former president of the Winston-Salem Branch and chairman of the 1960 Executive Board. Both of us hurried to the rally. He assured them of the support and cooperation of the local branch. I endorsed and complimented their spontaneous protest; advised them to continue their non-violent demonstrations; informed them of the technical difference between protest and boycott and insisted that they now announce and start an official boycott because of possible civil law violations. I cautioned the campus girls not to violate the college regulations—as to the hours they must be on campus—and encouraged the coed students to back up the boys when other girls had to be absent. I also assured them of the support and cooperation of the State and National Office. On February 11, Mr. Kelly Alexander made the following public endorsement: "The NAACP endorses unequivocally the orderly protests being made by college and high school students throughout the state in their effort to secure the right to use, on an equal basis, all facilities in places of public accommodation that solicit the patronage of the total population . . ."

At the big rally, the students voted to continue their passive resistance movement against segregated lunch counters in certain stores. The movement was formally organized with the following college students in charge of student participation: Mr. Jefferson T. Diggs, III, was named campus president; Mr. William Bright, executive vice-president, and a secretary was also elected. Mr. Carl Matthews was elected Executive Chairman of the overall movement in the city. The protest continued and chain store lunch counters remained closed; the counters used to display other merchandise.

Charlotte, N.C.

On February 9, students from Johnson C. Smith University occupied 60 seats at Woolworth's and 25 seats at Kress. Both stores closed their lunch counters. The student spokesman for the non-violent protest was Mr. Charlie Jones of Charlotte, N. C. Mr. Kelly Alexander served as student advisor to the group. A few days later, demonstrators moved to Sears Roebuck, McLellan, W. T. Grant and Leggett Drug Store; also to Belk's Department Store, a local chain store.

Fayetteville, N.C.

On February 9, a group of 18 students from Fayetteville State Teachers' College occupied seats at Woolworth's lunch counter. When it closed, they moved on to McCrory's lunch counter which also closed. The student spokesman is Mr. Harvey Daye. The protest is still active. Mr. Herbert Wright and I conferred with the Fayetteville Branch president and other officers. They assured us of their willingness to endorse, support and cooperate with the students' non-violent movement. The branch president and I conferred with Mr. Daye at a meeting he arranged for us. He asked for NAACP support and that we be ready to rush to their aid upon notice. We assured him that legal and financial assistance would be rendered upon notice. I proceeded to arrange for bond locally in case of any arrests without sufficient notice to me.

Raleigh, N.C.

On February 10, approximately 150 students from Shaw University and St. Augustine College took part in a non-violent demonstration at 10:30 a.m. by seeking service at the following Raleigh stores: Woolworth; McLellan; Hudson-Belk Department Store; Kress; Walgreen; Cromley and Sir Walter Drug Store. At each place, the counters were immediately closed when the Negro student asked for service. Signs were quickly brought out. They read, "Closed in the Interest of Public Safety," "Luncheonette Temporarily Closed" and "We Reserve the Right to Serve the Public As We See Fit." Lunch counters in several places were roped off and "No Trespassing" signs were hung. McLellan's closed its entire store at 2:00 p.m. and Walgreen's closed shortly after Negroes took their seats. Teenage whites moved from store to store—in front of the protesting students—to occupy the seats.

High Point, N.C.

On February 11, at 4:29 p.m., 26 teenage Negro students from William Penn High School took seats at Woolworth counters, which were closed immediately and, at 4:50, the manager closed the store for the day. McLellan's, next door to Woolworth's, closed before the demonstrators arrived. A few hours later, demonstrators caused the closing of Woolworth's and Eckard's Drug Store soda fountain at the College Village Shopping Center.

The adult spokesman for the students, Rev. B. Elton Cox and the vice-president of the High Point Branch, who accompanied them to the store, informed the store management that "the students will continue to sit until the counters are closed completely or until they are permitted to eat on an integrated basis. They will be back indefinitely." The demonstration by William Penn students marks the first entry of high school age youngsters into the spreading movement. All other affected cities have Negro colleges in their environs from which demonstrators have organized.

The William Penn students were accompanied by three adults, all of whom are active in Negro integration movements here and out-of-state. Rev. Cox indicated the students had decided early the previous week to follow the pattern of demonstrations occurring across the state and that they then came to him for advice. They were told, when they consulted him, "it seems in the realm of human dignity." He also told newsmen the students asked his advice on the legality of such demonstrations, but he declined to comment on what he told them.

Concord, N.C.

Fourteen students from Barber-Scotia College, on February 12, put on a demonstration at Belk's Department Store. The store closed its lunch counter. Officials of the local branch and Mr. Alexander are advising the students.

Elizabeth City, N.C.

On February 12, students from Elizabeth City State Teachers' College demonstrated at W. T. Grant's. The counters were immediately closed and the usual signs were displayed and the seats were later removed. The following day, W. T. Grant's closed five and one-half hours early. Massive gatherings of whites and Negro college students threatened trouble. Mr. Syralius Walston, Jr. is the student spokesman. There is no NAACP branch in Elizabeth City or Pasquotank County.

The demonstrations in the above cities have been non-violent to date. They were spontaneous, but after they started the student leaders turned to the NAACP for advice, legal assistance, necessary funds and assistance to carry on the protest. In all known cases, the necessary assistance was given. With few exceptions, the lunch counters have remained closed since the demonstrations started. A check is made on the stores daily. If a counter is opened, the demonstrators reappear. The counters are closed again. In Fayetteville and Greensboro, local committees have been appointed to try to work out a satisfactory solution and a truce is now in effect. It is reasonably certain that demonstrations will be resumed if the store managers refuse to integrate the lunch counters.

Short-lived demonstrations have been staged in Henderson, Monroe and Shelby by high school students.

The North Carolina State Conference, on February 13, scheduled a council meeting for students and leaders of sit-in strikes at the YMCA in Greensboro. The meeting was snowed out. Mr. Herbert Wright, who was in the state to attend the meeting, and I conferred with students and leaders at Winston, Fayetteville, Raleigh, Durham and Greensboro. C.O.R.E. and S.C.L.C. had scheduled a meeting in Durham for February 16 and invited students and their leaders. We informed the college chapters on the campuses of the colleges that had organized protest teams, except St. Augustime, Elizabeth City State Teachers' and Fayetteville State Teachers' Colleges. Mr. Wright was presented at the meeting. The leaders wanted some advice on protest procedure and information as to the assistance that was available from the NAACP. We arranged an informal meeting, especially for college chapter representatives, but welcomed all who wished to attend. The entire delegation did attend. C.O.R.E. representatives met with us and were vocal in our meeting.

Mr. Wright outlined and recommended a procedure to be followed by each college group in an effort to establish a line of communication with responsible local community citizens and the store management. Mr. Alexander reassured them of the state and national support. After our meeting, the students and their leaders appeared jubilant over the support—financial and legal—offered them by the NAACP and determined to continue. The colleges without NAACP chapters were assured of the same support as those with chapters. They were gratified and appreciative.

After returning to their colleges, most groups did follow through in attempts to make contact with local powers as Mr. Wright suggested. Not one reported success.

By this time, store managers realized that protests were beginning to crystalize, increase and gain public support. Lunch counters in stores where demonstrations were staged have closed down or made adjustments to meet present conditions. Some stores began serving lunch boxes to all customers to be eaten off premises, others removed seats and served customers standing. Picketing began at most stores where demonstrations were conducted. The stores that kept their counters open posted signs which read, "For Employees and Their Guests," which actually meant that any white customer was accepted as a guest. In Winston-Salem, the students at Winston-Salem Teachers' College accepted an invitation to be guests of students at Wake Forest Baptist College, which is also located in Winston-Salem. Both groups of students appeared at a Woolworth store. The Wake Forest students seated themselves at the lunch counter, leaving a vacant seat beside each of them. The students from Winston-Salem Teachers' College, who by that time were nearby, occupied the vacant seat. The white students ordered two items and, when they were served, passed one to the Negro student seated beside him. When they had finished eating, the police arrested 21 students for trespassing, nine whites and 12 Negroes. The warrants were signed by the manager. Their bail was set at $100 each. I arranged bail for all students. Rev. Hardge, branch president, and Dr. Jackson, chairman of the local board, were with me at the police station. When the Wake Forest College students' representative arrived, he informed me that he was prepared to post bond for the nine Wake Forest students. Bonds that were signed for those students were returned.

On Friday, February 12, several Negro students from St. Augustine College and Shaw University proceeded out to the Cameron Village, a suburban shopping center, presumably to demonstrate at the variety stores located there. They were arrested before arriving at the store and charged with trespassing. The police cited them and ordered them to leave the shopping center, informing them that it was private property. Before they had time to leave the so-called private property, the property manager asked for their arrest. Forty-one were arrested and charged with trespassing. Their bonds were set at $50 each. Attorney George Green of Raleigh, North Carolina and Attorney Jack Greenberg of New York City will represent the demonstrators in court.

Protesting students have been arrested at the following places for trespassing: New Bern, N. C., 23 high school students tried and convicted; cases appealed. Attorneys were supplied by State Legal Committee; Concord, N. C., nine Barber-Scotia College students tried and convicted; cases appealed. Attorneys were supplied by State Legal Committee; Statesville, N.C., 11 high school students charged with trespassing; trial postponed. Attorneys were supplied by State Legal Committee.

The protests are continuing in most of the cities. Two additions were added in March—Statesville and New Bern—March 15 and Goldsboro, March 19. All demonstrators are high school students.

Several city fathers have appointed good will committees to try to work out a solution satisfactory to the students and managers. All that have made reports have failed to find a solution; some are still working on it. Most protest groups cease during the weeks the conferences are being held. To date, they have all started again, as soon as the committee's failure is announced.

College final exams have reduced the number of participants and the length of time that the demonstrations can be carried on. It is feared that the close of colleges for summer vacation will bring a temporary halt to the demonstrations in college towns. There is some talk of high schools taking over for the summer. Just what will happen this summer is not yet known. Many college students are committing themselves to start protesting when they return next fall.

SUPPLEMENTARY REPORT ON SIT-IN LUNCH COUNTER STRIKES IN NORTH CAROLINA

The strikes and demonstrations are continuing in North Carolina. However, no additional communities have been added. The preparation for final exams and other activities, pertinent to the ending of the college year, have curtailed many of the demonstrations, but there is sufficient activity going on in most of the centers to show that the protests are still on.

The high school students are joining with local college students to continue demonstrations in Durham and Greensboro. The high school students have announced that they will continue the demonstrations in New Bern and Goldsboro during the school vacation.

On April 22, trespassing charges were dismissed in Wake County Superior Court against the 43 college students who were arrested, February 10, for being on the sidewalk of private property—Cameron Village—a private shopping center in which variety stores are located. The presumption was that the students were on their way to demonstrate in the stores. They were convicted in police court and each was ordered to pay fines of $10.00 and costs. The students were represented by Jack Greenberg and other attorneys. The case was appealed to the Superior Court, which handed down the dismissal ruling. The attorneys cited a 1946, U. S. Supreme Court, ruling to sustain their motion for dismissal. Judge Hooks granted the motion. Two other students, Albert Sampson and James A. Fox, convicted April 21 for trespassing at a white lunch counter in McLellan's store last March, were given a 30 day suspended jail sentence for two years or payment of $25 fine each and court costs. The sentences were appealed and they are free on $500 bond each.

The trial of the 45 A. & T. and Bennett College students in Greensboro included two white girls, who were charged with trespassing at Kress & Co., on April 21, have been continued.

In Durham, on May 6, forty-six students were arrested and, on May 11, fifty-seven students were arrested for trespassing. Many of the students were involved in both demonstrations. A total of 75 students—63 from North Carolina College and 12 from Duke University, plus 5 Durham Negroes—were arrested. Attorneys for the 80 students appeared before Recorder's Court Judge A. R. Wilson on May 19 and asked for trial by jury. A one hundred dollar bond was posted for each pending the Superior Court trial.

The Mayor's Committee appointed to negotiate the settlement of the strikes in Greensboro and High Point recommended that the chain stores desegregate the lunch counters, but the store managers refused to accept the recommendation and reopened the counters to whites only.

Mayor Marshall Kurfees of Winston-Salem appointed the city's Good Will Committee on April 1, 1960. It is composed of 10 whites, as follows: Gordon Hanes; Joe S. Rice, James G. Hanes; J. Ernest Yarbrough; Dr. Clarence H. Patrick; Paul Essex; Irving Carlyle; James A. Gray; E. S. Heefner and Dr. Mark Depp. The ten Negroes are as follows: Rev. Jenneth R. Williams; Curtis Todd; Rev. Jerry Drayton; Rev. D. R. Hedgley; A. H. Anderson; Sam Harvey; Edward E. Hill; C. I. Sawyer; Dr. E. L. Davis and Rev. H. W. Wiley.

All the Negroes are long-time members of the NAACP and three are members of the Winston-Salem Branch's Executive Board. They are as follows: Rev. H. W. Wiley; Dr. Jerry Drayton and Rev. David Hedgley—all local ministers. After their first meeting April 2, they asked that all demonstrations be stopped and the counters closed, but the protest, by way of withholding trade by Negroes, was continued on a voluntary basis and was noticeably effective.

On May 4, there was a rumor that the Mayor's Committee in Winston-Salem was about ready to recommend that the chain stores reopen their counters on a desegregated basis. It was also rumored that the chain store managers had said they would not accept the recommendation. The Mayor's Committee did not announce a recommendation, but the stores did reopen their lunch counters to whites only on May 5. Immediately, the demonstrations were reestablished by college students and reinforced by groups of high school students from Atkins High and Carver High Schools by May 10. The high school and college demonstrations had grown to 500, which not only closed the counters again but temporarily closed the stores. By May 10, the condition had become explosive and two arrests had been made. Donald Bradley, a college student, was arrested for violating a 1942, City Ordinance, Section 29–39 - "Parades and Congregations." "The congregation of persons or the marching in procession by persons upon the streets, sidewalks or other public places of the city or property of the city is hereby prohibited unless conducted in accordance with the provisions of this section." The law on parades reads, "No such congregation or parade shall be held or conducted unless permission shall first have been given in writing by the Chief of Police of the city and all persons participating in any congregation or parade without such a permit shall be guilty of a violation of this section . . . as to create public disturbance, or to operate as a nuisance, or to tend to create or threaten rioting, disorderly conduct or public or private mischief."

The mammouth demonstrations and the arrest of Bradley led to a conference of the city officials with protest leader, Carl Matthews, and others. In the conference, a temporary halt of demonstrations were called to give the city manager, John Gold, an opportunity to arrange a conference between the protest leaders and the store managers.

Apparently, the Mayor's Committee was stimulated to get back to work and try harder than ever before. On May 12, the Mayor's Good Will Committee met and decided to make a recommendation. On May 23, the store managers gave assurance that they would also make a decision by that date. The Committee announced that the store managers had agreed to keep their counters closed and requested the protestors to hold off all demonstrations of any kind through May 23.

The Executive Board of the Winston-Salem Branch, the protest leaders, the demonstrators and all Negroes were reluctant to commit themselves to honor the May 23 deadline, since the store managers broke their promise to the Mayor's Committee and opened their lunch counters to whites only on May 5. After much debate at the NAACP Protest Mass Meeting, on May 12, and the Executive Board Meeting, the decision was made to honor the May 23 deadline.

Bradley was released on $500 bond. He was convicted in Police Court on May 18, fined $50 and given 30 days suspended sentence for participating in an illegal parade. He was represented in court by Attorney Richard C. Erwin, who appealed the case. Bradley is out on bond. Bill Oren Speer, Assistant Manager of the F. W. Woolworth Company at 4th and Liberty Streets was charged with assault on Miss Asha Ralason, Teachers' College student from New York. She contended that Speer pushed her as he tried to close the door of the store the previous week during Negro demonstrations against segregation. Mr. Speer was tried in Police Court on May 19 where he pleaded not guilty and the case against him was dismissed.

On May 23, the twenty-member committee met and unanimously adopted the five-man subcommittee's recommendation to desegregate the lunch counters. The subcommittee had been working with the store managers.

The F. W. Woolworth manager of the store at 4th and Liberty Street, Mr. Herman A. Warren, age 58, had issued an ultimatium to the home office and the Committee to the effect that he would retire rather than desegregate his store, although retiring at this time would mean a financial sacrifice because his benefits would increase each year until he reached the age of 65.

The stores reopened their counters on a desegregated basis on Wednesday morning, May 25, without incident. Negroes are dining at the counters in moderate numbers, but in large enough numbers to be noticeable. Some of the Negro committee members reported that the store managers had asked them to stand by to assist in making a smooth transition. As of Thursday night, June 2—when Mr. Alexander spoke at a mass meeting here—it had not been necessary to call upon them. All observations and indications are that the adjustment is working well.

Conferences have been held with the leaders of the protest movement in other cities since the successful negotiations in Winston-Salem and we have been informed that some committees that were dormant have been reactivated. We believe that some other cities will soon follow the Winston-Salem example.

WINSTON-SALEM INTEGRATION

The following information report was received from one of the members of the five-man subcommittee of the Mayor's Good Will Committee of Winston-Salem, after he attended the first joint meeting of the subcommittee and the store managers and since the lunch counters were opened on a non-segregated basis two weeks ago.

The managers unanimously were not only pleased but enthusiastic in expressing their happiness and surprise at the public's ready adjustment to integrated lunch counters. They reported that their only regret was that they had not integrated earlier and

saved themselves all their worries, extra labor trying to defeat the integration movement and heavy sales losses during the past four months.

They further stated that their business was getting back to normal, but not quite up to par yet. The lunch counter business was reported to be growing the fastest because of the Negro patronage. To date, there had been nothing but pleasantness and satisfaction between the service personnel and the diners. One manager reported that his waitresses admitted that they had learned a lot since the counters opened, desegregated. One lesson was that Negroes tipped better than whites and some waitresses especially delighted in serving Negroes.

The Woolworth store, from which Mr. Warren resigned after managing the store for many years because he said he could not bow to opening his store's counters integrated against the will of his white customers, was reported by the new manager, according to the information given to him by the lunch counter personnel, to have more white people dining at the former Negro lunch counter than there were Negroes going to the former all-white lunch counter, which, in his words, "proves that somebody was lying when it was reported that white people generally were against integrating the counters." It was reported that stores from other cities are sending in their observers to view the transition.

OBSERVATIONS

Important NAACP Contributions to the Sit-In Demonstrators Which Are Building and Sustaining the Morale of the Protest Movement Throughout North Carolina and Some Specific Emergency Aids to Individual Students. The students from A. & T. College, under the leadership of Ezelle Blair, Jr., freshman, and the first student to begin the protest by seeking service at the Kress variety store in Greensboro, appealed to the

Greensboro Branch, NAACP, for help on the day they started the protest. Among the requests made, the most important was the assurance of bail bonds and legal aid. The NAACP gave that assurance immediately, named the bondsman and established a contact person for the students. Mr. Ezelle Blair, Sr. is chairman of the board.

The local branch also arranged for public mass meetings and generally served as a public relations medium for the demonstrators and the protest movement. The branch also provided expense monies for numerous necessities which constantly arose, such as transportation to and from the college to the downtown area and transportation and other necessary expenses to attend special meetings in the state. In every community in North Carolina where protests and demonstrations were conducted by college or high school students, the local NAACP has supplied substantially the same aid and support.

When an emergency arose, the contributing cause of which was activity in the protest movement or the individual students emergency, funds from the NAACP or representatives of the NAACP were available upon request to assist in making satisfactory adjustments. Some emergencies did arise. The following were great morale stimulants to the protest movement and placed the NAACP in an esteemed position, especially in the immediate communities and throughout the student population in North Carolina as the news reached many of them. However, there were no efforts to publicize emergency aid rendered to individual students.

Early in the sit-in demonstrations, Donald Bradley, a junior at Teachers College, Winston-Salem, N. C. and Miss Delois Reeves, also a junior, gave all indications that they would go the limit in demonstrating in the protest movement. They had lived up to every expectation, from the first of February to the middle of March. The first of March, Governor Hodges of North Carolina released a news story to the effect that he expected the college presidents to have sufficient control over their students as to pre-

vent them from continuing the sit-in demonstrations. The third quarter of college work was to begin in mid March and the seventeenth was the last day a student could enter class. Mr. Bradley and Miss Reeves had been extended all the credit possible by the college business office under state law. In fact, the state auditor was investigating the financial activity of the college business office at that time and was critical of the condition he found. Mr. Bradley and Miss Reeves had made it known to the Winston-Salem Branch, NAACP, that they would have to leave the college and consequently the protest demonstrations for lack of funds to pay their college entrance fee for the quarter. The treasury of the Winston-Salem Branch was sufficient to financially aid Miss Reeves only. The branch voted to pay her past due bills, which permitted her to register for the next quarter and continue demonstrating with the college students in the sit-in protest. The NAACP College Chapter was not financially able to rescue Mr. Bradley. He was still on the campus, but out of college because of his financial condition.

On March 16, a committee representing the men of the campus invited the Field Secretary to attend a special meeting of all the men students and faculty student advisor for the purpose of devising a way of paying Bradley's bill. Their argument was first that Bradley, once a popular basketball player, was the key man in keeping the protest morale high and that if he had to drop out, they were certain the protest would end for three reasons: (1) They would suffer the loss of his popularity (2) His personal determination to break down discrimination (he is a native of New Jersey) and (3) the threat of a student strike against the college because it would not permit Bradley to register for the third quarter. The threat was genuine as the students marched from the dining hall and noisily demonstrated in front of the president's residence that evening after dinner.

Rumors had already circulated that Mr. Bradley and Miss Reeves had been denied registration for the third semester because they were most active in the protest movement and that Teachers' College had bowed to Governor Hodges' suggestion that college presidents control the students in state supported institutions. The latter rumor was untrue. It is believed that it was started by the students to embarrass the president. There was a danger that the rumor would have gained support if the students had not registered. Newspaper publicity could have slowed down, if not curtailed, protest activity in every state supported college in North Carolina.

After all efforts to secure the funds needed for Bradley's registration had failed, the Field Secretary checked with the business office and found that the figures given ($279.00) were correct. A conference was held with the college president, who assured him that the rumors were false. In the name of the NAACP, a check was given to the president for Bradley's registration fee for the third semester.

Shaw University Student Rescued by the Raleigh Branch, NAACP

Mr. Mitchell, a foreign student at Shaw University and the leader of the Shaw University-St. Augustine College protest demonstrations in Raleigh, experienced a financial emergency the last of April which would have made it impossible for him to remain in college. Consequently, it would have seriously affected, if not brought to an end, the local demonstrations. Dr. Marguerite Adams, State Director of the Youth Program, a member of the faculty at Shaw University and active in helping the students direct their protest, told me of Mr. Mitchell's condition. On April 20, a conference was held with the Raleigh Branch leadership, including Rev. Ward, who was particularly active with the special fund-raising committee, to inform them of Mitchell's emergency and the importance of going to his rescue in order that he might remain in a position to continue his leadership in the sit-in demonstrations. His activity in

the movement was a matter of record and well known by the citizens of Raleigh. The NAACP, in cooperation with interested individuals, paid off the note, which was more than $300.

Winston-Salem Branch Finances Sit-In Demonstrations for Four Months

The Field Secretary was informed by Dr. F. W. Jackson, chairman of the Executive Board of the Winston-Salem Branch, that the last few days of the protest demonstration—when 500 or more college and high school students were participating—cost the branch approximately $150 a day for food, transportation and incidentals. When the lunch counters opened on a non-segregated basis on May 25, the branch provided funds to several student leaders, with which to buy lunch at a counter, as a token of appreciation and assurance that there would be at least a few desirable representatives visiting the counters that day. To date, the exact cost of the demonstrations is unknown, but we know several hundred dollars were expended by the Winston-Salem Branch during the four months of protests. Almost all of the expenses were paid for through the NAACP, however, many organizations helped to raise the funds.

Bail Bonds For Students Arrested in Statesville

When eleven students were arrested in Statesville, N. C., on trespassing charges, their bail was originally set at $100 each, cash bonds. The local NAACP branch was prepared to post the bonds. The warrants were changed to include "resisting an officer" to make the protest more expensive, it is believed, and the bonds were raised to a total of $3,300. The branch was not prepared to pay this amount. Mr. Mangrum, branch president, contacted an attorney in Winston-Salem who in turn contacted Attorney C. O. Pearson and the Field Secretary. We arranged for a bondsman to go to Statesville and post bond. The Statesville Branch paid the fee.

Message to the Grassroots

Malcolm X

We want to have just an off-the-cuff chat between you and me, us. We want to talk right down to earth in a language that everybody here can easily understand. We all agree tonight, all of the speakers have agreed, that America has a very serious problem. Not only does America have a very serious problem, but our people have a very serious problem. America's problem is us. We're her problem. The only reason she has a problem is she doesn't want us here. And every time you look at yourself, be you black, brown, red or yellow, a so-called Negro, you represent a person who poses such a serious problem for America because you're not wanted. Once you face this as a fact, then you can start plotting a course that will make you appear intelligent, instead of unintelligent.

What you and I need to do is learn to forget our differences. When we come together, we don't come together as Baptists or Methodists. You don't catch hell because you're a Baptist, and you don't catch hell because you're a Methodist. You don't catch hell because you're a Methodist or Baptist, you don't catch hell because you're a Democrat or a Republican, you don't catch hell because you're a Mason or an Elk, and you sure don't catch hell because you're an American; because if you were an American, you wouldn't catch hell. You catch hell because you're a black man. You catch hell, all of us catch hell, for the same reason.

So we're all black people, so-called Negroes, second-class citizens, ex-slaves. You're nothing but an ex-slave. You don't like to be

told that. But what else are you? You are ex-slaves. You didn't come here on the "Mayflower." You came here on a slave ship. In chains, like a horse, or a cow, or a chicken. And you were brought here by the people who came here on the "Mayflower," you were brought here by the so-called Pilgrims, or Founding Fathers. They were the ones who brought you here.

We have a common enemy. We have this in common: We have a common oppressor, a common exploiter, and a common discriminator. But once we all realize that we have a common enemy, then we unite—on the basis of what we have in common. And what we have foremost in common is that enemy—the white man. He's an enemy to all of us. I know some of you all think that some of them aren't enemies. Time will tell.

In Bandung back in, I think, 1954, was the first unity meeting in centuries of black people. And once you study what happened at the Bandung conference, and the results of the Bandung conference, it actually serves as a model for the same procedure you and I can use to get our problems solved. At Bandung all the nations came together, the dark nations from Africa and Asia. Some of them were Buddhists, some of them were Muslims, some of them were Christians, some were Confucianists, some were atheists. Despite their religious differences, they came together. Some were communists, some were socialists, some were capitalists—despite their economic and political differences, they came together. All of them were black, brown, red or yellow.

The number-one thing that was not allowed to attend the Bandung conference was the white man. He couldn't come. Once they excluded the white man, they found that they could get together. Once they kept him out, everybody else fell right in and fell in line. This is the thing that you and I have to understand. And these people who came together didn't have nuclear weapons, they didn't have jet planes, they didn't have all of the heavy armaments that the white man has. But they had unity.

They were able to submerge their little petty differences and agree on one thing: That there one African came from Kenya and was being colonized by the Englishman, and another African came from the Congo and was being colonized by the Belgian, and another African came from Guinea and was being colonized by the French, and another came from Angola and was being colonized by the Portuguese. When they came to the Bandung conference, they looked at the Portuguese, and at the Frenchman, and at the Englishman, and at the Dutchman, and learned or realized the one thing that all of them had in common—they were all from Europe, they were all Europeans, blond, blue-eyed and white skins. They began to recognize who their enemy was. The same man that was colonizing our people in Kenya was colonizing our people in the Congo. The same one in the Congo was colonizing our people in South Africa, and in Southern Rhodesia, and in Burma, and in India, and in Afghanistan, and in Pakistan. They realized all over the world where the dark man was being oppressed, he was being oppressed by the white man; where the dark man was being exploited, he was being exploited by the white man. So they got together on this basis—that they had a common enemy.

And when you and I here in Detroit and in Michigan and in America who have been awakened today look around us, we too realize here in America we all have a common enemy, whether he's in Georgia or Michigan, whether he's in California or New York. He's the same man—blue eyes and blond hair and pale skin—the same man. So what we have to do is what they did. They agreed to stop quarreling among themselves. Any

little spat that they had, they'd settle it among themselves, go into a huddle—don't let the enemy know that you've got a disagreement.

Instead of airing our differences in public, we have to realize we're all the same family. And when you have a family squabble, you don't get out on the sidewalk. If you do, everybody calls you uncouth, unrefined, uncivilized, savage. If you don't make it at home, you settle it at home; you get in the closet, argue it out behind closed doors, and then when you come out on the street, you pose a common front, a united front. And this is what we need to do in the community, and in the city, and in the state. We need to stop airing our differences in front of the white man, put the white man out of our meetings, and then sit down and talk shop with each other. That's what we've got to do.

I would like to make a few comments concerning the difference between the black revolution and the Negro revolution. Are they both the same? And if they're not, what is the difference? What is the difference between a black revolution and a Negro revolution? First, what is a revolution? Sometimes I'm inclined to believe that many of our people are using this word "revolution" loosely, without taking careful consideration of what this word actually means, and what its historic characteristics are. When you study the historic nature of revolutions, the motive of a revolution, the objective of a revolution, the result of a revolution, and the methods used in a revolution, you may change words. You may devise another program, you may change your goal and you may change your mind.

Look at the American Revolution in 1776. That revolution was for what? For land. Why did they want land? Independence. How was it carried out? Bloodshed. Number one, it was based on land, the basis of independence. And the only way they could get it was bloodshed. The French Revolution— what was it based on? The landless against the landlord. What was it for? Land. How did they get it? Bloodshed. Was no love lost, was no compromise, was no negotiation. I'm telling you—you don't know what a revolution is. Because when you find out what it is, you'll get back in the alley, you'll get out of the way.

The Russian Revolution—what was it based on? Land; the landless against the landlord. How did they bring it about? Bloodshed. You haven't got a revolution that doesn't involve bloodshed. And you're afraid to bleed. I said, you're afraid to bleed.

As long as the white man sent you to Korea, you bled. He sent you to Germany, you bled. He sent you to the South Pacific to fight the Japanese, you bled. You bleed for white people, but when it comes to seeing your own churches being bombed and little black girls murdered, you haven't got any blood. You bleed when the white man says bleed; you bite when the white man says bite; and you bark when the white man says bark. I hate to say this about us, but it's true. How are you going to be nonviolent in Mississippi, as violent as you were in Korea? How can you justify being nonviolent in Mississippi and Alabama, when your churches are being bombed, and your little girls are being murdered, and at the same time you are going to get violent with Hitler, and Tojo, and somebody else you don't even know?

If violence is wrong in America, violence is wrong abroad. If it is wrong to be violent defending black women and black children and black babies and black men, then it is wrong for America to draft us and make us violent abroad in defense of her. And if it is right for America to draft us, and teach us how to be violent in defense of her, then it is right for you and me to do whatever is necessary to defend our own people right here in this country.

The Chinese Revolution—they wanted land. They threw the British out, along with the Uncle Tom Chinese. Yes, they did. They set a good example. When I was in prison, I read an article—don't be shocked when I say that I was in prison. You're still in prison. That's what America means: prison. When I was in prison, I read an article in *Life* magazine showing a little Chinese girl, nine years old; her father was on his hands and knees and she was pulling the trigger because he was an Uncle Tom Chinaman. When they had the revolution over there, they took a whole generation of Uncle Toms and just wiped them out. And within ten years that little girl became a full-grown woman. No more Toms in China. And today it's one of the toughest, roughest, most feared countries on this earth—by the white man. Because there are no Uncle Toms over there.

Of all our studies, history is best qualified to reward our research. And when you see that you've got problems, all you have to do is examine the historic method used all over the world by others who have problems similar to yours. Once you see how they got theirs straight, then you know how you can get yours straight. There's been a revolution, a black revolution, going on in Africa. In Kenya, the Mau Mau were revolutionary; they were the ones who brought the word "Uhuru" to the fore. The Mau Mau, they were revolutionary, they believed in scorched earth, they knocked everything aside that got in their way, and their revolution also was based on land, a desire for land. In Algeria, the northern part of Africa, a revolution took place. The Algerians were revolutionists, they wanted land. France offered to let them be integrated into France. They told France, to hell with France, they wanted some land, not some France. And they engaged in a bloody battle.

So I cite these various revolutions, brothers and sisters, to show you that you don't have a peaceful revolution. You don't have a turn-the-other-cheek revolution. There's no such thing as a nonviolent revolution. The only kind of revolution that is nonviolent is the Negro revolution. The only revolution in which the goal is loving your enemy is the Negro revolution. It's the only revolution in which the goal is a desegregated lunch counter, a desegregated theater, a desegregated park, and a desegregated public toilet; you can sit down next to white folks—on the toilet. That's no revolution. Revolution is based on land. Land is the basis of all independence. Land is the basis of freedom, justice, and equity.

The white man knows what a revolution is. He knows that the black revolution is worldwide in scope and in nature. The black revolution is sweeping Asia, is sweeping Africa, is rearing its head in Latin America. The Cuban Revolution—that's a revolution. They overturned the system. Revolution is in Asia, revolution is in Africa, and the white man is screaming because he sees revolution in Latin America. How do you think he'll react to you when you learn what a real revolution is? You don't know what a revolution is. If you did, you wouldn't use that word.

Revolution is bloody, revolution is hostile, revolution knows no compromise, revolution overturns and destroys everything that gets in its way. And you, sitting around here like a knot on the wall, saying, "I'm going to love these folks no matter how much they hate me." No, you need a revolution. Whoever heard of a revolution where they lock arms, as Rev. Cleage was pointing out beautifully, singing "We Shall Overcome"? You don't do that in a revolution. You don't do any singing, you're too busy swinging. It's based on land. A revolutionary wants land so he can set up his own nation, an independent nation. These Negroes aren't asking for any nation—they're trying to crawl back on the plantation.

When you want a nation, that's called nationalism. When the white man became involved in a revolution in this country against England, what was it for? He wanted this land so he could set up another white nation. That's white nationalism. The American Revolution was white nationalism. The French Revolution was white nationalism. The Russian Revolution too—yes, it was—white nationalism. You don't think so? Why do you think Krushchev and Mao can't get their heads together? White nationalism. All the revolutions that are going on in Asia and Africa today are based on what?—black nationalism. A revolutionary is a black nation-

alist. He wants a nation. I was reading some beautiful words by Rev. Cleage, pointing out why he couldn't get together with someone else in the city because all of them were afraid of being identified with black nationalism. If you're afraid of black nationalism, you're afraid of revolution. And if you love revolution, you love black nationalism.

To understand this, you have to go back to what the young brother here referred to as the house Negro and the field Negro back during slavery. There were two kinds of slaves, the house Negro and the field Negro. The house Negroes—they lived in the house with master, they dressed pretty good, they ate good because they ate his food—what he left. They lived in the attic or the basement, but still they lived near the master; and they loved the master more than the master loved himself. They would give their life to save the master's house—quicker than the master would. If the master said, "We got a good house here," the house Negro would say, "Yeah, we got a good house here." Whenever the master said "we," he said "we." That's how you can tell a house Negro.

If the master's house caught on fire, the house Negro would fight harder to put the blaze out than the master would. If the master got sick, the house Negro would say, "What's the matter, boss, *we* sick?" *We* sick! He identified himself with his master, more than his master identified with himself. And if you came to the house Negro and said, "Let's run away, let's escape, let's separate," the house Negro would look at you and say, "Man, you crazy. What you mean, separate? Where is there a better house than this? Where can I wear better clothes than this? Where can I eat better food than this?" That was the house Negro. In those days he was called a "house nigger." And that's what we call them today, because we've still got some house niggers running around here.

This modern house Negro loves his master. He wants to live near him. He'll pay three times as much as the house is worth just to live near his master, and then brag about "I'm the only Negro out here." "I'm the only one on my job." "I'm the only one in this school." You're nothing but a house Negro. And if someone comes to you right now and says, "Let's separate," you say the same thing that the house Negro said on the plantation. "What you mean, separate? From America, this good white man? Where you going to get a better job than you get here?" I mean, this is what you say. "I ain't left nothing in Africa," that's what you say. Why, you left your mind in Africa.

On that same plantation, there was the field Negro. The field Negroes—those were the masses. There were always more Negroes in the field than there were Negroes in the house. The Negro in the field caught hell. He ate leftovers. In the house they ate high up on the hog. The Negro in the field didn't get anything but what was left of the insides of the hog. They call it "chitt'lings" nowadays. In those days they called them what they were—guts. That's what you were—gut-eaters. And some of you are still gut-eaters.

The field Negro was beaten from morning to night; he lived in a shack, in a hut; he wore old, castoff clothes. He hated his master. I say he hated his master. He was intelligent. That house Negro loved his master, but that field Negro—remember, they were in the majority, and they hated the master. When the house caught on fire, he didn't try to put it out; that field Negro prayed for a wind, for a breeze. When the master got sick, the field Negro prayed that he'd die. If someone came to the field Negro and said, "Let's separate, let's run," he didn't say "Where we going?" He'd say, "Any place is better than here." You've got field Negroes in America today. I'm a field Negro. The masses are the field Negroes. When they see this man's house on fire, you don't hear the little Negroes talking about *"our* government is in trouble." They say, "*The* government is in trouble." Imagine a Negro: "*Our* government"! I even heard one say *"our* astronauts." They won't even let him near the plant—and *"our* astronauts"! "*Our* Navy"—that's a Negro that is out of his mind, a Negro that is out of his mind.

Just as the slavemaster of that day used Tom, the house Negro, to keep the field Negroes in check, the same old slavemaster today has Negroes who are nothing but modern Uncle Toms, twentieth-century Uncle Toms, to keep you and me in check, to keep us under control, keep us passive and peaceful and nonviolent. That's Tom making you nonviolent. It's like when you go to the dentist, and the man's going to take your tooth. You're going to fight him when he starts pulling. So he squirts some stuff in your jaw called novocaine, to make you think they're not doing anything to you. So you sit there and because you've got all of that novocaine in your jaw, you suffer—peacefully. Blood running all down your jaw, and you don't know what's happening. Because someone has taught you to suffer—peacefully.

The white man does the same thing to you in the street, when he wants to put knots on your head and take advantage of you and not have to be afraid of your fighting back. To keep you from fighting back, he gets these old religious Uncle Toms to teach you and me, just like novocaine, to suffer peacefully. Don't stop suffering—just suffer peacefully. As Rev. Cleage pointed out, they say you should let your blood flow in the streets. This is a shame. You know he's a Christian preacher. If it's a shame to him, you know what it is to me.

There is nothing in our book, the Koran, that teaches us to suffer peacefully. Our religion teaches us to be intelligent. Be peaceful, be courteous, obey the law, respect everyone; but if someone puts his hand on you, send him to the cemetery. That's a good religion. In fact, that's that old-time religion. That's the one that Ma and Pa used to talk about: an eye for an eye, and a tooth for a tooth, and a head for a head, and a life for a life. That's a good religion. And nobody resents that kind of religion being taught but a wolf, who intends to make you his meal.

This is the way it is with the white man in America. He's a wolf—and you're sheep. Any time a shepherd, a pastor, teaches you and me not to run from the white man and, at the same time, teaches us not to fight the white man, he's a traitor to you and me. Don't lay down a life all by itself. No, preserve your life, it's the best thing you've got. And if you've got to give it up, let it be even-steven.

The slavemaster took Tom and dressed him well, fed him well and even gave him a little education—a *little* education; gave him a long coat and a top hat and made all the other slaves look up to him. Then he used Tom to control them. The same strategy that was used in those days is used today, by the same white man. He takes a Negro, a so-called Negro, and makes him prominent, builds him up, publicizes him, makes him a celebrity. And then he becomes a spokesman for Negroes—and a Negro leader.

I would like to mention just one other thing quickly, and that is the method that the white man uses, how the white man uses the "big guns," or Negro leaders, against the Negro revolution. They are not a part of the Negro revolution. They are used against the Negro revolution.

When Martin Luther King failed to desegregate Albany, Georgia, the civil-rights struggle in America reached its low point. King became bankrupt almost, as a leader. The Southern Christian Leadership Conference was in financial trouble; and it was in trouble, period, with the people when they failed to desegregate Albany, Georgia. Other Negro civil-rights leaders of so-called national stature became fallen idols. As they became fallen idols, began to lose their prestige and influence, local Negro leaders began to stir up the masses. In Cambridge, Maryland, Gloria Richardson; in Danville, Virginia, and other parts of the country, local leaders began to stir up our people at the grass-roots level. This was never done by these Negroes of national stature. They control you, but they have never incited you or excited you. They control you, they contain you, they have kept you on the plantation.

As soon as King failed in Birmingham, Negroes took to the streets. King went out to California to a big rally and raised I don't know how many thousands of dollars. He came to Detroit and had a march and raised some more thousands of dollars. And recall, right after that Roy Wilkins attacked King. He accused King of CORE [Congress Of Racial Equality] of starting trouble everywhere and then making the NAACP [National Association for the Advancement of Colored People] get them out of jail and spend a lot of money; they accused King and CORE of raising all the money and not paying it back. This happened; I've got it in documented evidence in the newspaper. Roy started attacking King, and King started attacking Roy, and Farmer started attacking both of them. And as these Negroes of national stature began to attack each other, they began to lose their control of the Negro masses.

The Negroes were out there in the streets. They were talking about how they were going to march on Washington. Right at that time Birmingham had exploded, and the Negroes in Birmingham—remember, they also exploded. They began to stab the crackers in the back and bust them up 'side their head—yes, they did. That's when Kennedy sent in the troops, down in Birmingham. After that, Kennedy got on the television and said "this is a moral issue." That's when he said he was going to put out a civil-rights bill. And when he mentioned civil-rights bill and the Southern crackers started talking about how they were going to boycott or filibuster it, then the Negroes started talking—about what? That they were going to march on Washington, march on the Senate, march on the White House, march on the Congress, and tie it up, bring it to a halt, not let the government proceed. They even said they were going out to the airport and lay down on the runway and not let any airplanes land. I'm telling you what they said. That was revolution. That was revolution. That was the black revolution.

It was the grass roots out there in the street. It scared the white man to death, scared the white power structure in Washington, D.C., to death; I was there. When they found out that this black steamroller was going to come down on the capital, they called in Wilkins, they called in Randolph, they called in these national Negro leaders that you respect and told them, "Call it off." Kennedy said, "Look, you all are letting this thing go too far." And Old Tom said, "Boss, I can't stop it, because I didn't start it." I'm telling you what they said. They said, "I'm not even in it, much less at the head of it." They said, "These Negroes are doing things on their own. They're running ahead of us." And that old shrewd fox, he said, "If you all aren't in it, I'll put you in it. I'll put you at the head of it. I'll endorse it. I'll welcome it. I'll help it. I'll join it."

A matter of hours went by. They had a meeting at the Carlyle Hotel in New York City. The Carlyle Hotel is owned by the Kennedy family; that's the hotel Kennedy spent the night at, two nights ago; it belongs to his family. A philanthropic society headed by a white man named Stephen Currier called all the top civil-rights leaders together at the Carlyle Hotel. And he told them, "By you all fighting each other, you are destroying the civil-rights movement. And since you're fighting over money from white liberals, let us set up what is known as the Council for United Civil Rights Leadership. Let's form this council, and all the civil-rights organizations will belong to it, and we'll use it for fund-raising purposes." Let me show you how tricky the white man is. As soon as they got it formed, they elected Whitney Young as its chairman, and who do you think became the co-chairman? Stephen Currier, the white man, a millionaire. Powell was talking about it down at Cobo Hall today. This is what he was talking about. Powell knows it happened. Randolph knows it happened. Wilkins knows it happened. King knows it happened. Every one of that Big Six—they know it happened.

Once they formed it, with the white man over it, he promised them and gave them $800,000 to split up among the Big Six; and told them that after the march was over they'd give them $700,000 more. A million

and a half dollars—split up between leaders that you have been following, going to jail for, crying crocodile tears for. And they're nothing but Frank James and Jesse James and the what-do-you-call-'em brothers.

As soon as they got the setup organized, the white man made available to them top public-relations experts; opened the news media across the country at their disposal, which then began to project these Big Six as the leaders of the march. Orginally they weren't even in the march. You were talking this march talk on Hastings Street, you were talking march talk on Lenox Avenue, and on Fillmore Street, and on Central Avenue, and 32nd Street and 63rd Street. That's where the march talk was being talked. But the white man put the Big Six at the head of it; made them the march. They became the march. They took it over. And the first move they made after they took it over, they invited Walter Reuther, a white man; they invited a priest, a rabbi, and an old white preacher, yes, an old white preacher. The same white element that put Kennedy into power—labor, the Catholics, the Jews, and liberal Protestants; the same clique that put Kennedy in power, joined the march on Washington.

It's just like when you've got some coffee that's too black, which means it's too strong. What do you do? You integrate it with cream, you make it weak. But if you pour too much cream in it, you won't even know you ever had coffee. It used to be hot, it becomes cool. It used to be strong, it becomes weak. It used to wake you up, now it puts you to sleep. This is what they did with the march on Washington. They joined it. They didn't integrate it, they infiltrated it. They joined it, became a part of it, took it over. And as they took it over, it lost its militancy. It ceased to be angry, it ceased to be hot, it ceased to be uncompromising. Why, it even ceased to be a march. It became a picnic, a circus. Nothing but a circus, with clowns and all. You had one right here in Detroit—I saw it on television—with clowns leading it, white clowns and black clowns. I know you don't like what I'm saying, but I'm going to tell you anyway. Because I can prove what I'm saying. If you think I'm telling you wrong, you bring me Martin Luther King and A. Philip Randolph and James Farmer and those other three, and see if they'll deny it over a microphone.

No, it was a sellout. It was a takeover. When James Baldwin came in from Paris, they wouldn't let him talk, because they couldn't make him go by the script. Burt Lancaster read the speech that Baldwin was supposed to make; they wouldn't let Baldwin get up there, because they know Baldwin is liable to say anything. They controlled it so tight, they told those Negroes what time to hit town, how to come, where to stop, what signs to carry, what song to sing, what speech they could make, and what speech they couldn't make; and then told them to get out of town by sundown. And every one of those Toms was out of town by sundown. Now I know you don't like my saying this. But I can back it up. It was a circus, a performance that beat anything Hollywood could ever do, the performance of the year. Reuther and those other three devils should get an Academy Award for the best actors because they acted like they really loved Negroes and fooled a whole lot of Negroes. And the six Negro leaders should get an award too, for the best supporting cast.

Press Releases by Malcolm X

Malcolm X

THE MUSLIM MOSQUE, INC.
HOTEL THERESA 2090 SEVENTH AVE., Suite 128 NEW YORK, N. Y.

May 15, 1964

Mr. Roy Wilkins
National Executive Secretary
NAACP
20 West 40th St.
New York, N. Y.

Dear Sir,

As you know, the Muslim Mosque Inc., provides a new vehicle in which free participation in the struggle for Freedom, Justice, and Equality for the 22 million Negroes can take place.

We have no restrictions on religious ties, political preferences nor organizational leanings of those who wish to participate with us.

Minister Malcolm has also made public his intentions not to attack any person or organization that is engaged in the struggle. He also asks forgiveness for the unkind things that he has said in the past.

Enclosed you will find two letters that have been disseminated as press releases. You will immediately become aware of the new areas for mutual cooperation that these releases mak possible. This is, of course, beneficial to all or our people and should considerably shorten our struggle.

Brother Malcolm will be back in America by May 23rd. We welcome any comments or suggestions that you may have concerning Minister Malcolm's new position. We pray that it will be attractive to you and herald in a new era for all of us.

Certainly he is looking forward to the day (in the near future) when all leaders and organizations will be able to present a United Action Front.

Source: Press Releases by Malcolm X, April 20, May 11, May 15, 1964. Copyright © 1964 NAACP. The author wishes to thank The National Association for the Advancement of Colored People for authorizing the use of this material.

May we hear from you soon?

Sincerely yours,
James Shabazz
Secretary

THE MUSLIM MOSQUE, INC.
HOTEL THERESA 2090 SEVENTH AVE.,
Suite 128 NEW YORK, N. Y.
May 11, 1964

For Immediate Release
FROM MALCOLM X IN LAGOS, NIGERIA
Each place I have visited, they have insisted that I don't leave. Thus I have been forced to stay longer than I originally intended in each country. In the Muslim world they loved me once they learned I was an American *Muslim*, and here in Africa they love me as soon as they learn that I am Malcolm X of the militant American Muslims. Africans in general, and Muslims in particular love militancy. I hope that my Hajj to the Holy City of Mecca will officially establish the religious affiliation of the Muslim Mosque, Inc. with the 750,000,000 Muslims of the World of Islam once and for all—and that my warm reception here in Africa will forever repudiate the American white man's propaganda that the Black man in Africa is not interested in the plight of the Black man in America.

The Muslim World is forced to concern itself from the moral point of view in its own religious concepts, with the fact that our plight clearly involves the violation of our *human rights.*

The Koran compels the Muslim World to take a stand on the side of those whose human rights are being violated, no matter what the religious persuasion of the victims are. Islam is a religion which concerns itself with the human rights of all mankind, despite race, color, or creed. It recognizes all (everyone) as part of one Human Family.

Here in Africa the 22 million American Blacks are looked upon as the long-lost brothers of Africa. Our people here are interested in every aspect of our plight, and they study our struggle for freedom from every angle. Despite western propaganda to the contrary, our African Brothers and Sisters love us, and are happy to learn that we also are awakening from our long "sleep" and are developing strong love for them.

(Signed)

El Hajj Malik El-Shabazz

THE MUSLIM MOSQUE, INC.
HOTEL THERESA 2090 SEVENTH AVE.,
Suite 128 NEW YORK, N. Y.
FROM MALCOLM X FOR IMMEDIATE RELEASE
Jedda, Saudi Arabia

April 20, 1964
Never have I witnessed such sincere hospitality and the overwhelming spirit of true brotherhood as is practiced by people *of all colors and races* here in this Ancient Holy Land, the home of Abraham, Muhammad and all the other prophets of the Holy Scriptures. For the past week I have been utterly speechless and spellbound by the graciousness I see displayed all around me by people *of all colors.*

Last night, April 19th, I was blessed to visit the Holy City of Mecca, and complete the "Omra", part of my pilgrimmage. Allah willing, I shall leave for Mina tomorrow, April 21st, and be back in Mecca to say my prayers from Mt. Arafat on Tuesday, April 22nd. Mina is about 20 miles from Mecca.

Last night I made my seven circuits around the Kaaba, led by a young Mutawif named Muhammad. I drank water from the well of Zem Zem, and then ran back and forth seven times between the hills of Mt. Al-Safa and Al-Marwah.

There were tens of thousands of pilgrims from all over the world. They were *of all colors,* from blue-eyed blonds to black-skinned Africans, but were all participating in the same ritual, displaying a spirit of unity and brotherhood that my experiences in America had led me to believe could never exist between the white and non-white.

America needs to understand Islam, because this is the one religion that erases the race problem from its society. Throughout my travels in the Muslim World, I have met, talked to, and even eaten with, people who would have been considered "white" in America, but the religion of Islam in their hearts has removed the "white" from their minds. They practice sincere and true brotherhood with other people irrespective of their color.

Before America allows herself to be destroyed by the "cancer of racism" she should become better acquainted with the religious philosophy of Islam, a religion that has already molded people of all colors into one vast family, a nation or brotherhood of Islam that leaps over all "obstacles" and stretches itself into almost all the Eastern countries of this earth.

The whites, as well as the non-whites who accept true Islam become a changed people. I have eaten from the same plate with people whose eyes were the bluest of blue, whose hair was the blondest of blond, and whose skin was the whitest of white - all the way from Cairo to Jedda and even in the Holy City of Mecca itself - and I felt the same sincerity in the words and deeds of these "white" Muslims that I felt among the African Muslims of Nigeria, Sudan and Ghana.

True Islam removes racism, because people of all colors and races who accept its religious principles and bow down to the One God, Allah, also automatically accept each other as brothers and sisters, regardless of differences in complexion.

You may be shocked by these words coming from me, but I have always been a man who tries to face facts, and to accept the reality of life as new experiences and knowledge unfolds it. The experiences of this pilgrimmage have taught me much, and each hour here in the Holy Land opens my eyes even more. If Islam can place the spirit of true brotherhood in the hearts of the "whites" whom I have met here in the Land of the Prophets, then surely it can also remove the "cancer of racism" from the heart of the white American, and perhaps in time to save America from imminent racial disaster, the same destruction brought upon Hitler by his racism that eventually destroyed the Germans themselves.

At present I am a State Guest of His Excellency, Prince Faisal, the ruler of Arabia.

I am most grateful to Dr. Mahmoud Youssef Shawarbi, Director of the Islamic Center of New York for helping me to understand true Islam, a religion that teaches brotherhood and tolerance between peoples of all colors and national origins. He was instrumental in opening my eyes to Islam's views concerning cooperation between peoples in solving mutual problems amicably. He always reminded me of the relevant verse in our *Holy Koran* which says:

"Call unto the way of the Lord with wisdom and fair exhortation and reason with them in the better way."

Holy Koran Ch. 16, Verse 125

Dr. Shawarbi's name and prestige have opened many doors for me here in the Muslim World. New York City should be proud that he is the Director of its Islamic Center in addition to being the Director of the Islamic Federation of the United States and Canada.

My experiences here in the Muslim World compel me to urge Americans of all colors to flock to this great religious man and drink of his spiritual wisdom.

In New York, Dr. Shawarbi had given me the book *"The Eternal Message of Muhammad"* by Abd-al-Rahman Azzam. I read this most inspiring book all the way to Jeddah and I must confess that its wealth of information, expressed in frank and simple terms, opened a new world of Islamic thought to me. It broadened my scope, and made me more open-minded.

Two nights ago I had the honor of meeting this noble man, the author of the book, at the home of his son, Dr. Omar Azzam, here in Jeddah. He seemed to be one of the most modern progressive and broad-minded humans I have ever met. In America he would be called a "white" man, but to me he was a Muslim, and his warm, friendly hospitality made me soon feel like one of his sons. Upon learning that I had no reservations in any hotel, this world traveler, UN diplomat, ambassador and companion of kings, gave me his own suite, at the Jeddah Palane Hotel.

This man who would be considered "white" in America, gave his bed to me, an American Negro. It was he who made Prince Faisal aware of my presence in Jeddah.

The very next morning, His Excellency's son, Muhammad Faisal, informed me personally that I was to be a State Guest, by the will and decree of his esteemed father.

The Deputy Chief of Protocol, took me before the Hajj Court, presided over by His Holiness Sheikh Muhammad Harkon with whom I had tea when I visited Jeddah in 1959. I was pleased that he remembered me. He okayed my visa to Mecca, gave me two books on Islam, with his personal seal and autograph, and told me he prayed I would

be a successful preacher of Islam in America. I felt very humble by the attention and honor they were bestowing upon me. It was an honor that in America would be bestowed upon a King—not a Negro.

They placed a car at my disposal, with a driver and a guide, making it possible for me to travel between Mecca and Jeddah almost at will. Never did I dream that I would be the recipient of such honors, especially being State Guest of the Prince who rules this Holy Land. All praise is due to Allah, the Lord of all the Worlds.

In my next letter I hope to tell you more about Mecca, and how Dr. Omar Azzam (the author's son) is modernizing these cities and the highway system that leads to all the Holy Places. They are even rebuilding the Great Mosque which houses the Kaaba in the Holy City of Mecca. It will be an architectural wonder that will rival the Taj Mahal in beauty, and the Pyramids in engineering skill when completed.

Text of letter dated April 19, 1964 from El-Hajj Malik El-Shabazz (Malcolm X)

The Civil Rights Act, 1964, and Voting Rights Act, 1965

THE CIVIL RIGHTS ACT

An act to enforce the constitutional right to vote, to confer jurisdiction upon the district courts of the United States to provide injunctive relief against discrimination in public accommodations, to authorize the Attorney General to institute suits to protect constitutional rights in public facilities and public education, to extend the Commission on Civil Rights, to prevent discrimination in federally assisted programs, to establish a Commission on Equal Employment Opportunity, and for other purposes*

---

*78 Stat. 241 (1964).

Be it enacted by the Senate and House of Representatives of the United States of America in Congress assembled, That this Act may be cited as the "Civil Rights Act of 1964."

TITLE I—VOTING RIGHTS . . .

Sec. 101. . . . "(2) No person acting under color of law shall—

"(A) in determining whether any individual is qualified under State law or laws to vote in any Federal election, apply any standard, practice, or procedure different from the standards, practices, or procedures applied under such law or laws to other individuals within the same county, parish, or similar political subdivision who have been found by State officials to be qualified to vote;

"(B) deny the right of any individual to vote in any Federal election because of an error or omission on any record or paper relating to any application, registration, or other act requisite to voting, if such error or omission is not material in determining whether such individual is qualified under State law to vote in such election; or —

"(C) employ any literacy test as a qualification for voting in any Federal election unless (i) such test is administered to each individual and is conducted wholly in writing, and (ii) a certified copy of the test and of the answers given by the individual is furnished to him within twenty-five days of the submission of his request made within the period of time during which records and papers are required to be retained and preserved pursuant to title III of the Civil Rights Act of 1960 (42 U.S.C. 1974—74e; 74 Stat. 88): *Provided, however,* That the Attorney General may enter into agreements with appropriate State or local authorities that preparation, conduct, and maintenance of such tests in accordance with the provisions as are necessary in the preparation, conduct, and main-tenance of such tests for persons who are blind or otherwise physically handicapped, meet the purposes of this subparagraph and constitute compliance therewith.

TITLE II—INJUNCTIVE RELIEF AGAINST DISCRIMINATION IN PLACES OF PUBLIC ACCOMMODATION

Sec. 201. (a) All persons shall be entitled to the full and equal enjoyment of the goods, services, facilities, privileges, advantages, and accommodations of any place of public accommodation, as defined in this section, without discrimination or segregation on the ground of race, color, religion, or national origin.

(b) Each of the following establishments which serves the public is a place of public accommodation within the meaning of this title if its operations affect commerce, or if discrimination or segregation by it is supported by State action:

(1) any inn, hotel, motel, or other establishment which provides lodging to transient guests, other than an establishment located within a building which contains not more than five rooms for rent or hire and which is actually occupied by the proprietor of such establishment as his residence;

(2) any restaurant, cafeteria, lunchroom, lunch counter, soda fountain, or other facility principally engaged in selling food for consumption on the premises, including, but not limited to, any such facility located on the premises of any retail establishment; or any gasoline station;

(3) any motion picture house, theater, concert hall, sports arena, stadium or other place of exhibition or entertainment; and

(4) any establishment (A) (i) which is physically located within the premises of any establishment otherwise covered by this subsection, or (ii) within the premises of which is physically located any such covered

establishment, and (B) which holds itself out as serving patrons of such covered establishment.

(c) The operations of an establishment affect commerce within the meaning of this title if (1) it is one of the establishments described in paragraph (1) of subsection (b); (2) in the case of an establishment described in paragraph (2) of subsection (b), it serves or offers to serve interstate travelers or a substantial portion of the food which it serves, or gasoline or other products which it sells, has moved in commerce; (3) in the case of an establishment described in paragraph (3) of subsection (b), it customarily presents films, performances, athletic teams, exhibitions, or other sources of entertainment which move in commerce; and (4) in the case of an establishment described in paragraph (4) of subsection (b), it is physically located within the premises of, or there is physically located within its premises, an establishment the operations of which affect commerce within the meaning of this subsection. For purposes of this section, "commerce" means travel, trade, traffic, commerce, transportation, or communication among the several States, or between the District of Columbia and any State, or between any foreign country or any territory or possession and any State or the District of Columbia, or between points in the same State but through any other State or the District of Columbia, or between points in the same State but through any other State or the District of Columbia or a foreign country.

(d) Discrimination or segregation by an establishment is supported by State action within the meaning of this title if such discrimination or segregation (1) is carried on under color of any law, statute, ordinance, or regulation; or (2) is carried on under color of any custom or usage required or enforced by officials of the State or political subdivision thereof; or (3) is required by action of the State or political subdivision thereof.

(e) The provisions of this title shall not apply to a private club or other establishment not in fact open to the public, except to the extent that the facilities of such establishment are made available to the customers or patrons of an establishment within the scope of subsection (b).

Sec. 202. All persons shall be entitled to be free, at any establishment or place, from discrimination or segregation of any kind on the ground of race, color, religion, or national origin, if such discrimination or segregation is or purports to be required by any law, statute, ordinance, regulation, rule, or order of a State or any agency or political subdivision thereof.

Sec. 203. No person shall (a) withhold, deny, or attempt to withhold or deny, or deprive or attempt to deprive, any person of any right or privilege secured by section 201 or 202, or (b) intimidate, threaten, or coerce, or attempt to intimidate, threaten, or coerce any person with the purpose of interfering with any right or privilege secured by section 201 or 202, or (c) punish or attempt to punish any person for exercising or attempting to exercise any right or privilege secured by section 201 or 202.

Sec. 204. (a) Whenever any person has engaged or there are reasonable grounds to believe that any person is about to engage in any act or practice prohibited by section 203, a civil action for preventive relief, including an application for a permanent or temporary injunction, restraining order, or other order, may be instituted by the person aggrieved and, upon timely application, the court may, in its discretion, permit the Attorney General to intervene in such civil action if he certifies that the case is of general public importance. Upon application by the complainant and in such circumstances as the court may deem just, the court may appoint an attorney for such complainant and may authorize the commencement of the civil action without the payment of fees, costs, or security.

TITLE III—DESEGREGATION OF PUBLIC FACILITIES

Sec. 301. (a) Whenever the Attorney General receives a complaint in writing signed by an individual to the effect that he is being deprived of or threatened with the loss of his right to the equal protection of the laws, on account of his race, color, religion, or national origin, by being denied equal utilization of any public facility which is owned, operated, or managed by or on behalf of any State or subdivision thereof, other than a public school or public college as defined in section 401 of title IV hereof, and the Attorney General believes the complaint is meritorious and certifies that the signer or signers of such complaint are unable, in his judgment, to initiate and maintain appropriate legal proceedings for relief and that the institution of an action will materially further the orderly progress of desegregation in public facilities, the Attorney General is authorized to institute for or in the name of the United States a civil action in any appropriate district court of the United States against such parties and for such relief as may be appropriate, and such court shall have and shall exercise jurisdiction of proceedings instituted pursuant to this section. The Attorney General may implead as defendants such additional parties as are or become necessary to the grant of effective relief hereunder.

TITLE IV—DESEGREGATION OF PUBLIC EDUCATION

Suits by the Attorney General

Sec. 407. (a) Whenever the Attorney General receives complaint in writing—

(1) signed by a parent or group of parents to the effect that his or their minor children, as members of a class of persons similarly situated, are being deprived by a school board of the equal protection of the laws, or

(2) signed by an individual, or his parent, to the effect that he has been denied admission to or not permitted to continue in attendance at a public college by reason of race, color, religion, or national origin, and the Attorney General believes the complaint is meritorious and certifies that the signer or signers of such complaint are unable, in his judgment, to initiate and maintain appropriate legal proceedings for relief and that the institution of an action will materially further the orderly achievement of desegregation in public education, the Attorney General is authorized, after giving notice of such complaint to the appropriate school board or college authority and after certifying that he is satisfied that such board or authority has had a reasonable time to adjust the conditions alleged in such complaint, to institute for or in the name of the United States a civil action in any appropriate district court of the United States against such parties and for such relief as may be appropriate, and such court shall have and shall exercise jurisdiction of proceedings instituted pursuant to this section, provided that nothing herein shall empower any official or court of the United States to issue any order seeking to achieve a racial balance in any school by requiring the transportation of pupils or students from one school to another or one school district to another in order to achieve such racial balance, or otherwise enlarge the existing power of the court to insure compliance with constitutional standards. The Attorney General may implead as defendants such additional parties as are or become necessary to the grant of effective relief hereunder.

(b) The Attorney General may deem a person or persons unable to initiate and maintain appropriate legal proceedings within the meaning of subsection (a) of this section when such person or persons are unable, either directly or through other interested persons or organizations, to bear the expense of the litigation or to obtain effective legal representation; or whenever he is satisfied that the institution of such litigation would jeopardize the personal safety, employment, or economic standing of such person or persons, their families, or their property.

TITLE V—COMMISSION ON CIVIL RIGHTS

Duties of the Commission

"Sec. 104. (a) The Commission shall—

1. "investigate allegations in writing under oath or affirmation that certain citizens of the United States are being deprived of their right to vote and have that vote counted by reason of their color, race, religion, or national origin; which writing, under oath or affirmation, shall set forth the facts upon which such belief or beliefs are based;

2. "study and collect information concerning legal developments constituting a denial of equal protection of the laws under the Constitution because of race, color, religion or national origin or in the administration of justice;

3. "appraise the laws and policies of the Federal Government with respect to denials of equal protection of the laws under the Constitution because of race, color, religion or national origin or in the administration of justice;

4. "serve as a national clearinghouse for information in respect to denials of equal protection of the laws because of race, color, religion or national origin, including but not limited to the fields of voting, education, housing, employment, the use of public facilities, and transportation, or in the administration of justice;

5. "investigate allegations, made in writing and under oath or affirmation, that citizens of the United States are unlawfully being accorded or denied the right to vote, or to have their votes properly counted, in any election of presidential electors, Members of the United States Senate, or of the House of Representatives, as a result of any patterns or practice of fraud or discrimination in the conduct of such election; and

6. "Nothing in this or any other Act shall be construed as authorizing the Commission, its Advisory Committees, or any person under its supervision or control to inquire into or investigate any membership practices or internal operations of any fraternal organization, any college or university fraternity or sorority, any private club or any religious organization."

TITLE VI—NONDISCRIMINATION IN FEDERALLY ASSISTED PROGRAMS

Sec. 601. No person in the United States shall, on the ground of race, color, or national origin, be excluded from participation in, be denied the benefits of, or be subjected to discrimination under any program or activity receiving Federal financial assistance.

TITLE VII—EQUAL EMPLOYMENT OPPORTUNITY

Discrimination Because of Race, Color, Religion, Sex, or National Origin

Sec. 703. (a) It shall be an unlawful employment practice for an employer—

1. to fail or refuse to hire or to discharge any individual, or otherwise to discriminate against any individual with respect to his compensation, terms, conditions, or privileges of employment, because of such individual's race, color, religion, sex, or national origin; or

2. to limit, segregate, or classify his employees in any way which would deprive or tend to deprive any individual of employment opportunities or otherwise adversely affect his status as an employee, because of such individual's race, color, religion, sex, or national origin.

(b) It shall be an unlawful employment practice for an employment agency to fail or refuse to refer for employment, or otherwise to discriminate against, any individual because of his race, color, religion, sex, or national origin, or to classify or refer for employment any individual on the basis of his race, color, religion, sex, or national origin.

(c) It shall be an unlawful employment practice for a labor organization—

1. to exclude or to expel from its membership, or otherwise to discriminate against, any individual because of his race, color, religion, sex, or national origin;

2. to limit, segregate, or classify its membership, or to classify or fail or refuse to refer for employment any individual, in any way which would deprive or tend to deprive any individual of employment opportunities, or would limit such employment opportunities or otherwise adversely affect his status as an employee or as an applicant for employment, because of such individual's race, color, religion, sex, or national origin; or

3. to cause or attempt to cause an employer to discriminate against an individual in violation of this section.

(d) It shall be an unlawful employment practice for any employer, labor organization, or joint labor-management committee controlling apprenticeship or other training or retraining, including on-the-job training programs, to discriminate against any individual because of his race, color, religion, sex, or national origin in admission to, or employment in, any program established to provide apprenticeship or other training.

(e) Notwithstanding any other provision of this title, (1) it shall not be an unlawful employment practice for an employer to hire and employ employees, for an employment agency to classify, or refer for employment any individual, for a labor organization to classify its membership or to classify or refer for employment any individual, or for an employer, labor organization, or joint labor-management committee controlling apprenticeship or other training or retraining programs to admit or employ any individual in any such program, on the basis of his religion, sex, or national origin in those certain instances where religion, sex, or national origin is a bona fide occupational qualification reasonably necessary to the normal operation of that particular business or enterprise, and (2) it shall not be an unlawful employment practice for a school, college, university, or other educational institution or institution of learning to hire and employ employees of a particular religion if such school, college, university, or other educational institution or institution of learning is, in whole or in substantial part, owned, supported, controlled, or managed by a particular religion or by a particular religious corporation, association, or society, or if the curriculum of such school, college, university, or other educational institution or institution of learning is directed toward the propagation of a particular religion.

(f) As used in this title, the phrase "unlawful employment practice" shall not be deemed to include any action or measure taken by an employer, labor organization, joint labor-management committee, or employment agency with respect to an individual who is a member of the Communist Party of the United States or of any other organization required to register as a Communist-action or Communist-front organization by final order of the Subversive Activities Control Board pursuant to the Subversive Activities Control Act of 1950.

(g) Notwithstanding any other provision of this title, it shall not be an unlawful employment practice for an employer to fail or refuse to hire and employ any individual for any position, for an employer to discharge any individual from any position, or for an employment agency to fail or refuse to refer any individual for employment in any position, or for a labor organization to fail or refuse to refer any individual for employment in any position, if—

1. the occupancy of such position, or access to the premises in or upon which any part of the duties of such position is performed, or is to be performed, is subject to any requirement imposed in the interest of the national security of the United States under any security program in effect pursuant to or administered under any statute of the United States or any Executive order of the President; and

2. such individual has not fulfilled or has ceased to fulfill that requirement.

(h) Notwithstanding any other provision of this title, it shall not be an unlawful employment practice for an employer to apply different standards of compensation, or different terms, conditions, or privileges of employment pursuant to a bona fide seniority or merit system, or a system which measures earnings by quantity or quality of production or to employees who work in different locations, provided that such differences are not the result of an intention to discriminate because of race, color, religion, sex, or national origin, nor shall it be an unlawful employment practice for an employer to give and to act upon the results of any professionally developed ability test provided that such test, its administration or action upon the results is not designed, intended or used to discriminate because of race, color, religion, sex or national origin. It shall not be an unlawful employment practice under this title for any employer to differentiate upon the basis of sex in determining the amount of the wages or compensation paid or to be paid to employees of such employer if such differentiation is authorized by the provisions of section 6(d) of the Fair Labor Standards Act of 1938, as amended (29 U.S.C. 206(d)).

Equal Employment Opportunity Commission

Sec. 705 (a) There is hereby created a Commission to be known as the Equal Employment Opportunity Commission, which shall be composed of five members, not more than three of whom shall be members of the same political party, who shall be appointed by the President by and with the advice and consent of the Senate. One of the original members shall be appointed for a term of one year, one for a term of two years, one for a term of three years, one for a term of four years, and one for a term of five years, beginning from the date of enactment of this title, but their successors shall be appointed for terms of five years each, except that any individual chosen to fill a vacancy shall be appointed only for the unexpired term of the member whom he shall succeed. The President shall designate one member to serve as Chairman of the Commission, and one member to serve as Vice Chairman. The Chairman shall be responsible on behalf of the Commission for the administrative operations of the Commission, and shall appoint, in accordance with the civil service laws, such officers, agents, attorneys, and employees as it deems necessary to assist it in the performance of its functions and to fix their compensation in accordance with the Classification Act of 1949, as amended. The Vice Chairman shall act as Chairman in the absence or disability of the Chairman or in the event of a vacancy in that office.

Prevention of Unlawful Employment Practices

Sec. 706. (a) Whenever it is charged in writing under oath by a person claiming to be aggrieved, or a written charge has been filed by a member of the Commission where he has reasonable cause to believe a violation of this title has occurred (and such charge sets forth the facts upon which it is based) that an employer, employment agency, or labor organization has engaged in an unlawful employment practice, the Commission shall furnish such employer, employment agency, or labor organization (hereinafter referred to as the "respondent") with a copy of such charge and shall make an investigation of such charge provided that such charge shall not be made public by the Commission. If the Commission shall determine, after such investigation, that there is reasonable cause to believe that the charge is true, the Commission shall endeavor to eliminate any such alleged unlawful employment practice by informal methods of conference, conciliation, and persuasion. Nothing said or done during and as a part of such endeavors may be made public by the Commission without the written consent of the parties, or used as evidence in a subsequent proceeding. Any officer or employee of the Commission, who shall make public in any manner whatever any information in violation of this subsection shall be deemed guilty of a misdemeanor and upon conviction thereof shall be fined not more than $1,000 or imprisoned not more than one year.

THE VOTING RIGHTS ACT, 1965

An act to enforce the Fifteenth Amendment to the Constitution of the United States, and for other purposes*

Be it enacted by the Senate and House of Representatives of the United States of America in Congress assembled, That this Act shall be known as the "Voting Rights Act of 1965"

Sec. 2. No voting qualification or prerequisite to voting, or standard, practice, or procedure shall be imposed or applied by any State or political subdivision to deny or abridge the right of any citizen of the United States to vote on account of race or color.

(c) If in any proceeding instituted by the Attorney General under any statute to enforce the guarantees of the fifteenth amendment in any State or political subdivision the court finds that violations of the fifteenth amendment justifying equitable relief have occurred within the territory of such State or political subdivision, the court, in addition to such relief as it may grant, shall retain jurisdiction for such period as it may deem appropriate and during such period no voting qualification or prerequisite to voting, or standard, practice, or procedure with respect to voting different from that in force or effect at the time the proceeding was commenced shall be enforced unless and until the court finds that such qualification, prerequisite, standard, practice, or procedure does not have the purpose and will not have the effect of denying or abridging the right to vote on account of race or color: *Provided,* That such qualification, prerequisite, standard, practice,

---

*79 Stat. 437 (1965).

or procedure may be enforced if the qualification, prerequisite, standard, practice, or procedure has been submitted by the chief legal officer or other appropriate official of such State or subdivision to the Attorney General and the Attorney General has not interposed an objection within sixty days after such submission, except that neither the court's finding nor the Attorney General's failure to object shall bar a subsequent action to enjoin enforcement of such qualification, prerequisite, standard, practice, or procedure.

Sec. 4. (a) To assure that the right of citizens of the United States to vote is not denied or abridged on account of race or color, no citizen shall be denied the right to vote in any Federal, State, or local election because of his failure to comply with any test or device in any State with respect to which the determinations have been made under subsection (b) or in any political subdivision with respect to which such determinations have been made as a separate unit, unless the United States District Court for the District of Columbia in an action for a declaratory judgment brought by such State or subdivision against the United States has determined that no such test or device has been used during the five years preceding the filing of the action for the purpose or with the effect of denying or abridging the right to vote on account of race or color: *Provided,* That no such declaratory judgment shall issue with respect to any plaintiff for a period of five years after the entry of a final judgment of any court of the United States, other than the denial of a declaratory judgment under this section, whether entered prior to or after the enactment of this Act, determining that denials or abridgments of the right to vote on account of race or color through the use of such tests or devices have occurred anywhere in the territory of such plaintiff.

. . . .

Sec. 10. (a) The Congress finds that the requirement of the payment of a poll tax as a precondition to voting (i) precludes persons of limited means from voting or imposes unreasonable financial hardship upon such persons as a precondition to their exercise of the franchise, (ii) does not bear a reasonable relationship to any legitimate State interest in the conduct of elections, and (iii) in some areas has the purpose or effect of denying persons the right to vote because of race or color. Upon the basis of these findings, Congress declares that the constitutional right of citizens to vote is denied or abridged in some areas by the requirement of the payment of a poll tax as a precondition to voting.

. . . .

Sec. 11. (a) No person acting under color of law shall fail or refuse to permit any person to vote who is entitled to vote under any provision of this Act or is otherwise qualified to vote, or willfully fail or refuse to tabulate, count, and report such person's vote. (b) No person, whether acting under color of law or otherwise, shall intimidate, threaten, or coerce, or attempt to intimidate, threaten, or coerce any person for voting or attempting to vote, or intimidate, threaten, or coerce, or attempt to intimidate, threaten, or coerce any person for urging or aiding any person to vote or attempt to vote, or intimidate, threaten, or coerce any person for exercising any powers or duties under section 3(a), 6, 8, 9, 10, or 12(e).

Program of the Chicago Freedom Movement

July, 1966

INTRODUCTION: THE PROBLEMS OF RACISM, GHETTOES, AND SLUMS

Racism, slums and ghettoes have been the essentials of Negro existence in Chicago. While the city permitted its earlier ethnic groups to enter the mainstream of American life, it has locked the Negro into the lower rungs of the social and economic ladder. The Negro in Chicago has been systematically excluded from the major rewards of American life; he is restricted in the jobs he may hold, the schools he may attend, and the places where he may live. In the year 1966 the Negro is as far behind the white as he was in the year 1940.

Chicago today is a divided city—segregated in all areas of social and economic activity, in employment, in education, in housing and in community organization. The Negro community is sectioned off from the larger metropolis into areas of the city that have been set aside for black ghettoes. Within these confines the Negro community is regulated from the outside like a colony— its potential economic resources underdeveloped, its more than one million inhabitants, the daily victims of personal rebuffs, insults and acts of prejudice, and its poorer citizens at the mercy of police, welfare workers, and minor government officials.

Racism in the large Northern cities has not featured lynchings, denial of the vote, or other clear injustices that could easily be removed as is the case in the South. Yet, racism in Chicago has been a stark reality, visible in many dimensions. It is reflected in the existence of the massive overcrowded ghetto that grows each year. It is reflected in the crime-infested slums where the living standards of the Negro poor often do not cover

Source: "Program of the Chicago Freedom Movement," July 1966. Mimeographed, no imprint (1966).

the bare necessities of urban living. It is reflected in the exploitation of Negroes by the dominant white society in higher rents and prices, lower wages and poorer schools.

Under the system of northern racism the Negro receives inferior and second-class status in every area of urban living. The Negro is concentrated in the low-paying and second-rate jobs. In housing, proportionately more Negroes live in substandard or deteriorating dwellings. In education, Negro schools have more inexperienced teachers, fewer classrooms, and less expenditures per pupil. In the maintenance of law and order Negroes are frequently the victims of police brutality and of stop and search methods of crime detection.

All Negroes in Chicago are confined to the ghetto and suffer second-class treatment regardless of their social or economic status. But the worst off are the Negro poor, locked into the slum which is the most deprived part of the ghetto. The forty (40) per cent of the Negro population who make up a black urban peasantry in the slums are the hardest hit victims of discrimination and segregation. Their incomes often have to be supplemented by welfare payments dispensed under procedures that are ugly and paternalistic. They are frequently unemployed. They are forced to live in rat infested buildings or in the Chicago Housing Authority's cement reservations. Their children are all but ignored by the school system. In short they have been frozen out of American society by both race and poverty.

The subjugation of Negroes in Chicago has not been the result of long-established legal codes or customs, like those that existed in the South. Although Chicago has not for a century had any segregation laws or discrimination ordinances, the subordination of Negroes in the North has been almost as effective as if there had been such laws. Northern segregation resulting from policies, in particular the decision-making procedures, of the major economic and social institutions. The employment policies of business firms and government, and practices of realtors, and the operation of the Chicago School System have all reinforced one another to keep the Negroes separate and unequal. The system of racial separation resulting from their interaction have become so strongly imbedded in the city's life that present racial patterns are passed on from generation to generation.

In many instances, although these restrictive policies have now been formally abolished or concealed, the effects of their operations over several decades remains. Very often, Negroes are no longer excluded consciously and deliberately. In employment, personnel men need not discriminate so long as Chicago's inferior schools send their pupils into the labor market less prepared than white graduates. Realtors can justify their discrimination when white parents rightfully fear that integrated schools eventually deteriorate because the school system considers them less important than white schools. School administrators can efficiently segregate by following neighborhood school policies in allocating school facilities.

In the past, the Negro's efforts to improve his living conditions have concentrated on going through the well-defined channels of white authority. Negroes for years have been asking, begging, and pleading that white employers, board presidents, bankers, realtors, politicians, and government officials correct racial patterns and inequities. The major lesson that the Negro community has learned is that racial change through this process comes only gradually, usually too late, and only in small measures.

In this rapidly changing world where technological changes may displace the unskilled workers, where affluence makes it possible to spend millions in waging wars in far away places like Vietnam, and where the elimination of poverty and racism have become National goals, Negroes no longer have the patience to abide by the old, unsuccessful gradualism of the respectable defenders of status-quo.

The present powerlessness of Negroes hinders them from changing conditions themselves or even in developing effective coalitions with others, but the time has now come for Negroes to set up their own instruments that will direct pressure at the institutions that still adhere to racism policies. Negroes must form their own power base from which Negro aspirations and goals can be demanded, a base from which they can make a strong common fight with others that can share their problems or their aspirations. Chicago will become an open city only when Negroes develop power in proportion to their numbers.

THE CHICAGO FREEDOM MOVEMENT

The Chicago Freedom Movement is a coalition of forces for the purpose of wiping out slums, ghettoes and racism. Its core is formed by the unity of the Southern Christian Leadership Conference (S.C.L.C.) and the Coordinating Council of Community Organizations (C.C.C.O.). S.C.L.C., operating under the leadership of Dr. Martin Luther King, Jr., was invited to Chicago by C.C.C.O. because of its dynamic work in the South. C.C.C.O. is a coalition of thirty-six (36) Chicago civil-rights and Negro community organizations. Cooperating with the Chicago Freedom Movement are a number of religious organizations, social agencies, neighborhood groups and individuals of good will.

Many groups in the Chicago region share with Negroes common problems of slum housing, welfare dependency, inferior education, police brutality, and color discrimination. Puerto Rican and Mexican Chicagoans are becoming increasingly vocal about these problems, and the Freedom Movement is seeking ways to join in a united effort with its Latin American brothers. Therefore, the Freedom Movement is making many proposals that provide for the improvement and upgrading of conditions of Latin Americans, other non-whites and some white minorities.

The Freedom Movement proposals and demands are designed to set the broad guidelines for a just and open city in which all men can live with dignity. Three interrelated goals set forth the direction to such a society:

1. To bring about equality of opportunity and of results.
2. To open up the major areas of metropolitan life of housing, employment, and education.
3. To provide power for the powerless.

Many will affirm these goals and wish that they could be achieved. But very little will happen unless Negroes, Latin Americans, other oppressed minorities and their white friends join hands and organize to bring about change—for power does not yield to pleading.

The Freedom Movement will achieve its goals through the organization of a non-violent movement which provides the power to participate in the decisions which now subjugates rather than elevates, which suppresses man's humanity rather than expresses it.

In order to generate the necessary power the movement will:

1. Organize a series of direct actions which will make the injustices so clear that the whole community will respond to the need to change.
2. Organize people in every sector of the ghettoes—in neighborhoods, in schools, in welfare unions, in public housing, in hospitals, to give the strength of numbers to the demands for change.
3. Strengthen the institutions which contribute to the goals of a just and open society and withdraw support from those institutions—banks, businesses, newspapers and professions—which drain the resources of the ghetto communities without contributing in return.
4. Demand representation of the organizations of the ghetto community (Chicago Freedom Movement) on decision-making bodies at every level of government, industry, labor, and church, affecting the lives of people in the ghetto.
5. Promote political education and participation so that the needs and aspirations of Negroes and other oppressed minorities are fully represented.

The Chicago Freedom Movement and its constituent organizations use many means to bring about change. Community organization, education, research, job development, legal redress and political education are all weapons in the arsenal of the Movement. But, its most distinctive and creative tool is that of non-violent direct action.

Non-violence is based on the truth that each human being has infinite dignity and worth. This truth, which is at the heart of our religious and democratic heritage, is denied by systems of discrimination and exploitation. The beginning of change in such systems of discrimination is for men to assert with simple dignity and humanity that they are men and human and that they will no longer be oppressed or oppressors. A just society is born when men cease to be accomplices in a system of degradation.

Then specific injustices and discriminations must be exposed by direct actions which reveal, without excuse or rationalization, the extent and nature of the problem. They bring into the open, as conflicts, social antagonisms that in the past had been hidden as subjugation or exploitation. The methodology of non-violence keeps attention focused on the real issues of injustice and discrimination rather than on false issues which arise when conflict becomes violent.

The non-violent movement seeks to create a community in which justice and equality provide the framework for all human relationships and are embodied in its institutions. The practice of justice is the evidence of a community based on respect for every person and of a society in which human values prevail over cash values. A genuine human community does not exist until all citizens are given an opportunity to participate to the fullest limits of their capacity. In this way each person contributes to the community's solution to its problems and fulfills himself as a member of the community.

The Chicago Freedom Movement commits itself to the struggle for freedom and justice in this metropolis and pledges our non-violent movement to the building of the beloved community where men will live as brothers and no group or class or nation will raise its hand against another.

AN OPEN AND JUST CITY

To wipe out slums, ghettoes, and racism we must create an *open* city with equal opportunities and equal results. To this end we have drawn up program proposals for employment and income, housing and metropolitan planning, education, financial services, police and legal protection. We only sketch the major ideas of the full program here as that document shall be released shortly.

Two different approaches are necessary to do the job. The first approach involves gigantic development programs for the slum ghettoes similar to those for underdeveloped nations. The second involves proposals for the various institutions of the whole metropolitan area.

We propose three major redevelopment program areas for three slum areas. The redevelopment projects will constitute a concrete application of the domestic Marshall Plan idea. A redevelopment authority, with majority control by persons and institutions in the area, will shape a unified plan for housing, employment, educational, social, and cultural development. Massive expenditures would create a climate for further public and private spending. The objective would be to make what are now the slum ghettoes as good places to live as any in Chicago.

In education our program is based on proposals that all schools should have at least the same expenditures as the best suburban public schools. Racial separation should be broken down by such new ideas as educational parks and city-suburban educational cooperation.

In employment our program proposals call for fair employment by the elimination of all forms of job bias and of all measures which screen out minority groups. The proposals call for full employment at decent wages by the creation of tens of thousands of new jobs in rebuilding our city and in new sub-professional positions in health, education, and welfare. We call for effective job training and retraining with the provision of a job at the successful completion of the program.

In housing our program calls for an open city in which no man is discriminated against. We call for adequate financing and programs for the redevelopment of slum and deteriorating housing and for the elimination of exploitation by slum lords. We call for humanization of the present public housing projects. We propose the development of a vastly increased supply of decent low and middle cost housing throughout the Chicago area.

In planning we call for the development of a metropolitan-wide land and transportation plan, including the City of Chicago, that will promote and facilitate access to jobs and housing for all men throughout the entire region; the plan would include the development of new areas, the irradication of slums and the redevelopment of these blighted areas both in Chicago and the older suburbs.

In welfare we call for the elimination of welfare dependency by a guaranteed adequate annual income as a matter of right with provision for payment in the most dignified manner possible. In the immediate future, pending the change in the manner of income distribution, we propose measures to humanize the welfare system and to strengthen the automony and rights of recipients.

In politics and governments we call for increased representation of Negroes, Latin Americans, and other exploited minorities.

We call for measures to equalize protection from police and the courts, including a citizen review board to monitor complaints of police brutality and arbitrary arrest.

The task of wiping out racism, slums, and ghettoes in order to make Chicago an "open city" is large, but necessary. We recognize

that many of the proposals in our full program are long-range ones—some of which will take a number of years before they are in full operation—and Chicago is receiving its total benefits. However, a good number of our proposals can be implemented this summer by the action of government and private executives; therefore, it is these proposals that constitute the demands for the summer campaign of the Chicago Freedom Movement.

Since people and organizations resist change, the Freedom Movement shall have to demonstrate by the tools of non-violent direct action that our summer demands can be implemented. We shall prove that the Chicago metropolitan area can be an open city. For this purpose we have chosen a small number of specific target demands, around which we shall organize non-violent direct action campaigns. With the creative help and pressure of the Freedom Movement, government and private organizations will find that the target demands can be met. Then they will be able to meet the other immediate summer demands.

SELECTED IMMEDIATE ACTION DEMANDS—SUMMER 1966

For our primary target we have chosen housing. As of July 10 we shall cease to be accomplices to a housing system of discrimination, segregation, and degradation. We shall begin to act as if Chicago were an open city. We shall act on the basis that every man is entitled to full access of buying or renting housing that is sound, attractive, and reasonably priced.

Demands for Open Housing

From the Real Estate Boards and Brokers:

1. All listings immediately available on a nondiscriminatory basis. This means that no realtor or real estate broker will handle a property that is not available to anyone, without regard to race, color, creed, or national origin.

2. Endorsement of, and support for open occupancy.

From the Banks and Savings Institutions:

1. Public statements of a non-discriminatory mortgage policy so that loans will be available to any qualified borrower without regard to the racial composition of the area, or the age of the area, a policy that takes into account years of discrimination against Negro borrowers.
2. Creation of special loan funds for the conversion of contract housing purchases to standard mortgages.

From the Chicago Housing Authority:

1. Program to rehabilitate present public housing, including such items as locked lobbies, restrooms in recreation areas, increased police protection and child care centers on every third floor.
2. No more public housing construction in the ghetto until a substantial number of units are started outside the ghetto.

From the Chicago Housing Authority and the Chicago Dwelling Association: A program to increase vastly the supply of low-cost housing on a scattered basis. The program should provide for both low and middle income families.

Enforcement of his Fair Practices Code, especially by revoking the licenses of real estate brokers who discriminate.

From the Illinois Public Aid Department and the Cook County Department of Public Aid: Direct the housing placement of welfare recipients so as to use the entire housing market.

From the Federal Government:

1. An executive order for Federal supervision of the non-discriminatory granting of loans by banks and saving institutions that are members of the Federal Deposit Insurance Corporation or by the Federal Savings and Loan Association.
2. Passage of the 1966 Civil Rights Act with a provision to make it illegal to discriminate in the sale or renting of property on the basis of race, color, creed, or national origin.

From the Mayor and City Council:

1. Ordinance giving ready access to the names of owners and investors for all slum properties.
2. A saturation program of increased garbage collection, street cleaning and building inspection services in the slum areas.

From Advertising Media: No advertising media will list either housing or jobs not available for every man.

Demands for Open Employment

From the Mayor and City Council:

1. Publication of headcounts of whites, Negroes, and Latin Americans for all city departments and for all firms from which city purchases are made.
2. A compliance program that checks on all contractors on a routine basis.
3. Revocation of contracts with firms that do not have a full-scale fair employment practice.

From Business:

1. Racial headcounts, including white, Negro, and Latin American, by job classification and income level, made public.
2. Radical steps to upgrade and to integrate all departments, at all levels of employment.

From Unions:

1. Headcounts in unions for apprentices, journeymen and union staff and officials by job classification.
2. A crash program to remedy any inequities discovered by the headcount.
3. Support for the organization of the unorganized minority workers since Negro and other minority workers are concentrated in the low paying, unorganized industries.
4. Indenture of at least 400 Negro and Latin American apprentices in the craft unions.

From the Governor of Illinois:

1. Prepare legislative proposals for a $2.00 State minimum wage law and for credit reform,

including the abolition of garnishment and wage assignment.
2. Publication of headcounts of whites, Negroes, and Latin Americans for all State departments and for all firms from which state purchases are made.

Welfare Demands

From the Illinois Public Aid Department and the Cook County Department of Public Aid:

1. Recognition of welfare unions and community organizations as bargaining agents for welfare recipients.
2. Regular meetings between representatives of the recipients and top department administrators.
3. Institution of a declaration of income system to replace the degrading investigation and means test for welfare eligibility.
4. Change in the rules and procedures to speed up the issuance of emergency checks and to eliminate withholding of checks pending investigation.

Education Demands

From the Chicago Board of Education:

1. Announce plan for desegregation of teachers in Chicago schools during 1966–67 school year.
2. Immediate publication of the achievement scores of all schools by grades.

From the Federal Government: Executive enforcement of Title VI of the 1964 Civil Rights Act regarding the complaint against the Chicago Board of Education.

Other Demands

From the Mayor and City Council: Creation of a citizens review board for grievances against police brutality and false arrests or stops and seizure.

From the Political Parties: The replacement of absentee precinct captains, with the requirement that precinct captains be residents of their precincts.

From the Federal Government: Direct funding of Chicago community organizations by the Office of Economic Opportunity.

Demands of Ourselves

From the People:

1. Financial support of the Freedom Movement.
2. Selective buying from firms that do not practice racial discrimination in hiring and upgrading of employees.
3. Deposit money in banks and savings institutions with clean records on hiring and lending policies.
4. Selective buying campaigns against businesses that boycott the products of Negro-owned companies.
5. Participation in the Freedom Movement target campaigns for this summer, including volunteer services and membership in one of the Freedom Movement organizations.

On Black Power

Stokely Carmichael

This is 1966 and it seems to me that it's "time out" for nice words. It's time black people got together. We have to say things nobody else in this country is willing to say and find the strength internally and from each other to say the things that need to be said. We have to understand the lies this country has spoken about black people and we have to set the record straight. No one else can do that but black people.

I remember when I was in school they used to say, "If you work real hard, if you sweat, if you are ambitious, then you will be successful." I'm here to tell you that if that was true, black people would own this country, because we sweat more than anybody else in this country. We have to say to this country that you have lied to us. We picked your cotton for $2.00 a day, we washed your dishes, we're the porters in your bank and in your building, we are the janitors and the elevator men. We worked hard and all we get is a little pay and a hard way to go from you. We have to talk not only about what's going on here but what this country is doing across the world. When we start getting the internal strength to tell them what should be told and to speak the truth as it should be spoken, let them pick the sides and let the chips fall where they may.

Now, about what black people have to do and what has been done to us by white people. If you are born in Lowndes County, Alabama, Swilling-chit, Mississippi or Harlem, New York and the color of your skin happens to be black you are going to catch it. The only reason we have to get together is the color of our skins. They oppress us because we are black and we are going to use that blackness to get out of the trick bag they put us in. Don't be ashamed of your color.

A few years ago, white people used to say, "Well, the reason they live in the ghetto is they are stupid, dumb, lazy, unambitious, apathetic, don't care, happy, contented," and the trouble was a whole lot of us believed that junk about ourselves. We were so busy trying to prove to white folks that we were everything they said we weren't that we got so busy being white we forgot what it was to be black. We are going to call our black brothers hand.

Now, after 1960, when we got moving, they couldn't say we were lazy and dumb and apathetic and all that anymore so they got sophisticated and started to play the dozens with us. They called conferences about our mamas and told us that's why we were where we were at. Some people were sitting up there talking with Johnson while he was talking about their mamas. I don't play the dozens with white folks. To set the record straight, the reason we are in the bag we are in isn't because of my mama, it's because of what they did to my mama. That's why I'm where I'm at. We have to put the blame where it belongs. The blame does not belong on the oppressed but on the oppressor, and that's where it is going to stay.

Don't let them scare you when you start opening your mouth—speak the truth. Tell them, "Don't blame us because we haven't ever had the chance to do wrong." They made sure that we have been so blocked-in we couldn't move until they said, "Move." Now there are a number of things we have

Source: Stokely Carmichael, "On Black Power." From *Notes and Comment.* Copyright © 1966 Student Nonviolent Coordinating Committee.

to do. The only thing we own in this country is the color of our skins and we are ashamed of that because they made us ashamed. We have to stop being ashamed of being black. A broad nose, a thick lip and nappy hair is us and we are going to call that beautiful whether they like it or not. We are not going to fry our hair anymore but they can start wearing their hair natural to look like us.

We have to define how we are going to move, not how they say we can move. We have never been able to do that before. Everybody in this country jumps up and says, "I'm a friend of the civil rights movement. I'm a friend of the Negro." We haven't had the chance to say whether or not that man is stabbing us in the back or not. All those people who are calling us friends are nothing but treacherous enemies and we can take care of our enemies but God deliver us from our "friends." The only protection we are going to have is from each other. We have to build a strong base to let them know if they touch one black man driving his wife to the hospital in Los Angeles, or one black man walking down a highway in Mississippi or if they take one black man who has a rebellion and put him in jail and start talking treason, we are going to disrupt this whole country.

We have to say, "Don't play jive and start writing poems after Malcolm is shot." We have to move from the point where the man left off and stop writing poems. We have to start supporting our own movement. If we can spend all that money to send a preacher to a Baptist convention in a Cadillac then we can spend money to support our own movement.

Now, let's get to what the white press has been calling riots. In the first place don't get confused with the words they use like "antiwhite," "hate," "militant" and all that nonsense like "radical" and "riots." What's happening is rebellions not riots and the extremist element is not RAM. As a matter of fact RAM is a very reactionary group, reacting against the pressures white people are putting on them. The extremists in this country are the white people who force us to live the way we live. We have to define our own ethic. We don't have to (and don't make any apologies about it) obey any law that we didn't have a part to make, especially if that law was made to keep us where we are. We have the right to break it.

We have to stop apologizing for each other. We must tell our black brothers and sisters who go to college, "Don't take any job for IBM or Wall Street because you aren't doing anything for us. You are helping this country perpetuate its lies about how democracy rises in this country." They have to come back to the community, where they belong and use their skills to help develop us. We have to tell the Doctors, "You can't go to college and come back and charge us $5.00 and $10.00 a visit. You have to charge us 50¢ and be thankful you get that." We have to tell our lawyers not to charge us what they charge but to be happy to take a case and plead it free of charge. We have to define success and tell them the food Ralph Bunche eats doesn't feed our hungry stomachs. We have to tell Ralph Bunche the only reason he is up there is so when we yell they can pull him out. We have to do that, nobody else can do that for us.

We have to talk about wars and soldiers and just what that means. A mercenary is a hired killer and any black man serving in this man's army is a black mercenary, nothing else. A mercenary fights for a country for a price but does not enjoy the rights of the country for which he is fighting. A mercenary will go to Viet Nam to fight for free elections for the Vietnamese but doesn't have free elections in Alabama, Mississippi, Georgia, Texas, Louisiana, South Carolina and Washington, D.C. A mercenary goes to Viet Nam and gets shot fighting for his country and they won't even bury him in his own home town. He's a mercenary, that's all. We must find the strength so that when they start grabbing us to fight their war we say, "Hell no."

We have to talk about nonviolence among us, so that we don't cut each other on Friday nights and don't destroy each other but move to a point where we appreciate and love each other. That's the nonviolence that has to be talked about. The psychology the man has used on us has turned us against each other. He says nothing about the cutting that goes on Friday night but talk about raising one finger-tip towards him and that's when he jumps up. We have to talk about nonviolence among us first.

We have to study black history but don't get fooled. You should know who John Hullett is, and Fanny Lou Hamer is, who Lerone Bennett is, who Max Stanford is, who Lawrence Landry is, who May Mallory is and who Robert Williams is. You have to know these people yourselves because you can't read about them in a book or in the press. You have to know what Mr. X said from his own lips not the Chicago *Sun-Times.* That responsibility is ours. The Muslims call themselves Muslims but the press calls them black Muslims. We have to call them Muslims and go to their mosque to find out what they are talking about firsthand and then we can talk about getting together. Don't let that man get up there and tell you, "Oh, you know those Muslims preach nothing but hate. You shouldn't be messing with them." "Yah, I don't mess with them, yah, I know they bad." The man's name is the Honorable Elijah Muhammad and he represents a great section of the black community. Honor him.

We have to go out and find our young blacks who are cutting and shooting each other and tell them they are doing the cutting and shooting to the wrong people. We have to bring them together and spend the time if we are not just shucking and jiving. This is 1966 and my grandmother used to tell me, "The time is far spent." We have to move this year.

There is a psychological war going on in this country and it's whether or not black people are going to be able to use the terms they want about their movement without white peoples blessing. We have to tell them we are going to use the term "Black Power" and we are going to define it because Black Power speaks to us. We can't let them project Black Power because they can only project it from white power and we know what white power had done to us. We have to organize ourselves to speak from a position of strength and stop begging people to look kindly upon us. We are going to build a movement in this country based on the color of our skins that is going to free us from our oppressors and we have to do that ourselves.

We have got to understand what is going on in Lowndes County, Alabama, what it means, who is in it and what they are doing so if white people steal that election like they do all over this country then the eyes of black people all over this country will be focused there to let them know we are going to take care of business if they mess with us in Lowndes County. That responsibility lies on all of us, not just the civil rights workers and do-gooders.

If we talk about education we have to educate ourselves, not with Hegel or Plato or the missionaries who came to Africa with the Bible and we had the land and when they left we had the Bible and they had the land. We have to tell them the only way anybody eliminates poverty in this country is to give poor people money. You don't have to headstart, uplift and upwardbound them into your culture. Just give us the money you stole from us, that's all. We have to say to people in this country, "We don't really care about you. For us to get better, we don't have to go to white things. We can do it in our own community, ourselves if you didn't steal the resources that belong there." We have to understand the Horatio Alger lie and that the individualist, profit-concept nonsense will never work for us. We have to form cooperatives and use the profits to benefit our community. We can't tolerate their system.

When we form coalitions we must say on what grounds we are going to form them, not white people telling us how to form them. We must build strength and pride amongst ourselves. We must think politically and get power because we are the only people in this country that are powerless. We are the only people who have to protect ourselves from our protectors. We are the only people who want a man called Willis removed who is a racist, that have to lie down in the street and beg a racist named Daley to remove the racist named Willis. We have to build a movement so we can see Daley and say, "Tell Willis to get that," and by the time we turn around he is gone. That's Black Power.

Everybody in this country is for "Freedom Now" but not everybody is for Black Power because we have got to get rid of some of the people who have white power. We have got to get us some Black Power. We

don't control anything but what white people say we can control. We have to be able to smash any political machine in the country that's oppressing us and bring it to its knees. We have to be aware that if we keep growing and multiplying the way we do in ten years all the major cities are going to be ours. We have to know that in Newark, New Jersey, where we are 60% of the population, we went along with their stories about integrating and we got absorbed. All we have to show for it is three councilmen who are speaking for them and not for us. We have to organize ourselves to speak for each other. That's Black Power. We have to move to control the economics and politics of our community....

The Detroit Rebellion of 1967

On Saturday evening, July 22, the Detroit Police Department raided five "blind pigs." The blind pigs had had their origin in prohibition days, and survived as private social clubs. Often, they were after-hours drinking and gambling spots.

The fifth blind pig on the raid list, the United Community and Civic League at the corner of 12th Street and Clairmount, had been raided twice before. Once 10 persons had been picked up; another time, 28. A Detroit Vice Squad officer had tried but failed to get in shortly after 10 o'clock Saturday night. He succeeded, on his second attempt, at 3:45 Sunday morning.

The Tactical Mobile Unit, the Police Department's Crowd Control Squad, had been dismissed at 3:00 A.M. Since Sunday morning traditionally is the least troublesome time

Source: "A Narrative of the Detroit Disorders of 1967." From *Report of the National Advisory Committee on Civil Disorders* (New York: Bantam Books edition, 1968), pp. 84–109.

for police in Detroit—and all over the country—only 193 officers were patrolling the streets. Of these, 44 were in the 10th Precinct where the blind pig was located.

Police expected to find two dozen patrons in the blind pig. That night, however, it was the scene of a party for several servicemen, two of whom were back from Vietnam. Instead of two dozen patrons, police found 82. Some voiced resentment at the police intrusion.

An hour went by before all 82 could be transported from the scene. The weather was humid and warm—the temperature that day was to rise to 86—and despite the late hour, many people were still on the street. In short order, a crowd of about 200 gathered.

In November of 1965, George Edwards, Judge of the United States Court of Appeals for the Sixth Circuit, and Commissioner of the Detroit Police Department from 1961 to 1963, had written in the *Michigan Law Review:*

It is clear that in 1965 no one will make excuses for any city's inability to foresee the possibility of racial trouble. . . . Although local police forces generally regard themselves as public servants with the responsibility of maintaining law and order, they tend to minimize this attitude when they are patrolling areas that are heavily populated with Negro citizens. There, they tend to view each person on the streets as a potential criminal or enemy, and all too often that attitude is reciprocated. Indeed, hostility between the Negro communities in our large cities and the police departments, is the major problem in law enforcement in this decade. It has been a major cause of all recent race riots.

At the time of Detroit's 1943 race riot, Judge Edwards told Commission investigators, there was "open warfare between the Detroit Negroes and the Detroit Police Department." As late as 1961, he had thought that "Detroit was the leading candidate in the United States for a race riot."

There was a long history of conflict between the police department and citizens. During the labor battles of the 1930's, union members had come to view the Detroit Police Department as a strike-breaking force. The 1943 riot, in which 34 persons died, was the bloodiest in the United States in a span of two decades.

Judge Edwards and his successor, Commissioner Ray Girardin, attempted to restructure the image of the department. A Citizens Complaint Bureau was set up to facilitate the filing of complaints by citizens against officers. In practice, however, this Bureau appeared to work little better than less enlightened and more cumbersome procedures in other cities.

On 12th Street, with its high incidence of vice and crime, the issue of police brutality was a recurrent theme. A month earlier the killing of a prostitute had been determined by police investigators to be the work of a pimp. According to rumors in the community the crime had been committed by a Vice Squad officer.

At about the same time, the killing of Danny Thomas, a 27-year old Negro Army veteran, by a gang of white youths, had in-

flamed the community. The city's major newspapers played down the story in hope that the murder would not become a cause for increased tensions. The intent backfired. A banner story in the *Michigan Chronicle,* the city's Negro newspaper, began: "As James Meredith marched again Sunday to prove a Negro could walk in Mississippi without fear, a young woman who saw her husband killed by a white gang, shouting: "Niggers keep out of Rouge Park," lost her baby.

"Relatives were upset that the full story of the murder was not being told, apparently in an effort to prevent the incident from sparking a riot."

Some Negroes believed that the daily newspapers' treatment of the story was further evidence of the double standard: playing up crimes by Negroes, playing down crimes committed against Negroes.

Although police arrested one suspect for murder, Negroes questioned why the entire gang was not held. What, they asked, would have been the result if a white man had been killed by a gang of Negroes? What if Negroes had made the kind of advances toward a white woman that the white men were rumored to have made toward Mrs. Thomas?

The Thomas family lived only four or five blocks from the raided blind pig. A few minutes after 5:00 A.M., just after the last of those arrested had been hauled away, an empty bottle smashed into the rear window of a police car. A litter basket was thrown through the window of a store. Rumors circulated of excess force used by the police during the raid. A youth, whom police nicknamed "Mr. Greensleeves" because of the color of his shirt, was shouting: "We're going to have a riot!" and exhorting the crowd to vandalism.

At 5:20 A.M. Commissioner Girardin was notified. He immediately called Mayor Jerome Cavanagh. Seventeen officers from other areas were ordered into the 10th Precinct. By 6:00 A.M. police strength had grown to 369 men. Of these, however, only 43 were committed to the immediate riot area. By that time the number of persons on

12th Street was growing into the thousands and widespread window-smashing and looting had begun.

On either side of 12th Street were neat, middle-class districts. Along 12th Street itself, however, crowded apartment houses created a density of more than 21,000 persons per square mile, almost double the city average.

The movement of people when the slums of "Black Bottom" had been cleared for urban renewal had changed 12th Street from an integrated community into an almost totally black one, in which only a number of merchants remained white. Only 18 percent of the residents were home-owners. Twenty-five percent of the housing was considered so substandard as to require clearance. Another 19 percent had major deficiencies.

The crime rate was almost double that of the city as a whole. A Detroit police officer told Commission investigators that prostitution was so wide-spread that officers made arrests only when soliciting became blatant. The proportion of broken families was more than twice that in the rest of the city.

By 7:50 A.M., when a 17-man police commando unit attempted to make the first sweep, an estimated 3,000 persons were on 12th Street. They offered no resistance. As the sweep moved down the street, they gave way to one side, and then flowed back behind it.

A shoe store manager said he waited vainly for police for two hours as the store was being looted. At 8:25 A.M. someone in the crowd yelled "The cops are coming!" The first flames of the riot billowed from the store. Firemen who responded were not harassed. The flames were extinguished.

By mid-morning, 1,122 men—approximately a fourth of the police department—had reported for duty. Of these, 540 were in or near the six-block riot area. One hundred and eight officers were attempting to establish a cordon. There was, however, no interference with looters, and police were refraining from the use of force.

Commissioner Girardin said: "If we had started shooting in there . . . not one of our policemen would have come out alive. I am convinced it would have turned into a race riot in the conventional sense."

According to witnesses, police at some roadblocks made little effort to stop people from going in and out of the area. Bantering took place between police officers and the populace, some still in pajamas. To some observers, there seemed at this point to be an atmosphere of apathy. On the one hand, the police failed to interfere with the looting. On the other, a number of older, more stable residents, who had seen the street deteriorate from a prosperous commercial thoroughfare to one ridden by vice, remained aloof.

Because officials feared that the 12th Street disturbance might be a diversion, many officers were sent to guard key installations in other sections of the city. Belle Isle, the recreation area in the Detroit River that had been the scene of the 1943 riot, was sealed off.

In an effort to avoid attracting people to the scene, some broadcasters cooperated by not reporting the riot, and an effort was made to downplay the extent of the disorder. The facade of "business as usual" necessitated the detailing of numerous police officers to protect the 50,000 spectators that were expected at that afternoon's New York Yankees-Detroit Tigers baseball game.

Early in the morning a task force of community workers went into the area to dispel rumors and act as counter-rioters. Such a task force had been singularly successful at the time of the incident in the Kercheval district in the summer of 1966, when scores of people had gathered at the site of an arrest. Kercheval, however, has a more stable population, fewer stores, less population density, and the city's most effective police-community relations program.

The 12th Street area, on the other hand, had been determined, in a 1966 survey conducted by Dr. Ernest Harburg of the Psychology Department of the University of

Michigan, to be a community of high stress and tension. An overwhelming majority of the residents indicated dissatisfaction with their environment.

Of those interviewed, 93 percent said they wanted to move out of the neighborhood; 73 percent felt that the streets were not safe; 91 percent believed that a person was likely to be robbed or beaten at night; 58 percent knew of a fight within the last 12 months in which a weapon had been employed; 32 percent stated that they themselves owned a weapon; 57 percent were worried about fires.

A significant proportion believed municipal services to be inferior: 36 percent were dissatisfied with the schools; 43 percent with the city's contribution to the neighborhood; 77 percent with the recreational facilities; 78 percent believed police did not respond promptly when they were summoned for help.

United States Representative John Conyers, Jr., a Negro. was notified about the disturbance at his home, a few blocks from 12th Street, at 8:30 A.M. Together with other community leaders, including Hubert G. Locke, a Negro and assistant to the commissioner of police, he began to drive around the area. In the side streets he asked people to stay in their homes. On 12th Street, he asked them to disperse. It was, by his own account, a futile task.

Numerous eyewitnesses interviewed by Commission investigators tell of the carefree mood with which people ran in and out of stores, looting and laughing, and joking with the police officers. Stores with "Soul Brothers" signs appeared no more immune than others. Looters paid no attention to residents who shouted at them and called their actions senseless. An epidemic of excitement had swept over the persons on the street.

Congressman Conyers noticed a woman with a baby in her arms; she was raging, cursing "whitey" for no apparent reason.

Shortly before noon Congressman Conyers climbed atop a car in the middle of 12th Street to address the people. As he began to

speak he was confronted by a man in his fifties whom he had once, as a lawyer, represented in court. The man had been active in civil rights. He believed himself to have been persecuted as a result, and it was Conyers' opinion that he may have been wrongfully jailed. Extremely bitter, the man inciting the crowd and challenging Conyers: "Why are you defending the cops and the establishment? You're just as bad as they are!"

A police officer in the riot area told Commission investigators that neither he nor his fellow officers were instructed as to what they were supposed to be doing. Witnesses tell of officers standing behind saw-horses as an area was being looted—and still standing there much later, when the mob had moved elsewhere. A squad from the commando unit, wearing helmets with face-covering visors and carrying bayonet-tipped carbines, blockaded a street several blocks from the scene of the riot. Their appearances drew residents into the street. Some began to harangue them and to question why they were in an area where there was no trouble. Representative Conyers convinced the police department to remove the commandos.

By that time a rumor was threading through the crowd that a man had been bayoneted by the police. Influenced by such stories, the crowd became belligerent. At approximately 1:00 P.M. stonings accelerated. Numerous officers reported injuries from rocks, bottles, and other objects thrown at them. Smoke billowed upward from four fires, the first since the one at the shoe store early in the morning. When firemen answered the alarms, they became the target for rocks and bottles.

At 2:00 P.M. Mayor Cavanagh met with community and political leaders at police headquarters. Until then there had been hope that, as the people blew off steam, the riot would dissipate. Now the opinion was nearly unanimous that additional forces would be needed.

A request was made for state police aid. By 3:00 P.M. 360 officers were assembling at the armory. At that moment looting was spreading from the 12th Street area to other main thoroughfares.

There was no lack of the disaffected to help spread it. Although not yet as hard-pressed as Newark, Detroit was, like Newark, losing population. Its prosperous middle-class whites were moving to the suburbs and being replaced by unskilled Negro migrants. Between 1960 and 1967 the Negro population rose from just under 30 percent to an esti-mated 40 percent of the total.

In a decade the school system had gained 50,000 to 60,000 children. Fifty-one percent of the elementary school classes were over-crowded. Simply to achieve the statewide average, the system needed 1,650 more teachers and 1,000 additional classrooms. The combined cost would be $63 million.

Of 300,000 school children, 171,000, or 57 percent, were Negro. According to the De-troit Superintendent of Schools, 25 different school districts surrounding the city spent up to $500 more per pupil per year than De-troit. In the inner city schools, more than half the pupils who entered high school became dropouts.

The strong union structure had created excellent conditions for most working men, but had left others, such as civil service and government workers, comparatively disad-vantaged and dissatisfied. In June the "Blue Flu" had struck the city as police officers, forbidden to strike, had staged a sick-out. In September, the teachers were to go on strike. The starting wages for a plumber's helper were almost equal to the salary of a police officer or teacher.

Some unions, traditionally closed to Ne-groes, zealously guarded training opportu-nities. In January of 1967 the school system notified six apprenticeship trades it would not open any new apprenticeship classes un-less a large number of Negroes were in-cluded. By fall, some of the programs were still closed.

High school diplomas from inner city schools were regarded by personnel direc-tors as less than valid. In July, unemploy-ment was at a five-year peak. In the 12th Street area it was estimated to be between 12 and 15 percent for Negro men and 30 per-cent or higher for those under 25.

The more education a Negro had, the greater the disparity between his income and that of a white with the same level of educa-tion. The income of whites and Negroes with a seventh grade education was about equal. The median income of whites with a high school diploma was $1,600 more per year than that of Negroes. White college graduates made $2,600 more. In fact, so far as income was concerned, it made very little difference to a Negro man whether he had attended school for 8 years or for 12. In the fall of 1967, a study conducted at one inner city high school, Northwestern, showed that, although 50 percent of the dropouts had found work, 90 percent of the 1967 graduating class was unemployed.

Mayor Cavanagh had appointed many Negroes to key positions in his administra-tion, but in elective offices the Negro popu-lation was still under-represented. Of nine councilmen, one was a Negro. Of seven school board members, two were Negroes.

Although federal programs had brought nearly $360 million to the city between 1962 and 1967, the money appeared to have had little impact at the grassroots. Urban re-newal, for which $38 million had been allo-cated, was opposed by many residents of the poverty area.

Because of its financial straits, the city was unable to produce on promises to correct such conditions as poor garbage collection and bad street lighting, which brought constant complaints from Negro residents.

On 12th Street Carl Perry, the Negro pro-prietor of a drug store and photography stu-dio, was dispensing ice cream, sodas, and candy to the youngsters streaming in and out of his store. For safekeeping he had brought the photography equipment from his studio, in the next block, to the drug store. The youths milling about repeatedly assured him that, although the market next door had been ransacked, his place of business was in no danger.

In mid-afternoon the market was set afire. Soon after, the drug store went up in flames.

State Representative James Del Rio, a Negro, was camping out in front of a building he owned when two small boys, neither more than 10 years old, approached. One prepared to throw a brick through a window. Del Rio stopped him; "That building belongs to me," he said.

"I'm glad you told me, baby, because I was just about to bust you in!" the youngster replied.

Some evidence that criminal elements were organizing spontaneously to take advantage of the riot began to manifest itself. A number of cars were noted to be returning again and again, their occupants methodically looting stores. Months later, goods stolen during the riot were still being peddled.

A spirit of carefree nihilism was taking hold. To riot and to destroy appeared more and more to become ends in themselves. Late Sunday afternoon it appeared to one observer that the young people were "dancing amidst the flames."

A Negro plainclothes officer was standing at an intersection when a man threw a Molotov cocktail into a business establishment at the corner. In the heat of the afternoon, fanned by the 20 to 25 m.p.h. winds of both Sunday and Monday, the fire reached the home next door within minutes. As residents uselessly sprayed the flames with garden hoses, the fire jumped from roof to roof of adjacent two and three-story buildings. Within the hour the entire block was in flames. The ninth house in the burning row belonged to the arsonist who had thrown the Molotov cocktail.

In some areas residents organized rifle squads to protect firefighters. Elsewhere, especially as the wind-whipped flames began to overwhelm the Detroit Fire Department and more and more residences burned, the firemen were subjected to curses and rock-throwing.

Because of a lack of funds, on a per capita basis the department is one of the smallest in the nation. In comparison to Newark, where approximately 1,000 firemen patrol an area of 16 square miles with a population of 400,000. Detroit's 1,700 firemen must cover a city of 140 square miles with a population of 1.6 million. Because the department had no mutual aid agreement with surrounding communities, it could not quickly call in reinforcements from outlying areas, and it was almost 9:00 P.M. before the first arrived. At one point, out of a total of 92 pieces of Detroit fire fighting equipment and 56 brought in from surrounding communities, only four engine companies were available to guard areas of the city outside of the riot perimeter.

As the afternoon progressed the fire department's radio carried repeated messages of apprehension and orders of caution:

> There is no police protection here at all; there isn't a policeman in the area. . . . If you have any trouble at all, pull out! . . . We're being stoned at the scene. It's going good. We need help! . . . Protect yourselves! Proceed away from the scene. . . . Engine 42 over at Linwood and Gladstone. They are throwing bottles at us so we are getting out of the area. . . . All companies without police protection—all companies without police protection—orders are to withdraw, do not try to put out the fires. I repeat—all companies without police protection orders are to withdraw, do not try to put out the fires!

It was 4:30 P.M. when the firemen, some of them exhausted by the heat, abandoned an area of approximately 100 square blocks on either side of 12th Street to wait protection from police and National Guardsmen.

During the course of the riot firemen were to withdraw 283 times.

Fire Chief Charles J. Quinlan estimated that at least two-thirds of the buildings were destroyed by spreading fires rather than fires set at the scene. Of the 683 structures involved, approximately one-third were residential, and in few, if any, of these was the fire set originally.

Governor George Romney flew over the area between 8:30 and 9:00 P.M. "It looked like the city had been bombed on the west side and there was an area two-and-a-half miles by three-and-a-half miles with major fires, with entire blocks in flames," he told the Commission.

In the midst of chaos there were some unexpected individual responses.

Twenty-four-year-old E. G., a Negro born in Savannah, Georgia, had come to Detroit in 1965 to attend Wayne State University. Rebellion had been building in him for a long time because,

> You just had to bow down to the white man. . . . When the insurance man would come by he would always call out to my mother by her first name and we were expected to smile and greet him happily. . . . Man, I know he would never have thought of me or my father going to his house and calling his wife by her first name. Then I once saw a white man slapping a young pregnant Negro woman on the street with such force that she just spun around and fell. I'll never forget that.

When a friend called to tell him about the riot on 12th Street, E. G. went there expecting "a true revolt," but was disappointed as soon as he saw the looting begin: "I wanted to see the people really rise up in revolt. When I saw the first person coming out of the store with things in his arms, I really got sick to my stomach and wanted to go home. Rebellion against the white suppressors is one thing, but one measly pair of shoes or some food completely ruins the whole concept."

E. G. was standing in a crowd, watching firemen work, when Fire Chief Alvin Wall called out for help from the spectators. E. G. responded. His reasoning was: "No matter what color someone is, whether they are green or pink or blue, I'd help them if they were in trouble. That's all there is to it."

He worked with the firemen for four days, the only Negro in an all-white crew. Elsewhere, at scattered locations, a half dozen other Negro youths pitched in to help the firemen.

At 4:20 P.M. Mayor Cavanagh requested that the National Guard be brought into Detroit. Although a major portion of the Guard was in its summer encampment 200 miles away, several hundred troops were conducting their regular weekend drill in the city. That circumstance obviated many problems. The first troops were on the streets by 7:00 P.M.

At 7:45 P.M. the mayor issued a proclamation instituting a 9:00 P.M. to 5:00 A.M. curfew. At 9:07 P.M. the first sniper fire was reported. Following his aerial survey of the city, Governor Romney, at or shortly before midnight, proclaimed that "a state of public emergency exists" in the cities of Detroit, Highland Park, and Hamtramck.

At 4:45 P.M. a 68-year-old white shoe repairman, George Messerlian, had seen looters carrying clothes from a cleaning establishment next to his shop. Armed with a saber, he had rushed into the street, flailing away at the looters. One Negro youth was nicked on the shoulder. Another, who had not been on the scene, inquired as to what had happened. After he had been told, he allegedly replied: "I'll get the old man for you!"

Going up to Messerlian, who had fallen or been knocked to the ground, the youth began to beat him with a club. Two other Negro youths dragged the attacker away from the old man. It was too late. Messerlian died four days later in the hospital.

At 9:15 P.M. a 16-year-old Negro boy, superficially wounded while looting, became the first reported gunshot victim.

At midnight Sharon George, a 23-year-old white woman, together with her two brothers, was a passenger in a car being driven by her husband. After having dropped off two Negro friends, they were returning home on one of Detroit's main avenues when they were slowed by a milling throng in the street. A shot fired from close range struck the car. The bullet splintered in Mrs.

George's body. She died less than two hours later.

An hour before midnight a 45-year-old white man, Walter Grzanka together with three white companions, went into the street. Shortly thereafter a market was broken into. Inside the show window a Negro man began filling bags with groceries and handing them to confederates outside the store. Grzanka twice went over to the store, accepted bags, and placed them down beside his companions across the street. On the third occassion he entered the market. When he emerged, the market owner, driving by in his car, shot and killed him.

In Grzanka's pockets police found seven cigars, four packages of pipe tobacco, and nine pairs of shoelaces.

Before dawn four other looters were shot, one of them accidently while struggling with a police officer. A Negro youth and a National Guardsman were injured by gunshots of undetermined origin. A private guard shot himself while pulling his revolver from his pocket. In the basement of the 13th Precinct Police Station a cue ball, thrown by an unknown assailant, cracked against the head of a sergeant.

At about midnight three white youths, armed with a shotgun, had gone to the roof of their apartment building, located in an all-white block, in order, they said, to protect the building from fire. At 2:45 A.M. a patrol car, carrying police officers and National Guardsmen, received a report of "snipers on the roof." As the patrol car arrived, the manager of the building went to the roof to tell the youths they had better come down.

The law enforcement personnel surrounded the building, some going to the front, others to the rear. As the manager, together with the three youths, descended the fire escape in the rear, a National Guardsman, believing he heard shots from the front, fired. His shot killed 23-year-old Clifton Pryor.

Early in the morning a young white fireman and a 49-year-old Negro homeowner were killed by fallen power lines.

By 2:00 A.M. Monday, Detroit police had been augmented by 800 State Police officers and 1,200 National Guardsmen. An additional 8,000 Guardsmen were on the way. Nevertheless, Governor Romney and Mayor Cavanagh decided to ask for federal assistance. At 2:15 A.M. the mayor called Vice President Hubert Humphrey, and was referred to Attorney General Ramsey Clark. A short time thereafter telephone contact was established between Governor Romney and the attorney general.*

There is some difference of opinion about what occurred next. According to the attorney general's office, the governor was advised of the seriousness of the request and told that the applicable federal statute required that, before federal troops could be brought into the city, he would have to state that the situation had deteriorated to the point that local and state forces could no longer maintain law and order. According to the governor, he was under the impression that he was being asked to declare that a "state of insurrection" existed in the city.

The governor was unwilling to make such a declaration, contending that, if he did, insurance polices would not cover the loss incurred as a result of the riot. He and the mayor decided to re-evaluate the need for federal troops.

Contact between Detroit and Washington was maintained throughout the early morning hours. At 9:00 A.M., as the disorder still showed no sign of abating, the governor and the mayor decided to make a renewed request for federal troops.

Shortly before noon the President of the United States authorized the sending of a task force of paratroopers to Selfridge Air Force Base, near the city. A few minutes past

---

*A little over two hours earlier, at 11:55 P.M. Mayor Cavanagh had informed the U.S. Attorney General that a "dangerous situation existed in the city." Details are set forth in the Final Report of Cyrus R. Vance, covering the Detroit Riots, released on September 12, 1967.

3:00 P.M. Lt. General John L. Throckmorton, commander of Task Force Detroit, met Cyrus Vance, former Deputy Secretary of Defense, at the air base. Approximately an hour later the first federal troops arrived at the air base.

After meeting with state and municipal officials, Mr. Vance, General Throckmorton, Governor Romney, and Mayor Cavanagh, made a tour of the city, which lasted until 7:15 P.M. During this tour Mr. Vance and General Throckmorton independently came to the conclusion that—since they had seen no looting or sniping, since the fires appeared to be coming under control, and since a substantial number of National Guardsmen had not yet been committed—injection of federal troops would be premature.

As the riot alternately waxed and waned, one area of the ghetto remained insulated. On the northeast side the residents of some 150 square blocks inhabited by 21,000 persons had, in 1966, banded together in the Positive Neighborhood Action Committee (PNAC). With professional help from the Institute of Urban Dynamics, they had organized block clubs and made plans for the improvement of the neighborhood. In order to meet the need for recreational facilities, which the city was not providing, they had raised $3,000 to purchase empty lots for playgrounds. Although opposed to urban renewal, they had agreed to co-sponsor with the Archdiocese of Detroit a housing project to be controlled jointly by the archdiocese and PNAC.

When the riot broke out, the residents, through the block clubs, were able to organize quickly. Youngsters, agreeing to stay in the neighborhood, participated in detouring traffic. While many persons reportedly sympathized with the idea of a rebellion against the "system," only two small fires were set— one in an empty building.

During the daylight hours Monday, nine more persons were killed by gunshots elsewhere in the city, and many others were seriously or critically injured. Twenty-three-year old Nathaniel Edmonds, a Negro, was sitting in his back yard when a young white man stopped his car, got out, and began an argument with him. A few minutes later, declaring that he was "going to paint his picture on him with a shotgun," the white man allegedly shotgunned Edmonds to death.

Mrs. Nannie Pack and Mrs. Mattie Thomas were sitting on the porch of Mrs. Pack's house when police began chasing looters from a nearby market. During the chase officers fired three shots from their shotguns. The discharge from one of these accidentally struck the two women. Both were still in the hospital weeks later.

Included among those critically injured when they were accidentally trapped in the line of fire were an 8-year-old Negro girl and a 14-year-old white boy.

As darkness settled Monday, the number of incidents reported to police began to rise again. Although many turned out to be false, several involved injuries to police officers, National Guardsmen, and civilians by gunshots of undetermined origin.

Watching the upward trend of reported incidents, Mr. Vance and General Throckmorton became convinced Federal troops should be used, and President Johnson was so advised. At 11:20 P.M. the President signed a proclamation federalizing the Michigan National Guard and authorizing the use of the paratroopers.

At this time there were nearly 5,000 Guardsmen in the city, but fatigue, lack of training, and the haste with which they had had to be deployed reduced their effectiveness. Some of the Guardsmen traveled 200 miles and then were on duty for 30 hours straight. Some had never received riot training and were given on-the-spot instructions on mob control—only to discover that there were no mobs, and that the situation they faced on the darkened streets was one for which they were unprepared.

Commanders committed men as they became available, often in small groups. In the resulting confusion, some units were lost in the city. Two Guardsmen assigned to an intersection on Monday were discovered still there on Friday.

Lessons learned by the California National Guard two years earlier in Watts regarding the danger of overreaction and the necessity of great restraint in using weapons had not, apparently, been passed on to the Michigan National Guard. The young troopers could not be expected to know what a danger they were creating by the lack of fire discipline, not only to the civilian population but to themselves.

A Detroit newspaper reporter who spent a night riding in a command jeep told a Commission investigator of machine guns being fired accidentally, street lights being shot out by rifle fire, and buildings being placed under seige on the sketchiest reports of sniping. Troopers would fire, and immediately from the distance there would be answering fire, sometimes consisting of tracer bullets.

In one instance, the newsman related, a report was received on the jeep radio that an Army bus was pinned down by sniper fire at an intersection. National Guardsmen and police, arriving from various directions, jumped out and began asking each other: "Where's the sniper fire coming from?" As one Guardsman pointed to a building, everyone rushed about, taking cover. A soldier, alighting from a jeep, accidentally pulled the trigger of his rifle. As the shot reverberated through the darkness an officer yelled: "What's going on?" "I don't know," came the answer. "Sniper, I guess."

Without any clear authorization or direction someone opened fire upon the suspected building. A tank rolled up and sprayed the building with 50 caliber tracer bullets. Law enforcement officers rushed into the surrounded building and discovered it empty. "They must be firing one shot and running," was the verdict.

The reporter interviewed the men who had gotten off the bus and were crouched around it. When he asked them about the sniping incident he was told that someone had heard a shot. He asked "Did the bullet hit the bus?" The answer was: "Well, we don't know."

Bracketing the hour of midnight Monday, heavy firing, injuring many persons and killing several, occurred in the south-eastern sector, which was to be taken over by the paratroopers at 4:00 A.M. Tuesday, and which was, at this time, considered to be the most active riot area in the city.

Employed as a private guard, 55-year-old Julius L. Dorsey, a Negro, was standing in front of a market when accosted by two Negro men and a woman. They demanded he permit them to loot the market. He ignored their demands. They began to berate him. He asked a neighbor to call the police. As the argument grew more heated, Dorsey fired three shots from his pistol into the air.

The police radio reported: "Looters, they have rifles." A patrol car driven by a police officer and carrying three National Guardsmen arrived. As the looters fled, the law enforcement personnel opened fire. When the firing ceased, one person lay dead.

He was Julius L. Dorsey.

In two areas—one consisting of a triangle formed by Mack, Gratiot, and E. Grand Boulevard, the other surrounding Southeastern High School—firing began shortly after 10:00 P.M. and continued for several hours.

In the first of the areas, a 22-year-old Negro complained that he had been shot at by snipers. Later, a half dozen civilians and one National Guardsman were wounded by shots of undetermined origin.

Henry Denson, a passenger in a car, was shot and killed when the vehicle's driver, either by accident or intent, failed to heed a warning to halt at a National Guard roadblock.

Similar incidents occurred in the vicinity of Southeastern High School, one of the National Guard staging areas. As early as 10:20 P.M. the area was reported to be under sniper fire. Around midnight there were two incidents, the sequence of which remains in doubt.

Shortly before midnight Ronald Powell, who lived three blocks east of the high school and whose wife was, momentarily, expecting a baby, asked the four friends with whom he had been spending the evening to take him home. He, together with Edward

Blackshear, Charles Glover, and John Leroy climbed into Charles Dunson's station wagon for the short drive. Some of the five may have been drinking, but none was intoxicated.

To the north of the high school they were halted at a National Guard roadblock, and told they would have to detour around the school and a fire station at Mack and St. Jean Streets because of the firing that had been occurring. Following orders, they took a circuitous route and approached Powell's home from the south.

On Lycaste Street, between Charlevoix and Goethe, they saw a jeep sitting at the curb. Believing it to be another roadblock, they slowed down. Simultaneously a shot rang out. A National Guardsman fell, hit in the ankle.

Other National Guardsmen at the scene thought the shot had come from the station wagon. Shot after shot was directed against the vehicle, at least 17 of them finding their mark. All five occupants were injured, John Leroy fatally.

At approximately the same time firemen, police, and National Guardsmen at the corner of Mack and St. Jean Streets, two and one-half blocks away, again came under fire from what they believed were rooftop snipers to the southeast, the direction of Charlevoix and Lycaste. The police and Guardsmen responded with a hail of fire.

When the shooting ceased, Carl Smith, a young firefighter, lay dead. An autopsy determined that the shot had been fired at street level, and, according to police, probably had come from the southeast.

At 4:00 A.M. when paratroopers, under the command of Col. A. R. Bolling, arrived at the high school, the area was so dark and still that the colonel thought, at first, that he had come to the wrong place. Investigating, he discovered National Guard troops, claiming they were pinned down by sniper fire, crouched behind the walls of the darkened building.

The colonel immediately ordered all the lights in the building turned on and his troops to show themselves as conspicuously as possible. In the apartment house across the street nearly every window had been shot out, and the walls were pockmarked with bullet holes. The colonel went into the building and began talking to the residents, many of whom had spent the night huddled on the floor. He reassured them no more shots would be fired.

According to Lt. Gen. Throckmorton and Colonel Bolling, the city, at this time, was saturated with fear. The National Guardsmen were afraid, the residents were afraid, and the police were afraid. Numerous persons, the majority of them Negroes, were being injured by gunshots of undetermined origin. The general and his staff felt that the major task of the troops was to reduce the fear and restore an air of normalcy.

In order to accomplish this, every effort was made to establish contact and rapport between the troops and the residents. Troopers—20 percent of whom were Negro—began helping to clean up the streets, collect garbage, and trace persons who had disappeared in the confusion. Residents in the neighborhoods responded with soup and sandwiches for the troops. In areas where the National Guard tried to establish rapport with the citizens, there was a similar response.

Within hours after the arrival of the paratroops the area occupied by them was the quietest in the city, bearing out General Throckmorton's view that the key to quelling a disorder is to saturate an area with "calm, determined, and hardened professional soldiers." Loaded weapons, he believes, are unnecessary. Troopers had strict orders not to fire unless they could see the specific person at whom they were aiming. Mass fire was forbidden.

During five days in the city, 2,700 Army troops expended only 201 rounds of ammunition, almost all during the first few hours, after which even stricter fire discipline was enforced. (In contrast, New Jersey National Guardsmen and State police expended 13,326 rounds of ammunition in three days in Newark.) Hundreds of reports of sniper fire—most of them false—continued to pour into police headquarters; the Army logged only 10. No paratrooper was injured by a gunshot. Only one person was hit by a shot fired by a trooper. He was a young Negro who was killed when he ran into the line of fire as a trooper, aiding police in a raid on an apartment, aimed at a person believed to be a sniper.

General Throckmorton ordered the weapons of all military personnel unloaded, but either the order failed to reach many National Guardsmen, or else it was disobeyed.

Even as the general was requesting the city to relight the streets, Guardsmen continued shooting out the lights, and there are reports of dozens of shots being fired to dispatch one light. At one such location, as Guardsmen were shooting out the street lights, a radio newscaster reported himself to be pinned down by "sniper fire."

On the same day that the general was attempting to restore normalcy by ordering street barricades taken down, Guardsmen on one street were not only, in broad daylight, ordering people off the street, but off their porches and away from the windows. Two persons who failed to respond to the order quickly enough were shot, one of them fatally.

The general himself reported an incident of a Guardsman "firing across the bow" of an automobile that was approaching a roadblock.

As in Los Angeles two years earlier, roadblocks that were ill-lighted and ill-defined—often consisting of no more than a trash barrel or similar object with Guardsmen standing nearby—proved a continuous hazard to motorists. At one such roadblock, National Guard Sergeant Larry Post, standing in the street, was caught in a sudden cross fire as his fellow Guardsmen opened up on a vehicle. He was the only soldier killed in the riot.

With persons of every description arming themselves, and guns being fired accidentally or on the vaguest pretext all over the city, it became more and more impossible to tell who was shooting at whom. Some firemen began carrying guns. One accidentally shot and wounded a fellow fireman. Another injured himself.

The chaos of a riot, and the difficulties faced by police officers, are demonstrated by an incident that occurred at 2:00 A.M. Tuesday.

A unit of 12 officers received a call to guard firemen from snipers. When they arrived at the corner of Vicksburg and Linwood in the 12th Street area, the intersection was well-lighted by the flames completely enveloping one building. Sniper fire was directed at the officers from an alley to the north, and gun flashes were observed in two buildings.

As the officers advanced on the two buildings, Patrolman Johnie [sic] Hamilton fired several rounds from his machinegun. Thereupon, the officers were suddenly subjected to fire from a new direction, the east. Hamilton, struck by four bullets, fell, critically injured, in the intersection. As two officers ran to his aid, they too were hit.

By this time other units of the Detroit Police Department, state police, and National Guard had arrived on the scene, and the area was covered with a hail of gunfire.

In the confusion the snipers who had initiated the shooting escaped.

At 9:15 P.M. Tuesday, July 25, 38-year-old Jack Sydnor, a Negro, came home drunk. Taking out his pistol, he fired one shot into an alley. A few minutes later the police arrived. As his common-law wife took refuge in a closet, Sydnor waited, gun in hand, while the police forced open the door. Patrolman Roger Poike, the first to enter, was shot by Sydnor. Although critically injured, the officer managed to get off six shots in return. Police within the building and on the street then poured a hail of fire into the apartment. When the shooting ceased, Sydnor's body, riddled by the gunfire, was found lying on the ground outside a window.

Nearby, a state police officer and a Negro youth were struck and seriously injured by stray bullets. As in other cases where the origin of the shots was not immediately determinable, police reported them as "shot by sniper."

Reports of "heavy sniper fire" poured into police headquarters from the two blocks surrounding the apartment house where the battle with Jack Sydnor had taken place. National Guard troops with two tanks were dispatched to help flush out the snipers.

Shots continued to be heard throughout the neighborhood. At approximately midnight—there are discrepancies as to the precise time—a machine gunner on a tank, startled by several shots, asked the assistant gunner where the shots were coming from. The assistant gunner pointed toward a flash in the window of an apartment house from which there had been earlier reports of sniping.

The machine gunner opened fire. As the slugs ripped through the window and walls of the apartment, they nearly severed the arm of 21-year-old Valerie Hood. Her 4-year-old niece, Tonya Blanding, toppled dead, a .50 caliber bullet hole in her chest.

A few seconds earlier, 19-year-old Bill Hood, standing in the window, had lighted a cigarette.

Down the street, a bystander was critically injured by a stray bullet. Simultaneously, the John C. Lodge Freeway, two blocks away, was reported to be under sniper fire. Tanks and National Guard troops were sent to investigate. At the Harlan House Motel, ten blocks from where Tonya Blanding had died a short time earlier, Mrs. Helen Hall, a 51-year-old white businesswoman, opened the drapes of the fourth floor hall window. Calling out to other guests, she exclaimed: "Look at the tanks!"

She died seconds later as bullets began to slam into the building. As the firing ceased, a 19-year-old Marine Pfc., carrying a Springfield rifle, burst into the building. When, accidentally, he pushed the rifle barrel through a window, the firing commenced anew. A police investigation showed that the Marine, who had just decided to "help out" the law enforcement personnel, was not involved in the death of Mrs. Hall.

R. R., a white 27-year-old coin dealer, was the owner of an expensive, three-story house on "L" Street, an integrated middle class neighborhood. In May of 1966, he and his wife and child had moved to New York and had rented the house to two young men. After several months he had begun to have problems with his tenants. On one occasion he reported to his attorney that he had been threatened by them.

In March of 1967, R. R. instituted eviction proceedings. These were still pending when the riot broke out. Concerned about the house, R. R. decided to fly to Detroit. When he arrived at the house, on Wednesday, July 26, he discovered the tenants were not at home.

He then called his attorney, who advised him to take physical possession of the house and, for legal purposes, to take witnesses along.

Together with his 17-year-old brother and another white youth, R. R. went to the house, entered, and began changing the locks on the doors. For protection they brought a .22 caliber rifle, which R. R.'s brother took into the cellar and fired into a pillow in order to test it.

Shortly after 8:00 P.M., R. R. called his attorney to advise him that the tenants had returned, and he had refused to admit them. Thereupon, R. R. alleged, the tenants had threatened to obtain the help of the National Guard. The attorney relates that he was not particularly concerned. He told R. R. that if the National Guard did appear he should have the officer in charge call him (the attorney).

At approximately the same time the National Guard claims it received information to the effect that several men had evicted the legal occupants of the house, and intended to start sniping after dark.

A National Guard column was dispatched to the scene. Shortly after 9:00 P.M., in the half-light of dusk, the column of approximately 30 men surrounded the house. A tank took position on a lawn across the street. The captain commanding the column placed in front of the house an explosive device similar to a firecracker. After setting this off in order to draw the attention of the occupants to the presence of the column, he called for them to come out of the house. No attempt was made to verify the truth or falsehood of the allegations regarding snipers.

When the captain received no reply from the house, he began counting to 10. As he was counting, he said, he heard a shot, the origin of which he could not determine. A few seconds later he heard another shot and saw a "fire streak" coming from an upstairs window. He thereupon gave the order to fire.

According to the three young men, they were on the second floor of the house and completely bewildered by the barrage of fire that was unleashed against it. As hundreds of bullets crashed through the first and second-story windows and ricocheted off the walls, they dashed to the third floor. Protected by a large chimney, they huddled in a closet until, during a lull in the firing, they were able to wave an item of clothing out of the window as a sign of surrender. They were arrested as snipers.

The firing from rifles and machine guns had been so intense that in a period of a few minutes it inflicted an estimated $10,000 worth of damage. One of a pair of stone columns was shot nearly in half.

Jailed at the 10th Precinct Station sometime Wednesday night R. R. and his two companions were taken from their cell to an "alley court," police slang for an unlawful attempt to make prisoners confess. A police officer, who has resigned from the force, allegedly administered such a severe beating to R. R. that the bruises still were visible two weeks later.

R. R.'s 17-year-old brother had his skull cracked open, and was thrown back into the cell. He was taken to a hospital only when other arrestees complained that he was bleeding to death.

At the preliminary hearing 12 days later the prosecution presented only one witness, the National Guard captain who had given the order to fire. The police officer who had signed the original complaint was not asked to take the stand. The charges against all three of the young men were dismissed.

Nevertheless, the morning after the original incident, a major metropolitan newspaper in another section of the country composed the following banner story from wire service reports:

> DETROIT, July 27 (Thursday)—Two National Guard tanks ripped a sniper's haven with machine guns Wednesday night and flushed out three shaggy-haired white youths. Snipers attacked a guard command post and Detroit's racial riot set a modern record for bloodshed. The death toll soared to 36, topping the Watts bloodbath of 1966 in which 35 died and making Detroit's insurrection the most deadly racial riot in modern U.S. history. . . .
>
> In the attack on the sniper's nest, the Guardsmen poured hundreds of rounds of .50 caliber machine gun fire into the home, which authorities said housed arms and ammunition used by West Side sniper squads.
>
> Guardsmen recovered guns and ammunition. A reporter with the troopers said the house, a neat brick home in a neighborhood of $20,000 to $50,000 homes, was torn apart by the machine gun and rifle fire.
>
> Sniper fire crackled from the home as the Guard unit approached. It was one of the first verified reports of sniping by whites. . . .
>
> A pile of loot taken from riot-ruined stores was recovered from the sniper's haven, located ten blocks from the heart of the 200-square block riot zone.
>
> Guardsmen said the house had been identified as a storehouse of arms and ammunition for snipers. Its arsenal was regarded as an indication that the sniping—or at least some of it—was organized.

As hundreds of arrestees were brought into the 10th Precinct Station, officers took it upon themselves to carry on investigations and to attempt to extract confessions. Dozens of charges of police brutality emanated from the station as prisoners were brought in uninjured, but later had to be taken to the hospital.

In the absence of the precinct commander, who had transferred his headquarters to the riot command post at a nearby hospital, discipline vanished. Prisoners who requested that they be permitted to notify someone of their arrest were almost invariably told that: "The telephones are out of order." Congressman Conyers and State Representative Del Rio, who went to the station hoping to coordinate with the police the establishing of a community patrol, were so upset by what they saw that they changed their minds and gave up on the project.

A young woman, brought into the station, was told to strip. After she had done so, and while an officer took pictures with a Polaroid camera, another officer came up to her and began fondling her. The negative of one of the pictures, fished out of a waste basket, subsequently was turned over to the mayor's office.

Citing the sniper danger, officers throughout the department had taken off their bright metal badges. They also had taped over the license plates and the numbers of the police cars. Identification of individual officers became virtually impossible.

On a number of occasions officers fired at fleeing looters, then made little attempt to determine whether their shots had hit anyone. Later some of the persons were discovered dead or injured in the street.

In one such case police and National Guardsmen were interrogating a youth suspected of arson when, according to officers, he attempted to escape. As he vaulted over the hood of an automobile, an officer fired his shotgun. The youth disappeared on the other side of the car. Without making an investigation, the officers and Guardsmen returned to their car and drove off.

When nearby residents called police, another squad car arrived to pick up the body. Despite the fact that an autopsy disclosed the youth had been killed by five shotgun pellets, only a cursory investigation was made, and the death was attributed to "sniper fire." No police officer at the scene during the shooting filed a report.

Not until a Detroit newspaper editor presented to the police the statements of several witnesses claiming that the youth had been shot by police after he had been told to run did the department launch an investigation. Not until three weeks after the shooting did an officer come forward to identify himself as the one who had fired the fatal shot.

Citing conflicts in the testimony of the score of witnesses, the Detroit Prosecutor's office declined to press charges.

Prosecution is proceeding in the case of three youths in whose shotgun deaths law enforcement personnel were implicated following a report that snipers were firing from the Algiers Motel. In fact, there is little evidence that anyone fired from inside the building. Two witnesses say that they had seen a man, standing outside of the motel, fire two shots from a rifle. The interrogation of other persons revealed that law enforcement personnel then shot out one or more street lights. Police patrols responded to the shots. An attack was launched on the motel.

The picture is further complicated by the fact that this incident occurred at roughly the same time that the National Guard was directing fire at the apartment house in which Tonya Blanding was killed. The apartment house was only six blocks distant from and in a direct line with the motel.

The killings occurred when officers began on-the-spot questioning of the occupants of the motel in an effort to discover weapons used in the "sniping." Several of those questioned reportedly were beaten. One was a Negro ex-paratrooper who had only recently been honorably discharged, and had gone to Detroit to look for a job.

Although by late Tuesday looting and fire-bombing had virtually ceased, between 7:00 and 11:00 P.M. that night there were 444 reports of incidents. Most were reports of sniper fire.

During the daylight hours of July 26th, there were 534 such reports. Between 8:30 and 11:00 P.M. there were 255. As they proliferated, the pressure on law enforcement officers to uncover the snipers became intense. Homes were broken into. Searches were made on the flimsiest of tips. A Detroit newspaper headline aptly proclaimed: "Everyone's Suspect in No Man's Land."

Before the arrest of a young woman IBM operator in the city assessor's office brought attention to the situation on Friday, July 28th, any person with a gun in his home was liable to be picked up as a suspect.

Of the 27 persons charged with sniping, 22 had charges against them dismissed at preliminary hearings, and the charges against two others were dismissed later. One pleaded guilty to possession of an unregistered gun and was given a suspended sentence. Trials of two are pending.

In all, more than 7,200 persons were arrested. Almost 3,000 of these were picked up on the second day of the riot, and by midnight Monday 4,000 were incarcerated in makeshift jails. Some were kept as long as 30 hours on buses. Others spent days in an underground garage without toilet facilities. An uncounted number were people who had merely been unfortunate enough to be on the wrong street at the wrong time. Included were members of the press whose attempts to show their credentials had been ignored. Released later, they were chided for not having exhibited their identification at the time of their arrests.

The booking system proved incapable of adequately handling the large number of arrestees. People became lost for days in the maze of different detention facilities. Until the later stages, bail was set deliberately high, often at $10,000 or more. When it became apparent that this policy was unrealistic and unworkable, the Prosecutor's office began releasing on low bail or on their own recognizance hundreds of those who had been picked up. Nevertheless, this fact was not publicized for fear of antagonizing those who had demanded a high-bail policy.

Of the 43 persons who were killed during the riot, 33 were Negro and 10 were white. Seventeen were looters, of whom two were white. Fifteen citizens (of whom four were white), one white National Guardsman, one white fireman, and one Negro private guard died as the result of gunshot wounds. Most of these deaths appear to have been accidental, but criminal homicide is suspected in some.

Two persons, including one fireman, died as a result of fallen power lines. Two were burned to death. One was a drunken gunman; one an arson suspect. One white man was killed by a rioter. One police officer was felled by a shotgun blast when his gun, in the hands of another officer, accidentally discharged during a scuffle with a looter.

Action by police officers accounted for 20 and, very likely, 21 of the deaths. Action by the National Guard for seven, and, very likely, nine. Action by the Army for one. Two deaths were the result of action by store owners. Four persons died accidentally. Rioters were responsible for two, and perhaps three of the deaths; a private guard for one. A white man is suspected of murdering a Negro youth. The perpetrator of one of the killings in the Algiers Motel remains unknown.

Damage estimates, originally set as high as $500 million, were quickly scaled down. The city assessor's office placed the loss—excluding business stock, private furnishings, and the buildings of churches and charitable institutions—at approximately $22 million. Insurance payments, according to the State Insurance Bureau, will come to about $32 million, representing an estimated 65 to 75 percent of the total loss.

By Thursday, July 27, most riot activity had ended. The paratroopers were removed from the city on Saturday. On Tuesday, August 1, the curfew was lifted and the National Guard moved out.

Police Statement on Black Panthers in Riots, Civil, and Criminal Disorders

TESTIMONY OF LT. WILLIAM L. OLSEN

The CHAIRMAN. Identify yourself for the record, please.

Lieutenant OLSEN. My name is William L. Olsen. I am a lieutenant with the Chicago Police Department.

The CHAIRMAN. How long have you been a lieutenant?

Lieutenant OLSEN. For approximately 2 years, a little over 2 years.

The CHAIRMAN. You have been on the police department 13 years?

Lieutenant OLSEN. I have.

The CHAIRMAN. At the present time you are in command of what unit?

Lieutenant OLSEN. The subversive unit of the intelligence division.

The CHAIRMAN. How long have you been in charge of that unit?

Lieutenant OLSEN. Approximately 9 months.

The CHAIRMAN. About 9 months.

Do you have a prepared statement?

Lieutenant OLSEN. I do, sir.

The CHAIRMAN. You may proceed with it.

Black Panther Party: History, Aims and Objectives

Lieutenant OLSEN. I intend to testify first on the Black Panther Party.

The Black Panther Party had its origin in Chicago, as best we can tell, on about November 1, 1968. It is our understanding that sometime in June 1968 several people got together and began making their inroads to the Black Panther Party national headquarters in Berkeley, Calif., seeking a charter for Chicago, Ill.

Source: From *Riots, Civil and Criminal Disorders: Hearings Before the Permanent Sub-committee on Government Operations.* U.S. Senate, 91st Congress, First Session, June 26, 30, 1969. Part 20, pp. 4434–4438.

Further, our information is that about October 1968 one of the current Black Panther Party members, a high official within the Black Panther Party in Illinois, traveled to California, sometime in October 1968, and at this time established contact with the National BPP office. The Illinois BPP chapter was subsequently recognized by the national central committee and officially opened their party headquarters at 2350 West Madison on November 1, 1968.

Within the party itself, the highest ranking official is the minister of defense, the imprisoned Huey P. Newton. Bobby Lee Rush, the Illinois deputy minister of defense, has stated that this rank is highest because the Panthers are at war with the power structure. During "peacetime," the chairman of the party will assume the No. 1 position. Currently, the national chairman of the party is Bobby George Scale, and locally it is Fred Allen Hampton. Fred Hampton is currently doing a 2- to 5-year term in the penitentiary for robbery.

Before the above ranks come, in descending order, the minister of information, the chief of staff, the communication secretary, the field secretaries or field marshals, and the various ministers. Except for those on the national central committee, all officers at the chapter level have their titles preceded by the qualifying term "Deputy."

The Black Panther Party has openly adopted the philosophy of the Chinese Communists.

I offer in exhibit an article that appeared in the Chicago Sun Times on May 25 wherein Fred Hampton was quoted as saying:

Question: Your goal is the socialist society?
Answer: That's our goal. That would be our first move.

The CHAIRMAN. What? I didn't quite understand you. What would be his first move?

They need a program that's geared toward some good issues—like our free school breakfasts for children program. We're feeding almost 3,000 children a week at our three centers—1441 N. Cleveland, 500 E. 37th and 1512 S. Pulaski—and we're opening up another center now at 3906 W. Lexington. They're open from 7 a.m. to 9 a.m. every school day. Anybody who comes there we'll feed.

Q. When did you start this?

A. We started April 1. We started because it's a primary way of teaching the people the works of socialism. And people might say it's fundamental. But that's the way you start off—fundamentally.

Q. Somebody in the Blackstone Rangers [renamed the Black P Stone Nation], said recently that all Black Disciples are Panthers and all Panthers are Black Disciples.

A. Right.

Q. You have a coalition?

A. We have a coalition.

Q. What is the nature of that coalition?

A. The Black Disciples recognize the Black Panther Party as being the vanguard party of the revolutionary struggle.

Q. Some people are saying you've recruited the Disciples in opposition to the Rangers, or the Black P Stone Nation Organization.

A. We're not at war with the Black P Stone Rangers. As a matter of fact we're at peace with the Black P Stone Rangers, contrary to what a lot of people might try to interject. The problem is, the pigs (police) are trying to make us believe that the Black P Stone Rangers are our enemies and they're trying to make the Black P Stone Rangers believe that we're their enemies. But from what I hear from the leaders of the Black P Stone Nation, when I talk to them myself, these attempts by the pigs are failing.

Q. Why would the police want to set you against each other?

A. It sets up a better atmosphere for breaking into the office. And it sets up a better atmosphere for shooting Panthers in the back when the people believe that the Panthers and the P Stone Rangers and the Disciples are nothing but gangs. None of these organizations is a gang. But they put this gangland image on us and tell people we're out killing each other. Then when one of us gets shot in the head by the pigs, the pigs say: "Well, they were nothing but a gang anyway." And the people say: "That's right. I read about it."

I just went to a wake where a young man had been shot in the head by a pig. And you know, this is bad. But it heightens the contradictions in the community. These things a lot of times in fact organize the people better then we can organize them ourselves.

Q. Do the Panthers believe in forcing confrontations for that purpose, to radicalize people?

A. Well, we believe in heightening contradictions. Because when you heighten contradictions it heightens the awareness of the people, you know. But I don't see where any confrontation has to be forced—in the city of Chicago or anywhere else. I think that Mayor Daley's a walking contradiction himself.

Q. On the Rangers, though. The Rangers are here. Then you come to town. And you say you're an elite, a vanguard unit. Isn't there inevitably going to be some friction in a case like that?

A. No, no, no. That's not true. I'm saying that we're all about the same thing. That's one of the largest groups of young warriors in the city. And we're talking about war. How would we come into conflict with people with the same interests? I'm not afraid to admit that I'm at war with the pigs. Why would I be afraid to admit that I'm at war with the Black P Stone Rangers? There's more pigs than P Stone Rangers.

Q. Your coalition with the Young Patriots and the Young Lords is basically a coalition of poor people, isn't it? And aren't the poor a minority in this country? In this class struggle you talk about, how can a minority win a revolution without enlisting the nonpoor working class and a labor movement that is more interested in shop issues than it is in political abstractions?

A. The people haven't really turned away from class struggle. They've never been turned on to class struggle. And racism is what has put the laboring forces in the situation they're in. Now we're out here in an attempt to eliminate priority being placed on the race question and to place that same priority on the class question.

But we are fighting some tremendous forces of pigs. We are fighting forces that come out in the papers and say that the Black Panther Party is a racist organization. They say we believe in black supremacy, and they talk about the Black Panther Party as a gang, and they try to make the Black . . . gangs. We understand what a problem this is.

It's going to take some time. Nobody's trying to fool themselves. It's going to take some time to educate these people right out here on streets.

But we're saying that as soon as these people come together and unite with real friends, for the purpose of attacking real enemies, that will be the end of all this racism within the labor unions.

You have to understand, it's just like trying to convince somebody that he's tall and short at the same time, or he's fat and skinny at the same time. You can not be a capitalistic society and have the masses benefit. And whether you want to believe it or not, the Black Panther Party is a humanitarian organization. We deal with the masses of the people. And we know where the masses are at.

We have not, you know, made overwhelming amounts of progress in the laboring front right here in Chicago. But I am saying very simply that we do have plans, and some of these plans can not be exposed. We do have ways of revolutionizing unions. But that's a subjective thing. We have to be believed on what we say.

Q. You say Panthers have to purge themselves of racism or be purged from the party. Did you have to do it personally?

A. Yes.

Q. When did you do it?

A. I did it after the line of the party was run down, and after we did a lot of intensive studying. We all study together. And we studied the Marx and Lenin theory and put their theory in practice, and we didn't have any trouble doing it.

Q. It wasn't hard to do?

A. It was nothing. If you've got an open mind, and somebody tells you something that's true then you find out it's true—you just do it. There ain't no big thing about that.

Lieutenant OLSEN. The question by the reporter was "Your goal is a Socialist society?"

Fred Hampton replied:

That is not our goal. That would be our first move. When we got into a socialist society, then that would have to evolve into a Communist society.

The CHAIRMAN. So the so-called new social order is a step toward a Communist society?

Lieutenant OLSEN. That is correct, sir.

The CHAIRMAN. That is according to the highest ranking leader in Chicago at this time?

Lieutenant OLSEN. That is correct, sir.

The next question that was asked by this reporter was:

You are Maoists, aren't you? You prefer Chinese socialism to Russian socialism?

His reply was:

Russia is not a people's republic. We think that China is a people's republic.

The Chairman. That may be received as an exhibit.

(The document referred to was marked "Exhibit No. 634" for reference and follows:)

Exhibit No. 634: The Illinois Black Panthers: Leader Talks About His Aims

[From the Chicago *Sun-Times*, May 25, 1969]

(By William Braden)

The Illinois Black Panther Party appeared on the Chicago scene last Nov. 1, when it opened a headquarters office at 2350 W. Madison.

The Panthers are a national phenomenon, and it is possible they represent a significant shift in the strategy and philosophy of at least some militant blacks—a new phase in the post civil rights movement.

They have armed themselves. And they speak of revolution.

But what kind of revolution?

An answer to that question might be found in some of the alliances the Panthers have recently formed with other Chicago groups—with Puerto Ricans and (improbable as it might seem) with Appalachian whites.

To find out what the coming of the Panthers might mean for Chicago, a *Sun-Times* reporter visited their heavily guarded office and interviewed 20-year-old Fred Hampton, state chairman of the Panthers. Here is part of that interview.

Q. What are the Black Panthers?

A. The Black Panthers Party is an armed propaganda unit. People need to understand politics better, so we're out there every day trying to educate them to the works of politics. There have been many attacks made upon the Black Panther Party, so we feel it's best to be an *armed* propaganda unit. But the basic thing is to educate.

Q. You're also a revolutionary unit, aren't you?

A. Whenever you talk about educating people, then you're a revolutionary party. Revolution is nothing but a change, because man is always evolving. And we're saying that the state has to evolve at the same level that man has evolved, and the contradiction now is capitalism and socialism. We think it's time for the state to evolve into a socialistic state.

Q. Your goal is a socialist society?

A. That's not our goal—that would be our first move. When we got into a socialist society, then that would have to evolve into a Communist society.

Q. You're Maoists, aren't you? You prefer Chinese socialism to Russian socialism?

A. Russia is not a people's republic. We think that China is a people's republic.

Q. Are you necessarily talking about an armed revolution?

A. No. But, by what this country has done to nonviolent leaders like Martin Luther King—I think that objectively this says there's going to have to be an armed struggle. People have to be armed to have power, you see.

Q. The Panthers say they reject black racism. Aren't you trying now to ally yourself with radical whites?

A. We're saying there's a difference between people that are white and people that are radical whites. We say that if a man can take on revolutionary ideologies, if he can take on the Marxist-Lenin theory—not only in theory but also in practice—then that man can be a friend to us. We believe that the reason we have not been successful in the revolutionary struggle in this country is because—in the past—we've failed to unite with real friends for the purpose of attacking real enemies.

Q. Along those lines you recently formed a coalition with the Young Lords, who are Puerto Rican, and the Young Patriots, a group of white Appalachians from the Uptown area. Is that correct?

A. That's correct. This coalition took place, I'd say, around four or five months ago. We had a section chief who was working out on the North Side, and he ran into these people. He worked with them. We gave them books to read, and things like that, and they started, you know, to come along those lines. We talked about common interests, and common enemies, and when we found we had these things in common we decided to form a coalition.

The coalition was also to show that we believe in solidarity in practice. A lot of people are running around talking about fighting fire with fire. They say they're going to fight racism with racism. But we claim that you fight fire best with water. We say you fight racism with solidarity. We say you don't fight capitalism with black capitalism. You fight capitalism with socialism.

This race question has got people so divided they don't even have a chance to come together and talk. If they did come together, they'd understand very clearly that this is a class struggle.

We're all in that same class. That makes us all friends. The other people who are oppressing us are all in the same class. That makes them real enemies.

Q. Is it true you purge Panthers who show racist tendencies?

A. Right. Because many people in the Black Panther Party can't make the move. They can't step up when the party's ideology steps up. A lot of times we have to regear our program as the time changes, you see, and people that can't make these changes are purged from the party. A lot of people have been purged, and a lot of people are being purged, and there are many more who are going to have to be purged.

Why? Because the people are educated by the vanguard. So that makes the vanguard the elite group of the revolutionary struggle. All the people may form an army one day, but the Black Panther Party will be the vanguard of that army. So what we're saying is that everybody can not be in the vanguard. And there's nothing wrong with that.

Q. You're an elitist group?

A. Right.

Q. Another newspaper reported that your coalition includes the Students for a Democratic Society, the SDS. That's not true, is it?

A. They're not part of our coalition. We work very close with the SDS, and they help us out in many ways, and we try to help them out in as many ways as we can. On many political questions and on many methods we and SDS go down the same path—as far as theory goes.

Q. But you're basically trying to put together a coalition of poor people. Is the SDS—a student movement—really fundamental to what you're doing?

A. I see anybody that recognizes the vanguard party—the Black Panther Party being the vanguard party. And you understand what that means? It means that . . . provide the leader-ship for all oppressed people. It's up to us what happens. We paid the cost of being the boss. We were the ones in this class that were oppressed the most. But we've never had any hangups with the SDS over this.

Q. What do you think of the Rev. Jesse Jackson and his Operation Breadbasket approach?

A. In operation Breadbasket, most of the things they have—Black Easter and Black Christmas—these programs are to benefit businessmen. It's not geared toward the masses. It couldn't be geared to the masses, because it's capitalistic.

Keep on Pushin': Rhythm & Blues as a Weapon

Rolland Snellings

In the Lash Years when we wore the chains of our dishonor, we were a defiant, spirited people. So much so, that there occurred a slave revolt on the average of once every three weeks. The slave revolts were the outward PHYSICAL manifestations of the inner SPIRIT of the captive people. The inner SPIRIT was also manifested in what were to become the rudiments or foundations of African-american culture: the spirituals, hollers, field-chants, etc.

The African-american spiritual was an ingenius instrument molded in the fires of oppression—disguised as mere "sacred songs," the spiritual was a vessel which carried the message of resistance, escape, or revolt. Resistance, escape, or revolt, the message of the spiritual, has been handed down through the years, in the collective memory of our people, in the "double-talk" of the parables, folk-tales, folksongs, etc. of the Black Man.

Given the primary powerlessness of our people to Whitey's brute force, we had to create a subtle instrument which would increase our "value" to the Beast while "taking care of business" for ourselves. "Boy, those niggers sure can sing; gather 'em up at the big house tonight from all over the plantation, so they can serenade us." So, the "get togethers" were very instrumental in providing many coded messages, details, etc. to the Underground Railroad and networks developing throughout the South.

From the period of "Reconstruction," where the neo-colonialism of White America was exposed for what it was, down to the outright betrayal and institution of color segregation, our people shifted their emphasis to the painful irony of the Blues (or Country Blues) to describe or "run down" our philosophy, attitudes, and outlooks. It is recorded that when Gertrude "Ma" Rainey gave a show in the Southern "back country," the Black farmers and sharecroppers (landless peasants) came from miles around, from neighboring districts and counties, to view the scene.

Such songs as "Backwater Blues" (describing the tragedy of the floods), "Yellow

Source: Rolland Snellings, "Keep on Pushin': Rhythm & Blues as a Weapon," *Liberator*, Vol. V, October 1968.

Dog Blues," and others were the crystallized philosophies, hopes, and aspirations voice FOR our people by their PRIEST-PHILOSO-PHERS: the Black singers and musicians. (This attitude of the Black musician and poet as priest-philosoper goes back to the indigenous African civilizations, where the artist-priest had a functional role as the keeper or guardian of the spirit of the nation—as well as the ancestors.) This attitude, curiously enough, has remained among us despite the dehumanization of chattel slavery and the "white-washing" of the Western Missionary Educational System. It has, of course been either ignored or by-passed by bourgeois "negro" sociologists, either through ignorance of heritage or fear of being classified "alien" to American cultural standards.

ONCE MORE: We are a defiant, spirited people who have a history of over three hundred years of constant slave revolts, in which our music played a vital role. Our main philosophical and cultural attitudes are displayed through our MUSIC, which serves as the ROOT of our culture; from which springs our art, poetry, literature, etc. Our creative artists—especially singers and musicians—function as PRIESTS, as PHILOSOPHERS of our captive nation; a holdover from our ancient past.

> "I got to keep on pushin', can't stop now. Move up a little higher, some way, some how.
> 'Cause I got my strength, don't make sense: Keep on pushin'!"

In the smoldering epoch of our times, eruptions of the Captive Nation are once again reflected in the songs of Black Folks. In the period of the early Fifties, JAZZ, which had been a vital part of Black people's music, was taken over by the racketeers and moved downtown into the clubs and bars of the middle-class pleasure-seekers, away from the roots, away from the Heart, the Womb, away from the home of the people: uptown-ghetto! With JAZZ—Bird, Diz, Miles, Max, Lady Day, Lester Young—JAZZ all gone away: Rhythm and Blues was the only music left to sing out the aspirations and soul stirrings of Blacks folks uptown N.Y. and "uptown-ghetto" across the face of the land. This was, at first, a blow to the Soul Folks: What would they possibly DO without BIRD, DIZ, MILES or LADY DAY or LESTER YOUNG to make them "feel alright" deep down in the nitty-gritty of their hearts? But, being a people raised on change, raised with the insecurities of change throbbing in the nerve-ends of their lives, they ADAPTED themselves to expression with their only cultural weapon or potential weapon: Rhythm and Blues.

Yes, JAZZ, fine JAZZ, great JAZZ was gone away, gone away, away into the Ofay night, away from the warm earth smell of their rhythms and soul vibrations, to make the cash registers clang and sing, ring and pile up green capital for the "negroes' 'FRIEND' " and sponsor "downtown" in the air-conditioned nightmares of the West.

The Fifties, the early Fifties, the later Fifties of suicidal Johnny Ace, Big Mabel, Chuck Willis, Chuck Jackson: all legendary Blues People, scorched with the pain reflected in bleary red-eyed heartbreak sweat-stained songs and tears flooding into the "Ebb-tide" of Roy Hamiltons or the Moon-glows; Clyde McPhatter and the Drifters blown to the "White Cliffs of Dover" on the "Wind" of the Diablos; "Crying in the Chapels" of the Orioles; or shot down, cut and beaten up in "Smokey Joe's Cafe."

These were OUR songs, OUR lives reflected in a thousand blue notes, notes of hopelessness marked with thicker calluses on black hands, more muscle cramps in mama's knees, more heartache and unemployment for our fathers and brothers, as Korea loomed distantly and we went away to slaughter up the Yellow race for Whitey's cause.

My people, YES, a million lonely eyes burning to touch Happiness, to touch Human Sympathy, Brotherhood, Justice: all those BIG words that BIG white learned men invented to taunt us into dissatisfaction with eight kids to a room, bedside roach-crawl and rats gnawing at the eight kids to a room on gloom street, on your street, my street: Ghetto-up-town U.S.A.!

My people, YES, my love, my Fifties of Martin Luther King, minister of youth: Large liquid eyes then searching for the Gandhi-secret Freedom-message looming huge and idealistic from Southern horizons bleeding in the sun of a thousand lynch-fires; echoing whitely in the poison-voice of Eastland, Talmadge, Russell, Earl Long and other Favorite Sons of the "Land of the Tree." (In those years of Martin Luther King, bus boycotts and other evidence of our growing struggle, we grew up, developed, expanded our souls, our minds churning to the beat of our people's only music, Rhythm and Blues. We lived it; sang it in vocal groups, in cabarets, on street corners: junkies nodding in the rain. We didn't call it "culture," didn't call it "negro art," it was just OUR music, OUR soul, like OUR girl-friends, OUR comrades, OUR families who didn't understand. It, again, was OUR voice, OUR ritual, OUR understanding of those deep things far too complicated to put into words—except those of Fats Domino, Little Richard, Ray Charles, Dinah Washington, Faye Addams, Ruth Brown, Lloyd Price and many more.)

> "Look, a look a 'yonder: what's that I see?
> Great big stone wall standing straight ahead of me.
> But I've got my pride, move the wall aside:
> Keep on pushin'!"

The Sixties, roaring in like a rocket, roaring through the Southland with freedom riders, more boycotts, sit-ins, wade-ins, stand-ins, kneel-ins; Black Muslims rising in the Northland new angry voice, young copper-skinned Malcolm X shaking up the psyche of the nations—Black and White. Lumumba, the U.N. Congo demonstrations, Robert Williams defends a Southern town against the Klan. WE are on the move, WE are moving to a New Tempo, to a New Dynamism—like Coltrane blowing SCREAMING in the downtown nightclubs: "Afro-Blue," "Blue Trane," "Africa," "Out of

This World;" and we hear in his screams the bloody Whiplash moans and screams of our great-grandfathers and grandmothers bending low; eyes ablaze with terror at castration, rape, mutilation, SCREAMING into the Raven Universe, SCREAMING into the coming generations, SCREAMING into the Womb of Mother Africa violated and crushed by the Roman Prophylactic: AAAAAAAIIIIIIIEEEEEEE! AAAAAAAIIII-IIIEEEEEEE!

We sing in our young hearts, we sing in our angry Black Souls: WE ARE COMING UP! WE ARE COMING UP! And it's reflected in the Riot-song that symbolized Harlem, Philly, Brooklyn, Rochester, Patterson, Elizabeth; this song, of course, "Dancing in the Streets"—making Martha and the Vandellas legendary. Then FLASH! it surges up again: "We Gonna' Make It" (to the tune of Medgar Evers gunned down in Mississippi: POW! POW! POW! POW!) "Keep On Trying" (to the tune of James Powell gunned down in Harlem: POW! POW! POW! Gonna' Come" (to the tune of Brother Malcolm shot down in the Audobon: POW! POW! POW! POW! POW! POW! POW! POW!)

THIS is, once again, a people's music, THIS is the reflection of their rising aspirations, THESE are the Truths sung by their modern PRIESTS and PHILOSOPHERS: We are on the move and our music is MOVING with us. WE are expressing our heartfelt anger, conjuring up strong Black Armies marching to the tune of "The Same Old Song" while gas bombs and myths explode in Watts, Los Angeles, explode into the putrid white heart of the racist hell that has us STILL IN CHAINS! YES, IN CHAINS! Look at our Rhythm and Blues singers! Look at the musicians! WHO own their contracts? WHO are their agents, managers; WHO speaks for them? CHAINS! CHAINS! MORE CHAINS! WHITE CHAINS CLANKING IN OUR SOULS! But we are coming out, we are coming up (WHITE AMERICA: DO YOU HEAR?), we are coming out from the chains that bind us: whether culture, economics, politics, military chains: WE ARE COMING OUT! FORGET about his computers, jetplanes, rocketships, blue-eyed troops; FORGET about atomic bombs, police-dogs, cattle-prods and dynamite. OUR songs are turning from "love," turning from being "songs," turning into WAYS, into WAYS, into "THINGS." We are making BLACK magic, BLACK NIGGER magic with our SONGS, with our LIVES: this is our BOMB, our BLACK BOMB, our TIME BOMB, our TIME BOMB which will bring on the "DESTRUCTION OF AMERICA," A PLAY BY LEROI JONES. This Social Voice of Rhythm and Blues is only the beginning of the end. Somewhere along the line, the "Keep On Pushin' " in song, in Rhythm and Blues is merging with the Revolutionary Dynamism of COLTRANE of ERIC DOLPHY of BROTHER MALCOLM of YOUNG BLACK GUERRILLAS STRIKING DEEP INTO THE HEARTLAND OF THE WESTERN EMPIRE. The Fire is spreading, the Fire is spreading, the Fire made from the merging of dynamic Black Music (Rhythm and Blues, Jazz), with politics (GUERRILLA WAR-FARE) is spreading like black oil flaming in Atlantic shipwrecks spreading like Black Fire: the Black Plague spreads across Europe in the Middle Ages—raining death. WORK your magic, BLACK magic, NIGGER magic across the Empire to the beat, to the dynamism of Social-conscious RHYTHM AND BLUES, NEW JAZZ, BLACK POETRY: WORK your NIGGER MAGIC in the sweaty smile of the Boston Monkey, "SUGAR PIE, HONEY-BUNCH:" twist and shimmy frug monkey down the Empire with thick ruby lips grinning like MAD like BLAZING RED EYES LURKING IN THE MOON.

EACH TIME a Black song is born, EACH TIME a Black Sister has another child, EACH TIME Black Youth says NO! to the racist draft boards, EACH TIME someone remembers Brother Malcolm's smile, EACH TIME we write a poem an essay as a Way into "Things," EACH TIME we love each other a little more: THIS THING QUAKES! WE are moving forward, WE are on the move, WE record it all in Rhythm and Blues, New Jazz, Black Poetry, WE—the Captive Nation listening to its priests and wisemen; growing stronger; donning Black Armor to get the job done so Rhythm and Blues can once again sing about "Love," "mellow" black women, and happy children: after it sings this Empire to the grave, after it sings the Sun of the Spirit back into the lonely heart of man. (For Dinah Washington, Sam Cooke, Nat Cole, Eric Dolphy, James Chaney, James Powell, Medgar Evers, Brother Malcolm, Leon Ameer, Walter Bowe, Khaleel Sayyed, Robert Collier: Many Thousand Gone!)

Maybe someday, I'll reach that higher goal.
I know I can make it with just a little bit of soul.
'Cause I've got my strength, don't make sense:
Keep on Pushin'!
Ha-al-lelujah! Ha-al-lelujah!:
Keep on Pushin'!
Keep on Pushin'!

Archie Shepp: Four for Trane

BILL SMITH: *Are people beginning to treat you as a more traditional artist these days?*

Source: Archie Shepp "Four for Trane." *Coda* Magazine, October 1, 1985, pp. 20–22. Copyright © 1985. Reprinted by permission of Archie Shepp.

ARCHIE SHEPP: Well yes, it's hard to accept me that way, but I suppose they are. I think music, especially this kind of music, is very much involved with the time or the period in which it's played, so people grow up with it, unlike Western classical music. They develop almost an allegiance to a certain style of music. For example you have people who listen to Louis Armstrong in the nineteen-twenties and say he didn't play anything after that. It's unfortunate because it doesn't allow us the same flexibility in this area to change, even to re-create music from past eras. People feel you've defected somehow from your generation. I think it's all about generations, this music. I notice my audience, at least the hard core, the old guys, are all getting grey and bald like me. The kids who are coming out have not heard a lot of this music, so in order to form a kind of connection I do try to play some of the more melodic things, and the kinds of things they have some reference to.

BS: *Yesterday I was reading a quote by the composer Edgar Varese and he said the musicians are always in the time that they are in, and the audience is always in the past. They don't become part of it exactly when it's happening.*

AS: Especially contemporary audiences. People expect re-created music; you go through all the styles or periods of the artist, but in a music like this that is being created on the spot, you might say, there are other social factors involved.

BS: *In the early times when you first became a player, in 1960 with Cecil Taylor, that was considered in its day to be a revolutionary music, by the audiences.*

AS: Yes I think so, and by my own standards I still consider it so given the organisation of those pieces and the fact that they were being done for the first time. Also Cecil [Taylor] writes quite differently to Ornette [Coleman] or John Coltrane. Both John and Ornette were primarily dealing with short forms of music — haiku, 32-bar, but Cecil I think broke that by bringing to the small group a concept of larger structures.

BS: *Have you listened in recent times to those Candid records?*

AS: Not recently, but I still remember them very vividly.

BS: *Because in retrospect, which is an easy way to judge something, they sound very melodic.*

AS: They probably sound "inside" now, whereas at the time they were breaking new ground. Since groups like Anthony Braxton and the Art Ensemble of Chicago and David Murray, who evolved out of that period, it's sort of standard fare — in a way. People have become more sophisticated, those who listen to that sort of music. Unfortunately not a lot of people listen to that kind of music.

BS: *There was a great deal of difficulty in that time even to be recorded at all. Because Nat Hentoff had the possibility to record you for labels like Candid — that was the only reason you got recorded.*

AS: That's right. Archie Blier, who I think was working with Jackie Gleason, was making a lot of money and he decided to invest in this jazz label. So I got the chance to record, because I had just joined Cecil Taylor's group.

BS: *In that same period you were seriously beginning to be a writer of plays and poetry.*

AS: I had a piece that was produced off-Broadway, originally entitled "The Communist." It was produced under the title "June Bug Graduates Tonight." It's now published in the Black Drama Anthology, a good anthology published by Signet Books. As a written work.

BS: *One of the other people in that period who had access to record companies was Bill Dixon — Savoy Records.*

AS: Right. Actually I might have turned Bill onto Savoy. He became a good friend of the assistant producer there. Bill did some artwork for them and stayed on there for quite a while.

We had a good quartet, a good idea during that time [1962]; I think we produced a lot of good music.

BS: *It gave you the chance to play original music. Didn't Bill write quite a lot of the music in that period?*

AS: Yes, in fact Bill was very helpful to me in learning how to write. I didn't write at all during that time, and he did quite a bit of writing, as well as copying for George Russell. He and Roswell Rudd were very helpful to me in learning how to notate music. I used to have a lot of problems with it. Still do — I still notate in a personal way as far as academically-trained musicians are concerned. It seems as though I can never satisfy them. But I think it's improved a bit since those days.

BS: *You were one of the first musicians to take the music into Europe and introduce the new music of that period to European audiences with the New York Contemporary Five [1963].*

AS: That's right. John Tchicai was very instrumental in that. He did a lot to help put the group together, in fact we impacted very strongly on the European audiences. Much stronger than I thought we would. We had a lot of confidence and we had good musicians. J.C. Moses (drums) — Don Moore (bass) — John Tchicai (alto saxophone) — and of course

Don Cherry. It took place mostly in Copenhagen, Denmark, and we were also in Sweden; although we did not get up as far as Norway and Finland.

BS: *How would you come upon a Danish player like John Tchicai?*

AS: Quite fortuitously. John had come to the United States seeking to make it as a musician. At the time the lady who was his wife worked for the Danish Embassy. John was a chef in a Swedish restaurant. Word got around downtown that there was this cat who sounded like Ornette, but he sounded like two Ornettes. So I really wanted to hear this guy and when I heard him he really knocked me out. He was playing with Don Cherry and that's how the idea began. We were all very young and all very excited. The criticism they all had of me — the one that's lingered through the years — was that I was playing too long. The drummer and I used to get into big arguments; God bless him, J. C., I really love the guy, he used to shout on the bandstand: "Next man — next man!" You know. To tell me to stop playing. We had really terrible arguments about that.

BS: *It wasn't so common for improvisation to be so long. In this same period, which I think is the development period of the so-called American "new music," of course we come upon the Jazz Composers Orchestra [1964], and the Jazz Composers Guild. You were actively involved in that.*

AS: Yes I was. That was a very crucial time for new music. Albert Ayler, Paul Bley, Carla Bley, Sun Ra, there were a lot of people. The idea was essentially Bill Dixon's. Bill you know, has a very creative mind that way, especially organisationally. When I met him he was working for the United Nations. He's a person who is well accustomed to putting together group situations, and he managed to organise this setting, which I thought was very positive. That's the one draw-back: we were all struggling at the time, and I had just, through the good graces of John Coltrane, been offered a contract with ABC Records (Impulse), and the group charter had decided that we were not going to record, we were going to withold our services. Well this turned out to be perhaps one of the biggest debates in the organisation because people thought that guys like me were scabbing out. But I explained that as the father of four children, and most of these people were single, and when they were married

they didn't have any children, so they didn't understand my position at all. I was on welfare, and I had struggled for years, for just this chance, and as I advised them, by our holding out on the record companies we were by no means going to stop the jazz record industry from recording. We were not going to break them. So as it turned out I did hold on to my record contract, and I think it was a good decision, because the Guild eventually broke up. It was a good idea, but to make those kinds of demands of musicians was somewhat unrealistic. This was a record contract with Impulse and John Coltrane had helped me to get that, and Bob Thiele [producer] had been very impressed by my first record "Four For Trane."

BS: *People often refer to you being very influenced by John Coltrane, both as a player and a spiritual person. Would that be true?*

AS: Well certainly as a musician, and certainly I feel influenced by his perception and the perspective that he brought to music, from a social political standpoint. He seemed to understand a lot about generations: the fact that in order for this music to evolve, and I think it's been proven correct, by the things we see today — older players, players who had some stake in this, today guys like Miles Davis who made money, have to begin to invest their time, energy and so on into the bringing up of younger players of newer experiences in the music. He [John Coltrane] was perhaps the only one who saw and anticipated that this music would change, and was flexible enough, at least in his outlook, to have a philosophy that would have accomodated that change.

BS: *And so the first record that you did for Impulse. "Four For Trane," is a thank-you to him.*

AS: It's a strange thing. Bob Thiele had been very averse to my recording for Impulse. In fact he didn't like the so-called "new music" at all. He accepted John's innovations because they sold, and they had a lot of money, but the young guys who were coming out of him, who often played a lot less melodically, he couldn't understand that. It turns out that John had offered the prospect to record to a then-young saxophone player, Byron Allen, and Byron had known Trane through his brother, or something like that, and Trane had offered him the possibility to record for Impulse. Then he met with Bob Thiele, who had this gimmick he would use. He would tell all the new players

— "Well if you are going to take this option to record that Trane has offered you, you've got to play all his music." Which would usually turn most of these avant gardists away. But I had been a student of Coltrane's music for years, and I really liked his music, so when I heard that Byron had turned down the record date — which he did, because he wanted to do all original music — I remember very well I had a conversation with Bill Dixon, it was perhaps just after I'd had a big blowout with Miles [Davis] in the Village Vanguard (he wouldn't let me sit in; of course we became friends later, but I was young then and I reacted very sensitively to the way he treated me). The next day I was talking to Bill Dixon. Bill's about ten years older than I am, and he was a confidant as well as a colleague, and I was telling him how on welfare it was hard for me and my family and I was trying so hard to get a record date but Bob Thiele, whom I used to call up with my welfare money — I lived on a fifth floor walkup, I would take a dollar a day in dimes and I would call Bob ten times a day, this went on for months — and he was never in according to his secretary. This evening after this blowout with Miles, I was talking with Bill and he said, "Well why don't you ask John Coltrane to get you a record date?" he said sort of gruffly — "He's supposed to be a friend of yours isn't he?" As a young man I had never really thought of it, but then I remembered this story of Byron Allen having been offered the record date and having turned it down — so why the hell not, I'll ask John. Because I wouldn't mind recording his tunes at all.

So I went to the Half Note where he was playing and on his intermission, I wanted to ask him, but I was really very shy, so I hemmed and hawed, and he sort of looked me down — he said "Shepp what are you trying to ask me" so I said, John, I want to get a record date, can you help me. And for the first time he looked at me in a way that was rather stern and he sort of looked through me and he said, "You know a lot of people take advantage of me because they think I'm easy." That's what he said — he looked me straight in the eye like that. So I trembled because I didn't want him to think I was thinking he was easy. But it was an insight into John that I had never seen, he had never talked to me that way before. Then he said, "Okay — I'll see what I can

do." The next day I called Bob Thiele and I got him on the phone for the first time ever. That was the start of a ten-year association with the company. In fact, when he made the gimmick, the deal, you are going to have to do John's tunes, I said I've got them all arranged, we've been rehearsing, we're ready. That was the "Four For Trane" date.

BS: *In that period [1965] you did something that also was not happening, apart from Langston Hughes. Leroi Jones and Charles Mingus, you presented poetry with music on record.*

AS: Of course Duke [Ellington] had done some things earlier — "Peter And The Wolf" and those kinds of things, and he had done some monologues that I had found very impressive, but also my theatre training in college was very helpful. I had heard Ezra Pound and T.S. Eliot, which showed me records had dimensions other than musical works.

BS: *One of the great ones is the poem for Malcolm X, "Malcolm, Semper Malcolm." He was a very strong political force for young black musicians and artists in America at that time.*

AS: No question about it. I was very moved by the assassination of Malcolm X. However I would say my earlier training since I was born in the south, I am a southern negro as Cecil Taylor always points out, it made me first aware of Martin Luther King and I was always very close to the things that Dr. King was trying to do. Because I felt that if you put King and Malcolm together you had a real political solution for black people in the United States.

BS: *Considering what we were just talking about, about how difficult it was originally for you to record on Impulse, eventually when John Coltrane made the record "Ascension" [1965], which was a very startling record, it seems almost impossible to think now, based on what you've told me, that such a record would ever take place.*

AS: John was a nexus, a connection between his generation, of so-called "beboppers" and what he himself was about to create. What they call the avant garde today. I say he created it because in a sense he was able to synthesize in his work, perhaps the most important innovations of Ornette Coleman and Cecil Taylor, and to maintain the basic elements that we consider vital to the organisation of black music. Namely — swing. Because Trane was never an intellectual or academic musician, he was always a real hard swinger. I think what upset a lot of people is that he could combine all the theoretical, the most innovative qualities of his time and his peers into the context of "hot music."

All the guys he chose for "Ascension" felt very sympathetique with his efforts because, like Coleman Hawkins before him, I think he was very much in touch with the tenor of the time, so a record like "Ascension," if I think of an analogy: there was a baseball game, the American League Championship, and they asked one of the players, a black player who was an outfielder — was he scared when the ball was hit out there to him, and it was the last ball of the game, and it was the winning catch? And he said, "no man I was just waiting on it to get there." That was the feeling of the "Ascension" date, that many of the people there, we were right on time.

Text of Black Studies Proposal

RECOMMENDATIONS OF COMMITTEE ON AFRO-AMERICAN STUDIES

The committee on Afro-American Studies, in accordance with its mandate from the administration, is pleased to make the following recommendations:

That a formal academic department, to be known as the W.E.B. Dubois Department of Afro-American Studies be established at the university.

This department will offer an undergraduate major in Afro-American studies as well as courses of studies essential to non-majors intending to play some role in the black community.

It is our view that DETAILED and SPECIFIC requirements of the department and the structure of its program should be left to the department after it has been established but that the general scope of the department will be as follows:

a. The department must concern itself with the wide range of questions pertaining to the political and cultural history, the present situation as well of the future aspirations and possibilities of Black America. This means that the work offered in the department must run across traditional boundaries of the various disciplines including studies in History, Social Sciences, Literature, the Arts, languages and other areas relevant to the black experience.

b. This cohesive and comprehensive approach to the area means that there must be consideration not only of the black community in the United States but of the experience of the black communities of Africa and other parts of this hemisphere. This international scope must be reflected in the faculty and students of the department.

c. The program of the department must involve traditional approaches of study and scholarship, and beyond that, must involve the student in research and non-traditional work study programs in the black community as a basic element of his education.

d. Part of the Department's mandate must be to initiate discussions and negotiations with the other colleges of the area to determine the feasibility of a Five College Department which would be able to coordinate the development of Black Studies in the area utilizing the unique resources of all Five Colleges.

e. That an essential element of the department will be a black cultural center offering courses of instruction and training in the literary and performing arts. This center will concern itself with preserving, developing and presenting to the general community the various expressions of the cultural life of the black community.

The full report and proposal of the Committee follows.

Traditionally, American institutions of higher education have embodied and reflected within their institutional structure and functions the effects of social and economic ideas and developments within the general society. To this extent they have been the creatures of society, being defined by social forces rather than the definers and shapers of events and developments within the society.

Now, however, for a number of disparate but converging reasons colleges and universities throughout the nation have become one of the arenas in which the large social issues and changes which are currently affecting the general society are finding sharp focus in the form of increasingly bitter confrontations. This situation is inevitable and generally healthy. The situation is not, as many educators have suggested, that "the university is being pilloried for deep-seated social failures for which they are not responsible and over which they can exert no control." It is rather, that the universities are being challenged to accept responsibility for the very real role that they have accepted and are playing in creating and perpetuating national social conditions.

As the national black community intensifies its struggle to liberate itself from the oppressive conditions imposed by centuries of racism, the extent to which not only blacks but other non-Caucasian ethnic minorities have been excluded from the central institutions which structure the American experience become more evident. The extent to which Blacks have been excluded not only from the campus but have been systematically denied their historical and cultural role in the records of the society, as expressed by the curricula of the universities, is outlined in increasingly sharp focus. Thus, for reasons that go much deeper than their traditional function as conduits of immigrant minorities into the "American mainstream," the American university is faced with a necessity to re-

spond in a much more innovative manner to sweeping social changes in the general society.

In fact, it seems clear, that in an increasingly complicated technically oriented society, the institutions of higher learning are being called to a much more vital and definitive role in the solution of social problems. We are witnessing a domestic social revolution which can only intensify in the years to come. The overt and visible symptoms of this social crisis are easily evident: major cities are periodically immobilized by what can only be termed urban guerilla warfare with an ever-increasing toll in human life and property and a deepening and bitter polarization of the country along racial and class lines. While it is not so immediately clear exactly what is to be done if a traumatic and potentially irreconcilable racial confrontation is to be avoided some quite precise and specific adjustments are beginning to emerge.

It is now fashionable—following the Kerner Commission report—to attribute the present domestic distress to the effects of "white racism." What is not so clearly present is any general willingness on the part of the dominant institutions of American life to examine fully and with uncompromising candor the implications of the phrase. We do not detect any serious, informed action-oriented debate taking place within those institutions which affect and define the patterns of social, economic and political relationships in the nation. There is much talk, portentious platitude, pious handwringing and even tokenism, but the kinds of rigorous self-scrutiny and reappraisal of time-honored practices and assumptions which is essential to any real effort to solve the problems facing the society, seems only rarely to be present. It is in the spirit of this kind of committed dialogue and from a pervasive sense of urgency that this proposal is made.

In the matter of the traditional exclusion and oppression of Black Americans, no institution—whatever its particular role in American life might be—is without responsibility. This includes the great public universities. And in the same manner that these institutions must accept, by virtue of their traditional record of insensitivity, moral myopia and neglect, a major culpability for the current crisis, they must now accept a major responsibility and a leading role in its solution.

The University of Massachusetts, its recent gropings towards the inclusion of Black people not-withstanding, is on its record one of the least committed and responsive of the large public universities in the country at the present time. In almost a hundred years of existence it had, until last year—and only on the initiative of its handful of Black faculty members—demonstrated little specific concern for the educational needs of the Black Community of this state.

But it is not our intention to belabor the errors and injustices of the past. We, speaking in behalf of the Black community of the University, are concerned with present realities and the possibilities of the future. At present there are more Black students at the Universities of Mississippi and Alabama than at the University of Massachusetts. Until the past academic year with the initiation of the CCEBS program, there were more students on this campus from Africa and Asia than from the black communities of Boston and Springfield. The proposal which follows is predicated on the assumption that the CCEBS program is in evidence of the University's increased awareness of the inadequacy of its record and its commitment to correcting this situation in the future. We assume that the program will be expanded and broadened to include other minorities, specifically the native Indian and Puerto Rican communities and much greater numbers of black students than has generally been the case. If this is not to be done then there is quite literally no contribution that this institution can make to the needs of the future so far as the country's racial crisis is concerned and it would be well advised to abandon any such hope that it might entertain.

However, the mere presence of Black students in the physical environment of the campus is merely a beginning. There are certain necessary adjustments that any previously almost exclusively white institution which was conceived, structured and run without any thought to the specific educational and psychological needs and expectations of the present generation of Black students.

The persistence of white racism as a dominant social force in the society is evidence of, among other things, a basic failure on the part of the educational system. It is evidence of an ethnic and cultural rigidity, a narrow, provincial racial and cultural chauvinism which pervades the curriculum offerings of these institutions. Universities in which the cultural pluralism which is the reality of America finds adequate reflection in the course offerings are very few indeed. And when courses that essay to relate an accurate assessment of the history, cultural heritage and contemporary situation of the Black community exist, they are sporadic individual efforts inserted into a white curricula without adequate context or continuity.

So long as universities continue to conduct their business, make up their curricula, and structure the information they dispense as though the country were simply a collection of white suburban enclaves and the history of the country merely the record of the destruction or assimilation of inferior cultures by the dominant Anglo-Saxon minority, then the unfortunate ignorance, prejudice and misunderstanding that currently marks the relationship between the various ethnic groups will continue. The immediate victim of this procedure is the student, but in the long term it is the peace and stability of the society that suffers.

For the white student, this racial and cultural chauvinism has functioned to defraud him of any sophisticated and accurate vision of his nation's reality. For the Black student it has been a damaging and embittering fact of life. This failure of perception, intelligence and indeed of morality on the part of the schools has had a damaging effect on the Black community which has come, in turn, to suspect and in many cases reject "whitey's education." Because these schools have been traditionally the purveyors of white middle-class values and assumptions which are by definition of the Kerner Commission Report racist, the university-educated Black person has been frequently lost to the Black community. Quite literally his education served to make it impossible for him to find a useful and creative role in that community. It is because this generation of Black students and many of their counterparts of the faculty are not inclined to participate in the perpetuation of this pattern, that this proposal is being written. It presumes the willingness of this University to undertake significant and expensive changes in, and additions to, the intellectual and cultural environment of the school, that the education offered here be effectively responsive to the practical needs of the Black community and psychological needs of the young Black students who have been deprived by the society and its educational system of any positive sense of the history and culture of their people. Also, the presence and availability of the department and curriculum that we are proposing will inevitably serve to expand the white student's consciousness of the history and current reality of his country and society.

Toward this end we propose that the University immediately undertake the formation of a Department of Afro-American Studies, to be in full operation by September of 1972. The department will prepare and offer to the University a series of course sequences in various disciplines which will in combination present the social, cultural and political history of the Afro-American people in a comprehensive and structurally integrated manner. The courses will involve studies in the following disciplines: African Languages, Literature, History, Anthropology, Political Science, Economics, Psychology, Music and the Fine Arts. Fully staffed and functioning, the department will offer an interdisciplinary major in Afro-American studies available to students interested in careers in education and scholarship.

In addition, the department will offer course sequences which will represent a basic part of the academic programs of Black students in each of the named disciplines, whatever their major academic field or vocational interest may be. These course sequences will be further discussed but the primary purpose is to provide the student with an approach and perspective towards his major field which is based on concerns, experience and needs of the Black community.

Clearly, a few of these objectives might be achieved by an expansion of the scope and a structuring of existing departments. The mere addition of Black faculty is not sufficient, however. And on the evidence of history, it is equally clear that existing departments lack either the will, ability or energy to undertake the extensive reorientation of their personnel and procedures that would make the function that we are describing possible to them. And, even if this were not the case, such an effort, even at its most effective, would simply continue and institutionalize the disjointed, fragmented, and unsatisfactory approach to the subject that has prevailed.

What is necessary, and what is being proposed here is a cohesive department which as a formally centralized unit with its own resources of teaching, administrative and research personnel, can plan, develop, and coordinate such a program. WHAT IS BEING PROPOSED IS A BLACK EDUCATIONAL entity which can initiate the necessary relationship to the Black community—both national and international—which is neither possible or appropriate for any EXISTING BODY OR AGENCY OF THE UNIVERSITY AT PRESENT. There is, quite literally, nothing in the existing structures of the university which fills or is capable of filling such a role.

In addition to the regular teaching function of the department, it will move into the existing vacuum and become a focus for the expression of Black academic and cultural concerns. Thus, it will be responsible for bringing to the campus for varying periods of time lecturers, scholars, writers and artists from the national Black community and the Third World. It must have the autonomy and resources to negotiate exchange programs for

Black faculty and students from this university with other universities in this country, Africa, the Carribbean and other communities of African-descended peoples. Thus it will meet a need, which is important in the total educational experience, for a BLACK ACADEMIC AND CULTURAL PRESENCE in what is at present a completely white oriented environment. Nothing short of such an institution can meet the needs and expectations of this and future generations of Black students.

SUGGESTED READINGS

Jack M. Bloom, *Class, Race, and the Civil Rights Movement* (Bloomington, Ind. 1987)

Taylor Branch, *Parting the Waters: America in the King Years, 1954–1963* (New York, 1988)

Taylor Branch, *Pillar of Fire: America in the King Years, 1963–1965* (New York, 1998)

Clayborne Carson, *In Struggle: SNCC and the Black Awakening of the 1960s* (Cambridge, Mass., 1981)

Robert Conot, *Rivers of Blood Years of Darkness* (New York, 1967)

Vicki Crawford, et al., Jacqueline Anne Rouse and Barbara Woods eds., *Women in the Civil Rights Movement: Trailblazers and Torchbearers, 1941–1965* (Brooklyn, N.Y., 1993)

John Dittmer, *Local People: The Struggle for Civil Rights in Mississippi* (Urbana, Ill., 1994)

John Egerton, *Speak Now Against the Day: The Generation Before the Civil Rights Movement in the South* (New York, 1994)

Adam Fairclough, *Race and Democracy: The Civil Rights Struggle in Louisiana, 1915–1972* (Athens, Ga., 1995)

Peter Louis Goldman, *The Death and Life of Malcolm X* (Urbana, Ill., 1979)

Joanne Grant, *Ella Baker: Freedom Bound* (New York, 1998)

Michael K. Honey, *Southern Labor and Black Civil Rights: Organizing Memphis Workers* (Urbana, Ill., 1993)

Charles Jones, ed., *The Black Panther Party (Reconsidered): Reflections and Scholarship* (Baltimore, 1998)

Richard Kluger, *Simple Justice: The History of Brown vs. Board of Education and Black America's Struggle for Equality* (New York, 1975)

Chana Kai Lee, *For Freedom's Sake: The Life of Fannie Lou Hammer* (Urbana, Ill., 1999)

August Meier and Elliot Rudwick, *Core: A Study in the Civil Rights Movement, 1942–1968* (New York, 1973)

Aldon Morris, *The Origins of the Civil Rights Movement: Black Communities Organizing for Change* (New York, 1984)

Lynne Olson, *Freedom's Daughters: The Unsung Heroines of the Civil Rights Movement, 1930–1970* (New York, 2001)

Charles M. Payne, *I've Got the Light of Freedom: The Organizing Tradition and the Mississippi Freedom Struggle* (Berkeley, Calif., 1995)

Harvard Sitkoff, *The Struggle for Black Equality, 1954–1980* (New York, 1981)

Mark V. Tushnet, *The NAACP's Legal Strategy Against Segregated Education, 1925–1950* (Chapel Hill, N.C., 1987)

Timothy B. Tyson, *Radio Free Dixie: Robert F. Williams and the Roots of Black Power* (Chapel Hill, N.C., 1999)

The Million Man March, Washington, D.C., October 16, 1995. (Photo by Ron Byrd.)

Chapter 11

And Still We Are Not Saved

In the decades since the end of the Civil Rights movement, the black community has evolved in a number of different ways. Despite the demise of legal segregation and disfranchisement, the failure of the larger society to address the more vexing aspects of racial inequality resulting from a lack of equal employment opportunity, access to capital, poor housing and schools, and lack of adequate health care ensured that the struggle for black equality would continue. The reemergence of conservatism as a backlash against the gains of the Civil Rights movement has forced African Americans to defend even the tenuous progress made during the 1960s. Within the African American community, the 1970s witnessed the rise of black feminism as an intellectual and political force and of prominent individual women and organizations. The first two documents reveal how black feminism generated discussions of gender relations, sexual preferences, and the issue of homophobia in the black community. The interview with Samuel R. Delany, a distinguished science fiction writer and literary critic, relates his experiences of growing up gay in the black community.

In a retreat from the sympathetic decisions of the Warren court, the Supreme Court decisions of the 1980s limited the scope of the judicial and legislative victories of the Civil Rights movement. The attempt to roll back affirmative action was a central plank of the modern conservative platform. At the same time, conservative white southern Democrats moved to the Republican Party, and the political influence of African Americans within the Democratic Party grew. Of special significance were the elections of black mayors in a number of cities throughout the country and the historic campaigns of Jesse Jackson in 1984 and 1988 for the Democratic nomination for President. Included in the selection of documents are Muhammad Ahmad's analysis of the Jackson campaign and Chicago Mayor Harold Washington's plan for urban restoration. Further advances in the political arena and the effort to deal with the problems of urban black communities were stymied by the politics of fiscal conservatism and racial backlash. Though affirmative action did allow the development of a significant black middle class based in government service, positions in private industry among skilled workers and in the new high-tech industries have not kept pace. The continued failures of integration in housing, education, and employment have created a political space for the caustic criticisms of Louis Farrakhan and the Nation of Islam that call into question the nation's commitment to racial equality. The contradiction between Farrakhan's inflammatory rhetoric attacking white society and his relatively conservative program of black self-help and redemption is represented in his 1984 interview and the "Pledge" taken at the Million Man March. The nomination of Clarence Thomas to the Supreme Court revealed the birth of a new black conservatism that echoes the market values and social conservatism of the mainstream American right. An unprecedented response to his nomination was the fullpage advertisement entitled "African American Women in Defense of Ourselves."

In striking contrast to the picture of continued inequality and conservative backlash is the dominance of African American athletes and entertainers in the realm of popular culture and in mass media. Black athletes are in the majority in the sports of basketball and football and are the most admired of sports figures in games such as baseball and even tennis and golf. Moreover, hip hop is the dominant form of cultural expression among the nation's youth, and Rap artists are among the most successful figures in the music industry today. "Friends of the Court" is a revealing article that describes the lifestyle and cultural values of young male basketball players.

James Spady's "The Hip Hop Vision" is an early attempt to explore the implications of rap music and hip hop culture. The introduction by Sonia Sanchez expresses the great influence of hip hop on young black poets. One of the unexpected achievements of black cultural nationalism has been the institutionalization of Kwanzaa as a national African American holiday. The document included here describes the origins, tenets, and early history of the ceremony.

At the dawn of the new millenium, African American activism seems to have come full circle with the attempts to obtain reparations for slavery. Lawsuits and legislative attempts to address the question of centuries of unpaid labor proliferate. We have included Representative John Conyer's proposed bill, HR40, to set up a federal commission to study this issue. Regardless of the outcome of this particular or any other struggles, the concluding document by Derrick Bell is a call to African Americans as individuals or in groups to continue the long and difficult struggle to achieve racial equality and justice.

A Black Feminist Statement

The Combahee River Collective

We are a collective of black feminists who have been meeting together since 1974.[1] During that time we have been involved in the process of defining and clarifying our politics, while at the same time doing political work within our own group and in coalition with other progressive organizations and movements. The most general statement of our politics at the present time would be

that we are actively committed to struggling against racial, sexual, heterosexual, and class oppression and see as our particular task the development of integrated analysis and practice based upon the fact that the major systems of oppression are interlocking. The synthesis of these oppressions creates the conditions of our lives. As black women we see black feminism as the logical political movement to combat the manifold and simultaneous oppressions that all women of color face.

We will discuss four major topics in the paper that follows: (1) The genesis of contemporary black feminism; (2) what we be-

---

Source: "A Black Feminist Statement" The Combahee River Collective. April, 1977. Copyright © 1977 Combahee River Collective.

[1]This statement is dated April 1977.

lieve, i.e., the specific province of our politics; (3) the problems in organizing black feminists, including a brief herstory of our collective; and (4) black feminist issues and practice.

1. THE GENESIS OF CONTEMPORARY BLACK FEMINISM

Before looking at the recent development of black feminism, we would like to affirm that we find our origins in the historical reality of Afro-American women's continuous life-and-death struggle for survival and liberation. Black women's extremely negative relationship to the American political system (a system of white male rule) has always been determined by our membership in two oppressed racial and sexual castes. As Angela Davis points out in "Reflections on the Black Woman's Role in the Community of Slaves," black women have always embodied, if only in their physical manifestation, an adversary stance to white male rule and have actively resisted its inroads upon them and their communities in both dramatic and subtle ways. There have always been black women activists—some known, like Sojourner Truth, Harriet Tubman, Frances E. W. Harper, Ida B. Wells-Barnett, and Mary Church Tersell, and thousands upon thousands unknown—who had a shared awareness of how their sexual identity combined with their racial identity to make their whole life situation and the focus of their political struggles unique. Contemporary black feminism is the outgrowth of countless generations of personal sacrifice, militancy, and work by our mothers and sisters.

A black feminist presence has evolved most obviously in connection with the second wave of the American women's movement beginning in the late 1960s. Black, other Third World, and working women have been involved in the feminist movement from its start, but both outside reactionary forces and racism and elitism within the movement itself have served to obscure our participation. In 1973 black feminists, primarily located in New York, felt the necessity of forming a separate black feminist group. This became the National Black Feminist Organization (NBFO).

Black feminist politics also have an obvious connection to movements for black liberation, particularly those of the 1960s and 1970s. Many of us were active in those movements (civil rights, black nationalism, the Black Panthers), and all of our lives were greatly affected and changed by their ideology, their goals, and the tactics used to achieve their goals. It was our experience and disillusionment within these liberation movements, as well as experience on the periphery of the white male left, that led to the need to develop a politics that was antiracist, unlike those of white women, and antisexist, unlike those of black and white men.

There is also undeniably a personal genesis for black feminism, that is, the political realization that comes from the seemingly personal experiences of individual black women's lives. Black feminists and many more black women who do not define themselves as feminists have all experienced sexual oppression as a constant factor in our day-to-day existence.

Black feminists often talk about their feelings of craziness before becoming conscious of the concepts of sexual politics, patriarchal rule, and, most importantly, feminism, the political analysis and practice that we women use to struggle against our oppression. The fact that racial politics and indeed racism are pervasive factors in our lives did not allow us, and still does not allow most black women, to look more deeply into our own experiences and define those things that make our lives what they are and our oppression specific to us. In the process of consciousness-raising, actually life-sharing, we began to recognize the commonality of our experiences and, from that sharing and growing consciousness, to build a politics that will change our lives and inevitably end our oppression.

Our development also must be tied to the contemporary economic and political position of black people. The post–World War II generation of black youth was the first to be able to minimally partake of certain educational and employment options, previously closed completely to black people. Although our economic position is still at the very bottom of the American capitalist economy, a handful of us have been able to gain certain tools as a result of tokenism in education and employment that potentially enable us to more effectively fight our oppression.

A combined antiracist and antisexist position drew us together initially, and as we developed politically we addressed ourselves to heterosexism and economic oppression under capitalism.

2. WHAT WE BELIEVE

Above all else, our politics initially sprang from the shared belief that black women are inherently valuable, that our liberation is a necessity not as an adjunct to somebody else's but because of our need as human persons for autonomy. This may seem so obvious as to sound simplistic, but it is apparent that no other ostensibly progressive movement has ever considered our specific oppression a priority or worked seriously for the ending of that oppression. Merely naming the pejorative stereotypes attributed to black women (e.g., mammy, matriarch, Sapphire, whore, bulldagger), let alone cataloguing the cruel, often murderous, treatment we receive, indicates how little value has been placed upon our lives during four centuries of bondage in the Western Hemisphere. We realize that the only people who care enough about us to work consistently for our liberation is us. Our politics evolve from a healthy love for ourselves, our sisters, and our community, which allows us to continue our struggle and work.

This focusing upon our own oppression is embodied in the concept of identity politics. We believe that the most profound and potentially the most radical politics come directly out of our own identity, as opposed to working to end somebody else's oppression. In the case of black women this is a particularly repugnant, dangerous, threatening, and therefore revolutionary concept because it is obvious from looking at all the political movements that have preceded us that anyone is more worthy of liberation than ourselves. We reject pedestals, queenhood, and walking ten paces behind. To be recognized as human, levelly human, is enough.

We believe that sexual politics under patriarchy is as pervasive in black women's lives as are the politics of class and race. We also often find it difficult to separate race from class from sex oppression because in our lives they are most often experienced simultaneously. We know that there is such a thing as racial-sexual oppression that is neither solely racial nor solely sexual, e.g., the history of rape of black women by white men as a weapon of political repression.

Although we are feminists and lesbians, we feel solidarity with progressive black men and do not advocate the fractionalization that white women who are separatists demand. Our situation as black people necessitates that we have solidarity around the fact of race, which white women of course do not need to have with white men, unless it is their negative solidarity as racial oppressors. We struggle together with black men against racism, while we also struggle with black men about sexism.

We realize that the liberation of all oppressed peoples necessitates the destruction of the political-economic systems of capitalism and imperialism as well as patriarchy. We are socialists because we believe the work must be organized for the collective benefit of those who do the work and create the products and not for the profit of the bosses. Material resources must be equally distributed among those who create these resources. We are not convinced, however, that a socialist revolution that is not also a feminist and antiracist revolution will guarantee our liberation. We have arrived at the necessity for developing an understanding of class relationships that takes into account the specific class position of black women who are generally marginal in the labor force, while at this particular time some of us are temporarily viewed as doubly desirable tokens at white-collar and professional levels. We need to articulate the real class situation of persons who are not merely raceless, sexless workers, but for whom racial and sexual oppression are significant determinants in their working/economic lives. Although we are in essential agreement with Marx's theory as it applied to the very specific economic relationships he analyzed, we know that this analysis must be extended further in order for us to understand our specific economic situation as black women.

A political contribution that we feel we have already made is the expansion of the feminist principle that the personal is political. In our consciousness-raising sessions, for example, we have in many ways gone beyond white women's revelations because we are dealing with the implications of race and class as well as sex. Even our black women's style of talking/testifying in black language about what we have experienced has a resonance that is both cultural and political. We have spent a great deal of energy delving into the cultural and experiential nature of our oppression out of necessity because none of these matters have ever been looked at before. No one before has ever examined the multilayered texture of black women's lives.

As we have already stated, we reject the stance of lesbian separatism because it is not a viable political analysis or strategy for us. It leaves out far too much and far too many people, particularly black men, women, and children. We have a great deal of criticism and loathing for what men have been socialized to be in this society: what they support, how they act, and how they oppress. But we do not have the misguided notion that it is their maleness, per se—i.e., their biological maleness—that makes them what they are. As black women we find any type of biological determinism a particularly dangerous

and reactionary basis upon which to build a politic. We must also question whether lesbian separatism is an adequate and progressive political analysis and strategy, even for those who practice it, since it so completely denies any but the sexual sources of women's oppression, negating the facts of class and race.

3. PROBLEMS IN ORGANIZING BLACK FEMINISTS

During our years together as a black feminist collective we have experienced success and defeat, joy and pain, victory and failure. We have found that it is very difficult to organize around black feminist issues, difficult even to announce in certain contexts that we are black feminists. We have tried to think about the reasons for our difficulties, particularly since the white women's movement continues to be strong and to grow in many directions. In this section we will discuss some of the general reasons for the organizing problems we face and also talk specifically about the stages in organizing our own collective.

The major source of difficulty in our political work is that we are not just trying to fight oppression on one front or even two, but instead to address a whole range of oppressions. We do not have racial, sexual, hetero-sexual, or class privilege to rely upon, nor do we have even the minimal access to resources and power that groups who possess any one of these types of privilege have.

The psychological toll of being a black woman and the difficulties this presents in reaching political consciousness and doing political work can never be underestimated. There is a very low value placed upon black women's psyches in this society, which is both racist and sexist. As an early group member once said, "We are all damaged people merely by virtue of being black women." We are dispossessed psychologically and on every other level, and yet we feel the necessity to struggle to change our condition and the condition of all black women. In "A Black Feminist's Search for Sisterhood," Michele Wallace arrives at this conclusion:

> We exist as women who are black who are feminists, each stranded for the moment, working independently because there is not yet an environment in this society remotely congenial to our struggle—because, being on the bottom, we would have to do what no one else has done: we would have to fight the world. [2]

Wallace is not pessimistic but realistic in her assessment of black feminists' position, particularly in her allusion to the nearly classic isolation most of us face. We might use our position at the bottom, however, to make a clear leap into revolutionary action. If black women were free, it would mean that everyone else would have to be free since our freedom would necessitate the destruction of all the systems of oppression.

Feminism is, nevertheless, very threatening to the majority of black people because it calls into question some of the most basic assumptions about our existence, i.e., that gender should be a determinant of power relationships. Here is the way male and female roles were defined in a black nationalist pamphlet from the early 1970s.

> We understand that it is and has been traditional that the man is the head of the house. He is the leader of the house/nation because his knowledge of the world is broader, his awareness is greater, his understanding is fuller and his application of this information is wiser. . . . After all, it is only reasonable that the man be the head of the house because he is able to defend and protect the development of his home. . . . Women cannot do the same things as men—they are made by nature to function differently. Equality of men and

women is something that cannot happen even in the abstract world. Men are not equal to other men, i.e., ability, experience, or even understanding. The value of men and women can be seen as in the value of gold and silver—they are not equal but both have great value. We must realize that men and women are a complement to each other because there is no house/family without a man and his wife. Both are essential to the development of any life. [3]

The material conditions of most black women would hardly lead them to upset both economic and sexual arrangements that seem to represent some stability in their lives. Many black women have a good understanding of both sexism and racism, but because of the everyday constrictions of their lives cannot risk struggling against them both.

The reaction of black men to feminism has been notoriously negative. They are, of course, even more threatened than black women by the possibility that black feminists might organize around our own needs. They realize that they might not only lose valuable and hard-working allies in their struggles, but that they might also be forced to change their habitually sexist ways of interacting with and oppressing black women. Accusations that black feminism divides the black struggle are powerful deterrents to the growth of an autonomous black women's movement.

Still, hundreds of women have been active at different times during the three-year existence of our group. And every black woman who came, came out of a strongly felt need for some level of possibility that did not previously exist in her life.

When we first started meeting early in 1974 after the NBFO first eastern regional conference, we did not have a strategy for organizing, or even a focus. We just wanted

[2]Michele Wallace. "A Black Feminist's Search for Sisterhood," *Village Voice*, 28 July 1975, 6–7.

[3]Mumininas of Committee for Unified Newark, *Mwanamke Mwananchi (The Nationalist Woman)*, Newark, NJ, c. 1971, 4–5.

to see what we had. After a period of months of not meeting, we began to meet again late in the year and started doing an intense variety of consciousness-raising. The overwhelming feeling that we had is that after years and years we had finally found each other. Although we were not doing political work as a group, individuals continued their involvement in lesbian politics, sterilization abuse, and abortion rights work, Third World Women's International Women's Day activities, and support activity for the trials of Dr. Kenneth Edelin, Joan Little, and Inez Garcia. During our first summer, when membership had dropped off considerably, those of us remaining devoted serious discussion to the possibility of opening a refuge for battered women in a black community. (There was no refuge in Boston at that time.) We also decided around that time to become an independent collective since we had serious disagreements with NBFO's bourgeois-feminist stance and their lack of a clear political focus.

We also were contacted at that time by socialist feminists, with whom we had worked on abortion rights activities, who wanted to encourage us to attend the National Socialist Feminist Conference in Yellow Springs. One of our members did attend and despite the narrowness of the ideology that was promoted at that particular conference, we became more aware of the need for us to understand our own economic situation and to make our own economic analysis.

In the fall, when some members returned, we experienced several months of comparative inactivity and internal disagreements which were first conceptualized as a lesbian-straight split but which were also the result of class and political differences. During the summer those of us who were still meeting had determined the need to do political work and to move beyond consciousness-raising and serving exclusively as an emotional support group. At the beginning of 1976, when some of the women who had not wanted to do political work and who also had voiced disagreements stopped attend-

ing of their own accord, we again looked for a focus. We decided at that time, with the addition of new members, to become a study group. We had always shared our reading with each other, and some of us had written papers on black feminism for group discussion a few months before this decision was made. We began functioning as a study group and also began discussing the possibility of starting a black feminist publication. We had a retreat in the late spring, which provided a time for both political discussion and working out interpersonal issues. Currently we are planning to gather together a collection of black feminist writing. We feel that it is absolutely essential to demonstrate the reality of our politics to other black women and believe that we can do this through writing and distributing our work. The fact that individual black feminists are living in isolation all over the country, that our own numbers are smart, and that we have some skills in writing, printing, and publishing makes us want to carry out these kinds of projects as a means of organizing black feminists as we continue to do political work in coalition with other groups.

4. BLACK FEMINIST ISSUES AND PRACTICE

During our time together we have identified and worked on many issues of particular relevance to black women. The inclusiveness of our politics makes us concerned with any situation that impinges upon the lives of women, Third World, and working people. We are of course particularly committed to working on those struggles in which race, sex, and class are simultaneous factors in oppression. We might, for example, become involved in workplace organizing at a factory that employs Third-World women or picket a hospital that is cutting back on already inadequate health care to a Third World ommunity, or set up a rape crisis center in a black neighborhood. Organizing around welfare or day-care concerns might also be a focus. The work to be done and the countless issues that this work represents merely reflect the pervasiveness of our oppression.

Issues and projects that collective members have actually worked on are sterilization abuse, abortion rights, battered women, rape, and health care. We have also done many workshops and educationals on black feminism on college campuses, at women's conferences, and most recently for high school women.

One issue that is of major concern to us and that we have begun to publicly address is racism in the white women's movement. As black feminists we are made constantly and painfully aware of how little effort white women have made to understand and combat their racism, which requires among other things that they have a more than superficial comprehension of race, color, and black history and culture. Eliminating racism in the white women's movement is by definition work for white women to do, but we will continue to speak to and demand accountability on this issue.

In the practice of our politics we do not believe that the end always justifies the means. Many reactionary and destructive acts have been done in the name of achieving "correct" political goals. As feminists we do not want to mess over people in the name of politics. We believe in collective process and a nonhierarchical distribution of power within our own group and in our vision of a revolutionary society. We are committed to a continual examination of our politics as they develop through criticism and self-criticism as an essential aspect of our practice. As black feminists and lesbians we know that we have a very definite revolutionary task to perform, and we are ready for the lifetime of work and struggle before us.

All of Who I Am in the Same Place: The Combahee River Collective

Duchess Harris

The Combahee River Collective statement has been printed in numerous publications since it was written in 1977, but a history of the organization or information about its members has yet to be documented. In its first years, the Collective was active in such projects as support work for Kenneth Edelin, a Black doctor at Boston City Hospital who was arrested for manslaughter for performing a legal abortion. Collective members were involved in the case of Ella Ellison, a Black woman who was accused of murder because she had been seen in the area in which a homicide was committed. They also picketed with the Third World Workers Coalition to ensure that Black laborers would be hired for the construction of a new high school in the Black community. This is only a short synopsis of what the group did over a five-year period. The Collective was

Source: Duchess Harris, "All of Who I Am in the Same Place" *The Womanist,* Vol. 2, No. 1 (Fall, 1999), pp. 9–17, 20–21. Copyright © 1999 Duchess Harris. Used by permission.

made up of highly educated Black Lesbian feminists, six of whom—Barbara Smith, Sharon Page Ritchie, Cheryl Clarke, Margo Okizawa Rey, Gloria Akasha Hull, and Demita Frazier—I have interviewed and will describe in this article.

BARBARA SMITH

Re-entering the world of activism was something that Barbara Smith did not think she would do. She did her first political work in the Civil Rights Movement, where she thought there was going to be a revolution. After that disappointment, she did not have hope that the Black women's movement would be much different. Quoting her:

I think that I felt my status change so much from having been raised Colored/Negro to becoming Black in the space of a short lifetime. And what those names, those labels, represent is a world of difference. There is a difference between our naming ourselves and other people declaring who we were with an insulting label. When I entered college in 1965, I thought that by the time I got out of college things would be basically, "fixed," you know and since that didn't happen, I don't know if I thought we were on a verge of a revolution. It's hard to look at history with hindsight because you realize so much more than when you were actually experiencing it. I think one of the things that I was so happy about is that I had thought that I would never be involved in political work after I graduated from college because that was the height of Black Nationalism and I felt like I just wasn't permitted to be the kind of person I was in that context. I was supposed to marry someone or not marry them, who cares, but my job was to have babies for the Nation and to walk seven paces behind a man and basically be a maidservant. I didn't get involved in the women's movement for a few years after it became very visible because my perception was that it was entirely white.

After attending the National Black Feminist Organization meeting in New York in 1973,

Barbara Smith felt she could do more in the Boston community because she was doing it from a Black feminist base. When she returned from the NBFO conference, she met with people from Boston and started trying to build a Boston NBFO chapter. She met Demita Frazier a few weeks later, in early 1974, and when Smith and Frazier began to meet regularly they discovered that their vision was more radical than that of the National Black Feminist Organization. According to a 1994 interview with Demita Frazier:

We wanted to talk about radical economics. Some of us were thinking that we were socialists. We thought that we needed to have an economic analysis. We were also concerned that there be a voice for Lesbians in Black women's organizations and we weren't certain where NBFO was going, even though they had been founded by women who were Lesbians. So, after one of our members (and I do believe it was Barbara) went to the Socialist Feminist Organizing Conference that was held at Oberlin College in Ohio, we decided that we wanted to be a collective and not be in a hierarchy organization because it was antithetical to our beliefs about democracy and the need to share. We also felt that we had a more radical vision. And so we decided [to send] a letter saying that we were no longer going to be the National Black Feminist Organization chapter in Boston. Towards the middle of 1975, we were having serious discussions about our relationship to the National Black Feminist Organization and we made a decision during that summer.

The organization got its new name from Barbara Smith, who had a small book published by Left Press entitled *Harriet Tubman, Conductor on the Underground Railroad* by Earl Conrad. The Combahee River is where the abolitionist Harriet Tubman planned and led the only military campaign in U.S. history organized by a woman. Smith wanted to name the collective after a meaningful historical event that was meaningful to African American women.

There were women's groups all over the country named for Harriet Tubman and Smith wanted to do something different. She liked the idea of naming the group for a collective action, as opposed to one heroic person's feats. She chose the name of the river where 750 slaves escaped to freedom:

The boats were out there; the Yankee Union boats were out there and they [the slaves] were running, literally, to get on them, I guess, during this battle–but the thing is that it wasn't just one person who did something courageous, it was a group of people. The Combahee River is an incredible militant chapter of U.S. history, not just of Black history, of world history. In fact, at the time when people looked at their conditions and they fought back, they took great risks to change their situation; and for us to call ourselves the Combahee River Collective, that was an educational [tool] both for ourselves and for anybody who asked, "So what does that mean, I never heard of that?" It was a way of talking about ourselves being on a continuum of Black struggle, of Black women's struggle.

In the summer of 1994, Barbara Smith was filmed by the Combahee River in South Carolina. When the videographer asked about the importance of the collective, this was her response:

Combahee was really so wonderful because it was the first time that I could be all of who I was in the same place. That I didn't have to leave my feminism outside the door to be accepted as I would in a conservative Black political context. I didn't have to leave my lesbianism outside. I didn't have to leave my race outside, as I might in an all-white-women's context where they didn't want to know all of that. So, it was just really wonderful to be able to be our whole selves and to be accepted in that way. In the early 1970s, to be a Black lesbian feminist meant that you were a person of total courage. It was almost frightening. I spent a lot of time wondering if I would ever be able to come out because I didn't see any way that I could be Black and a feminist and a lesbian. I wasn't thinking so much about being a feminist. I was just thinking about how

could I add lesbian to being a Black woman. It was just like no place for us. That is what Combahee created, a place where we could be ourselves and where we were valued. A place without homophobia, a place without racism, a place without sexism.

SHARON PAGE RITCHIE

Sharon Page Ritchie became involved with the Combahee River Collective through her connection to Margaret Sloan of the NBFO, whom she met at the University of Chicago. Ritchie grew up in a little house on the South Side of Chicago, where her father worked for the city as a building inspector and her mother was a public schoolteacher:

When I talk about my family, I say that I come from a long line of teachers and social workers, so education was a critically important value in my family. Literacy, reading, writing, ideas . . . my mother's house was nice because it was filled with books and magazines, and it was always more important that we should be interested in them than that we should be perfect little housekeepers. We had an education, but we didn't have much money. My mother and my aunts were Deltas. I wasn't a Delta because I was a lesbian. However, I was a Links debutante. I wore three hairpieces and a white dress. Other girls in the cotillion were the daughters of the doctors, lawyers, and probably the undertakers, and so people like my mother always talked about the rich dentist like that was his name. So, financially speaking, we were not in that class. There was more focus on the arts and literature and those things in my family and less so on furs.

The church is really not a very big thing to me, and I really don't remember people talking about it very much. It may have been, but I don't remember. My feeling was growing up in Chicago that sort of traditional strict Baptist church thing and the moral judgements that came out of that about how men were supposed to be and women were supposed to be, in my family that was presented as something that people of our class didn't go for. That was more of a country thing, more of a Southern thing, more of a working-class thing. So, I did not think of the women who I thought of as feminists, intellectuals, or writers, or any of that kind of thing, to have come from a very strong religious background.

Connected to the Northeastern Collective through people she had known in Chicago, Ritchie met Demita Frazier at a Chicago Lesbian Liberation meeting when she was in her late teens. When Demita Frazier and another member, Linda Powell, moved to the East Coast, Ritchie was doing temp work which she realized that she could do anywhere. If she moved to the Eastern seaboard, she could be close to a supportive community of friends.

CHERYL CLARKE

Cheryl Clarke was born in Washington, D.C., in 1947 and grew up there. She did her undergraduate work at Howard University, and then left Washington in 1969 to do graduate work at Rutgers in New Brunswick, New Jersey, where she still lives. Her mother was born in North Carolina in 1916 and migrated to Washington via Detroit around 1920. Her father was born in Washington in 1913; and the only time he was ever out of D.C. was in the service during World War II. She characterized her family as lower-middle-class people whose forebears were laborers. Her mother's mother had been in domestic service. Her father was a dishwasher. Her father's parents had a little bit more mobility: his mother worked for the federal government for years and retired in the late 50's. Widowed early, she was the bastion and sole support of the family; but they had a large extended family, so she had much help. She had three children, in addition to Cheryl.

By the time Cheryl was born, both her parents were working for the government. Her mother worked for the city government in Washington as a recorder of deeds, and her father worked as a security guard at the Bureau of Standards. Both of them retired in the mid to late 70's after thirty-five years in government. She told me:

We were always told we were poor, but I always had security—my basic needs were met, and I had a very sheltered upbringing. I remember at one point telling my mother that I wanted to be a nurse, and she said, "I don't care what you want to be if you are going to college first." So we sort of grew up knowing that. Also, they nurtured a kind of independence in the house. My mother said, "I want you to get your education so you don't have to be dependent on anybody." And that was how we were raised and sort of pushed. They gave us dance lessons, piano lessons, took us to museums. Basically, it was like my mother who took charge of those kinds of things, because she wanted to cultivate some kind of appetite for other than material kinds of things—or, at least, that was in terms of how I see my upbringing.

In 1965, Clarke went to Howard where she and Paula Giddings were classmates:

We were in the same major. Paula was the editor of the undergraduate journal, and she was always a leader. She was always articulating a position. Extremely smart and extremely well-liked, as she still is now. We were in our last year; well, the Spring of 1968 to the Spring of 1969 involved in a writing workshop, and there were other people, plus two or three faculty members who were involved where you would meet every other Sunday. And I was writing poetry then, and we were reading our work to one another, and it is very interesting—the results of that activity enabled us to know how to have a public voice.

Now, I was not an activist when I was in college. I had other interests, and was much more shy than I am now. But because of that workshop, we met editors from Random House who met with us and encouraged us. We met Toni Morrison, who was an editor at Random House at that time and one of my teachers. Howard exposed me to the richness of Afro-American culture, which I have particularly focused on in the literature in terms of my own intellectual development. And began really myself in literature in 1968 when I took Arthur Davis' course, Negro Literature in America, which was only offered once a year. But I watched a whole transformation of the curriculum in Howard during the time that I was there because there were many scholars at Howard who had specialized in Afro-American study who were ostracized-people like Sterling Brown, people like E. Franklin Frazier, people like Chancellor Williams, most of them historians and sociologists.

And during that whole Black Power thing, students really began to bring those people out of the woodwork. So, by the time I graduated, the courses that addressed Afro-American issues came to the foreground and, you know, Afro-American studies began to become a hot thing, and you could hardly get into Afro-American history courses. It became an intellectual hotbed as well as a political hotbed, and it was a real process for me to grapple with the Black nationalist issues. I have never really been a nationalist because I have always considered it impractical and negative and limited. And remember, I told you, they always nurtured independence in us, so I did not want to be constrained by narrow politics. I loved Howard because of how it opened another world to me in terms of Afro-American culture.

MARGO OKIZAWA REY

Margo Okizawa Rey was born in Japan in 1949 to an upper-middle-class Japanese woman and an African American G.I. from working-class Chicago. Rey told me that she obtained her class identity from her father and her cultural identity from her mother:

Women's class is very much connected to the men they are attached to; my mother's class background didn't really have an impact on how we lived our lives. So, I would say I grew up working-class, lower-middle-class, but with definite sort of Japanese cultural sensibilities as well African American. I think my father has gotten more politicized in his old age, but when we were together, you know, he was

sort of a "pull yourself up by your bootstraps" kind of guy. He was one of those people who thought that you just have to be the best person you can be. He didn't talk about race that much, and it is ironic that my mother, who is Japanese and didn't know much about American culture, instilled—but that was more of a private thing. I think the thing that is interesting about my mother is that she is a feminist, although she would never use the term. The men in her family just seemed to get everything. The boys got to do things first, like eat, take baths. Her father got to do everything first; her mother was just kind of waiting on him hand and foot. She said to herself that she was not going to let any man boss her around, which is completely counter to traditional Japanese culture. Somehow, she met my father, and one of the things that she was struck by was these American men would say "ladies first," and she thought [that] was wonderful; but, of course, she didn't understand the sexist underlying stuff. She thought America must be a wonderful place if ladies get to go first. So, that sort of captured their imagination, and they got together. So, my early feminist leanings come from her.

GLORIA HULL

Gloria Hull grew up in a three-room shotgun house in Shreveport, Louisiana. Neither of her parents finished grammar school. Her mother was a cook and a domestic. Her father was disabled, but did whatever kind of work he could pick up as a carpenter. She considered her upbringing to be working poor:

I remember very clearly that my mother made three dollars a day. She did that so that my brother and sister and I would be able to go on trips at school, or have a white dress at graduation. Early memories that situate me class-wise were that there was no liquid money, so we kept a running tab going with the Italian grocer at the end of the block. We were paying very high prices for whatever we bought, but were able to pay him with the little bit of money that did come in. I remember that the days that we bought food were really the high point of the weekdays. Food was essential.

Hull graduated from Booker T. Washington High School in 1962 as the valedictorian of her class. She went to Southern University, and then won a National Defense Education Act fellowship to the University of Illinois at Urbana to study English literature:

What I really wanted to do was be a journalist. The first time I got out of the South and saw a little bit of the larger world was between my junior and senior years [of college]. There was this program where Black kids from Southern colleges were brought to Northern campuses, and I spent the summer at Yale working with the New Haven Human Relations Council. I had written for the high school newspaper, the college newspaper, so I said journalism, that's really what I want to do. I had heard that Columbia was one of the best journalism schools in the country. When I was in New Haven, I figured out how to get myself to New York City and I had an interview with the assistant dean at the Columbia School of Journalism. This is the summer of '65. I'm just walking around with no sense that I'd be afraid or anything; I'm just doing this. It was a really good interview, and I feel that I might have gotten somewhere with it, but no one encouraged me. The highest aspiration anybody could see me doing or achieving was being a teacher. With the grades and the fellowship, "teacher" got translated into "college teacher," but still a teacher. So, that is how I ended up in graduate school for English.

Before Hull went to graduate school, she married her college sweetheart, who had graduated the year before her from Southern and had gone to pursue a Ph.D. in Chemistry at Purdue University in Lafayette, Indiana. He came from a family that was even more economically disadvantaged than hers: he had one pair of jeans that he had to wash out at night and dry in front of a space heater, iron, and put on the next morning. There were twelve children in his family. After spending one semester at Urbana, Hull gave up her fellowship and went to be with her husband at Purdue, where she became a teaching assistant. Her husband got a job at the University of Delaware when Hull was

finishing her dissertation and looking for a job:

When I look back on this, I laugh about how tremendously naive I was. I mean naive in the sense of not knowing the protocol for academic professionalism. I went down there to see the chairman of the English Department at the University of Delaware with my husband, with my son on my lap, dressed up in my Sunday School-type chic dress, little heels. I didn't know from beans, so they offered me this position. I didn't know that I could bargain or anything. The reason he was just sitting there amazed is that a Black woman had dropped in their laps. Another little index of it is that I didn't even know how to do a professional vita. I had on it stuff like, I played piano for the Black Baptist church that I grew up in. There was no Black woman to say, "This is how you do it"; nobody took me under her wing. It is so different now.

During three years in Delaware, Hull made connections that would change her life and inevitably link her to the Combahee River Collective. She ended up working on the Feminist Reprints Committee, where she met Florence Howe and Alice Walker. Although she had done her dissertation on Byron and English dramatic poetry, she had become interested in Black women writers and African American literature, particularly the women writers of the Harlem Renaissance. When she went to the annual meeting of the Modern Language Association in New York City in 1974, she met Barbara Smith. Having met Smith and the rest of the Boston women, she began to attend Combahee retreats to expand her network of Black feminist thinking.

DEMITA FRAZIER

Demita Frazier, who is from Chicago, brought issues of urban poverty to the Combahee discussions. Frazier arrived in Boston intending to organize Black women around feminist issues, but it took about a year to find others who might be interested in doing Black feminist consciousness-raising:

> We each got our names from different people, and we all had been involved in the National Black Feminist Organization. When we arrived, it took a while, but that first meeting when we met at my house in Dorchester, Massachusetts, . . . was quite something, because we were strangers to one another. We had gotten phone numbers and said, "Let's try to have a meeting and talk about what we could do in terms of organizing an NBFO chapter here in Boston." We were actually saying we were feminists. We were proud of that. We were not worried about flack from anybody else. It was a moment of power because, I think, we all recognized very quickly on that meeting in my living room that we were at the precipice of something really important. That was literally how it started, sitting in someone's living room, having a discussion about the issues, and it wasn't even the issues so much as getting to know one another and what our issues were, what brought us to think of ourselves as feminists. Where did we get these ideas? What books did we read? And then, of course, there was a sense of sharing. We were interested in so many similar things, even though we came from very different places. Most of us came from an academic background. Others had been really involved in organizing from the cities that we had come from. It was quite something for us. It was really very different for men.

The Boston chapter of the NBFO started with four Black women sitting in Frazier's living room discussing what had brought them to think of themselves as feminists. Boston in the 1970s was in turmoil over court-ordered busing to desegregate its schools. Barbara Smith describes the racial tensions:

> I moved to Boston in about 1972, and there were many places in Boston that to this day I have never ventured into. It was absolutely known that as a Black person you did not go to South Boston. You did not go to East Boston. You did not go to Chelsea. Those are a few of the names of neighborhoods that I remember

right off the top of my head. Sometimes on the way to somewhere else, like to trying to get to Dorchester, one might get lost in South Boston, and on those occasions it was always like, "Uh oh, I really need to get out of here." It was really frightening, if indeed one got lost in those neighborhoods trying to go from one place to another. But, in general, one knew that one did not go.

> For example, there was an attorney named Ted Landsmark who was down in City Hall Plaza, which is this very modern setting. It doesn't look like colonial Boston. So, he was down there for business, I am sure. And he was attacked by a group a white men, and they used an American flag to beat him up. I don't know who was there on the spot with the camera, but that picture went out over the wire services all over the country, probably all over the world, to show what this country was all about—and that was only about twenty years ago.

> Another example was a high school student who was playing football; and I don't remember what neighborhood they were playing in, if it was one of those places where one dare not venture if one was Black, but he was shot from the stands, and he was paralyzed for life. So, that was the kind of atmosphere that we lived in. Going into a store and being followed. When I went into a store the assumption was that I came in to rob it.

In a 1994 interview with Susan Goodwillie, Demita Frazier described the political climate of Boston in the 1970s:

> I think what drew a lot of us here was the chance to really establish identities that were our own, apart from family and apart from the communities or origin that we came from. So, you can picture us in 1973 and 1974, coming together as women in a city where there was so much political activity going on in Boston at that time. If you think about it, some of it wasn't progressive. Busing was just beginning at that time. The desegregation order had come down, and so the busing was beginning in Boston and . . . was causing a lot of political foment. There was a lot of discussion about

race and about class. So, we arrived in that atmosphere. And for those of us who had been feminists before we came to the city, and for those of us who had been organizers, we were thrilled at the chance to be in a city where there seemed to be a lot of discussion. There was a feeling that you could talk about nearly anything, and you could raise issues about just anything.

COMING TOGETHER: THE COMBAHEE RIVER COLLECTIVE RETREATS

We are actively committed to struggling against racial, sexual, heterosexual, and class oppression and see as our particular task the development of integrated analysis and practice based upon the fact that major systems of oppression are interlocking. The synthesis of these oppressions creates the condition of our lives. As Black women we see Black feminism as the logical political movement to combat the manifold and simultaneous oppressions that all women of color face.

—The Combahee River Collective Statement

The Combahee River Collective held retreats throughout the Northeast between 1977 and 1979. The first retreat was held 8–10 July 1977. The retreat was held at 10 Jewett Lane at a private home in South Hadley, Massachusetts. The purpose of the retreat was to assess the state of the movement, to share information about the participants' political work, and to talk about possibilities and issues for organizing Black women (24 May 1977 letter authored by Demita Frazier, Barbara Smith, and Beverly Smith). Subsequent retreats were meant to foster unity because of geographic separation. The twenty Black feminists who were invited were asked to bring copies of any written materials relevant to Black feminism—articles, pamphlets, papers, their own creative work—to share with the group. Frazier, Smith, and Smith, who organized the retreats, hoped that they would foster political stimulation and spiritual rejuvenation. They encouraged the participants to come ready to talk, laugh, eat,

dance, and have a good time. According to the interviews that I conducted, this is what occurred:

> Audre Lorde was involved in the retreats. I had just met her and I asked her to come and she was thrilled; and that is really how we got to become friends, because we would see each other periodically at these retreats. We would call them retreats, but, in fact, they were political meetings that had lots of different elements. So, it was a way for people who were separated to be in the same place and do some political work with each other.

The discussion schedule included five sections. The group met on Friday evening for a discussion entitled, "What's Been Done, What's Happening Now, What We Want for the Future." During this session, the group discussed political activities in which they had been involved over the past few years. On Saturday morning between 10 a.m. and noon the group's topic was "Theory and Analysis." They discussed the Combahee River Collective Statement as a means of focusing the first part of the session, then moved to the need to develop a Black feminist economic analysis, the question of violence, and lesbian separatism. After lunch there were two sessions on organizing. In the next session the group approached several questions: Is there a Black feminist movement? How to develop new organizing skills for Black feminist revolution? How to build new institutions? What about barriers to organizing such as antifeminism, repression, class, the backlash, heterosexism, racism, ageism, and sexism? Also, can publishing be used as a tool for organizing? Is it a viable Black feminist mode? How do we work out the knots for coalitions between white women and Black women? After this two-hour discussion, the group focused for another two hours on sterilization abuse, Black women's health, and battered women. They spent between 11 a.m. and 4 p.m. on Sunday discussing the effects and remedies of isolation.

The second Black feminist retreat was held 4–5 Nov. 1977 in Franklin Township, New Jersey, at Cassie Alfonso's home. The seven items on the agenda were the following: 1) trust between lesbian and nonlesbian feminists; 2) socialism and a Black feminist ideology; 3) lesbian separatism and the Black liberation struggle; 4) Black feminist organization versus Black feminist movement; 5) Black feminist scholarship; 6) class conflicts among Black women; and 7) love between women—lesbian, nonlesbian, Black and white (25 Aug. 1977 letter written by Cheryl Clarke and Cassie Alfonso). The participants were asked to bring something that would make a statement about themselves: a picture, a poem, or a journal excerpt. The retreat had five sessions that addressed the issues: the personal is political, political definitions, political realities—from analysis to action, and "Where do we go from here?" There were also two bodywork/ exercise sessions scheduled.

The third Black feminist retreat was scheduled for 24–26 March 1978. The fourth retreat met 21–23 July 1978. After these retreats occurred, the participants were encouraged to write articles for the Third World women's issue of *Conditions*, a journal edited by Lorraine Bethel and Barbara Smith. The importance of publishing was emphasized in the fifth retreat, held 8 July 1979. They discussed contributing articles for a lesbian herstory issue of two journals, *Heresies* and *Frontiers*. Both Beverly and Barbara Smith had been approached to compile an anthology on Black feminism. It is interesting to note that *All the Women are White, All the Blacks are Men, But Some of Us Are Brave* (1982) was edited by two Combahee members.

The fifth retreat was important because they catalogued the following indicators that Black feminism had grown between 1977 and 1979: There were now two Black feminist groups in Boston; Black academic women were organizing nationally in the field of history, and at the Modern Language Association, and had formed *Sojourner*, a Third World

Women's Studies research newsletter. A group for Black women in publishing was organizing in New York. Art collaborations were happening in New York. CRISIS, a Black women's "grassroots" organization, had formed in 1979 to combat murders in Boston. Coalitions between lesbian and straight Black women mothers in Kansas City had been established. Contacts had been made with Black social service workers in New Jersey and in Minneapolis. The women at the fifth retreat also discussed the growth of Black feminist and lesbian culture as evidenced by the performance groups Varied Voices Tour, Sweet Honey in the Rock, and Black Earth Sisters. The group noted that white feminists had begun to take responsibility for dealing with their racism, which lightens the load of Black feminists. And they went to two important poetry readings: at the Solomon Fuller Mental Health Center in Boston to hear Audre Lorde, Kate Rushin, and Fahamisha Shariat Brown; and at Sanders Theater at Harvard to hear Audre Lorde and Adrienne Rich.

Participants at the sixth retreat dealt with two literary events in the 1970s. They discussed articles in the May/June 1979 issue of *The Black Scholar* collectively titled, "The Black Sexism Debate," written in response to Robert Staples' "The Myth of Black Macho: A Response to Angry Black Feminists" in the previous issue. They also discussed the importance of writing to *Essence* to support an article in the September 1979 issue entitled "I am a Lesbian," by Chirlane McCray. McCray was a Combahee member, and the importance of the article was that at this time *Essence* had a policy on publishing articles and fiction about lesbians. The group was hoping that their positive letters would counteract the homophobic letters that they expected *Essence* to receive. The seventh retreat was held in Washington, D.C., 16–18 Feb. 1980. According to Smith:

> The retreats were multidimensional, multimedia events. They were so many different things. Of course, it was a time to talk politics. It was a time to have parties. It was a time to

flirt, for some. It was a time to have these incredible meals. We used to bring literature and things that we had read, articles, we would bring enough copies for everyone. We would have stuff laid out on the table. Now, having been a publisher for thirteen years for the only press of women of color in this country, I think how a part of that was bringing Xerox copies, because that was all we had then, if we wanted to read about ourselves in any fashion or read things that were relevant to us.

What I really see is Black feminism as a building block. I think that we always felt a kinship, sisterhood, and solidarity with not just women of color, but with people of color, generally. That is articulated in the statement and certainly in the kinds of things that we move on to work on and do political work on; but it is like building blocks. Our major felt contradiction is/was as Black women, there will be the White women's movement. So, if we were going to build something, it was going to be the opposite of what existed—in other words, Black, which was who we were.

The retreats were wonderful. They sort of came about as a brainstorm. We realized we wanted to meet with more Black feminists. In Boston, we had a very large group; but we knew that there was organizing going on in New York and in New Jersey and in Chicago and very similar places. So, we put a call out and called our friends and basically that is what we did. We called everybody we knew who we thought might be interested in spending a weekend talking politics, playing cards, eating good food, and spending time together to give you the support and also to give ourselves a sense of a broader community. So I don't remember what the year was. It might have been 1976, 1977. 1976, we organized our first Black feminist retreat. And we didn't advertise, we just did word of mouth. And we met with twenty-five or thirty women at the first one, sleeping over on a weekend in Western Massachusetts in South Hadley, Massachusetts. It was wonderful. First of all, we had, at that point, we had been organizing for a couple of years, and while we were feeling isolated, we did feel hungry for more. We wanted different perspectives. We wanted to hear from other people. The thrill of having people arriv-

ing, car load after car load of women who knew each other, but some who didn't know we were being brought together by five different women. We were just thrilled. There were so many colors, so many faces, so many bodies, from all over, and a chance to hear what was going on in different cities. [We were] standing around and looking at us all standing on that lawn, and realizing we are all women who are taking this big risk, because it was risky to be a feminist in the Black community. We realized it was risky and there we were, all these risk takers, all these ground breakers. It was very powerful for us, and it was wonderful also, because we had the opportunity at that first meeting to go around and talk about—from sort of an autobiographical perspective—how we all came to be feminists; and we got to tell our stories, fascinating places. Very interesting. One thing that I think we all had in common was again, we were all—it seemed like almost of all us—were women who never quite fit any sort of stereotype about wherever we were. We weren't appropriate little girls, necessarily. And if we were appropriate little girls, we weren't very appropriate teenagers. We were girls who were rebellious, and if we weren't rebellious in act, we were definitely rebellious in thought. We were girls who early on either had been sexually abused or physically assaulted and never wanted that to happen to us again. So, we were bringing a sort of reality politics like, "You know, I don't want this to happen to me or my children. There must be a way to talk about this."

COMMUNITY ACTIVISM

All of the Combahee women were involved in other Civil Rights and women's issues groups. For example, several belonged to the Committee to End Sterilization Abuse. There was cross-pollination between Combahee and other organizations to which the members belonged. When they first organized in the Combahee River Collective, there were no battered women's shelters in Boston or in the Boston area; but soon after they began, Transition House opened, and women were organizing the night marches. They were providing the information that a woman can bring a rape charge and not be viewed as the perpetrator.

When the collective became involved with the case of L. L. Ellison, a Black woman at Framingham State Prison who defended herself against a sexual assault by murdering a guard, it brought them into a circle of people who were fighting the death penalty in the state. This interaction helped them to form coalitions with other community activists, and brought them into another sector of the Black community: women's church groups, including the auxiliaries of Baptist churches. They were asked to speak about what Black feminist politics meant for Black women. According to Barbara Smith, they were very successful, because even though they caused upheaval, they brought the question of violence against Black women to the table:

> We would show up ready to create our discussion, [to] talk about consciousness-raising and the importance of looking into the issues of violence against Black women. And also, [to frame] an analysis about what it meant for us to take one step back and what it meant to support Black men. Did we have to necessarily walk behind Black men to be supportive of Black men and therefore, supportive of our whole community? So, things got very hot and heavy at this meeting. We were being told, "What made you think you represent all Black women? You don't represent me, necessarily." It wasn't a hostile group, but people were feeling, "What does this mean? How can you say this represents that you are representing us?" An older Black woman (she must have been in her sixties or seventies) said, "Well, from what I can understand, what they are saying sounds right to me, so they represent me." And that was, again, one of those moments when we've got affirmation [from] someone who [you] would respect, because you were taught to respect older Black people as a child. You were just taught to respect your elders, and it was so affirming to have her say that. And it sort of really put other women—it sort of gave other women—the permission to say that they could understand and support the issues.

The simple truth is . . . : she didn't have anything to lose. She is an older woman who has had a whole lifetime of experience. And I see it in my own mother now. You just don't have to lie anymore after you get past a certain age as woman, and she was just very clear. She worked in people's houses—cleaning them—and primarily White people's, and she talked about having to fend off the husband or the older son when she was a young woman doing that work and what it meant for her. She lost many jobs and understood—she understood—sexual politics. . . . It is so funny. If you knew the people involved, you would understand that it [sexual orientation] was never an issue. We were Lesbians. We were not going to be repressed or oppressed in a group that we were organizing for. We had a couple of women who were bisexual in the group, and they were fine with us. At least, I can say they were fine with me. Because the women who were integral to organizing Combahee were Lesbians, it was done just as it was. We were the women who came together, and we made it a part of our politics that we thought that we were open to all women: Lesbians, straight women, and bisexual women. So, at that time, it was as far as we were concerned, it wasn't an issue. People always act as if homophobia is something the Black community invented. We all know that that is not true. We didn't find that women were completely closed to the idea of being in a room with a group of Lesbians talking about feminist politics. We just, we were a group of women trying to come together to talk about what it meant to be Black and female and Lesbians on the spectrum. So, that is just how it was.

I don't ever remember us going anywhere and people saying things like, "Here come the bull daggers" or "Here come those dikes." We didn't have that problem. It also may have been because in the venues that we found ourselves—we took ourselves—to, we were involved with progressive people and progressive organizations. It is different when you are going out to do a speaking engagement, to talk about Black feminist organizing, because inevitably we would always say, as an organization, we support and respect the right for women to make the decisions about themselves, their sexuality, their lives, whatever. And so, we always stated that and it would create some interesting discussions, but it was not as if we went someplace and got stoned, or we went to a meeting in a church and had people threaten to nail us to the cross and set us on fire. It just didn't happen that way. We had, there was, also a certain amount of respect that you get as a political activist. I found this to be true when you are working with people of color. Because we were really focusing on the issues and these were life and death, bread and butter issues. And we just acted as if it were perfectly all right for us to be who we were and be respected for who we were. So, we didn't have problems as a group going into situations like that, which is not to say, as individuals, we didn't have problems in the community. But I never did.

SIMULTANEITY OF OPPRESSION: DEFINING A POLITIC

The women of the Combahee River Collective created a theory that was more polyvocal than the theories espoused by the Kennedy Commission women and the National Black Feminist Organization. The theory that they were able to provide is a useful tool to analyze the position of Black women in the 1990s:

I think we came up with the term "identity politics." I never really saw it anywhere else, and I would suggest that people–if they really want to find the origin of the term–that they try to find it in any place earlier than in the Combahee River Collective statement. I don't remember seeing it anywhere else. But what we meant by "identity politics" was a politics that grew out of our objective material experiences as Black women. This was the kind of politics that had never been done or practiced before, to our knowledge, although we began to find out that there were Black feminists in the early part of this century, and also, perhaps, in the latter part of the nineteenth century. But it had never been quite formulated in the way that we were trying to formulate it, particularly because we were talking about homophobia, lesbian identity, as well.

So, there were basically politics that worked for us. There were politics that took everything

into account as opposed to saying, "Leave your feminism, your gender, your sexual orientation–you leave that outside. You can be Black in here, but you can't be a lesbian, you can't be a feminist; or, you can be a feminist in here, but you can't be Black. That's really what we meant. We meant politics that came out of the various identities that we had that really worked for us. It gave us a way to move, a way to make change. It was not the reductive version that theorists now really criticize. It was not being simplistic in saying I am Black and you are not. That wasn't what we were doing.

It was remarkable that without a clear model, without a huge amount of applause from the stands or whatever, that we took this on. We took on the contradictions of being in the U.S. and living in U.S. society under this system. We took on race, class, sexual orientation, and gender. And we said, instead of being bowled over by it and destroyed by it, we are going to make it into something vital and inspiring. I have to say that I really did know what we were doing when we were doing it. I think that because I have such a grounding in Black history and in Black culture, I was quite aware that we were doing something new.

One of the things that I used to feel was the lack of role models for myself. I used to feel like, if only Lorraine [Hansberry] hadn't died so early, then there would be someone who is older than me who is trying to carve out the territory. Audre [Lorde] was important to me in that way. Being able to look over to and up to someone who had been here more years than I, who shared the same kind of vision in politics, but I was very aware that we were doing something new because I knew enough about history and about political organizing to know that we were doing something that was never attempted before. But that doesn't mean that I felt competent at every moment. It was absolutely daunting work. It was depressing. It was frightening. It was exhausting. Yes, I think, that metaphor of a river that begins in a dark swamp and small spaces and opens out, I think that is quite apt. I was excited because I assumed that the 80's would be similar in their degree of growth and energy as the 70's had been. But as it turned out, I was not right about that.

The 1980s turned out to be the Reagan years, and organizing became much more difficult. Public sentiment moved to the right, and the economic situation became even worse for those who were supposed to have benefited from trickle-down economics. Nevertheless, when twelve Black women were murdered in Boston in 1979, the Black feminist agenda went into full effect.

THEORY, PRACTICE, AND ACTION: TWELVE MURDERS—THE FINAL ACT

The only research that has been done to date about the activism of the Combahee River Collective in response to the time when twelve Black women were murdered in Boston in 1979 is Jamie Grant's unpublished article, "Who Is Killing Us?" According to Grant, between 28 January and 30 May 1979, thirteen women, twelve Black and one white, were murdered within a two-mile radius in the city of Boston. All but one of the victims were found in predominately Black neighborhoods in the contiguous districts of Roxbury, Dorchester, and the South End. Many of the women were strangled, with bare hands or a scarf or cord, and some were stabbed; two were buried after they were killed, and two were dismembered. Several of the women had been raped.

Notorious at the time for its poor treatment of Blacks with the busing situation, the Black attorney who had been stabbed with an American flag, and for an attack on a Black high school football player, Boston reflected this social climate in its major newspaper, the *Globe*. The 30 January 1979 edition noted the discovery of the bodies of the first two murder victims, then unidentified, beside the racing forms on page thirty, in a four-paragraph description headlined, "Two bodies found in a trash bag." On 31 January, the murder of Gwendolyn Yvette Stinson

was noted on page thirteen under the head, "Dorchester girl found dead." Caren Prater's death, on 6 February, finally warranted a small block on the front page, followed by a confusing article about community outrage and police resources. On 7 February, on the eighth page of its Metro report, the *Globe* covered a community meeting with Mayor White at the Lee School in Dorchester, which more than 700 people attended.

The *Globe* took no responsibility for its complicity in the lack of public attention to the murders. When it did focus attention on the crimes, it was to attack the Black community's response. Except for a small 17 February article on the murders, the *Globe* remained silent about the crisis until 21 February, when Daryl Ann Hargett was found in her apartment. Then, inside a small box in the lower left-hand corner of the front page, the *Globe* reported the death of the fifth Black woman in thirty days, misspelling Hargett's first name. In contrast to the *Globe*, the *Bay State Banner*, the Black community weekly, ran full-blown coverage of the situation from 1 February, and reported on the Black community's response. The *Banner* continued detailed, front-page coverage throughout the year.

On 1 April, following the deaths of six Black women, fifteen hundred people took to the streets to mourn the losses of their sisters, daughters, mothers, friends. The memorial march commenced in Boston's South End at the Harriet Tubman House, and paused first at the Wellington Street apartment of Daryl Ann Hargett, the fifth victim, who was found strangled on the floor of her bedroom:

> By that time in April, six women had been murdered and there was a memorial march in the South End about the murders. It was a protest march. It was also trying to commemorate them, and there was a rally at the Stride-Rite factory field, and you heard things that had already been said, but the message came across—loud and clear from the almost entirely Black male speakers—that what Black women needed to do was stay in the house. That's the way you saved yourself from being murdered.

You stayed in the house and/or you found a man to protect you. If you were going to leave the house, you had to find a man to go with you to take care of you. And also, the murders were being viewed at time as being completely racial murders. It was all women, and some of the women had been sexually assaulted, but they were still seen as racial murders. There were a lot of feminist lesbians at that rally; so, there were at least some people there that, when they heard this message that these were just racial murders, our ears perked up, stood up, whatever, and we were thinking, "No, no, I don't think so," because there was something called violence against women that we were all too familiar with; and we just felt so-it was just such a difficult afternoon because at one level, we were grieving because Black women were being killed; we felt like we were at risk. We knew we were, in fact. We were scared. It was a very frightening time to be a Black woman in Boston. So, there was that kind of collective shared grieving, and then there was this real feeling of real fury. It was just infuriating, because we knew that it was not a coincidence that everybody who had been murdered was female, and as it turned out, by the time it was over, twelve Black women had been murdered. When the marchers reached the Stride Rite factory on Lenox Street in Roxbury, where the bodies of the first two women were found, Lorraine Bethel, who eventually co-edited *Conditions Five* with Barbara Smith, was there. Smith remembers Lorraine saying, "This is just horrible; we've got to do something."

Smith's anger and frustration at the rally speakers' failure to acknowledge sexism as a factor in the deaths of the women propelled her into action. She returned to her apartment in Roxbury and began developing a pamphlet that would speak to the fears of Black women in Boston:

I said, "I think we really need to do a pamphlet. We need to do something." So, I started writing a pamphlet that night and I thought of the title—"Six Black Women: Why Did They Die?"—and I wrote it up. I always write everything longhand to begin with, and then I typed it. I had a little Smith-Corona electric portable at that time. And by the next morning, it was basically done. I called other people in the Collective. The Collective was never huge, so I am not talking about called twenty people. But I called other people in the group and I read it to them. This was before faxes and all that madness. I read it to them and then I also called up Urban Planning Aid in Boston and went down there and got assistance with laying out the pamphlet, using my actual typing from my own typewriter at home.

Basically, what we wanted to say—and did say—in the pamphlet is that we had to look at these murders as both racist and sexist crimes and that we really needed to talk about violence against women in the Black community. We needed to talk about those women who did not have men as a buffer. Almost no woman has a man as a buffer between them and violence, because it doesn't make any difference if you are married or heterosexual, whatever, all kinds of women are at risk for attack in different kinds of circumstances. And, in fact, most women are attacked by the men they know. So, obviously, having a man isn't going to protect you from violence. But we really wanted to, first of all, get out that sexual political analysis about these murders. We wanted to do some consciousness-raising about what the murders meant. We also wanted to give women hope. So, the pamphlet had the statement, the analysis, the political analysis, and it said that it had been prepared by the Combahee River Collective. That was a big risk for us, a big leap to identify ourselves in something that we knew was going to be widely distributed. It also had a list of things that you can do to protect yourself. In other words, self-defense methods. I remember consulting with people, like some of the violence-against-women organizations, to really check out to make sure that the things that we were suggesting were usable and good and then, also, we had a list of organizations that were doing work on violence against women in Boston.

We got great support from the community churches. We got a lot of support from very diverse groups of people, but I must say, the larger white feminist community was incredibly supportive. It was a real opportunity to do some coalition-building, and we were able to mobilize hundreds and hundreds of people to come out and to speak out, to talk about the issue. We were able to bring together very diverse groups of people around the issue of violence against women. And we never felt that it had lost the focus on the fact that the women were Black. One thing we did say, though, is that "These are Black women who were being murdered. They could have been you." It could have been any of us.

LIFE AFTER THE COMBAHEE RIVER COLLECTIVE

Throughout the interviews I conducted, there were numerous reasons cited for the eventual disintegration of the Combahee River Collective. What seemed to come to the surface after much investigation were accusations that the group was less egalitarian than they claimed to be. Several of the interviewees alluded to the fact that, although hierarchies were not supposed to exist, indeed they did. There was also mention of love relations that went awry, leaving at least one member of the partnership not wanting to attend retreats.

It seems that the Collective was most cohesive and active when the murders in Boston were occurring. Having an event to respond to and collectively to organize around gave them a cause to focus on, which distracted them from the in-fighting that existed over power struggles and broken hearts. Also, according to Margo Okizawa Rey, who had attended graduate school at Harvard, this was a time in many of their twenty-something lives that geographical disbursement was bound to happen. By the early 1980s, several of the members had left the Boston area to begin the next phase of their lives. Most of the women continued the work of the collective through academia. Rey and Hull are examples of two members who ended up in California teaching race/class/gender theory at San Francisco State and Santa Cruz, respectively. Sharon Page Ritchie plans to join the California University system to study clothing design. Cheryl Clarke is working on her dissertation (which is about contemporary Black women poets) at Rutgers University, where she is an administrator and advocate for the gay/lesbian/bisexual students on campus. Barbara Smith is working on a gay and lesbian studies anthology and resides in New York, and Demita Frazier has returned to Chicago to practice law. Although they no longer operate as a collective, they left a legacy for Black feminists of the 1990s to continue.

Mayor Washington's Action Agenda for Chicago's Future, 1987–1991

Mayor Harold Washington

MAYOR HAROLD WASHINGTON'S VISION FOR THE FUTURE OF CHICAGO

Fellow Chicagoans: We in Chicago share a dream that this city's wonderful mosaic of peoples and communities can live, work and build together. You and I believe that all neighborhoods are important and should flourish. We believe that all people should be able to find productive work, feed their families, and have adequate shelter. We are all united in the desire that our children have hope for the future.

We can achieve this dream by building together the only kind of unity that will last in our city, a unity based on fairness, openness, mutual respect, and a true sharing of both the responsibilities and rewards of government. It is on this foundation that I have built my vision of Chicago and how we will bring it about.

The best way to communicate the future Chicago that I envision is to take you there, to show you what I want and will work for:

- Neighborhoods throughout the city in which a new generation of Chicagoans is raising families in safe and clean environments, and where property values and taxes are reasonable and stable.
- A world-class downtown Chicago with a bustling North Loop and Theater District, a new central library, a colossal financial district, and a newly-developed riverfront.

Source: Mayor Washington's Action Agenda for Chicago's Future, 1987–1991. Chicago: Committee to Re-Elect Mayor Washington, 1987.

- Thriving new industrial parks that provide jobs for neighborhood residents and space for new home-grown businesses. Companies remain in Chicago to take advantage of our capable labor force, our research and educational facilities, and our overall quality of life.
- New affordable housing, as well as an array of quality health care and human services that are accessible to those who need them.
- Public meetings being held throughout the city at which people are helping to plan the future of their neighborhoods. Street repaving, local zoning decisions, new shopping malls—all will be debated by our residents.
- All students enrolling in public schools graduate—and then find work or go to college.
- A world-renowned Chicago International Cultural Festival that celebrates the diversity and richness of Chicago and the world with art, music, theater and food.

I have an Action Agenda that will move us closer to this Chicago over the next four years. It builds on the foundation we have established during my first term. Many of the resources we have used to create a government that is fair, efficient and free of corruption may now be channeled into building a stronger, more unified, and more prosperous Chicago.

Our task will not be easy because resources are limited and we face continued opposition by some. Despite these obstacles, the progress we have made during the past four years gives me confidence and hope for our future.

We have done what you asked us to do. You asked us to open City Hall to all the people of this city and to take advantage of their diverse talents and ideas—and we have. You asked us to end a system of patronage that sold city jobs and contracts for political gain—and we have. You asked us to reinvest in the many neighborhoods of Chicago—and we have. You asked us to respond to those with special needs, such as our children, the homeless, the elderly, and the disabled—and we have. You asked us to modernize an antiquated bureaucracy and run government responsibly and efficiently—and we have. You asked us to take politics out of the school system and the police department—and we have. And you asked us to provide leadership to make Chicago work together—we have done that, too.

Together, we have made an impressive beginning. But much remains to be accomplished. My next term will provide the leadership and programs to move us closer to a Chicago that will be emulated by cities throughout the world as a model of good government, economic opportunity, cultural richness, and racial and ethnic harmony.

We can fashion Chicago into an even more beautiful mosaic. As you read this agenda, you will find the specifics of what we can achieve by working together over the next four years. Our record of "promises made, promises kept" in the first term demonstrates that we can do even more in the second term.

Please join me.

Harold Washington

Mayor Harold Washington

MAYOR HAROLD WASHINGTON'S ACTION AGENDA: 1987–1991

I. Introduction

Mayor Washington will lead Chicago with his Action Agenda, a platform that continues in the direction he set in his first term. During those four years the Mayor estab-

lished a fair distribution of government benefits, open information to all citizens, and widespread participation in formulating public policies. Chicago can now forge ahead with confidence.

Mayor Washington's Action Agenda focuses on three vital functions of our city:

A City of Opportunity for Its People providing all Chicagoans with basic opportunities for a decent job and a quality education.

A City of Thriving Neighborhoods through physical improvements, increased affordable housing, public safety, and a clean and healthy environment.

An International City improving Chicago's stature throughout the world by implementing key projects, strengthening our transportation network, and promoting our cultural riches.

These programs will be achieved with a foundation of fair and effective government and four basic strategies for action:

- Fiscal Reform
- Planning
- Partnerships
- Leadership

II. Programs for Our Future

A. Chicago: A City of Opportunity for Its People The greatness of a city can be measured by the basic employment and education opportunities that are provided to its people. Mayor Washington is committed to providing these opportunities to every Chicagoan. Here is how he will act on this commitment during the next four years.

Jobs Mayor Washington's goal of a decent job for every Chicagoan requires practical leadership, working partnerships, and a strong legislative agenda if we are to retain and expand Chicago's base of quality jobs. Mayor Washington will enhance Chicago's recent economic rebound by increasing business confidence in Chicago and fighting for federal and state job creation and training resources. If national economic trends continue, the number of employed Chicagoans will increase at the same pace as in the past four years—or as many as 100,000 more working Chicagoans.

The city's own resources are not adequate to address our large need for jobs. Chicago requires its fair share of federal and state funding to assist in operating its own programs. People on welfare need support for job training, child care, and health insurance in order to get back into the labor market. Federal policy is also essential to expand the number of jobs by promoting the economy and by putting people to work to meet currently neglected public needs. Mayor Washington will use his leadership with other mayors in the State and the nation to promote an expanded jobs policy.

In the next four years, Mayor Washington will increase job opportunities for all Chicagoans by building on partnerships with business, labor, schools, neighborhoods, and other governments to leverage resources, promote balanced economic development, improve the skills of Chicago's workforce, retain Chicago's existing manufacturing base, and link economic development benefits to neighborhoods and their residents. Since smaller businesses account for most of today's job growth, the Mayor's agenda will emphasize small business expansion.

Education/Youth Chicago has a vital stake in the future of our youth. Only by giving our children the support and guidance needed to grow to their fullest potential can we ensure that Chicago will meet the challenges of the 21st century. The future of our youth depends on three interrelated factors: the guidance and assistance we provide for their development, the education we make available, and the economic climate we create for them.

During his next term, Mayor Washington will focus on three areas. He will work with the Board of Education and Chicago City Colleges to develop and implement policies to provide a quality education for all students. He will expand City programs that provide support services for youth. The Mayor will work with other government and community agencies to provide employment and training opportunities and literacy programs.

B. Chicago: A City of Thriving Neighborhoods After many decades of neglect, Chicago's people and their neighborhoods are gaining strength. By insisting on fairness in the way public resources are distributed, Mayor Harold Washington has ensured that neighborhoods throughout Chicago are finally receiving their fair share of public resources. However, we still have far to go before the Mayor's vision of a city of working neighborhoods, strong in their physical structure and social fabric is achieved.

Mayor Washington will strengthen neighborhoods during his next term by focusing on five priority areas: neighborhood improvements, housing, public safety, energy, and health and environment.

Neighborhood Improvements During his first term in office, Mayor Washington established policies that have worked to strengthen our neighborhoods. These include balancing investments between Chicago's downtown and the neighborhoods, using partnerships to create new funding sources for neighborhood development, and empowering neighborhoods—providing residents, businesses and their organizations with the resources and capacity to participate in guiding the development of their own communities. These same policies will guide his second term investment in neighborhoods.

Housing Mayor Washington will take significant steps to increase the availability of affordable housing in the next four years despite sustained federal cutbacks. Significant progress must be made to expand our citywide approach to protect and upgrade Chicago's housing stock by coordinating housing court, building codes and inspections, tax policies, housing abandonment prevention, and other city activities that affect affordable housing. City government must also work with the CHA and its residents to stabilize the authority financially, improve services to residents, and involve residents in CHA planning and operations.

To increase affordable housing over the next four years, Mayor Washington will:

- Expand housing partnerships to leverage resources for affordable housing construction, rehabilitation, and energy conservation.
- Find permanent solutions to homelessness by lobbying for state and federal rental subsidies. In the interim, the Mayor will seek funding for additional homeless shelters.
- Develop the City's first low income housing trust fund.
- Advocate for the State of Illinois to create a new Low Income Housing Trust Fund, provide mortgage insurance and foreclosure protection, and redirect state reserves to fund low and moderate housing programs.

Public Safety Mayor Washington is bringing safety to our neighborhoods by putting more police on the streets, confronting the youth gang program, and improving overall public safety. His second term initiatives will:

- Intensify our successful fight against gang crime.
- Continue to improve police handling of sexual assault and domestic violence.
- Continue Mayor Washington's war on drugs through prevention, enforcement and treatment.
- Free more police officers to be on the street rather than behind desks.
- Increase the use of citizen volunteers in the Police and Fire Departments.
- Modernize the city's public safety communication system.
- Expand emergency medical services with more paramedics and ambulances.

Energy Chicago's neighborhoods need affordable energy if they are to thrive. In the past four years, Mayor Washington has shown extraordinary leadership in fighting unjust utility rate increases, initiating programs to cut home energy costs, and exploring lower cost energy options for the future.

During the next four years, Mayor Washington will:

- Achieve the best energy bargain for Chicagoans by renegotiating the city's franchise agreement with Commonwealth Edison.
- Implement waste-to-energy facilities that provide low-cost energy.
- Reduce energy costs to city government.
- Provide maximum support for energy conservation programs such as the Chicago Energy Savers Fund.
- Spearhead a regional energy planning alliance of government, utilities and consumers to seek lowest cost energy.

Health and Environment Mayor Washington envisions a Chicago with a healthy population, a clean environment, and a thriving industrial base. He is confident that this can be achieved if we take steps now to safeguard the health of our people, restore the purity of our air, land and water, and prevent new enviromental hazards. Mayor Washington will work with health agencies, neighborhood organizations, environmental protection groups and local industry to protect our environment. He will also protect the public's health by focusing on disease prevention as well as treatment, and providing quality health care for the medically indigent.

C. Chicago: An International City Chicago's mosaic of neighborhoods and people from all parts of the world is fitting for a city that has a prominent international role in business, culture, and transportation and is the leading city of its region. As an international city, Chicago is the home of world-class cultural institutions, a center of commerce and finance, a transportation hub for the world, and vibrant ethnic neighborhoods and celebrations.

Mayor Washington will continue to increase Chicago's stature as an international city in the next four years by investing in our central area, culture and entertainment facilities, and our transportation network.

Central Area

- Make rapid progress on North, West, and South Loop, as well as River North and Cityfront Center projects that are expanding Chicago's downtown as a center of world-class commercial, cultural, recreational, and residential activities.
- Begin construction on a new central library.

International Business

- Promote Chicago as a world center of finance, commerce, and commodity trading.
- Open world markets for small and medium sized businesses.
- Revive exports and imports through the Port of Chicago.

Culture and Entertainment

- Invite the world to Chicago's remarkable summer festivals, cultural institutions, diverse architecture, and beautiful lakefront.
- Implement the City's first cultural plan.
- Ensure that quality facilities are available for theater, dance and music.
- Develop additional public support for major museums and cultural organizations.
- Continue redevelopment of Navy Pier as a recreational and cultural facility of international significance.

Transportation

- Launch the next phase of the $1.6 billion expansion of O'Hare International Airport, and develop adjacent city-owned property through intergovernmental agreements with neighboring suburbs. This will generate thousands of jobs and millions of dollars in city revenues.
- Continue to revitalize Midway Airport to attract additional commercial carriers, and develop adjacent properties with commercial and hotel facilities.
- Build the Southwest Transit Line to connect downtown Chicago with Midway Airport.
- Expand CTA and RTA programs and services to help give city residents access to suburban jobs.

Regional Partnerships

- Cooperate to solve regional environmental issues such as solid and toxic waste disposal and shoreline protection.
- Ensure that the Chicago area becomes a national center of research and technological innovation through such efforts as obtaining the proposed super-collider.
- Market the Chicago region as a cultural center and the most competitive location for business and new investment.

III. Strategies For Action

Mayor Washington's "Action Agenda" is an ambitious four-year plan, but it can be achieved because the Mayor has already spent four years reconstructing city government and fighting for resources for Chicago in all legislative arenas. During his next term Mayor Washington will promote the same standards that he used during his first term to make city government more fair and effective. These include:

- Affirmative action policies to ensure the fair representation of all Chicagoans in the workforce and public purchasing of goods and services.
- A code of ethics to guide city employees and mayoral appointees.
- Professional management and personnel systems to improve service delivery.
- Computerized record-keeping and auditing.
- Expanded competitive bidding, cost containment, and increased fiscal integrity.
- Collective bargaining and fairly administered grievance procedures.
- "Chicago First" hiring policy to ensure that Chicagoans have access to jobs created with their tax dollars.
- Intergovernmental coordination to improve the efficiency of service delivery.

- Public participation and freedom of information on policy-making and budgeting.

Mayor Washington has identified four strategies for city government that will move his agenda forward:

- Fiscal Reform
- Planning
- Partnerships
- Leadership

A. Fiscal Reform Mayor Washington has brought fiscal stability to Chicago to ensure the future vitality of our city and other local governments. During his next term, Mayor Washington will focus on replacing lost federal funds and improving revenue collection systems. Through the Financial Planning Committee he has drawn on the expertise of the business community to better understand these problems. He will seek the advice of business, labor, and community groups to develop solutions.

Mayor Washington is developing Chicago's first long-term, financial plan to move Chicago toward a more diverse revenue mix, linking revenue sources with expenditures, and stabilizing our tax base to encourage economic development. Above all, fiscal reform must end regressive taxation, level the playing field for business, and achieve a fair return to Chicago from the state and federal governments.

B. Planning Mayor Washington is making Chicago a model of effective planning. He has undertaken a variety of planning efforts that involve all relevant interests. Mayor Washington will set comparable planning standards for other units of government, such as the CTA and the Park District. In the next four years these plans will be coordinated for the first time.

The Chicago Works Together development plan and cultural plan have strategic goals and objectives that facilitate government decision making. Under Mayor's Washington's leadership, strategic assess-

ments have been developed in areas as diverse as infant mortality, solid waste management, land use, the steel and apparel industries, and long-term care for the elderly. Work is currently underway to improve the management and the capital improvement planning processes, and to initiate a long-term, financial plan.

C. Partnerships Mayor Washington has articulated an agenda to bring us closer to his vision for Chicago's future—but only Chicagoans can make it happen. Chicagoans must work together as partners to enhance limited resources, balance competing goals, design projects that fit community needs, and get more done with less.

The partnership approach to effective government has been fundamental to Mayor Washington's administration and is a foundation for his Action Agenda. It has been used for large and small issues, ranging from the steel industry to homelessness, and has involved public, private, community, and labor leaders. Partnerships have brought new actors together to discuss resource constraints and public standards for fair and effective public action.

- In the next four years Mayor Washington will continue to use many of the 50 public/private partnerships he formed during his first term. Following are a few examples:
  Economic Development Commission (EDC): A revitalized EDC with energetic business, community, and labor leaders will plan for Chicago's long-term development.
  Educational Summit: A partnership involving the Board of Education, Chicago City Colleges, community organizations, and public and private employers is exploring innovative ways to improve public education, job skills, and youth employment.
  Chicago Housing Partnership: This partnership between the City of Chicago, developers, and major financial institutions will leverage new financial resources for affordable housing development, primarily by neighborhood housing developers.

Collective Bargaining: Collective bargaining agreements with City of Chicago employees and their trade unions promise to give fairness, opportunity, and efficiency real meaning for city government. As partners, the City of Chicago, its employees, and their respective unions will continue to make Chicago work.

D. Leadership The Mayor of a great city has to provide leadership in the city, state, and federal arenas, and must provide guidance to other units of local government. Mayor Washington has achieved remarkable legislative success despite City Council opposition, and he has proven to be a leader among urban mayors against President Reagan's war on urban programs. He also has set high standards for the effective and fair operation of government.

During the next four years Mayor Washington will continue his efforts to make Chicago's City Council a deliberative legislative body. He will work with the Council to improve the budget making process so that it represents the needs and priorities of all Chicago in a way that unifies the city and enhances effective government. Modernization of the municipal and zoning codes will increase efficiency and make it easier for citizens to carry out their business.

At the regional, state, and federal levels he will form working coalitions to bring Chicago its fair share of available resources. Finally, Mayor Washington will actively participate in a regional partnership to solve shared problems and to promote the entire Chicago region. He will continue working with other Illinois cities to develop a statewide Municipal Agenda.

Mayor Washington will also exercise his leadership with the many separate units of government that provide specific services for Chicagoans. These include the Board of Education, Chicago Park District, Chicago Housing Authority, Chicago City Colleges, and Chicago Transportation Authority. The Mayor of Chicago has the responsibility to appoint, with City Council approval, competent board members who agree with the high public standards he has established for the effective and fair performance of government.

During the next four years, Mayor Washington will work directly with these special purpose governments, as well as through his appointees, to set clear agency missions, goals and policies, in order to establish mechanisms that ensure fairness, effectiveness, accountability, and openness.

IV. Conclusion

This comprehensive action agenda for the next four years will make Chicago work better as a city of opportunity for its people, a city of thriving neighborhoods, and an international city. While this agenda is straightforward, practical, and innovative, its implementation will not be easy. It will take more than one term to develop permanent solutions to limited resources and policital obstructionism.

Mayor Washington will rely on the same standards to implement his "Action Agenda" that he used to initiate reform. This means having a plan and a program for the hundreds of different problems and services that must be addressed every day. It means strong partnerships, effectiveness and efficiency, balancing limited resources with important human needs, and skillful leadership.

Chicago can be proud of what has been accomplished during the past four years. While we have far to go, we have seen that fairness, openness and public participation work to make government more effective.

The first term record also demonstrates that he has the skill and determination to make government work for all Chicagoans. We have highlighted some of his accomplishments in the appendix to show that Mayor Washington has built a strong foundation for a second term of action and progress, and to illustrate that Mayor Washington keeps his promises to Chicago.

APPENDIX THE WASHINGTON RECORD: 1983–1987

Promises Made

During his first term, Mayor Washington made and kept his promises to:

- Involve Chicagoans in government decision making.
- Reverse decades of neglect by rebuilding Chicago's neighborhoods.
- Reverse the decline in jobs and affordable housing.
- Bring fairness and honesty to all aspects of city government.
- Respond to all communities of Chicago and work with them to solve their problems.
- End patronage and support collective bargaining for all city workers.
- Open the closed doors of City Hall to make government accessible and accountable.
- End waste and mismanagement while improving Chicago's finances.
- Forge strong partnerships with business, community organizations, and labor.
- Confront the problem of hunger, homelessness, infant mortality and youth gang crime.
- Fight for Chicago at the state and federal levels and put urban needs back on the national agenda.

Promises Kept

Chicagoans can take pride that Mayor Washington translates promises into programs. His first term produced a set of accomplishments that have improved the quality of life for Chicagoans, have led the city forward, and have made city government more fair and effective. They are highlighted below:

Improving Peoples' Lives

- Implemented the largest neighborhood reconstruction program in Chicago's history—and completed it under budget and on schedule.
- Tripled the number of community-based organizations receiving funds to deliver vital services in Chicago's neighborhoods.

- Quadrupled police foot patrol in the neighborhoods.
- Instituted a moratorium on solid waste landfills and worked with business and community groups to develop long-range solutions.
- Increased home delivered meals to seniors and disabled Chicagoans.
- Reduced the infant mortality rate.
- Started long overdue rehabilitation to make City Hall and other public facilities more accessible to the disabled.
- Formed the Chicago Alliance Against Drugs and opened Chicago's only public in-patient program for teenage drug abusers.
- Fought successfully against utility rate hikes.
- Doubled the number of food boxes delivered to the hungry and increased by ten-fold the number of shelter beds.
- Commissioned an Education Summit to develop and implement programs designed to improve skill levels of all youth and give them better access to job and higher education opportunities.
- Combined state, federal, and local dollars to launch a citywide AIDS Information Project.
- Supported home ownership opportunities through city-sponsored low-interest mortgages.
- Worked with the City Council to pass the Tenant Landlord Bill of Rights.
- Established the Chicago Housing Partnership between the city and the private sector, which leveraged new dollars to support low-income housing.
- Saved over 1,500 housing units through the new housing abandonment prevention program which was developed in cooperation with community organizations.
- Saved lives through a new trauma ordinance and an improved emergency hotline which for the first time provides services in 40 different languages.
- Created the "Hire the Future" program which placed 75,000 youth in summer jobs.
- Created a new small business loan program which created or retained 20,000 jobs.
- Began training women and minorities for non-traditional jobs from which they were previously excluded.
- Expanded neighborhood festivals from 12 in 1983 to over 80 in 1986 by working in partnership with community groups.

- Doubled funding to neighborhood arts programs.
- Led the nation in banning leaded gasoline.
- Reduced police brutality.

Leading the City Forward

- Made substantial progress in the O'Hare Airport Expansion and the revitalization of Midway Airport.
- Expanded the internationally acclaimed Chicago Jazz Fest, Taste of Chicago, and initiated the Blues and Gospel Fests.
- Competed successfully for over $70 million in federal support for business and housing development projects.
- Secured $496 million to build the Southwest Rapid Transit Line.
- Enhanced Chicago's international stature by initiating new sister-city ties in Asia, Europe, and Latin America; and expanded the international business program.
- Successfully passed a $130 million bond issue which will fund the nation's largest urban public library in Chicago's South Loop.
- Saved the Chicago Theater and reopened Navy Pier.
- Broke logjams in the North Loop Redevelopment Project and moved several projects forward.
- Led the effort to keep the White Sox in Chicago.
- Was in the forefront in passing a $28 million educational reform bill in the state legislature.
- Passed substantial legislative reforms through the Chicago City Council.
- Led the fight against federal revenue sharing cuts by launching a Fair Share Return campaign throughout Illinois and the nation.

Making Government Effective

- Eliminated the $168 million dollar deficit and balanced the budget every year.

- Opened the doors to City Hall through the city's first Freedom of Information Order and Open Budget Executive Orders.
- Successfully fought institutionalized corruption through the Mayor's Ethics Executive Order and finally, achieved a unanimous passage of the Ethics Ordinance.
- Created the city's first Department of Revenue which collected over $20 million from delinquent parking tickets, more than $11 million from overdue water and sewer bills, and more from other fees and fines.
- Received a "Financial Leadership Award" for outstanding financial management practices from the U.S. Conference of Mayors.
- Ended patronage through implementation of a professional hiring system as included in the Shakman decree.
- Increased city contracts to minorities and women from 4% in 1983 to 34%—or $70 million—in 1986.
- Fulfilled a promise to support collective bargaining rights for all city employees.
- Brought fairness to hiring and purchasing practices, and reversed past discrimination.
- Saved millions of dollars through increased competitive bidding and other innovative purchashing practices.
- For the first time, made Chicago government represent the diversity of Chicago by appointing people from all neighborhoods, all ethnic groups, and all walks of life to government jobs and to boards and commissions.
- Worked cooperatively with the private sector to form the following partnerships and task forces that address Chicago's pressing needs: the Financial Planning Committee, the Chicago Housing Partnership, Partnerships in Health, Chicago Energy Savers Fund, the Mayor's Apparel and Fashion Industry Task Force, and many more.
- Created the city's first mayoral commission on Latino affairs.

Jesse Jackson, the People's Candidate: A Reply to Obafemi Senghor

Muhammad Ahmad

A. JESSE'S LEGACY

Twenty years ago, Dr. Martin Luther King, Jr., was supporting a strike for better wages/working conditions by garbage workers who were predominantly black in Memphis, Tenn. This was to be a prelude for his intended Poor People's Campaign; a campaign that intended to unite all oppressed minorities of all races with poor whites, scheduled to be held in the spring of 1968 in Washington, D.C.

From sources who were close to Dr. King, it has been passed on that Dr. King was beginning to recognize the importance of class struggle and had intended to ask the AFL-CIO to call a *general strike* in support of the Memphis workers. Of course, if this had happened, all sectors of American society would have been polarized. Not since the 1960's has an African-American leader become the focal point of American politics. Jesse Jackson, who marched, organized and struggled with Dr. King, now inherits that legacy. Some call Jesse an opportunist but when we criticize we must first start with ourselves; *what have we done to contribute to the liberation of African-Americans, not just in words but also in deeds?* Many of us who were revolutionaries in the 1960's criticized Dr. King because we were out on the "firing line" the most, suffering the most casualities and saw weakness in his strategy but still supported him because we knew he was progressive and was moving people towards a revolutionary transformation.

Much has transpired in the past twenty years during which time the conservative right wing of the capitalist ruling class waged a war of genocide against Black America.

One of the reforms won by the civil rights movement was the passage of the Voting Rights Act in 1965. In 10 years following its (VRA) passage, voter registration among African-Americans doubled. The movement for black political empowerment began to grow with the electing of black mayors in major cities numbering approximately 303; 34 of them in cities with 50,000 plus population today. Between 1974 and 1980 the number of African-Americans holding public office doubled in six southern states. In Louisiana the number of black elected officials increased by 143%; in North Carolina by 55%.

The idea of a black presidential candidate seems to have started as a symbolic protest to racial and political inequalities in the U.S. economic and political systems. The growth of the idea of a black presidential candidate evolved along with the growth and maturation of the black electorate and democratization of the political process in America. In 1960, Reverend Clennon King and Reginald Carter announced their candidacies for president and vice president on the Afro-American party ticket but the idea did not catch on. In 1964 Clifton DeBerry ran for president on the Socialist Workers Party ticket and in 1968 Charlene Mitchell ran for president for the Communist Party becoming the first black woman to run for president. Eldridge Cleaver in '68, then Minister of Information of the Black Panther Party was candidate for president of the Peace and Freedom Party. Cleaver got on the ballot in over 19 states and won nearly 200,000 votes. Dick Gregory also ran for president and received almost 150,000 votes.[1]

The motion toward electing black political officials took various organizational forms. In various communities black political conventions were held endorsing candidates. In 1970 the Congress of African People (CAP) convened to harness the motion.[2] As CAP degenerated more into cultural nationalism, the National Black Political Convention was held in Gary, Indiana. While many nationalist activists were calling for an independent black political party many veteran civil rights activists including Jesse Jackson were calling for building an anti-racist, progressive wing inside of the Democratic Party. The progressive resistance forces inside the Democratic Party have continuously challenged the racism internal to the Democratic Party and have strove to implement "Peace and Justice" issues into the Democratic Party platform.

The National Black Political Assembly (NBPA) grew out of the National Black Political Convention and raised a progressive program for black candidates to address. An idea does not take root among the masses until it corresponds with the objective experience of the masses and is grasped by them consciously seizing upon the historical time.

Congresswoman Shirley Chisholm paved the way for the forward motion of running a black presidential candidate when she ran for president in 1972 inside ten of the Democratic Party primaries.[3]

In 1976 NBPA developed a campaign 76 strategy designed to run an independent black presidential campaign. The campaign called on Rep. Ron Dellums (D-Calif.) to run for president. Dellums declined and not much came of the campaign. In 1980 several hundred activists met to form the National Black Independent Party (NBIP). As a new black political movement began to take shape in the early 1980's, many African-American political activists began to see coalition building and cross ethnic alliances as the key to winning political victories.

The coalition built in Chicago around the election of Harold Washington for mayor and bucking the racist Democratic Party was used as a model for the progressive electoral strategy.[4] The new political upsurge represents a new juncture in the black liberation movement.

The efforts to strengthen the resistance camp among Black elected officials and to forge broader alliances in the electoral process are promising developments for the progressive and working class movements more generally. They reveal the potential for the emergence of a serious left opposition within the Democratic Party, anchored firmly among Black elected officials. Such an opposition bloc is a crucial element in the long-term consolidation of a progressive coalition in the U.S. with the capacity to impact national policy.[5]

The democratization of the political process is pertinent to restructuring America because while African-Americans constitute 25% of the population in Alabama, only 5.7 of the elected officials are African-Americans. One third of Mississippians are

[1]Manning Marable, *Black American Politics* [London: Verso, 1985] pp. 248–249.

[2]"Unity and Struggle"-History of the Revolutionary Communist League (M_LM)", *Forward*, No. 3., January 1980, pp. 120–135.

[3]Hanes, Walter, Jr. *Invisible Politics* [Albany, New York: State University of New York Press, 1985] p. 93.

[4]Abdul Alkalimat and Doug Gills, "Black Power vs. Racism: Harold Washington becomes Mayor" in Rod Bush (ed), *The New Black Vote* [San Francisco: Synthesis Publications, 1984] pp. 55–179.

[5]Black Liberation Commission/Line of March, *Jesse Jackson's Challenge*, June 1984, p. 7.

African-Americans but only 7.3% of the elected officials are. In Georgia, three quarters of the counties with an African-American population of 20% or more have no African-American elected officials at all.

Between the 1980 and '84 elections, more than two million blacks were added to voter rolls; an increase of 24 percent. African-Americans', between ages 18 and 24, registration rates caught up to Anglo-Americans of the same age in 1984 and passed Anglo-Americans in 1986 (46% for blacks and 42% for whites). In 11 southern states African-Americans added 695,000 voters to the rolls between '84 and '86, while Anglo-Americans lost 227,000. Even so there are only 12 million registered African-Americans out of a potential of 19 million voters.

Historically the stage was set for the emergence of a black progressive challenge within the Democratic Party. On November 3, 1983, Jesse Jackson announced he would seek the Democratic nomination for President of the United States. The Jackson campaign came at a time when the black movement for national democratic rights was undergoing a transition. For 15 years the movement had retreated into accommodationist politics aligning itself with the liberal wing of the Democratic Party. But beginning with the August 27th March on Washington in 1983 and culminating with the election of Harold Washington in Chicago and Wilson Goode in Philadelphia, a new motion of black politics began to take shape.

Building on his base built in Operation Push and black churches, Reverend Jesse Jackson entered into an alliance with Minister Louis Farrakhan, leader of the Nation of Islam. With the charismatic speakers of the NOI and the eloquent Minister Farrakhan, the Jackson campaign was able to mobilize "the masses" of African-Americans even to overcome the neo-colonist opposition; "the toms of a new type," Andy Young of Atlanta, Coleman Young of Detroit, Wilson Goode of Philadelphia, and most of the traditional black democratic office holders who were tied to the white liberal democratic machine.

This remains exemplary, in fact, that in the 1984 presidential campaign 80–85% of all blacks voted for Jesse in the primary; he received 17% of the Asian and Latin vote in California, and 33% in New York and 20% of the overall Democratic primary vote. Even with the Farrakhan factor, which we will discuss later, Jesse won some impressive victories in '84, winning over 3.5 million popular votes and over 60 Congressional districts, 30 of them in the south, winning most of the major urban centers, north and south, taking the popular vote in the states of Louisiana, South Carolina, Mississippi, Virginia and the District of Columbia. Cesse Cackson came in fourth out of eight in New Hampshire which is 98% white, won almost 15% of the caucus votes in Vermont where less than 1,000 African-Americans live. Jesse won such places as Homestead, Pennsylvania, was endorsed by farmers in Columbia, Missouri, where farmers had to put sacks over their heads for fear of reprisal from the government. The Apache Nation in Arizona endorsed the Jackson campaign, and Jesse won every Hispanic district in New York City, even though all of the elected Hispanic leadership went with Mondale.

Jesse Jackson developed a new foreign policy of unity towards the Third World. He went to Syria and met with President Asaad and secured the release of American flyer Lt. Goodman. He went to Cuba, met with Fidel Castro and negotiated the release of political prisoners.

In February 1984 Milton Coleman, a Negro reporter released to his white colleagues that Jesse Jackson had made a racial remark about Jews referring to them as "Hymies" and New York as "Hymietown." This story broke in the Washington Post and was carried nationwide. The majority of the Jewish community made an all out attack on Jesse and Minister Louis Farrakhan of the Nation of Islam. But the white establishment press did not talk about the basis of the attack. The majority of the Jewish community (6 million) who have risen to become the richest and most powerful minority, who once were liberal and left being Zionist, supporting the state of Israel, have become conservative. This political transition of the Jewish community has occurred in the last 40 years, Jews who once were Black America's allies have in the last 20 years aligned themselves with the forces of reaction to become enemies on many occasions. Jesse, having a progressive position for the establishment of a Palestine state, is the reason for the attack.

Minister Farrakhan's defense of Jesse and his further attacks on Zionism brought a barrage of white reaction to such a point that Jesse had to sever his ties with Minister Farrakhan in order to maintain the Rainbow Coalition. During the last four years Jesse Jackson has become a people's advocate going to so many picket lines, protest marches and strikes that its too many to account for. Beginning in 1983 Jesse led the get-out-the-vote for increasing voter registration which led to 2 million new voters which in 1986 provided the margin of victory for eight Southern Democratic Senators, not one of whom received the majority of the white vote in their state. This returned the Senate to a Democratic majority. And, when the black electorate opposed the nomination of conservative Robert Bork to the U.S. Supreme Court, their political clout was felt with his defeat.

Between 1984 and 1987 Jesse helped build the Rainbow Coalition into an embryo political organization with a membership of 20,000. Jesse Jackson has become the most articulate spokesperson for a coherent alternative to Reaganism or conservative reaction. The success of Jesse's populist message has helped slow the rightward drift of the Democratic Party. Jesse entered the 1988 primary season as the "progressive" candidate who speaks for an ever-widening sector of the American population who, by virtue of their class and social status, have become victims of the Reagan counter-revolution. The Rainbow Coalition, being a progressive political organization, which is attempting to unite the entire American working class to struggle on an 'economic common ground' poses to be an open challenge to the conservative right.

The polarization of political forces and the general political drift to the right in the United States makes it necessary to intensify the struggle against racism and imperialism.

The Republican party has become the political voice of the reactionary sector of financial capital. The Republicans though they have suffered a temporary setback in the November (1986) election have set the country (the majority of white workers) to the right by espousing a conservative philosophy that has been viewed as the only alternative to maintain the American standard of living (labor benefits of imperialism); have forced the liberal-democrats on the political defensive.

The traditional east coast/mid-west liberal democrats who have been previously the left center forces are capitulating to the rising racism in sectors of the white working class and are moving the political center towards the right [the support for fiscal cuts (social services, military support of the contra's support for the imperialist attack on Nicaragua, Libya, Grenada, etc.)], and the Democratic leadership council led by Nunn, Gephart, Babbitt and Robb, also want to take the Democratic party to the right.

The United States capitalist ruling class seems to be opting to align its forces (influences, capital and power) with the ultra right (open fascistic) political groups, are fanning racisim in the white working class during the present structural crisis in order to keep it from uniting, reaching class consciousness and carrying out class warfare. The white United Front represented by its extreme nationalist wing, the KKK, Aryan Nations, Contra·De Posse and other paramilitary ultra-right groups represented a million plus Americans who are prepared to fight to bring in fascism and to be military counter-revolutionaries to stop socialism. These groups are in alliance with the legal religious ultra-right front groups, such as Moral Majority, Jerry Falwell, Pat Robertson and others who use Christianity as a cover to support the political motion (trend) towards fascism and aggressive military support of U.S. imperialism.

The social populist democrats now appear on the political stage as the new popular center forces in opposition to fascism/conservatism. The Rainbow Coalition as the progressive wing inside the Democratic party represents the most explosive politcal force to challenge the traditional democratic leadership at the next Democratic convention.

With Jesse's message of "economic violence," he has either been the front runner or the No. 2 contender in the 1988 Democratic primaries. Going against a negative image projected by a racist/conservative news media and having little money to spend for TV advertisements, Jesse Jackson's campaign in 1988 has been a historical phenomenon. Having the strongest message and less money, Jesse has won the minds and hearts of millions of Americans of all races, creeds, and strata, using the Charles Bibbs, Sr., formula of MMO—Message, Money, Organization, Jackson took 20% in the Minnesota caucus, which is about 96% white, 23% in the Maine caucus, and 27% in the Vermont primary. Jesse edged out Paul Simon and Dick Gephardt early as Albert Gore hung in until New York. To show the impact of the Jackson campaign, Jesse received 10% of the vote in Iowa (a predominantly white state). In 1984 Jesse got only 1.5% of the vote in Iowa. On Super Tuesday, Jesse Jackson won five states and finished a strong second place in 11 states. Jesse took Louisiana, Mississippi, Alabama, Georgia and Virginia. In the final count, Jesse captured 97% of the black vote and 10% of the white. Jesse placed second in most of the rest of the states including Texas, Hawaii, and other contenders' home states.

It should be noted that African-Americans comprise almost one-fourth of the Democratic vote across the South, and they make up nearly half the electorate in such Deep South states as Alabama and Mississippi.

Super Tuesday: How They Voted

With the momentum from Super Tuesday, Jesse grabbed a first place in South Carolina and Alaska and then captured second place to Paul Simon in Illinois. But the turning point in the campaign showing its potential to transforming America was Jesse Jackson's stunning victory over Michael Dukakis in the Michigan caucuses. Jesse's resounding upset gaining 55% of the vote worried the U.S. capitalist class ruling circles, its political representatives, and the Democratic party establishment. They now felt they had to do something to stop a people's democratic revolt. The Democratic party establishment began to show its racist teeth and lined into a Stop-Jackson campaign. While Gov. Michael Dukakis is the liberal bourgeoisie's candidate, Mayor Ed Koch endorsed Gore and used him as a shield to launch his racist attack on Jesse in New York. Though Dukakis won in Wisconsin, New York, Pennsylvania, Indiana, and Ohio, while Jackson won in D.C., and Califormia is up for grabs, the race is not over. In fact, the real politicking on a historical basis just begun. Jesse will go to Atlanta to the National Democratic Convention in July with more political clout than any black man or progressive has ever had in history inside of the Democratic party. Already the Jesse Jackson campaign has altered the issues Dukakis relates to. Jackson Action is setting the agenda for the entire Democratic party. Even many whites who did not vote for Jesse admit he is the best man for the job. For many of them they know they are voting against their class interests but cannot seem to help themselves because of the old racial blindspot. The Jesse Jackson campaign has pushed the entire Democratic party to the left.

Jesse will go into Atlanta with a well-organized voter base with a minimum of 1,000 delegates and more than twice the number he had in 1984. More than anything else, the Jesse Jackson campaign has set the stage for a new politics and reflects the present state of political consciousness of Black and progressive America.

B. UNDERSTANDING THE PRESENT STATE OF POLITICAL CONSCIOUSNESS OF BLACK AMERICA

In attempting to understand the underpinnings of the present political consciousness of the majority of African-Americans, one must take a sober look at the state of Black America.

Though there were gains won in voting rights and equal access to accommodations from the civil rights movement, the general overall economic condition of African-Americans has qualitatively depreciated in relation to Anglo (white) Americans. The response of the black electorate to the new black politics represented on a national scale by the Jesse Jackson campaign and the Rainbow Coalition is an attempt to affect state (government) policy domestically and internationally to basically alter that condition.

While the percentage of African-Americans earning more than $35,000 a year rose in constant dollars, from 15.7% in 1970 to 21.2% in 1986 and 8.8% African-Americans now earn more than $50,000 a year, a two-prong gap is widening between black America and white America and also between the black middle class, the black working class, and the black underclass. Three times as many African-Americans live in poverty than whites. On the average, the African-American medium income is 57% that of Anglo-Americans, a decline of about four percent since the early 70's. In 1980, 23.7% of all black families headed by persons with at least four years of college earned less than $15,000 annually, while 26.1% of householders in white families who only had four years of high school received a comparable annual salary. In 1981, 54.8% of black families had annual incomes of less than $15,000, while only 27.9 percent of white families were similarly situated. The income distrib-

ution overall of black families whose heads have completed four years of college parallels the income distribution for white families headed by high school graduates more closely than it does white families headed by college students. Add the cost of sending children to college, educational capital and the black-white gap totals where middle income whites make ten times as much as the majority of black America. While there was an increase in African-Americans obtaining professional, technical and craft positions, simultaneously unskilled labor jobs in industry have been exported to the Third World Newly Industrialized Countries (NIC's).

In 1960, 11 percent of black workers were employed in professional and technical and craft positions; by 1980 their proportion had almost doubled to 21 percent. Between 1972 and 1982 the percentage of employed blacks working in professional and technical positions increased from 8.2 to 11.8 percent. Black women professionals increased from 11 percent of all employed black women in 1972 to nearly 14 percent of the total in 1980. Approximately one-fourth of black workers employed in the public sector have federal government jobs, half work for city and county governments, and the remaining one-fourth are employed in state government. Between 1975 and 1984 African-Americans employed full-time by city government expanded from 260,254 to 302,726; and their median annual income rose from $9,342 in 1975 to $17,144 in 1984. The total number of full-time black county employees was 95,727 in 1975 and 131,793 by 1984. During that period the median annual income of black county workers grew from $8,260 to $15,004. One third (34 percent) of black male managers and half (51 percent) of black male professionals work for the government. Similarly, two-fifths (41 percent) of black female managers and two-thirds (69 percent) of black female professionals have jobs in the public sector.[4] This has gone along with a big increase generally in black public sector employment for all classes, which rose from 1.6 million in 1970 to 2.5 million in 1980. Black women clerical employment expanded from 7.5 percent of employed blacks in 1950 to 30.8 percent in 1970. The employment gains of black women are not as impressive when one considers that clerical jobs are the lowest paid of the "white collar" positions, with an annual income in 1980 of only $11,717 for full-time workers.

Though the black middle class has experienced gradual progress, the black working class which was expanding, gathering strength with 3.3 million in unions have been seriously setback with the de-industrialization of America. There are approximately 9 million African-American workers not organized (non-union). Most of these non-unionized black workers are in the south where there still is domestic industrial growth because of low wages.

> Between 1975 and 1984 alone, the Southeast gained 5.2 million jobs—a 32% rise—and it is projected that over the next thirty years, there will be another jump of 50%.[6]

Of the 12 million black workers, 6.6 million are black female workers. The de-industrialization of America is swelling the ranks of the hard-core unemployed strata of the black working class nominally called the black underclass. In 1983, 9.9 million African-Americans—approximately 36 percent of the black population—lived in poverty, the highest black poverty rate since the government began reporting data on black poverty in 1968. Of all black families headed by women, 56.7% are below the poverty level, as compared with 29.8% of similarly situated white families. Over the past couple of decades, between 1960 andf 1982, the proportion of black men not participating in the labor force rose from 7.0 percent to 28.1 percent, compared to an increase from 15.8 percent to 22.2 percent for white men.

As the civil rights movement began to falter due to the U.S. government's conspiracy (COINTELPRO-counter-intelligence program) against the black liberation movement and internal dissent over direction and who was going to lead; direct action (mass civil disobedience) as a strategy began to be replaced by the drive of black electoral politics. In the 1980's African-American activity in the electoral arena has increased. The black liberation movement being a product of history does not skip stages; though its ultimate cumulative development will be towards an revolutionary program, this has not and will not occur without the black liberation movement exhausting the bourgeois democratic process.

> . . . the current attempt to bring the poltical weight of Black America to bear in the electoral arena—and on the terrain of the Democratic Party—represents a significant maturation of the spontaneous Black liberation movement and signals a new stage in its development. And second, because the Black liberation movement stands at the intersection of the class and racial contradictions under U.S. capitalism, this new stage of development promises to have a profound impact in the decades ahead on the shape and direction of working class politics overall and in fact offers the best hope of leading a working class breakaway from the Democratic Party.[7]

This new development of political consciousness of Black America has several features; first, its base rests on the active mobilization of the African-American masses who have previously had a passive if not apathetic relation to the electoral process; second, it is evident with the Harold Washington and Jesse Jackson campaigns that an embryonic "people's" political program is beginning to formulate, one which clearly

---

[6]Gordon Dillahunt, "Key to Social Change, A Southern Strategy," *Forward Motion*, January-February 1988, Vol. 7, No. 1, p. 11.

[7]Line of March, "The New Motion in Black Politics and the Electoral Arena," *Line of March*, #15, Spring 1984, p. 11.

stands to the left of the bourgeois political spectrum, in opposition to institutionalized racism and encompassing social/political questions affecting the entire multi-national working class. Third, this new tendency in political consciousness is becoming a black insurgency inside the Democratic Party that is challenging its conservative leadership, stimulating the labor movement and pressuring the accommodationist black political uncle tom leaders.

There are now 6,625 black elected officials in the United States, representing 1.5 percent of all elective offices. There is a potential for 55,000 black elected officials. The South has 53 percent of the nation's African-American population and 63.8 percent of all black elected officials. There are 4200–4500 black elected officials in the South; 521 black elected officials in the state of Mississippi. Black elected officials increased more than 300 percent between 1970 and 1982, and their numbers have continued to grow. Black mayors have increased from 48 in 1973 to 223 in 1983; ten of eighteen largest cities in the U.S., now have black mayors—such cities as Detroit, Atlanta, Oakland, Philadelphia, Chicago, and Washington, D.C.

The institution that is the base of the drive for black elective empowerment is the black Christian Church. The church has approximately 10 million voters. As of 1984 there were 6 million black registered Democrats. There are generally 8.5 million black baptists, 3.7 million in the Pentecostal Church of God in Christ, 2 million in the AME, 1.3 million black Catholics, most of whom live in Louisiana, and others in different denominations. So to understand to a very large extent the state of political consciousness of the organized majority of black Americans; 10 million out of 19 million potential black votes and 30 million people, one has to take a serious look at the political consciousness of black ministers, the theology of liberation and how that is manifesting as political clout in the Democratic party in order to determine how it can be transformed into a politics of liberation.

C. JESSE'S MESSAGE AND THE NEW POLITICS

The workers of the world must unite because slave labor anywhere is a threat to organized labor everywhere.

One thing is clear in 1988 only one candidate, Jesse Jackson, is discussing the class, race, gender and political aspects of oppression affecting all sectors of American society. Since 1984 when Jesse Jackson's program for the Democratic party was abolition of runoff primaries, the end of the U.S. first strike option, normalization of relations with Cuba, a major cut in arms spending and support for affirmative action, Jesse has broadened his message and increased his activities as a people's advocate. In the last four years Jesse has been on almost every picket line in support of union struggles against concessions. Jesse has not only opposed the government's imperialist intervention in Grenada, the bombing of Libya, U.S. South African policy, U.S. support of the right wing in El Salvador and support of military aggression (contras) against Nicaragua but also U.S. policies in the Middle East. Jesse Jackson has called for support of the right to self determination everywhere. He says he wants to raise the minimum wage, institute comparable-worth wages for women, build affordable housing financed from pension funds and "stop drugs from coming in, stop jobs from going out." This message now hits millions of people of all races that are known as the "working poor." Fifteen percent of America is in poverty—34 million people. Of the 34 million, 23 million are white, 11 million black, Hispanic, Asian and youth. There are 9 million poor adults who work. Between 1978 and 1986, the number of poor adults age 22 to 64 who averaged 30 weeks or more of work a year rose 52 percent to include almost 7 million Americans. As of 1986, 2 million Americans worked full time throughout the year and were still poor which was an increase of more than 50 percent since 1978.

The working poor include members of households in which the wage earners who work part time or full time during the year but still have incomes below the poverty line—set now at $11,203 in annual cash income for a family of four. Most poor families in which one or more members who are white, and the majority are two-parent families.[8]

From 1981 to 1986 approximately 5 million Americans who had held their jobs for three years or more lost them through plant closings or layoffs. The increase in the working poor and the growing gap between the rich and poor is largely due to the overseas expansion of U.S. capital and the scientific and technological revolution which has underminded the status of the U.S. working class and its privileged position in the basic industries.

This new so-called industrial revolution which has been pushed by U.S. industrialists has leveled downward the living standards of the more privileged sectors of the workers to the status of the lower-paid workers, who have become more numerous with each new technological advance.

Accompanying this are plant office closings, runaway factories, out sourcing and the growth of a service sector composed of African-American, Latino, Asian and Native peoples together with women and the ever-growing displaced workers resulting from the introduction of high technology. This displacement has led to the deterioration in the position of men who did not graduate from college. In the early 1970's, a 30-year-old male college graduate earned only about 15 to 20 percent more than a 30-year-old male high school graduate. This 15 to 20 percent earnings gap held steady throughout the end of 1970. But the overseas flight of U.S. companies hurt non-college men badly. The gap between college and non-college graduates grew until it now stands at 40 percent—$26,250 for college graduates versus $17,250 for high school graduates.

High tech has reduced wages and has been used by the U.S. capitalist class to bust unions. This fact is beginning to breakout in the political arena with the Jackson candidacy.

Politics has a special place in social life, notably in economic life. Its special place is determined first, by the fact that in contrast to the other elements of the superstructure (law, art, ethics, etc.) politics most directly reflects the economics, the economic interests of classes. Second, politics reflects the main aspects of economic relations in a society, their class nature, and the character of property in the means of production. This makes it possible to regard politics not just as a reflection of economics, but as its concentrated expression.[9]

Jesse goes on to describe U.S. multi-national corporations' expansion into the Third World. Jesse says in the last seven years, 11 million new jobs were created under Reagan but six million pay $7,000 a year or less. The capitalists drove down the standard of living for workers and drove down prices for farmers. Jesse teaches Americans that "Your jobs didn't go from white to black, from male to female, from New York to South Carolina. Your jobs went to South Korea and Taiwan and South Africa and Haiti and Chile." At the same time Jesse Jackson says it is not the fault of workers in these countries that jobs went there but the U.S. multi-national corporations' and that workers in these countries should be paid equal pay of American workers and have the right to organize unions. While Jesse's program of workers' rights describe the situation, he does not call for a remedy to the problem; that is the nationalization of basic industries; the U.S. multi-national corporation with the resources going to the benefit of the working people. Though this may be an eventual program of a social

[8]*U.S. News and World Report*, Jan. 11, 1988, p. 19.

[9]Yuri Popov, *Essays in Political Economy: Imperialism and the Developing Countries.* [Moscow: Progress Publishers, 1984] p. 52.

democratic party, Jesse has given the outline for a workers' Bill of Rights.

A Rainbow Worker's Bill of Rights

Workers Have a Right to a Job: People need jobs and there are jobs which need to be done. We can build the housing, roads, bridges that we need as well as providing care for this nation's people. We can end plant closings without notice and unemployment without hope.

Workers Have a Right to a Union: All workers, including public employees, should be able to organize themselves into unions, have those unions recognized and work under a collective bargaining agreement.

Workers Have a Right to a Living Wage: People who work full-time should be able to rise out of poverty on their pay. American families need family wages. Young workers (youth) need opportunity.

Workers Have a Right to Fair Competition: International trade needs a level playing field. Recognition of the basic democratic rights of workers at home and abroad to organize, bargain collectively and to have enforced work place standards. Free labor cannot "compete" with slave labor.

Workers Have a Right to Freedom from Discrimination: Affirmative action for those locked out of better jobs. Pay equity for those locked into low wages.

Workers Have a Right to Education that Works: Basic education for basic skills. Vocational education for current jobs. Life long education for a changing economy.

Workers Have a Right to Respect: The contributions of workers, past and present, deserve a prominent place in the education of future workers. Those who give a life of labor deserve to have the companies for whom they work reinvest in their industry, in their community and in their country.

(Excerpted from a presentation by Rev. Jesse Jackson, Labor Day 1987.)

Redefine Our Relationship to the Third World

Real Security requires a new direction in policy towards the Third World based on the three principles of the Jackson doctrine.

Support and strengthen the rule of international law. The Ayatollah is wrong when he mines the waters of the Persian Gulf and threatens world trade by preventing the free navigation of international waters. But President Reagan is wrong—and loses the moral authority to challenge him—when he illegally mines the harbors in Nicaragua. Because our interests are so broad the U.S. has the most to gain in a world that respects the rule of law in international relations.

Promote self-determination and human rights. The 130 countries of the Third World have different histories, cultures and economic conditions. They necessarily will have different social and political experiments. They have the right to choose their own destiny—to find their own ways to cope with poverty, illiteracy, and political representation. We must respect that right, confident that democracy and freedom are spreading in the world. We should condition our own aid and trade benefits on their respect for democratic rights, including the protection of the right of workers to organize.

Support international economic justice and development. Growth andprospertiy in the U.S. requires raising the standard of living in the Third World, not lowering our own. We must work with Japan, West Germany, and other trade surplus countries to fund a new 'International Marshall Plan' for Third World development. By our providing capital and debt relief Third World economies will grow, their standard of living will increase, and trade with the U.S. will be revitalized creating millions of jobs for Americans.

When we seek to determine the outcome of upheaval or revolution, we expend our resources and our reputation on an impossible task. Thus we should sharply reduce our military forces designed for intervention abroad. We should cancel all new aircraft carrier task forces—saving $40 billion. We should immediately halt U.S. aid to the contras in Central America and to UNITA in Angola. We should implement full economic sanctions against South Africa while promoting the economic development of the Frontline states. We must support a comprehensive political settlement in the Middle East which benefits both Arabs and Israelis and thus ensures the long-run prosperity of all countries in the region.

Our military should not be used to prop up undemocratic governments abroad which provide a 'better' environment for multinational corporations to operate in. We should condition our foreign aid and trade benefits on other countries' respect for democratic rights, including the protection of the right of workers to organize. Slave labor anywhere is a threat to organized labor everywhere.

(Jesse Jackson campaign literature, 1988).

Issue Highlights from the Jackson Program

Workers' Bill of Rights

- The right to a job, to organize unions, to a living wage.
- Affirmative action and pay equity
- Vocational education

Civil Rights

- Affirmative action in education and employment
- Equal opportunity in access to jobs, job training and job mobility
- Enforce the Voting Rights Act
- Pass the ERA
- Pass the Lesbian/Gay Rights Bill
- Ban anti-gay discrimination in the federal government, in the military, in immigration policy

Social Welfare

- Double the federal education budget
- Fund bilingual education
- Adult literacy and education campaigns

- Restore college grants and loans
- Teen parenting services
- Eliminate hunger by increased funding and more effective programs
- Meet the nutritional needs of Native Americans and immigrants
- National health care program

Drugs

- Trade sanctions against drug-producing nations
- Block narcotic entry points
- Expand drug education and treatment programs

AIDS

- Increase funding for AIDS research and education
- Special AIDS outreach for drug users, prostitutes, prisoners and the homeless
- Increase funding for medical and social support for people with AIDS and their families
- End AIDS-related discrimination

Family Benefits

- Comprehensive national child care policy
- Minimum poverty-line benefit for needy families
- Increase funding for family planning, prenatal and maternal health care
- Restore Medicaid funding for abortion

Family Farm

- Moratoriums on family farm foreclosures
- Fair price to farmers to meet production costs
- Debt restructuring, soil conservation and affirmative action for minority farmers
- Make foreclosed acreage available at long-term, low-interest rates

Foreign Policy

- Respect international law and strengthen the U.N. and the World Court
- Respect the right of nations to determine their social systems

- Reduce U.S. forces in Europe/reduce the defense budget at least $100 billion
- Moratorium on the testing and deployment of nuclear weapons
- Adhere to the ABM treaty
- Stop the development and deployment of Star Wars
- Halt U.S. aid to Central America contras and UNITA in Angola
- Full economic sanctions against South Africa
- Support the economic development of the Frontline states
- Respect the right of the Palestinians to self-determination, including an independent state
- Respect the right of Israel to secure borders
- End the U.S. military build-up in the Persian Gulf
- Restructure the international debt
- Halt the IMF austerity programs

Jesse Jackson's populist message is setting the stage for a new "Peace and Justice" politics. Rather than concentrating on anti-communism which is reactionary "conservative" politics, the new politics centers around the real causes of the forms of oppression affecting the American people; drugs which are controlled by right wing "conservative" gangsters and politicians that prop up the capitalist system with its billions in illegal profit with laundered money, run-away corporations who set up subsidiary operations in Third World countries to control their economies through technological neo-colonialism (controlling the economy through technology produced by U.S. corporations), producing goods at phenomenally cheap wages, reducing the wages of workers in the U.S. by busting unions and selling the products back to American workers, rendering the American economy into a high tech service economy. What is happening through the scientific and technological revolution, is the capitalist class has developed a new social re-division of labor worldwide. By making the Third World the industrial base, they get profits from labor which has yet to become organized into unions and at the same time weaken organized labor (unions) in the western capitalist nations, super-exploiting the entire world. The only answer in the immediate future is to politically struggle to gain "people's" control of the corporations by writing a clause in the U.S. Constitution that every American worker has the right to a guaranteed job and adequate housing.

The political maturation of the mass of African-Americans will come through political/class struggle in the electoral arena, community and at the point of production. Much of this political maturation will develop around the struggle to advance reforms in the political system. The political radicalization of the majority of 6.6 million African-Americans who are registered Democrats will develop from political ruptures or polarizations over issues and principles that affect the historical relationship of African-Americans to the capitalist system.

Jesse Jackson and the Rainbow Coalition with its alliance with farmers, labor unions and oppressed nationalities, and the poor, poses to be the cataclysmic agent to raise advance democratic demands inside the Democratic party which may cause the rupture or polarization that will set the motion forward towards the development of a third labor/people's party. While many progressives have remained outside of the ranks of the capitalist party, many need to take the struggle inside the Democratic party to galvanize a progressive people's bloc to force the KKK and conservative racist imperialist politicians either out of the Democratic party or to a political showdown thereby impacting on the local, regional and national political arena. The progressive "Rainbow" movement inside the Democratic party (moreso than in the trade union movement as it currently exists) promises to give rise to concrete programs, forms of organization, institutions, trained cadres, leading political figures, etc., that will sooner or later split the Democratic party and propel not only the black liberation struggle but the working class and people's movement more generally toward a political expression which is truly independent of the bourgeois political parties. *The potential for the development of an independent working class party will require a protracted process of consoli-*

dation of a progressive wing in the Democratic Party and a series of polarizations with the forces of reaction over the forecoming years.

The Jackson campaign represents a new trend in politics with a comprehesive progressive agenda:

> Though Jackson's campaign is not organizationally independent of the Democratic Party, his politics do represent a serious challenge to the traditional alliances that have been at its core. In this sense Jackson's program serves as the basis for the development of a self-conscious progressive bloc, independent of the old liberal-labor power brokers, within the organizational context of the Democratic Party.[10]

Much of this new trend in politics will be acted out at the forthcoming Democratic convention and beyond.

D. THE CHALLENGE: SELF DETERMINATION AT HOME: AFTER 88 WHICH ROAD FORWARD?

Jesse has defined three basic political schools of thought in mainstream America:

> There are three such schools: conservatives who want things to stay as they are; liberals, who want to reform what is; and progressives who want to change things. Our Rainbow represents the progressive school of thought.[11]

Jesse Jackson goes on to explain that everyone who went to jail in the South during the Civil Rights Movement and who marched with Dr. King was not progressive.

Not in 40 years, since 1948 when Henry Wallace ran on the anti-racist, anti-imperialist Progressive Party ticket for President has progressive politics played a major role in the electoral arena. At the turn of the century the Socialist party became a force to be recognized electing 1,200 local officials and fielding a presidential candidate five times.[12]

With Jesse going into the Democratic convention as the No. 2 contender, historical precedence has been set. Whatever the options, if Jesse becomes a vice presidential nominee or whether he brokers for various demands and serves as a people's advocate, the struggle will be advanced.

The Jackson campaign presents the possibility for the movement for people's empowerment of combining electoral work with other forms of organizing and of electing representatives who can articulate and fight for the concerns of the poorest sectors of the black and working class community. The Jesse Jackson campaign has given rise to an embryonic poltical program which stands clearly on the left of the borugeois political spectrum; one which causes a sharp polarization with institutionalized racism, but raises other political questions as well. This motion puts the neo-colonialist, uncle-tom-of-a-new-type, Negro accommodationalist politicians on the defensive and isolates them from the masses. The motion represented by the Jackson campaign represents a new stage of political maturation for the black community. Though led by African-Americans, this new stage of development promises to have a profound impact in the decades ahead on the shape and direction of working class politics overall and in fact offers the best hope of leading a working class breakaway from the Democratic Party. It is important in this sense to see electoral politics as a crucial arena of the class struggle and a place where the poltical maturation of

---

[10]Gerald Lenoir; "The Democrats Dilemma," *Frontline*/Special Supplement, Vol. 5, No. 20, April 11, 1988.

[11]Jesse Jackson, "The Rainbow Coalition is Here to Stay," *The Black Scholar*, September/October 1984, p. 73.

[12]Sheila Collins, *The Rainbow Challenge.* [New York: Monthly Review Press, 1986] p. 303.

the working class movement also takes place. To have an ultra-left sectarian position of not taking up the struggle inside the bourgeois political arena is to isolate the progressive forces and become right-wing opportunists. With the absence of a genuine mass based-revolutionary party to represent their interests, revolutionaries need to utilize the electoral process, i.e., the Democratic party to attempt to stretch its apparatus as far as possible until there is a mass break (conscious) with the one-party capitalist system and create a working class people's party, representing the interests of the working class and other progressive strata. So the next stage of struggle legally will be to struggle through the electoral process to form a coalition government prior to socialist revolution.

The concerns of Obafemi Senghor and the 200–250 black political prisoners now incarcerated in America's prisons to demand their immediate release due to the U.S. Government's unjust war against Black America can best be addressed if it is raised in the context of the legal poltical super-structure along with the question of African-Americans' right to self determinatifon and reparations first.

The challenge after '88 for Jesse Jackson and the Rainbow Coalition is to organize the momentum of the '88 campaign whether a Democratic or Republican administration is elected. It is a protracted struggle of electing a Rainbow (progressive) government by the year 2000. Jesse and the Rainbow must also educate the hundreds of millions of Americans to the questions which will lead to a revolutionary transformation of America. Dr. King said, "White America must recognize that justice for Black people cannot be changed without radical changes in the structure of our society."

Political portional representation will be meaningless if it is not matched with economic equity. Reparations for Native Americans, Asian-Americans, who were put in concentration camps during World War II, Mexican-Americans and African-Americans

are key to rectifying economic and political injustices which are the basis to political and economic inequality today.

A decade ago James Foreman raised the question of reparations for us in light of the black experience in America. Many people reacted negatively and tried to dismiss the thought; but he was correct. We need to repair for the damage done to us because of slavery, segregation and discrimination. We need not apologize for seeking reparations. Creative justice demands reparations. If reparations are still being given to Israel by Germany for damage imposed on Jews under Hitler, and if because of an uneasy conscience America is giving $5 million a day to Israel in reparations, then reparations are justified for us. Court cases clearly show the government can be sued for reparations when it is found to be abusive.[13]

In order to make Reparations real for the masses of African-American people, tactics must go from defensive political action "fightback" to the offensive, *political revolutionary action*. Mass revolutionary action means taking the political offensive. It means agitating both within and outside of the capitalist political structure to isolate and politically overthrow, vote out of office the racist-conservative politicians and to cause a political polarization/realignment of political forces inside the U.S. Though this may occur on a limited scale at first, it would serve tremendous educational value in raisng the class consciousness of African-Americans and all workers. This can be done on the local levels by supporting the insurgent political parties, tickets, blocs, caucuses, that are anti-establishment and anti-macho. Also by uniting with the Rainbow Coalition, pushing the Rainbow to polarize the Democratic party, progressives should organize people's referendums and build a constitutional recall movement of conservative/racist politicians around their "anti-people" voting records.

[13]Rev. Jesse L. Jackson, *Straight from the Heart* [Philadelphia: Fortress Press, 1987] pp. 300–301.

This could entail convening a "democratic" people's convention, people's courts, political tribunals and civil lawsuits for genocide. From below; that is outside of the electoral capitalist poltical structure, political "reparations" demonstrations by the "army of the unemployed" who demand full employment and workers who call for a general strike could convene teachings concerning racist-conservative-imperialist politicians' "voting records"/deals/conspiracies to crush the people's movement.

Part of this broad coalition effort would be the Reparations and Self Determination Bill through petition drives demanding land and capital as partial repayment for years of genocide. This petition should be presented to the Congressional Black Caucus to be initiated in Congress as a bill. Also, on the local level each black progressive Congress person should be petitioned to present Reparations in the form of a bill. This would be to get the question before the board masses and the world as a mass issue. Also important, with continuous offensive political agitation would be political re-education and building

the independent political party to candidates who will raise the demands of self determination, Reparations for African-Americans and economic democracy. It is within this context of mass revolutionary action that African-Americans can take their demand of Reparations and Self Determination with a mass march on the United Nations and send representatives around the world calling for international support for the African-American National liberation movement.

Recent estimates state that in the next 20 years, by the year 2000, blacks, Hispanics, Native Americans, Asian-Americans, and other Third World people will make up 50 to 60 percent of the total population of the United States. African-Americans and Hispanics alone will make up 30% of the U.S. population. With the appeal to an economic common ground, the new progressive politics is paving the way towards a people's America; as Jesse says, "A people united will never be defeated.

We Will Win!

Spring, 1988

The Possibility of Possibilities

A Written Interview with Samuel R. Delany, by Joseph Beam

Joseph Beam: *I'm certain that there are many black gay male writers who write only "heterosexually." You and James Baldwin, in recent times, are the only two major writers who*

Source: Interview with Samuel R. Delany, "The Possibility of Possibilities." Copyright © 2002 by Samuel R. Delany. Reprinted by permission of Samuel R. Delaney and his agents, Henry Morrison, Inc.

have dared write about black gay men and from a black gay male perspective. What has allowed and enabled and enabled you to write as a black, openly gay man? What events precipitated that courageous choice?

Samuel R. Delany: Courage doesn't have much to do with it. Rather, I think, it's a kind of education. I don't mean school. I mean the social education you get in the world—what the Nineteenth Century called an education of the sentiments. Also, remember, my first five science fiction novels were written as "heterosexually" as any homophobe could wish. It must have been sometime in the late fifties, when I was still in my teens, that it hit me: if everybody knew that *all* of us were queer—that's the word I used, thinking about it to myself then—nobody could blackmail us any more. Today, with the Annual Gay Pride Day March, and a widely distributed gay press (and not so well-distributed books such as this one), and the Phil Donahue Show, we forget the biggest fear we used to have as gay men, in the forties and fifties, black or white, was of someone's finding out: anyone who knew you were gay, especially if they were straight, had life-and-death power over you. That person could lose you your job, get you evicted, or have you generally hounded out of town. The House Un-American Activities Committee was hunting up gays right along with Communists back in the early fifties—because we were more susceptible to blackmail, and therefore bigger security risks! Well, it went through a lot of people's minds that if it *was* all out, this awful power any straight person immediately assumed over every gay person would vanish. I don't know when or where, a few years later in the sixties, I first read this detailed clearly—it was well before Stonewall.

But the reason I can't recall the particular article is that by the time I'd read it, it was such a frequently rehearsed idea. The specific piece merely confirmed something I—and many other gay people—had thought many times.

In terms of any long-range, large-scale program, as many of us making ourselves known to as many people as possible was the only sane political alternative to end our greatest fear and oppression. And the more people who did it, the safer it would be for the rest of us. It's still not easy, but it's easier now than it was in 1960.

As a black man, I tended to straddle worlds: white and black. As a gay man, I straddled them too: straight and gay. I'd been leading a pretty active gay sexual life from the time I was seventeen. But on my second or third heterosexual experiment, I found myself on my way to being a father. So, at nineteen I got married. Although my wife was wholly aware of my sexual orientation (and we'd discussed the possibility of a then-illegal abortion), we decided to marry anyway and have the baby. And I found myself with all the privileges and pressures of a heterosexual coupling. My wife miscarried a few months later. But we stayed married for the next thirteen years—till after, indeed, we had another child.

Anyway.

My father, who died about ten months before I dropped out of City College to run off to Detroit and get myself hitched with this brilliant, eighteen-year-old Jewish poet, had owned a funeral home in Harlem. The organist who played for the services when I was a kid was a brown, round, roly-poly, irrepressibly effeminate man named Herman. It was an open secret Herman was gay. The adults in my family joked about it all the time. Herman certainly never tried to hide it—I don't know whether he could have.

Herman was very fond of me and my younger sister. From somewhere, he'd gotten the idea that I liked shad roe. (I didn't. What seven or eight year old does? But then, perhaps he was teasing. He was so flamboyant in his every phrase and gesture, there was no way to be sure.) From various trips to see one sister in Baltimore, or another in Washington, D.C., Herman would bring back large, oval tins of shad roe as a present for me. And Sundays my mother would serve it for breakfast, exhorting me to eat just a taste, and, later, on some visit, while I waited, silent and awed at her untruth, would tell Herman how much I'd *loved* it!

In August, bent nearly double, his shirt sleeves rolled up over wet, teak-colored arms, some black delivery man would push a bronze and mahogany casket on the collapsible rubber-tired catafalque slowly and step by step into the chapel, where Herman, in his navy suit and scarlet tie, was practicing. (At the actual service a black tie would replace it. But, during practice, as he put it, "Mother needs *some* color about her or things will be just *too* dreary—don't you think?") Herman would glance over, see the man, break into an organ fanfare, rise from the bench, clasp both hands to his heart, flutter them and his eyelids, roll his pupils toward heaven, and exclaim: "Oh, my smellin' salts! Get me my smellin' salts! Boy, you come in here and do that to a woman like me, lookin' like that? My heart can't take it! I may just faint right here, you pretty thing!"

If the delivery man had been through this before, he might stop, stand up over the coffin with sweat drops under his rough hair, and say: "What's a' matter with you, Herman? You one of them faggots that likes men?"

But Herman's eyes would widen in astonishment, and, drawing back, one hand to his tie, he'd declare: "Me? Oh, chile, chile, you must be ill or something!" Then he would march up, take the young man's chin in his hand, and examine his face with peering eyes. "Me? One of *them?* Why, you must have a fever, boy! I swear, you must have been workin' out in the heat too long today. I do believe you must be sick!" Here he would feel the man's forehead, then, removing his hand, look at the sweat that had come off on his own palm, touch his forefinger to his tongue, and declare: "Oh, my lord, you *are* tasty! Here," he would go on before the man could say anything, putting both his hands flat on the delivery man's chest, between the open shirt buttons, and push the shirt back off the dark arms, "let me just massage them fine, strong muscles of yours and relax you and get you all comfortable so them awful and hideous ideas about me can fly out of your head forever and ever and ever, Amen! Don't that feel good? Don't you want a nice, lovely massage to relax all them big, beautiful muscles you got? *Umm?* Boy, how did you get so strong? Now don't tell me you don't like that! That's lovely, just lovely the way it feels, isn't it? Imagine, honey! Thinkin' such nastiness like that about a woman like me! I mean, I just might faint right here, and you gonna have to carry me to a chair and fan me and bring my smellin' salts!" Meanwhile, he would be rubbing the

man's chest and arms. "*Ooooh*, that feels so good, I can hardly stand it myself!" His voice would go up real high and he'd grin. "Honey, you feelin' a little better now?"

In the chapel corner the floor fan purred, its blades a metallic haze behind circular wires. In seersucker shorts and sandals, on the first row of wooden folding chairs painted gold with maroon plush seats, I sat, watching all this.

Different men would put up with Herman's antics for different lengths of time; and the casket delivery man (or the coal man or the plumber's assistant) would finally shrug away, laughing and pulling his shirt back up: "Aw, Herman, cut it out, now . . . !" and my father, in his vest and shirt sleeves, would come from the embalming room at the chapel back, chuckling at the whole thing, followed by a smiling Freddy, Dad's chief embalmer.

I'd smile, too. Although I wasn't sure what exactly I was smiling at.

One thing I realized was that this kind of fooling around (the word "camping" I didn't hear for another half dozen years or more) was strictly masculine. It was 1948 or '49. And if my mother or another woman were present, Herman's horseplay stopped just as assuredly as would my father's occasional "goddamn," "shit," or "nigger, this" or "nigger, that." Yet the change of rhetoric did not seem, with Herman, at all the general male politeness/shyness before women as was the case with my father and his other, rougher friends. Herman was, if anything, more attentive to my mother than any of the others. And she was clearly fond of him. With her, he was always full of questions about us children and advice on paint and slipcovers, and consolation, sympathy, and humor about any of her domestic complaints (not to mention cans of shad roe, packages of flowered stationary, and bags of salt-water taffy from Atlantic City), all delivered with his balding, brown head far closer to my mother's, it seemed when they talked over coffee upstairs in the kitchen, than my father's or anyone else's ever got.

A few years later, when I was fourteen or fifteen, I remember Herman, bent over, sweating, fat, stopping in to visit Freddy or my father at the funeral parlor, walking slowly, carrying some bulging shopping bag. (He no longer played the organ for us.) I would ask him how he was, and he would shake his head and declare: "I ain't well, honey. I ain't a well woman at *all!* Pray to the Lord you never get as sick as I been most of the last year! But you lookin' just wonderful, boy! Wonderful! *Mmmm!*" And when I was seventeen or eighteen, I remember going to look at him, grown from fat to obese, squeezed into his own coffin in the back chapel—the one time he got to wear his red tie at a service, which only added to that uneasy feeling always haunting the funerals of friends that this was not real death, only practice. I also realized I had no notion what actual sexual outlets there'd been in Herman's life. Had he gone to bars? Had he gone to baths? Had he picked up people in the afternoon in Forty-Second Street moviehouses or in the evenings along the benches beside Central Park West? Once a month, did he spend a night cruising the halls in the YMCA, over on 135th Street, where, on Saturday afternoons I used to go so innocently swimming? Had there been a long-term lover, waiting for him at home, un-met by, and un-mentioned to, people like my father he worked for? Or had his encounters been confined to the touch teased by some workman; or had it even been his arm around my shoulder, his thigh against my own, when, years before, beside me on the organ bench, he'd taught me the proper fingering for the scale on the chapel console, before running to my parents to exclaim: "You *must* get that boy some piano lessons! You must! There's so much talent in his little hands, I tell you, it just breaks my heart!"—an exhortation my parents took no more seriously than they did any of his other outrageousness. (I was already studying the violin.) I had no way to know. Herman was fat and forty when, as a child, I met him. By his fifties he was dead of diabetic complications.

Herman's funeral was among the many my father was never paid for, which changed him, in Mom's mind, from a dear and amusing friend to one of the "characters" she claimed were always latching on to my father, to live off him, to drain him of money and affection, and finally to die on him.

Today, I like shad roe a lot. And, somehow, by the time I was nineteen and married, I had decided—from Herman and several other gay black men I'd seen or met—that *some* blacks were more open about being gay than many whites. My own explanation was, I suppose, that because we had less to begin with, in the end we had less to lose. Still, the openness Herman showed, as did a number of other gay men, black and white, never seemed an option for me. But I always treasured the image of Herman's outrageous and defiant freedom to say absolutely anything. . . .

Anything except, of course, I *am* queer, and I like men sexually better than women.

At the time I would have analyzed my own "lack of options" this way: I wasn't personally attracted to effeminate men. Therefore, I couldn't imagine the men I would *be* attracted to attracted in turn to someone who *was* effeminate. *Ergo*, I'd better *not* swish—not if I wanted the kind of sexual partners I thought I did, Q.E.D.*

Today, of course, my "*ergo*" looks pretty shaky. What was really going on was closer to this: I wasn't particularly attracted to effeminate men—okay, we'll take that as a given. But the second assumption was: since I was terrified someone might find out I was gay, I just assumed any male I was attracted to would be equally terrified of discovery. Therefore, no swishing for *either* of us! If nothing else, his would get me in trouble; mine would get him in trouble. And when I

Ergo means 'therefore'. Q.E.D. stands for *quod errat demonstrandum*, which means, 'thus it is proven'; this was once traditionally written at the end of mathematical proofs.

look back on it now, it's pretty hard to separate that terror of discovery from the initial sexualization of "straight looking" (whatever that is) men in the first place.

It's kind of sad, isn't it?

But, for better or worse, that's the kind of sentimental education on which what was to come was based.

The next big step came when I was about twenty-two. I'd been married for three years. I'd already published four novels, with a fifth due out soon. Then, I had a kind of breakdown and was in a city mental hospital, where I was in a ward-wide therapy group. Each of the group's eighteen patients had individual therapy once a week with Dr. Grossman. But daily, all together, we had a group session. My group had blacks, Hispanics, and whites in about equal numbers. In my individual hour, the first thing I brought up with Dr. Grossman was my homosexuality. After all, homosexuality was a "mental problem," if not a "mental illness"—at least in 1964. But in group sessions, I didn't mention it. Not talking about something like that in a therapy session seemed to me, then, a contradiction in terms. I discussed it with Dr. Grossman, who said, bless his soul, that if talking to the group about my homosexuality made me uncomfortable, he didn't feel there was any pressing need for it. But that felt wrong to me; I decided to bring it up anyway.

Was I scared? Yes!

But I was also scared not to. My breakdown had frightened me. I had no idea, at twenty-two, if group therapy in a mental hospital would help. But since I was there, it seemed idiotic to waste the therapy if it was available. Therapy to me meant talking precisely about such things.

Therefore, talk, I decided, is what I'd better do.

Most of the group didn't threaten me. One Hispanic woman was there because she'd killed her baby and had somehow ended up in the hospital, rather than in jail. One poor, pear-shaped, working class white man was obsessed with his stomach—

should he walk around with it held out (rich and successful men always seemed to do this), or should he hold it in (because sometimes that's what it seemed they did)? While he was there, he never did quite get that his problem *was* his problem—rather than his inability to resolve it. His earliest memory, he told us, was of his father bloodying his mother's nose with a punch, while she clutched him, as an infant, in her arms and the blood gushed down over him. And there was an elderly Jewish woman who had flipped out, apparently, when her 86-year-old and terminally-ill mother had committed suicide in the Park Avenue apartment downstairs from hers. She's been placed in the hospital by her husband, to be "cured" by the time his vacation came around. And, indeed, the day the vacation began, he sumarily removed her from the hospital, over the protests of the doctors. I remember she left us, on her husband's arm, babbling on about how of course she was better, she had to be better, it was time to go on vacation, and, yes, she was really much better now, she felt perfectly fine, oh, she'd be just wonderful, she'd be really fine once they got started on the drive to Colorado, everything would be wonderful, they'd have a wonderful time, he'd see how much better she was—then she'd bite viciously at the lace-rimmed handkerchief pulled tight around her fore-knuckle, and try to squeeze back the tears, grinding her teeth loud enough for us to hear across the lobby, while her white-haired, pin-striped husband tugged her, stumbling, toward the glass doors and the waiting car outside. Also in the group was an older, white-haired man, named Joe, who, from his demeanor, manicure, and sweaters, I just assumed was gay, though he'd mentioned it in group session no more than I had. There was also a black twenty-year old named Beverly. Endless arguments and fights between her mother and a succession of her mother's lovers had finally driven her to live on her apartment house roof—which is where she'd been found before she had been brought into Mt. Sinai. In all the non-therapy programs, Beverly presented herself as a ballsy black dyke. But, with the same people, during the group session she withdrew into paralyzed silence, though she claimed to have no problems talking to Dr. Grossman in her weekly individual hour; although his presence, along with slightly more formal seating arrangement, was the only difference in the gathering she'd seemed so comfortable with minutes before the official therapy hour, or, indeed, minutes afterwards.

Next to these guys, I guess, I just felt pretty sane.

My fear of talking about my own homosexuality, however, centered on one patient. Call him Hank.

Hank was white, about my age, and a pretty aggressive fellow. Once a young woman patient had become hysterical because she didn't want to take some medication. Nurses, orderlies, and a resident had physically restrained her to give her an injection—when Hank had rushed up at her screams and started punching, putting a very surprised psychiatric resident on the floor. His own problem, as I recall, was something wrong with his feet. They were perpetually sore, and it was sometimes painful for him to walk. Nothing physical had been found wrong with them, and he'd been transferred to the mental ward for observation on the chance his ailment was psychosomatic. Aside from occasional moments of belligerence, he was a pretty affable guy. I rather liked him and, I guess, wanted him to like me. But his affability also included the odd "faggot" joke, which left me dubious over talking with him about being gay, even in "group."

Nevertheless, I'd made up my mind.

So, Monday morning, when the eighteen of us were seated around on our aluminum folding chairs, I launched in: as I recall, it was the most abject of confessions. I explained the whole thing, looking fixedly at the white and black floor tile. I had this problem—I was homosexual, but I was really "working on it." I was sure that, with

help, I could "get better." I went on and on like this for about five minutes, and finally glanced up at Hank—whom I'd been afraid to look at since I'd started, and for whom, in a kind of negative way, the whole performance was geared.

And I saw something:

First, he wasn't paying much attention. He was squiggling around in his chair. And you could tell: his feet hurt him a *whole* lot. Now I explained that I'd really been most worried about *his* reaction—to which, as I recall, he was kind of surprised. He looked up at me, a little bemused, and said that homosexuality was just something that, Gee, he didn't know too much about.

Joe, I remember, made a measured comment during one of the silences in the discussion that followed:

"I've had sexual experiences with men before," he began. Maybe this is just something you're going through, Chip. I mean you're married—comparatively happily, I gather—and you say you don't have any sexual problems there. Perhaps it's just something you're trying out. Soon it'll be behind you. And it won't worry you any more."

"No," I said. "No, I don't think so. First off, I've been going through it ever since I was a kid. And, second, I don't want it to stop. I like it too much. But . . . "

Which returned us to that unanswerable silence that seemed, if anything, more and more the heart of my "therapeutic" confession.

Hank's only real comment came about an hour later, when most of us from group were now in another room, making our potholders or picture frames. Hank suddenly turned to Joe (in his lavender angora sweater) and baldly announced, "Now, you see I figured *you* were that way—" while Joe raised a silvery eyebrow in a refined Caucasian version of Herman's grandly black and preposterous protest so many years before.

It was lost on Hank. "But you?" He turned to me. "Now that really surprised me. I just never would have figured that for somebody like you. That's real strange."

I don't know about Joe; but that was when I made the connection with that all-but-forgotten article; I began to suspect that perhaps the "therapeutic" value of my confession, after all, may not have been psychological so much as sociological. Certainly Hank wasn't any *less* friendly to me after that, as we continued through lunch and the various occupational sessions for the rest of the day. But he didn't tell any more "faggot" jokes—not when Joe or I was around.

The most important part of the lesson resolved for me that night however, while I was lying in bed, thinking over the day:

Thanks to my unfounded fear of Hank's anger (the guy—like most of the world—just had too many problems of his own), I'd talked like someone miserable, troubled, and sick over being gay; and that just wasn't who I was. On the contrary, my actual feeling was that, despite my marriage, the gay aspects of my life, from the social to the sexual, were the most educational, the most supportive, the most creative, and the most opening parts of my life. Being gay had meant everything to me from the fact that I knew I could survive on my own fairly comfortably in just about any medium-sized or large American city, to an exposure to aspects of art, theater, and literature I simply never would have gotten had I been straight. Where had all the things I'd said that morning come from?

I began to understand where they'd come from that night. They'd come from a book by the infamous Dr. Burgler I had read as a teenager that had explained how homosexuals were psychically retarded. They came from an appendix to a book by another psychologist that told how homosexuals were all alcoholics who committed suicide. They had come from the section on "Inversion" by Havelock Ellis in *Psychopathia Sexualis* that I'd also read; some of it had come from Vidal's *The City and the Pillar* and some from Andre Tellier's *The Twilight Men*. Some of it had come from the pathos of Theodore Sturgeon's science fiction story "The World Well Lost" and his Western story, "Scars." And

some had come from Cocteau's *The White Paper* and some came from Gide's *Corydon*. Some, even, had come from Baldwin's *Giovanni's Room*.

When you talk about something openly for the first time—and that, certainly, was the first time I'd talked to a public *group* about being gay—for better or worse you use the public language you've been given. It's only later, alone in the night, that maybe, if you're a writer, you ask yourself how closely that language reflects your experience. And that night I realized my experience had been betrayed.

For all their "faggot" jokes, the Hanks of this world just weren't *interested* in my abjection and my apologies, one way or the other. They'd been a waste of time. They only wounded my soul—and had misinformed anyone who'd actually bothered to listen.

I thought about Herman. I thought about any number of other gay men, black and white, some friends, some casual sex partners among the many, many hundred's I'd had over the last six years since I was seventeen. I also thought about Baldwin and Vidal and Gide and Cocteau and Tellier again. They, at least, *had* talked about it. And however full of death and darkness their accounts had been, they'd at least essayed a certain personal honesty. And the thing about honesty is that all of ours is different. Maybe I just had to try my own.

The next day, at the hospital, it happened that I was to be interviewed by a bunch of medical students and interns interested in going into psychiatry. While the white-smocked students listened and took notes, the chief psychiatrist, an iron-haired, balding man in his late forties, asked the questions.

The whole effect was very different from the one of the day before.

I explained to them that I was a writer, I was black, I was homosexual, I was married, I was twenty-two, and I had published four novels—but whatever problems I had, they didn't *seem* to lie in the sexual area. While I was talking, I felt pretty self-assured, and probably sounded it—I remember wondering, vaguely, if that made me sound to them even *more* disturbed; but since it was the truth, it was their problem, not mine. And I talked, of course, about what I thought to be the actual pressures that had contributed to my breakdown. The questioning psychiatrist's tongue kept slipping and he would accidently call me "Dr. Delany . . ." The students would laugh, and, embarrassed, he would correct himself and call me "Mr." for a while, till his tongue slipped again. And again they'd laugh.

Later, to my therapy group, I even explained what I felt had happened with my "confession"—how I'd needlessly and inaccurately presented myself so much as a victim, in order not to offend them and to assuage their (i.e., Hank's) imagined anger.

Straight, white Hank wasn't much more interested in *that* than he'd been in the original confession!

A few days later the suicide of another patient (Deirdre was not in our group; still, some of us had known her: she was the woman Hank had tried to defend from the doctors who'd been trying to force medication on her) shifted us all into another mode. Deirdre had been eighteen; she was pregnant by another patient, and suffered from grueling headaches. Another victim of the law then in place against abortions, she had not been able to get the doctors to authorize a therapeutic abortion for her: she was too "unstable," they claimed, for such a "psychologically difficult" operation—though she had wanted one desperately. Refused one once again, she had hung herself in the third-floor bathroom with a towel from the shower-curtain pole.

Her death broke up a number of people in our group, especially Hank and Beverly.

A week later, I was released from the program.

Maybe six weeks after that, I was crossing Cooper Square.

At Astor Place, when I heard someone call: "Hey! Hello!" I looked back, to recognize Hank, waving at me with a Great grin and hobbling forward.

"Guess what!" was the first thing he said to me. "It's physical, Chip! They finally found some goddamned pinched nerve, which is why my feet hurt me all the time! So I'm not crazy after all! Isn't that great? Can you imagine, after all that, it turns out to be *physical?*"

"That's great!" I said.

He was a very happy young man, very happy to be telling me about it; and I was, indeed, happy for him.

Well, it was my next novel that I decided I wanted to base at least some sections of it on some of my real experiences. In this case, it was in the middle of a very satisfying triple relationship with my wife and another man, where we all lived quite pleasantly together and slept—quite actively—in the same bed. It's not in the foreground of the book.* It's just used as a kind of decoration. But I wonder if it's an accident that *that's* the first of my SF novels anyone paid any real attention to, when it appeared, a year or so later.

JB: *Poet Sonia Sanchez writes from midnight to 3 a.m., after her twin sons have gone to sleep; and novelist Maya Angelou rents a hotel room where she writes from 7 a.m. until 2 p.m. How do you fit writing into your life?*

SRD: Back there in my twenties, I used to keep to Lord Byron's romantic schedule. You know: rise at one in the afternoon, socialize till five, dine till nine, then start to work and continue writing all through the night, till dawn paled in the eastern window—then I'd crash . . . starting all over again next afternoon. It didn't do Byron much good either—he was dead at thirty-six. About a dozen years back, however, I became a parent: that pretty much foxed the sybaritic routine. For maybe half the time since, I've been a one-parent family. So for the past dozen years, it's been up at four or five in the morning and work till one or two in the afternoon—with an hour out to get my kid to school. Then, once she comes home, it's on to corre-

---

*Babel=17 (Ace Books, 1966), by Samuel R. Delany, Vintage Books, New York: 2002.

spondence, essays, interviews and the like (generally things that can be interrupted by homework and the real world). Somewhere in the middle of it, I cook dinner.

And I'm in bed by 9:30.

It sounds more organized than it is. But it's the only way to get anything done if you have a kid, unless you have a wife (of whatever sex) and/or servants. And I don't have or want either.

JB: Poet Judy Grahn, in her recent book, *Another Mother Tongue: Gay Worlds, Gay Words* speaks of gay and lesbian people as society's visionaries and seers. She maintains that gay people have been present in most cultures and have often fulfilled respected, honorable functions such as village magicians, tribal shamans, and medicine women. As a creator of futuristic cultures and worlds, a visionary by literal definition, what is your personal vision?

SRD: I don't have *a* personal vision. I have any number, many of them quite contradictory. I distrust people with only one—especially if it's too complete, and they want to thrust everyone else into it.

Some of my very fragmentary and incomplete visions are quite bleak and scary. There's room for those too, you know.

Others are optimistic as hell.

When, in a science fiction story, one or another of my vision's is doing its job best, then it's engaging in heated dialogue with *your* visions, which I assume are just as plural, fragmentary, and alive as mine. The way to start that dialogue is, of course, by reading some of my SF stories or SF novels and letting them engage you.

Now if you just mean how would I like to see life improved—well, that doesn't require anything so grandiose as a "vision."

There's lots of small, local problems I'd like to see remedied by the application of some local institutional and collective energy.

I think it's a societal flaw when social forces nudge gay people toward a single (or limited group of) social function(s). And it doesn't matter whether that social function is that of the medicine woman in one society, or that of the hairdresser in another, or that of the prostitute in a third. No matter how great an individual's contribution is in any of these fields, if the choice for gay people is conceived of as singularly limited by the general populus, then none of the three societies provide real freedom.

And that's what we should be talking about, no?

In a recent sword and sorcery tale of mine, there's a gay male character who, for a while, works as a leather tanner in the particular society he lives in. Halfway through the story, you learn that, in his culture, the tanning industry is almost wholly gay: everyone knows that leather tanners are "that way," and, indeed, in that society, many of them are. I hope my readers—gay and straight—will, first, recognize the syndrome involved. At the same time I hope that, because of the distance the fantasy setting provides, they get at least an inkling of how wasteful, oppressive, and arbitrary it is to have all gays herded toward any one (or any one kind of) profession.

The dialogue of multiple, partial, plural visions is great political training—training for that most difficult of political tasks: dealing with new problems in practical terms when they come along. But the training comes from considering one vision, *then* another. It comes from going back and forth *between* visions, from ferreting out the parts that are coherent, from recognizing the parts that are contradictory, and locating the parts that are incomplete as one vision highlights another. That's what's really valuable—far more so than the content of any single one.

Writing about the uses of criticism, T. S. Eliot says somewhere: "About someone so great as Shakespeare, it is probable that we can never be right; and if we can never be right, it is better that we should from time to time change our way of being wrong." Well, the world is even more complicated than Shakespeare. Individual personal visions of the best way to organize the future—whether Marx's, Jefferson's, Fourier's, or

Spengler's—just aren't going to *be* entirely right. Therefore the needed talent is to be able to move from vision to vision, to get the little benefits that fall out of each.

There's a simple fact we science fiction writers know a bit better than anyone else: You really *can't* predict what the world will be like in five or fifty years. If any individual science fiction story happens to coincide, in part, with something that comes to pass, it's a scatter-shot effect: with *all* the various SF visions of the future, one or another *will* turn out correct—at least if you look at it with the proper squint. But nobody's going to know which one till after the fact.

The visionaries' job is, I think, to provide mental practice in dealing with a whole *range* of different situations (at least the SF visionaries')—situations different from what we have now *and* different from one another.

But in the same way that courage is a small part of writing about your own life situations honestly (when compared to the obvious social disasters that accrue to writing about them dishonestly or not writing about them at all), single, prophetic visions are a very small part of writing about the future—compared to the social gain in mental flexibility that comes from contemplating a range of possible futures in a real world where the future is as unpredictable as ours.

JB: *You've known Harlem Renaissance artist-writer Bruce Nugent since you were about 17. Will you talk about your friendship with him?*

SRD: Well, Bruce was born in 1905, and I wasn't born till 1942. When I met him in '58 or '59, he was already a man in his fifties. We met at the West End Avenue apartment of some friends of mine, Bernard and Iva Kay. Bernie and Bruce had been friends since they were, respectively, nineteen and twenty-three. Bernie had prepared me for the meeting by showing me some of Bruce's privately printed and beautifully illustrated pamphlets. That spring or summer afternoon, while I was sitting around in the living room, and Bruce dropped over, I remember him as a tall, coffee-complected

black man, with an extraordinarily delicate voice, which moved from gentle humor to an equally gentle intensity, over just about everything he talked of. Bruce had spent some time in Italy, living in Florence and Rome. He spoke Italian, and was enamoured of (almost) all things Italianate. Bernie had spent some time living off Puerto Rico, near Ponce, and was equally enamoured of things Hispanic. Years later, when Bernie was running a translation bureau, Bruce worked there doing the Italian translations, and when I would drop into the Forty-second Street offices to say hello, they would be at their respective desks, working away at those appalling international business letters—usually about machine parts, invoices, or die castings.

About four years ago, Bruce was honored with a symposium at the home of some Harlem Renaissance scholars, here in New York at the Hatch-Billops Collection, in an industrial part of the city. After the reception, Bruce was interviewed, in the long, narrow, semi-loft apartment that houses that famous library of African-American drama and art, one 75-foot wall lined with books, while a lot of his old and new friends sat around and, when the interview opened up to questions, also asked questions and gave their own comments and reminiscences.

Bernie was ill with lung cancer, but he insisted on going. So I and my lover drove him down; it was a wonderful afternoon, and for the first time I saw actual copies of *Fire* and other Harlem Renaissance publications. But at one point early in the interview, Bruce told the man with the recording microphone: "You really should be interviewing Bernie, there. We've been friends since we were *children!* He knows much more about me than *I* do!" Bernie had a spectacular memory for anecdotes. (I have about twenty hours of his reminiscences on tape. Bruce may have been right.) At one point in the symposium Bernie told us about Bruce's giving his shoes away to a cold and barefoot black man one winter night in the twenties, then walking barefoot in the snow to get another pair from Bernie—and I realized this was the incredible kind and heroically sensitive black artist that I had known, however slightly, for the past twenty-five years. (White American writers seldom *have* to give their shoes away to their fellows.) Bernie also used to say that for every piece of writing or work of art by Bruce that survived, five or ten had been lost or given to people who would probably do little or nothing to preserve them.

Bruce of course was sixty back in 1965. And it was very easy to see the gay activism of the late sixties and the early seventies as leaving men like Bruce (and Bernie) behind. A number of times I heard Bruce say, in passing, "I just don't see why everyone has to be labeled. I just don't think words like homosexual—or gay—*do* anything for anybody." And I would hold my counsel and rack it up to age. But later, when young historians, like David Lewis, Robert Hemingway, Eric Garber and half a dozen others discovered what a treasure of information and insight Bruce was (you run into his name today as a research source in practically every work on the Harlem Renaissance that gets published), it was astonishing—and warming—to watch him catch up; and, indeed, to be able to provide first-hand historical insight into what *is* going on today thanks to his astute observations on what was going on thirty to fifty and sixty years back.

I last saw Bruce at Bernie's memorial service, three years ago. We arrived early and had coffee together at the Olympia Coffee Shop around on Broadway. After the service, when actor Earl Hymen's beautiful eulogy was over (though Bernie was a white New Englander with impeccable religious connections in New Hampshire, two of his three eulogists were black, and over half the mourners at the memorial service were black or Hispanic), I walked with Bruce from the church, while he cried openly and unabashedly for his dead friend. Since then, I've spoken to him a few times on the phone.

But, sadly, I haven't made the trip over to Hoboken to see him.

JB: *In your interview with Christopher Casper, which appeared in Donald Keller's In-scape (Seattle, 1983), you speak of "the possibility of possibilities." Often, as black men, the only dreams we are permitted to pursue are those of the athletic star, entertainer, or lotto winner. Will you elaborate on this notion?*

SRD: In that interview I said that the possibility of possibilities is what we had to teach our people. The fact that, in large part, we don't is something I remember my father complaining about at least as far back as when I was ten years old.

But for all my father's complaints, for all mine, the black kid on the street today just doesn't know about black scientists and inventors like Benjamim Banneker, Ernest E. Just—or, today, even George Washington Carver, with his peanuts and nectarines. They don't know about black Captain Hugh Mulzac; maybe one out of twenty knows the first man killed in the American Revolution was a black man, Crispus Attucks; but do one out of a hundred know the first man to reach the North Pole was a black explorer, Matthew Henson—part of Admiral Peary's discovery expedition? I mean, it was only two weeks ago *I* first learned that black opera singer Leontyne Price's brother was *General* Price—and I'm supposed to be more or less informed! I suppose you have to put things like that in some perspective: what is it? Six out of ten Americans don't know for sure the name of the President of the United States? But the fact is, white people can afford to be that stupid. *We* can't. When we are, we pay far more heavily.

A point I made in the interview you cited, and that I'd like to make again: a simple *list* of black achievments and black achievers won't do it. What's necessary is some understanding of how they relate to each other. When I was eight my parents, as did the parents of how many other Harlem children, took me to *meet* Mr. Henson, the great North Pole explorer. A small, frail, brown old man, not unlike my mother's gentle father, Mr. Henson lived with his daughter in the Dunbar Houses. Standing before his armchair, with my hands folded in front of me, while the sunlight from the venetian blinds made bars over the taupe wall, I asked, very tentatively, what the North Pole had been like. He smiled at me over his pipe and said, "Well, it was *very* cold." But my parents wanted me to know that the man who had first set foot on the North Pole was black, was real, and lived in Harlem like I did . . . and they hoped, as did a lot of other black parents who took their children to meet him, that I just might make the mental leap: Therefore, *I* can do something memorable in the world, too. That goes double for, say, a list of black gay male achievers. Lists alone are very ephemeral. Over the years names drop off them with appalling frequency. Only a clear understanding of relationships and real historical processes, events, and influences can hold them in their right constellations with any permanency.

That's why it's such a joy to see the burgeoning of interest, research, and scholarship in that wonderful period of black writing, the Harlem Renaissance—a good number of whose writers were gay as well.

JB: *If you had one minute in which to address (via satellite, phone lines, computer terminals, etc.) the entire world, what would you say?*

SRD: Understand, you're talking to a guy who deeply distrusts that sort of totalizing gesture. To me, the question falls in with, "What are the ten greatest novels in the world?" or "What's the greatest minute of symphonic music ever written?" To do anything but laugh at such questions is simply to betray one's vast naivete about the range and complexity of excellences available in the field one is presuming to judge.

The fact is, even if all practical translation problems were solved, I don't think there *is* anything to say in one minute that everyone in the world would understand—if only because of the huge societal differences that make up our world—differences that are, themselves, constitutive of world society; there's certainly not much you could say in a minute that would *change* things. *Your* question betrays, I suspect, a somewhat naive vision of the world as much smaller (and much more homogenized) than it could possibly be—a vision that *one* of my "personal" visions, as you'll find it in some of my recent science fiction, is specifically and heartedly in contest with. I think it's important to have both images—so the argument can occur.

Still, that doesn't stop me from believing one side's right and one side's wrong.

Look, I don't even know what I'd want to say to all the gay black males in the very small United States of America. Let me see. How about, "There're maybe a couple of million of us, and we have a tough row to hoe, brother. But don't let the bastards get you down"? Somehow, I don't think that's saying anything most of us don't know already. And as far as everybody in the whole, very wide *world* . . . ?

I'd rather trade my "minute with the world" for, say, half an hour with the people currently heading the Times Square redevelopment and rehabilitation program.*

For some time now that historic strip of sleazy entertainments has been slated for demolition. Office towers will replace most of the movie houses and sex shops. Much of what's left will be squeezed into a mall at one end—and a *very* few of the theaters are supposed to be renovated! This week's *Village Voice* has a cover story explaining that there's as much corruption, tax favoring, and general mismanagement in this urban project as there usually is in any such— maybe a little more.

The victims the article cites are the usual: the elderly, the black, the Hispanic, and the young. Delaying suits have been filed. But nowhere does the article even mention that this area has traditionally been a center for *much*, to put it mildly, of New York City's

---

*Fourteen years after this interview, in 1999 Delany published *Times Square Red, Times Square Blue* (New York University Press), which addresses the problems of the Times Square make-over that closed out the century.

homosexual activity. And much of that activity is among black and brown working-class gay men. Indeed, in the area slated for demolition and replacement by offices stands one of the city's most established black gay bars: Blue's. The neighborhood hosts a half a dozen other gay bars with a larger or smaller black and Hispanic presence, from Trix and Hombres, to La Fiesta, Cats, and Dirty Edna's. As well there are more than half a dozen movie houses, both pornographic and legitimate, which serve as meeting places for gay men. If I *were* given that half an hour, I'd need to do about two or three weeks' research before I got what I wanted to say together. But you can be sure there's something to *be* said there. And I think it might have a better chance of doing some good than a minute-long world-wide homily.

But I really believe the answer to a better world is lots of local groups putting out lots of local energy into solving the immediate local problems by which oppression manifests itself. (A political program that doesn't start by dealing with your problems and my problems in the particular part of the world *we* live in, here an now, is no political program for you and me!) Only then will the solutions link up, support, and stabilize larger patterns of liberation. That we inhabit a country in which, for all its murderously real problems, this is a feasible vision is a great privilege . . . especially when you envision it in world terms.

New York, 1985

African American Women in Defense of Ourselves

As women of African descent, we are deeply troubled by the recent nomination, confirmation and seating of Clarence Thomas as an Associate Justice of the U.S. Supreme Court. We know that the presence of Clarence Thomas on the Court will be continually used to divert attention from historic struggles for social justice through suggestions that the presence of a Black man on the Supreme Court constitutes an assurance that the rights of African Americans will be protected. Clarence Thomas' public record is ample evidence this will not be true. Further, the consolidation of a conservative majority on the Supreme Court seriously endangers the rights of all women, poor and working class people and the elderly. The seating of Clarence Thomas is an affront not only to

African American women and men, but to all people concerned with social justice.

We are particularly outraged by the racist and sexist treatment of Professor Anita Hill, an African American woman who was maligned and castigated for daring to speak publicly of her own experience of sexual abuse. The malicious defamation of Professor Hill insulted all women of African descent and sent a dangerous message to any woman who might contemplate a sexual harassment complaint.

We speak here because we recognize that the media are now portraying the Black community as prepared to tolerate both the dismantling of affirmative action and the evil of sexual harassment in order to have any Black man on the Supreme Court. We want to make clear that the media have ignored or distorted many African American voices. We will not be silenced.

Many have erroneously portrayed the allegations against Clarence Thomas as an

Source: "African American Women in Defense of Ourselves." *New York Times,* November 17, 1991.

issue of either gender or race. As women of African descent, we understand sexual harassment as both. We further understand that Clarence Thomas outrageously manipulated the legacy of lynching in order to shelter himself from Anita Hill's allegations. To deflect attention away from the reality of sexual abuse in African American women's lives, he trivialized and misrepresented this painful part of African American people's history. This country, which has a long legacy of racism and sexism, has never taken the sexual abuse of Black women seriously. Throughout U.S. history Black women have been sexually stereotyped as immoral, insatiable, perverse: the initiators in all sexual contacts—abusive or otherwise. The common assumption in legal proceedings as well as in the larger society has been that Black women cannot be raped or otherwise sexually abused. As Anita Hill's experience demonstrates, Black women who speak of these matters are not likely to be believed.

In 1991, we cannot tolerate this type of dismissal of any one Black woman's experience or this attack upon our collective character without protest, outrage, and resistance.

As women of African descent, we express our vehement opposition to the policies represented by the placement of Clarence Thomas on the Supreme Court. The Bush administration, having obstructed the passage of civil rights legislation, impeded the extension of unemployment compensation, cut student aid and dismantled social welfare programs, has continually demonstrated that it is not operating in our best interests. Nor is this appointee. We pledge ourselves to continue to speak out in defense of one another, in defense of the African American community and against those who are hostile to social justice no matter what color they are. No one will speak for us but ourselves.

This ad represents a grassroots initiative of the 1603 women of African descent whose names appear herein. We also thank the hundreds of people of conscience—women and men of differing racial and ethnic backgrounds—who have contributed to make our statement possible. We welcome contributions to help defray the cost of this ad and similar ads in African American newspapers. We would also like to hear from those interested in establishing a progressive network among women of African descent so that we may more effectively make our voices heard in the future. To send contributions or communications, write African American Women In Defense of Ourselves, 317 S. Division St., Suite 199, Ann Arbor, Michigan 48104; or phone our Chicago voice mailbox (312) 918-2702.

The Hip Hop Vision: Password: Nation Conscious Rap

James G. Spady

Source: James G. Spady, "Hip Hop Vision: Password: Nation Conscious Rap." In *Nation Conscious Rap*, pp. 401–415, © 1991. Used by permission of James G. Spady.

"The Black world has changed so dramatically since before World War II that it would be impossible for a youth coming up today to have the same view of the world and himself which his father had. In the turbulent cities of America, the rhythm of life is quicker and more varied, and complex for the masses. Life becomes a game in which one has to learn at an early age to be flexible, to scheme and hustle if he is to survive . . .

It is clear that the black nation today is in a state of profound flux. The collective conscience of the people is being shaken to the very core of its being, thereby causing black music and black culture to take off into so many different directions. The pathos, violence, and disorder involved in this period of severe cultural and social disruption are often shocking to older generation Negroes."

—Peter Labrie, "The New Breed"

Rap music is an externalization of highly charged inner feelings shared commonly by young black people. It is the cultural manifestation of this epoch in the pristine history of Black people. It is both old and new, old because it is one with the black man's existence; new, because it is fresh and contemporary. There is an inner need to express something new and exciting, outrageous and engaging. Exuberant, bright, charismatic and endothermic, it is capable of both producing and absorbing heat. This is indicative of its *dynamic* power.

When Chuck D. employed young bloods, "Don't Believe The Hype," he was functioning both diacritically and dialectically. By diacritical we mean superior ability to distinguish or discern. In other words this generation is one of keen insight, capable of cutting through a lot of the hype. Why do we say aspects of rap music are dialectical? Is it not marked by an inner tension, conflict and interconnectedness of varied elements? Who could argue against the rappers' ability to use language as a weapon against the turbulence engulfing their lives.

Their are many cogent, philosophical principles underlying the music now called rap. Yet, little attention has been given to an examination of that growing body of rappers who are in the forefront of Nation Conscious Rap.

The poet, dramatist, literary and music critic, Larry Neal, rightly asserted: "The black artist must link his work to the struggle for his liberation and the liberation of his brothers and sisters. But, he will have executed an essential aspect of his role if he makes even a small gesture in the manner outlined. He will be furthering the psychological liberation of his people, without which, no change is even possible.

The artist and the political activist are one. They are both shapers of the future reality. Both understand and manipulate the collective myths of the race. Both are warriors, priests, lovers and destroyers. For the first violence will be internal . . . the destruction of a weak spiritual self for a more perfect self. But it will be a necessary violence. It is the only thing that will destroy the double consciousness, the tension that is in the souls of black folk."

Writing in the Password to his landmark anthology, *Black Fire,* Larry Neal captures the essence of that long term relationship between the artist and political activist. He moved in on the righteous tip, "and Shine Swam on." Fully conversant with Afro-American urban toasts, Neal rightly draws upon the pristine mythology of Black America to explore and explode the tension that is in the souls of black folk. That was twenty years ago.

The 1990's signal flack, space is cleared for the new Jack: "My mission, to sum it up, is to teach young people that there is a way out by coming into a knowledge of themselves. Once they come into a knowledge of who they really are theologically, biologically, that they are the first . . . I want to ask you a question. Who was the first man to walk on the moon? Neil Armstrong. Who was the second? Nobody ever remembers the second. See, they always remember the first. If the Black Man was the original man, the maker, the owner, the cream of the planet Earth then that tells you that everything he's doing is according to God's will. We invented every other living being. Without Black you couldn't have no other color. So I look at all of those actual facts and say that it's important for the young minds to get acquainted with themselves. The best knowledge is self knowledge, and once they get acquainted with themselves then they won't have to worry about selling drugs, they won't have to worry about working for the Caucasian for a living."

That is the voice of a Nation Conscious Rapper from Chicago; Prince Akeem. Here is a 22 year old black man who knows that knowledge of self is the beginning of coherence. Is it not why he emphasizes the levels of congruence between the origins of man and the prescience of the African? Anthropologists, archaeologists, biologists, geneticists, and historians now agree that the earliest evidence of man and woman is found in Africa. Therefore they are considered the mothers and fathers of civilization. Prince Akeem further argues teleologically i.e. that divine Providence is pertinent to the outcome of Blacks. It is his belief that the will of God is supreme. Therefore he sees his own mission as quite clear.

"My name is Akeem. Akeem means strong and independent young warrior. I've always been alone. I don't rely on nothing but God. I will fight anybody. I've been a fighter all of my life. I'm just saying this with deep sincerity. I'm a lover of my people. Why not? I'm Black. I'm not just a Muslim. See our problem as a people is this. When you say Muslim then they expect you to wear turbans and all of that stuff. If you want to learn martial arts, then you want to be Chinese when you're black. It's not like that. Kung Fu is an Arabic name. It was a black man that originated that, and we don't want to look into that. A lot of people tell me to shutup, because I have something to say. I don't plan on rapping too long. Can I tell you something? Deeply, deep inside Allah is channeling my mind." Many of the younger rap artists are not aware of the strong tradition of powerful black and muslim artistry prior to the emergence of Nation Conscious. What a creative source to tap into.

HIP HOP'S POWER, CONSCIOUSNESS AND VISION

The power and consciousness of the Hip Hop movement flow through the circle of leadership they offer to the current generation. It is imperative that we recognize that it is not coincidental that this cultural movement explodes after a full decade of cultural implosion. Deep inside we felt the spirits moving in the live nuclei. It is evident from the very presence of the X-Clan, Poor Righteous Teachers, Lakim Shabazz, Public Enemy and Leaders of the New School that there are many social, political, intellectual and cultural forces that shape, form and provide coherence for their youthful impulses. They are the ones charged with the awesome responsibility of building a new society.

Initially, there were some who did not recognize the Hip Hop cultural explosion as part of a long continuum of black artistic expressions. Could it be because they raised the black urban toast to a new level of receptivity? Was it not Larry Neal [naw, we don't mean Larry Larr] who signaled this emergence twenty years earlier by opening the closing of *Black Fire,* "And Shine Swam On," with the message about the black urban toast? *(BUT)?* If the *Ninja Man* can continue to hang in the Caribbean memory, clearly *Shine* will be around for some time here. Dance Hall down criers continue to realize that once you move on the floor you are entering an area of cultural confluence. Shabba Ranks, Cutty Ranks teamed with Dennis Brown, Big Youth and U Roy and the oldsters to further solidify the cultural forces.

As the Hip Hop artists of the United States and elsewhere begin to discover Alicia Johnson, Amiri Baraka, Marvin X, Amus Mor and Larry Neal, "Rap" will explore new streets. They have only begun to explore the private mythology of black folk. That is what lies near the very heart and souls of black folk.

Larry Neal rightly and righteously observed that the private mythology of Black America is central to the whole discourse. "Its symbolism is direct and profound. Shine is US. We have been below-deck stoking the ship's furnaces. Now the ship is sinking, but where will we swim? Jamming belly up you immediately recognize the difference between IVAN D and IVAN VAN. Watch out for the criminals, the Rude Boys and the

Jazabelles. Not Labelle or Patti Labelle in the land of sunshine. Blue waters welcome Yemanga. Goddess of the deep blue seas. Sea Deep. See, I told you.

"There is a tension throughout our communities. The ghosts of that tension are Nat Turner, Martin Delaney, Booker T. Washington, Frederick Douglass, Malcolm X, Garvey, Monroe Trotter, Dubois, Fanon and a whole panoply of mythical heroes from Brer Rabbit to Shine. These ghosts have left us with some very heavy questions about the realities for black people in America." Larry Neal is dropping the heavy science like Just Ice Just-Ernest Just.

IMAGE REVERSAL

Amiri, the poet, once said, "What a culture produces is, and refers to, is an image—a picture of a process, since it is a form of a process; movement seen. The changing of images, of references, is the Black man's way back to the racial integrity of the captured African, which is where we must take ourselves, in feeling, to be truly the warriors we propose to be. To form an absolutely rational attitude toward West man, and West thought. Which is what is needed. To see the white man as separate and as enemy. To make a fight according to the absolute realities of the world as it is." Later Baraka writes, "The song title, 'A White Man's Heaven Is A Black Man's Hell' describes how complete an image reversal is necessary in the West. Because for many Black people, the white man has succeeded in making this hell seem like heaven. But black youth are much better off in this regard than their parents. They are the ones who need the least image reversal."

Against this historical background it was most appropriate for Amiri Baraka's son, Ras Baraka, to deliver a Hip Hop Manifesto at the opening of the 1st Annual Hip Hop Conference at Howard University in February, 1991. It was on that same campus during the 1950's that Amiri began a necessary image reversal. Memories of the capstone:

"The frats and yellow folks ran Howard's official student life. Everything else was improvisation. We'd find ourselves trailing through black night in Southwest Washington headed for parties. Dudes would say, "Some a them D.C. boys gonna split your heads open!" But we, being officially fearless, would go on and come to a joint that looked just like those sets we'd left back home." Thirty years on movement sets had transformed the old capstone to just a stone. Therefore in the Spring of '90, the young bloods (congregated in the Nia Force) encircled the stoney brook faces of the Naughty by Nature.

HIP HOP IS A GREAT LIGHT

Moving toward the center force were Hip Hop artists like 'Two Kings In A Cipher' and 'Defiant Giants.' Cognizant that 'Daffy was a Black man,' Two Kings in a Cipher moves up them hills like Trinidad Reel. Turning to the mighty voice of the Defiant Giants we hear, "Hip Hop is a light. It's like the sun and the light of the sun which strikes the Earth and causes the Earth to rotate. Just as the sun is burning at a temperature of 14,072 degrees, it sends out light at 1,086 miles per second, striking the Earth at its very center, causing it to revolve and rotate at 1,037 miles per hour." Continuing to drop the heavy science, in motion. "The best of hip hop is like the sun, because it's hot. When it's a dope beat it pumps you up, heats you up, it causes you to sweat. And when you have light giving, revolutionary, spiritual lyrics, that light travels and it strikes you in your mind, and it causes your mind to rotate like the earth, causing you to think differently, causing you to act differently, causing you to bring down the world of white supremacy in your mind. Hip Hop is a great light, and it is also God's music today, when it's in its proper form."

Speaking near the city of Refuge where light and sound seldom enter, the mighty Defiant Giants continue to explore sources of

Nation Conscious Rap. ". . . Let us not forget the root of our light. When you hear the Poor Righteous Teachers, when you hear X-Clan, Public Enemy, Paris, the Defiant Giants, Brand Nubians, Kool Moe Dee; when you hear them rap of black consciousness, they rap from our father, all of our fathers, the lessons of the Honorable Elijah Muhammad. That's where we rap from. This great black man. When you hear these rappers rap, when you hear us rap on the radio, when you see our video, that is Elijah rapping, that is Elijah speaking to you. He lives today. We have also been inspired by the boldest black man here in America, who has made his sojourn throughout this nation and throughout the world, the boldest leader on the planet earth today, the Honorable Minister Louis Farrakhan. We all owe him a great debt of gratitude."

When Mister Cee was asked to identify leaders that had influenced him in his personal life he replied, "Brothers like Dr. Martin Luther King, Malcolm X, Minister Louis Farrakhan, Elijah Muhammad, W.E.B. Dubois, Frederick Douglass."

If Yo Yo, Isis or Sister Souljah would rediscover Ruby McCollum, the woman in Florida's Suwannee Jail, they could bring their foremothers and foresisters back into the continuum. Walking briskly with an expressionless face, Ruby wore a bright green camel's hair coat. Stories, stories and more stories that enliven their historical memory.

GANGSTARR IN THE ARENA

Gangstarr's, "Step In The Arena" is moving in a solid hip hop fashion. Had to be using a Jem Fogger. Call him Guru Keith E. The modern usage of the term guru as acronym suggests, 'Gifted, Unlimited, Rhymes, Universal,' and that is what you hear. "Just To Get A Rep" is righteously, endemically hardcore. So reel is their motion that either banned entirely or presented as an expurgated visual text. It is powerful. D.J. Premier kicks it like this, "Not everyone is into real rap, that's including those people that are signing rap acts. They're telling some groups that they have to write certain types of songs to get radio air play. Conditioned at an early age to see clearly, G. Keith reveals the genesis. "Everyday stuff is what makes me want to write. Some stuff has a more worldly view, but I don't want to get deep into that. I like to paint a more mellow picture. Part of my youth was in the Nation of Islam, and that still reflects in my writing. But I'm not involved in that right now. I consider us hardcore jazzfunk. The street is hardcore, but we're smoothed out more in a way lyrically. I don't like to shout, but it's still hardcore."

THE STREETS

The street is hardcore and it is the rhythmic locus of the Hip Hop world. At one time, it was just the Hip world. At another time, the streets were cold, cold locus of the dance world. People were doing the Funky Chicken, the Freeze, the Down in the Middle Split, Slide, Bicycle. It was the locus of the Bop World years ago. Dark glasses kept you from seeing what wasn't happening. Dark Knights of existence. Parked upon Belmont Plateau.

The house was sitting on a highly inclined section of that street. They got high inside. Living. Living just enough for the city. Along, along those bloodpaved streets were the occupants of this city refuge. Siren. Lights. Ducking behind and under cars. Night sticks beat the senses out of scenic bloods. Your moms called you one-two-three times. The cool breeze of summer continued to blow. Kurtis.

She stood on the curve where cars passed daily. Mid daylight. Her body slid closer to the curve to check out the inside of the passing car. "Where you going?" "What you want to do?" "$5? What about $3? Triad. Father, Son of Bazerk and Holy Ghosts. The Trinity as train. Daylight falls in the bottom, too. Not yet 16 and the streets are blazing hot. Beeper signifying another connexion.

Streets. Money. Money and **Mo' Money.** There is a 14-year-old trying to make it to Mickey Dees. Three dollars a wop or $3 per hour. Either way, they are getting paid. But somebody has got to spot! Offer a way out. Can I kick it? [A Tribe Called Quest]:

To all the people who can quest like
a tribe does
Before this
Did you really
Know what life was?
Comprehend to the track for it's wide
cuz
Getting mentioned on the tip of the
vibe buzz
Rock 'n Roll to the beat of the funk fuzz
Wipe your feet really good on the rhythm
rug
If you feel the urge to freak, do the jitterbug.

Dancing and Profiling. The streets remain the locus of the Hip Hop world. On the corners lessons are learned, reasoning done. You can dance to stop from freaking out. Not a lot of space here. So they run to the corner to get a cold beer. All while the *world* is closing in on them. Spinning, sinning and all the while defending.

Changing. Those streets of yesteryear are no more. Now it is crack-filled and gang-banged. Loose and cracked. Yet, most of our people walk straight through these streets night and day. Risking lives. But this is a risque world. The deafening sound of ultra-sonic beat box blasts DJ Jazzy Jeff and the Fresh Prince's **"Summertime."** Riding along that silver crest B.M.W. (Black Man's Wheels) with the dope sunset hookup playing Aretha Franklin's "What You See Is What You Sweat" L.P. Hotter Than July. Now you may even hear Bebe and CeCe's "Lifestyle," especially if its the Eagles' quarterback cruising through the streets. Further to the curve, somebody calls out "How you living?" Quiet voice replies, **LARGE!** Flourescent mint green convertible, with green mag wheels.

It's reel. Filmic. Whole. Endothermic. Half-hearted. Ragged. Dressed. Clean. Whole.

These are the streets of Philly in the 1990's. They might be "In Search of the Last Trump of Funk." Sometimes names and faces are swirling in some bar. Air condition makes it a hot, funky cool but in the SAAB it is cold cool. The street is hardcore and it is the locus of the Hip Hop world.

ONE LOVE MONIE

The street is hardcore, and it is the rhythmic locus of the Hip Hop world. Cruising down those mean streets in the hyped drive. People are down to earth with "Monie In The Middle." Coming out of England with those deep Jamaican roots, Monie Love chose to explore less observed activities in this domain. She says, "When I was living in Brooklyn. I wrote a lot of material, because I lived on a busy block. As far as what I choose to write about, I think we have enough people covering the political end. I figure I'll get lost in the bunch of people that are already doing that kind of stuff. I write about things that are less strenuous on the brain. Like little things that might go on in the streets, I don't really excel in any one area. I have a different type twist to my story lines. I pick real situations to talk about." Once settling in the United States Monie entered the heavy light circle of the Jungle Brothers (never to far from the Calypso Monarch) and De La Soul. Electrifying the world audiences with 'Monie In The Middle' she moved, *Down to Earth* in short order.

Carol Luther imagined another Brooklyn 20 years ago

Peaches in open markets
in Brownsville, Bed-Stuy and
The Coast Village
remind me of summers in
Memphis
where peaches grew on trees
and we shook them down

Moving through the streets of North Philly, Mark Traylor presaged the Hip Hop generation by 20:

them hard-looking
hard-talking
hard-looking
cool black-dudes
and
them fine-looking
fine-walking
fine-talking
fine-loving
them, fine soul sisters

The literary critic, poet and teacher Eugene Redmond clearly identifies the mission of Afro-American Poetry in his *Drum Voices*. Turning to the Philly poets Gene opined, "Philadelphia poets explore city life and Africa, and exalt blackness. There is, too, the rage and vehemence often found in New York and Chicago poetry. "Cool Black Nights" (by Traylor, who died at age twenty-two) also captures driving street rhythms and rough rhymes." We published poets Straight Outta Philly in the early 1970's. Black Mu Poetry forums provided young street wise writers a platform to dissect the Treacherous Terrordome of their lives. Rap and Reason there you locate the Birth of Brightness.

PHILLY AS A CENTER OF HIP HOP PHILOSOPHY

The earliest expression of Hip Hop lyrics germane to Philly was written by Brother Smooth- Larry Neal, the regal predecessor of Larry Larr who is definitely in our mighty traveled tradition. Can I tell you this story or will you send me through all kinds of changes?

Setting: Streets of Philly. Time: Fluid but often located in the 50's and early 60's with way back memories. Already the driving street rhythms are present. Had to be those unspeakable Philly images. That gave rise to, "Yo! MTV Raps" and the video revolution. Had to see what we were talking about. Philly rappers are known for their tragicomic imagination. They are feigning ignorance, acting like they really don't know. Included in this diverse field of players is The Fresh Prince playing like

he's in Belair when his terribly noble quest for wholeness can only be found in the streets of Philly. Just at the moment when the crassest elements of those Nigguh paved streets realized their were no ambulances for Niggers Tonight, Jazzy Jeff and The Fresh Prince entered the American conscience. Witty and adroit with a full grasp of tragic conventions and an inner circle of tragicomic elements- The Fresh Prince brought comic relief in the midst of seriousness. No need to dis what was being done by other rappers. It was a clever, clearing of space for other dramaturgical African American experiences.

And now we return to Larry Neal whose poem "Can I Tell You This Story Or Will You Send Me Through All Kinds Of Changes" ushers in the modern voice of Philly hip hop lyricists. That is why Hip Hop Majesty Pharoah appreciated Larry's deep, dark emblematic rendering of Philly black asphalt streets in our times:

In those days, the avenues were
nigger cops, like Rudy who thought he was
the Durango kid;
we shot him in the doorway of a mean loud
    party.
These were the days of the bebopping
house of blue lights.

Bird gained weight: we meet our
turnpike death clutching our instruments.
Places got turned out then
heads were busted and lips swelled purple;
we were blind.
We stayed high on Mexican marijuana,
drank wine in narrow alleys
and Lady melody, the blues spirit breezed
in every now and then.

We were killed in weird ways,
picked guts, stabbed heads, bleeding marcels
cursing each other's mothers and fathers and
sisters and brothers;
old dripple-lipped drunks high on tokay
    spewing
and pissing on themselves.
And Daddy Grace mad with powers, shoving
    pigfeet
and barbecue down the throats of shouting
    soul stirrers.

Preachers dreamed yellow Cadillacs
waiters pretending doctor,
mailmen pretending lawyer
doctor and lawyer pretending Negro society.

How can one continue to ask the origins of this current generation? Actually they are the natural byproducts of previous generations. Even more direct, didactic and diacritical. There is no way to miss the potency of their messages.

Cryptic, Staccato, livid lives. Another Philly Rapper appropriately called Schooly D enters the squared circle.

What's up
What's going on
Before we start this next record
I gotta put my shades on
So I can feel cool
Remember that law?
When you had to put your shades on to feel
    cool?
Well, it's still a law
Gotta put your shades on
So I can't see
what you ain't doing
and you ain't doing nothing.

Or to empower it further you gotta listen for the 'Black Man' cut. Cuz it's on the razor, J.B. Style. Styling and profiling. Cruising and oozing. Elements of style in Philly streets. Black-speak here is terse, located in a distanting zone, The Phase. Everybody wore a variation of the Phase. Understated. New words for a new people. Counterpoint as melodic phraser. Empowering logic, often outside of the article of reason. But they be reasoning with the brethren. Verbal skills are built on many Philly stoops. Getting the last deadly word in. Careful listeners. Word smith. A turn of phrase. Inversion is an index to inner vision. These elements are concretized in the heavy d cell wisdom of Schooly D and Larry N.

So dense is the philly intalk and so laden with wisdom is the philosophy that undergirds the intalk that the editors of Nation

Conscious Rap went to an indigenous north Philly philosopher whose careful assessment deserves our attention. Talking about Eugene Rivers. One of the two trained North Philly philosophers formerly on the painterly scene in Philly town before going to New Haven, Cambridge and Kingston, Jamaica.

"Philly had a whole group of radical black intellectuals who were at the cutting edge of phenomenal amounts of stuff. Cruse. The Panther stuff. C.L.R. James, Eric Williams, Padmore, Martin Sostre, George Jackson, Fanon. The entire range. Phenomenal stuff . . . . The theoretical broadness and the catholicism of the intellectual orientation was absolutely unparalled . . . . There is a certain level of adversity that is a precondition for artistic and intellectual creativity and independence. In Philly it is among the urban working class to middle class black males that this creativity emerges . . . . my sense is that Philly was unique because there is a certain homogenized urban working class experience that the black males go through. It is part of a collective experience. Philly is much more homogenous, not as diversified and differentiated as New York City or Chicago with a much more southern kind of thing. Philly has got an interesting old, urban solid working class. Dubois alludes to it in the middle of the 1860's. You've got this interesting urbanization process with this kind of homogenized, collective black consciousness which is very tough. That toughness translates itself into the artistic and intellectual realm. Relating to that toughness is a sense of fraternity based on the collective black male experience versus the white experience. In my experience there were whiteys and there were the bloods. The gang experience was part of the rites of passage which was very fraternal. Admittedly there were sociopathic dimensions. But there was a very strong male binding thing because of the commonality of the experience."

Continuing in the Philly Langue. "My experience was that all of the brothers always wanted the brothers to make it. Brothers would sometime get sacked down into the more destructive dimensions of the experience but by the same token the achievers were encouraged." He goes on to describe that kinetic, intellectually vibrant atmosphere in Philadelphia, "There was a much more cosmopolitan intellectual thing steeped in a philly jitterbug hipster tradition. There is a jitterbug, hipster, cosmopolitan intellectual aesthetic . . . . What do we do with this aesthetic, this whole vision of the world? Philly has a smooth brother style; interesting enough, it is noted from here to Boston . . . . There is a style and an aesthetic that is uniquely referred to as the *Philly* style, is a whole hipster, jitterbug, irreverent, desparately contemptuous vision of the white world. The women are awed. Here is the synthesis of the physical and the mental, the spiritual, physical, intellectual integrated organic unit which is *Black*, authentically black. *Blue Black Blurple*. That becomes the basis for the aesthetic. The Blue Black: The Blue Black Blurple." What he is talking about is the Blurble aesthetic.

Philly bloods have that utterly seditious sense of independence, of autonomy. Actually that is part of the reason why they are not recorded as often in the Hip Hop domain. They know what they want and they don't want no stuff. You can't stuff them easily. People are overwhelmed by the image. Rivers explained that many people can't fathom this strange species of Philly bloods who "have the view that the European thing must be fully comprehended because that is the only way to appreciate the opposition, out of a sense of warfare you study them, out of a commitment to engage your opposition at every level, psychologically, culturally, ideologically and intellectually. For that reason you study them with a vengeance. You study them out of your contempt for the brutality of their legacy."

Rivers rightly asserted characteristics evident not only in the Philly black aesthetic but also some aspects of today's hip hop cultural movement: There is an almost ontological aversion to the Eurocentric hegemony.

This young philosopher noted, "my organizing metaphors and symbols came out of the Nation of Islam. The notion that knowledge of self is a precondition for coherence, the originality of the Black man a la Leakey or Gould . . . the first man is a driving force. The fact that life is a jihad. Existence itself is a jihad against the cycle of death are all principles in the Nation of Islam's philosophy. Is it any surprise that the most pronounced influence on this current generation of Nation Conscious Rappers is the Nation of Islam's philosophy, especially as articulated by the early Malcolm X and Minister Louis Farrakhan.

The pathos, violence and disorder in the American society generally finds another avenue of expression in some rap lyrics. The noted black urban planner, Peter Labrie, provides useful insight into the basis for what appears to be a drastic change from the previous generation to the current one. The presence of Niggas With Attitudes (N.W.A.) can be understood within the changing society so powerfully described by Labrie over twenty years ago. He said, "our purpose here is to inquire into some of the vital internal forces that have traditionally structured the black community in America. Outside of a few exceptional cases, it is widely acknowledged that black people, from slavery to at least World War II, lived in a severly limited, isolated and relatively static world. The general orientation of his life and of his subjective mind was that which had been shaped by the slave-like conditions of the Southern plantation system. Although after World War I many black people migrated to cities, even those in the cities remained, by and large, a Southern people. The moral habits and cultural norms internalized in their consciences were essentially the same as those shared by their relatives and friends left behind in the South. . . . However, between the pre-World War II period and now, many things have come to pass: the Depression, two major wars, erratic but large scale occurences of industrialization and urbanization, economic and employment stagnation, etc. It would be impossible to measure the influence which all these complex societal forces had upon the black community, but one result is obviously, namely, that most black people have acquired a different basis for their existence of their community life." How is this difference manifested? "With his experiences under oppression and into the deeper and more subjective realms of life, with his knowledge of the white world around him, it becomes almost impossible for him to be moral in any conventional sense. To have someone tell him to go to college so that he can get a good job, to be patient and grateful until some 'charity' organization gives him something, is an insult. If he wants something, he will take it whatever way he can and by any means necessary. This is his will to power which goes beyond conventional morality."

When it comes to assessing N.W.A.'s lyrics in the context of 'conventional morality," it is problematic. Eazy E expresses what is a conscious anticonventional perspective. "When we first started, everybody was black this, black that. The whole positive black thing we said f . . . that—we wanted to come out in everybody's face. Something that would shock people." This is further evidenced by their current album "Niggaz 4 Life." It is obviously in response to the high decibel criticism they've received especially inside of the black community. Like this, "Why not call myself a nigger? It's better than pulling the trigger and going up the river/and then I get called nigger anyway. . . . I guess I'll be a nigger for life." The attitudes, dispositions and raw street talk signifies a declaration of "outsiderness," an opting out of what are known as the values and mores of conventional Afro-American life. There is an obvious predilection toward *outragedness* both as metaphor and as life. What is the value system that generates this violent response to perceived female insubordination? Which sociopolitical variables interact with intrapsychic forces on the real side? Downpression in the neocolonial settings of Blackurban enclaves has produced

unique challenges. Eazy E lays it out like this in WHPK's (University of Chicago) house magazine. "I was getting my record company rolling and Dr. Dre said, 'why don't you go on and rap?' I said, I ain't never rapped in my life. So the first record I ever did was 'Boyz in the Hood'. I used to be a DJ—me and Dre. So really, Dre got me started into everything." When asked how crazy record sales has changed his life Eazy E responds, 'No No big change, really. I mean, the only change in it is that it's legal. 'Cause the shit I was doing before that other thing, you know, selling drugs." Rapping provided Eazy E an alternative to working in the informal economy. Writing lyrics and speaking out of the everydayness of their experiences, NWA keeps pumping those graphic brakes. Ren: "Compton is wild man. It's like you can't even stand outside. There's people riding by in Compton with guns, shooting, daylight, nighttime. Your mama can't water the grass whatever. You got to just constantly watch your back. There's people out there that's crazy. And the police, they just fuck with you 'cause they think you're part of a gang. . . . I got shot being in the wrong place at the wrong time, that's how it is. . . . And it ain't only Compton. It's Watts. South Central L.A. They've got the biggest drive-by shootings going on. Everynight on the news, you hear about somebody getting took out."

Street Knowledge. Straight Outta Compton where if the word is not the weapon, the weapon is. Little research has been done on the mental pathology of the people inhabiting those war zones. What kind of cultural expression comes out of this existence. *In Wretched of the Earth*, the Martinician psychiatrist, Dr. Frantz Fanon observed the following about the Algerians who faced daily acts of repression in the old colonial regime. Fanon; "The Algerian, exposed to temptations to commit murder every day—famine, eviction from his room, because he has not paid the rent, the mother's dried up breasts, children like skeletons, the building yard which has closed down, the unemployed that hang about the foreman like crows—the native comes to his neighbor as a relentless enemy." There are parallel acts of microaggression that one finds in the Compton's, South Central L.A.'s, Harlem's and Philly's of the world. As Fanon points out the victim strikes out against those closest to him—his neighbor, his woman, his mother, her father, her friends, etc. This is a crucial stage in the decolonization process. "Fanon puts it correctly, The colonized man will first manifest this aggressiveness which has been deposited in his bones against his own people. This is the period when the niggers beat each other up, and the police and magistrates do not know which way to turn when faced with the astonishing waves of crime in North Africa [substitute for L.A. or Compton]. . . . When the native is confronted with the colonial order of things, he finds he is in a state of permanent tension. The settler's world is a hostile world, which spurns the native, but at the same time it is a world of which he is envious. We have seen that the native never ceases to dream of putting himself in the place of the settler—not of becoming the settler, but of substituting himself for the settler. This hostile world, ponderous and aggressive because it fends off the colonized masses with all the hardness it is capable of, represents not merely a hell from which the swiftest flight possible is desirable, but also a paradise close at hand which is guarded by terrible watch dogs."

Given this background it is not at all surprising to see the emergence of a particular type of rap called variedly Gangsta Rap, Hardcore Rap, etc. It reflects a national culture under colonial domination. Elsewhere in the circle of reasoning is the group of Nation Conscious Rappers who have taken on the responsibility of addressing their own people. The body of literature produced under the aegis can rightly be called a literature of combat. The people's contact with the new movement gives rise to a new rhythm of life and to forgotten muscular tensions. It develops the imagination. Fanon is right "It

is only from that moment that we can speak of a national literature. Here there is, at the level of literary creation, the taking up and clarification of themes which are typically nationalistic. This may properly be called a literature of combat, in the sense that it calls on the whole people to fight for their existence as a nation. It is a literature of combat, because it molds the national consciousness, giving it form and contours and flinging open before it new and boundless horizons; it is a literature of combat because it assumes responsibility and because it is the will to liberty expressed in terms of time and space."

PHILOSOPHICAL DIMENSIONS OF RAP

The emergence of Nation Conscious Rappers at this juncture in our history is most significant. The fact that a mass national cultural movement has grown organically out of disparate Black communities is a musical phenomenon worthy of further exploration. In examining rap as a socio-communicative and idiomatic manifestation, the philosopher George Yancy states, "Philosophically, the lyrically expressed music found in rap has profound ontological implications. For the analysis of a lyrically expressed rap demonstrates a certain existential, socio-ontological and groundational significance for the emical self understandings of a culture, society, community, etc. On one level rap is *descriptive* of a certain fluid everydayness (alltaglich): tales of concrete situations, (reminiscent of folklore); distinctive styles of dress; shared plights; shared socio historical realities; shared unconscious associations, etc. On another level, however rap is *prescriptive* (as anyone knows who has listened to Public Enemy, Poor Righteous Teachers et al.) But rap as a modality of prescriptive didacticism and socio-political discontent is nevertheless couched in a mode of linguistically intrinsic to a sociality of shared experience. In short whether viewed as a form of description or prescription, rap presupposes the contention that discourse is fundamentally a form of praxis."

RAP AS RHYTHMIC PRAXIS DISCOURSE

Concluding his brief but dense essay, "Rapese," Yancy notes, "Now given that rap grows out of a cultural matrix, and nexus of meanings peculiar to African-Americans, idiomatic expressions found in rap are quite suggestive of African-American life stylizations. By treating rap as fundamentally a groundational phenomenon, we participate in the shared vision of Larry Neal concerning the need to emphasize the rootedness and situatedness of African-American cultural objectivations (aesthetics, music, literature, sculpture, etc.) Hence rap as *musical*

literature (or rhythmic-praxis discourse) as it were, is an integral and functional pact of the African-American community lifestlye."

NATION CONSCIOUS RAP: THE HIP HOP VISION

Drums. Bronx. Trumpet. Brooklyn. Keyboard. Long Island. This book captures the tune, texture, lore and history of this important cultural movement. Their shared vision. Groundational sources. High hat symbols. Like Big Daddy Kane said, "Words are powerful, words can change the world . . . myths are built with words, too. But instead of building you up, they beat you down. Just like a bass drum." Drums. Philly. Drums. Chicago. Drums. Bronx. Locus of the Hip Hop World.

Foreword

Sonia Sanchez

What I remember about reading the first time to an audience is that I was stricken at how the words stayed on the page. And how at the same time I remembered the language of my grandmother and the language of my father and jazz musicians, how their language/sounds bounced off paper, went into some sacred space of broken tongues, re-entered the atmosphere at such a pace that their re-entry burned the edges of our souls

and our ears as we listened. Went home, again.

When I first heard some of the older poets in the anthology read, their words sped from the paper to our ears and back to their pages. And among those of us who listened, there was a recognition of poems well-done, executed. Poems in keeping with the times, on-time poems, necessary poems, history/herstory poems. I think when they finally heard some of us read, they saw us look at the word, splice it, look up at the word and jazz it up, look backwards at the word and decide to disconnect and reconnect it at the end, stretch it, moan it, groan it, peel it, and then finally, redress the world and say, "See, this is a poem." And I saw other poets, I saw white poets, begin to come

Source: Sonia Sanchez, Foreword from *bum rush the page* by Tony Medina and Louis Reyes Rivera. Copyright © 2001 by Bone Bristle, LLC., Tony Medina and Louis Reyes Rivera. Used by permission of The Three Rivers Press, a division of Random House, Inc.

and listen to how we read because people didn't read like that, or had not read in that fashion before. And our generation of Black Arts poets began to show poets how to read.

These new poets, these hip-hop poets heard the sound and picked it up. And they did the same thing we did with poetry and sound, they did the sound, the pace, the pace of sound, the swiftness of sound, the discordant way of looking at the world of sound, the blackness of sound, the color of sound, the beat of sound, but above all it was that fast beat. It was what I called the new bebopic beat. Because when the bebop people started to play nobody could keep up with them. It was so fast you couldn't even hear. I would always say to my kids when I first heard hip-hop, "I can't hear it. I don't understand." And the same kind of thing when Dizzy and Max were playing; nobody could play it except them, and nobody could hear it. You had to have a fast ear to hear it cuz otherwise they would play it and done been gone. Same thing that happened with rap. It came at a fast pace and if you turned your head, you missed it. It was gone. The bebop, the bam, and the hip hop.

Each generation brings something new to this thing called craft, to this thing called poetry. What we did when we looked at Margaret Walker and Gwendolyn Brooks, we went back into their herstory and history and pulled back from Langston Hughes, Sterling Brown, Dudley Randall, and Robert Hayden, that whole group. We pulled from them the craft of writing, the discipline of writing and the history and herstory of our people. Then we said, "Let's bring it to a new sense of history. Let's in a sense 're-word' history, refocus history with these new words and a new way of looking at the world." So we employed what they gave us along with what was going on in the world: the politics of being Black, from civil rights to Black Power, to the new sense of self, to the new sense of who we are/were. And we came up with poems that did similar things that Miss Margaret and Sister Gwen and Brother Sterling Brown did. But we also, I

think, began to give it a new modern sound that was part of a twentieth century sound. And I guess what I'm saying is that at some point you had to look and see that their poetry was viable, but it was another sound. It was a different sound. When Baraka, Askia, and I scatted, used the music of Monk, Coltrane, Dizzy, the blues of our people we cut the century in half, re-entered the century with the good news that the Africans were all alive and living in the Diaspora. This is the very modernist way we looked at poetry. The world not ending with a whimper, but being full of ideas and sound and music that challenged everyone.

What we have to learn, it seems to me, in this 21st century, is that we have been history, and we are history. And we have to unearth the history. To me, this 21st century is a serious time to look at ourselves because there's a possibility that some of us will disappear in this 21st century as a significant force in world history. I would not have said that in the 20th century. But because we have not understood our history, we have allowed ourselves to be bought and killed out of history. I mean, there are people who allow us to be bought out of history. So at some point, it is necessary, it is incumbent upon us to look and see as poets still poeting in the 21st century, *how do I go out of my skin and return again with friends who will have something relevant to say?*

It might not be a new discussion, but it's something that comes up time and time again. And each poet has got to respond to it some kind of way. Once when I was teaching, some of the little black kids were being chased home by some of the older white children who were calling them nigger. And so I went home and wrote a poem: ". . . nigger/ that word ain't shit to me/ don't you know where you at when you call me nigger/ I'll say it slow for you—niiiigggger./ I know I'm black,/ beautiful with meaning nigger, my man/ you way behind the set." Those children memorized that poem and when they were chased again, they stopped the chasers and they turned and said, "That word don't turn me on man/ I know I'm black." And they flaunted their blackness in the streets. And the white kids stopped in their tracks. And this is important: If they could chase someone with just one word, then they have the power, but if you could stop the word's importance by replacing it with something new, then you had the power. I tried to reinvent the word to give them the new power. And that's what you have to do. I empowered those children.

They were being chased with a word. They were running. And when they stopped and turned with their interpretation of the word nigger, they were at a new place with themselves. They put the white kids on pause. A safe place to be, lovin' themselves in the middle of the 20th century. And what I feel in this anthology is the love these young people have for language. Their tongues caress the words with humor and irony and love.

Friends of the Court

L. Jon Wertheim

It had been a brutal NBA road trip for the Seattle SuperSonics, five cities in eight days. On March 5, still feeling the effects of the travel, Marty White, Trevor Pope and Glen King arrived at Seattle's Key Arena later than usual for the first home game in nearly two weeks. They dropped off their black Chevy Silverado truck with the attendant in the team's parking lot, then entered the arena through a VIP door. Dressed in billowy sweaters and leather jackets, they strutted confidently into the locker room area, giving ushers and team employees a wink or a warm hello. At the lip of the tunnel leading to the court, a guard smiled at the threesome. "Good luck tonight, guys," he said.

Despite appearances to the contrary, White, Pope and King do not play for the Sonics. Pope and White are boyhood friends of Seattle's star point guard, Gary Payton.

King is Payton's older cousin. The three men all live in Seattle, where they work for Payton, serving as his personal assistants, chauffeurs, de facto bodyguards and nearly constant companions—the Glove's gloves, so to speak. They accompany him to All-Star Games, summer workouts in Las Vegas, autograph signings, commercial shoots. They travel to all of Seattle's 41 road games; at home games they sit either in Payton's private luxury box or in the club seats opposite the Seattle bench. "Them's my boys," says Payton, his raspy voice full of affection. "The Sonics are my team, but in a way these guys are my team too. They go everywhere with me."

It's no exaggeration. A few years ago Sonics season-ticket holders Mark and Nikki Mahan paid $17,000 for Payton and teammate Vin Baker to come to their house and cook them dinner. The money went to Payton's charitable foundation. For that, the Mahans could have expected an intimate meal with two of their favorite players. When Payton showed up, Pope and White were in tow. Were the Mahans surprised by the extra

Source: L. Jon Wertheim, "Friends of the Court." *Sports Illustrated* (April 8, 2002), pp. 52–56, 58, 60, 62.

company? "Not really," says Nikki. "Vin had arrived about five minutes earlier and brought a few of his guys too."

I

Call them what you will: posses, crews, peeps, boyz, bobos, personal assistants. "How about just saying, 'friends and family'?" suggests Detroit Pistons guard Jerry Stackhouse. From NBA stars to scrubs, veterans to rookies, scores of players find comfort in numbers. One need only look down the corridor outside the locker room—where dozens of friends and relatives congregate after a game and wait for players to emerge—to realize how de rigueur the entourage has become. "They're like contracts," adds Charles Oakley, the Chicago Bulls forward and the NBA's unofficial social critic. "Everyone's got one. Some are just bigger than others."

How big? When Stephon Marbury played for the New Jersey Nets, he once invited 64 of his closest relatives and acquaintants to descend on the green room reserved for friends and family at Continental Airlines Arena. (Shortly thereafter the team quietly told players they would be limited to four lounge passes apiece.) During the NBA's All-Star weekend, on Feb. 8–10 in Philadelphia, the 60 or so players invited to participate in various festivities booked more than 300 rooms for their guests—and that was at just one hotel. "Sometimes I could swear that the entourages have entourages," says one Eastern Conference coach. "That's how out of control it's gotten."

What these acolytes actually *do* runs the gamut. Some athletes, such as Shaquille O'Neal, have "car guys" who warm up their vehicles after games and shield them from the horror of climbing into an SUV in which music isn't already blaring. Baron Davis, the Charlotte Hornets' All-Star guard, even has a personal deejay at home—Erin (Alcatraz) Blunt, best known for having played the role of Ahmad Abdul Rahim in *The Bad News*

Bears. Some players retain "jewelry guys," who make sure that all their chains, earrings, medallions and bracelets are properly polished. Other crew members feed the athletes' addiction to competition, serving as training partners in the NBA's off-court triathlon of PlayStation, pool and Pop-a-Shot.

What some other posse members do, however, is a mystery. When Benoit Benjamin, that notorious flake, was signed by the Vancouver Grizzlies in 1995, he arrived for a media session in a white limousine filled with friends. One wore a jacket emblazoned with the logos of every team for which Benjamin had played. The man introduced himself to Steve Frost, Vancouver's p.r. director, as "the CEO" and handed Frost a business card that read simply: CEO. "CEO of what?" Frost asked.

"Benoit Benjamin Inc.," the man responded. That was the last Frost saw of him. Thirteen games later Benjamin was traded to the Milwaukee Bucks, and one can only assume that the CEO added another logo to his jacket.

Mysterious or not, what all posse members do is imbue the athletes with a sense of importance. "It's become a status symbol to have an entourage," says Alvin Poussaint, a professor of psychiatry at Harvard Medical School. "It illustrates how famous and wealthy you are: *Look at me. People want to travel in my circle and bask in my glow.*"

Chicken Littles around the league cite posses as yet another example of the inexorable decline of professional basketball. Entourage members are gangsters, thugs, huns, injecting an excess of "street" into the image-conscious league. They are hangers-on trying to ride the (untucked) shirttails of unsuspecting players. In pre-draft interviews some NBA teams ask prospects if they maintain entourages. Publicly, the league has expressed support for entourages. "As a rule the posse thing has been a plus for us," commissioner David Stern said last year. But choosing your friends judiciously is a topic covered at the league's mandatory rookie orientation seminar. While working as a career consultant for the Nets in 1999, Dana London saw firsthand how the NBA tried to scuttle the players' relationships with these associates. "The entourages pose a problem for people interested in maintaining control," she says.

Some of the hand-wringing is justified. The various crimes and misdemeanors committed by cohorts of the Philadelphia 76ers' Allen Iverson have been well documented. In his first two seasons in the NBA, Indiana Pacers guard Ron Artest nearly went bankrupt lavishing cash, gifts and even cars on more than 30 family members and friends. "Probably wasted a couple of million or so," Artest says. "It seemed like the right thing to do. I wanted to take care of my friends." Other players have deployed their buddies on less-than-wholesome missions. A former Dallas Mavericks forward spent considerable time on the injured list and attended games in street clothes. At one point he purchased a two-way radio to keep in his sleeve as he sat on the bench, then dispatched members of his crew to comb the arena for attractive women. When they located potential consorts, they contacted the player on the bench, told them their whereabouts and waited for his sign of approval.

Those, however, are the exceptions. Behind their shroud of mystique, entourages are actually as innocuous as tattoos and baggy shorts. The dirty little secret is that posses often do NBA players far more good than harm.

II

Let's be clear: The entourage is not the sole preserve of sports, let alone the NBA. Roadies and toadies are fixtures in the music world—at the height of his popularity, in the early '90s, rapper M.C. Hammer had more than 100 dancers, body-guards and friends on tour with him—and Hollywood stars are notorious for flying their associates to location shoots. For years athletes, boxers in particular, have had coteries to swaddle them in adoration, run errands, procure women and provide a sense of home no matter where they are. Muhammad Ali's followers were so ubiquitous that some, such as Ferdie Pacheco and Drew (Bundini) Brown, became quasicelebrities in their own right.

Sugar Ray Robinson may have had the first big-time entourage in sports. In the '50s he toured Europe in a flamingo-pink Cadillac, joined by a motley crew that included, by turns, his manager, barber, voice teacher, drama coach, golf pro, shoeshine boy and a French midget who served as a translator. (Perhaps not coincidentally, Robinson died virtually penniless.) Yet today's NBA is particularly fertile ground for posses for a variety of reasons.

- **Youth** As NBA players get ever younger, increasingly forgoing college, they are more in need of support groups. Four years of college are an ideal transition from the near-total dependence of life at home to the near-total independence of life in the NBA. It is a rare 18-year-old who can successfully move to a new city and take up a demanding and highly public full-time job. Days after graduating from high school in Houston, forward Rashard Lewis was drafted by the Sonics. Soon he was more than 1,000 miles from home, in a new climate, adjusting to the unfamiliar role of bench warmer. When his homesickness became chronic, Lewis summoned his best friend, Travis Eskridge, to live with him. "Suddenly I had someone who knew me, used the same slang and knew the same people," says Lewis, who is now in his fourth year. "When Travis came, it was like getting a little bit of home."

  After the Minnesota Timberwolves drafted Kevin Garnett out of high school, in 1995, management was deeply concerned about his adjustment. "Lots of other guys on the team had families and kids," recalls coach Flip Saunders. "Are they going to want to hang out with an 18-year-old, and vice versa?" To the Timberwolves' surprise, Garnett showed up with his own sizable peer group, a mix of siblings, a girlfriend and friends from his old neighborhood in Mauldin, S.C. Like a post-modern Brady Bunch, they were one clan living all together in Garnett's manse. They even had a name: OBF, short for Official Block Family. Seven years later Garnett credits this support network with contributing to his success as a player.

- **Culture Shock** More than in any other professional team sport, NBA players come from urban, often destitute families. It is a shock to go from indigence to vast wealth literally overnight; the presence of old friends is one way to reduce the dissonance. "You're in your early 20s and you're a millionaire, but you're still not respected as such by society—no one is asking you to join the country club," says London. "An entourage is a way for these guys to validate themselves."

This is compounded by the hip-hop ethos of many players, which says that there is no faster way to lose your street cred than failing to "keep it real." The social circle of the Hornets' Davis, for example, still comprises cousins, friends and former AAU teammates from his old neighborhood in South Central Los Angeles. While Davis lives alone in Charlotte, he frequently flies his friends out to watch him play on the road, and he returns to his childhood home in South Central in the off-season. Davis is adamant that, although he has switched tax brackets, he hasn't changed his social class. "You're not going to abandon your homeboys because you've made it," he says. "Let me get this straight: I'm in the NBA and making money, so I'm supposed to start kicking it at Yale and Harvard with Poindexter and Penderpuss? Nuh-uh. That's not me."

- **Sharing the Wealth** The simplest explanation for the rise of the posse, however, is money. "The big contracts came," says Hornets coach Paul Silas, "and all the boys came out of the woodwork." Put less cynically, players have never been in a better financial position to look after their families and friends. Not all that long ago it wasn't feasible for a player to subsidize an entourage. Today the average NBA salary exceeds $4 million a year—a fourfold increase over the past decade—and money is seldom an issue.

Payton, for one, has been exceedingly generous with various friends and relatives from Oakland who have joined him in Seattle throughout his career. He has paid the college tuition of two friends and given others seed money to start up their own businesses. One friend, Clarence Johnson, once a regular in Seattle, is now back in Oakland running a franchise of Gary Payton Wireless. Payton flies his associates on private planes, treats them to lavish dinners and fetes them on his 80-foot yacht. In short, he has helped elevate them to a social status they may never have known otherwise. "I can open doors," Payton says. "Once the doors are open, it's up to them to make the most of the opportunity, but I want to put them in a position to get real comfortable."

III

Lorenzen (Ren) Wright is a solid but unremarkable player for the Memphis Grizzlies. The Wright Stuff, as he bills his crew, includes his business manager, Aric (A-One) Whaley; Wright's best friend and personal trainer, Rewis (Raw Dawg) Williams; his brother Lou Wright; cousin Emanuel (E-Man) Wright; and two security staffers, Tim Green and Dennis McNeil. In addition to paying each of them a salary, Wright provides them with a five-bedroom house and a "company car," a green Ford Expedition. He picks up the tab when he and the guys go bowling, go out to eat or go to the casino in Tunica, Miss. Earlier this year, when each member of the Wright Stuff had his own last name tattooed on his forearm, the player treated. The expenses add up fast, but given that Wright is midway through a seven-year, $42 million contract . . . well, no harm, no foul. "My guys make me feel comfortable, and they take care of the little things so I can concentrate on basketball," Wright says. "If anything, it's a good investment."

That said, Wright is also making good on a promise. A decade ago he was the star forward for Memphis's Booker T. Washington High School, and Raw Dawg was a quicksilver guard. After games and practices the two best friends would cruise their blighted neighborhood in Wright's dilapidated Volvo. If they had $5 between them, they'd drive to Taco Bell. One night, over a 10-pack of tacos, they made a pact. "If one of us blew up, he'd take care of the other," recalls Raw Dawg. "Of course, to us at the time that meant buying nice shoes."

Raw Dawg stopped growing at 5' 9" and went to tiny Tougaloo (Miss.) College. He was supposed to play ball there, but it didn't work out, and he eventually left school. Wright, meanwhile, became a star at Memphis State and, in 1996, a Los Angeles Clippers lottery pick. Since then he has seen to it that Raw Dawg has never wanted for anything. Raw Dawg accompanied Wright to L.A., where they befriended Whaley. When Wright was traded to Atlanta, in 1999, Raw Dawg trailed along and lived in Wright's house. "Those were good times," says Raw Dawg, 24. "But when Ren was traded to Memphis, our hometown, last summer, it was too good to be true."

Raw Dawg's typical day is loosely structured. Every morning he drives from the group house to Wright's monstrous house in the swanky Southwind district to wake up his friend at 9:15. (Though Wright lives with his wife, Sherra, and their five kids, they're usually out of the house by the time he likes to arise.) Raw Dawg then makes Wright breakfast or starts him on a workout. Raw Dawg's duties also include helping out Wright's father, Herb, a former rec center director who has been partially paralyzed since 1984, when he was shot by a man he had kicked out of the gym. In the afternoon R-Dawg might put Wright through another workout. Or rebound while Wright shoots jumpers. Or drive him to a stylist, where they both get their braids done. "My day is pretty much up to Ren," says Raw Dawg, who still has athletic eligibility left and might return to college this summer. "The biggest thing is that I be on time."

Game nights are when Raw Dawg truly earns his keep, an estimated $2,000 per month. Seated with the rest of the Wright Stuff a dozen rows behind Memphis's bench, Raw Dawg spends most of his time yelling, his distinct voice echoing through the Pyramid. Using a lexicon intelligible to few others in the premium seating, Raw Dawg constantly encourages Wright with "get in his grill, Ren!" The encouragement clearly reaches Wright's ears. Several times a game, he looks to his crew and smiles.

Among other fringe benefits, each member of Wright's entourage has a key to his mansion. Its crown jewel is the third floor, which is taken up entirely by the mother of all rec rooms, a shrine to arrested development replete with a flat-screen television, a PlayStation, an X-Box, classic video-game consoles, a pool table and a state-of-the-art sound system. Even when Wright is on the road, any member can come and go as he pleases, as long as he doesn't disturb Sherra and the children. The Wright Stuff also uses the third floor to hold competitions against the entourages of other Grizzlies.

Watching Raw Dawg—shod in stylish black Kenneth Cole loafers, by the way—and the rest of the crew luxuriate on the third floor, Wright swells with pride. "They've been with me all the way, and I feel that we've made it, not that I've made it," he says. "Maybe I'm the one in the NBA, but I know that if the roles were reversed, they would have done the same for me."

IV

Not that it's all PlayStation wishes and SUV dreams. Marty White, who is 6' 5'' and built like Mount Rainier, asserts that in a decade in Seattle he has never come to blows protecting Payton but he might with anyone brazen enough to suggest that he's a Payton flunky whose professional duties range from lingering to loitering. "I know the perception, and I hate it," says White, who just took an exam to become a licensed real estate broker in the state of Washington. "People assume that we're Gary's hang-out buddies. I see that and think, If only you knew. . . ."

As a boss Payton is just as unrelenting as he is on the court, likely to give his employees written warning for tardiness. There's even a fitness clause in the lengthy employment contract he makes his crew members sign. ("Got to look good and be in shape if you're going to roll with GP," Payton cackles.) King, Pope and White have work spaces in the Seattle offices of Payton's agents, Eric and Aaron Goodwin. Payton expects his crew to join him on the road. ("I hate being by myself," he says.) The three, prohibited by Sonics management from boarding team flights, fly commercial to every city, and Payton puts them up at the team hotel, often a $300-per-night Ritz-Carlton. But Payton also demands that they go ahead of him to the next city or back to Seattle and be there waiting when he arrives. The upshot? King, Pope and White rack up 200,000 frequent-flier miles a year, but they often have to miss the road games to beat Payton home.

"People say, 'What's it like hanging out with Gary?'" says King. "I tell them it's work. We earn every dime. There's no spoon-feeding going on here."

Indeed, while members of various entourages are paid as much as $2,000 weekly, most have specific duties. Bulls guard Jalen Rose, for instance, expects his boyhood friend Rizz Scott to cook all his meals. Jack Miles, a former Philadelphia deputy sheriff and U.S. Marines boxer, provides 24-hour security for Bucks forward Tim Thomas. (Miles has been so diligent that Milwaukee recently hired him to moonlight as the team's director of security.) Stackhouse's brothers and nephews wash his cars, feed his dogs, pay his bills, stock his fridge and pick up his dry cleaning.

"I realize how this is going to sound," says Grizzlies rookie forward Shane Battier, "but the NBA schedule is so demanding that you need someone to take care of the details, whether it's shipping a package or picking up milk at the store." After going without a personal assistant for the first half of the season, Battier retained one in January. ("I'm not sure I'd quite call it an entourage," he says. "It's a she. And she's a retired FedEx employee. I ride with a tough crowd.")

It can also fall to friends and relatives to watch games and critique their employer. Four of Stackhouse's brothers and nephews

call themselves the Regulars and sit courtside in The Palace at Auburn Hills, razzing the refs and the opposing team at each game. "They won't use profanity," says Stackhouse, "but I expect them to be loud during the game and tell me what I did right and wrong afterward." (Stackhouse does extra promotional work for the team in exchange for his crew's seats.) Friends of Baron Davis catch all the Hornets' games, either in person or on satellite, and send Davis text messages on his two-way pager about particular plays. There might be a dozen messages awaiting him when he returns to the locker room after the game.

"These guys know basketball, and they know my game better than anyone," says Davis. "They tell me what I need to hear, not what I want to hear."

One can't help wonder what it's like when your homeboy doubles as your boss, when the brother with whom you once shared a bedroom is suddenly responsible for your livelihood. Don't feelings of gratitude and indebtedness distort the dynamic? Not one of the dozens of entourage members interviewed for this story expressed that concern. King says the solution to the dilemma is simple: Draw a line between work and play. "When I'm on the clock, Gary's my boss," he says. "When we're just hanging out, G's a guy I can say anything to and slap him upside the head."

V

At the 2002 Winter Olympics, the coach, parents and five siblings of gold medal skater Sarah Hughes followed her around. There was scant talk of her having a posse. Instead we were told ad nauseam that the 16-year-old Hughes has a close-knit family. When 17-year-old Ty Tryon made his PGA Tour debut earlier this year, he was ringed by an 11-member brigade that included a trainer, a yoga instructor, an image consultant, an agent, a sports shrink and two massage therapists. It was a retinue to rival any rapper's, but there was no hue and cry. For years hangers-on and self-styled gurus have been native fauna on the tennis circuit. No one has cared much. Why is there so much consternation when basketball players bring along similar phalanxes?

One answer: The NBA, unlike individual sports, has team dynamics that might be disrupted by entourages. In Philadelphia during the 1996–97 season, the entourages of Stackhouse (then a 76er) and Iverson reportedly engaged in a brawl that became part of NBA lore. The source of the purported conflict was that each crew claimed the other's "guy" was taking too many shots. Stories also abound about entourage members accosting coaches and team officials to complain about substitution patterns or the way their player was or wasn't being used.

What's more, good team chemistry usually requires that players bond. How much social interaction can a player have with teammates when he's perpetually surrounded by his own set of friends? As Charles Barkley grouses, "It used to be your teammates were your posse. Now everyone has his own circle."

On the other hand, taking steps to exclude an entourage can also ruffle feathers. Two seasons ago Seattle management barred entourage members (as well as the media) from attending team practices, claiming that their presence was a distraction. When Nate McMillan took over as coach last season, he went a step further, barring entourage members from the training facility. Those assigned to pick up players are made to wait in the parking lot, their cars idling. In the Payton camp, at least, this was taken as an affront. Responds McMillan, "I don't have a problem with [entourages] as long as they understand the boundaries. But you can't be hanging around the locker room or practice or riding the bus."

Then there's this nettlesome question: Would there be any such angst if the entourage members weren't black and didn't wear billowy jeans and copious jewelry? No, says Poussaint, the Harvard psychiatrist, "these are African-Americans making lots of money, and having these entourages looks like loose spending, and I think that turns people off."

The posse cited most by critics is Iverson's, which he calls Cru Thik. It's composed mostly of Iverson's childhood friends, whom he imported to Philadelphia from his hometown of Newport News, Va. At times the crew has had more than a dozen members, not including Iverson's personal hair stylist from New Jersey, whom he flies to most road games. Some members have shown themselves to have something less than sterling characters. In 1998, for instance, Michael Powell, who was convicted of felony possession of cocaine in 1990 and weapons possession in '92, was pulled over while in Iverson's car and charged with cocaine possession. (The charge was dismissed.)

Two seasons ago Iverson took his friends along on a road trip to Miami. After a night of partying on South Beach, Iverson missed a morning practice and was suspended by the 76ers for one game. At the time Iverson's friend Alonzo Mourning, the Miami Heat center, said, "I don't think [Allen] has the right people around him." (Mourning should know. In April 1996 federal investigators raided his house in Potomac, Md., and seized guns, ammunition and more than $40,000 in cash as part of a drug search. The subject of the sting was Earl Lee Nolton Jr., a Mourning associate who had been living off and on in the house. Nolton later pleaded guilty to distributing crack and was sentenced to 21 years in prison.)

While Iverson stands steadfastly by his entourage—among his panoply of tattoos one reads CRU THIK and another is the Japanese characters for loyalty—its members haven't always reciprocated. One "friend" allegedly charged a $7,000 watch to Iverson's credit card. Even so, one would be hard-pressed to argue that Cru Thik has had a harmful effect on the play of the league's reigning MVP. Besides, Cru Thik has thinned; Iverson seems to have pruned his social circle recently. These days Iverson's closest confidants—yes, even the inner circles can have concentric rings—are Henry (Que) Gaskins, a Northwestern M.B.A., and Gary Moore, Iverson's former youth football coach. "Things have really calmed down," says Miles, who got to know Cru Thik when Iverson and Tim Thomas were teammates. "Like a lot of young guys Allen had to figure out who really had his best interests at heart. When you find those who don't, it's time to make some changes."

Fortunately, for decamped aides-decamp there is a secondary labor market. A few seasons ago in Minneapolis, a member of Garnett's OBF decided he wasn't getting sufficient respect, so he switched over to Marbury's entourage. Then there is the case of former guard Vernon Maxwell, who is somewhat akin to the National Basketball Development League of entourages. When Maxwell played in Philly in the mid-'90s, he was joined by, among others, his friend Brian (Cigar) Thompson. When Maxwell was traded to San Antonio, Cigar stayed, got in good with the Iverson crowd and is now a peripheral member of Cru Thik. Similarly, when Maxwell was traded to Seattle in 1999, he hung out with Mandrell Hall. Maxwell was cut by the Sonics after the season, but Hall stayed around the Pacific Northwest and now bills himself as an assistant to Vin Baker.

"Like all the guys. I hang with, Mandrell can help make my life easier, and I can help make his life easier," says Baker. "I hear it all the time, 'Vin's entourage this, Vin's entourage that.' But I'm telling you, if people took the time to see what we're really about, they'd realize that it's a win-win situation." Put another way, like so many NBA players, Baker is not worried about staying one step ahead of the posse.

The Million Man March Pledge

Louis Farrakhan

I pledge that from this day forward, I will strive to love my brother as I love myself.

I, from this day forward, will strive to improve myself spiritually, morally, mentally, socially, politically, and economically for the benefit of myself, my family, and my people.

I pledge that I will strive to build businesses, build houses, build hospitals, build factories, and enter into international trade for the good of myself, my family, and my people.

I pledge that from this day forward, I will never raise my hand with a knife or a gun to beat, cut, or shoot any member of my family or any human being except in self-defense.

I pledge from this day forward, I will never abuse my wife by striking her, disrespecting her, for she is the mother of my children and the producer of my future.

I pledge that from this day forward, I will never engage in the abuse of children, little boys, or little girls for sexual gratification. I will let them grow in peace to be strong men and women for the future of our people.

I will never again use the B-word to describe any female—but particularly, my own Black sister.

I pledge from this day forward that I will not poison my body with drugs or that which is destructive to my health and my well-being.

Source: Louis Farrakhan, "The Million Man March Pledge," Washington, D.C. October 16, 1995. Copyright © 1995 Louis Farrakhan.

I pledge from this day forward, I will support Black newspapers, Black radio, Black television. I will support Black artists who clean up their act to show respect for their people and respect for the heirs of the human family.

I will do all of this, so help me God.

Black Church Burnings in the South: Six Month Preliminary Investigation

In 1969, according to some Black community leaders, white supremacists were riding through Mississippi, in and around Meridian, torching Black churches. Twelve African American churches burned to the ground during a wave of terror that led to increased racial tensions. Some African American leaders report that neither local nor federal authorities took the burnings of the churches seriously until the white supremacists changed their strategy and firebombed a Jewish synagogue. "All of a sudden there were orders from a local law enforcement official to shoot to kill anyone that goes near Black or Jewish churches" recalled one community leader who remembers these events quite vividly.

The historical precedent was set. This time, however, we're not waiting for any more churches to be firebombed. "The time is now to seek justice and protection," Mississippi community leader.

The Center for Democratic Renewal (CDR) is a national, multi-racial, non-profit organization dedicated to working for social justice. Our mission is to promote a diverse and just society, free of racism and bigotry. For 17 years we have researched, monitored and analyzed hate groups and hate group activities so that we could better educate activists and communities on ways to combat hatred and lessen its impact. Through the years we have

moved from counting hate crimes to developing effective long-term strategies to counter their effects. While our focus has been and continues to be white supremacy and its manifestations on mainstream America, our purpose is to eradicate its influence on basic institutional and social structures, and more importantly, individuals.

When we became aware of the increased attacks on Southern Black churches, we began to investigate the extent of the bombings, burnings and vandalisms taking place in the 1990s. We have found that the greatest number of church burnings are happening in nine Southern states: Georgia, Alabama, South Carolina, North Carolina, Tennessee, Arkansas, Mississippi, Louisiana and Virginia.

For the last six months, the Center for Democratic Renewal, in partnership with the National Council of Churches and the Center for Constitutional Rights, has traveled thousands of miles to more than 30 different church sites. The delegation has conducted hundreds of interviews, provided technical assistance, spiritual guidance, legal advice, and worked to develop an ongoing strategy to identify resources to begin the rebuilding and restoration of these historically Black and multiracial landmarks. We've collectively engaged in this initiative to offer immediate and long-term support to the victims, to accurately record each case in its proper historical context, and to capture the essence of the fears, frustrations and concerns of each victim and church family. We

---

Source: "Report of Six Month Preliminary Investigation: Black Church Burnings in the South." Center for Democratic Renewal, June 10, 1996. Copyright © 1996 Center for Democratic Renewal.

have collected information and established a central repository, where data related to the burnings of Black churches in the South, including reports, photographs, video and audio tapes, can be permanently archived.

The results of our six months of work are summarized in this report. Our findings focus on four areas that surfaced as recurring themes in each community: the response of victims to federal involvement, concerns expressed by some victims that the use of terror and intimidation to move them off their land may be motives for the torching of their churches, the contemporary climate of white supremacy in the South, and an up-to-date count of actual church arsons.

This report is not an attempt to be critical of the federal government's involvement in these cases. Nor does this document express in totality the breadth and scope of the issues and concerns shared by the victims. It is intended to chronicle these incidents of domestic terrorism in ways that lift up the remarkable expressions of church families who have unwillingly become victims of some of the most heinous acts of white supremacy in this country. It will shed some light on how church burnings, including racially motivated acts of physical violence, can and most often do go unnoticed if local authorities are determined not to report them as hate crimes. This report illustrates how retaliation and intimidation remain an integral part of the Black church communities struggles long after the church burns. And finally, it will reflect the incredible strength and determination of church families who are committed to protecting the sanctity of the Black church as the center of spiritual growth in the African American community.

BLACK CHURCH BURNINGS: STATISTICS

Today, CDR's records show that 80 mostly rural, historically Black and multiracial churches have been firebombed, burned or vandalized since January 1990. Of that number, 28 have occurred since January 1996, at a rate of what appears to be about one per week. CDR's data show that generally, the attacks occur between the hours of 12 midnight and 7:00 a.m., and in most cases, firebombs or other types of accelerants were used to destroy the structures. Of those persons arrested and/or prosecuted for destruction to African American houses of worship, the majority have been white males between the ages of 14 and 45. Most travel in groups ranging from two to five, and many come from middle class suburban families. Our data also shows that since 1990 at least 13 of these arsons took place in January, around the Martin Luther King holiday.

According to information released by the Department of Justice, there are currently 200 federal agents from the ATF and FBI assigned to the various fire investigations. The Bureau of Alcohol, Tobacco and Firearms (ATF) is the arson investigative agency of the federal government. ATF derives its authority to investigate arson incidents from 18 U.S.C. Section 844(i) which makes it a federal crime to use explosives or fire to destroy property affecting interstate commerce. The legislative history of this law makes it clear that Congress intended it to cover churches and synagogues. During the 1950s and 60s, there was no federal agency with the specialized skill needed for investigating complex arson cases.

Since January 1995, ATF has conducted 51 church fire investigations. Twenty-five of these investigations are arsons which occurred at predominately African American churches. As of May 1, 1996, only four months into the year, DOJ received reports of fires at 24 churches, seventeen of which occurred at churches in which membership is predominately African American. As of May 20, 1996, the FBI had 42 pending investigations involving church arsons or suspected arsons which occurred in 15 states. Of this total, 33 churches were predominately African American.

For more detailed statistics and information on the latest data on the church attacks, please turn to the back of this report.

CONCERNS ABOUT FEDERAL INVESTIGATIONS

The Clinton Administration has what appears to be an incredible mountain to climb as concerns about the federal government's handling of these investigations on the local level remain topics of front porch conversations in many rural communities. While there seems to be a broad consensus that federal authorities have put forth a good faith public response in their efforts to effectively coordinate investigative and prosecutorial initiatives, this effort is being undermined at best by the ATF's credibility factor. The integrity of federal investigations in Tennessee and Alabama are being viewed as suspect, particularly around investigations into the January 8, 1996, firebombing of the Inner City Church and the Greene County Church fires in Boligee, Alabama.

In South Carolina, the state with the largest number of reported Black church burnings, there are allegations that in the past, a lack of real cooperation between the State Law Enforcement Division (SLED) and federal agents has hampered investigatory efforts involving such a massive undertaking. This relationship, as well as suspicions about whether an accurate account of Black church burnings in South Carolina was being released was called into question in May 3, 1996, when an article appeared in the *State Newspaper* reporting that according to ATF statistics, there had been 100 church fires in South Carolina since 1991. This figure was quickly refuted by the State Law Enforcement Division.

This section raises many clear and compelling points that must be addressed by the Clinton Administration as they reflect what appears to be escalating points of tension in communities across the South.

QUESTIONABLE INVESTIGATIONS

One area that has not been given widespread attention in the cases of Black church burnings, is the issue of whether or not local volunteer fire departments may be playing a key role in obstructing the course of federal investigations in many of the church fires in the South. This issue coupled with issues of suspect state and federal investigations continue to stir community debate.

- June 6, 1994, the Jerusalem Branch Baptist Church in Aiken, South Carolina burned to the ground. Local fire officials concluded that the cause of the fire was electrical. Experts brought in by Jerusalem's insurance company, the Southern Mutual Church Insurance Company, determined the cause of the fire to be arson. To date, there is no indication that federal authorities initiated an arson investigation.

  Reactions to the church burnings by local officials in some areas range from indifference to outright hostility towards the victims. Personal attitudes play a large part in the type of investigation that takes place in some regions, which translates into questionable investigations. In many cases, local authorities spent little time or effort investigating the fires, often refusing to recognize the possibility of arson. In some cases an even worse type of negligence has been exhibited when church members were accused of burning down their own churches, their sacred "home away from home." The following examples illustrate the propensity of local authorities to dismiss the need to take seriously the investigation:

- When the Mount Zion AME Church in Greeleyville, S.C., burned to the ground on the morning of June 20, 1995, the pastor was informed by a firefighter working on the scene that the cause of their church burning was an electrical fire. When the pastor asked the question, "How can that be so?" he was again advised that the fire was electrical. On the same night, the nearby Macedonia Baptist Church in Manning burned to the ground. When local and state authorities began their investigation, the cause of the fire was changed to arson. Two young white males with admitted connections to the Christian Knights of the Ku Klux Klan, one of the most active white supremacist groups in South Carolina, were later arrested and charged with arson in these cases. The cause of the fires was later determined to be racially motivated.

- In Lauderdale, Mississippi, when St. Paul's Primitive Baptist Church burned to the ground, local and state authorities first determined that the church burning was arson. Later, after interviewing the deacon of the church, and discovering that he smokes, officials determined that the cause was a cigarette butt that was thrown against the church building.

The deacon, who had been a part of the church family for more than 20 years, had just finished cutting the grass and cleaning the church in preparation for Easter Sunday services. Although he is a smoker, his pastor had instructed the parishioners not to smoke in the church, and the deacon insists that he was in the parking lot near his truck when he smoked his cigarette. When called to the Sheriff's Department to be interviewed by local and federal authorities, the deacon stated that one of the agents thoroughly interrogated him while another agent began to quote scripture to him. Then everyone left the room, except the individual who recorded the deacon's statement. It was at that point that the deacon reportedly broke into tears. "The deacon cried, not because he burned down the church, but because he loved his church and felt extremely humiliated that he would be accused of burning it down," stated a local NAACP official. During a May 1996 news conference, the Meridian County Chapter of the NAACP supported the deacon and the church, and challenged the findings of the investigation. Many feel that the investigation was cut short when an easy answer to the cause of the fire was found. In Mississippi, six church fires have been identified since 1993. Four of those fires took place within the last two months. The Lauderdale church fire was the most recent.

Another reason for authorities to look further than church family members in their investigations is evident in the Lauderdale Church fire. Not too far away, the trailer home of a Black family was burned to the ground within two or three days of the church fire. Their trailer home was located near a church where a small African-American congregation worshipped. According to residents, it took a long time for the volunteer fire department to reach the home. This family claims to have never been contacted by local, state or federal law enforcement authorities, despite the fact that a white male was seen leaving the scene of the fire, as the home burned to the ground.

- In West Point Mississippi, the Living Manner Baptist Church sits on a major highway across from a public school. The pastor and his congregates left the church site shortly after Sunday worship service on March 10, 1996. All electrical power to the church was shut off. At approximately seven o'clock that evening, the pastor was called and told that the church was on fire. According to fire officials, the ceiling furnace caused the church to catch fire, despite the fact that the furnace was not on.

- In Dallas County, Alabama on March 25, 1996, the Central Baptist Church was destroyed by fire. State and federal authorities determined in a matter of days that the church was burned to the ground after a violent rain and electrical storm. Members of the congregation, a small family church of about 25–30, cooperated fully with investigators, and believed that they were doing a fine job. According to certain members of the church, federal authorities from Birmingham were brought in to investigate the fire. Shortly after the case was ruled as natural (struck by lightning), local authorities began to interview members of the congregation, inquiring as to whether or not there were problems within the church and problems with the church finances. Federal authorities began to show up unannounced at the homes and on the jobs of some parishioners. Eventually the District Attorney subpoenaed the church's financial records. When asked the question, "If the state and federal authorities concluded that the church was burned by natural causes, then why is there what appears to be a local and federal probe into the church's affairs?" No one could answer that question. The church family was forced to incur the cost of hiring an attorney to represent them.

ALLEGATIONS OF FEDERAL HARASSMENT OF CHURCH MEMBERS

We've found, in our investigation, that local fire and police officials are not the only ones to quickly "blame the victims" of these church burnings. Church members often put a great deal of trust in federal authorities when local

authorities fail them. But in some cases, illustrated below, federal investigators seemed as
eager as local officials to dismiss the idea of
deliberate arson from outside forces and
the wider overarching pattern of Southern
church burnings. Church members, rather
than being assured of a fair investigation by
federal officials, instead felt harassed by
them, particularly when they themselves became the targets of federal probes.

- On February 21, 1996, the Glorious Church of
  God of Christ in Richmond, Virginia was
  nearly destroyed by fire. The 2-story granite
  structure, built in 1908, received more than
  $300,000–400,000 in damage. The incident was
  reported to church members around 6:30 am
  on a very foggy morning. The fire was investigated by the city fire inspector, state police
  and the ATF. The fire was reportedly started
  when someone turned on the gas stoves, after
  saturating the sofa and lounge with gasoline.
  The fire department questioned parishioners,
  asked about squabbles within the church, and
  even did checks on church members who had
  left years earlier.
      In May, the ATF came back, as is appropri-
  ate for a proper investigation. ATF agents informed church members that all of the outside
  leads were dead, and insinuated that church
  members had burned down their own church.
- On May 21, 1996, Rev. Algie Jarrett testified
  before Congress that a federal agent, when investigating the burning of the Mount Calvary
  Church of God in Bolivar, Tennessee, showed
  up at the high school of a seventeen year-old
  student, harshly questioning and interrogating her. She felt that the investigator was trying to get her to say something that was not
  true.
- While investigating the arson of the Inner City
  Baptist Church in Knoxville, Tennessee, federal authorities have polygraphed pastors,
  fingerprinted church members, shown up
  unannounced at job sites and homes, and implied that church members burned their own
  church.
- Members of the Gays Hill Baptist Church in
  Millen, Georgia were subjected to intense
  questioning by federal agents more than two
  months after the church burned to the
  ground. Among other questions the agent(s)
  reportedly inquired about the only white female who attended the church, using references that church members found offensive.
  At one point agents accused church members
  of not allowing Mexicans to worship with
  them.
- Nearly three months after someone set fire to
  the Sweet Home Baptist Church in Baker,
  Louisiana, what church members describe as a
  team of investigators appeared one day and
  began interviewing every member of the
  church. The Sweet Home Baptist Church is
  a small family of 30–35 people. According to
  one church member, "I had never been through
  anything like that in my life. The way they were
  asking us questions, it seemed liked they were
  saying that we set fire to our own church."
- On Monday, May 14, 1996, the day after a National Council of Churches' delegation traveled to Tennessee to meet with local ministers,
  the 100-year-old Mount Pleasant Baptist
  Church in Tigrett, Tennessee, was completely
  destroyed. This was the fifteenth Black church
  to be burned in Tennessee since August 1994.
  The fire was reported to the fire department
  around noon. Based on local reports, agents
  from the Federal Bureau of Investigation
  spent all afternoon and evening in the neighborhood. Some residents report that agents
  went door-to-door, questioning residents.
  Federal Agents reportedly asked questions
  such as, "Do you know if the fire was set?"
  and "Did you see anybody taking things out
  of the church?" Church members felt as if
  they were being accused.
      On Wednesday, June 5, 1996, certain mem-
  bers of the church received subpoenas from
  the state fire marshall requesting their presence at the police department for questioning.
  Those who were ordered to appear were
  scheduled for different times and asked to
  bring church documents with them, implying
  that they, and the church itself, were under investigation.

CHURCH OFFICIALS CLAIM NO KNOWLEDGE OF STATE OR FEDERAL INVESTIGATION

In some cases, church officials appear to have
been virtually ignored by local, state, and federal officials. The burned out churches provoked so little interest, that only a cursory

investigation has taken place, if any at all. Church members are left wondering why so little has been done when their spiritual homes have been destroyed.

- On March 8 & 9, 1995, during the early morning hours, the interior structure of the Hammond Grove Baptist Church in Aiken, South Carolina was almost destroyed by vandals, causing nearly $20,000 worth of damage. Two young white males, 14 and 15 years of age, left a path of destruction that included racist graffiti of every hate-filled phrase imaginable—"Kill Niggers, Satan Rules, White Aryan race"—plus the drawing of a noose with the word "nigger" pointing to the inside. Despite widespread local coverage and the evidence that this was a racially motivated act, never once did members of this church receive as much as a phone call from state or federal authorities. It is believed that these young men may have connections to a white supremacist group that reportedly organized on the local school campus. The church is located in a majority white community.
- The New Hope Missionary Baptist Church in Marianna, Arkansas burned to the ground on the third Sunday in January 1996 (January 21). The exact time the fire stared is unknown, though church members have reason to believe the fire started sometime after midnight and before daybreak. The state fire marshall conducted the investigation into the cause of the fire, but to date the results have not been released. One of the church deacons was asked to do a recorded interview with the insurance adjuster. The deacon asked several simple questions that have yet to be answered. He asked questions such as, "Who called the fire department? Was the call made from a pay telephone or a residence phone?" The pastor is still puzzled that neither he nor any members of the church were called. After the initial visit from the fire department, church members never heard from officials again. Despite all of the media coverage about Black church burnings in the South, this church fire received no media coverage and little official attention.
- On March 31, 1996, one week before Easter Sunday, Butler Chapel AME Church in Orangeburg, South Carolina, burned to the ground. This was the final, and fatal, attack on

the church that had earlier experienced several incidents of vandalism and fires. The first attack on the church were vandals who simply came into the church and destroyed things by tearing them up. In the second attack, the tablecloth on the communion table was burned. A second tablecloth was burned one week before the church was totally burned and destroyed.

Church members were told by representatives of the local fire department that the fire was deliberately set. Something yet unidentified was thrown into the church to start the fire. Officially stating that the church was a victim of "vandalism," the insurance company has declared the church a total loss. Church members know of no state or federal investigation, even though the church is located within a 50-mile radius of other South Carolina church fires in the Denmark/Barnwell area.

SUSPICIONS OF PROPERTY/ FINANCIAL MOTIVATIONS

Some of the churches, located in small towns or rural areas, have been in the same place, on the same land, for a number of years. As the town has grown up around the churches, or as the community changes, the land that the churches occupy has become valuable to local residents. Some church members feel that the arsons are a deliberate attempt to frighten the church families into moving from the land and selling off their heritage.

- The Mount Zion AME Church in Greeleyville, S.C., was burned to the ground on June 20, 1995. Prior to the church arson, some church leaders had been approached by individuals in the community interested in the sale or swap of their land. The nearly 80-year-old structure was completely destroyed by fire.
- The St. John's Baptist Church in the Dixiana Community in South Carolina burned on August 15, 1995, after 10 years of repeated acts of vandalism, defacement to gravesites, and destruction. The church site, surrounded by encroaching development, has a state road that reportedly runs across the front of what was

the old church site. Because of the prolonged period of racist terror aimed at the church, the question of whether someone is attempting to run this church family off their land continues to come up over and over again in local discussions.

- The Living Manna Baptist Church in West Point, Mississippi, burned extensively on Sunday, March 10, 1996. Officials determined the fire to be accidental—caused by the ceiling furnace. The church, located on a major highway directly across from a public school, reportedly sits on prime land in this small Mississippi town. Some sources have reported that church leaders frequently get offers to buy their land. A similar offer was presented shortly after the church burning incident.
- The Rock Hill Baptist Church in Aiken, S.C., burned down to the ground February 19, 1994. The church arson, which remains unsolved, literally destroyed the nucleus of the church family as it existed. Without money to rebuild, the site today remains empty of what used to be a thriving small family church. Some say that, "It got to the point where the elders were dying off and the children began to sell property that had been in their families for years. I believe they were trying to run us off. That's what I believe."
- The Butler Chapel AME Church is located on a dirt road in a predominately white community in Orangeburg, S.C. For many years the community was all African American, but as Blacks moved out, whites moved in. We own the land and will keep it but we will not rebuild on the same site. We will not move our cemetery. Over 100 years of history rests here and we will not be forced off our land.

CONTINUING THREATS AND INTIMIDATION

The burnings of Black churches are deliberate acts of threat and intimidation to whole Black communities. Sometimes, however, that's not enough for some members of the community, and individual ministers are threatened.

- When the Mount Zion AME Church in Greeleyville, South Carolina, was burned, the persons charged with the crime attended a preliminary hearing where they claimed involvement in the Christian Knights of the Ku Klux Klan. After the hearing, a terroristic threat was made to the pastor. Someone approached him outside the courthouse building saying, "I'm going to get you Nigger." The same threat was reportedly made a second time under different circumstances. Both incidents were reported to federal authorities.
- Immediately following the burning of the Inner City Church in Knoxville, Tennessee, on January 8, 1996, pastors from the church, along with their family members, began to receive threatening phone calls at their homes. During one such incident the caller reportedly threatened, "Your wife is going to leave home one day and not come back." Although each incident was forwarded to federal authorities, family members received no response. "They acted as if it just didn't matter" stated one pastor.

WHITE SUPREMACY AND BLACK CHURCH BURNINGS

- On May 17, 1992, three Black churches located in southeastern Arkansas were burned by two white males from Desha County, who wanted to "get" African Americans. Both men pleaded guilty to one count of violating Title 18 United States Code, Section 371, Conspiracy. They were sentenced to 37 months.
- On April 3, 1993, in Pike County Mississippi, on the anniversary of the death of Dr. Martin Luther King, Jr., two African American churches were destroyed. The Springhill Freewill Baptist Church and the Rocky Point Missionary Baptist Church in rural southern Mississippi were burned to the ground by three white males who wanted to teach the "niggers" a lesson. On October 1, 1993, all three men pled guilty to federal charges. Two of the defendants were sentenced to 37 months and one was sentenced to 46 months in federal prison.
- The Mount Zion AME Church in Greeleyville, S.C. was burned on June 21, 1995 and the Macedonia Baptist Church in Bloomville was destroyed the next day. One of the men arrested, Timothy Adron Welch, carried a card certifying that he was a member of the Christian Knights of the Ku Klux Klan. Both Welch

and Gary Christopher Cox, who was also arrested for the arsons, reportedly attended KKK rallies that were held near the Mount Zion Church.

- Three white men were convicted of the firebombing of two Black churches in Columbia, Tennessee in 1995. The men reportedly attacked the churches because they wanted to teach Blacks a lesson after one of the men discovered his daughter was involved in an interracial relationship.
- Three white males in Sumter County, Alabama, pled guilty to destroying three Black churches in the area, Buck's Chapel Church, Oak Grove Missionary Baptist Church and Pine Top Baptist. The three were prosecuted in state court on criminal charges motivated by hate on the basis of religion and race.
- In Clarksville, Tennessee, three white males between the ages of 15 and 18 were charged with civil rights violations, arson, possession of firearms, and were convicted in federal court for the firebombings of two homes and the Benevolent Lodge. They claimed to be members of a group they called the Aryan Faction.
- Ernest Pierce, state leader of the Knights of the Ku Klux Klan, was indicted and prosecuted for the December 1991 burning of the Barren River Baptist Church in Bowling Green, Kentucky.

CONCLUSION

Domestic Terrorism is defined by the FBI as the "unlawful" use of force or violence against persons or property to intimidate or coerce the government, the civilian population or any segment thereof in furtherance of political or social objectives."

House Bill 2703 defines "terrorism" as state and federal crimes such as kidnapping, killing, serious assaults, and illegal property damage that creates a substantial risk of serious bodily injury when such crimes involve conduct in both the United States and abroad; meet a jurisdictional base and are certified by the attorney General as "terrorism" because the crime is calculated to retaliate against the government, or influence government conduct by intimidation or coercion, and is a violation of one or a number of federal statues. Under this broad definition, virtually every serious crime involving conduct both within and outside of the United States is a federal crime of "terrorism" when the Attorney General says it is.

According to the Hate Crimes Statistics Act, a Hate Crime is defined as any crime that manifests evidence of prejudice on the basis of race, religion, national origin, which includes but is not limited to murder, aggravated assault, rape, and destruction to property.

The Center for Democratic Renewal, along with the National Council of Churches and the Center for Constitutional Rights, maintains that these attacks against Black churches are acts of domestic terrorism and hate crimes. The perpetrators of these acts must be sought out and prosecuted to the fullest extent of the law. The seriousness of these arsons cannot be underemphasized. The growing numbers of church burnings and bombings have reached epidemic proportion.

A Ten Point Plan to Mobilize the Churches

1. Establish 4–5 church cluster-collaborations which sponsor "Adopt-A-Gang" programs to organize and evangelize youth in gangs, inner-city churches would serve as drop-in centers providing sanctuary for troubled youth.

2. Commission missionaries to serve as advocates and ombudsmen for black and Latino juveniles in the courts. Such missionaries would work closely with probation officers, law enforcement officials, and youth streetworkers to assist at-risk youth and their families. They would also convene summit meetings between school superintendents, principals of public middle and high schools, and black and Latino pastors to develop partnerships that will focus on the youth most at-risk. We propose to do pastoral work with the most violent and troubled young people and their families. In our judgment this is a rational alternative to ill-conceived proposals to substitute incarceration for education.

3. Commission youth evangelists to do street-level one-on-one evangelism with youth involved in drug trafficking. These evangelists would also work to prepare these youth for participation in the economic life of the nation. Such work might include preparation for college, the development of legal revenue-generating enterprises, and acquisition of trade skills and union membership.

4. Establish accountable, community-based economic development projects that go beyond "market and state" visions of revenue generation. Such an economic development initiative will include community and trusts, microenterprise projects, worker cooperatives, and democratically run community development corporations.

5. Establish links between suburban and downtown churches and front-line ministries to provide spiritual, human resource, and material support.

6. Initiate and support neighborhood crimewatch programs within local church neighborhoods. If, for example, 200 churches covered the four corners surrounding their sites, 800 blocks would be safer.

7. Establish working relationships between local churches and community-based health centers to provide pastoral counseling for families during times of crisis. We also propose the initiation of drug abuse prevention programs and abstinence-oriented educational programs focusing on the prevention of AIDS and sexually transmitted diseases.

8. Convene a working summit meeting for Christian black and Latino men and women in order to discuss the development of Christian brotherhoods and sisterhoods that would provide rational alternatives to violent gang life. Such groups would also be charged with fostering responsibility to family and protecting houses of worship.

9. Establish rape crisis drop-in centers and services for battered women in churches. Counseling programs must be established for abusive men, particularly teenagers and young adults.

10. Develop an aggressive black and Latino curriculum, with an additional focus on the struggles of women and poor people. Such a curriculum could be taught in churches as a means of helping our youth understand that the God of history has been and remains active in the lives of all people.

NTLF MISSION

NTLF's primary mission is to help provide African-American Christian churches with the strategic vision, programmatic structure, and financial resources necessary to save at-risk inner-city youth from child abuse and neglect, street violence, drug abuse, school failure, teen-age pregnancy, incarceration,

---

Source: National Ten Point Leadership Foundation and the Ella J. Baker House, Boston, "A Ten-Point Plan to Mobilize the Churches" by Reverend Eugene Rivera. Copyright © 2002 National Ten Point Leadership Foundation. Used with permission.

chronic joblessness, spiritual depravity, and hopelessness about the future.

Executive Director Jacqueline C. Rivers and her husband, Rev. Eugene F. Rivers 3d also run the Azusa Christian Community, a church located in Boston's most economically distressed Dorchester neighborhood. Inspired by the half-century of work done in Philadelphia by Pastor Benjamin Smith of Deliverance Evangelistic Church, NTLF grew directly out of the Rivers' own decade-plus of nationally-acknowledged, faith-centered, street-level work with some of America's most severely at-risk inner-city children, including juvenile probationers.

In Boston, NTLF acts in partnership with local synagogues and the Catholic Church, and runs programs in cooperation with social service agencies and law enforcement authorities.

While working diligently to attract the full-time staff and raise the money needed to deepen and expand its youth and community outreach ministry in Dorchester and throughout Boston, NTLF has established on-going ties to many national research institutions, think tanks, universities, and seminaries including The Institute for Civil Society, the New York Theological Seminary, Harvard University, Public/Private Ventures, the Brookings Institution, the Manhattan Institute, and others.

Kwanzaa

Kwanzaa was created in 1966 by M. Ron Karenga. But to appreciate the real value and purpose of **Kwanzaa** for Black people and to save it from becoming a fad and dying the inevitable and undignified death of all fads—it must be clearly separated from the myths and distortions that have grown up around it. The first myth is that **Kwanzaa** is a continental African holiday rather than an African-American one. But the fact is that there is nowhere on the African continent a holiday named **Kwanzaa.** Nor is there any holiday celebrated on the continent with the same symbols, practices or principles. **Kwanzaa,** is an African-American holiday which by its very definition reflects the dual character of the identity and experience of the African-American people.

Karenga put emphasis on the African roots of the holiday rather than its African-American roots and content for four basic reasons. First, we, African-Americans, are an African people and thus, our creations are African both in terms of our racial type and historical and cultural continuity. Karenga did not mean to suggest in any way that **Kwanzaa** was a continental African holiday rather than African-American one. On the contrary, he always stressed that although **Kwanzaa** has some historical roots in Africa, it is essentially a product of the particular social conditions and self-determined needs of the African-American people.

Secondly the concept of **Kwanzaa** as a holiday of the "first fruits" comes directly out of the tradition of agricultural peoples in Africa, who celebrated and gave thanks for harvests at designated times during the year. Although African-Americans are essentially an urban people and thus, have no crops to harvest, the concept of "ingathering and celebration" formed a conceptual basis for **Kwanzaa.**

Thus, **Kwanzaa** is a time for the gathering in of our people, celebration of ourselves and our achievements and rededication to greater achievements and fuller more meaningful lives in the future. Moreover, the collective values, spirit and practices which pervade the **Kwanzaa** holiday, have their historical and cultural roots in Africa.

It is true that **Kwanzaa** is derived from the Swahili word, **Kwanza,** which means first and is part of the phrase "Matunda ya Kwanza" (first fruits). However, Maulana Ron Karenga added the extra **a** to distinguish the name of the holiday **Kwanzaa** from the word **Kwanza** which simply means first and does not convey the distinct identity and purpose of the holiday.

I. Meaning

Kwanzaa is a word meaning "First" or in this case it signifies the **First Fruits.** Celebration of harvesting the first crops or first fruits is traditional in Africa. At this time of year our people in Africa came together to make joyful noises, give thanks and enjoy the blessing of living, and acting together for the community. Everyone brought what he grew or made to contribute to the Karamu (feast) that took place in the celebration. Songs were sung, dances danced, food was eaten and drinks were drunk, in a word—life was lived in sheer enjoyment.

II. Symbols of Kwanzaa

A. **Mkeka** (Mikeka)—The **Mkeka** is a straw mat on which all other items are placed. It is a traditional item and therefore symbolizes tradition as the foundation on which all else rests.

B. **Kinara** (Vinara)—The **Kinara** is a candle-holder which holds seven candles and represents the original stalk from which we all sprang. For it is traditionally said that the first-born was like a stalk of corn which produces corn which in turn becomes stalks which reproduce in the same manner so that there is no ending to us.

C. **Mshumaa** (Mishumaa)—The seven candles represent the Seven Principles (Nguzo Saba) on which the first-born set up

our society in order that our people might get the maximum from it. They are Umoja (Unity); Kujichagulia (Self-Determination); Ujima (Collective Work and Responsibility); Ujamaa (Co-operative Economics); Nia (Purpose); Kuumba (Creativity); and Imani (Faith).

The number of candles used as explained above are seven and include one black, three red and three green candles. The black candle is placed in front on the **kinara;** the three red candles are placed on the left and the three green candles are placed on the right of the **kinara.** Each day a candle is lit to symbolize one of the **Nguzo Saba.** After it is lit, it is explained by the person lighting it and used as the main topic of discussion for that day.

The Black candle is the center candle because it represents Black people in unity, and unity is the central or foundational principle. Also, the black candle is the first candle lit, because it is the first principle of the **Nguzo Saba.** Beginning with the second day, the candles are lit on the left and the right alternately. This is done because the candles on the left are red and represent struggle which comes before a green future can be assured. Thus, the practice of lighting the red and then the green candle is a statement and reinforcement of the fact that there can be no future unless and until there's struggle. Finally, each candle which has been lit is relit along with the candles of the day until the last candle has been lit on the last day of **Kwanzaa.**

D. **Kibunzi** (Vibunzi)—The ear of corn represents the offspring or produce (the children) of the stalk (the parents of the house). It signifies the ability or potential of the offspring themselves to become stalks, i.e. parents, and thus produce their offspring—a process which goes on indefinitely and insures the immortality of the Nation. To illustrate this we use as many ears of corn as we have children which again signifies the number of potential stalks i.e. parents. Every house has at least one ear of corn, for there is always the potential even if it has not yet been realized.

III. Dates and Procedures

A. The dates are December 26 thru January 1.

B. Dedication to Work and Study—

December 26 thru January 1 is the dedication period in which we commit ourselves to work and study for the World Liberation of African People now and forever, for as long as the moon follows the sun.

C. Procedures

On each day of the week of **Kwanzaa,** when asked, "Habari Gani, (What's the news?)", the answer will not be "Njema (Good)", but one of the Seven Principles—depending upon whether or not it is the first, second, onto the 7th day, i.e. on the fifth day if someone asks, "Habari Gani?", the answer would be "Nia," which is the fifth principle.

Approximately a week before the 26th, decorations should be put up and arranged. **First,** we should use a Red, Black and Green color scheme. The Red is for the blood of our ancestors which has not been shed in vain, Black is for our faces and the jobs we must do, and Green is for the land, youth, and new ideas. **Secondly,** the main table should have as its center piece, a straw basket of mixed tropical fruits and vegetables. **Thirdly,** either the floor or a low table should be used to place the **mkeka** and other items. After the **mkeka** has been spread out, place the **kinara** in the center. Then place the ear(s) of **kibunzi** around or on the sides of it. Place the **Zawadi** on the **mkeka** in any creative arrangement. The **Zawadi** can be placed whenever they are available. Finally, the **mishumaa** should be placed in the kinara. And at dinner, it should be brought to the table, lit and explained in terms of the principle it represents. The children should explain it as far as possible, since it is for them that this is done, therefore, on the first day one **mshumaa** should be lit, and so on until the seventh day on which all are lit. Each night the **kinara** should be replaced on the **mkeka** after dinner and the **mishumaa** should be blown out that night.

Finally, on the day of Kwanzaa the seventh day, January 1, the **Zawadi** should be opened. Moreover, it is important that a large dinner be prepared that day, and that at the table the last Principle is explained and discussed and that the children's commitments for the coming year be heard. It would be good to play African music all that day if records or tapes are available.

Please Note that the children should do as much in preparation and celebration of the holiday as they are able to do, i.e. decorate, cook, place items, etc.

Suggested Kwanzaa Decorations

The following symbols are suggested for Kwanzaa decorating:

Candles—(in windows) Red/Black/Green. Red is the flame. Black is for the kinara (candle-holder) and Green is for the Candle.

Ankh—(in small windows) represents life and man. Black/Brown/Yellow/Red.

Sun—represents Creation and Growth. Yellow/Orange/Red.

Corn—represents the offspring or the potential offspring.

Horn of Plenty—Harvest/Fruits of our labor.

IV. **Karamu** (The Feast)

The night of the feast is for the community. It is a part of the Kwanzaa celebration and takes place on the 31st of December. The Karamu consists of the seven main things that feasts usually consist of: food, drink, music, dance, conversation, laughter, and ceremony. All of the things mentioned are provided by the different Houses that make up our Community, i.e. the families. The women together, decide what is needed and the men come up with the necessary money and or material. They prepare everything by the third Principle of the Nguzo Saba which is Ujima. (Collective Work and Responsibility). We bring out pillows and we sit on the floor, dance dances, listen to African music, tell African stories, make our traditional tambiko (sacrifice offering) and drink from the **kikombe** (unity cup), drinking from which we shall each say "Harambee!"

The decoration for the Karamu should be the same as for the rest of **Kwanzaa.** It should be at the largest house and should be donated for the Karamu. A long low table should be used to place the food on. Again, the color scheme and the center piece should be used, as well as the other symbols which the House should already have.

V. The **Zawadi** (Gifts)

This is the special day for the watoto (our children). The gifts are given to the children the last day of Kwanzaa, January 1st. The presents represent: 1) the fruits of the labor of the parents, and 2) the rewards of the seeds sown by the children. For parents must commit their children to goodness which to us is beauty. We must commit them to goodness, good thoughts, good grades, etc., for the coming year and reward them according to how well they live up to their commitments. Goodness again, is beauty and beauty is that which promises happiness to the family and community. For all acts, thoughts and values are invalid if they do not in some way benefit the community.

This is in brief our holiday which we decided on, using tradition and reason as is our custom. To us it is a sign of self-determination and self-respect. And it is one of the legacies that we leave our children so that they will not turn to each other and say "our fathers have left us nothing." And finally, we do it because we are creative and we enjoy creating images and the foundations upon which these images rest. For it is the wisdom of our fathers that no matter how well an image is made it must stand on something. Surely, by things like this, we provide that something of value.

PRONUNCIATION GUIDE

Swahili pronunciation is extremely easy. The vowels are pronounced like those of Spanish and the consonants, with only a few exceptions like those of English. The vowels are as follows: a=ah as in father; e=a as in day; I=ee as in free; o=o as in go; u=oo as in too. The accent is almost always on the penultimate, i.e., next to the last syllable, except for a few words borrowed from Arabic which are irrelevant here.

The singular and plurals of the Swahili words used in Kwanzaa are as follows (with singulars first and plurals second):

1. Mkeka, Mikeka
2. Kinara, Vinara
3. Kibunzi (Vibunzi)
4. Zawadi (Singular & Plural)
5. Mshummaa, Mishumaa
6. Nguzo (Singular & Plural)
7. Karamu (Singular & Plural)

The Commission to Study Reparations Proposals for African Americans Act

John Conyers, Jr.

MAJOR ISSUES—REPARATIONS

The Commission to Study Reparations Proposals for African American Act: In January of 1989, I first introduced the bill H.R. 40, Commission to Study Reparation Proposals for African Americans Act. I have re-introduced HR 40 every Congress since 1989, and will continue to do so until it's passed into law.

One of the biggest challenges in discussing the issue of reparations in a political context is deciding how to have a national discussion without allowing the issue to polarize our party or our nation. The approach that I have advocated for over a decade has been for the federal government to undertake an official study of the impact of slavery on the social, political and economic life of our nation.

Over 4 million Africans and their descendants were enslaved in the United States and its colonies from 1619 to 1865, and as a result, the United States was able to begin its grand place as the most prosperous country in the free world.

It is un-controverted that African slaves were not compensated for their labor. More unclear however, is what the effects and remnants of this relationship have had on African-Americans and our nation from the time of emancipation through today.

I chose the number of the bill, 40, as a symbol of the forty acres and a mule that the United States initially promised freed slaves.

Source: Congressman John Conyers, Jr., "The Commission to Study Reparations Proposals for African Americans Act, House Rule 40." (January 1989).

This unfulfilled promise and the serious devastation that slavery had on African-American lives has never been officially acknowledged by the United States Government.

My bill does four things:

1. It acknowledges the fundamental injustice and inhumanity of slavery
2. It establishes a commission to study slavery, its subsequent racial and economic discrimination against freed slaves;
3. It studies the impact of those forces on today's living African Americans; and
4. The commission would then make recommendations to Congress on appropriate remedies to redress the harm inflicted on living African Americans.

The commission established would also shed light on the capture and procurement of slaves, the transport and sale of slaves, the treatment of slaves in the colonies and in the United States. It would examine the extent to which Federal and State governments in the U.S. supported the institution of slavery and examine federal and state laws that discriminated against freed African slaves from the end of the Civil War to the present.

Many of the most pressing issues, which have heretofore not been broached on any broad scale, would be addressed. Issues such as the lingering negative effects of the institution of slavery, whether an apology is owed, whether compensation is warranted and, if so, in what form and who should be eligible would also be delved into.

H.R. 40 has strong grass roots support within the African American community, including major civil rights organizations, religious organizations, academic and civic groups from across the country. This support is very similar to the strong grassroots support that proceeded another legislative initiative: the Martin Luther King, Jr. Holiday bill. It took a full 15 years from the time I first introduced it on April 5, 1968 to its passage in the fall of 1983. Through most of those 15 years, the idea of a federal holiday honoring an African American civil rights leader was considered a radical idea.

Like the King Holiday bill, we have seen the support for this bill increase each year. Today we have over 40 co-sponsors, more than at any time in the past. What is also encouraging is the dramatic increase in the number of supporters for the bill among Members of Congress who are not members of the Congressional Black Caucus. Just this past month my Colleague Tony Hall, from Ohio introduced a bill calling for an apology as well as the creation of a reparations commission. So now, for the first time we now have two bills in Congress that call for the creation of a commission.

We are also encouraged by the support of city councils and other local jurisdiction that have supported our bill. Already the city councils in Detroit, Cleveland, Chicago and Atlanta have passed bills supporting H.R. 40. And just this past month a councilman in Los Angeles, the site of our 2000 convention has introduced a bill with the strong support of the Los Angeles community. Also, there are presently two bills in the Michigan State House of Representatives addressing the issue of reparations.

It is a fact that slavery flourished in the United States and constituted an immoral and inhumane deprivation of African slaves' lives, liberty and cultural heritage. As a result, millions of African Americans today continue to suffer great injustices.

But reparation is a national and a global issue, which should be addressed in America and in the world. It is not limited to Black Americans in the US but is an issue for the many countries and villages in Africa, which were pilfered, and the many countries, which participated in the institution of slavery.

Another reason that this bill has garnered so much resistance is because many people want to leave slavery in the past—they contend that slavery happened so long ago that it is hurtful and divisive to bring it up now. It's too painful. But the concept of reparations is not a foreign idea to either the U.S. government or governments throughout the world.

Though there is historical cognition for reparations and it is a term that is fairly well known in the international body politic, the question of reparations for African Americans remains unresolved. And so, just as we've discussed the Holocaust, and Japanese interment camps, and to some extent the devastation that the colonists inflicted upon the Indians, we must talk about slavery and its continued effects.

Last year the Democratic Party included this issue in the platform it asks that country engage in a discussion at the federal legislative level would send an important signal to the African American community and other people of goodwill.

Commission to Study Reparation Proposals for African-Americans Act (Introduced in the House)

HR 40 IH
107th CONGRESS
1st Session
H. R. 40

To acknowledge the fundamental injustice, cruelty, brutality, and inhumanity of slavery in the United States and the 13 American colonies between 1619 and 1865 and to establish a commission to examine the institution of slavery, subsequently de jure and de facto racial and economic discrimination against African-Americans, and the impact of these forces on living African-Americans, to make recommendations to the Congress on appropriate remedies, and for other purposes.

IN THE HOUSE OF REPRESENTATIVES
January 3, 2001

Mr. CONYERS (for himself, Mr. FATTAH, Mr. HASTINGS of Florida, Mr. HILLIARD, Mr. JEFFERSON, Ms. EDDIE BERNICE JOHNSON of Texas, Mrs. MEEK of Florida,

Mr. OWENS, Mr. RUSH, and Mr. TOWNS) introduced the following bill; which was referred to the Committee on the Judiciary

A BILL

To acknowledge the fundamental injustice, cruelty, brutality, and inhumanity of slavery in the United States and the 13 American colonies between 1619 and 1865 and to establish a commission to examine the institution of slavery, subsequently de jure and de facto racial and economic discrimination against African-Americans, and the impact of these forces on living African-Americans, to make recommendations to the Congress on appropriate remedies, and for other purposes.

Be it enacted by the Senate and House of Representatives of the United States of America in Congress assembled,

SECTION 1. SHORT TITLE.

This Act may be cited as the 'Commission to Study Reparation Proposals for African-Americans Act'.

SEC. 2. FINDINGS AND PURPOSE.

(a) FINDINGS- The Congress finds that—
   (1) approximately 4,000,000 Africans and their descendants were enslaved in the United States and colonies that became the United States from 1619 to 1865;
   (2) the institution of slavery was constitutionally and statutorily sanctioned by the Government of the United States from 1789 through 1865;
   (3) the slavery that flourished in the United States constituted an immoral and inhumane deprivation of Africans' life, liberty, African citizenship rights, and cultural heritage, and denied them the fruits of their own labor; and
   (4) sufficient inquiry has not been made into the effects of the institution of slavery on living African-Americans and society in the United States.

(b) PURPOSE- The purpose of this Act is to establish a commission to—
   (1) examine the institution of slavery which existed from 1619 through 1865 within the United States and the colonies that became the United States, including the extent to which the Federal and State Governments constitutionally and statutorily supported the institution of slavery;
   (2) examine de jure and de facto discrimination against freed slaves and their descendants from the end of the Civil War to the present, including economic, political, and social discrimination;
   (3) examine the lingering negative effects of the institution of slavery and the discrimination described in paragraph (2) on living African-Americans and on society in the United States;
   (4) recommend appropriate ways to educate the American public of the Commission's findings;
   (5) recommend appropriate remedies in consideration of the Commission's findings on the matters described in paragraphs (1) and (2); and
   (6) submit to the Congress the results of such examination, together with such recommendations.

SEC. 3. ESTABLISHMENT AND DUTIES.

(a) ESTABLISHMENT- There is established the Commission to Study Reparation Proposals for African-Americans (hereinafter in this Act referred to as the 'Commission').

(b) DUTIES- The Commission shall perform the following duties:
   (1) Examine the institution of slavery which existed within the United States and the colonies that became the United States from 1619 through 1865. The Commission's examination shall include an examination of—
      (A) the capture and procurement of Africans;

(B) the transport of Africans to the United States and the colonies that became the United States for the purpose of enslavement, including their treatment during transport;

(C) the sale and acquisition of Africans as chattel property in interstate and instrastate commerce; and

(D) the treatment of African slaves in the colonies and the United States, including the deprivation of their freedom, exploitation of their labor, and destruction of their culture, language, religion, and families.

(2) Examine the extent to which the Federal and State governments of the United States supported the institution of slavery in constitutional and statutory provisions, including the extent to which such governments prevented, opposed, or restricted efforts of freed African slaves to repatriate to their homeland.

(3) Examine Federal and State laws that discriminated against freed African slaves and their descendants during the period between the end of the Civil War and the present.

(4) Examine other forms of discrimination in the public and private sectors against freed African slaves and their descendants during the period between the end of the Civil War and the present.

(5) Examine the lingering negative effects of the institution of slavery and the matters described in paragraphs (1), (2), (3), and (4) on living African-Americans and on society in the United States.

(6) Recommend appropriate ways to educate the American public of the Commission's findings.

(7) Recommend appropriate remedies in consideration of the Commission's findings on the matters described in paragraphs (1), (2), (3), and (4). In making such recommendations, the Commission shall address, among other issues, the following questions:

(A) Whether the Government of the United States should offer a formal apology on behalf of the people of the United States for the perpetration of gross human rights violations on African slaves and their descendants.

(B) Whether African-Americans still suffer from the lingering effects of the matters described in paragraphs (1), (2), (3), and (4).

(C) Whether, in consideration of the Commission's findings, any form of compensation to the descendants of African slaves is warranted.

(D) If the Commission finds that such compensation is warranted, what should be the amount of compensation, what form of compensation should be awarded, and who should be eligible for such compensation.

(c) REPORT TO CONGRESS- The Commission shall submit a written report of its findings and recommendations to the Congress not later than the date which is one year after the date of the first meeting of the Commission held pursuant to section 4(c).

SEC. 4. MEMBERSHIP.

(a) NUMBER AND APPOINTMENT- (1) The Commission shall be composed of 7 members, who shall be appointed, within 90 days after the date of enactment of this Act, as follows:

(A) Three members shall be appointed by the President.

(B) Three members shall be appointed by the Speaker of the House of Representatives.

(C) One member shall be appointed by the President pro tempore of the Senate.

(2) All members of the Commission shall be persons who are especially qualified to serve on the Commission by virtue of their education, training, or experience, particularly in the field of African-American studies.

(b) TERMS- The term of office for members shall be for the life of the Commission. A vacancy in the Commission shall not affect the powers of the Commission, and shall be filled in the same manner in which the original appointment was made.

(c) FIRST MEETING- The President shall call the first meeting of the Commission within 120 days after the date of the enactment of this Act, or within 30 days after the date on which legislation is enacted making appropriations to carry out this Act, whichever date is later.

(d) QUORUM- Four members of the Commission shall constitute a quorum, but a lesser number may hold hearings.

(e) CHAIR AND VICE CHAIR- The Commission shall elect a Chair and Vice Chair from among its members. The term of office of each shall be for the life of the Commission.

(f) COMPENSATION- (1) Except as provided in paragraph (2), each member of the Commission shall receive compensation at the daily equivalent of the annual rate of basic pay payable for GS-18 of the General Schedule under section 5332 of title 5, United States Code, for each day, including travel time, during which he or she is engaged in the actual performance of duties vested in the Commission.

(2) A member of the Commission who is a full-time officer or employee of the United States or a Member of Congress shall receive no additional pay, allowances, or benefits by reason of his or her service to the Commission.

(3) All members of the Commission shall be reimbursed for travel, subsistence, and other necessary expenses incurred by them in the performance of their duties to the extent authorized by chapter 57 of title 5, United States Code.

SEC. 5. POWERS OF THE COMMISSION.

(a) HEARINGS AND SESSIONS- The Commission may, for the purpose of carrying out the provisions of this Act, hold such hearings and sit and act at such times and at such places in the United States, and request the attendance and testimony of such witnesses and the production of such books, records, correspondence, memoranda, papers, and documents, as the Commission considers appropriate. The Commission may request the Attorney General to invoke the aid of an appropriate United States district court to require, by subpoena or otherwise, such attendance, testimony, or production.

(b) POWERS OF SUBCOMMITTEES AND MEMBERS- Any subcommittee or member of the Commission may, if authorized by the Commission, take any action which the Commission is authorized to take by this section.

(c) OBTAINING OFFICIAL DATA- The Commission may acquire directly from the head of any department, agency, or instrumentality of the executive branch of the Government, available information which the Commission considers useful in the discharge of its duties. All departments, agencies, and instrumentalities of the executive branch of the Government shall cooperate with the Commission with respect to such information and shall furnish all information requested by the Commission to the extent permitted by law.

SEC. 6. ADMINISTRATIVE PROVISIONS.

(a) STAFF- The Commission may, without regard to section 5311(b) of title 5, United States Code, appoint and fix the compensation of such personnel as the Commission considers appropriate.

(b) APPLICABILITY OF CERTAIN CIVIL SERVICE LAWS- The staff of the Commission may be appointed without regard to the provisions of title 5, United States Code, governing appointments in the competitive service, and without regard to the provisions of chapter 51 and subchapter III of chapter 53 of such title relating to classification and General Schedule pay rates, except that the compensation of any employee of the Commission may not exceed a rate equal to the annual rate of basic pay payable for GS-18 of the General Schedule under section 5332 of title 5, United States Code.

(c) EXPERTS AND CONSULTANTS- The Commission may procure the services of experts and consultants in accordance with the provisions of section 3109(b) of title 5, United States Code, but at rates for individuals not to exceed the daily equivalent of the highest rate payable under section 5332 of such title.

(d) ADMINISTRATIVE SUPPORT SERVICES- The Commission may enter into agreements with the Administrator of General Services for procurement of financial and administrative services necessary for the discharge of the duties of the Commission. Payment for such services shall be made by reimbursement from funds of the Commission in such amounts as may be agreed upon by the Chairman of the Commission and the Administrator.

(e) CONTRACTS- The Commission may—

(1) procure supplies, services, and property by contract in accordance with applicable laws and regulations and to the extent or in such amounts as are provided in appropriations Acts; and

(2) enter into contracts with departments, agencies, and instrumentalities of the Federal Government, State agencies, and private firms, institutions, and agencies, for the conduct of research or surveys, the preparation of reports, and other activities necessary for the discharge of the duties of the Commission, to the extent or in such amounts as are provided in appropriations Acts.

SEC. 7. TERMINATION.

The Commission shall terminate 90 days after the date on which the Commission submits its report to the Congress under section 3(c).

SEC. 8. AUTHORIZATION OF APPROPRIATIONS.

To carry out the provisions of this Act, there are authorized to be appropriated $8,000,000.

Risks, Rewards, and Reaffirmation

Derrick Bell

Two decades ago, or more, the *New Yorker* magazine published a short story about a group of black trash collectors and their unbearably arrogant white supervisor. In the story, Jake, one of the black workers, is always trying to give his boss good advice

Source: Derrick Bell, "Risks, Rewards, and Reaffirmation," from *Confronting Authority: Reflections of an Ardent Protestor.* Copyright © 1994 by Derrick Bell. Reprinted by permission of Beacon Press, Boston.

about how to run his business. The supervisor resents the unsolicited suggestions and finally dismisses Jake. The other black workers shake their heads. "Well, we knew it would happen. Ole Jake done gone and got his damn self fired trying to teach the white folks."

Jake's assertiveness/subservience dilemma will strike a familiar chord for many Americans regardless of race, including some holding positions far loftier than manual laborer. If Jake had clowned around with his co-workers and followed his boss's orders to the letter—even when they were stupid—he would have kept his job, though at great cost to his self-respect. The soul-saving alternative that Jake selected, candidly telling his boss what he thought, cost him his position; unless he found another quickly—a difficult task his boss would not make any easier—he would not be able to care for his family, and his self-respect would be threatened along with everything else.

The moral contained in Jake's story became an important touchstone during my thirty years of marriage to Jewel Bell. Permanently ingrained in my memory is her predictable response whenever I sought her counsel before launching some protest that would likely jeopardize my job and outrage my colleagues. She would shake her head and sigh, "There you go again. After all these years, still trying to teach the white folks."

Jewel was not attempting to discourage my periodic crusades against what I deemed some manifestation of racist excess. She understood that the soul is sometimes sustained by action even when that action borders on the absurd. Rather, she was suggesting the difficulty and, often, the futility of trying to propagate my views about racial discrimination to those who already possessed quite different, and equally deeply held views about white entitlement. My heartfelt protests might annoy, but they would seldom undermine the authority or power of those I confronted. "Teaching the white folk" is thus both a manifestation of faith and an exercise in folly. I might believe that I was doing what I thought "right," but Jewel's admonition was a gentle reminder that I was not necessarily doing "good." That is, my good intentions might well translate into results that—at least in part—might be the very opposite of what I intended.

The discrepancy between doing what one thinks "right" and doing "good" can be applied profitably to an assessment of civil rights efforts over the last dozen or so years. Few will deny that the racial equality goals that a few decades ago seemed in sight are now further away than ever. Equality, experi-

ence tells us, did not follow the enactment of civil rights laws or victories in the courts. Similarly, the plight of the poor and the disadvantaged is not much eased by social programs, which no matter how ambitiously undertaken, seem able to deliver only food without nutrition, welfare without well-being, job training without employment opportunities, and legal services without justice. In fact, the minimum relief we provide to the needy serves mainly to dissipate the organizing and protesting potential generated by deprivation and thus ensures maximum status stability for the already well-off.

I am certain that when Thurgood Marshall argued in the school segregation decisions for an end to formal racial segregation, neither he nor the hundreds of civil rights advocates urging similar relief realized that the society was much more ready to move beyond Jim Crow signs and blatant racial exclusion than it was actually to provide equal opportunity and access without regard to race. We learned the hard way that commitment to white dominance could both survive official segregation and gain in effectiveness under the equal opportunity standard we civil rights lawyers had urged on courts and the country.

While earlier, blacks could be excluded simply because of their race, in the post-*Brown* world discrimination took a more subtle and more formidable form. Courts began finding that if a challenged rule or law did not overtly bar blacks, and if the rule was intended to further some arguably valid function, then civil rights challenges would fail in the absence of hard-to-obtain proof that the rule was intended or administered—despite its neutral language—to discriminate on the basis of race. Proof that in its functioning the rule had the effect of excluding or burdening more blacks than whites was admissible but was not alone sufficient. Otherwise, as one Supreme Court opinion put it, civil rights suits "would raise serious questions about, and perhaps invalidate, a whole range of tax, welfare, public service, regulatory, and licensing statutes." Even worse, rules enacted to help blacks are manipulated to preserve whites' interests at blacks' expense.

Thus, rather than eliminate racial discrimination, civil rights laws have only driven it underground, where it flourishes even more effectively. While employers, landlords, and other merchants can no longer rely on rules that blatantly discriminate against minorities, they can erect barriers that, although they make no mention of race, have the same exclusionary effect. The discrimination that was out in the open during the Jim Crow era could at least be seen, condemned, and fought as a moral issue. Today, statistics, complaints, even secretly filmed instances of discrimination that are televised nationwide—real estate agents steering black customers to black neighborhoods, schools relegating minority students to remedial tracks, and police officers harassing young black men—upset few people because, evidently, no amount of hard evidence will shake the nation's conviction that the system is fair for all.

Given the intransigence of discrimination, civil rights campaigns aimed at changing the rules, without affecting the underlying status quo, have proved counterproductive even when their original goals were achieved. If this is paranoia, it is spurred and sustained by history. Nor is it limited to racial issues. Doing good in this racially charged, economically disparate environment is not simply difficult, it may not be possible. As Jake's experience teaches, even those who are willing to risk their jobs in order to do good may invite disaster. Is it any wonder that racial reform efforts fail?

Given the existence of so many obstacles, the question posed by my late wife, Jewel, "Why does it always have to be you?", takes on new significance. As I have demonstrated, there is slight chance that a solo protest will either succeed itself or lead others to join the protest. On the other hand, the protest almost certainly will alienate those powers against whom it is aimed, and probably will harm, or at least upset, those on whose behalf it was undertaken. Those at a distance may applaud, but those close to the protester are likely to remain silent or be openly critical.

If you or people close to you are wronged, the only way to preserve your sense of self is to respond vigorously. The price of the challenge, though high, is often worth it. The writer Alice Walker told me that when she was still relatively unknown, a major magazine commissioned her to write an autobiographical piece about growing up in the deep South. Publication would, she knew, not only bring her writing to a national public but also provide a substantial amount of much-needed money. The magazine's editors, after perusing her manuscript, met her for lunch at an expensive New York restaurant, where they insisted on changes that she felt altered the character—as well as the accuracy—of her piece. Walker discussed her reservations about what they wanted, but the editors were adamant. "Listen to us, Alice," one of them finally told her with some exasperation. "If you want us to publish your article, you *have* to make these changes." Walker gathered together her manuscript and stood up to leave. "Listen to me," she told them, "all I *have* to do in life is save my soul."

Obviously, her determination to protect her integrity as a writer did not destroy, and almost certainly enhanced, the success Alice Walker later achieved. Surely, she knew that for anyone, but particularly for a black woman writing about race, a commitment to guarding one's artistic integrity at all costs is both essential and extremely difficult. The rewards for those blacks willing to tell whites only what they want to hear have always been both a temptation and a destructive trap.

But the need to confront authority knows no racial limits, nor is the willingness to do so a character trait that manifests itself only when one's job or career is on the line. Every day, in countless ways, people endure without response the affronts we all encounter. Tolerance may be a prerequisite for life in a civilized society, but those who make it a rule to let the small indignities pass without complaint can become so worn down by their treatment and so conditioned to remain silent that they will find themselves unable to fight the more serious battles. Far from insignificant, it is the willingness to take on the small challenges of daily life that prepares one to take a stand when people's basic rights are threatened.

Everyone knows firsthand the frustration of standing in a long, slowly moving line, whether it be at the bank, the supermarket, or any government agency issuing licenses, permits, and—especially—any form of public assistance. The scenario is familiar. One lone person is working at a counter designed for several clerks. At the bank, most of the tellers' windows are vacant. At the market, the check-out aisles are closed. The tellers are checking their receipts. Cashiers, if present at all, are stocking shelves. Sometimes those who might be aiding long-waiting standees are huddled over in a corner gossiping, seemingly oblivious of the ever-lengthening line of unhappy customers. Every now and then— not invariably, you understand—but occasionally, when I find myself in such a line, my patience exhausted, I will take a deep breath and speak out in a firm voice: "Attention, management. We have all been waiting in this line for a very long time. We would appreciate you doing something to speed things up. Thank you very much." Almost always, in reluctant response to my loud call for service, three things will happen. First, those near me in line will disassociate themselves from me. They will turn away, avert their eyes, even take a step or so away, whatever they think necessary to indicate to others that they are not my companions in this disturbance. It is not they who are making a scene out of so ordinary an inconvenience as standing in a slow-moving line. Second, a manager or someone in charge will appear, offer an apology or explanation for the delay, and request that more booths be opened. The line begins to move more speedily. Third, at least one person in the line, after glancing about to ensure

none of the others are watching, will look toward me, make eye contact, and nod appreciatively. I smile back, acknowledging the thanks.

This little scenario reflects in microcosm the order of events in challenges to authority of much greater significance. On-the-spot protests to long lines, of course, involve no real confrontation with authority. Managers understand that unhappy customers can become former customers. But, unless a few of those customers are willing—usually without the support of their fellow sufferers—to register vigorous complaints, long lines and other annoyances become routine.

Yet, rather than risk challenging any authority—however benign—most people will defer to it. The typical reaction to the inconvenience and delay of a long line is not a protest to management, but passive acceptance. This response was dramatized in a television commercial touting a Caribbean vacation as an escape from the frustration and stress of urban living. It showed a prospective passenger standing in line at her bank. She is mightily upset with the teller who, in her view, is the cause of the long line. The woman is ready to explode with frustration, but calms herself by remembering that by that evening, she will be flying off on vacation. To calm her frazzled nerves, she savors in advance the Caribbean's beautiful weather and warm beaches. Then she realizes that the line has not moved during her reverie. She becomes furious, but again gains relief by reminding herself that by evening, she will be on the plane, fleeing from all such hassles. Watching that commercial, I remembered my even longer waits in bank lines in Jamaica and other Caribbean vacation sites. How, I wonder, will this woman handle her bank-line frustrations there? I wonder as well how she responds to the other, small annoyances we all encounter: the landlord who fails—despite repeated requests—to make much-needed repairs, or the doctor who keeps her waiting despite the fact that she made an appointment, carefully wedged into a very busy day. More important, how does she handle the more direct denials of her dignity and worth at her job? What if she is over-worked and underpaid, passed over for pro-motion, even subjected to unwelcome sexual comments by her supervisor? Does she re-press it all by thinking about her next Caribbean vacation? If she wanted to break her pattern of resigned acceptance of mis-treatment, would she know when and how to do it? Would she know how to assess the risks and maximize the likelihood that her confrontation will bring a much-desired change in her treatment, in her status, in her well-being? In other words, if one is not born with the motivation to confront authority, can one acquire it? And if one has it, does it wither away if not exercised?

Protest is, as Gloria Steinem suggests in her book *Revolution from Within,* a form of re-volt. Self-esteem, Steinem maintains, is the most revolutionary of qualities. Obedience is created by systems and ideological con-structs that weaken a person's belief in his or her own merit. She quotes a civil rights worker, H. Jack Geiger, a physician and a prime spokesperson for the Physicians for Social Responsibility: "Of all the injuries in-flicted by racism on people of color, the most corrosive is the wound within, the internal-ized racism that leads some victims, at un-speakable cost to their own sense of self, to embrace the values of their oppressors." As the saying goes, in order to free the body, one must first free the mind. Those who value themselves will have the courage and sense of self-worth to demand to be treated fairly and respectfully. Whatever the re-sponse, the demand in itself is liberating.

This is a difficult feat even for those African Americans who have not only achieved much, but are seen to have done so. For exam-ple, Arthur Ashe, in his book, *Days of Grace: A Memoir,* written with Arnold Rampersad just before Ashe's untimely death, reports that long ago he made peace with his home state, Virginia, and the South, and adds:

But segregation had achieved by that time what it was intended to achieve: it left me a marked man, forever aware of a shadow of contempt that lay across my identity and my sense of self-esteem. Subtly the shadow falls on my reputation, the way I know I am per-ceived; the mere memory of it darkens my most sunny days. I believe that the same is true for almost every African American of the slightest sensitivity and intelligence. . . . I don't want to overstate the case. I think of myself, and others think of me, as supremely self-con-fident. . . . Still, I also know that the shadow is always there; only death will free me, and blacks like me, from its pall.

For a black man who achieved so much both as a tennis player, author, broadcaster, businessman, activist, and as a caring citi-zen, this is a remarkable statement. The mark of oppression that Ashe recognized is widespread, destructive to many, and poses a constant challenge to our sense of who we are. It is the source of so much of the patho-logical behavior that society identifies as vir-tually a genetic trait of blacks, rather than the result of lifelong deprivation, exclusion, and the resulting self-hate. As its victims, blacks should be acutely aware of the causes of such behavior, and yet precisely because of the mark of oppression, we are often more unforgiving than whites.

The Pulitzer Prize–winning author James Alan McPherson tells a poignant story about his father, which reflects the tendency of blacks to condemn the antisocial behavior that results from racism while ignoring its causes. McPherson's father, a master electri-cian in Savannah, Georgia, had destroyed his life with alcohol. For long years, McPher-son hated his father and blamed him alone for failing his family. After becoming suc-cessful himself, McPherson was invited back to his hometown to present a prestigious lec-ture and sought through his speech to show that he had forgiven his father for the alco-holism he could still not understand or excuse.

After the lecture, a long-time friend admonished him: "I found it incredible, totally unbelievable, that you could remember *no* specific incidents of oppression, to yourself or others around you. It is *impossible* for you to have been born in the South of the forties and not have experienced specific incidents of racial oppression. You may have suppressed those experiences in your subconscious, but they happened." The friend continued: "You sharply forgot to mention that time and time again, your father had been unjustly denied an electrician's license—and he was the best. Yes, Mr. Mac was the best, or so my father and mother told me. My father and mother also told me, and my brother and sister, that the lily-white test administrators would never release your father's test results. This refusal by *white folks* to grant your father an electrician's license and release his test scores, along with scores of other rejections and humiliations— the inheritance of all black people—caused your father irrevocable pain. The pain may have even caused him to masquerade—as many unpleasantries have undoubtedly caused you to masquerade—his hostilities toward whites. He turned to drink for relief, you turn to ideas. . . . Those black folk who did not have other escape mechanisms, had to masquerade, or face the sure prospect of being blown to pieces, physically and psychologically. Believe me, your father's alleged status as the first black master electrician in Georgia came at a terrible drain on his inner resources. His effort to become an electrician, much less a master electrician, was a great leap from the abyss of despair."

Revealing the frustrating nature of so much of the progress blacks have made over the years, McPherson reports that his brother, who had his father's genius for things electrical and mechanical, is a mechanic for a major airline. For years now, he has been the only black mechanic in his shop. He once expected to be promoted to foreman. He took the standardized tests and outscored his peers. The rule was changed to make the election of a foreman democratic. He played politics, made friends, did favors. Finally, a somewhat friendly white peer told him, "Mac, your only trouble is your father was the wrong color." After every new foreman is elected, McPherson reports that his brother still receives calls at his home during off hours. These calls are from his peers, and they need help with technical problems that they cannot solve. They ask, "Mac, what should we do?"

The question, "What should we do?" is one more appropriately posed to the modern day Macs who have obtained positions, prestige, and influence denied to McPherson's father, his brother, and to millions of other blacks as well. Like it or not, we are the Timurs selected for the Citadel, representatives for those who didn't make it, couldn't make it. Yes, we even are the representatives for those who, because they lack our skills and opportunities, or who, robbed of the motivation and good fortune that helped us along the way, now don't care whether they make it or not.

We must not forget, particularly those of us who are "first blacks," that our elections, appointments, and promotions were not based simply on our credentials, ability, or experience. As important—likely more important— than merit is the fact that we came along at just the right time. My faculty position at Harvard is far from unique in this regard. It was clear that outstanding black lawyers . . . — Charles Houston, William Hastie, William Coleman—all deserved positions they were denied because they were black. For them, there were no Tamars in the Citadel. They, unlike those of us who made it into the academic ranks, had neither the thrust of the civil rights movement, nor the perhaps unconscious, but no less motivating mandate of the urban riots to parlay their talent into a position.

These facts do not deny individual accomplishment, they simply require recognition that every black person in this society—and far more whites than are willing to acknowledge it—achieved success with the aid of good luck, connections, or both. What is the obligation then of black people who have achieved place, position, and prestige? It is simply not to forget that every step we take up the ladder provides white society with another example that what they wish to believe about racism's demise is actually fact. This knowledge should not discourage achievement, but should serve as a continuing challenge to do as much to help our people as our success unintentionally serves to worsen their plight.

My friend the Reverend Peter Gomes gave me the key to what I view as my obligation. He advised me back in 1980, as I was leaving Harvard to become dean of the University of Oregon Law School. "Derrick," he said, "as a dean, you must look in the mirror each morning and say, 'I am an evil.' For you will have authority and sometimes you will disappoint expectations you should reward and will reward those expectations you should disappoint. There is no way you can avoid such mischief. So, each morning upon arising, you must look at yourself in the mirror, and remind yourself, 'I am an evil.' Then you must ask, 'But today, can I be a necessary evil?' "

It did not take me long to learn that Gomes was sadly wrong about the authority available—for either good or mischief—to a law school dean. But his admonition is most appropriate for successful blacks whose success unintentionally makes life harder for the many blacks whom they would like to help. For all of us, each day provides another opportunity to become, as Peter Gomes would put it, "a necessary evil." That is, we must not become so caught up in career advancement that we fail either to remember ourselves or remind those in authority that our individual advancement is not synonymous with group progress.

This is a principal point in Judge A. Leon Higginbotham's open letter to Justice Clarence Thomas:

> When I think of your appointment to the Supreme Court, I see not only the result of your own ambition, but also the culmination

of years of heartbreaking work by thousands who preceded you. I know you may not want to be burdened by the memory of their sacrifices. But I also know that you have no right to forget this history. Your life is very different from what it would have been had these men and women never lived. . . . This history has affected your past and present life.

Higginbotham's strong admonition is applicable to a wider group of blacks who maintain that they did make it on their own and vigorously assert that the subordinate status of blacks is the result, not of racial discrimination, but of personal and group inadequacy. As we saw in the last chapter, even Paul Robeson, W.E.B. Du Bois, and Martin Luther King, generally regarded as heroes, were criticized severely by other black leaders for their harsh statements *against* white authority, which other blacks feared would worsen conditions for the black race. But blacks feel even more threatened by other blacks who, for whatever reason, take positions *supporting* authority. Robeson, Du Bois, and King were deemed to have "gone too far." But blacks who are thought to have "sold out" or "betrayed the race" by making statements about racial issues that comfort and reassure whites are condemned as traitors and "Uncle Toms." No one will deny that self-help is a component of programs and policies intended to rescue the millions of blacks mired in poverty and despair, but the assertion that the problems of the poor will be solved by self-help alone is such an extreme position it suggests that those blacks willing to make such arguments do so for the public attention they gain. Such individuals are particularly disturbing to successful blacks because we know that—to some extent—our achievements are grounded in a willingness to work for or otherwise identify with individuals and institutions whose racial policies are far from commendable.

Writer Jill Nelson makes clear how difficult it is to maintain one's ethical bearings in the job market. Describing a series of interviews at a major white newspaper that was considering her as a reporter, she reports:

I've been doing the standard Negro balancing act when it comes to dealing with white folks, which involves sufficiently blurring the edges of my being so that white folks don't feel intimidated and simultaneously holding on to my integrity. There is a thin line between Uncle Tomming and Mau-Mauing. To step over that line can mean disaster. On one side lies employment and self-hatred, on the other, the equally dubious honor of unemployment with integrity. In the middle lies something like employment with honor, although I'm not sure exactly how that works.

Given the tightrope act blacks must perform to make it in this country, those blacks who deny that race plays any part in our success or failure are involved—at the very least—in serious denial. And yet the alienation from the community that blacks who confront their communities suffer is disquietingly similar to the rejection suffered by those who confront authority. I confess that I have at times been quick to condemn black professionals who have opted for the easy road to success for minorities, namely, ignoring the continuing perversity of racism and acting as though the law is fair and color-blind. While authority figures with favors to grant reward blacks whose views serve to legitimate the society's rose-colored assumptions about race, motivations may be as complex for those who comfort as they certainly are for those of us who confront authority.

I have railed at the appointment of Justice Clarence Thomas, whose major qualification for replacing the late Justice Thurgood Marshall on the Supreme Court is his willingness to kick black folks when they are down. Because his votes and opinions in his first few terms on the Court have shown no more racial sensitivity than his pre-Court positions, Thomas is now publicly condemned even by some blacks who—despite his positions opposing affirmative action and condemning civil rights leaders—supported his nomination under the rubric: "give the brother a chance." But just as confrontations with authority sometime produce unexpected, positive results, perhaps even Justice Thomas's

regrettable performance will prove of some benefit to blacks he seems so willing to reject and who—in turn—have surely rejected him. At the least, Thomas's presence on the nation's highest Court provides black people with a continuing reminder that what many of us condemn as a serious deficiency in him is, as well, a constant temptation in us.

This willingness to seek instruction even in travesty comes naturally to the protester. In my case, while I have been a civil rights litigator, administrator, and for the last quarter of a century, a law professor and writer, I have really been a teacher. I have learned over the years that while knowledge and understanding of the law are important, they are secondary to the essence of teaching, which Peter Gomes defines as the ability "to communicate not only subject, but self."

Gomes, in one of his justly famous Sunday morning sermons, reminded the congregation of what we all know, that the memorable teachers in our lives hold that status even though we do not recall a single thing they taught us. Rather, we remember them as individuals who spurred us to learn on our own, both the subject matter and ourselves. Gomes quoted a description of such a great teacher in England about whom it was said, "He taught as a learner, led as a follower, and so set the feet of many in the way of life."

Gomes pointed to a plaque at the front of the Memorial Church erected in memory of Andrew Preston Peabody, the third Plummer Professor of Christian Morals at Harvard, who served in that post for thirty-three years during the nineteenth century. The plaque states that the Reverend Peabody was remembered as author, editor, teacher, and preacher, and as helper of all whom he met. His worth was summed up in the statement: "His precept was glorified by his example."

A marvelous model for a teacher, but what of the individual teacher-protesters who rise and, with all the odds stacked against them, challenge authority? How find a lesson in the hostility of those in power or the negative reactions from a great many whom one counts as allies, if not friends? Often, the lone protester—abandoned (or worse) by associates and unable to reach his or her goal—will feel less like a teacher than the mythical Sisyphus, forever pushing to the top of the mountain the rock that, upon nearing the heights, only rolls back down to the bottom. At a first reading of Sisyphus, it is hard to escape the despairing, existential angst that accompanies any realization of the futility of struggle. But the French philosopher Albert Camus puts a different face upon Sisyphus' tragic fate. Rather than hopelessness, Camus sees incredible courage and even liberation in this timeless story. He sees strength in Sisyphus' course, not because Sisyphus continues to push the rock to the mountain's top, but because he returns to the bottom to retrieve it—knowing he will never get it to the top. "At each of those moments when he leaves the heights and gradually sinks toward the lairs of the gods, he is superior to his fate. He is stronger than his rock."

In appraising Sisyphus' dilemma, Camus has offered the protester cum teacher a lesson that transcends the bounds of philosophy and enters the realm of art. For, in the final analysis, art is an expression that provides a heightened meaning and appreciation of the human experience. The artist in the vanguard seldom works in an environment of acceptance. Faced often with rejection and ridicule, he or she pushes against the bounds of convention in an effort to create a new convention, sometimes building on, but more often exceeding and threatening accepted conventions.

Alice Walker opens her essay "Saving the Life That Is Your Own: The Importance of Models in the Artist's Life" with a letter to Emile Bernard from Vincent Van Gogh.

> However hateful painting may be, and however cumbersome in the times we are living in, if anyone who has chosen this handicraft pursues it zealously, he is a man of duty, sound and faithful.

> Society makes our existence wretchedly difficult at times, hence our impotence and the imperfection of our work. . . . I myself am suffering under an absolute lack of models. What I am doing is hard, . . . but that is because I am trying to gather new thoughts by doing some rough work, and I'm afraid abstractions would make me soft.

Thus, Van Gogh captures in words the similarity of his work to that of the individual protester. Both seek to communicate the feelings of life and thereby more fully experience and give meaning and substance to one's existence. Just as the artist may hope for recognition, so the protester hopes that assertive action may bring about reform. Such hopes, though, supplement rather than fuel the main creative urge: expression of self through a medium—painting or protest—that communicates a view of "what is" against a background of *what might be*.

It was in that spirit that I presented what was to be my last speech to Harvard law students as a faculty member, early in 1992. At bottom, I reminded them, my protest leave was undertaken less to change the school than to influence students through example as well as through exhortations of perhaps the most important lesson my life experience has taught: commitment to change must be combined with readiness to confront authority. Not because you will always win, not because you will always be right, but because your faith in what you believe is right must be a living, working faith, a faith that draws you away from comfort and security and toward risk, when necessary, through confrontation.

The underlying lesson in all my courses is that individuals must gain control of their lives, not by attaining riches or power or fame, but by confronting and trying to remedy a few of the evils and wrongs that we witness every day. The opportunity to illustrate my commitment to that belief has been worth the sacrifices I have made—which, in fact, have been few. I say this even if the warnings are borne out that my protest at

Harvard in fact retards the progress toward diversity the faculty all claim to support in principle.

Daring to risk. That is tough. After all, there is at Harvard, as in the rest of our modern world, a distressing commitment to the unwritten commandment: "Thou shalt conform and not confront." The seeking of security seems to be a priority at Harvard, where faculty members are tenured, most key staff are equally secure, and students—compared to most of their counterparts around the country—are well off, indeed. In asserting the supremacy of the University, the members of its community are seldom meek or humble or submissive. Nor, in my experience, are they tolerant of those within their midst who dare venture beyond accepted procedures in an effort to bring change and reform. In this, the Harvard community is not significantly different from centers of power the world over.

Eventually, the Harvard Law School will hire and tenure its first woman of color. If my experience is a guide, even that event will not herald the adoption of policies intended to ensure either diversity or merit in the hiring process. It is even more certain that social reform, when it comes, at Harvard or elsewhere—will be borne on the scary wings of risk. In the very grasp of that fear, we must commit ourselves to reform, and retain that commitment while staring in the face of overwhelming evidence that the change we seek will be difficult—even impossible—to achieve.

Chiding the large group that had turned out for my talk, I reminded them that they must move beyond the trappings of reform—attending rallies, applauding speeches, and enjoying the camaraderie of the moment. I warned them about equating their presence at these events with the kind of commitment that enables one to struggle for change that may not come and to persevere despite the opposition that will come. All of us, I advised, can learn from my enslaved forebears that in the commitment to living, to warding off oppressors, harassing them when we can, helping others, there is the stuff of triumph, recognizable even in defeat.

The analogy with slavery is less remote than it might appear. Like the slaves, law students—and likely a substantial portion of the citizenry in general—must live their lives under the debilitating weight of subordination and abuse—not physical certainly—but mental and emotional. The effort to get ahead or, at least, to hold one's own, extracts a fearful price in diminishing freedoms that are no less lost for being voluntarily surrendered.

Americans of all races have been in denial about our history of African slavery. Whites fear blacks will use it to provoke guilt, and blacks fear whites will use it to enhance their superior status. But lost in this collective amnesia is an uplifting example, one of great potential value in our modern world. Again, the enslavement of African peoples in this country was infinitely worse than anything that occurs at Harvard or elsewhere, but out of lives transformed by law into property, the slaves created models of fortitude and faith. The lives of this oppressed people and their legacy of music, art, and religion defy their awful condemnation to lives in bondage. They insisted on their humanity despite a hostile world's conviction that they were chattel, nothing more.

As the slave singers raised their voices to freedom, they must have known that there was no escape, no way out—in this world. The lyrics of their songs dreamed of a "City Called Heaven," but while they lived, they continued to engage themselves in the creation of humanity. Here is our model. We need do no more—and surely must do no less—than seek to emulate what they have done.

SUGGESTED READINGS

Arthur R. Ashe, Jr., *A Hard Road to Glory: A History of the African American Athlete Since 1946.* 3 Volumes. (New York, 1988)

Derrick Bell, *And We Are Not Saved: The Elusive Quest for Racial Justice* (New York, 1987)

Bob Blauner, *Black Lives, White Lives: Three Decades of Race Relations in America* (Berkeley, Calif., 1989)

Obie Clayton Jr., ed., *An American Dilemma Revisited: Race Relations in a Changing World* (New York, 1996)

Cathy J. Cohen, *The Boundaries of Blackness: AIDS and the Breakdown of Black Politics* (Chicago, 1999)

Michael C. Dawson, *Behind the Mule: Race and Class in African American Politics* (Princeton, N.J., 1994)

Mattias Gardell, *In the Name of Elijah Muhammad: Louis Farrakhan and the Nation of Islam* (Durham, N.C., 1996)

Patricia Gurin, Shirley Hatchett and James S. Jackson, *Hope and Independence: Blacks Response to Electoral and Party Politics* (New York, 1989)

Patricia Gurin and Edgar Epps, *Black Consciousness, Identity and Achievement: A Study of Students in Historically Black Colleges* (New York, 1975)

Herbert Hill and James E. Jones, eds., *Race in America: The Struggle for Equality* (Madison, Wis., 1993)

Gerald David Jaynes and Robert M. Williams, Jr., *A Common Destiny: Blacks and American Society* (Washington, D.C., 1989)

J. Morgan Kousser, *Colorblind Injustice: Minority Voting Rights and the Undoing of the Second Reconstruction* (Chapel Hill, N.C., 1999)

Manning Marable, *Race, Reform, and Rebellion: The Second Reconstruction in Black America, 1945–1990* (Jackson, Miss., 1984)

Toni Morrison, ed., *Race-ing Justice, En-gendering Power: Essays on Anita Hill, Clarence Thomas, and the Construction of Social Reality* (New York, 1992)

Carl Husemoller Nightingale, *On The Edge: A History of Poor Black Children and Their American Dreams* (New York, 1993)

William Eric Perkins, ed., *Droppin' Science: Critical Essays on Rap Music and Hip Hop Culture* (Philadelphia, 1996)

Robert J. Powell, *Black Art and Culture in the 20th Century* (New York, 1997)

Beverly Guy-Sheftall, ed., *Words of Fire: An Anthology of African American Feminist Thought* (New York, 1995)

Carol B. Stack, *All Our Kin: Strategies for Survival in a Black Community* (New York, 1974)

Thomas J. Sugrue, *The Origins of the Urban Crisis: Race and Inequality in Postwar Detroit* (Princeton, N.J., 1996)

Hanes Walton, *African American Power and Politics: The Political Context Variable* (New York, 1997)